Active Server Pages
In Plain English

Timothy Eden
Patricia Hartman

M&T Books
An imprint of IDG Books Worldwide, Inc.

Foster City, CA • Chicago, IL • Indianapolis, IN • New York, NY

Active Server Pages In Plain English

Published by
M&T Books
An imprint of IDG Books Worldwide, Inc.
919 E. Hillsdale Blvd., Suite 400
Foster City, CA 94404
www.idgbooks.com (IDG Books Worldwide Web site)

ISBN: 0-7645-4745-3

Printed in the United States of America

10 9 8 7 6 5 4 3 2 1

1O/TR/QR/QR/FC

Distributed in the United States by IDG Books Worldwide, Inc.

Distributed by CDG Books Canada Inc. for Canada; by Transworld Publishers Limited in the United Kingdom; by IDG Norge Books for Norway; by IDG Sweden Books for Sweden; by IDG Books Australia Publishing Corporation Pty. Ltd. for Australia and New Zealand; by TransQuest Publishers Pte Ltd. for Singapore, Malaysia, Thailand, Indonesia, and Hong Kong; by Gotop Information Inc. for Taiwan; by ICG Muse, Inc. for Japan; by Intersoft for South Africa; by Eyrolles for France; by International Thomson Publishing for Germany, Austria, and Switzerland; by Distribuidora Cuspide for Argentina; by LR International for Brazil; by Galileo Libros for Chile; by Ediciones ZETA S.C.R. Ltda. for Peru; by WS Computer Publishing Corporation, Inc., for the Philippines; by Contemporanea de Ediciones for Venezuela; by Express Computer Distributors for the Caribbean and West Indies; by Micronesia Media Distributor, Inc. for Micronesia; by Chips Computadoras S.A. de C.V. for Mexico; by Editorial Norma de Panama S.A. for Panama; by American Bookshops for Finland.

For general information on IDG Books Worldwide's books in the U.S., please call our Consumer Customer Service department at 800-762-2974. For reseller information, including discounts and premium sales, please call our Reseller Customer Service department at 800-434-3422.

For information on where to purchase IDG Books Worldwide's books outside the U.S., please contact our International Sales department at 317-572-3993 or fax 317-572-4002.

For consumer information on foreign language translations, please contact our Customer Service department at 800-434-3422, fax 317-572-4002, or e-mail rights@idgbooks.com.

For information on licensing foreign or domestic rights, please phone + 1-650-653-7098.

For sales inquiries and special prices for bulk quantities, please contact our Order Services department at 800-434-3422 or write to the address above.

For information on using IDG Books Worldwide's books in the classroom or for ordering examination copies, please contact our Educational Sales department at 800-434-2086 or fax 317-572-4005.

For press review copies, author interviews, or other publicity information, please contact our Public Relations department at 650-653-7000 or fax 650-653-7500.

For authorization to photocopy items for corporate, personal, or educational use, please contact Copyright Clearance Center, 222 Rosewood Drive, Danvers, MA 01923, or fax 978-750-4470.

Library of Congress Cataloging-in-Publication Data

Hartman, Patricia A.
Active Server Pages in plain English / Timothy Eden, Patricia Hartman.
   p. cm.
   Includes index.
   ISBN 0-7645-4745-3 (alk. paper)
   1. Active server pages. 2. Web sites. 3. Web servers--Computer programs. I. Eden, Timothy, 1959- II. Title.
   TK5105.8885.A26 H36 2001
   005.2'76--dc21   00-053415

 is a registered trademark or trademark under exclusive license to IDG Books Worldwide, Inc. from International Data Group, Inc. in the United States and/or other countries.

 is a trademark of IDG Books Worldwide, Inc.

ABOUT IDG BOOKS WORLDWIDE

Welcome to the world of IDG Books Worldwide.

IDG Books Worldwide, Inc., is a subsidiary of International Data Group, the world's largest publisher of computer-related information and the leading global provider of information services on information technology. IDG was founded more than 30 years ago by Patrick J. McGovern and now employs more than 9,000 people worldwide. IDG publishes more than 290 computer publications in over 75 countries. More than 90 million people read one or more IDG publications each month.

Launched in 1990, IDG Books Worldwide is today the #1 publisher of best-selling computer books in the United States. We are proud to have received eight awards from the Computer Press Association in recognition of editorial excellence and three from Computer Currents' First Annual Readers' Choice Awards. Our best-selling ...For Dummies® series has more than 50 million copies in print with translations in 31 languages. IDG Books Worldwide, through a joint venture with IDG's Hi-Tech Beijing, became the first U.S. publisher to publish a computer book in the People's Republic of China. In record time, IDG Books Worldwide has become the first choice for millions of readers around the world who want to learn how to better manage their businesses.

Our mission is simple: Every one of our books is designed to bring extra value and skill-building instructions to the reader. Our books are written by experts who understand and care about our readers. The knowledge base of our editorial staff comes from years of experience in publishing, education, and journalism — experience we use to produce books to carry us into the new millennium. In short, we care about books, so we attract the best people. We devote special attention to details such as audience, interior design, use of icons, and illustrations. And because we use an efficient process of authoring, editing, and desktop publishing our books electronically, we can spend more time ensuring superior content and less time on the technicalities of making books.

You can count on our commitment to deliver high-quality books at competitive prices on topics you want to read about. At IDG Books Worldwide, we continue in the IDG tradition of delivering quality for more than 30 years. You'll find no better book on a subject than one from IDG Books Worldwide.

John J. Kilcullen

John Kilcullen
Chairman and CEO
IDG Books Worldwide, Inc.

IDG is the world's leading IT media, research and exposition company. Founded in 1964, IDG had 1997 revenues of $2.05 billion and has more than 9,000 employees worldwide. IDG offers the widest range of media options that reach IT buyers in 75 countries representing 95% of worldwide IT spending. IDG's diverse product and services portfolio spans six key areas including print publishing, online publishing, expositions and conferences, market research, education and training, and global marketing services. More than 90 million people read one or more of IDG's 290 magazines and newspapers, including IDG's leading global brands — Computerworld, PC World, Network World, Macworld and the Channel World family of publications. IDG Books Worldwide is one of the fastest-growing computer book publishers in the world, with more than 700 titles in 36 languages. The "...For Dummies®" series alone has more than 50 million copies in print. IDG offers online users the largest network of technology-specific Web sites around the world through IDG.net (http://www.idg.net), which comprises more than 225 targeted Web sites in 55 countries worldwide. International Data Corporation (IDC) is the world's largest provider of information technology data, analysis and consulting, with research centers in over 41 countries and more than 400 research analysts worldwide. IDG World Expo is a leading producer of more than 168 globally branded conferences and expositions in 35 countries including E3 (Electronic Entertainment Expo), Macworld Expo, ComNet, Windows World Expo, ICE (Internet Commerce Expo), Agenda, DEMO, and Spotlight. IDG's training subsidiary, ExecuTrain, is the world's largest computer training company, with more than 230 locations worldwide and 785 training courses. IDG Marketing Services helps industry-leading IT companies build international brand recognition by developing global integrated marketing programs via IDG's print, online and exposition products worldwide. Further information about the company can be found at www.idg.com.   1/26/00

Credits

Acquisitions Editor
Debra Williams Cauley

Project Editor
Terri Varveris

Technical Editor
Greg Guntle

Copy Editor
Luann Rouff

Project Coordinator
Joe Shines
Danette Nurse

Quality Control Technician
Dina F Quan

Graphics and Production Specialists
Robert Bihlmayer
Rolly Delrosario
Jude Levinson
Ramses Ramiriz
Victor Pérez-Varela

Book Designer
Kurt Krames

Illustrator
Gabriele McCann

Proofreading and Indexing
York Production Services

Cover Image
© Noma/Images.com

About the Authors

Timothy Eden is a lead e-commerce developer for ExtremeStyle (www.extremestyle.com) in Jacksonville, Florida. Timothy has over 10 years programming experience. In addition to programming in the world of Active Server Pages, Timothy has also written several articles on the Java language. He is a graduate of Auburn University War Eagle! Timothy can be reached at tim@extremestyle.com or timothyeden@mediaone.net.

Patricia Hartman has written a number of books related to computer databases as well as worked in a civil service environment where she supervised a computer network support staff and developed applications in Basic and database languages. Dr. Hartman holds graduate degrees from the University of Minnesota and has taught at state universities in Minnesota and California. She is a Certified Netware Engineer and is currently consulting in networking and Web design services, as well as authoring books and other publications. She lives in North San Diego County with her husband, two Rottweilers, a cat, and their computer network.

*To my husband, William Rupp, and my family
(Mark, Craig, Karina, Deborah, Kent, Serena,
Laurissa, Ryan, Sam, Giovanna, Deanna,
Laithe, Andrew and Aunt Florence)
whose patience and understanding
helped me along the way.
– Patricia Hartman*

*To my wife, Amy, who gave me the time
and encouragement to write this book.
Thank you Bunn. To Tim and Lori Chesser
and Bob and Mary Barker thank you
for your friendship.
– Timothy Eden*

Preface

Welcome to *Active Server Pages In Plain English!*

Active Server Pages (ASP) is a must for today's Internet programmers. These days, it isn't enough to program in a computer language such as C++ or Visual Basic. Windows NT and Windows 2000 Servers that run the Internet Information Server (IIS) are used for many corporate and other large Web sites. In order to carry out SQL queries against large databases and complete the transactions needed by a production Web site, you need to understand and use ASP.

What Window server programmers who use ASP need is a good ASP reference combined with a tutorial that shows you how to use ASP. *Active Server Pages In Plain English* provides this. The reference material offers documentation on ASP and the languages used with ASP: HTML, VBScript, and SQL. The coverage in the reference material, although extensive, focuses primarily on what ASP programmers need.

The tutorial chapters complement the reference material, adding practical information to this book. These chapters cover creating an ASP, using VBScript with ASP, ASP objects needed to create an application, working with databases (the ADO Server object), creating server-side ActiveX COM objects, and relating Visual Basic to ASP.

Information in this book is literally at your fingertips. Tables are provided that organize all of the keywords covered in the reference sections by category. The tables include page numbers where the keywords can be located in their respective reference section. An alphabetical listing of each ASP keyword is also provided along with a page reference to where it is located in the ASP Core Reference section. So that you can access information quickly, numerous cross-references are provided throughout the tutorial chapters and reference material, also with page numbers. In addition, the edges of each page in the reference sections contain thumb tabs to help you find what you need easily.

What You Need to Get Started

To begin, you need a PC that runs the Personal Web Server (Windows 98) or Internet Information Server 4 or higher. Ideally you should have a Pentium II or equivalent processor and 64 MB of RAM, a 2GB hard drive, CD-ROM drive. You will need Internet access if you intend to upload your work to an Internet server.

Organization of the Book

Active Server Pages In Plain English has two reference parts and one tutorial part. The three parts are described in the following sections.

Part I: ASP Reference

This part consists of the following reference sections:

- ASP In Plain English: This is a table that displays a number of typical tasks an ASP programmer might face, along with the pages in the book where an explanation may be found.

- ASP By Category: A table that orgainizes each keyword — method, object, property — covered in the ASP Core Reference section by category. Page numbers where each keyword can be found in the book are provided.

- ASP A to Z: This is an alphabetical list of the keywords covered in the ASP Core Reference section. Page numbers where each keyword can be found in the book are provided.

- ASP Core Reference: Extensive documentation for the ASP keywords, including objects and collections.

Part II: Languages Used with the ASP Reference

This part covers languages used with ASP. It includes the following reference sections:

- A complete reference of the HTML tag syntax
- A complete reference of VBScript language
- A complete reference of the SQL language

Part III: The Tutorial

This part contains six tutorial chapters. They provide many examples that demonstrate the use of ASP, including the additional languages commonly used in the process of creating ASP applications. The following list describes the coverage of each tutorial chapter:

- The first chapter gets you started with ASP. It covers the four most important objects you will use to create all your applications: ADO, Response, Request, and Server objects.
- Chapter two deals with VBScript and how it is used with ASP, including both client-side and server-side scripting.
- Chapter three shows how to use the global.asa file; the Session, Application, and StaticObject collections; and the MTS component. These are all ASP objects you need to create an application.
- Chapter four focuses on working with databases, using the ActiveX Data object. This chapter primarily concentrates on the ADO COM object, since a large part of ASP deals with database access.
- Chapter five shows how to create server-side objects in the Component Object Model (COM) and how Visual Basic interfaces with ASP.
- Chapter six continues the tutorial by demonstrating how to create classes and ActiveX controls as well as ActiveX documents. It concludes with a discussion of COM and the advantages of server-side scripting and how to package and deploy your application in Visual Basic.

There is a bonus appendix available on-line at `http://catalog.` `hungryminds.com/0764547453/extras/`. It contains additional information about the enumerated constants mentioned in this book.

Conventions Used in This Book

The language conventions in the reference sections are oriented toward the method of use. The language keywords are organized alphabetically within the key reference sections. A Purpose, Syntax, and Example section are provided for just about every keyword. Each term and its purpose is declared. This is then followed by the syntax needed to use the element and a practical example of its usage.

Monospace type is used throughout. It designates in-text code and the names of properties, methods, collections, objects, statements, parameters, and constants.

Reach Out

We (Patricia Hartman and Timothy Eden) and the publisher would like your feedback. After you have had a chance to use this book, please take a moment to register this book on the `http://my2cents.` `idgbooks.com` Web site. (Details are listed on the my2cents page in the back of the book.)

Also, feel free to send us any errors that you find in the book. You can contact us directly at:

`aspipe@hitekdesigns.com`

Acknowledgments

We would like to thank David Fugate of Waterside Produc-tions for providing support and assistance with this project.

We are also grateful to Debra Williams Cauley for giving us the opportunity to write *Active Server Pages In Plain English* — a reference and tutorial for Internet programmers using Windows NT and Windows 2000 systems.

Finally, we want to thank the editors, Terri Varveris and Greg Guntle, for assisting us in this prodigious project. We appreciate their diligence in ensuring the high quality of the work and the guidance and direction we received in this regard.

Contents at a Glance

Preface ix
Acknowledgments xiii

Part I: ASP Reference 2

ASP in Plain English. 5
ASP by Category 9
ASP A to Z 23
ASP Core Reference. 35

Part II: Languages Used with the ASP Reference 310

HTML by Category 313
HTML Reference 319
VBScript by Category. 393
VBScript Reference 399
SQL by Category 461
SQL Reference 467

Part III: The Tutorial 530

Chapter 1: Getting Started with Active Server Pages. 533
Chapter 2: VBScript and Active Server Pages. 569
Chapter 3: Objects Used for ASP Applications 593
Chapter 4: Working with the Database: The ADO Object 611
Chapter 5: Creating Server-Side ActiveX COM Objects 675
Chapter 6: Visual Basic and Active Server Pages 699

Index 733

Contents

Preface. ix

Acknowledgments xiii

Part I: ASP Reference 2

ASP in Plain English 5

ASP by Category 9

ASP A to Z 23

ASP Core Reference 35

    Application Object 36

    AspError Object 42

    Command Object 46

    Connection Object 56

    Connection Collections Object 74

    Dictionary Object 76

    Drive Object 84

    Error Object 91

    Field Object 97

    Fields Collections Object 108

    File Object 114

    FileSystemObject Object 121

    Folder Object 141

    Folder Collection Object 153

    Parameter Object 156

    Property Object 164

    Properties Collection Object 170

    Record Object 172

    RecordSet Object 186

    Request Object 224

    Response Object 241

    Server Object 259

    Session Object 268

    Stream Object 276

    TextStream Object 298

Part II: Languages Used with the ASP Reference 310

HTML by Category 313

HTML Reference 319

VBScript by Category. 393

VBScript Reference. 399

SQL by Category 461

SQL Reference 467

Part III: The Tutorial 530

Chapter 1: Getting Started with Active Server Pages 533

Installing the Internet Information Server 534
  IIS and Windows 98 534
  IIS and Windows NT 4.0 Option Pack 535
  IIS and Windows 2000 Server 538
Creating Your First Active Server Page 540
  Learning the Syntax of ASP 540
  Using VBScript with an ASP. 541
Getting Started with ASP Components. 542
  The Response Object 543
  The Request Object. 546
  The Server Object. 554
Using Server-Side Include Files. 561
  Using ASP as Server-Side Include Files 562
  Using VBScript Subs and Functions. 563

Chapter 2: VBScript and Active Server Pages 569

What Is VBScript? 569
  Browser Support 570
  Support Considerations. 571
  VBScript Features. 571
Using VBScript for Client Scripting. 573
  Building Applications with VBScript 574
  Integrating VBScript into HTML Documents. 575
More Client-Side VBScript Examples. 577
  Validating Entries with VBScript 577
  Referencing the History List with VBScript 579
Installing the Personal Web Server and IIS. 581
  Installing the Personal Web Server 582
  Installing IIS. 584

Using VBScript and Active Server Pages for
Server-Side Scripting 586
 Creating a Random Number Effect 588
 Requesting Server Information 589

Chapter 3: Objects Used for ASP Applications 593
 Maintaining State on the Internet. 593
 Starting an ASP Application: The Global.asa File 594
 Scope of Applications: Application and Session Objects . . . 596
  Application-Level Scope: The Application Object 596
  Session-Level Scope: The Session Object 597
 Session Object Properties and Methods 599
  SessionID Property 599
  TimeOut Property 600
  LCID Property 600
  CodePage Property 600
  Abandon Method 600
  Session.Contents.Remove Method. 600
  Session.Contents.RemoveAll Method 601
 Application Object Methods 601
  Lock Method 601
  UnLock Method 602
  Application.Contents.Remove Method 602
  Application.Contents.RemoveAll Method. 603
 Application and Session Object Collections 603
  Contents Collection. 603
  Contents Collection Application Object Example 603
  Contents Collection Session Object Example. 604
 Storing Global Information in Arrays 605
  Storing Global Information in Arrays at
   the Application Level 605
  Storing Global Information in Arrays at
   the Session Level 606
 StaticObjects Collection 607
  StaticObjects Application Object Example 607
  StaticObjects Session Object Example. 608

Chapter 4: Working with the Database: The ADO Object 611
 What is OLE DB? 612
 The ADO Model 612
 General Overview of Getting a Connection 621
  Creating a Connection to a Datasource 621
  Creating a DSN with the ODBC 622
 The Connection Object 628
  Establishing a Connection with the Connection Object . . 628

Executing Transactions Against a Data
Source with the Connection Object 630
Freeing Resources with the Connection Object 631
The RecordSet Object 631
Understanding Isolation, Locking, and Cursor Types . . . 632
Navigating the Recordset. 636
Adding, Updating, and Deleting a Recordset 638
Viewing Recordset Changes with
Resync and Requery 639
Checking the Status of a RecordSet Action 640
Turning a Recordset into an Array. 640
Displaing a Recordset in an HTML Page 641
Filling in a Drop Down List Box with a Recordset. 643
The Field Object 644
The Error Object and Error Collection 645
The Command Object 647
Passing Parameters to a Stored Procedure via
the CommandText Property 648
Passing Parameters via the parameter_array Argument . . 649
Using Other Command Object Properties 650
Storing a Procedure from a SQL Server 652
The Parameter Object and Collection 653
The Property Object and Collection 655
The Record Object 659
GetChildren Method 663
CopyRecord, MoveRecord, and DeleteRecord Methods . . 664
The Stream Object 665
The Remote Data Services 667
DataFactory Object 668
DataSpace Object 670
DataControl Object 670
RDS References 671

Chapter 5: Creating Server-Side ActiveX COM Objects 675

Understanding the COM Object and ActiveX Objects 676
COM+ and TIP. 676
Objects and Classes. 677
Uses of ActiveX Objects 677
Using Visual Basic to Create an ActiveX COM Object 678
The ActiveX DLL Project. 678
Changing the Name of the Project and Class Module . . . 680
Creating a Function in the Class Module 683
Completing and Running Your ActiveX Com Object 683
Using Microsoft Visual Interdev to Write ASP Code. . . . 683
Using Microsoft FrontPage to Write ASP Code 688

Registering the ActiveX COM Object. 690
Creating an ActiveX COM Object to Divide Numbers 693
Objectives of Component Development 696

Chapter 6: Visual Basic and Active Server Pages 699

What is Visual Basic? 699
    Elements of Visual Basic. 700
    Visual Basic and VBScript 700
Scripting an ActiveX Automation Object. 701
    Linking and Embedding Objects. 701
    Writing a String Test Function 704
    Writing a Conversion Function 707
Creating Classes in Visual Basic 707
Creating ActiveX Controls in Visual Basic. 708
    Adding Features to the UserControl. 710
    Writing the Code and Testing the Control 712
Creating ActiveX Documents in Visual Basic 713
    Organizing an ActiveX Document. 713
    Building a UserDocument 714
Data Access in Visual Basic 718
The COM, Visual Basic, and ASP. 718
    COM. 719
    Visual Basic 719
    ASP 719
ActiveX, MAPI, and OLE 720
    ActiveX 720
    MAPI 720
    OLE 721
Advantages of ASP and Server-Side Scripting 722
    Advantages of ASP 722
    A Simple Server-Side Script 722
Packaging and Deploying Applications in Visual Basic 724
    Packaging Your Control. 724
    Deploying the Control 728

Index **733**

Active Server Pages

Pages

In Plain English

ASP Reference

The ASP Reference part contains the following reference sections:

IN THIS PART

- ASP in Plain English
- ASP by Category
- ASP A to Z
- ASP Core Reference

in plain english in pl
sh in plain english in
glish in plain english
in plain english in pl
sh in plain english in
glish in plain english
in plain english in pl
glish in plain english
in plain english in pl
sh in plain english in
glish in plain english
in plain english in pl
sh in plain english in
glish in plain english
in plain english in pl
lish in plain english
in plain english in pl
sh in plain english in
glish in plain english
in plain english in pl
sh in plain english in
lish in plain english
in plain english in pl
glish in plain english

ASP in Plain English

This section is for those who have a specific task that they need to get done or a problem they need solved, but are not sure where in the book to find a solution. The following table displays a number of typical challenges an ASP programmer might face, along with the pages in the book where an explanation may be found.

This reference also helps if you have used a particular method in the past, but have forgotten details about it. The table jogs your memory by giving you references where that method is described or discussed.

If you want to...	Use this keyword	Located on these pages
create a database connection	Connection Object	Ch. 4 (628)
create a System DSN	ODBC Data Connection	Ch. 4 (622)
connect to a database	ActiveX Data Object	Ch. 4 (621)
get data from a database	RecordSet Object	Ch. 4 (636)
create an ActiveX Component	Component Object Model	Ch. 5 (678)
query a database	SQL	SQL Syntax (519)
join database tables	Join	SQL Syntax (514)
obtain information submitted to a web server on an HTML form	Request Object	Ch. 1 (546), ASP Core Reference (224)
allow a user to send information back to the browse.	Response Object	Ch. 1 (543), ASP Reference (241)
integrate VBScript with HTML documents	VBScript, HTML	Ch. 2 (575), Ch. 5 (675), Ch. 6 (699), VBScript Reference (399), HTML Reference (319)
install the Personal Web Server	Personal Web Server (PWS)	Ch. 2 (582)
Install the Internet Information Server	Internet Information Server (IIS)	Ch. 1 (534)
set up a global.asa file	ASP Objects	Ch. 3 (594)
set properties for a user on the fly	Session Object	Ch. 3 (597), ASP Core Reference (268)
check for errors	Error Object	Ch. 4 (645), ASP Core Reference (92)
process transactions	Connection Object	Ch. 4 (621), ASP Reference (60)
register a COM Object	RegSrv32.DLL	Ch. 5 (690)
write an ActiveX script	ActiveX COM and HTML	Ch. 2 (589), Ch. 4 (611), Ch. 5 (687),
detect the client's browser	Server-side scripting	Ch. 5 (675), Ch. 6 (700)

If you want to...	Use this keyword	Located on these pages
package and ship components	Visual Basic Packaging and Deployment	Ch. 6 (708)
send information to a client	Response Object	Ch. 1, (543), ASP Core Reference (241)
use an editor to write ASP	Visual Interdev, HTML Editors	Ch. 5 (683), Ch. 6 (716)

ASP by Category

The following table lists the ASP keywords that you can use to find any method, property or object pertaining to the core of the Active Server Page technology. The leftmost column contains the keyword, while the center column states the category that the keyword is a part of.

Keyword	Category	Page Number in ASP Core Reference Section
Abandon	Session Object Method	270
AbsolutePage	Recordset Object Property	208
AbsolutePosition	Recordset Object Property	208
ActiveCommand	Recordset Object Property	209
ActiveConnection	Command Object Property	49
ActiveConnection	Record Object Property	182
ActiveConnection	Recordset Object Property	209
AbsolutePage	Recordset Object Property	208
ActualSize	Field Object Property	100
Add	Dictionary Object Method	76
AddHeader	Response Object Method	244
AddNew	Recordset Object Method	186
Append	Field Collection Object Method	108
Append	Parameter Object Collection Method	162
AppendChunk	Field Object Method	98
AppendChunk	Parameter Object Method	156
AppendToLog	Response Object Method	245
Application_OnEnd	Application Object Event	39
Application_OnStart	Application Object Event	38
ASPCode	ASPError Object Property	42
ASPDescription	ASPError Object Property	42
AtEndOfLine	Text Stream Object Property	307
AtEndOfStream	Text Stream Object Property	307
Attributes	Connection Object Property	65
Attributes	Field Object Property	100
Attributes	File Object Property	114
Attributes	Folder Object Property	145
Attributes	Parameter Object Property	157
Attributes	Property Object Property	164
AvailableSpace	Drive Object Property	84
BeginTrans	Connection Object Method	57

Keyword	Category	Page Number in ASP Core Reference Section
BinaryWrite	Request Object Method	246
BinaryRead	Request Object Method	228
Bof	RecordSet Object Property	210
Bookmark	RecordSet Object Property	211
Buffer	Response Object Property	250
BuildPath	FileSystemObject Method	122
ClientCertificate	Request Object Property	225
CacheControl	Response Object Property	252
Cachesize	RecordSet Object Property	211
Cancel	Command Object Method	47
Cancel	RecordSet Object Method	187
Cancel	Connection Object Method	58
Cancel	Record Object Method	172
Cancel	Stream Object Method	277
CancelBatch	RecordSet Object Method	188
CancelUpdate	Field Collection Object Method	109
CancelUpdate	RecordSet Object Method	188
Category	ASPError Object Property	43
Charset	Response Object Property	253
Charset	Stream Object Property	291
Clear	Error Object Method	95
Clear	Response Object Method	247
ClientCertificate Collection	Request Object Collection	225
Clone	RecordSet Object Method	189
Close	Record Object Method	173
Close	RecordSet Object Method	190
Close	Text Stream Object Method	299
Close	Connection Object Method	59
Close	Stream Object Method	278
CodePage	Session Object Property	271
CopyFile	FileSystemObject Method	122

Continued

ASP by Category

Keyword	Category	Page Number in ASP Core Reference Section
CopyFolder	FileSystemObject Method	123
CopyRecord	Record Object Method	174
CopyTo	Stream Object Method	279
Column	ASPError Object Property	43
Column	Text Stream Object Property	308
CommitTrans	Connection Object Method	60
CommandText	Command Object Property	50
CommandTimeout	Command Object Property	51
CommandTimeout	Connecting Object Property	66
CommandType	Command Object Property	51
CommitTrans	Connection Object Method	60
CompareBookmarks	RecordSet Object Method	190
CompareMode	Dictionary Object Property	81
ConnectionString	Connection Object Property	67
ConnectionTimeout	Connection Object Property	68
Contents	Session Object Collection	274
Contents	Application Object Collection	36
Contents.Remove	Application Object Method	40
Contents.Remove	Session Object Method	270
Contents.RemoveAll	Application Object Method	40
Contents.RemoveAll	Session Object Method	271
ContentType	Response Object Property	253
Cookies Collection	Response Object Collection	241
Cookies Collection	Request Object Collection	230
Count	Dictionary Object Property	82
Count	Error Collection Object Property	96
Count	Field Collection Object Property	113
Count	Properties Collection Object Property	171
Count	Parameter Object Collection Property	163
Copy	Folder Object Method	141

Keyword	Category	Page Number in ASP Core Reference Section
CreateParameter	Command Object Method	47
CreateFolder	FileSystemObject Method	124
CreateObject	Command Object Method	46
CreateObject	Server Object Method	259
CreateTextFile	Folder Object Method	142
CreateTextFile	FileSystemObject Method	125
CursorLocation	RecordSet Object Property	212
CursorLocation	Connection Object Property	68
Cursortype	RecordSet Object Property	212
DateCreated	File Object Property	115
DateCreated	Folder Object Property	146
DateLastAccessed	File Object Property	116
DateLastAccessed	Folder Object Property	146
DateLastModified	File Object Property	116
DateLastModified	Folder Object Property	147
DefaultDatabase	Connection Object Property	69
DefinedSize	Field Object Property	101
Delete	Field Collection Object Method	110
Delete	Folder Object Method	143
Delete	Parameter Object Collection Method	162
Delete	RecordSet Object Method	191
DeleteFile	FileSystemObject Method	126
DeleteFolder	FileSystemObject Method	126
DeleteRecord	Record Object Method	176
Description	ASPError Object Property	44
Description	Error Object Property	92
Direction	Parameter Object Property	158
Drive	File Object Property	117
Drive	Folder Object Property	147
DriveLetterName	Drive Object Property	85

Continued

ASP by Category

Keyword	Category	Page Number in ASP Core Reference Section
DriveType	Drive Object Property	85
Drives	File System Object Property	140
Drives	Folder Collection Object Property	153
EditMode	RecordSet Object Property	213
End	Response Object Method	248
Eof	Recordset Object Property	210
Eos	Stream Object Property	292
Errors	Connection Object Collection	74
Execute	Connection Object Method	65
Execute	Command Object Method	48
Execute	Server Object Method	266
Exists	Dictionary Object Method	77
Expires	Response Object Property	254
ExpiresAbsolute	Response Object Property	255
Fields	RecordSet Object Property	223
File	ASPError Object Property	44
Files	Folder Object Property	148
Files	Folder Collection Object Property	154
FileExists	FileSystemObject Method	127
FileSystem	Drive Object Property	86
Filter	RecordSet Object Property	214
Find	RecordSet Object Method	192
Flush	Response Object Method	249
Flush	Stream Object Method	290
Folders	Folder Collection Object Property	155
FolderExists	FileSystemObject Method	128
Form	Request Object Collection	231
FreeSpace	Drive Object Property	87
GetAbsolutePathName	FileSystemObject Method	129
GetBaseName	FileSystemObject Method	129

Keyword	Category	Page Number in ASP Core Reference Section
GetChildren	Record Object Method	177
GetChunk	Field Object Method	99
GetDrive	FileSystemObject Method	130
GetDriveName	FileSystemObject Method	131
GetExtensionName	FileSystemObject Method	132
GetFile	FileSystemObject Method	132
GetFileName	FileSystemObject Method	133
GetFolder	FileSystemObject Method	134
GetLastError	Server Object Method	265
GetParentFolderName	FileSystemObject Method	135
GetRows	RecordSet Object Method	194
GetSpecialFolder	FileSystemObject Method	135
GetString	RecordSet Object Method	195
GetTempName	FileSystemObject Method	136
HTMLEncode	Server Object Method	261
Index	RecordSet Object Property	215
Inherited	Property Object Property	165
IsClientConnected	Response Object Property	255
IsolationLevel	Connection Object Property	70
IsReady	Drive Object Property	87
IsRootFolder	Folder Object Property	148
Item	Dictionary Object Property	83
Item	Error Object Property	97
Item	Field Collection Object Property	113
Item	Properties Collection Object Property	171
Items	Dictionary Object Method	78
Key	Dictionary Object Property	84
Keys	Dictionary Object Method	79
LCID	Session Object Property	272
Line	ASPError Object Property	45

Continued

ASP by Category

Keyword	Category	Page Number in ASP Core Reference Section
Line	Text Stream Object Property	309
LineSeparator	Stream Object Property	293
LoadFromFile	Stream Object Method	280
Lock	Application Object Method	41
LockType	RecordSet Object Property	216
MapPath	Server Object Method	262
MarshalOptions	RecordSet Object Property	216
MaxRecords	RecordSet Object Property	217
Mode	Connection Object Property	70
Mode	Record Object Property	182
Mode	Stream Object Property	293
Move	Folder Object Method	144
Move	RecordSet Object Method	197
MoveFile	FileSystemObject Method	137
MoveFirst	RecordSet Object Method	197
MoveFolder	FileSystemObject Method	138
MoveLast	RecordSet Object Method	198
MoveNext	RecordSet Object Method	198
MovePrevious	RecordSet Object Method	199
MoveRecord	Record Object Method	177
Name	Field Object Property	102
Name	File Object Property	117
Name	Folder Object Property	149
Name	Parameter Object Property	159
Name	Property Object Property	166
Name	Command Object Property	52
Name	Property Object Property	166
NativeError	Error Object Property	92
NextRecordset	RecordSet Object Method	199
Number	Error Object Property	93
Number	ASPError Object Property	45
NumericScale	Field Object Property	102

Keyword	Category	Page Number in ASP Core Reference Section
NumericScale	Parameter Object Property	159
Open	Connection Object Method	61
Open	RecordSet Object Method	201
Open	Record Object Method	179
Open	Stream Object Method	281
OpenSchema	Connection Object Method	63
OpenTextFile	FileSystemObject Method	139
OriginalValue	Field Object Property	103
PageCount	RecordSet Object Property	218
PageSize	RecordSet Object Property	218
ParentFolder	File Object Property	118
ParentFolder	Folder Object Property	150
ParentURL	Record Object Property	183
Path	Drive Object Property	88
Path	File Object Property	119
Path	Folder Object Property	150
PICS	Response Object Property	257
Position	Stream Object Property	294
Precision	Field Object Property	103
Precision	Parameter Object Property	159
Prepared	Command Object-Property	52
Properties	RecordSet Object Property	224
Provider	Connection Object Property	72
QueryString	Request Collection	232
Read	Text Stream Object Method	299
Read	Stream Object Method	283
ReadAll	Text Stream Object Method	300
ReadLine	Text Stream Object Method	301
ReadText	Stream Object Method	284
RecordCount	RecordSet Object Property	219
RecordType	Record Object Property	184

Continued

Keyword	Category	Page Number in ASP Core Reference Section
Redirect	Response Object Method	249
Refresh	Error Object Collection Method	96
Refresh	Field Collection Object Method	111
Refresh	Parameter Object Collection Method	163
Refresh	Properties Collection Object Method	170
Remove	Dictionary Object Method	80
RemoveAll	Dictionary Object Method	81
Requery	RecordSet Object Method	202
Resync	Field Collection Object Method	111
Resync	RecordSet Object Method	203
RollBackTrans	Connection Object Method	64
RootFolder	Drive Object Property	89
Save	RecordSet Object Method	204
SaveToFile	Stream Object Method	285
ScriptTimeout	Server Object Property	267
SerialNumber	Drive Object Property	89
ServerVariables	Request Object Collection	234
SessionID	Session Object Property	273
Session_OnEnd	Session Object Events	269
Session_OnStart	Session Object Events	268
SetEOS	Stream Object Method	286
ShareName	Drive Object Property	90
ShortName	File Object Property	119
ShortName	Folder Object Property	151
ShortPath	File Object Property	120
Size	Parameter Object Property	160
Size	File Object Property	120
Size	Folder Object Property	151

Keyword	Category	Page Number in ASP Core Reference Section
Size	Stream Object Property	295
Skip	Text Stream Object Method	302
SkipLine	Text Stream Object Method	303
SkipLine	Stream Object Method	287
Sort	RecordSet Object Property	219
Sorce	ASPError Object Property	46
Source	Record Object Property	184
Source	RecordSet Object Property	220
Source	Error Object Property	94
SQLState	Error Object Property	94
State	Command Object Property	53
State	Connection Object Property	72
State	Record Object Property	185
State	Stream Object Property	296
State	RecordSet Object Property	221
StaticObjects Collection	Session Object	275
StaticObjects Collection	Application Object	37
Status	Field Object Property	104
Status	RecordSet Object Property	222
Status	Response Object Property	256
StayinSync	RecordSet Object Property	223
SubFolders	Folder Object Property	152
Supports	RecordSet Object Method	205
Timeout	Session Object Property	274
TotalBytes	Request Object Property	229
TotalSize	Drive Object Property	90
Transfer	Server Object Method	264
Type	Field Object Property	105
Type	File Object Property	121
Type	Folder Object Property	152
Type	Parameter Object Property	161
Type	Property Object Property	167

ASP by Category

Continued

ASP by Category

Keyword	Category	Page Number in ASP Core Reference Section
Type	Stream Object Property	298
Type	Property Object Property	167
UnderlyingValue	Field Object Property	106
Unlock	Application Object Method	41
Update	Field Collection Object Method	112
Update	RecordSet Object Method	206
UpdateBatch	RecordSet Object Method	207
URLEncode	Server Object Method	263
Value	Field Object Property	107
Value	Parameter Object Property	162
Value	Property Object Property	168
Version	Connection Object Property	73
VolumeName	Drive Object Property	91
Write	Response Object Method	250
Write	Text Stream Object Method	304
Write	Stream Object Method	288
WriteBlankLine	Text Stream Object Method	306
WriteLine	Text Stream Object Method	305
WriteText	Stream Object Method	289

in plain english in p
sh in plain english in
glish in plain english
in plain english in p
sh in plain english in
glish in plain english
in plain english in p
glish in plain english
in plain english in p
sh in plain english in
glish in plain english
in plain english in p
sh in plain english in
glish in plain english
in plain english in p
lish in plain english
in plain english in p
sh in plain english in
glish in plain english
in plain english in p
sh in plain english in
lish in plain english
n plain english in p
glish in plain english

ASP A to Z

This reference is a table of the terms and keywords covered in the ASP Core Reference section. This table is an alphabetically ordered list of Active Server Pages keywords. It also lists the page number where each term or keyword can be found in the ASP Core Reference section.

Keyword	Located on this page in the ASP Core Reference section
Abandon	270
Absolute Page	208
Absolute Position	208
ActiveCommand	209
ActiveConnection	49
ActiveConnection	182
ActiveConnection	209
ActualSize	100
Add	76
AddHeader	244
AddNew	186
Append	108
Append	162
AppendChunk	98
AppendChunk	156
AppendToLog	245
Application.Contents.Remove	40
Application.Contents.Remove.All	40
Application_OnEnd	39
Application_OnStart	38
AspCode	42
AspDescription	42
AtEndOfLine	307
AtEndOfStream	307
Attributes	65
Attributes	100
Attributes	114
Attributes	145
Attributes	157
Attributes	164
AvailableSpace	84
BeginTrans	57
BinaryRead	228

ASP A to Z

Keyword	Located on this page in the ASP Core Reference section
BinaryWrite	246
BOF	210
Bookmark	211
Buffer	250
BuildPath	122
CacheControl	252
CacheSize	211
Cancel	47
Cancel	58
Cancel	172
Cancel	187
Cancel	277
CancelBatch	188
CancelUpdate	109
CancelUpdate	188
Category	43
Charset	253
Charset	291
Clear	95
Clear	247
ClientCertificate	225
Clone	189
Close	59
Close	173
Close	190
Close	278
CodePage	271
Column	43
Column	308
CommandText	50
CommandTimeout	51
CommandTimeout	66

Continued

ASP A to Z

ASP A to Z

Keyword	Located on this page in the ASP Core Reference section
CommandType	51
CommitTrans	60
CompareBookmarks	190
CompareMode	81
ConnectionString	67
ConnectionTimeout	68
Contents	36
Contents	274
Contents.Remove	270
Contents.RemoveAll	271
ContentType	253
Cookies	230
Cookies	241
Copy	141
CopyFile	122
CopyFolder	123
CopyRecord	174
CopyTo	279
Count	82
Count	96
Count	113
Count	163
Count	171
CreateFolder	124
CreateObject	259
CreateParameter	47
CreateTextField	126
CreateTextFile	142
CursorLocation	68
CursorLocation	212
CursorType	212
DateCreated	115
DateCreated	146

Keyword	Located on this page in the ASP Core Reference section
DateLastAccessed	116
DateLastAccessed	146
DateLastModified	116
DateLastModified	147
DefaultDatabase	69
DefinedSize	101
Delete	110
Delete	143
Delete	162
Delete	191
DeleteFile	126
DeleteFolder	126
DeleteRecord	176
Description	44
Description	92
Direction	158
Drive	117
Drive	147
DriveLetter	85
Drives	140
Drives	153
DriveType	85
EditMode	213
End	248
EOF	210
EOS	292
Errors	74
Execute	48
Execute	266
Exists	77
Expires	254
ExpiresAbsolute	255

ASP A to Z

Continued

Keyword	Located on this page in the ASP Core Reference section
Fields	223
File	44
FileExists	127
Files	148
Files	154
FileSystem	86
Filter	214
Find	192
Flush	249
Flush	290
FolderExists	128
Folders	155
Form	231
FreeSpace	87
GetAbsolutePathName	129
GetBaseName	129
GetChildren	177
GetChunk	99
GetDrive	130
GetDriveName	131
GetExtensionName	132
GetFile	132
GetFileName	133
GetFolder	134
GetLastError	265
GetParentFolderName	135
GetRows	194
GetSpecialFolder	135
GetString	195
GetTempName	136
HTMLEncode	261
Index	215
Inherited	165

ASP A to Z

Keyword	Located on this page in the ASP Core Reference section
IsClientConnected	255
IsolationLevel	70
IsReady	87
IsRootFolder	148
Item	83
Item	97
Item	113
Item	171
Items	78
Key	84
Keys	79
LCID	272
Line	45
Line	309
LineSeparator	293
LoadFromFile	280
Lock	41
LockType	216
MapPath	262
MarshalOptions	216
MaxRecords	217
Mode	70
Mode	182
Mode	293
Move	144
Move	197
MoveFile	137
MoveFirst	197
MoveFolder	138
MoveLast	198
MoveNext	198
MovePrevious	199

Continued

ASP A to Z

Keyword	Located on this page in the ASP Core Reference section
MoveRecord	177
Name	52
Name	102
Name	117
Name	149
Name	159
Name	166
NativeError	92
NextRecordSet	199
Number	45
Number	93
NumericScale	102
NumericScale	159
Open	61
Open	179
Open	201
Open	281
OpenSchema	63
OpenTextFile	139
OriginalValue	103
PageCount	218
PageSize	218
Parameters	53
ParentFolder	118
ParentFolder	150
ParentURL	183
Path	88
Path	119
Path	150
PICS	257
Position	294
Precision	103
Precision	159

Keyword	Located on this page in the ASP Core Reference section
Prepared	52
Properties	54
Properties	75
Properties	224
Provider	72
QueryString	232
Read	283
ReadAll	300
ReadLine	301
ReadText	284
Record Object Method	172
RecordCount	219
RecordSet Object Method	186
RecordSet Object Properties	208
RecordType	184
Redirect	249
Refresh	96
Refresh	111
Refresh	163
Refresh	170
Remove	80
RemoveAll	81
Requery	202
Request Object Collection	224
Request Object Properties	229
Resync	111
Resync	203
RollbackTrans	64
RootFolder	89
Save	204
SaveToFile	285
ScriptTimeout	267

ASP A to Z

Continued

Keyword	Located on this page in the ASP Core Reference section
SerialNumber	89
ServerVariables	234
Session Object Event	268
Session_OnEnd	269
Session_OnStart	268
SessionID	273
SetEOS	286
ShareName	90
ShortName	119
ShortName	151
ShortPath	120
Size	120
Size	151
Size	160
Size	295
Skip	302
SkipLine	287
SkipLine	303
Sort	219
Source	46
Source	94
Source	184
Source	220
SQLState	94
State	53
State	72
State	185
State	221
State	296
StaticObjects	37
StaticObjects	275
Status	104

Keyword	Located on this page in the ASP Core Reference section
Status	222
Status	256
StayinSync	223
SubFolders	152
Supports	205
Timeout	274
TotalBytes	229
TotalSize	90
Transfer	264
Type	105
Type	121
Type	152
Type	161
Type	167
Type	298
UnderlyingValue	106
Unlock	41
Update	112
Update	206
UpdateBatch	207
URLEncode	263
Value	107
Value	162
Value	168
Version	73
VolumeName	91
Write	250
Write	288
Write	304
WriteBlankLines	306
WriteLine	305
WriteText	289

ASP A to Z

ASP Core Reference

The ASP Core Reference material is the heart of this book. This section covers the details for all the methods and properties associated with the objects involved with Active Server Pages (ASP).

The ASP keywords are organized alphabetically within the 26 ASP object categories. The ASP object categories begin with the Application object and end with the TextStream object. This section covers the following objects: Application, AspError, Command, Connection, Dictionary, Drive, Error, Error Object Collection, Field, Fields Collection, File, FileSystemObject, Folder, Folder Collection, Parameter, Parameter Object Collection, Property, Properties Collection, Record, RecordSet, RecordSet Collection, Request, Response, Session, Stream and TextStream objects.

Application Object

Purpose

The Application object is used to create variables and objects that are applied to all users of an ASP project. These variables and objects are loaded into memory the first time any user accesses the application. They are in memory until the Web server shuts down.

Syntax

```
Application.Collection
Application.Property
Application.Method
Application("variable")
```

Contents	Application Object Collection

Purpose

Use this collection to obtain the names of all items associated with the Application object.Syntax

```
Application.Contents(NameOfContent)
```

Table 1 lists the argument associated with the Contents collection.

Table 1 *Arguments for the Contents Collection*

Value	Required	Type	Description
NameOfContent	Yes	String	The name of the item in the collection

Example

The following example shows you how to retrieve all the items assoicated witht the Application object:

```
<%
For each Thing in Application.Contents
    Response.Write Thing
    Response.Write "<BR>"
Next
%<


'If you want to use the Application Content's Count method
'to list 'all the objects in the Application Content then use
' this code.
```

```
<% For   j = 0 to Application.Contents.Count
     Response.Write Application.Contents.Key(j)
     Response.Write "<BR>"
     Response.Write Application.Contents.Item(j)
Next%>
```

StaticObjects   Application Object Collection

Purpose

Use this collection when you need to determine the value of a specific property for an object. The objects created with the <OBJECT> tags represent
everything within the scope of the Application object.

●─CROSS-REFERENCE

The <OBJECT> tag is covered in the HTML Syntax Reference section.

Syntax

```
Application.StaticObjects(NameOfObject)
```

Table 2 lists the arguments associated with the StaticObjects collection.

Table 2 *Arguments for the StaticObjects Collection*

Value	Required	Type	Description
NameOfObject	Yes	String	The name of the item in the collection

Examples

The following example shows two objects being created with application
scope in the global.asa file. Then, in a different Web page, the Application
object's StaticObjects collection is used to find the names of the
Application objects created with the <OBJECT> tag.

In the global.asa file:

```
<OBJECT RUNAT=Server SCOPE=Application ID=MyInfo
PROGID="MSWC.MyInfo">
</OBJECT>
<OBJECT RUNAT=Server SCOPE=Application ID=TheAdRot
PROGID="MSWC.AdRotator">
</OBJECT>
```

In any other ASP:

```
<%
For each key in Application.StaticObjects
    Response.Write key
    Response.Write "<BR>"
Next
%>
```

```
This is the result of running the Application.StaticObjects.
MyInfo
TheAdRot
```

Application_OnStart   Application Object Event

Purpose

Use this event to execute whenever any user starts your ASP application for the first time. You place the code to this event in the global.asa file. This event is called only one time.

Syntax

```
<SCRIPT LANGUAGE=ScriptLanguage RUNAT=Server>
Sub Application_OnStart
. . . your code
End Sub
</SCRIPT>
```

Example

The following example shows you how to initialize the application variables CompanyName, CompanyAddress, and WebAddress when the Application_object's OnStart event occurs in the global.asa file. In addition, the example shows you how to use to store an array as an application variable in the Application object's On_Start event.

```
<SCRIPT LANGUAGE=ScriptLanguage RUNAT=Server>
Sub Application_OnStart
Application("CompanyName") = "ExtremeStyle INC"
Application("CompanyAddress") = "Jacksonville Florida"
Application("WebAddress") = www.extremestyle.com

Dim appExtremePeople(6)
AppExtremePeople(0) = "Robert Futrell"
AppExtremePeople(1) = "Ray "
```

```
AppExtremePeople(2) = "Jenn"
AppExtremePeople(3) = "Eric"
AppExtremePeople(4) = "Steve"
AppExtremePeople(5) = "Kitty Boo"
Application("ExtremeP") = appExtremePeople

End Sub
</SCRIPT>
```

Application_OnEnd   Application Object Event

Purpose

Use this event to execute whenever the Web server shuts down. The down-side of this event is that the Session, Response, and Request objects are closed before this event is executed; therefore, you can not use any of these objects in this event. There really isn't much you can do when this event executes.

Syntax

```
<SCRIPT LANGUAGE=ScriptLanguage RUNAT=Server>
Sub Application_OnEnd

. . .
End Sub
</SCRIPT>
```

Example

The following example destroys the application variable Abarray before the Application_object's OnEnd event finishes:

```
<SCRIPT LANGUAGE=ScriptLanguage RUNAT=Server>
<Object RUNAT = Server Scope=Application ID= MyObj PROGID =
"MSWC.AdRotator">

Sub Application_OnStart
End Sub


Sub Application_OnEnd
    Set Application("Abarray") = nothing
End Sub
</SCRIPT>
```

ASP Core Reference

Application.Contents.Remove | Application Object Method

Purpose

Use this method to delete an item from the Contents collection.

Syntax

```
Application.Contents.Remove(NameOfVarible |
NameOfVariableIndex)
```

Table 3 lists the arguments associated with the Application.Contents. Remove method.

Table 3   *Arguments for the Application.Contents.Remove Method*

Value	Required	Type	Description
NameOfVariable	Yes	String	The name of the application variable

Example

This example adds two application variables to the Application.Contents collection and then removes one:

```
<%
    Application("strA")=("A Item")
    Application("strB")=("B Item")
    Application.Contents.Remove(strA)
%>
```

Application.Contents. RemoveAll | Application Object Method

Purpose

Use this method to remove all items that have been added to the Application.Contents collection.

Syntax

```
Application.Contents.RemoveAll ()
```

Example

The following example removes all the items in the Application.Contents collection:

```
<%
Application.Contents.RemoveAll()
%>
```

ASP Core Reference

Lock	**Application Object Method**

Purpose

Use this method to lock an application variable from being changed.

Syntax

```
Application.Lock
```

Example

The following example uses the Application object's Lock method to allow only one user to change the application variable Password. Once the application variable has been changed, then the script uses the UnLock method to release the lock.

```
<%
Application.Lock
Application("Password") =
"www.ExtremeStyle.com"
Application.Unlock
%>
```

Unlock	**Application Object Method**

Purpose

Use this method when you need to allow other users to change the Application object variables after the object is locked with the Lock method. If you do not call this method, the Web server unlocks the Application object when the .asp file stops executing.

Syntax

```
Application.Unlock
```

Example

The following example uses the Application object's Unlock method to release the lock that is placed on the program while the application variable "Location" is changed. Until Unlock executes, no one can change any Application variables.

```
<%
'change the connection object's
Application.Lock
Application("Location") = "Warner Robins, Georgia"
Application.Unlock
%>
```

ASP Core Reference

AspError Object

Purpose

This is a new object for Internet Information Server (IIS) 5.0. There are no events or methods with the AspError object, only properties

●─CROSS-REFERENCE────────────────────

Chapter 1 in the Tutorial section covers the AspError object.

Syntax

ASPError.Property

AspCode	**AspError Object Property**

Purpose

Use this property to return an error code generated by IIS 5.0. A string data type returns from this property.

Syntax

AspErrorObject.ASPCode

Example

Use this code in the error page to which IIS 5.0 redirects errors:

```
<%
'this returns the last ASPError object
Set AspError = Server.GetLastError()
If AspError.ASPCode > "" then
    Response.Write "The AspCode is "
    Response.Write AspError.ASPCode
End if
%>
```

AspDescription	**AspError Object Property**

Purpose

Use this property to return a detailed description of an ASP-related error. This property returns a string.

Syntax

AspErrorObject.AspDescription

Example

In the page to which IIS 5.0 redirects errors, use the following code to find the AspCode property:

```
<%
'this returns the last AspError object
Set AspError = Server.GetLastError()
If AspError.AspDescription > "" then
    Response.Write "The
AspDescription is "
    Response.Write
AspError.AspDescription
End if
%>
```

Category   AspError Object Property

Purpose

Use this property to determine if the source of the error was internal to your ASP application, the scripting language, or an object in your code. This property returns a string.

Syntax

```
AspErrorObject.Category
```

Example

Use this code in the error page to which IIS 5.0 redirects errors:

```
<%
'this returns the last AspError object
Set AspError = Server.GetLastError()
If AspError.Category > "" then
    Response.Write "The Category is "
    Response.Write AspError.Category
End if
%>
```

Column   AspError Object Property

Purpose

Use this property to indicate the column number within an .asp file that generated an error. This property returns a long integer data type.

Syntax

```
Long integer = AspErrorObject.Column
```

Example

Use this code in the error page to which IIS 5.0 redirects errors:

```
<%
'this returns the last ASPError object
Set AspError = Server.GetLastError()
If AspError.Source > "" then
    Response.Write "The Column Number is "
    Response.Write AspError.Column
End if
%>
```

Description   AspError Object Property

Purpose

Use this property to return a short description of the error.

Syntax

```
String = AspErrorObject.Description
```

Example

In the page to which IIS 5.0 redirects errors, use the following code to find
the AspCode property:

```
<%
'this returns the last ASPError object
Set AspError = Server.GetLastError()
If AspError.Description > "" then
    Response.Write "The Description is "
    Response.Write AspError.Description
End if
%>
```

File   AspError Object Property

Purpose

Use this property to determine the name of the .asp file that is involved in
the error.

Syntax

```
String = AspErrorObject.File
```

Example

Use this code in the error page to which IIS 5.0 redirects errors:

```
<%
'this returns the last AspError object
Set AspError = Server.GetLastError()
If AspError.File > "" then
    Response.Write "The File is "
    Response.Write AspError.File
End if
%>
```

Line
AspError Object Property

Purpose

Use this property to determine the line number that generated the code inside an .asp file. This property returns a long integer.

Syntax

```
LongInteger = AspErrorObject.Line
```

Example

Use this code in the error page to which IIS 5.0 redirects errors:

```
<%
'this returns the last AspError object
Set AspError = Server.GetLastError()
If AspError.Source > "" then
    Response.Write "The Line number the error
occurred at is "
    Response.Write AspError.Line
End if
%>
```

Number
AspError Object Property

Purpose

Use this property to return the standard COM error code.

Syntax

```
AspErrorObject.Number
```

Example

Use this code in the error page to which IIS 5.0 redirects errors:

```
<%
'this returns the last AspError object
Set AspError = Server.GetLastError()
If AspError.Number > "" then
    Response.Write "The Number is "
    Response.Write AspError.Number
End if
%>
```

Source	AspError Object Property

Purpose

Use this property to return the source code of the line that caused the error. This property returns a string data type.

Syntax

```
String = AspErrorObject.Source
```

Example

Use this code in the error page to which IIS 5.0 redirects errors:

```
<%
'this returns the last AspError object
Set AspError = Server.GetLastError()
If AspError.Source > "" then
Response.Write "The source of the
error is "
Response.Write AspError.Source
End if
%>
```

Command Object

Purpose

Use the Command object to pass parameters to a stored procedure. However, you can also use this object to pass SQL queries to your database.

Syntax

```
Set CommandObject =
Server.CreateObject("ADODB.Command")
```

```
CommandObject.Collection
CommandObject.Property
CommandObject.Method
```

Cancel   Command Object Method

Purpose
Use this method to cancel the execution of a pending Execute method call.

Syntax

```
CommandObject.Cancel
```

If the ExecuteOptionEnum constant adExecuteAsync option is not used with the Execute call, a run-time error will be generated.

Example
This script shows you how to cancel a pending Execute method call:

```
Set CmdObj = Server.CreateObject("ADODB.Command")
CmdObj.CommandText = "Select * From SomeTable"
CmdObj.ActiveConnection = YourConnectionObject
CmdObj.Execute
CmdObj.Cancel
```

CreateParameter   Command Object Method

Purpose
Use this method to pass arguments to stored procedures. The direction argument needs a ParameterDirectionEnum constant.

●—CROSS-REFERENCE
The ParameterDirectionEnum constants are available at the URL noted in the Preface.

Syntax

```
Set Parameter = CommandObject.CreateParameter( Name, Type,
Direction, Size,
Value)
```

Table 4 lists the arguments associated with the CreateParameter method.

ASP Core Reference

Table 4 *Arguments for the CreateParameter Method*

Value	Required	Type	Description
Name	No	String	The name that you want to give the parameter
Type	No	DataTypeEnum	The data type of the parameter. The datatype can be any of the DataType enumerated constants. The default is adEmpty.
Direction	No	Parameter DirectionEnum	This indicates which way the parameter is going: in, out, or both ways. The default is adParamInput.
Size	No	Long	The maximum size that the parameter value can be in character or bytes. The default is 0.
Value	No	Variant	The value you want to set the parameter to.

Examples

This script shows you how to use the CreateParameter method:

```
Set ComandObj = Server.CreateObject("ADODB.Command")
'create the parameter object
Set Para = ComandObj.CreateParameter("MyPara",adLong,
adParamInput, 9,125)
```

Or, you can do this:

```
Set Para = CommandObj.CreateParameter
Para.Name = "MyPara"
Para.Type = adLong
Para.Direction = adParamInput
Para.Size = 9
Para.Value = 125
```

Execute   Command Object Method

Purpose

Use this method to execute a query, SQL statement, or stored procedure that you set in the CommandText property.

Syntax

```
Set RecordSet = CommandObject.Execute(RecordAffected,
Parameters, Options)
```

Table 5 lists the arguments associated with the Execute method.

Table 5   *Arguments for the Execute Method*

Name	Required	Type	Description
RecordsAffected	No	Long	This is a variable that you provide. When this method executes the number of records affected by the Command object will be stored in this variable.
Parameters	No	Variant	An array of parameter values passed with a SQL statement. Output parameters will not return correct values if passed here.
Options	No	Long	You tell the database provider how to interpret the CommandText property of the Command object.

Example

The following example shows you how to use the RecordAffect variable:

```
CommObj.CommandText = "Update Name Set
FName = 'Rats'
Where LastName = 'Smith'"
CommandObj.Execute myNumOfRecsAff
Response.Write "Number of Records Changed "
Response.Write myNumOfRecsAff
```

Parameter values passed in the Parameters argument will override any previously set values.

ActiveConnection   Command Object Property

Purpose

Use this property to get or set the currently opened Connection object.

Syntax

To set the ActiveConnection property, use the following code:

```
Set CommandObject.ActiveConnection = ConnectionObject
```

To get the ActiveConnection property, use this code:

```
String = Command.ActiveConnection
```

Example

The following example sets the Command object's ActiveConnection property to the Connection object's active connection. For the purposes of this example, we will assume that the Connection object already has an active connection and the name of that active connection is DataConn.

```
'Assume the DataConn is the Connection object
'set the commandobject
Set CommandObj = Server.CreateObject ("ADODB.Command")
CommandObj.ActiveConnection = DataConn
```

● TIP

Always try to use an existing data connection.

CommandText	Command Object Property

Purpose

Use this property to get or set the command text. The CommandText is the string that contains either a SQL statement or the call to a stored procedure.

Syntax

```
CommandObject.CommandText = "some sql statement" or "stored
procedure"
```

Examples

The following code shows you how to set the Command object's CommandText property with a SQL statement:

```
CommandObj.CommendText("Select * From AnyTable")
Or
CommmandObj.CommandText("Insert Into AnyTable (col1)
values('auburn')")
Command.Excute
```

The following example shows you how to retrieve the Command object's CommandText property:

```
Dim strComText
StrComText = CommandObj.CommandText
```

CommandTimeout   Command Object Property

Purpose

Use this property to either set or get the amount of time (in seconds) that you will allow a command to execute before an error is generated. The property is set to seconds.

Syntax

```
CommandObject.CommandTimeout = time in seconds
Long  = CommandObject.CommandTimeout
```

Example

Use the following to get the CommandTimeout property:

```
Set CmdObj = Server.CreateObject("ADODB.Command")
Long = CmdObj.CommandTimeout
```

Use this next example to set the CommandTimeout property to 20 seconds:

```
CmdObj.CommandTimeout = 20
```

Once the command exceeds the 20 seconds, an error is generated.

●—NOTE

The Command object's CommandTimeout property has nothing to do with this property.

CommandType   Command Object Property

Purpose

Use this property to let the database provider know what type of command is being executed before the command actually executes.

This property can help you a lot. By setting this property before using the Execute method, you can improve the processing of the command. This property either returns a CommandTypeEnum constant or is set with a CommandTypeEnum constant.

Syntax

```
CommandTypeEnum = CommandObject.CommandType
CommandObject.CommandType = CommandTypeEnum
```

●—CROSS-REFERENCE

The CommandType enumeration constants are available at the URL noted in the Preface.

Example

If you know that no records will be returned from a command, use the adExecuteEnum constants adCmdStoredProc + adExecuteNoRecords:

```
CommandObj.CommandType = adCmdStoredProc + adExecuteNoRecords
```

By notifying the database provider that no records will be returned, the provider can go directly to its internal code, thereby increasing the speed of the process.

Name   Command Object Property

Purpose

Use this property to either set or return the Command object's actual name (such as Susan or Hal.) You know Hal, don't you? He nearly killed Dave in "2001: A Space Odyssey."

Syntax

```
CommandObject.Name
```

Examples

Use the following to set the name:

```
CommandObject.Name = "Hal"
```

Use this to get the name:

```
String = CommandObject.Name
```

Prepared   Command Object Property

Purpose

Use this property to determine whether the ADO should create a compiled version of the CommandText before executing it. This property is set to either True or False. False is the default setting.

Syntax

```
CommandObject.Prepared
```

Example

The following example sets the Prepared property to True:

```
CommandObj.Prepared = True
```

The next example gets the Boolean value of the Prepared property:

```
Dim tboolean
Tboolean = CommandObj.Prepared
```

Not all database providers can create a complied version of the commandText. If the database provider cannot support it, when you try to get the state of the `Prepared` property, a False will be returned.

State	**Command Object Property**

Purpose

Use this property to determine the state of a command object. The state of a Command object is open, closed, or currently being processed. This property returns an `ObjectStateEnum` constant.

Syntax

```
ObjectStateEnum = CommandObject.State
```

●—**CROSS-REFERENCE**————————————————————————————

The `ObjectState` enumeration constants are available at the URL noted in the Preface.

Example

The following example shows you how to use the `State` property to determine if the Command object is in a state of executing:

```
'to find out if the Command object is in
'a state of executing.
If CommandObject.State = adStateExecuting then
    Response.Write "command executing"
End if
```

Parameters	**Command Object Collection**

Purpose

Contains the entire `Parameters` collection contained in a Command object.

Syntax

```
Parameters = CommandObject.Parameters
```

Examples

The Command object uses the `Parameters Object Collection` to pass arguments to a stored procedure. The `Parameter` object's `Append` method (p. 162) is used to add a `Parameter` object to the collection. The following code shows you how to add a Parameter object named "ParameterObject" to the Parameters collection:

```
'CommandObj1 is the Command object already created
Set ParameterObject =
CommandObj1.CreateParameter("MyPara1",adInteger, adParamInput,
8,
120)
CommandObject.append ParameterObject
```

If you want to find out the name and type of all the Parameter objects in the Command collection, use the following script.

```
For each Pobject in CommandObj1
Response.Write CommandObj1.Name
Response.Write Type
Next
```

Properties	Command Object Collection

Purpose

This collection contains all the Properties objects for a Command object.

Syntax

```
Properties = Command.Properties
```

Example

The following example shows you how to determine all the properties in a Command object :

```
set conn4 = Server.CreateObject("ADODB.Connection")
conn4.Open Application("db_ConnectionString")
set CommObj = Server.CreateObject("ADODB.Command")
CommObj.ActiveConnection = conn4
CommObj.CommandText = "sp_getStates"
For each Item in CommObj.Properties
    Response.Write Item.Name
    Response.Write " = "
    Response.Write Item.Value
    Response.Write "<BR>"
Next
CommObj.Execute
'destroy the objects

set CommObj = nothing
set conn4 = nothing
```

The following list is typical of what you might retrieve:

```
Preserve on Abort = False
Blocking Storage Objects = True
Use Bookmarks = False
Skip Deleted Bookmarks = False
Bookmark Type = 1
Fetch Backwards = False
Hold Rows = False
Scroll Backwards = False
Column Privileges = False
Command Time Out = 30
Preserve on Commit = False
Delay Storage Object Updates = False
Immobile Rows = True
Literal Bookmarks = False
Literal Row Identity = True
Maximum Open Rows = 0
Maximum Pending Rows = 0
Maximum Rows = 0
Notification Phases = 31
Others' Inserts Visible = False
Others' Changes Visible = False
Own Inserts Visible = False
Own Changes Visible = False
Quick Restart = False
Reentrant Events = True
Remove Deleted Rows = False
Report Multiple Changes = False
Row Privileges = False
Row Threading Model = 1
Objects Transacted = False
Updatability = 0
Strong Row Identity = False
IAccessor = True
IColumnsInfo = True
IColumnsRowset = True
IConnectionPointContainer = False
IRowset = True
IRowsetChange = False
IRowsetIdentity = False
IRowsetInfo = True
IRowsetLocate = False
IRowsetResynch = False
```

```
IRowsetScroll = False
IRowsetUpdate = False
ISupportErrorInfo = True
ISequentialStream = False
Column Set Notification = 3
Row Delete Notification = 3
Row First Change Notification = 3
Row Insert Notification = 3
Row Resynchronization Notification = 3
Rowset Release Notification = 3
Rowset Fetch Position Change Notification = 3
Row Undo Change Notification = 3
Row Undo Delete Notification = 3
Row Undo Insert Notification = 3
Row Update Notification = 3
Change Inserted Rows = True
Return Pending Inserts = False
IConvertType = True
Notification Granularity = 1
Access Order = 1
Bookmark Information = 0
Unique Rows = False
Query Based Updates/Deletes/Inserts = False
Generate a Rowset that can be marshalled = False
Position on the last row after insert = False
IRowsetChangeExtInfo = False
ODBC Cursor Type = 0
ODBC Concurrency Type = 15
BLOB accessibility on Forward-Only cursor = False
Include SQL_FLOAT, SQL_DOUBLE, and SQL_REAL in QBU where
clauses = False
Force SQL Server Firehose Mode cursor = False
Force no parameter rebinding when executing a command = False
Force no command preparation when executing a parameterized
command = False
Force no command reexecution when failure to satisfy all
required properties = False
Bookmarkable = False
```

Connection Object

Purpose

Use the Connection object to handle the creation of a connection to a data-source.

Syntax

```
Set ConnectionObject = Server.CreateObject
("ADODB.Connection")
ConnectionObject.Collection
ConnectionObject.Property
ConnectionObject.Method
```

BeginTrans   Connection Object Method

Purpose

Use this method to begin a database transaction. Anytime you use a
Structured Query Language (SQL) Insert, Update or Delete statement, a
database transaction occurs. If an error occurs during the transaction, you
don't want a change to the database to happen. That's why database transactions take an "all or nothing" approach — either the database gets changed or
nothing is done.

A visual representation of the database transaction process is shown in the
figure. The first step in starting a database transaction is the BeginTrans
method. Once this method is called, any changes to a database are cached
until the transaction is rolled backed or committed.

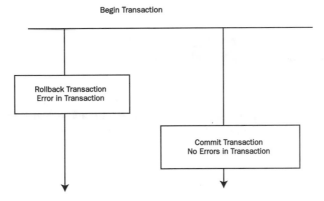

Begin Transaction

Rollback Transaction
Error in Transaction

Commit Transaction
No Errors in Transaction

The database transaction process

Syntax

```
Transaction Nesting Level = Connectionobject.BeginTrans()
BeginTrans returns a Long data type.  The returned value
indicates the nesting level of the transaction.
```

Example

The following example makes a change to the table Baseball. Thus, a transaction will take place if the SQL statement executed on the Connection object
DataConn is sucessful. In order to start the transaction process, the method

BeginTrans is executed before the Connection object DataConn. finishes. Once the SQL statement is executed, we test for errors in the Connection object. If errors exist, changes to the table Baseball are changed back to the way they were before the SQL statement was executed. If no errors exist, the changes are commited to the table.

```
Dim DataConn
Dim SqlString
Set DataConn = Server.CreateObject ("ADODB.Connection")
DataConn.ConnectionString = connString
DataConn.Open
'Start the Transaction
DataConn.BeginTrans
SqlString = "Delete * From Baseball Where RBI < 30 "
DataConn.Execute (SqlString)
If DataConn.Errors.Count > 0 then
    For each error in DataConn.Errors
        Response.Write Error.number
    Next
    DataConn.RollbackTrans
Else
    DataConn.CommitTrans
End if
```

Cancel	**Connection Object Method**

Purpose

Use this method to stop any pending, asynchronous Execute or Open operation. If you supply the Connection object's Open method Option argument with one of the three following enumerated constants, then you have created a asynchronous connection. The three enumerated constants are adAsync Connect, adAsysncExecute, or adAsyncFetch. Therefore, if you need to stop a connection to a database, use this method.

Syntax

```
ConnectionObject.Cancel
```

Example

The following example attempts to open an aynchronous connection by placing the enumerated constant adAsyncConnect in the Option argument of the Connection object's Open method. The Open method will contain a connection string, a password, a user Id, and the adAsyncConnect, which is equal to 16. The code tests to see if a connection has been established after 9 seconds. The Connection object property State will test to see if a connection is opened. If the connection is not opened, the connection will be canceled.

```
Dim DataConn
Dim SqlString
Dim password, userid,ConnString

userid = "EricCone"
password = "FSU"
Set DataConn = Server.CreateObject ("ADODB.Connection")
ConnString = "DSN=MYDSN_MAIN"


DataConn.ConnectionString = connString


'the number 16 is the value of the adAsyncConnect constant
'supplied to the Option argument of the Connection object's
'Open method.
DataConn.Open connString, userid, password,16

'We are going to give the connection 10 seconds to 'complete.
If not completed then we will cancel the
'aynchronous connection.
Time = Second()

'wait 10 seconds
While (Time + 9 < Time1)
    Time1 = Second ()
Wend

'if connection not established after 9 seconds then
'cancel.
if DataConn.State <> 1 then
    DataConn.Cancel
end if
```

Close   Connection Object Method

Purpose

Use this method to close any open Connection objects.

Syntax

```
ConnectionObject.Close
```

Examples

The following example closes an open conection:

```
'DataConn is your connection
DataConn.close
```

Even though the connection is now closed, the Connection object still exists in memory. Therefore, we need to remove the Connection object from memory:

```
'then free up resource by destroying the object
Set DataConn = nothing
```

If you want to make sure that the object has been destroyed, use one of the object state enumeration constants.

```
If DataConn.State = adStateOpen then
    DataConn.close
End if
Set DataConn = nothing
```

CommitTrans	Connection Object Method

Purpose

Use this method to complete any transaction started with the BeginTrans method. You must have a BeginTrans method at the beginning of the transaction in order to use this method.

Syntax

```
ConnectionObject.CommitTrans
```

Example

This script shows you how to use the CommitTrans method in a transaction:

```
'DataConn is your connection
DataConn.CommitTrans
```

●—CAUTION

If you use nested transactions, then for every BeginTrans method, you must have a corresponding CommitTrans method.

```
'set Boolean var to false
blnFatalError = false
'DataConn is your Connection object
Sql1 = "Insert into TableA (col1, col2)Values("a","b")"
Sql2 = "Delete * From TableB"
```

```
'this BeginTrans method surrounds the two transactions
DataConn.BeginTrans
        'the first transaction
DataConn.BeginTrans
DataConn.Execute (Sql1)
If DataConn.Errors.Count > 0 then
    For each error in DataConn.Errors
        Response.Write Error.number
    Next
            blnFatalError = true
    DataConn.RollbackTrans
Else
    DataConn.CommitTrans
End if
'the second transaction
DataConn.BeginTrans
DataConn.Execute (Sql2)
If DataConn.Errors.Count > 0 then
    For each error in DataConn.Errors
        Response.Write Error.number
    Next
blnFatalError = true
DataConn.RollbackTrans
Else
    DataConn.CommitTrans
End if
If blnFatalError = True then
    DataConn.RollbackTrans
else
    DataConn.CommitTrans
End if
```

Open	**Connection Object Method**

Purpose

Use this method to open a connection to a data source.

Syntax

```
Connection.Open  ConnectionString, UserId, Password, Options
```

Table 6 lists the arguments associated with the Open method.

Table 6   *Arguments for the Open Method*

Value	Required	Type	Description
ConnectionString	No	String	The connection string
UserId	No	String	User Id needed for the database
Password	No	String	Password to the database
Option	No	Connection OptionEnum	Extra connection option; it takes one of the ConnectionOption enumeration constants

The ODBC provider supplies the ConnectionString argument. Using Microsoft's Access as a data source, a connection string might look something like the following:

```
"DSN=IceCompany;DBQ=c:\IceCompany.mdb;DriverId=281;FIL=MS
Access;MaxBufferSize=2048;PageTimeout=5;"
```

Some connection strings will contain the user ID and password; therefore, you don't need to supply those elements in that case. But if the connection string does have a user ID and password, putting a value in the UserId or Password argument will override those items in the connection string.

The Option argument takes the ConnectOption enumeration constant. Currently, ADO 2.0 has two constants in ConnectOptionEnum. Table 7 lists the constants associated with the ConnectionOption enumeration constant.

Table 7   *ConnectOption Enumeration Constants*

Value	Required	Value	Description
adAsyncConnect	No	16	Opens a connection asynchronously
adConnectUnspecified	No	−1	The connection mode is unspecified

●—CROSS-REFERENCE

The ConnectOption enumeration constants are available at the URL noted in the Preface.

Example

The following example shows how to open a connection to a database using the Open method.

```
connString = "DSN=
IceCompany;DBQ=c:\IceCompany.mdb;DriverId=281;FIL=MS
Access;MaxBufferSize=2048;PageTimeout=5;"


Dim DataConn
Set DataConn = Server.CreateObject ("ADODB.Connection")
DataConn.ConnectionString = connString
DataConn.Open
```

OpenSchema — Connection Object Method

Purpose

Use this method to find out metadata information about an open database's *schema*. A schema is a series of database objects that are owned by a database. This method returns a recordset of database information.

Syntax

```
Recordset = Connection.OpenSchema
(QueryType, Criteria, SchemaId)
```

Table 8 lists the arguments associated with the OpenSchema method.

Table 8 *Arguments for the OpenSchema Method*

Value	Required	Type	Description
QueryType	Yes	SchemaEnum	The schema type query to run
Criteria	No	Variant	The array of query constraints
SchemaID	No	Variant	The GUID for a provider

ASP Core Reference

● CROSS-REFERENCE

You can find the list of Schema enumeration constants at the URL noted in the Preface.

Examples

The following example shows how to find out all the table names in a schema:

```
Set RsSchema = DataConn.OpenSchema (adSchemaColumns)
While Not RsSchema.EOF
    Response.Write RsSchema ("TABLE_NAME")
    RsSchema.MoveNext
Wend
```

Use the following to find out column information on the first table in a schema:

```
Set RsSchema = DataConn.OpenSchema (adSchemaColumns)
While Not RsSchema.EOF
    Response.Write RsSchema ("TABLE_NAME")
    RsSchema.MoveNext
Wend
```

The next bit of code shows you how to determine the character sets that your Connection object supported. The enumerated constant that you would use is adSchemaCharacterSets.

```
//Conn is the connection object
Set RsSchema = Conn.OpenSchema (adSchemaCharacterSets)
While Not RsSchema.EOF
    Response.Write RsSchema ("CHARACTER_SET_CATALOG")
    Response.Write RsSchema ("CHARACTER_SET_SCHEMA")
    Response.Write RsSchema ("CHARACTER_SET_NAME")
    Response.Write RsSchema ("FORM_OF_USE")
  Response.Write RsSchema ("NUMBER_OF_CHARACTERS")
    Response.Write RsSchema ("DEFAULT_COLLATE_NAME")
    RsSchema.MoveNext
Wend
```

●—**NOTE** ────────────────────────────────────

Not every database provider supports every enumerated constant. For example, Sybase does not support adSchemaAsserts.

RollbackTrans | **Connection Object Method**

Purpose

Use this method to cancel any changes made to the database. This is effective if any errors occur while a transaction is executing.

Syntax

```
ConnectionObject.RollbackTrans
```

Example

This script shows you how to use the RollbackTrans method in a transaction. Once the RollbackTrans method is used, the pending changes to a database are canceled and the affected rows are returned to their formal values.

```
Dim DataConn
Dim TransNestLevel
```

```
Dim SqlString
Dim connString
connString =  "DSN=
IceCompany;DBQ=c:\IceCompany.mdb;DriverId=281;FIL=MS
Access;MaxBufferSize=2048;PageTimeout=5;"

Set DataConn = Server.CreateObject ("ADODB.Connection")
DataConn.ConnectionString = connString
DataConn.Open
TransNestLevel = DataConn.BeginTrans
SqlString = "Delete * From AnyTable"
DataConn.Execute (Sql)
If DataConn.Errors.Count > 0 then
   For each error in DataConn.Errors
       Response.Write Error.number
   Next
   DataConn.RollbackTrans
Else
   DataConn.CommitTrans
End if
```

Attributes   Connection Object Property

Purpose
Use this property if you want to start a new transaction after each transaction completes. This property tells you the kinds of transactions your Connection object can perform. The property returns an adXactAttribute enumerated constant.

Syntax
```
ConnectionObject.Attributes = adXactAttributeEnum constant
Long = ConnectionObject.Attributes
```

Examples
The following example shows you how to get the Attributes property from a Connection object. The Attributes property returns a Long value.

```
'we are making the
Dim DataConn,Myatt
connString =  "DSN=
IceCompany;DBQ=c:\IceCompany.mdb;DriverId=281;FIL=MS
Access;MaxBufferSize=2048;PageTimeout=5;"

Set DataConn = Server.CreateObject ("ADODB.Connection")
```

ASP Core Reference

```
DataConn.ConnectionString = connString
DataConn.Open
Myatt = ConnectionObject.Attributes
```

If you want to ensure that any new transactions are automatically started after a CommitTrans method, then use this script:

```
//DataConn is the Connection object
DataConn.Attributes = adXactCommitRetaining
DataConn.open connectString
```

Use the next script if you want to ensure that any new transactions are automatically started after both a Rollback and a CommitTrans method are started:

```
DataConn.Attributes = adXactCommitRetaing AND
adXactAbortRetaining
```

● CROSS-REFERENCE

The adXactAttribute enumerated constants are available at the URL noted in the Preface.

CommandTimeout	**Connection Object Property**

Purpose

Use the CommandTimeout property to set the time (in seconds) that you have to wait before terminating a command and generating an error. The default is 30 seconds.

Syntax

```
ConnectionObject.CommandTimeout
```

Examples

The following code sets the CommandTimeout property to five seconds. Remember that you must set this property before issuing the Connection object's Open or Execute method.

```
//DataConn is the Connection object
DataConn.CommandTimeout = 5
DataConn.Open
```

Use this script to find the value of the CommandTimeout property. The return value is a Long value.

```
Long = DataConn.CommandTimeout
```

ConnectionString

Purpose

Use the ConnectionString property to hold the string that contains the information enabling a connection to a database. You must set this property before attempting to open a connection.

Syntax:

```
ConnectionObject.ConnectionString
```

A connection string is always part of an URL. It can be composed of four parts. A connection string will always have at least one of these parts:

- The *provider* gives the name of the database provider.
- The *file name* gives the database provider a specific file containing connection information. The file name is normally the Date Source Name (DSN) that you create to connect to a datasource.
- The *remote provider* gives the name of a database provider that should be used when opening a client-side connection. (This applies to the Remote Data Source, or RDS.)
- The *remote server* gives the path of the server that should be used when opening a client-side connection. (This applies to the RDS.)

●—CROSS-REFERENCE

Chapter 4, which covers connecting the ADO to a database, shows you some different ways the connection string can be formed.

Example

The following example shows you a possible connection string to a Microsoft Access database:

```
ConnString =  "Driver={Microsoft Access Driver (*.mdb)};"
ConnString = ConnString & "Dbq=\somepath\mydb.mdb;"
ConnString = ConnString & "Uid=Admin;"
ConnString = ConnString & "Pwd=;"
```

The next code shows you a possible connection string for an Oracle database:

```
ConnString =  "Driver={Microsoft ODBC for Oracle};"
ConnString = ConnString & "Server=OracleServer.world;"
ConnString = ConnString & "Uid=demo;"
ConnString = ConnString & "Pwd=demo;"
```

ASP Core Reference

ConnectionTimeout
Connection Object Property

Purpose

Use this property to set the time in seconds that your ASP can try to establish a connection to a database. If the time is exceeded, an error occurs. The default time is 15 seconds.

Syntax

```
ConnectionObject.ConnectionTimeout
```

Example

Use this script to set the ConnectionTimeout property:

```
'ConnectionTimeout is set with a variant of Type Long
DataConn.ConnectionTimeout = 10

'ConnectionTimeout returns a variant of Type Long
Dim Long Ln
Ln = DataConn.ConnectionTimeout
```

●─TIP

You cannot reset the ConnectionTimeout property once a connection has been established.

If no connection is made to the database before the value of the ConectionTimeout property is exceeded, an error is generated.

```
The following bit of code shows you how to set the Connection
object's ConnectionTimeout property. In this example, the value
is set to 0.//if you want to wait forever then set the
//ConnectionTimeout to 0
DataConn.ConnectionTimeout = 0
```

CursorLocation
Connection Object Property

Purpose

Use this to property set or return the location of the cursor engine. What is a cursor engine? The Client Cursor engine is a set of data structures that caches in memory (or temporarily on disk for large sets of data) the set of query results retrieved from a Database Management System (DBMS), as well as client updates to those results. Remote Data Services calls the Client Cursor Engine to perform various tasks for you automatically.

The Client Cursor Engine contains buffers for metadata, such as tables, rows, columns, keys, and time stamps, as well as the actual table data itself. To manage the cache, the Client Cursor Engine can do the following:

- Create and delete temporary tables
- Populate tables
- Manage updates to the data values
- Provide schema information (such as base tables, key columns, update-able columns, special columns, and computed columns)
- Provide the mechanism to send batched updates to the server with min-imum network traffic, by sending only the modified records.

The CursorLocation property returns a CursorLocation enumeration con-stant.

●—CROSS-REFERENCE

The CursorLocation enumerated constants are available at the URL noted in the Preface.

Syntax

```
CursorLocationEnum = ConnectionObject.CursorLocation
ConnectionObject.CursorLocation = CursorLocationEnum
```

Examples

The following code gets the cursor location:

```
CursorLocationEnum = ConnectionObject.CursorLocation
```

The next code sets the cursor location:

```
ConnectionObject.CursorLocation = CursorLocationEnum
```

DefaultDatabase	**Connection Object Property**

Purpose

You use this property to determine the default database for your Connection object.

Syntax

```
ConnectionObject.DefaultDatabase
```

Examples

The following code finds the default database. The return value is a String data type.

```
String = ConnectionObject.DefaultDatabase
```

The next code sets the default database to the database `MyRecords`:

```
ConnectionObject.DefaultDatabase = "MyRecords"
```

IsolationLevel   Connection Object Property

Purpose

Use this property to indicate the level of transaction isolation for a `Connection` object. What exactly does that mean in plain English? Well, transactions enable you to change information in a table. However, if two users try to change that data at the same time, problems could result, with one user overwriting data in the table before the other user can commit the other transaction. Thus, the need for *concurrency control* is vital. That is, if two users act on the same data, each transaction must be allowed to go to completion without interference from the other transaction.

The setting does not take effect until the next time you call the `Connection` object's `BeginTrans` method (p. 57). If the level of isolation you request is unavailable, the provider may return the next-greater level of isolation. This property returns an `IsolationLevel` enumeration constant.

●—CROSS-REFERENCE

The `IsolationLevel` enumerated constants are available at the URL noted in the Preface.

Syntax

```
ConnectionObject.IsolationLevel
```

Examples

The following code retrieves the isolation level. The return type is an `IsolationLevelEnum` constant.

```
IsolationLevelEnum = ConnectionObject.IsolationLevel
```

The following code sets the `IsolationLevel` property with an `Isolation Level` enumerated value. Remember that you must set this property before the connection is made.

```
ConnectionObjectIsolationLevel = IsolationLevelEnum
```

Mode   Connection Object Property

Purpose

Use this property to determine the available permissions for modifying the data retrieved in a `Connection`, `Record`, or `Stream` object. The property returns a `ConnectionMode` enumeration constant.

●—CROSS-REFERENCE

The ConnecMode enumerated constants are available at the URL noted in the Preface.

Syntax

```
ConnectionObject.Mode
```

Examples

The following code uses the Mode property to determine if the Connection object allows read/write permission.

```
Dim DataConn
Set DataConn = Server.CreateObject ("ADODB.Connection")
DataConn.ConnectionString = connString
DataConn.Open

If DataConn.Mode = adModeReadWrite then
    Response.Write "Permissions is Read/Write"
End if
```

The folowing code uses the Mode property to set the Connection object's permission to read-only. Remember that you must set this property before the connection is made.

```
Dim DataConn
Set DataConn = Server.CreateObject ("ADODB.Connection")
DataConn.ConnectionString = connString
DataConn.Mode adModeRead
DataConn.Open
```

If you want, you can create a DSN-less connection string. For instance, you could use the following code if you were using an Oracle data source located on an Internet Service Provider (ISP) with a domain server name of "OracleServer.world":

```
Dim DataConn
Set DataConn = Server.CreateObject ("ADODB.Connection")
ConnString = "Driver={Microsoft ODBC for Oracle};"
ConnString = ConnString & "Server=OracleServer.world;"
ConnString = ConnString & "Uid=demo;
Pwd=demo;"DataConn.ConnectionString = connString
DataConn.Open
```

ASP Core Reference

Provider
Connection Object Property

Purpose

Use this property to return the name of the database provider for the connection.

Table 9 lists the return values for the different data source providers.

Table 9   *Return Values for Different Data Source Providers*

Return Value	Data Source
MSDASQL	Microsoft Access or the provider is unknown
MSIDXS	Microsoft Index Server
SQLOLEDB	Microsoft SQL Server
MSDAORA	Oracle
MS Remote	When the data source is on a server at another IP address
MSDAIPD.DSO	Internal Publishing
Microsoft.JET.OLEDB.4.0	Microsoft JET

Syntax

```
ConnectionObject.Provider
```

Example

The following code finds the database provider:

```
Dim DataConn
Set DataConn = Server.CreateObject("ADODB.Connection")
Response.Write " DataConn.Provider is "
Response.Write DataConn.Provider
```

State
Connection Object Property

Purpose

Use this property to determine if your Connection object is open or closed. The return value will be one of the ObjectStateEnum constants.

●─CROSS-REFERENCE

The ObjectState enumerated constants are available at the URL noted in the Preface.

Syntax

```
ConnectionObject.State
```

Examples

If you want to find out if you successfully got a connection, use the following code:

```
'Connection object is DataConn
DataConn.Open
If DataConn.State = adStateOpen then
    Response.Write "open connection"
Else
    Response.Write "no connection object"
    DataConn.Close
    Set DataConn = nothing
End if
```

If you want to find out if you successfully closed a connection, use this code:

```
If DataConn.State = adStateClosed then
    Response.Write "connection DataConn is closed"
End if
```

Version   Connection Object Property

Purpose

Use this property to indicate the ADO version number.

Syntax

```
ConnectionObject.Version
```

Examples

The following code finds the version of ADO that you are using:

```
Dim DataConn
Set DataConn = Server.CreateObject("ADODB.Connection")
Response.Write " DataConn.Version is "
Response.Write DataConn.Version
```

●─NOTE─────────────────────────────

If the version is ADO 2.1, the property will return 2.1.

ASP Core Reference

Connection Collections Object

Purpose

Use the Connection Object Collection to investigate errors and properties associated with the Connection object. Both the Errors Collection and Properties Collection have two properties associated with them — Count and Item.

●—CROSS-REFERENCE————————————————

A details to the Error Collection and Properties Collection are given on pages 95 and 170, respectively, in this section (The Asp Core Reference).

Syntax

```
ConnectionObject.Errors
ConnectionObject.Properties
```

Errors	**Connection Object Collection**

Purpose

Use the Errors collection to handle any errors that occur during the execution of an ADO operation. You may have noticed that there is an Error object associated with the ADO, and then there is an errors collection associated with the Connection object. This is because when an error occurs during an ADO operation, the Error object is added to the Connection object's Errors collection. The Errors collection will describe the errors for that one operation, and then will be cleared when another ADO operation occurs.

Syntax

```
ConnectionObject.Errors
```

Example

This example shows you how to obtain the individual Error object's from the Connection object's Errors Collection:

```
'DataConn is your connection object
DataConn.BeginTrans
SqlString = "Delete * From AnyTable"
DataConn.Execute (Sql)
'if the count of Error object in the Collection
'is greater than zero
If DataConn.Errors.Count > 0 then
    For each error in DataConn.Errors
        'Write out the individual Error object property
        Response.Write Error.number
```

```
    Next
    DataConn.RollbackTrans
Else
    DataConn.CommitTrans
End if
```

Properties   Connection Object Collection

Purpose

Use this collection to contain all of the Property objects for a Connection object. Each property consists of a string name.

Syntax

```
Properties = ConnectionObject.Properties
```

Examples

The following example retrieves all the Name and Value properties of the Connection object's Properties Collection and runs the following script:

```
 'Open a create a connection object
Set DataConn = Server.Connection("ADODB.Connection")
'connString is a connection string
DataConn.ConnectionString = connString
DataConn.Open
For Each item In DataConn.Properties
    Response.Write item.Name
    Response.Write "-"
    Response.Write item.Value
    Response.Write "<BR>"

Next
```

The following is a typical list of some of the properties that you will find when you execute the preceding code:

```
Active Sessions-64
Asynchable Commit-False
Catalog Location-1
Catalog Term-DATABASE
Catalog Usage-13
Column Definition-0
NULL Concatenation Behavior-1
Data Source Name-IceTech
Read-Only Data Source-True
DBMS Name-ACCESS
```

ASP Core Reference

```
DBMS Version-03.50.0000
GROUP BY Support-2
Heterogeneous Table Support-0
Identifier Case Sensitivity-4
Maximum Index Size-255
Maximum Row Size-2096
Maximum Row Size Includes BLOB-False
Maximum Tables in SELECT-16
```

Dictionary Object

Purpose

Use the Dictionary object the same way you would use an array. The Dictionary object allows you to add and delete from a list of items. However, in the case of the Dictionary object, each item has an associated key name.

Syntax

```
DictionaryObject.Property
DictionaryObject.Method
```

Add	**Dictionary Object Method**

Purpose

Use this method to add a key value pair to a Dictionary object. Treat this method just as you would when adding an element to an array. If you put a value in the second element of the array with a value of "Kansas", then the key value would be 2 and the item would be "Kansas". If the key already exists, an error will occur.

Syntax

```
DictionaryObject.Add  TheKey,TheItem
```

Table 10 lists the arguments associated with the Add method.

Table 10 *Arguments for the Add Method*

Value	Required	Type	Description
TheKey	Yes	String	The name of the key value to set and recall the value by
TheItem	Yes	String	The value to associate with TheKey

Example

The following example will add six key/item pairs to a Dictionary object:

```
<%
Dim dictObj
Set dictObj = CreateObject("Scripting.Dictionary")
dictObj.Add "People1","GregEdenfield"
dictObj.Add "People2","RonCarroll"
dictObj.Add "People3","DebbieWhite"
dictObj.Add "People4","LoriTappanSly"
dictObj.Add "People5","SteveZeuner"
dictObj.Add "People6", "VirginiaWright"
%>
```

Exists   Dictionary Object Method

Purpose

Use this method to determine if a certain key exists. This method returns a True or False.

Syntax

```
DictionaryObject.Exists("TheKey")
```

Table 11 lists the argument associated with the Exists method.

Table 11 *Argument for the Exists Method*

Value	Required	Type	Description
TheKey	Yes	String	This is the name of the key that you want to find if it exists or does not exist.

Example

The following example indicates whether one of the keys created in the Add method exists or not.

```
<%
'we are going to assume that the dictObj Dictionary 'object
already has been created.
If dictObj.Exists("LoriTappan") then
    Response.Write "LoriTappan key exists"
End if
%>
```

Items
Dictionary Object Method

Purpose

Use this method to get the array containing all the items in a Dictionary object.

Syntax

```
Dim AnArrayVar
AnArrayVar = DictionaryObject.Items
```

Table 12 lists the argument associated with the Items method.

Table 12 *Argument for the Items Method*

Value	Required	Type	Description
AnArrayVar	Yes	Array	The variable that will contain the Items array. You can pick any variable name; just make sure that there is a Dim statement to initialize the variable.

Example

The following code will first create a Dictionary object, and then add three key/item pairs to the object's array of key/item pairs. After these pairs have been added, the code uses the Items method to retrieve all the pairs via an array. The Response object's Write method is used to output the pairs.

```
<%
Dim bay, dictObj, J
Set dictObj = CreateObject("Scripting.Dictionary")
dictObj.Add "Friend1", "JohnNeel"
dictObj.Add "Friend2", "KathleenNeel"
dictObj.Add "Friend3", "AllisonHumphrey"
dictObj.Add "Friend4", "DarrelKing"

'place the Items array into J
J = dictObj.Items

For each item in J
    Response.Write "<BR>"
    Response.Write item
```

```
Next
%>
```

The browser will return the following

```
JohnNeel
KathleenNeel
AllisonHumphrey
DarrelKing
```

Keys   Dictionary Object Method

Purpose

Use this method to get the array containing all the keys in a Dictionary object.

Syntax

```
Dim AnArrayVar
AnArrayVar = DictionaryObject.Keys
```

Table 13 lists the argument associated with the Keys method.

Table 13   Argument for the Keys Method

Value	Required	Type	Description
AnArrayVar	Yes	Array	The variable that will contain the Keys array. You can pick any variable name; just make sure that there is a Dim statement to initialize the variable.

Example

The following code will first create a Dictionary object, and then add three key/item pairs to the object's array of key/item pairs. After these pairs have been added, the code takes the Keys and places them into the array J. Next the keys in the array J become output.

```
<%
Dim bay, dictObj, J
Set dictObj = CreateObject("Scripting.Dictionary")
dictObj.Add "Friend1", "JohnNeel"
dictObj.Add "Friend2", "KathleenNeel"
```

```
dictObj.Add "Friend3", "AllisonHumphrey"

'place the Keys array into J
J = dictObj.Keys

For each item in J
    Response.Write "<BR>"
    Response.Write item
Next
%>
```

The browser will return the following output..

```
Friend1
Friend2
Friend3
```

Remove   Dictionary Object Method

Purpose

Use this method to remove a single key/item pair from the Dictionary object.

Syntax

```
DictionaryObject.Remove("TheKey")
```

Table 14 lists the argument associated with the Remove method.

Table 14   Argument for Remove Method

Value	Required	Type	Description
TheKey	Yes	String	The name of the individual key to remove from the Dictionary object

Example

The following example will remove one of the key/item pairs created in the Add method:

```
<%
'we are going to assume that the dictObj Dictionary 'object
```

```
already has been created.
dictObj.Remove("RonCarroll")
'see the updated list of keys in the Dictionary object
bay = dictObj.Keys
for each item in bay
    Response.Write "<BR>"
    Response.Write item
next

%>
```

RemoveAll	Dictionary Object Method

Purpose
Use this method to remove all the key/item pairs from the Dictionary object.

Syntax
```
DictionaryObject.RemoveAll
```

Example
The following code removes all the key/item pairs from the Dictionary object:

```
<%
'we are going to assume that the dictObj Dictionary 'object
already has been created.
dictObj.RemoveAll
%>
```

CompareMode	Dictionary Object Property

Purpose
Use this property to set and get the comparison mode for comparing string keys in a Dictionary object.

Syntax
```
DictionaryObject.CompareMode  = CompareValue
```

Table 15 lists the argument associated with the CompareMode property.

ASP Core Reference

Table 15   *Argument for the CompareMode Property*

Value	Required	Type	Description
CompareValue	No	Number	If provided, compare is a value representing the comparison mode used by VBScript functions such as StrComp. Following are the values that you can use for this property:
			VbUseCompareOption = -1
			VbBinaryCompare = 0
			VbTextCompare = 1
			VbDatabaseCompare = 2

Example

The following script shows you how to set and obtain the value for the CompareMode property from the Dictionary object:

```
<%
Dim dictObj
Set dictObj = CreateObject("Scripting.Dictionary")
'we are going to set the comparison mode to binary
DictObj.CompareMode = 0
Response.Write "The CompareMode is "
Response.Write DictObj.CompareMode
%>
```

Count   Dictionary Object Property

Purpose

Use this property to find the number of elements in the Keys array and Items array of the Dictionary object.

Syntax

```
DictionaryObject.Count
```

Example

The following code retrieves the number of elements in the Keys array:

```
<%
Dim bay, dictObj, Jarray,J
Set dictObj = CreateObject("Scripting.Dictionary")
```

```
dictObj.Add "Friend1", "JohnNeel"
dictObj.Add "Friend2", "KathleenNeel"
dictObj.Add "Friend3", "AllisonHumphrey"

'place the Keys array into J
Jarray = dictObj.Keys
'use the Count property to count out element of array
For J = 0 to dictObj.Count -1
    Response.Write "<BR>"
    Response.Write Jarray(J)
Next
%>
```

Item   Dictionary Object Property

Purpose

Use this property to set or get the value of an the Dictionary object's Item property.

Syntax

```
DictionaryObject.Item(TheKey) = NewItemValue
```

Table 16 lists the arguments associated with the Item property.

Table 16   *Arguments for the Item Property*

Value	Required	Type	Description
TheKey	Yes	String	The name of the individual key to set or get from the Dictionary object
NewItemValue	If setting value	String	The value to set the Item

Example

The following example sets the item "Red" to the key "Color".

```
<%
'we are going to assume that the dictObj Dictionary 'object
already has been created.
dictObj.Item("Color") = "Red"
%>
```

Key — Dictionary Object Property

Purpose
Use this property to set or get the value of a key.

Syntax

```
DictionaryObject.Key(TheKey) = Item Value
```

Table 17 lists the arguments associated with the Key property.

Table 17   *Arguments for the Key Property*

Value	Required	Type	Description
TheKey	Yes	String	The name of the individual key to set or get from the Dictionary object
Item Value	Yes	String	The value to set the key

Example
The following example sets a key named "College" to the value "DeltaState":

```
<%
'we are going to assume that the dictObj Dictionary 'object
already has been created.
dictObj.Key("College") = "DeltaState"
%>
```

Drive Object

Purpose
Use the Drive object to obtain information about a local or network drive.

Syntax

```
DriveObject.property
```

AvailableSpace — Drive Object Property

Purpose
Use this property to find the amount of available space on a specific drive. The Drive object's FreeSpace property (p. 87) does the same thing as the Available Space property. It is unclear why you would need two properties to do the same thing.

Syntax

```
DriveObject.AvailableSpace
```

Example

The following example opens the `FileSystemObject` object, and then creates a `Drive` object from a local hard drive "C:" Once the `Drive` object is created, the `AvailableSpace` property is used to find the free memory on the hard drive.

```
<%
Dim FSObj,DrvObj
Set FSObj = Server.CreateObject("Scripting.FileSystemObject")
Set DrvObj = FSObj.GetDrive("C:")
Response.Write DrvObj.AvailableSpace
%>
```

DriveLetter   Drive Object Property

Purpose

Use this property to find the drive letter of the `Drive` object.

Syntax

```
DriveObject.DriveLetter
```

Example

The following example opens the`FileSystemObject` object, and then creates a `Drive` object from a network mapped drive "G:" Once the `Drive` object is created, the `DriveLetterName` property is used to find the name of the drive.

```
<%
Dim FSObj,DrvObj
Set FSObj = Server.CreateObject("Scripting.FileSystemObject")
Set DrvObj = FSObj.GetDrive("G:")
Response.Write DrvObj.DriveLetter
%>
```

The value G will be returned.

DriveType   Drive Object Property

Purpose

Use this property to indicate the type of drive the `Drive` object is. There are six values that this property can return:

```
0 — Unknown
1 — Removable
```

```
2 — Fixed
3 — Network
4 — CD-ROM
5 — RAM Disk
```

Syntax

```
DriveObject.DriveType
```

Example

The following example opens the FileSystemObject object, and then creates a Drive object from a network mapped drive "G:" The G: drive is a CD-ROM drive. Once the Drive object is created, the DriveType property is used to indicate the type of drive.

```
<%
Dim FSObj,DrvObj
Set FSObj = Server.CreateObject("Scripting.FileSystemObject")
Set DrvObj = FSObj.GetDrive("G:")
Select Case DrvObj.DriveType
Case 0
    Response.Write "Unknown DriveType"
Case 1
    Response.Write "Removable DriveType"
Case 2
    Response.Write "Fixed DriveType"
Case 3
    Response.Write "Network Drive"
Case 4
    Response.Write "CD-ROM Drive"
Case 5
    Response.Write "RAM DISK Drive"
End Select
%>
```

FileSystem | Drive Object Property

Purpose

Use this property to determine the type of file system that the Drive object contains. Possible return values are FAT, FAT32, NTFS, or CDFS.

Syntax

```
DriveObject.FileSystem
```

Example

The following example opens the FileSystemObject object, and then creates a Drive object from a network mapped drive "G:" The G: drive is a CD-ROM drive. Once the `Drive` object is created, the `FileSystem` property is used to indicate the type of file system associated with the `Drive` object.

```
<%
Dim FSObj,DrvObj
Set FSObj = Server.CreateObject("Scripting.FileSystemObject")
Set DrvObj = FSObj.GetDrive("G:")
Response.Write "FileSystem Type is "
Response.Write DrvObj.FileSystem
%>
```

FreeSpace   Drive Object Property

Purpose

Use this property to determine the amount of available space on a specific drive. The `Drive` object's `AvailableSpace` property (p. 84) does the same thing as the `FreeSpace` property. Again, it is unclear why you would need two properties to do the same thing.

Syntax

```
DriveObject.FreeSpace
```

Example

The following example opens the `FileSystemObject` object, and then creates a `Drive` object from a local hard drive "D:" (Normally, D: is your CD reader or another device, but we got tired of using C: in the examples.) Once the `Drive` object is created, the `FreeSpace` property is used to determine the amount of free memory on the drive.

```
<%
Dim FSObj,DrvObj
Set FSObj = Server.CreateObject("Scripting.FileSystemObject")
Set DrvObj = FSObj.GetDrive("D:")
Response.Write DrvObj.FreeSpace
%>
```

IsReady   Drive Object Property

Purpose

Use this property to determine whether the drive in the `Drive` object is ready or not. A True or False will be returned.

Syntax

```
DriveObject.IsReady
```

Example

The following example opens the FileSystemObject object, and then creates a Drive object from a local hard drive "G:" Normally, G: for this example is a network drive. Once the Drive object is created, the IsReady property is used to determine whether the drive is ready to be used or not.

```
<%
Dim FSObj,DrvObj
Set FSObj = Server.CreateObject("Scripting.FileSystemObject")
Set DrvObj = FSObj.GetDrive("G:")
If DrvObj.IsReady then
    Response.Write "<BR>Drive is Ready"
Else
    Response.Write "<BR>Drive is NOT Ready"
End if
%>
```

Path   Drive Object Property

Purpose

Use this property to determine the specific path for a drive.

Syntax

```
DriveObject.Path
```

Example

The following example opens the FileSystemObject object, and then creates a Drive object from a local hard drive "C:" Once the Drive object is created, the Path property is used to determine the path of the drive.

```
<%
Dim FSObj,DrvObj
Set FSObj = Server.CreateObject("Scripting.FileSystemObject")
Set DrvObj = FSObj.GetDrive("C:")
Response.Write "The path of the drive is "
Response.Write DrvObj.Path
%>
```

The example returns C.

RootFolder   Drive Object Property

Purpose

Use this property to get the Folder object for the root folder of the Drive object. Once you estalish the Folder object, you can start to use the Folder object's properties.

●─CROSS-REFERENCE────────────────

The Folder object's properties are listed on page 141.

Syntax

```
DriveObject.RootFolder
```

Example

The following example opens theFileSystemObject object, and then creates a Drive object from a local hard drive "C:" Once the Drive object is created, the code uses the RootFolder property to obtain the Folder object for the root, which of course is C in this example.

```
<%
Dim FSObj,DrvObj,RootFolderObj
Set FSObj = Server.CreateObject("Scripting.FileSystemObject")
Set DrvObj = FSObj.GetDrive("C:")
RootFolderObj = DrvObj.RootFolder
Response.Write RootFolderObj
%>
```

SerialNumber   Drive Object Property

Purpose

Use this property to obtain the serial number that idenifies a disk volume.

Syntax

```
DriveObject.SerialNumber
```

Example

The following example opens theFileSystemObject object, and then creates a Drive object from a local hard drive "C:" After the script obtains the Drive object, the SerialNumber property obtains the serial number of the disk.

```
<%
Dim FSObj,DrvObj,RootFolderObj
Set FSObj =
Server.CreateObject("Scripting.FileSystemObject")
```

ASP Core Reference

```
Set DrvObj = FSObj.GetDrive("C:")
Response.Write"The SerialNumber
 of the Disk is "
Response.WriteDrvObj.SerialNumber
%>
```

ShareName
Drive Object Property

Purpose

Use this property to get the network share name of the specified drive. It should go without saying (that means we have to say it) that in order to use this property, you need a Drive object in a network environment. Otherwise, the value returns a blank.

Syntax

```
DriveObject.ShareName
```

Example

The following example opens theFileSystemObject object, and then creates a Drive object from a local hard drive "C:" After the script obtains the Drive object, the ShareName property obtains the share name of the Drive object for the network.

```
<%
Dim FSObj,DrvObj,RootFolderObj
Set FSObj = Server.CreateObject("Scripting.FileSystemObject")
Set DrvObj = FSObj.GetDrive("C:")
'if ShareName not blank
If len(DrvObj.ShareName) > 0 then
Response.Write "The ShareName of the Disk is "
  Response.Write DrvObj.ShareName
Else
  Response.Write "This drive is not shared"
End if
%>
```

TotalSize
Drive Object Property

Purpose

Use this property to determine the total size of the Drive object.

Syntax

```
DriveObject.TotalSize
```

Example

The following example opens theFileSystemObject object, and then creates a Drive object from a local hard drive "C:" Once the Drive object is created, the script uses the Response object's Write method to indicate the total size of the Drive object.

```
<%
Dim FSObj,DrvObj,RootFolderObj
Set FSObj = Server.CreateObject("Scripting.FileSystemObject")
Set DrvObj = FSObj.GetDrive("C:")
Response.WriteWrite "Total Size of the Drive is "
Response.WriteWrite DrvObj.TotalSize

%>
```

VolumeName	Drive Object Property

Purpose

Use this property to determine the name of the volume. You must be in a network environment to use this property; otherwise, if you try using this property on your local hard drive, you will receive a run-time error.

Syntax

```
DriveObject.VolumeName
```

Example

The following example opens theFileSystemObject object, and then creates a Drive object from a local hard drive "C:" For this example, we are assuming C is a network drive. Once the Drive object is created, the script uses the Response object's Write method to indicate the VolumeName property of the drive.

```
<%
Dim FSObj,DrvObj,RootFolderObj
Set FSObj = Server.CreateObject("Scripting.FileSystemObject")
Set DrvObj = FSObj.GetDrive("C:")
Response.Write"Volume Name of the Drive is "
Response.WriteDrvObj.VolumeName

%>
```

Error Object

Purpose

Use the Error object to find information about an individual error that is stored in the Errors Collection.

Syntax

```
Error.property
```

Description   Error Object Property

Purpose

Use this property to return the text message describing the error.

Syntax

```
String = Error.Description
```

Example

The following example shows you how to use the Error object's Description property:

```
'DataConn is your connection
DataConn.BeginTrans
SqlString = "Select * From AnyTable"
Set RS = DataConn.Execute (Sql)
If DataConn.Errors.Count > 0 then
    For each error in DataConn.Errors
        Response.Write Error.Description
    Next
Else
    If Not RS.Eof and Not RS.Bof then
    Response.Write"The Value of the First Column"
    Response.WriteRS(0).Value
    End If
End if
```

NativeError   Error Object Property

Purpose

Use this property to return the error number specific to the data provider.

Syntax

```
Long = Error.NativeError
```

Example

This script shows you how to use the NativeError property.:

```
'DataConn is your connection
DataConn.BeginTrans
SqlString = "Select * From AnyTable"
```

ASP Core Reference

```
Set RS = DataConn.Execute (SqlString)
If DataConn.Errors.Count > 0 then
    For each error in DataConn.Errors
        Response.Write Error.Description
        Response.Write "<BR>" &
Error.NativeError
    Next
Else
    If Not RS.Eof and Not RS.Bof then
    Response.Write"The Value of
the First Column"
Response.WriteRS(0).Value
    End If
End if
```

Number   Error Object Property

Purpose

Use this property to return the actual number of the error thrown by the database provider.

Syntax

```
ErrorObject.Number
```

Example

To see the error numbers from an Error object, use the following script:

```
'DataConn is your connection
SqlString = "Select * From AnyTable"
Set RS = DataConn.Execute (SqlString)
If DataConn.Errors.Count > 0 then
'Sometimes the error with be a negative number
    If DataConn.Errors.Number > 0 then
        For each error in DataConn.Errors
            Response.Write Error.Description
        Next
    End if
Else
    If Not RS.Eof and Not RS.Bof then
        Response.Write "The Value of the First Column"
        Response.Write RS(0).Value
    End If
End if
```

Source	**Error Object Property**

Purpose

Use this property to determine which object generated the error.

Syntax

```
ErrorObject.Source
```

Example

To get the error source, use the following script:

```
'DataConn is your connection
'the Correct Table is States, Suppose you put the
'table name State1 — the error that you will get
'is presented at the bottom of the code
SqlString = "Select * From State1"
Set RS = DataConn.Execute (SqlString)
If DataConn.Errors.Count > 0 then
    For each error in DataConn.Errors
        Response.Write Error.Description
        'Describes the Source of the Error
        Response.Write Error.Source
    Next
Else
    If Not RS.Eof and Not RS.Bof then
        Response.WriteWrite "The Value of the First Column"
        Response.WriteWrite RS(0).Value
    End If
End if
```

The message generated from the preceding code might look something like the following:

```
Microsoft OLE DB Provider for ODBC Drivers error '80040e37'
[Microsoft][ODBC SQL Server Driver][SQL Server]Invalid object
name 'States1'.
```

SQLState	**Error Object Property**

Purpose

Use this property to determine the SQLState for a given Error object. Not all database providers provide this property. Normally, this property returns a five-character SQL error code.

Syntax

```
ErrorObject.SQLState
```

Example

The following example shows you how to use the Error object's SQLState property. The SQLState error codes are defined by the SQL Access Group.//DataConn is your connection

```
SqlString = "Select * From AnyTable"
Set RS = DataConn.Execute (SqlString)
If DataConn.Errors.Count > 0 then
'Sometimes the error with be a negative number
    If DataConn.Errors.Number > 0 then
        For each error in DataConn.Errors
            Response.Write Error.SQLState
        Next
    End if
Else
    If Not RS.Eof and Not RS.Bof then
        Response.WriteWrite "The Value of the First Column"
        Response.WriteWrite RS(0).Value
    End If
End if
```

Clear	Error Object Collection Method

Purpose

Use this method to remove all the Error objects from the Error collection. The Active Data Object (ADO) automatically calls this method when an error occurs.

Syntax

```
ErrorObject.Clear
```

Example

Because this method is automatically called when an error occurs, no example is necessary. However, the example below calls the Clear property after all the Error object's in the Connection object's Errors Collection are investigated for the SQLState property.

```
'DataConn is your connection
SqlString = "Select * From AnyTable"
Set RS = DataConn.Execute (SqlString)
If DataConn.Errors.Count > 0 then
'Sometimes the error with be a negative number
    For each error in DataConn.Errors
```

ASP Core Reference

```
    Response.Write Error.SQLState
Next

    DataConn.Errors.Clear
End if
```

Count   Error Object Collection Property

Purpose

Use this property to determine the number of Error objects in the collection. This property returns a Long variant.

Syntax

```
Long = Errors.Count
```

Example

This script shows the use of the Error object's Count property:

```
'DataConn is your connection
SqlString = "Select * From AnyTable"
Set RS = DataConn.Execute (SqlString)
'go through the error if count greater than 0
If DataConn.Errors.Count > 0 then
'Sometimes the error with be a negative number
If DataConn.Errors.Number > 0 then
    'Updates the Error Collection with lastest info
    DataConn.Errors.Refresh
    For each error in DataConn.Errors
        Response.Write Error.SQLState
    Next
End if
```

Refresh   Error Object Collection Method

Purpose

Use this method to refresh the Errors Collection object with latest information from the database provider.

Syntax

```
ErrorObject.Refresh
```

Example

This script shows you how to use the Refresh method to update the Errors collection object with the latest information about errors:/DataConn is your connection

```
SqlString = "Select * From AnyTable"
Set RS = DataConn.Execute (SqlString)
If DataConn.Errors.Count > 0 then
'Sometimes the error with be a negative number
    If DataConn.Errors.Number > 0 then
        'Updates the Error Collection with lastest info
        DataConn.Errors.Refresh
        For each error in DataConn.Errors
            Response.Write Error.SQLState
        Next
    End if
End if
```

Item	Error Object Collection Property

Purpose

Using this property enables you to index the Error objects in the Errors collection. This way, you can sort through the objects.

Syntax

```
ErrorObject = Errors.Item(Index)
```

Example

This script shows the use of the Error object's Count property:

```
'DataConn is your connection
SqlString = "Select * From AnyTable"
Set RS = DataConn.Execute (SqlString)
'go through the error if count greater than 0
If DataConn.Errors.Count > 0 then
'Sometimes the error with be a negative number
    For j = 0 to DataConn.Errors.Count - 1
        Response.Write Error.Item(j)
    Next
End if
```

Field Object

Purpose

Use the Field object to identify a field (another name for field is column) in a RecordSet object. The Field object is denoted by a ordinal number in the RecordSet object or by the Field object's name.

Syntax

```
FieldObject.Property
FieldObject.Method
```

AppendChunk   Field Object Method

Purpose

Use this to method to append data to a large or binary Field object.

Syntax

```
Field.AppendChunk(Data)
```

Table 18 lists the argument associated with the AppendChunk method.

Table 18   *Argument for the AppendChunk Method*

Value	Required	Type	Description
Data	Yes	Variant	The data to be appended to the Field object.

Example

The following example gets a recordset from the table named photos. The table stores the photos as binary data. The data in this case is in the field bwphoto. Through the use of the ActualSize property, the code is able to determine what size to use with the AppendChuck method. The binary data is then placed into the Field object's Image. The data in the photo table is output to the browser through the Response object's BinaryWrite method.

```
<%
Set DataConn = Server.CreateObject("ADODB.Connection")

DataConn.Open Application("dbConnectionString"),
'set Connection = server.createobject("ADODB.Connection")
'Connection.Open "DatabaseDSN", "UserName", "Password"
set Result = server.createobject("ADODB.Recordset")
sql = "SELECT bwphoto FROM photos WHERE ImageId ='" & ImageID
&"'"

Result.Open sql, Connection, adOpenKeyset
if not (Result.eof and Result.bof) then
    'get the length of the contentns
    fldsze = Result.ActualSize("bwphoto")
    'Appendchuck or getchuck will work here
```

```
    Image = Result("bwphoto").AppendChuck(fldsze)
    Response.Buffer = true
    Response.ContentType = "image/gif"
    Response.BinaryWrite Image
else
    Response.Write "Nothing in database"
end if
Result.Close
Connection.Close
Response.End
%>
```

GetChunk   Field Object Method

Purpose
Use this method to return the contents of a large or binary Field object.

Syntax
```
Field.GetChunk(Length)
```

Table 19 lists the argument associated with the GetChunk method.

Table 19 *Argument for the GetChunk Method*

Value	Required	Type	Description
Length	Yes	Long	The number of bytes or characters to be retrieved

ASP Core Reference

Example
The following example uses the GetChunk method to obtain the contents of the Field object ImageData. This field contains binary data of .GIF files. The difference between the GetChunk and AppendChunk (p. ___) methods is that GetChunk or AppendChunk can be used to initially get the binary data, but only AppendChunk can add data.

```
<%
Set DataConn = Server.CreateObject("ADODB.Connection")
DataConn.Open Application("dbConnectionString"),
'set Connection = server.createobject("ADODB.Connection")
'Connection.Open "DatabaseDSN", "UserName", "Password"
set Result = server.createobject("ADODB.Recordset")
sql = "SELECT ImageData FROM Images WHERE ImageID=" & ImageID
```

```
Result.Open sql, Connection, adOpenKeyset
if not (Result.eof and Result.bof) then
    Image = Result("ImageData ").GetChunk(1024000)
    Response.Buffer = true
    Response.ContentType = "image/gif"
    Response.BinaryWrite Image
else
    Response.Write "nothing in database"
end if
Result.Close
Connection.Close
Response.End
%>
```

ActualSize   Field Object Property

Purpose

Use this property to determine the length of a Field object's value. The
datatype that is assigned to this property is a Long.

Syntax

```
Long = Field.ActualSize
Field.ActualSize = Long
```

Example

To find the actual size of all the fields in a recordset, use the following code:

```
'assume DataConn is the Connection object
SqlStm = "Select CollegeName From Colleges"
RS = DataConn.Execute("SqlStm")
'open a recordset with the Connection object execute 'method
RS = DataConn.Execute(SqlStm)
For j = 0 to RS.Fields.Count - 1
    Response.Write RS(j).ActualSize
Next
DataConn.close
Set DataConn = nothing
```

Attributes   Field Object Property

Purpose

Use this property to determine one or more characteristics of a Field object.
This method returns a FieldAttribute enumeration constant.

CROSS-REFERENCE

The `FieldAttribute` enumeration constants are available at the URL noted in the Preface.

Syntax

```
FieldAttributeEnum = Field.Attributes
```

Example

The following example shows you how use the `Attributes` property to determine if a field named "FirstName" can be set to null:

```
Set FldObj = RecordSetObject.Fields("FirstName")
If (FldObj.Attributes andadFldMaybeNull) = adFldUnknownUpdatable
then
     Response.WriteWrite "This field can be set to Null"
End if
```

DefinedSize	Field Object Property

Purpose

Use this property to determine the defined size of the `Field` object. The `Field` object's `ActualSize` property (p. 100) tells you the real size of the field versus the defined size, which is the size defined in the data schema.

Syntax

```
Long = Field.DefinedSize
```

Example

To find the defined field size for all fields in a result set greater than 5, use the following script:

```
Set DataConn = Server.CreateObject("ADODB.Connection")
DataConn.Open Application("dbConnectionString"),
'set Connection = server.createobject("ADODB.Connection")
'Connection.Open "DatabaseDSN", "UserName", "Password"
set Result = server.createobject("ADODB.Recordset")
sql = "SELECT CollegeName From Colleges"

RS.Open sql, Connection, adOpenKeyset

For I = 0 to RS.Fields.Count − 1
    If RS(I).DefinedSize > 5 then
        Response.WriteWrite "Defined Field Size is greater than
5"
    End if
Next
```

ASP Core Reference

Name

Purpose

Use this property to determine the name of the Field object.

Syntax

```
String = Field.Name
```

Example

To display the Field object's name, use the following script:

```
'DataConn is the Connection object
Set DataConn = Server.CreateObject("ADODB.Connection")
Set RS = Server.CreateObject("ADODB.Recordset")
SqlStm = "Select * From Colleges"
'open with a adDynamic which is 3.
RS.Open SqlStm, DataConn, 3, 1
'List out all the name of the Field
For j = 0 to RS.Fields.Count - 1
    Response.WriteRS(j).Name
Wend
```

NumericScale

Purpose

Use this property to determine how many digits to the right of the decimal point this Field object has.

Syntax

```
Byte = Field.NumericScale
```

Example

This script determines the number of digits to the right of the decimal point for all numeric fields in a result set.

```
Set DataConn = Server.CreateObject("ADODB.Connection")
DataConn.Open Application("dbConnectionString"),
'set Connection = Server.createobject("ADODB.Connection")
set Result = Server.createobject("ADODB.Recordset")
sql = "SELECT CollegeName From Colleges"

RS.Open sql, Connection, 2 , 1

For I = 0 to RS.Fields.Count — 1
    'if the field type is decimal
```

```
If RS(I).Type = adDecimal then
    Response.WriteRS(I).NumericScale
End if
```

Next

OriginalValue   Field Object Property

Purpose
Use this property to determine the value of the Field object from the data source before any changes happened.

Syntax
```
Field.OriginalValue
```

Example
To see the original value after a record has been changed, use the following script:

```
'DataConn is the Connection object
Set DataConn = Server.CreateObject("ADODB.Connection")
Set RS = Server.CreateObject("ADODB.Recordset")
SqlStm = "Select CollegeName From Colleges"
'open with a adDynamic which is 3.
RS.Open SqlStm, DataConn, 3, 1
'Move to the 5th record
RS.Move 5
'if college value is auburn then store in variable
'else change value to clemson.
If RS.Fields("College").Value = "Auburn" then
OValue = RS.Fields("College").OriginalValue
Else
RS.Update "College", "Clemson"
End if
```

Precision   Field Object Property

Purpose
Use this property to determine the maximum number of digits that can be used. A byte length is returned.

Syntax
```
Byte = Field.Precision
```

Example

The following example shows you how to find the maximum number of digits that the Deposits and Withdrawals fields can use by examining the Precision property:

```
'DataConn is the connection object
set Result = server.createobject("ADODB.Recordset")
sql = "SELECT Deposits,Withdrawals From BankDeposits"
RS.Open sql, DataConn, 2, 1

For I = 0 to RS.Fields.Count - 1
    'if the field type is decimal
    If RS(I).Type = adDecimal or RS(I).Type = adDouble or
RS(I).Type = adCurrency or RS(I).Type = adNumeric then
    Response.Write RS(I).Precision
    End if

Next
```

Status	Field Object Property

Purpose

Use this property to determine the status of a Field object, such as whether a field can be null, or whether the data type is defined in the database to be read-only. The value returns a FieldStatus enumeration constant such as adFieldIsNull or adFieldOk. The constant adFieldOk — which is 0 — is the default.

●—CROSS-REFERENCE

The FieldStatus enumerated constants are available at the URL noted in the Preface.

Syntax

```
Long = Field.Status
```

Example

The following example retrieves the names of employees from the table ExtremeStyleEmployees. The code then determines if the field FirstName is unavailable to be read by testing the value of the Field object's Status property. If the value of the Status property shows that the field "FirstName" is available, then we read the field.

```
<%
set DataConn = Server.CreateObject("ADODB.Connection")
```

```
DataConn.Open Application("db_ConnectionString")
sqlstm = "Select FirstName From ExtremeStyleEmployees"
'Open a connection
Dim RSetObj
Set RSetObj = Server.CreateObject("ADODB.Recordset")
RSetObj.Open sqlstm , DataConn , 1 , 1
Do while NOT EOF
'check to see if field is avaiable
    If RSetObj("FirstName").Status = adFieldUnavaiable then
    Response.Write "field is FirstName not avaiable to be read"
else
    Response.Write RSetObj("FirstName")
End if
RSetObj.MoveNext
Loop
%>
```

Type   Field Object Property

Purpose

Use this property to determine the variant type of the field. A DataTypeEnum
constant returns when you query this property.

●—CROSS-REFERENCE

The DataType enumeration constants are listed on-line.

Syntax

```
DataTypeEnum = Field.Type
```

Example

To find the Field object's Type property for each field in a recordset, use the
following script.

```
'-a list of the DataType enumeration constants are given--
Const adFldUpdatable = &H00000004
Const adFldUnknownUpdatable = &H00000008
Const adFldIsNullable = &H00000020
Const adUnsignedTinyInt = 17
Const adBoolean = 11
Const adLongVarChar = 201
Const adLongVarWChar = 203
Const adBinary = 128
Const adVarBinary = 204
```

```
Const adLongVarBinary = 205
Const adVarChar = 200
Const adWVarChar = 202
Const adBSTR = 8
Const adChar = 129
Const adWChar = 130
'___- CursorTypeEnum Values ___-
Const adOpenForwardOnly = 0
Const adOpenKeyset = 1
Const adOpenDynamic = 2
Const adOpenStatic = 3

Set DataConn = Server.CreateObject("ADODB.Connection")

'DataConn is the connection object
set Result = server.createobject("ADODB.Recordset")
sql = "SELECT Deposits,Withdrawals From BankDeposits"
'this opens a recordset using one of the constants
RS.Open sql, DataConn, adOpenKeyset, 1

For I = 0 to RS.Fields.Count - 1
    'if print out the field type
    Select Case RS(I).Type

    Case adLongVarBinary
        Response.Write "a binary"
    Case adUnsignedTinyInt
        Response.Write "unsigned Tiny int value"
    Case adBoolean, adUnsignedTinyInt
        Response.Write "boolean values"
    End Select
Next
```

UnderlyingValue   Field Object Property

Purpose

Use this property to determine the present value of the Field object. If the
field has been updated, the UnderlyingValue property will differ from the
Field object's OriginalValue property (p. 103).

Syntax

```
Variant = Field.UnderlyingValue
```

Example

To find the UnderlyingValue property of a field, use the following script:

```
Set DataConn = Server.CreateObject("ADODB.Connection")
Set RS = Server.CreateObject("ADODB.Recordset")
SqlStm = "Select F_Name,L_Name,City,State From Names"
RS.Open SqlStm, DataConn, adOpenDynamic
'Move to 7th Record
RS.Move 7
'print out the value of the 7th record
Response.Write "<BR>"& RS("F_Name").value
Response.Write "<BR>"& RS("L_Name").value
Response.Write "<BR>"& RS("City").value
Response.Write "<BR>"& RS("State").value

'change the value of the 7th Record
RS("F_Name").Value = "Tommy"
RS("L_Name").Value = "Erwin"
RS("City").Value = "Chiefland"
RS("State").Value = "Florida"
RS.Update

Response.Write "<BR>"& RS("F_Name").value
Response.Write "<BR>"& RS("L_Name").value
Response.Write "<BR>"& RS("City").value
Response.Write "<BR>"& RS("State").value

'this will print out the value before change
Response.Write "<BR>"& RS("F_Name").UnderlyingValue
Response.Write "<BR>"& RS("L_Name").UnderlyingValue
Response.Write "<BR>"& RS("City").UnderlyingValue
Response.Write "<BR>"& RS("State").UnderlyingValue
```

Value   Field Object Property

Purpose

Use this property to determine the value assigned, but not updated, to the Field object.

Syntax

```
Variant = Field.Value
```

Example

To find the value of a field, use the following code:

```
Set DataConn = Server.CreateObject("ADODB.Connection")
Set RS = Server.CreateObject("ADODB.Recordset")
SqlStm = "Select F_Name,L_Name,City,State From Names"
RS.Open SqlStm, DataConn, adOpenDynamic
'Move to 7th Record
'print out the value of the 7th record
Response.Write "<BR>"& RS("F_Name").Value
Response.Write "<BR>"& RS("L_Name").Value
Response.Write "<BR>"& RS("City").Value
Response.Write "<BR>"& RS("State").Value
```

Fields Collections Object

Purpose

Use the Fields Collection to add or obtain information about individual Field objects contained in a RecordSet object.

Syntax

```
RecordSetObject.Fields.Property
RecordSetObject.Fields.Method
```

Append	Fields Collections Object Method

Purpose

Use this method to add a Field object to the Fields collection. The cursor location property must be set to adUseClient before calling this method.

Syntax

```
RecordSetObject.Fields.Append ( Name, Type, DefinedSize,
Attribute Constant )
```

Table 20 lists the arguments associated with the Append method.

Table 20 *Arguments for the Append Method*

Value	Required	Type	Description
Name	Yes	String	The name of the new Field object
Type	Yes	DataTypeEnum	The data type of the Field object

Value	Required	Type	Description
DefinedSize	No	Long	The size defined in the database
Attribute Constant	No		FieldAttributeEnum The attribute for the new field. The default is adFldDefault.

●—CROSS-REFERENCE

The `DataType` and `FieldAttribute` enumeration constants are available on-line.

Example

The following code adds a `Field` object to the `Fields` collection:

```
Set DataConn = Server.CreateObject("ADODB.Connection")
Set RS = Server.CreateObject("ADODB.Recordset")
SqlStm = "Select F_Name,L_Name,City,State From Names"
RS.Open SqlStm, DataConn, adOpenDynamic
Rs.CursorLocation = adUseClient
'add this field object to the collection
RS.Fields.Append "Country", adVarChar, 50, adFldMayBeNull
RS.Fields.Refresh
```

CancelUpdate	Fields Collections Object Method

Purpose

Use this method to cancel any changes you have made to a new or existing record in the `RecordSet` object before issuing the `Update` method (p. 206). You can also use this method to cancel any changes to a `Fields` ollections object before issuing the update.

Syntax

```
RecordSetObject.Fields.CancelUpdate
```

Example

The following example cancels the new column that was added in the `Fields` collections `Append` method (p. 108). Then the change is stopped by issuing the `CancelUpdate` method on the Fields Collections.

```
<%
set DataConn = Server.CreateObject("ADODB.Connection")
```

ASP Core Reference

```
DataConn.Open Application("db_ConnectionString")
sqlstm = "Select * From Colleges"
'Open a connection
Dim Rs
Set Rs = Server.CreateObject("ADODB.Recordset")
SqlStm = "Select F_Name,L_Name,City,State From Names"
RS.Open SqlStm, DataConn, adOpenDynamic
Rs.CursorLocation = adUseClient
'add this field object to the collection
RS.Fields.Append "Country", adVarChar, 50, adFldMayBeNull
RS.Fields.Refresh
'cancel the update before issuing the RS.Update
RS.Fields.CancelUpdate
%>
```

Delete   Fields Collections Object Method

Purpose

Use this method to delete a Field object from the Fields collections.

Syntax

```
RecordSetObject.Fields.Delete(Field Object Index)
```

Table 21 lists the argument associated with the Delete method.

Table 21   *Argument for the Delete Method*

Value	Required	Type	Description
Field Object Index	Yes	Variant	The name of the column or the column number to be deleted

Example

This example deletes the Field object added in the Fields collection's Append method (p. 108):

```
Set DataConn = Server.CreateObject("ADODB.Connection")
Set RS = Server.CreateObject("ADODB.Recordset")
SqlStm = "Select F_Name,L_Name,City,State From Names"
RS.Open SqlStm, DataConn, adOpenDynamic
Rs.CursorLocation = adUseClient
'add this field object to the collection
```

```
RS.Fields.Delete("Country")
RS.Fields.Refresh
```

Refresh   Fields Collections Object Method

Purpose
Use this method to update the `Field` object in the `Fields` collections.

Syntax
```
RecordSetObject.Fields.Refresh
```

Example
The following code refreshes the `Field` object after the field "Country" is added to the Fields ollections:

```
Set DataConn = Server.CreateObject("ADODB.Connection")
Set RS = Server.CreateObject("ADODB.Recordset")
SqlStm = "Select F_Name,L_Name,City,State From Names"
RS.Open SqlStm, DataConn, adOpenDynamic
Rs.CursorLocation = adUseClient
'add this field object to the collection
RS.Fields.Append "Country", adVarChar, 50, adFldMayBeNull
RS.Fields.Refresh
```

Resync   Fields Collections Object Method

Purpose
Use this method to synchronize the `OriginalValue` (p. 103), `Value` (p. 107), and `UnderlyingValue` (p. 106) properties of the `Field` object in the `Fields` Collections. However, if you supply the `Resync` method with the `ResyncEnum` constant `adResyncUnderlyingValues`, then only the `UnderlyingValue` property will be synchronized.

If new rows have been added to the `Field` Collections, issuing this method will not affect the `Field` Collections `Count` property. Thus, if there are four items in the Collection before issuing the `Resync` method, there will still be four after issuing the `Resync` method, even if you added a new row to the Collection.

Syntax
```
RecordSetObject.Fields.Resync ( Resync Value)
```

Table 22 lists the argument associated with the `Resync` method.

Table 22 *Argument for the Resync Method*

Value	Required	Type	Description
Resync Value	No	ResyncEnum	This is a `Resync` enumeration constant.The default value is `adResynceAll Values`. If the value `adResyncUnderlyingValues` is used, then only the underlying value of the `Field` property will be synchronized.

●—**CROSS-REFERENCE**

The `Resync` enumeration constants are available at the URL noted in the Preface.

Example

The following example refreshes all the changes to the `Field` Collections object:

```
Set DataConn = Server.CreateObject("ADODB.Connection")
Set RS = Server.CreateObject("ADODB.Recordset")
SqlStm = "Select F_Name,L_Name,City,State From Names"
RS.Open SqlStm, DataConn, adOpenDynamic
Rs.CursorLocation = adUseClient
'add this field object to the collection
RS.Fields.Append "Country", adVarChar, 50, adFldMayBeNull
RS.Fields.Resync
```

Update	**Fields Collections Object Method**

Purpose

Use this method to save any changes you made to any items in the `Fields` Collections. One drawback about this method is that not every database provider supports it.

Syntax

```
RecordSetObject.Fields.Update
```

Example

The following example shows you how to use the `Update` method to update the `Fields` Collection. The code shows a new column being added to the recordset

RS through the use of the Fields Collections object's Append method. Once the column has been appended, then the Update method is called.

```
Set DataConn = Server.CreateObject("ADODB.Connection")
Set RS = Server.CreateObject("ADODB.Recordset")
SqlStm = "Select F_Name,L_Name,City,State From Names"
RS.Open SqlStm, DataConn, adOpenDynamic
Rs.CursorLocation = adUseClient
'add this field object to the collection
RS.Fields.Append "Country", adVarChar, 50, adFldMayBeNull
RS.Fields.Update
```

Count   Fields Collections Object Property

Purpose
Use this property to determine the number of Field objects in the Field Collections object. This property returns a long value.

Syntax
```
Long = RecordSetObject.Fields.Count
```

Example
The following code gets the field counts from the recordset RS:

```
Set DataConn = Server.CreateObject("ADODB.Connection")
Set RS = Server.CreateObject("ADODB.Recordset")
SqlStm = "Select F_Name,L_Name,City,State From Names"
RS.Open SqlStm, DataConn, adOpenDynamic
'to get count
Response.Write RS.Fields.Count
```

Item   Fields Collections Object Property

Purpose
Use this property to enable indexing of the Field object in the Fields Collection.

Syntax
```
Set Field = RecordSetObject.Fields.Item(Field Object Index)
```

Table 23 lists the argument associated with the Item property.

ASP Core Reference

Table 23 *Argument for Item Property*

Value	Required	Type	Description
Field Object Index	Yes	Variant	The name of the column or the column number to be indexed

Example

The following code uses the Item property to get the value of each column in the Field object. The line of code For I = 0 to RS.Fields.Count − 1 counts the number of fields in the recordset.

```
Set DataConn = Server.CreateObject("ADODB.Connection")
Set RS = Server.CreateObject("ADODB.Recordset")
SqlStm = "Select F_Name,L_Name,City,State From Names"
RS.Open SqlStm, DataConn, adOpenDynamic
'to get count
For I = 0 to  RS.Fields.Count − 1
    Response.Write RS.Fields.Item(I)
Next
```

File Object

Purpose

The File object allows the programmer to access information about a file such as the last time someone accessed the file.

Syntax

```
FileObject.PropertyName
```

Attributes   **File Object Property**

Purpose

Use this property to set or find the attribute of the file. The values that this property can return are given below. These are the same values as those for the Folder object.

```
0 — Normal
1 — ReadOnly
2 — Hidden
4 — System
8 — Volume
16 — Directory
```

```
32 — Archive
1024 - Alias
2048 - Compressed
```

Syntax

```
FolderObject.Attributes
```

Example

The following example opens the FileSystemObject object, and then creates a File object from the file C:\myfiles\DrWilliamEbauer.txt. Once the File object is created, the Attributes property is used to indicate the type of attributes for the file.

```
<%
Dim FSObj,FileObj
Set FSObj = Server.CreateObject("Scripting.FileSystemObject")
Set FileObj = FSObj.GetFile("C:\myfiles\DrWilliamEbauer.txt")
Select Case FileObj.Attributes
Case 0
Response.Write "Normal "
Case 1
Response.Write "ReadOnly"
Case 2
    Response.Write "Hidden"
Case 4
    Response.Write "System"
Case 8
    Response.Write "Volume"
Case 16
    Response.Write "Directory"
Case 32
    Response.Write "Archive"
Case 1024
    Response.Write "Alias"
Case 2048
    Response.Write "Compressed"
End Select
%>
```

DateCreated   File Object Property

Purpose

Use this property to determine when the file associated with the File object was created.

Syntax

```
FileObject.DateCreated
```

Example

The following example opens the `FileSystemObject` object, and then creates a `File` object from the file C:\myfiles.txt. Once the `File` object is created, the `DateCreated` property is used to determine when the file was created.

```
<%
Dim FSObj,FileObj
Set FSObj = Server.CreateObject("Scripting.FileSystemObject")
Set FileObj = FSObj.GetFile("C:\myfiles.txt")
Response.Write "The file was created on "
Response.Write FileObj.DateCreated
%>
```

DateLastAccessed   File Object Property

Purpose

Use this property to determine when the given directory was last accessed.

Syntax

```
FileObject.DateLastAccessed
```

Example

The following example opens the `FileSystemObject` object, and then creates a `File` object from the file C:\myfiles.txt. Once the `File` object is created, the code uses the `DateLastAccessed` property to determine when the file c:\myfiles.txt was last accessed.

```
<%
Dim FSObj,FileObj
Set FSObj = Server.CreateObject("Scripting.FileSystemObject")
Set FileObj = FSObj.GetFile("C:\myfiles.txt")
Response.Write "The Last Time this directory accessed was "
Response.Write FileObj.DateLastAccessed
%>
```

DateLastModified   File Object Property

Purpose

Use this property to determine when the last modification to the file associated with the `File` object occurred.

Syntax

```
FileObject.DateLastModified
```

Example

The following example opens the FileSystemObject object, and then creates a File object from a file c:\Auburn.txt. Once the File object is created, the code uses the DateLastModified property to determine when the last modification to this file occurred.

```
<%
Dim FSObj,FileObj
Set FSObj = Server.CreateObject("Scripting.FileSystemObject")
Set FileObj = FSObj.GetFile("c:\Auburn.txt")
Response.Write "Last Date Directory was Modified "
Response.Write FileObj.DateLastModified
%>
```

Drive   File Object Property

Purpose

Use this property to determine the drive letter on which the file in the File object resides.

Syntax

```
FileObject.Drive
```

Example

The following example opens theFileSystemObject object, and then creates a File object from a file c:\Georgia.txt. Once the File object is created, the Drive property is used to determine the drive letter associated with the File object.

```
<%
Dim FSObj,FileObj
Set FSObj = Server.CreateObject("Scripting.FileSystemObject")
Set FileObj = FSObj.GetFile("c:\Georgia.txt")
Response.Write "The Drive letter associated with the Folder
Object is "
Response.Write FileObj.Drive
%>
```

Following is the message that will appear in the browser:

```
The Drive letter associated with the Folder object is C.
```

Name   File Object Property

Purpose

Use this property to get the name of the file associated with the File object.

Syntax

```
FileObject.Name
```

Example

The following example opens the FileSystemObject object, and then creates a File object from a file c:\Georgia.txt. Once the File object is created, the Name property is used to determine the name of the file associated with the File object.

```
<%
Dim FSObj,FileObj
Set FSObj = Server.CreateObject("Scripting.FileSystemObject")
Set FileObj = FSObj.GetFile("c:\Georgia.txt")
Response.Write "The Name of the File in the File Object is "
Response.Write FileObj.Name
%>
```

Following is the message that will appear in the browser:

```
The Name of the File in the File Object is GEORGIA.TXT
```

ParentFolder   File Object Property

Purpose

Use this property to get the Folder object of the File object.

Syntax

```
FileObject.ParentFolder
```

Example

The following example opens the FileSystemObject object, and then creates a File object from a file c:\TombalTexas.txt. After the File object is created, the code uses the ParentFolder property to get the parent Folder object of c:\TombalTexas.txt.

```
<%
Dim FSObj,FileObj
Set FSObj = Server.CreateObject("Scripting.FileSystemObject")
Set FileObj = FSObj.GetFile("c:\TombalTexas.txt")
Response.Write "The ParentFolder of this File object is "
Response.Write FileObj.ParentFolder
%>
```

The message that will appear in the browser is as follows:

```
The ParentFolder of this File object is C:\
```

Path   File Object Property

Purpose
Use this property the determine the path of the File object.

Syntax
```
FileObject.Path
```

Example
The following example opens the FileSystemObject object, and then creates a File object from a file c:\SamHendrix.txt. After the File object is created, the code uses the Path property to obtain the path of the File object.

```
<%
Dim FSObj,FileObj
Set FSObj = Server.CreateObject("Scripting.FileSystemObject")

Set FileObj = FSObj.GetFile("c:\SamHendrix.txt")
Response.Write "The path of this file is "
Response.Write FileObj.Path
%>
```

The code will return the following message:

```
The path of this file is C:\SAMHENDRIX.TXT
```

ShortName   File Object Property

Purpose
Use this property to find the 8.3 version of the filename.

Syntax
```
FileObject.ShortName
```

Example
The following example opens the FileSystemObject object, and then creates a File object from the file c:\MaryEllenHendrix.txt. Once the File object is created, the code uses the ShortName property to obtain the version 8.3 name of the file.

```
<%
Dim FSObj,FileObj
Set FSObj = Server.CreateObject("Scripting.FileSystemObject")
Set FileObj = FSObj.Get File("c:\MaryEllenHendrix.txt")

Response.Write "ShortName of the File object is "
Response.Write FileObj.ShortName
%>
```

ASP Core Reference

The code will return the following message:

```
ShortName of the File object is MARYELLENHENDRIX
```

ShortPath
File Object Property

Purpose

Use this property to get the 8.3 version of the file path for the File object. Most of the time, the string returned will be identical to what is returned by the Path property.

Syntax

```
FileObject.ShortPath
```

Example

This example shows how to obtain the short path name of the File object. The following code creates a File object from the file c:\KelseyHendrix.txt. Once the File object is created, the code uses the ShortPath property to obtain the version 8.3 name of the path.

```
<%
Dim FSObj,FileObj
Set FSObj = Server.CreateObject("Scripting.FileSystemObject")

Set FileObj = FSObj.GetFile("c:\KelseyHendrix.txt")

Response.Write "ShortName of the File object is "
Response.Write FileObj.ShortName
%>
```

The code will return the following message:

```
ShortName of the File object is C:\KELSEYHENDRIX.TXT
```

Size
File Object Property

Purpose

Use this property to get the number of bytes in the File object.

Syntax

```
FileObject.Size
```

Example

This example shows how to obtain the size of the File object. The following code creates a File object from the file c:\JoyEbauer.txt. Once the File object is created, the code uses the Size property to obtain the size of the file.

```
<%
Dim FSObj,FileObj
Set FSObj = Server.CreateObject("Scripting.FileSystemObject")
Set FileObj = FSObj.GetFile("c:\JoyEbauer.txt")
Response.Write "Size of the File object is "
Response.Write FileObj.Size
%>
```

Type	File Object Property

Purpose

Use this property to get information about what type of file the File object
is. The value returned from this property is a string. Normally, for a file with
a .TXT extension, you will get the value TEXT DOCUMENT.

Syntax

```
FileObject.Type
```

Example

The following example associates a .PDF file — c:\WarnerRobinsHighClass77.
pdf — with a File object. Then, the Response object's Write method is used
to output the file type.

```
<%
Dim FSObj,FileObj
Set FSObj = Server.CreateObject("Scripting.FileSystemObject")
Set FileObj = FSObj.GetFile("c:\WarnerRobinsHighClass77.pdf")
Response.Write "The File Type is "
Response.Write FileObj.Type
%>
```

The code will return the following message:

```
The File Type is Adobe Acrobat Document
```

FileSystemObject Object

Purpose

This object deals with the creation and maintenance of a file.

Syntax

```
Set filesysobj = CreateObject("Scripting.FileSystemObject")
```

ASP Core Reference

BuildPath   FileSystemObject Method

Purpose

Use this method to add an additional directory path to an existing path.

Syntax

```
object.BuildPath(path, name)
FileSystemObject. BuildPath( TheNameofDir, theAddedPath)
```

Table 24 lists the arguments associated with the BuildPath method.

Table 24   *Arguments for the BuildPath Method*

Value	Required	Type	Description
TheNameofDir	Yes	String	The name of the path, such as c:\yourname\me
TheAddedPath	Yes	String	The value adds an additional path name you want to The NameofDir. This argument will add a slash "\" to the name of the path.

Example

The following example uses the BuildPath method to add the path \Gifs to the directory c:\MyImages:

```
<%
dim fso
Set fso = Server.CreateObject("Scripting.FileSystemObject")
Response.Write "The new path is "
Response.Write fso.BuildPath("c:\MyImages" ,"Gifs")
%>
```

The output that will appear in the browser is as follows:

```
The new path is C:\MyImages\Gifs
```

CopyFile   FileSystemObject Method

Purpose

Use this method to copy a file from one location to another location.

Syntax

```
FileSytemObject.CopyFile  Source, Destination, OverWrite
```

Table 25 lists the arguments associated with the CopyFile method.

Table 25   *Arguments for the CopyFile Method*

Value	Required	Type	Description
Source	Yes	String	The file that will be copied
Destination	Yes	String	The location where the file is to be copied to
OverWrite	No	Boolean	If the file already exists, do you want to overwrite the contents of that file with the new contents?

Example

The following example creates a copy of the file c:\WilliamEbauer.txt to the directory c:\friends. A FileSystemObject object is created, and then the code uses the CopyFile method to create the copy of c:\WilliamEbauer.txt in the directory c:\friends.

```
<%
dim fso
Set fso = Server.CreateObject("Scripting.FileSystemObject")
fso.CopyFile "c:\ WilliamEbauer.txt" ,"c:\ friends \"
%>
```

CopyFolder   FileSystemObject Method

Purpose

Use this method to copy the contents of a folder to a different location.

Syntax

```
FileSytemObject.CopyFolder  Source, Destination, OverWrite
```

Table 26 lists the arguments associated with the CopyFolder method.

Table 26   *Arguments for the CopyFolder Method*

Value	Required	Type	Description
Source	Yes	String	The directory that will be copied
Destination	Yes	String	The location where the directory is to be copied to

Continued

Table 26   *Continued*

Value	Required	Type	Description
OverWrite	No	Boolean	If the folder already exists, do you want to overwrite the contents of that folder with the new contents?

Example

The following example creates a copy of the contents of folder c:\MyImages\Gifs to the directory c:\OtherImages.

```
<%
dim fso
Set fso = Server.CreateObject("Scripting.FileSystemObject")
fso.CopyFolder " c:\MyImages\Gifs" ," c:\OtherImages"
%>
```

CreateFolder   FileSystemObject Method

Purpose

Use this method to create a new folder. You can also say that this method is used to create a new file directory.

Syntax

```
FileSytemObject.CreateFolder NameofNewDirectory
```

Table 27 lists the argument associated with the CreateFolder method.

Table 27   *Argument for the CreateFolder Method*

Value	Required	Type	Description
NameofNewDirectory	Yes	String	The directory that will be created

Example

The following example creates a new directory using the CreateFolder method. The directory is named c:\MyNewDirectory.

```
<%
dim fso
Set fso = Server.CreateObject("Scripting.FileSystemObject")
```

```
fso.CreateFolder "c:\MyNewDirectory"
%>
```

CreateTextFile   FileSystemObject Method

Purpose

Use this method to create a particular filename and return a TextStream object (p. 298) that can be used to read from or write to the file.

The Overwrite argument is optional; it is a Boolean value that determines if an existing file may be overwritten. The returned value will be True if the file can be overwritten, and False if it can't be overwritten; if absent, existing files will not be overwritten. The Unicode argument is an optional Boolean value that determines whether the file is created as a Unicode or ASCII file.

Syntax

```
object.CreateTextFile(filename[, overwrite[, unicode]])
```

Table 28 lists the arguments associated with the CreateTextFile method.

Table 28 *Arguments for the CreateTextFile Method*

Value	Required	Type	Description
FileName	Yes	String	The name of the file you want to create, including the path
Overwrite	No	Boolean	This option is used to overwrite an existing file
			True = you can overwrite an existing file
			False = you cannot overwrite an existing file. False is the default value.
Unicode	No	Boolean	Determines whether a file is created with ASCII or Unicode
			True = the file is created with Unicode
			False = the file is created with ASCII. The default value is False.

ASP Core Reference

Example

The following example shows you how to use the CreateTextFile method to create a text file. The full path of the text file is included in the filename. The example creates the file c:\AuburnTigers.txt.

```
<%
Dim filesystemobj,Myfile
Set filesystemobj =
CreateObject("Scripting.FileSystemObject",True)
Set Myfile =
filesystemobj.CreateTextFile("c:\AuburnTigers.txt",true,false)
%>
```

DeleteFile   FileSystemObject Method

Purpose

Use this method to delete a file.

Syntax

```
FileSystemObject.DeleteFile    NameofTheFileToDelete
```

Table 29 lists the argument associated with the DeleteFile method.

Table 29   Argument for the DeleteFile Method

Value	Required	Type	Description
NameofTheFileToDelete	Yes	String	This value is name of the file to be deleted.

Example

The following example deletes a file using the DeleteFile method. The file is named c:\MyNewTextFile.txt.

```
<%
dim fso
Set fso = Server.CreateObject("Scripting.FileSystemObject")
fso.DeleteFile " c:\MyNewTextFile.txt"
%>
```

DeleteFolder   FileSystemObject Method

Purpose

Use this method to delete a folder from a directory structure.

Syntax

```
FileSystemObject.DeleteFile    TheFolderToDelete
```

Table 30 lists the argument associated with the DeleteFolder method.

Table 30 *Argument for the DeleteFolder Method*

Value	Required	Type	Description
TheFolderToDelete	Yes	String	The name of the folder to be deleted. Remember to include the drive that it is to be deleted on, such as c:\.

Example

The following example deletes a folder using the DeleteFolder method. The folder to be deleted is c:\MyImages.

```
<%
dim fso
Set fso = Server.CreateObject("Scripting.FileSystemObject")
fso.DeleteFolder "c:\MyImages"
%>
```

FileExists   FileSystemObject Method

Purpose

Use this method to determine if a file exists. This method returns either a True or False value.

Syntax

```
FileSystemObject.FileExists NameOFFile
```

Table 31 lists the argument associated with the FileExists method.

Table 31 *Argument for the FileExists Method*

Value	Required	Type	Description
NameOFFile	Yes	String	The name of the file whose existence you want to confirm. Remember to include the drive that it is to be created on, such as c:\.

Example

The following example determines if the file c:\AmyEden.txt exists or not:

```
<%
dim fso
```

```
Set fso = Server.CreateObject("Scripting.FileSystemObject")
fso.FileExist
if (fso.FileExists "c:\AmyEden") then
    Response.Write "The file exists"
else
    Response.Write "The file does not exists"
end if
%>
```

FolderExists   FileSystemObject Method

Purpose

Use this method to determine if a folder exists. This method returns either a
True or False value.

Syntax

```
FileSystemObject.FolderExists NameofFolder
```

Table 32 lists the argument associated with the FolderExists method.

Table 32 *Argument for the FolderExists Method*

Value	Required	Type	Description
NameofFolder	Yes	String	The name of the folder whose existence you want to confirm. Remember to include the drive that it is to be created on, such as c:\.

Example

The following example determines if the folder c:\AuburnFootball exists
or not.

```
<%
dim fso
Set fso = Server.CreateObject("Scripting.FileSystemObject")
fso.FileExist
if (fso.FolderExists "c:\AuburnFootball") then
    Response.Write "The directory exists"
else
    Response.Write "The directory does not exists"
end if
%>
```

GetAbsolutePathName | FileSystemObject Method

Purpose
Use this method to determine the absolute path of a file.

Syntax
```
FileSystemObject.GetAbsolutePathName  Path
```

Table 33 lists the argument associated with the GetAbsolutePathName method.

Table 33 *Argument for the GetAbsolutePathName Method*

Value	Required	Type	Description
Path	Yes	String	The URL of the path, such as c:\

Example
The following example finds the absolute path name for the file c:\DavidMoore\JoyMoore.txt:

```
<%
dim fso
Set fso = Server.CreateObject("Scripting.FileSystemObject")
Response.Write "The AbsolutePath is "
Response.Write fso.GetAbsolutePathName "
c:\DavidMoore\JoyMoore.txt"
%>
```

The browser will return the following message:

```
The AbsolutePath is C:\DavidMoore\JoyMoore.txt
```

GetBaseName | FileSystemObject Method

Purpose
Use this method to get the base name of the file or directory.

Syntax

ho extension part.

```
FileSystemObject.GetBaseName Path
```

Table 34 lists the argument associated with the GetBaseName method.

Table 34 *TArgument for the GetBaseName Method*

Value	Required	Type	Description
Path	Yes	String	The URL of the path, such as c:\

Example

The following example finds the base name for the file c:\ScottHorne.txt:

```
<%
dim fso
Set fso = Server.CreateObject("Scripting.FileSystemObject")
Response.Write "The Base Name is "
Response.Write fso.GetBaseName " c:\ScottHorne.txt"
%>
```

The browser will return the following message:

```
The Base Name is ScottHorne
```

GetDrive   FileSystemObject Method

Purpose

Use this method to get the Drive object. Once the Drive object is obtained, you can use the properties contained in the Drive object.

●—CROSS-REFERENCE

Coverage of the Drive object's properties start on page 84.

Syntax

```
FSObj = Server.CreateObject("Scripting.FileSystemObject")
Set DriveObject = FSObj.GetDrive(TheDriveName)
```

Table 35 lists the argument associated with the GetDrive method.

Table 35 *Argument for the GetDrive Method*

Value	Required	Type	Description
TheDriveName	Yes	String	The name of the drive, such as c:\ or d:\

Example

The following example gets the Drive object. Then use the Drive object's SerialNumber property to display the serial number of the drive.

```
<%
dim fso,drvobj
Set fso = Server.CreateObject("Scripting.FileSystemObject")
Set drvobj = fso.GetDrive("c:\")
Response.Write "The Serial Number of the drive is "
Response.Write drvobj.SerialNumber
%>
```

GetDriveName   FileSystemObject Method

Purpose

Use this method to determine the name of the drive.

Syntax

```
FileSystemObject.GetDriveName Path
```

Table 36 lists the argument associated with the GetDriveName method.

Table 36 *Argument for the GetDriveName Method*

Value	Required	Type	Description
Path	Yes	String	The URL of the drive, such as c:\

Example

The following example finds the drive name for the file c:\DavidMoore:

```
<%
dim fso
Set fso = Server.CreateObject("Scripting.FileSystemObject")
Response.Write "The Drive Name is "
Response.Write fso.GetDriveName("c:\DavidMoore")
%>
```

The browser will return the following message:

```
The Drive Name is c:
```

GetExtensionName   FileSystemObject Method

Purpose
Use this method to find the extension on a file.

Syntax
```
FileSystemObject.GetExtensionName FileName
```

Table 37 lists the argument associated with the GetExtensionName method.

Table 37   Argument for the GetExtensionName Method

Value	Required	Type	Description
FileName	Yes	String	The URL of the file, such as c:\

Example
The following example will find the name of the extension for the file
c:\myname.pdf:

```
<%
dim fso
Set fso = Server.CreateObject("Scripting.FileSystemObject")
Response.Write "The Extension Name is "
Response.Write fso.GetExtensionName("c:\myname.pdf")
%>
```

The browser will return the following message:

```
The Extension Name is pdf
```

GetFile   FileSystemObject Method

Purpose
Use this method to obtain the File object. Once you get the File object, you
can use all the properties of the File object.

●—CROSS-REFERENCE
Coverage of the File object's properties starts on page 114.

Syntax
```
FSObj = Server.CreateObject("Scripting.FileSystemObject")
Set FileObject = FSObj.GetFile(TheFileName)
```

Table 38 lists the argument associated with the GetFile method.

Table 38   *Argument for the GetFile Method*

Value	Required	Type	Description
TheFileName	Yes	String	The name of the file

Example

The following example gets the File object that is created from the file c:\BaseballTeams.txt. Then use the File object's DateLastAccessed property (p. 116) to display the last time anyone accessed the file.

```
<%
dim fso,fileobj
Set fso = Server.CreateObject("Scripting.FileSystemObject")
Set fileobj = fso.GetFile("c:\BaseballTeams.txt")
Response.Write "The Last Time anyone accessed this file was "
Response.Write fileobj.DateLastAccessed
%>
```

GetFileName   FileSystemObject Method

Purpose
Use this method to obtain the name of the file.

Syntax
```
FileSystemObject.GetFileName FileName
```

Table 39 lists the argument associated with the GetFileName method.

Table 39   *Argument for the GetFileName Method*

Value	Required	Type	Description
FileName	Yes	String	The URL of the file, such as c:\

Example

The following example will find the name of the file for the file c:\myname.pdf:

```
<%
dim fso
Set fso = Server.CreateObject("Scripting.FileSystemObject")
Response.Write "The Name of the File is "
```

```
Response.Write fso.GetFileName("c:\myname.pdf")
%>
```

The browser will return the following message:

```
The Name of the File is myname.pdf
```

GetFolder	**FileSystemObject Method**

Purpose

Use this method to obtain the Folder object.

●—CROSS-REFERENCE————————————

You can find all the properties of the Folder object starting on page (p. 141).

Syntax

```
FSObj = Server.CreateObject("Scripting.FileSystemObject")
Set FolderObject = FSObj.GetFolder(TheDirectoryName)
```

Table 40 lists the argument associated with the GetFolder method.

Table 40   *Argument for the GetFolder Method*

Value	Required	Type	Description
TheDirectoryName	Yes	String	The name of the directory that will be associated with the Folder object, such as c:\anydirectory

Example

The following example will get the Folder object from the directory c:\Images\Gifs. Then use the Folder object's DateLastAccessed property (p. 116) to display the last time anyone accessed the directory.

```
<%
dim fso,folderobj
Set fso = Server.CreateObject("Scripting.FileSystemObject")
Set folderobj = fso.GetFolder("c:\Images\Gifs")
%>
```

GetParentFolderName

Purpose

Use this method to obtain the name of the parent directory of a subdirectory.

Syntax

```
FileSystemObject.GetParentFolderName NameofDirectory
```

Table 41 lists the argument associated with the GetParentFolderName method.

Table 41   *Argument for the GetParentFolderName Method*

Value	Required	Type	Description
NameofDirectory	Yes	String	The URL of the file, such as c:\anydirectory

Example

The following example will get the parent folder for the directory c:\Images\Gifs\:

```
<%
dim fso,folderobj
Set fso = Server.CreateObject("Scripting.FileSystemObject")
Set folderobj = fso.GetFolder("c:\Images\Gifs\")
Response.Write "The Parent Folder is "
Response.Write folderobj.GetParentFolderName
%>
```

The browser will return the following message:

```
The Parent Folder is c:\Images
```

GetSpecialFolder

Purpose

Use this method to return one of the "special" folders. Normally, these special folders are related to the c:\Windows directory.

Syntax

```
FileSystemObject.GetSpecialFolder (FolderOption)
```

Table 42 lists the argument associated with the GetSpecialFolder method.

Table 42   *Argument for the GetSpecialFolder Method*

Value	Required	Type	Description
FolderOption	Yes	Number	Windows directory that represents one of the following three options:
			MainWindowsDirectory — 0
			SystemWindowsDirectory — 1
			TempWindowsDirectory - 2

Example

The following example returns the special folder that represents option 1 from the table:

```
<%
dim fso
Set fso = Server.CreateObject("Scripting.FileSystemObject")
fso.GetSpecialFolder(1)
Response.Write "The Special Folder is "
Response.Write folderobj.GetSpecialFolder
%>
```

The browser will return the following message:

```
The Special Folder  is c:\Windows\System
```

GetTempName   FileSystemObject Method

Purpose

Use this method to randomly generate a temporary file or folder name. You can use this method whenever you need a place to hold a file for a short time. After you're finished using the temporary file or folder, delete it.

Syntax

```
Set temp = FileSystemObject.GetTempName
```

Example

The following code is used to randomly generate a temporary filename. That temporary filename is used to create a file.

```
<%
dim fso,tempfname
Set fso = Server.CreateObject("Scripting.FileSystemObject")
tempfname  = fso.GetTempName
```

```
fso.CreateTextFile tempfname
Response.Write "The Temporary File Name is "
Response.Write tempfname
%>
```

MoveFile — FileSystemObject Method

Purpose

Use this method to move a file from one location to another.

Syntax

```
FileSystemObject.MoveFile  TheFileToBeMove,
    TheLocationToMoveFileTo
```

Table 43 lists the arguments associated with the MoveFile method.

Table 43 Arguments for the MoveFile Method

Value	Required	Type	Description
TheFileToBeMove	Yes	String	The name of the file, including the directory that is to be moved. The directory will be something like c:\yourfile or d:\yourfile.
TheLocationToMoveFileTo	Yes	String	The path to the new location, such as c:\newlocation or g:\mycomputer\the-newlocation\. You must have a slash "\" at the end of your destination location.

Example

The following code moves the file c:\DonElwell.txt to a file location on a network drive. Remember that you must have a network envirnoment in order for this example to work; otherwise, use your local hard drive with this example. You must have a slash "\" at the end of your

```
<%
dim fso,tempfname
Set fso = Server.CreateObject("Scripting.FileSystemObject")
fso.MoveFile "c:\DonElwell.txt" , "g:\Net\SamHendrix\"
%>
```

| MoveFolder | FileSystemObject Method |

Purpose

Use this method to move a folder from one location to another. The File and Folder objects both have a Move method. (The Folder objects Move method is covered on p. 144.) We recommend you use this method instead.

Syntax

```
FileSystemObject.MoveFile  TheFileToBeMove,
TheLocationToMoveFileTo
```

Table 44 lists the arguments associated with the MoveFolder method.

Table 44 *Arguments for the MoveFolder Method*

Value	Required	Type	Description
TheFileToBeMove	Yes	String	The name of the file, including the directory that is to be moved. The directory will be something like c:\your-file or d:\yourfile.
TheLocationToMoveFileTo	Yes	String	The path to the new location, such as c:\newlocation or g:\mycomputer\the-newlocation\. You must have a "\" at the end of your destination location.

Example

The following code moves the folder c:\LoriSly to a file location on a network drive. The file on the network drive is g:\Net\SamHendrix\. Remember that you must have a network envirnoment in order for this example to work; otherwise, use your local hard drive.for this example You must have a "\" at the end of your

```
<%
dim fso,tempfname
Set fso = Server.CreateObject("Scripting.FileSystemObject")
fso.MoveFolder "c:\LoriSly" , "g:\Net\SamHendrix\"
%>
```

OpenTextFile   FileSystemObject Method

Purpose

Use this to method to open a particular file and return a `TextStream` object (p. 298) that can be used to read from, write to, or append to a file.

Syntax

```
FileSystemObject.OpenTextFile(filename[, inoutmode[,
create[, format]]])
```

Table 45 lists the arguments associated with the `OpenTextFile` method.

Table 45 *Arguments for TextFile Method*

Value	Required	Type	Description
Filename	Yes	String	The name of the file you're going to open
Inoutmode	No	Number	The input/output mode you want to use. Inoutmode can have any of the following settings: ForReading 1 Opens a file for reading only. You can't write to this file. ForWriting 2 Opens a file for writing only. You can't read from this file. ForAppending 8 Opens a file and writes to the end of the file.
CreateFile	No	Boolean	Tells you if a file will be created if the file doesn't exist. True – the file will be created False – the file will not be created
Format	No	Number	This value can have three states. TristateUseDefault -2 Opens the file using the system default. If no value is supplied to option, this is the default. TristateTrue -1 Opens the file as Unicode TristateFalse 0 Opens the file as ASCII

Example

The following example uses the OpenTextFile method to open a file for writing text. The file will be opened for reading only. The file is created if it doen't exist and the format for the file will be ASCII.

```
<%
Dim Fso, f
Set Fso = CreateObject("Scripting.FileSystemObject")
Set f = fso.OpenTextFile("c:\testfile.txt", 1, True, 0)
%>
```

Drives   FileSystemObject Property

Purpose

Use this property to get the Drive Collection object. This object contains all the drives on a local machine.

Syntax

```
DriveObject.Drives
```

Example

The following example uses the Drives property to obtain all the drives that exist in this Drive object. Once the example obtains this property, the code finds the number of drives on the server and outputs the drive letter.

```
<%
 Dim FSObj, DriveObject
Set FSObj = CreateObject("Scripting.FileSystemObject")

Set DriveObject = FSObj.Drives
'get the number of drives in the collection
Response.Write "The number of drives is "
Response.Write FSObj.Drives.Count
Response.Write "<BR>"
For each item in DriveObject
    Response.Write "<BR>Drive is ->"
    Response.Write item
Next
%>
```

```
The output in your browser would look something like the
following.
The number of drives is 2
Drive is -> A:
Drive is -> C:
```

Folder Object

Purpose

The Folder object allows you to create or maniputlate a folder. The folder is also known as a file directory.

Syntax

```
FolderObject.Method
FolderObject.Property
```

Copy	Folder Object Method

Purpose

Use this method to copy a directory associated with a Folder object from one location to another. We recommend that you *not* use this method, because in testing we found it doesn't work. Use the FileSytemObject object's CopyFolder method (p. 123) instead of this the Folder object's.

Syntax

```
FolderObject.Copy  Destination[, overwriteflag]
```

Table 46 lists the arguments associated with the Copy method.

Table 46   Arguments for the Copy Method

Value	Required	Type	Description
Destination	Yes	String	The place where you want to copy this directory to.
Overwriteflag	No	Boolean	Whether you can overwrite an existing folder
			True – you can overwrite
			False – you cannot overwrite

Example

As noted earlier, because the Folder object's Copy method is unreliable, we recommend you use the FileSystemObject CopyFolder method. The following example creates a copy of the contents of folder c:\MyImages\Gifs to the directory c:\OtherImages using the CopyFolder method. All the contents in the folder c:\MyImage\Gifs are copied to c:\OtherImages.

```
<%
dim fso
Set fso = Server.CreateObject("Scripting.FileSystemObject")
```

```
fso.CopyFolder " c:\MyImages\Gifs" ," c:\OtherImages"
%>
```

CreateTextFile   Folder Object Method

Purpose

Use this method to create a text file in the Folder object. We recommend using the FileSystemObject CreateTextFile method (p. 125) to create a text file, rather than the Folder object.

Syntax

```
FolderObj.CreateTextFile  Filename [,OverwriteExisting [,
Unicode]]
```

Table 47 lists the arguments associated with the CreateTextField method.

Table 47   Arguments for the CreateTextFile Method

Name	Required	Type	Description
FileName	Yes	String	The name of the text file you are going to create
OverwriteExisting	No	Boolean	Tells you if you can over-write a file that already has the same filename
			True – you can over-write the file
			False – you cannot over-write the file
Unicode	No	Boolean	Tells you if the text file is to be in Unicode or ASCII
			True – creates the file as Unicode
			False – creates the file as ASCII
			False is the default.

Example

The following example creates the file c:\myfiles\GaryAlbers.txt using the Folder object's CreateTextFile. When the file is created, it is placed in the folder of the Folder object. The file will be created in ASCII.

```
<%
dim fso
Set fso = Server.CreateObject("Scripting.FileSystemObject")
'create the folder object
Set FldObj = fso.GetFolder("c:\myfiles")
'create the file c:\myfiles\GaryAlbers.txt
FldObj.CreateTextFile "GaryAlbers.txt",True,False
%>
```

Delete   Folder Object Method

Purpose

Use this method to delete a directory associated with a Folder object. However, we recommend using the FileSystemObject DeleteFolder method (p. 126).

Syntax

```
FolderObject.Delete  Forcedelete
```

Table 48 lists the argument associated with the Delete method.

Table 48 *Argument for the Delete Method*

Value	Required	Type	Description
Forcedelete		No	Boolean Indicates whether a folder marked read-only can be forced to be deleted
			True – indicates the read-only folder can be deleted.
			False – indicates the read-only folder cannot be deleted.

Example

The following example opens the FileScriptingObject, and then creates a Folder object from a directory c:\myfiles. Once the Folder object is created, the Delete method is used to delete the directory associated with the Folder object.

```
<%
Dim FSObj,FldObj
Set FSObj = Server.CreateObject("Scripting.FileSystemObject")
Set FldObj = FSObj.GetFolder("C:\myfiles")
'delete the directory
FldObj.Delete True
```

ASP Core Reference

```
FSObj.Close
Set FSOjb = nothing
Set FldObj = nothing
%>
```

Move   Folder Object Method

Purpose

Use this method to move a directory associated with a `Folder` object to another location. We recommend using the `MoveFolder` method from the `FileSystemObject`.

Syntax

```
FolderObject.Move Destination
```

Table 49 lists the argument associated with the Move method.

Table 49   *Argument for the Move Method*

Value	Required	Type	Description
Destination	Yes	String	The place where you want to move this directory to.

Example

The following example opens the `FileScriptingObject`, and then creates a `Folder` object from a directory c:\myfiles\folder1. Once the `Folder` object is created, the directory c:\myfiles\folder1 is moved to c:\yourfiles using the Move method.

```
<%
Dim FSObj,FldObj
Set FSObj = Server.CreateObject("Scripting.FileSystemObject")
'create the folder object
Set FldObj = FSObj.GetFolder("c:\myfiles\folder1")
'move the directory
'move folder object to c:\yourfiles
FldObj.Move "c:\yourfiles"
FSObj.Close
Set FSOjb = nothing
Set FldObj = nothing
%>
```

Attributes	Folder Object Property

Purpose

Use this property to set or find the attribute of the folder. The values that this property can return are as follows:

```
0 — Normal
1 — ReadOnly
2 — Hidden
4 — System
8 — Volume
16 — Directory
32 — Archive
1024 - Alias
2048 - Compressed
```

Syntax

```
FolderObject.Attributes
```

Example

The following example creates a `FileScriptingObject` object, and then creates a `Folder` object from c:\myfiles. Once the `Folder` object is created, the `Attributes` property is used to indicate the type of attributes for the folder c:\myfiles.

```
<%
Dim FSObj,FldObj
Set FSObj = Server.CreateObject("Scripting.FileSystemObject")
'create the folder object
Set FldObj = FSObj.GetFolder("c:\myfiles")
Select Case FldObj.Attributes
Case 0
Response.Write "Normal "
Case 1
Response.Write "ReadOnly"
Case 2
    Response.Write "Hidden"
Case 4
    Response.Write "System"
Case 8
    Response.Write "Volume"
Case 16
    Response.Write "Directory"
Case 32
    Response.Write "Archive"
```

```
Case 1024
   Response.Write "Alias"
Case 2048
   Response.Write "Compressed"
End Select
%>
```

DateCreated   Folder Object Property

Purpose

Use this property to find out when the directory associated with the Folder object was created.

Syntax

```
FolderObject.DateCreated
```

Example

The following example opens the FileScriptingObject object, and then creates a Folder object from a directory c:\myfiles. Once the Folder object is created, the DateCreated property is used to find out when the directory c:\myfiles\ was created.

```
<%
Dim FSObj,FldObj
Set FSObj = Server.CreateObject("Scripting.FileSystemObject")
Set FldObj = FSObj.GetFolder("c:\myfiles")
Response.Write "The directory was created on "
Response.Write FldObj.DateCreated
%>
```

DateLastAccessed   Folder Object Property

Purpose

Use this property to find out when a directory was last accessed.

Syntax

```
FolderObject.DateLastAccessed
```

Example

The following example opens the FileScriptingObject object, and then creates a Folder object from a directory c:\myfiles. Once the Folder object is created, the DateLastAccessed property is used to determine when the directory c:\myfiles\ was last accessed.

```
<%
Dim FSObj,FldObj
Set FSObj = Server.CreateObject("Scripting.FileSystemObject")
Set FldObj = FSObj.GetFolder("c:\myfiles")
Response.Write "The Last Time this directory accessed was "
Response.Write FldObj.DateLastAccessed
%>
```

DateLastModified
Folder Object Property

Purpose
Use this property to find out when the last modification to the directory associated with the Folder object occurred.

Syntax
```
FolderObject.DateLastModified
```

Example
The following example opens the FileScriptingObject object, and then creates a Folder object from a directory c:\myfiles.Once the Folder object is created, the DateLastModified property is used to determine when this directory was last modified.

```
<%
Dim FSObj,FldObj
Set FSObj = Server.CreateObject("Scripting.FileSystemObject")
Set FldObj = FSObj.GetFolder("c:\myfiles")
Response.Write "Last Date Directory was Modified "
Response.Write FldObj.DateLastModified
%>
```

Drive
Folder Object Property

Purpose
Use this property to determine the drive letter of the Folder object.

Syntax
```
FolderObject.Drive
```

Example
The following example opens the FileScriptingObject object, and then creates a Folder object from a directory c:\myfiles. Once the Folder object is created, the Drive property is used to find the drive letter associated with the Folder object.

ASP Core Reference

```
<%
Dim FSObj,FldObj
Set FSObj = Server.CreateObject("Scripting.FileSystemObject")
Set FldObj = FSObj.GetFolder("c:\myfiles")
Response.Write "The Drive letter associated with
the Folder Object is "
Response.Write FldObj.Drive
%>
```

The message that will appear in the browser is as follows:

The drive letter associated with the Folder object is C.

Files	FolderObject Property

Purpose
This property returns a Files collection containing all the files in the Folder object.

Syntax
```
Set FileCollectionObject = FolderObject.Files
```

Example
The following example gets all the files in the Folder object created from c:\myfiles.

```
<%
Dim FSObj,FldObj
Set FSObj = Server.CreateObject("Scripting.FileSystemObject")
Set FldObj = FSObj.GetFolder("c:\myfiles")
'get the Files Collection object that contains all the
'files in the Folder object
Set FilesCollectionObj = FldObj.Files
'You can then see the file by using the item and count
'Files Collection properties
For j = 0 to FilesCollectionObj.count
    'the file object

Next
%>
```

IsRootFolder	Folder Object Property

Purpose
Use this property to determine if the Folder object is at the root. This property returns either a True or False value.

Syntax

```
FolderObject.IsRootFolder
```

Example

The following example opens the FileScriptingObject object, and then creates a Folder object from a directory c:\myfiles. Once the Folder object is created, the IsRootFolder property is used to determine if the Folder object is at the root.

```
<%
Dim FSObj,FldObj
Set FSObj = Server.CreateObject("Scripting.FileSystemObject")
Set FldObj = FSObj.GetFolder("c:\myfiles")
If (FldObj.IsRootFolder) then
    Response.Write "The Folder Object is at the root. "
Else
    Response.Write "The Folder Object is NOT at the root. "
End if
%>
```

Name   Folder Object Property

Purpose

Use this property to obtain the name of the directory associated with the Folder object.

Syntax

```
FolderObject.Name
```

Example

The following example opens the FileScriptingObject object, and then creates a Folder object from a directory c:\myfiles\dvd. Once the Folder object is created, the code uses the Name property to find the name of the folder associated with the Folder object.

```
<%
Dim FSObj,FldObj
Set FSObj = Server.CreateObject("Scripting.FileSystemObject")
Set FldObj = FSObj.GetFolder("c:\myfiles\dvd")
Response.Write "The Name of the directory associated with the
Folder Object is "
Response.Write FldObj.Name
%>
```

The message that will appear in the browser is as follows:

```
The Name of the directory associated with the Folder object is dvd
```

ParentFolder

Folder Object Property

Purpose

Use this property to return the Folder object of the parent to the Folder object; in other words, the directory that is above the directory you have associated with the Folder object.

Syntax

```
FolderObject.ParentFolder
```

Example

The following example opens the FileScriptingObject object, and then creates a Folder object from a directory c:\images\gifs. Once the Folder object is created, the ParentFolder property value can be found.

```
<%
Dim FSObj,FldObj
Set FSObj = Server.CreateObject("Scripting.FileSystemObject")
Set FldObj = FSObj.GetFolder("c:\images\gifs")
Response.Write "The parent directory is   "
Response.Write FldObj.ParentFolder
%>
```

The code will return the following message:

```
The parent directory is C:\images
```

Path

Folder Object Property

Purpose

Use this property the find the path of the Folder object

Syntax

```
FolderObject.Path
```

Example

The following example opens the FileScriptingObject object, and then creates a Folder object from a directory c:\myfiles. Once the Folder object is created, the Path property is used to find the path of the Folder object.

```
<%
Dim FSObj,FldObj
Set FSObj = Server.CreateObject("Scripting.FileSystemObject")
Set FldObj = FSObj.GetFolder("c:\myfiles")
Response.Write "The path of this folder is "
Response.Write FldObj.Path
%>
```

The code will return the following message:

```
The path of this folder is C:\myfiles
```

ShortName
Folder Object Property

Purpose
Use this property to find the 8.3 version of the folder name.

Syntax

```
FolderObject.ShortName
```

Example
The following example opens the FileScriptingObject object, and then creates a Folder object from a directory c:\myfiles. Once the Folder object is created, the code uses the ShortName property to obtain the Version 8.3 name of the file directory.

```
<%
Dim FSObj,FldObj
Set FSObj = Server.CreateObject("Scripting.FileSystemObject")
Set FldObj = FSObj.GetFolder("c:\myfiles")
Response.Write "ShortName of the Folder object is "
Response.Write FldObj.ShortName
%>
```

The code will return the following message:

ShortName of the Folder object is myfiles

Size
Folder Object Property

Purpose
Use this property to determine the size of all the files and subdirectories that the Folder object contains.

Syntax

```
FolderObject.Size
```

Example
The following code creates a Folder object from the directory c:\myfiles. Once the object is created, the code outputs the size in bytes of the all the files and directories under c:\myfiles.

```
<%
Dim FSObj,FldObj
Set FSObj = Server.CreateObject("Scripting.FileSystemObject")
```

```
Set FldObj = FSObj.GetFolder("c:\myfiles")
Response.Write "The Byte Size of all files and directory under
the Folder object is "
Response.Write FldObj.Size
%>
```

SubFolders   Folder Object Property

Purpose

Use this property to get the Folders Collection object for all the subdirectories under the Folder object.

Syntax

```
Set Var = FolderObject.SubFolders
```

Example

The following example obtains the Folders Collection object containing all the subdirectories under the directory c:\myfiles. Once the Folders Collection is obtained, the code uses the ShortName property to find all the Version 8.3 names of the subdirectories.

```
<%
Dim FSObj,FldObj,FldCollObj
Set FSObj = Server.CreateObject("Scripting.FileSystemObject")
Set FldObj = FSObj.GetFolder("c:\myfiles")
Set FldCollObj = FldObj.SubFolders
'find the number of subdirectories
Response.Write "<BR>The number of subdirectories
in collection is "
Response.Write FldCollObj.Count
For each item in FldCollObj
    Response.Write "<br>ShortName of Directory is "
    Response.Write item.ShortName
Next
%>
```

Type   Folder Object Property

Purpose

Use this property to obtain information about the Folder object. For a Folder object, the return value will be FILE.

Syntax

```
FolderObject.Type
```

Example

The following example outputs to your browser information about the Folder object. The directory c:\FriendOfMine contains text files.

```
<%
Dim FSObj,FldObj,FldCollObj
Set FSObj = Server.CreateObject("Scripting.FileSystemObject")
Set FldObj = FSObj.GetFolder("c:\FriendsOfMine")
Response.Write "The Type property returned ->"
Response.Write FldObj.Type
%>
```

The following is output in the browser:

```
The Type property returned FILE
```

Folder Collection Object

Purpose

Use the Folder Collection object to obtain information about individual Drive, Folder, and File objects. In plain English, you can use the Folder Collection object to get information about all the files and sub directories in a directory.

Syntax

```
FolderObject.Property
FolderObject.Method
```

Drives	Folder Collection Object Method

Purpose

Use the Drives method to find all the available drives contained in the Folder object. This method is associated with the FileSystemObject object's Drives property. The collection contains a Count and Item property.

Syntax

```
Set FSObj = Server.CreateObject("Scripting.FileSystemObject")
Set DrvCollObj =  FSObj.Drives
```

Example

The following example obtains the Drive Collection containing all the drives under on your computer's local hard drive. If your computer is tied into a network, then all the drives that your computer is mapped to will also be returned. The FileSystemObject object's GetDrives method is used to obtain the Drive collection. Once the Drive Collection is obtained, the

Folder Collection object's Count and Item property are used to list the drives in the collection.

```
<%
Dim FSObj,DrvCollObj
Set FSObj = Server.CreateObject("Scripting.FileSystemObject")
'use the FileSystemObject object Drives property to obtain
'the Drive Collection
Set DrvCollObj = FSObj.Drives
'find the number of subdirectories
Response.Write "<BR>The number of Drives in collection is "
Response.Write DrvCollObj.Count
For each item in DrvCollObj
    Response.Write "<br>Drive Name is "
    Response.Write item
Next
%>
```

Files	Folder Collection Object Property

Purpose

Use this property to find all the available files contained in a directory. This collection is associated with the FileSystemObject's Files Collection. The Folder object property SubFolder contains the same functionality as this collection. The collection contains a Count and Item property.

Syntax

```
Set FSObj = Server.CreateObject("Scripting.FileSystemObject")
Set folderobj = fso.GetFolder(file or drive)
Set FilesCollObj = folderobj.Files
```

Example

The following example uses the FileSystemObject's GetFolder method to obtain a folder object for the directory C:. Then the Files method is used to obtain the Files Collection, which contains all the files in the directory. The Name property of these files is output to the browser using the Response object's Write method.

```
<%
Dim FSObj,FolderObj,FileCollObj
Set FSObj = Server.CreateObject("Scripting.FileSystemObject")
Set FolderObj = FSObj.GetFolder("C:")
Set FileCollObj = FolderObj.Files
'find the number of files in Folder object
Response.Write "<BR>The number of Files in collection is "
```

```
Response.Write FileCollObj.Count
For each item in FileCollObj
    Response.Write "<br>File Name is "
    Response.Write item.Name
Next
%>
```

Folders   Folder Collection Object Property

Purpose

Use this property to find all the subdirectories contained inside a directory. Each of the subdirectories found under a directory will be a Folder object. Thus when you bundle all of these Folder objects together, they make a collection of Folder objects.

Syntax

```
Set FSObj = Server.CreateObject("Scripting.FileSystemObject")
Set folderobj = fso.GetFolder(file or drive)
Set FilesCollObj = folderobj. Folders
```

Example

The following example uses the FileSystemObject object's GetFolder method to obtain a folder object for the directory C:. Then the Folder object's SubFolder property is used to obtain all the subdirectories under the Folder object. All the subdirectories make up the collection. The Name property of these subdirectories is output to the browser using the Response object's Write method.

```
<%
Dim FSObj,FolderObj,FolderCollObj
Set FSObj = Server.CreateObject("Scripting.FileSystemObject")
Set FolderObj = FSObj.GetFolder("C:")
Set FolderCollObj = FolderObj.SubFolders
'find the number of files in Folder object
Response.Write "<BR>The number of Subdirectories in Folder
collection is "
Response.Write FolderCollObj.Count
For each item in FolderCollObj
    Response.Write "<br>Folder Name is "
    Response.Write item.Name
Next
%>
```

Parameter Object

Purpose

Use the Parameter object to pass parameters to a stored procedure.

Syntax

```
ParameterObject.Method
ParameterObject.Property
```

AppendChunk	Parameter Object Method

Purpose

Use this method to append data to a large or binary Parameter object. We recommend you use the Field object's AppendChunk method (p. 98) instead of the Parameter object's AppendChunk method to retrieve binary data from a database.

Syntax

```
ParameterObject.AppendChunk (the binary data)
```

Table 50 lists the argument associated with the AppendChunk method.

Table 50 *Argument for the AppendChunk Method*

Name	Required	Type	Description
The binary data	Yes		This is the binary data that will be added to the parameter object.

Example

Use this method to get images from tables. The SQL statement will retrieve the record from the table Images whose field ImageId is equal to 10. In order to initialize AppendChunk, the value 1024000 is used. There is nothing magic about the number 1024000; we just want a big enough number to initialize the method.

```
Set DataConn = Server.CreateObject("ADODB.Connection")
DataConn.Open Application("dbConnectionString")

Set Result = Server.createobject("ADODB.Recordset")
sql = "SELECT ImageData FROM Images WHERE ImageID= 10"
```

```
Result.Open sql, DataConn, adOpenKeyset
if not (Result.eof and Result.bof) then
    'put binary data into Field object Image using
    'the AppendChuck method
    Image = Result("ImageData").AppendChunk(1024000)
    Response.Buffer = true
    Response.ContentType = "image/gif"
    Response.BinaryWrite Image
else
    Response.Write "Photo not found"
end if
'close the recordset
Result.Close
'close the database connection
DataConn.Close
Response.End
```

Attributes	Parameter Object Property

Purpose

Use this property to determine the characteristics that a Parameter object
contains. This property is either set by or returns a ParameterAttributes
Enum constant.

●─CROSS-REFERENCE

The ParameterAttributes enumeration constants are available at
the URL noted in the Preface.

Syntax

```
ParameterAttributeEnum = ParameterObject.Attributes
ParameterObject.Attributes = ParameterAttributeEnum
```

Example

This example enables you to determine whether the attribute accepts the
signed values or null values:

```
If (ParameterObject.Attributes = adParamSigned or adParamNullable
) = adParamNullable then
    Response.Write "Attribute is nullable"
End if
```

Direction   Parameter Object Property

Purpose

Use this property to determine the direction in which a parameter is going: into a stored procedure, out of a stored procedure, or both in and out of a stored procedure. When setting or getting the value of the property, a ParameterDirectionEnum constant is involved.

●─CROSS-REFERENCE─────────────────────────

The list of ParameterDirection enumeration constants is available at the URL noted in the Preface.

Syntax

```
ParameterObject.Direction = ParameterDirectionEnum
ParameterDirectionEnum = Parameter.Direction
```

Example

This script shows you how to check the Parameter object's Direction property value.

```
set conn4 = Server.CreateObject("ADODB.Connection")
conn4.Open Application("db_ConnectionString")

set CommObj = Server.CreateObject("ADODB.Command")
CommObj.ActiveConnection = conn4
CommObj.CommandType = adCmdStoredProcedure


CommObj.CommandText = "sp_getStates"

Set ParaObj = CommObj.CreateParameter

ParaObj.Value = 2
ParaObj.Type = adInteger
ParaObj.Direction = adParamInputOutput
Commobj.Parameters.Append ParaObj

CommObj.Execute

set CommObj = nothing
set conn4 = nothing
```

Name   Parameter Object Property

Purpose

Use this property to set or get the name of a Parameter object.

Syntax

```
ParameterObject.Name
```

Examples

Use the following script to get the value of the Name property:

```
String = ParameterObject.Name
```

Use this script to set the value of the Name property:

```
ParameterObject.Name = "AuburnParameterObject"
```

If you are using several Parameter objects, it makes sense to name each one. Use names that will aid you in remembering the stored procedure that is associated with your Parameter object.

NumericScale   Parameter Object Property

Purpose

Use this property to indicate the number of digits to the right of the decimal point. You use a byte to set this value, and a byte is returned when you get the value of this property.

Syntax

```
Byte = ParameterObject.NumericScale
ParameterObject.NumericScale = Byte
```

Example

Use the following script to get the value of the NumericScale property:

```
Byte = ParameterObject.NumericScale
```

Use this script to set the NumericScale property to 2 (two digits to the right of the decimal point).

```
ParameterObject.NumericScale = 2
```

Precision   Parameter Object Property

Purpose

Use this property to determine how precise you want the numeric value in the Parameter object to be. This property sets the maximum number of digits

ASP Core Reference

that can be used to represent a numeric value. You use a byte to set this value, and a byte is returned when you get the value of this property.

Syntax

```
ParameterObject.Precision
```

Examples

This example shows you how to get the Precision property value:

```
Byte = ParameterObject.Precision
```

This script shows you how to set the Precision property value to a maximum of 15 digits:

```
ParameterObject.Precision = 15
```

Size	Parameter Object Property

Purpose

Use this property to set the maximum size (in bytes or characters) of a Parameter object.

Syntax

```
ParameterObject.Size = byte or characters
Long = ParameterObject.Size
```

Examples

Use this script to set the value of the Size property to 20 characters long:

```
ParameterObject.Size = 20
```

The following example uses the Size property to pass an integer to a stored procedure. The Parameter object's Size property for an integer value is 8.

```
'the connection object is DataConn
set CommObj = Server.CreateObject("ADODB.Command")
CommObj.ActiveConnection = DataConn
CommObj.CommandType = adCmdStoredProcedure
CommObj.CommandText = "sp_getStates"
        'create the parameter object
Set ParaObj = CommObj.CreateParameter
 'set the values for the parameter object
ParaObj.Value = 2
ParaObj.Type = adInteger
ParaObj.Direction = adParamInputOutput
ParaObj.Size = 8
Commobj.Parameters.Append ParaObj
CommObj.Execute
```

ASP Core Reference

```
set CommObj = nothing
set DataConn = nothing
```

Type   Parameter Object Property

Purpose

Use this property to determine the variable type that the Parameter object is
set to. The variable type is set using a value from the DataTypeEnum constants.

●—CROSS-REFERENCE

The DataType enumeration constants are available on-line.

Syntax

```
DataTypeEnum = ParameterObject.Type
ParameterObject.Type = adVarBinary
```

Example

The following example shows you how to display the value of the Parameter
object's Type property:

```
'the connection object is DataConn
set CommObj = Server.CreateObject("ADODB.Command")
CommObj.ActiveConnection = DataConn
CommObj.CommandType = adCmdStoredProcedure
CommObj.CommandText = "sp_getStates"
'create the parameter object
Set ParaObj = CommObj.CreateParameter
'set the values for the parameter object
ParaObj.Value = 2
ParaObj.Type = adInteger
ParaObj.Direction = adParamInputOutput
ParaObj.Size = 8
Commobj.Parameters.Append ParaObj
CommObj.Execute
'get the parameter object type
Response.Write "ParaObj.Type is "
Response.Write ParaObj.Type

set CommObj = nothing
set DataConn = nothing
```

ASP Core Reference

Value — Parameter Object Property

Purpose
Use this property to indicate the value of the Parameter object.

Syntax
```
ParameterObject.Value
```

Examples
The following script gets the value of the Parameter object's Value property:

```
Variant = ParameterObject.Value
```

The next example shows you how to set the Parameter object named "Me" to a value of "Warner Robins High School" using the Value property:

```
ParameterObject.Parameters("Me").Value = "Warner Robins High
School"
```

Append — Parameter Object Collection Method

Purpose
Use this property to add a Parameter object to the collection.

Syntax
```
ParameterCollection.Append(ParameterObject)
```

Example
The following script appends a Parameter object to the Parameter object's collection:

```
Set ParameterObj = CommandObj.CreateParameter
ParameterObj.Name = "ParaObj1"
ParameterObj.Type = adVarchar
ParameterObj.Direction = adParamInput
Dim str
Str = "Auburn Tigers"
ParameterObj.Size = Len(Trim(str))
ParameterObj.Value = Str
CommandObj.Parameters.Append Paramobj
```

Delete — Parameter Object Collection Method

Purpose
You use this method to delete a Parameter object from the collection. An index number is used to tell which Parameter object to delete from the Parameter object's collection.

ASP Core Reference

Syntax

```
ParametersObject.Delete(index)
```

Example

Suppose you had a Parameter object collection with the following object names in the collection: FirstParaObj, SecondParaObj, and ThirdParaObj. If you wanted to delete the Parameter object named SecondParaObj, you'd use the following code: The index number for the Parameter object named SecondParaObj is 2.

```
CommandObj.Parameters.Delete(2)
```

Refresh	Parameter Object Collection Method

Purpose

Use this method to update the objects in the Parameter object's collection. This method re-queries the database provider for information about the Parameter objects in the Parameter collection. Because of this, your server's performance could be affected. On the other hand, this method enables you to avoid repeatedly calling the Command object's CreateParameter method. Instead, you can generate a reusable piece of code.

Syntax

```
ParameterObject.Refresh
```

Example

The following code shows a function that refreshes a Parameter object in the Parameter Object Collection with a new name and value:

```
Function reuseParameter(ParameterObj, indexNum, val,name)
    ParameterObj.Refresh
    ParameterObj(indexNum).Value = val
    ParameterObj(indexNum).
    ParameterObj(indexNum).Name = name
End Function
```

Count	Parameter Object Collection Property

Purpose

Use this property to determine the number of Parameter objects in the Parameter object collection.

Syntax

```
Long = Parameters.Count
```

ASP Core Reference

Example

This example lists all the items in the Parameter object:

```
For each Item Parameter.Count
    Response.Write  Parameter.Item(0)
Next
```

Property Object

Purpose

Use this object to find attributes for a single property for one of the following four objects: Connection, Command, RecordSet, and Field.

Syntax

```
PropertyObject.Property
```

Attributes	Property Object Property

Purpose

Use this property to determine the behavior of the Property object. The value returned is a PropertyAttributes enumerated constant.

●─CROSS-REFERENCE

You can find the PropertyAttributes enumerated constants at the URL noted in the Preface.

Syntax

```
Object.PropertyObject.Attributes
Object.Properties.Item( index).Attributes
```

Example

The following example finds the Attributes property for a Command object run under Microsoft SQL Server 7.0. The connection string to the database is set in a fictitious application variable db_ConnectionString.

```
<%
Dim DataConn,RsetObj,CmdObj
set DataConn = Server.CreateObject("ADODB.Connection")
DataConn.Open Application("db_ConnectionString")

sqlstm = "Select EquipType From Equipment"
    'Open a connection
    Dim RSetObj
```

```
    Set RSetObj = server.CreateObject("ADODB.Recordset")

    RSetObj.Open SqlStm , DataConn , 1 , 1

    Set CmdObj = server.CreateObject("ADODB.Command")
CmdObj.ActiveConnection = DataConn


For each item in CmdObj.Properties
        Response.Write "<BR>"&item.Name&"->"
        Response.Write item.Value
        Response.Write "    ATTRIBUTE ->"
        Response.Write item.Attributes
        Response.Write "    TYPE -> "
        Response.Write item.type
next
%>
```

The partial list of values returned from the execution of this code might look
like the following:

```
Preserve on Abort->False ATTRIBUTE ->513 TYPE -> 11
Blocking Storage Objects->True ATTRIBUTE ->513 TYPE -> 11
Use Bookmarks->False ATTRIBUTE ->1537 TYPE -> 11
Skip Deleted Bookmarks->False ATTRIBUTE ->513 TYPE -> 11
Bookmark Type->1 ATTRIBUTE ->513 TYPE -> 3
```

The number beside the ATTRIBUTE is the value of a combination of Property
Attributes enumerated constants. For instance, the first line of the return
values shows an Attributes property of 513. This value is a combination of
adPropRequired (512) and adPropRead (1).

Inherited	Property Object Property

Purpose

Using this property returns a Boolean value that indicates whether a
Property object is inherited from an underlying object. This is a new property that is added to the Property object for ADO 2.5. Because the objects
that deal with the Property object in ASP are not inherited, the value for the
properties will be False.

Syntax

```
Object.PropertyObject.Inherited
Object.Properties.Item(index).Inherited
```

Example

The following example determines whether or not the Property object for the Connection object is inherited or not. Remember that you must be running ADO 2.5 to use this property.

```
<%
Dim DataConn,RsetObj,CmdObj
    set DataConn = Server.CreateObject("ADODB.Connection")
    DataConn.Open Application("db_ConnectionString")

For each item in DataConn.Properties
    Response.Write "<BR>"&item.Name&"->"
    Response.Write item.Inherited
next
%>
```

Name	Property Object Property

Purpose

Use this property to find the name of the Property object.

Syntax

```
Object.PropertyObject.Name
Object.Properties.Item( index). Name
```

Example

The following example finds the name of the Property object for a Connection object run under Microsoft SQL Server 7.0 . The connection string to the database is set in a fictitious application variable db_Connection String. For this example, we are connecting to a table called Equipment in the database.

```
<%
Dim DataConn,RsetObj,CmdObj
set DataConn = Server.CreateObject("ADODB.Connection")
DataConn.Open Application("db_ConnectionString")

sqlstm = "Select EquipType From Equipment"
'Open a connection
Dim RSetObj
Set RSetObj = Server.CreateObject("ADODB.Recordset")

RSetObj.Open SqlStm , DataConn , 1 , 1

Set CmdObj = Server.CreateObject("ADODB.Command")
```

```
CmdObj.ActiveConnection = DataConn

For each item in CmdObj.Properties
    Response.Write "<BR>"&item.Name&"->"
    Response.Write item.Value
next
%>
```

The partial list of values returned from the execution of this code might look like the following:

```
Current Catalog->
Active Sessions->
Asynchable Commit->
Catalog Location->
Catalog Term->
```

Type   Property Object Property

Purpose

Use this property to determine the data type of the Property object. This property returns a DataType enumerated constant indicating whether the value is a Boolean, date decimal, and so on.

●—CROSS-REFERENCE

You can find the DataType enumerated constants at the URL noted in the Preface.

Syntax

```
Object.Propertyobject.Type
Object.Properties.Item( index).Type
```

Example

The following example finds the name and the data type of the Property object for a Connection object run under Microsoft SQL Server 7.0. The connection string to the database is set in a fictitious application variable db_ConnectionString. For this example, we are connecting to a table called Equipment in the database.

```
<%
Dim DataConn,RsetObj,CmdObj
set DataConn = Server.CreateObject("ADODB.Connection")
DataConn.Open Application("db_ConnectionString")

sqlstm = "Select EquipType From Equipment"
```

ASP Core Reference

```
'Open a connection
Dim RSetObj
Set RSetObj = server.CreateObject("ADODB.Recordset")

RSetObj.Open SqlStm , DataConn , 1 , 1

    Set CmdObj = server.CreateObject("ADODB.Command")
CmdObj.ActiveConnection = DataConn

For each item in CmdObj.Properties
    Response.Write "<BR>"&item.Name&"->"
    Response.Write item.Type
Next
%>
```

The partial list of values returned from the execution of this code might look
like the following:

```
Current Catalog->8
Active Sessions->3
Asynchable Commit->11
Catalog Location->3
Catalog Term->8
```

In the list, an 8 represents a null-terminated character string. An 11 represents a Boolean value, and a 3 represents an integer.

Value | Property Object Property

Purpose

Use this property to find the value of the Property object. This is the one
property in the Property object that can be both set and get. Some properties
in a Properties Collection of the Connection, Command, RecordSet, or Field
objects will not allow you to set their value. Therefore, you need to determine whether a property can be set; you do this using the Property
Attributes enumerated constant adPropWrite.

●—CROSS-REFERENCE

You can find the PropertyAttributes enumerated constants at the
URL noted in the Preface.

Syntax

```
Object.Propertyobject.Value
Object.Properties.Item( index).Value
```

Example

The following example checks to see if the Property object named ObjAtt allows you to set the value of the property "Blocking Storage Object". If the values of the PropertyAttributesEnum constant for both the property "Blocking Storage Object" and adPropWrite are equal to the value of adPropWrite then we can change then Value property for the Property object "Blocking Storage Objects".

```
<%
Dim DataConn,RsetObj,CmdObj,ObjAtt
    set DataConn = Server.CreateObject("ADODB.Connection")
DataConn.Open Application("db_ConnectionString")

sqlstm = "Select EquipType From Equipment"
    'Open a connection
    Dim RSetObj
    Set RSetObj = Server.CreateObject("ADODB.Recordset")

    RSetObj.Open SqlStm , DataConn , 1 , 1

    Set CmdObj = Server.CreateObject("ADODB.Command")
CmdObj.ActiveConnection = DataConn

For each item in CmdObj.Properties
    Response.Write "<BR>"&item.Name&"->"

    ObjAtt = CmdObj.Properties("Blocking Storage
Objects").Attribute
    If (ObjAtt and adPropWrite) = adPropWrite Then
        ObjAtt.Properties("Blocking Storage Objects").Value =
        False
    End if
    Response.Write item.Type

Next
%>
```

Notice in the code that the reference to the property is found via the syntax ObjAtt.Properties("Blocking Storage Objects") Value. This is the syntax to reference an individual property by name for the Connection, Command, RecordSet, or Field objects.

Properties Collection Object

Purpose

Use the Properties Collection object to obtain information about the individual Property objects: Connection, Command, RecordSet, and Field. This collection contains either none or many Property objects.

Syntax

```
Object.Properties
```

Refresh	Properties Collection Object Method

Purpose

Use this method to update the Property Collection object if you change the database provider.

Syntax

```
Object.Properties.Refresh
```

Example

The following example first sets the DataConn method to one database provider, and then output the Name and Type of the Property objects in the Connection object's Properties Collection. Next, the code will then change database providers via a connection string stored in an application variable.

```
<%
Dim DataConn,DataConn1,RsetObj,CmdObj
    set DataConn = Server.CreateObject("ADODB.Connection")
DataConn.Open Application("db_ConnectionString")

sqlstm = "Select EquipType From Equipment"
    'Open a connection
    Dim RSetObj
    Set RSetObj = Server.CreateObject("ADODB.Recordset")

    RSetObj.Open SqlStm , DataConn , 1 , 1

    'REFRESH THE Properties Collection for the Connection
    'object
    DataConn.Properties.Refresh

'output the Properties Collection for the Connection object
For each item in DataConn.Properties
    Response.Write "<BR>"&item.Name&"->"
    Response.Write item.Type
```

```
Next
%>
```

| Count | Properties Collection Object Property |

Purpose
Use this property to determine the number of Property objects in the Properties Collection object.

Syntax
```
Object.Properties.Count
```

Example
The following example uses the Count property to find the number of Property objects in the Properties Collection.

```
<%
Dim DataConn,DataConn1,RsetObj,CmdObj,J
    set DataConn = Server.CreateObject("ADODB.Connection")
DataConn.Open Application("db_ConnectionString")

sqlstm = "Select EquipType From Equipment"
    'Open a connection
    Dim RSetObj
    Set RSetObj = Server.CreateObject("ADODB.Recordset")

    RSetObj.Open SqlStm , DataConn , 1 , 1

    Set CmdObj = Server.CreateObject("ADODB.Command")
CmdObj.ActiveConnection = DataConn
    'REFRESH THE COLLECTION
    CmdObj.Properties.Refresh

    'GET THE Number of Property object in Command
    'object
    Response.Write "The Number of Property Object is "
    Response.Write CmdObj.Properties.Count

%>
```

| Item | Properties Collection Property |

Purpose
Use this property to index the number of Property objects in a collection.

ASP Core Reference

Syntax

```
Object.Properties.Item( index )
```

Example

The following example uses the Count property in conjunction with the Item property to list the Property objects from the Connection object.

```
<%
Dim DataConn,DataConn1,RsetObj,CmdObj,J
set DataConn = Server.CreateObject("ADODB.Connection")
DataConn.Open Application("db_ConnectionString")

For j = 0 to DataConn.Properties.Count
    Response.Write "<BR>"&DataConn.Properties.Item(j).Name&"->"
    Response.Write DataConn.Properties.Item(j).Type
Next
%>
```

Record Object

Purpose

Use the Record object to interact with data sources, such as Oracle, that are not relational databases. The type of data sources that the Record object would deal with are text files. Since the Record object is new to ADO 2.5, there aren't many uses for it yet. One use is with the OLE DB Provider for Internet Publishing.

Syntax

```
RecordObject.Method
RecordObject.Property
```

Cancel	Record Object Method

Purpose

Use this method to end the execution of an asynchronous call. The Record object's Open (p. 179), CopyRecord (p. 174), MoveRecord (p. 177), and DeleteRecord (p. 176) methods have options that allow asynchronous calls.

● NOTE

Microsoft defines an *asynchronous operation* as one that returns control to the calling program without waiting for the operation to complete. Before the operation is complete, code execution continues.

Syntax

```
RecordObj.Cancel
```

Example

The following example uses the Open method to make an asynchronous call in opening a Record object. The directory www.extremestyle.com/Images will be associated with the Record object MyRecordobj. If it takes more that five seconds to open the Record object, the example will use the Cancel method to stop the Open method.

```
<%
Dim MyRecordobj
Dim Tdate, Sec
Tdate = Time()
Sec = Second(Time())
Set MyRecordobj = Server.CreateObject("ADODB.Record")
MyRecordobj.Open "Images","URL=http://www.extremestyle.com", , ,
adOpenAsync, ,
'wait 8 seconds to see if Record object opened
Do while Second(Time()) < Sec + 8
    'loop for 8 seconds
Loop
'use the Record State property to see if Record object is opened
if NOT MyRecordobj.State    then
    MyRecordObj.Cancel
end if

%>
```

Close   Record Object Method

Purpose

Use this method to undo the association between a file or directory and a Record object.

Syntax

```
RecordObj.Close
```

Example

The following example begins by associating the file CecilAllison.doc with a Record object. Then the example uses the Close method to remove the association between the Record object and CecilAllison.doc.

```
<%
Dim Recordobj
```

ASP Core Reference

```
Set Recordobj = Server.CreateObject("ADODB.Record")
Recordobj.Open " ",
"URL=http://www.anywebsite.com/CecilAllison.doc"
'now that the Record object is open, let's dissolve the
'tie between the file CecilAllison.doc with the
'Record object Recordobj.
Recordobj.Close
'free up resource by getting rid of object
Set Recordobj = nothing
%>
```

CopyRecord   Record Object Method

Purpose

Use this method to copy the files or directory associated with a Record object to another location. Remember that you may need a user ID or password to place the copy in the other location.

Syntax

```
RecordObject.CopyRecord    Source, Destination, UserName,
Password, Options, Async
```

Table 51 lists the arguments associated with the CopyRecord method.

Table 51 *Arguments for the CopyRecord Method*

Value	Required	Type	Description
Source	No	String	A string stating what file or directory associated with the Record object is to be copied. If the source argument is empty, the file or directory represented by this Record object will be copied.
Destination	No	String	A string containing the file or directory to which this Record object is to be copied. Normally, the file or directory is in the form of a URL.
UserName	No	String	The user name that the destination location needs for authorization
Password	No	String	The password that the destination location needs for authocation

Value	Required	Type	Description
Options	No	String	Value indicating how the Record object will be copied. This value is a CopyRecordOptions enumerated constant. The default value is adCopyUnspecified . Its numerical value is -1.
Async	No	Boolean	Value indicating whether or not this operation should be asynchronous. Value is either True or False.

● **CROSS-REFERENCE**

The CopyRecordOptions enumerated constants are available at the URL noted in the Preface.

Examples

The following example copies the Record object www.anywebsite.com\images to www.myfiles.com.

```
<%
Dim Recordobj
Set Recordobj = Server.CreateObject("ADODB.Record")
Recordobj.open "images","URL=http://www.anywebsite.com"
Recordobj.RecordCopy " ", "URL=http://www.myfiles.com"
%>
```

The next example copies the Record object www.anywebsite.com\images to www.myfiles.com, except a user ID and password are required by www.myfiles.com, and this operation will be asynchronous. The user ID will be Carmen, and the password will be Burgess. The Record object State property will check after eight seconds to see if the copying has finished. If it is not finished, the Cancel method will be issued, to stop the asynchronous operation.

```
<%
Dim MyRecordobj
Dim Tdate, Sec
'get the time
Tdate = Time()
Sec = Second(Time())
Set MyRecordobj = Server.CreateObject("ADODB.Record")
MyRecordobj.Open "Images","URL=http://www.myfiles.com"
Recordobj.RecordCopy " ",
```

ASP Core Reference

```
"URL=http://www.myfiles.com","Carmen","Burgess", ,True

'wait 8 seconds to see if Record object opened
Do while Second(Time()) < Sec + 8
Loop
'use the Record State property to see if Record object is opened
if NOT MyRecordobj.State    then
    MyRecordObj.Cancel
end if

%>
```

DeleteRecord   Record Object Method

Purpose

Use this method to delete a file or directory associated with a Record object.

Syntax

```
RecordObj.DeleteRecord Source, Async
```

Table 52 lists the arguments associated with the DeleteRecord method.

Table 52 *Arguments for the DeleteRecord Method*

Value	Required	Type	Description
Source	No	String	A string stating what file or directory associated with the Record object is to be deleted. If Source is empty, the file or directory represented by this Record object will be deleted.
Async	No	Boolean	A Boolean value indicating whether or not the deletion is asynchronous

Example

The following example creates a Record object from the source www.any-website.com/auburn.txt, and then uses the DeleteRecord method to delete this file.

```
<%
Dim Recordobj
Set Recordobj = Server.CreateObject("ADODB.Record")
Recordobj.Open "auburn.txt","URL=http://www.anywebsite.com"
```

```
'delete the file auburn.txt
Recordobj.DeleteRecord
%>
```

GetChildren   Record Object Method

Purpose

Use this method to place the directories and files of a Record object into a recordset.

Syntax

```
Set recset = RecordObject.GetChildren
```

Example

The following example contains a Record object that was created from the directory c:\inetpub\wwwroot\mywebsite. The URL for this Web site directory is http://www.anyname.com. The code below will list all the subdirectories using the GetChildren method.

```
<%
'the Parent Directory is c:
Dim recordobj,ChildRecordSet,j
Set recordobj = Server.CreateObject("ADODB.Record")
Recordobj.Open "mywebsite","URL = "http://www.anyname.com/"
Set ChildRecordSet = recordobj.GetChildren()
Response.Write "number of Fields in RecordSet is"
Response.Write ChildRecordSet.Fields.Count
For j = 0 to ChildRecordSet.Fields.Count-1
    Response.Write "<BR>"
    Response.Write "Name is "
    Response.Write ChildRecordSet.Fields(j).Name
    Response.Write "Value is "
    Response.Write ChildRecordSet.Fields(j).Value
    ChildRecordSet.MoveNext
Next
%>
```

MoveRecord   Record Object Method

Purpose

Use this method to move the files or directory associated with a Record object from one location to another. Remember that depending on the URL, you may need a user ID and password to move a Record object.

Syntax

```
RecordObject.MoveRecord  Source, Destination, UserName, Password,
Options, Async
```

Table 53 lists the arguments associated with the MoveRecord method.

Table 53 *Arguments for the MoveRecord Method*

Value	Required	Type	Description
Source	No	String	A string stating what file or directory associated with the Record object is to be copied. If Source is empty, the file or directory represented by this Record object will be copied.
Destination	No	String	A string containing the file or directory to which this Record object is to be copied. Normally, the file or directory is in the form of a URL.
UserName	No	String	The user name that the destination location needs for authorization.
Password	No	String	The password that the destination location needs for authorization.
Options	No	String	Value indicating how the Record object will be copied. This value is a CopyRecordOptions enumerated constant. The default is adCopy Unspecified. The numeric value for adCopyUnspecified is - -1.
Async	No	Boolean	A Boolean value indicating whether or not the deletion is asynchronous

CROSS-REFERENCE

The CopyRecordOptions enumeration constants are available at the URL noted in the Preface.

Example

The following example attaches the directory Images to the Record object MyRecordObject. This directory in located in the URL www.anywebsite.com.

The example uses the MoveRecord method to relocate this directory to
www.another.com. For the purposes of this example, the URL www.another.
com requires a user name and password for authentication. The user name
is "Melissa" and the password is "Chesser".

```
<%
Dim MyRecordObject
Set MyRecordObject = Server.CreateObject("ADODB.Record")
MyRecordObject.Open
"Images","URL=http://www.anywebsite.com"
MyRecordObject.MoveRecord " ", "http://www.another.com",
"Melissa","Chesser"
MyRecordObject.Close
Set MyRecordObject = nothing
%>
```

Open

Record Object Method

Purpose

Use this method to associate an existing file or directory with a Record
object, or to create a new file or directory that will be associated with a
Record object.

Syntax

```
RecordObject.Open Source, ActiveConnection, Mode, CreateOptions,
Options, UserName, Password
```

Table 54 lists the arguments associated with the Open method.

Table 54 *Arguments for the Open Method*

Value	Required	Type	Description
Source	No	String	This is the name of the file or directory that will be the source for the Record object.
			The source can be an absolute URL, a relative URL, or a RecordSet object that has already been opened. If you leave the ActiveConnection option empty, you must specify a value for the source.

Continued

ASP Core Reference

Table 54 *Continued*

Value	Required	Type	Description
Active Connection	No	String	This is the URL or file that Record the object will have an active connection with. Normally, the syntax to start this option is "URL = "
Mode	No	ConnectMode enumerated constant	Value determines the con nection mode. Use one of the ConnectionMode enu- meration constants. Four of the eight constants are given below. To see the other ConnectionMode val- ues, see the cross-refer- ence following this table.
			adModeUnknown (the default) – 0
			adModeRead – 1
			adModeWrite – 2
			adModeReadWrite – 3
Create Options	No	Record CreateOptions enumerated constant.	Value determines whether or not a file or directory should be opened or cre ated. This is a RecordCreateOption
			The default is adFailifNotExists - -1.
Options	No	RecordOpen Options enumerated constant	Value determines options for opening the Record object. This is a RecordOpenOptions enu- meration constant. The default is adOpenRecord Unspecified - -1.
UserName	No	String	The user name that a Web site needs if a user name and password are required for authentication
Password	No	String	The password that a Web site needs if a password is required for authentication.

CROSS-REFERENCE

The values for the `ConnectMode`, `RecordCreateOptions`, and `RecordOpenOptions` enumerated constants can be found at the URL noted in the Preface.

Examples

The following example associates an existing Web site directory http://localhost/mywebsite to a `Record` object:

```
<%
Dim recordobj
Set recordobj = Server.CreateObject("ADODB.Record")
Recordobj.Open "","URL= http://localhost/mywebsite"
%>
```

The preceding code is a simple example of placing a directory http://localhost/mywebsite into a `Record` object. But if the Web site requires authentication, you need a user name and password. The following example associates the URL www.terrieden.com to a `Record` object, and this Web site requires a user name and password in order to access the site. The example uses the user name and password option to associate the site with a `Record` object. The user name is RogerEden and the password is `MyFather`.

```
<%
Dim Recordobj
Set Recordobj = Server.CreateObject("ADODB.Record")
Recordobj.Open "","URL=http://www.terrieden.com" , , ,
,"RogerEden","MyFather"
%>
```

The following code shows you how to open the absolute URL http://www.anywebsite.com/RobertBerry.txt" as a record. The example uses the relative URL — RobertBerry.txt — in the Source option; and the absolute URL — http://www.anywebsite.com — in the `ActiveConnection` option.

```
<%
Dim Recordobj
Set Recordobj = Server.CreateObject("ADODB.Record")
Recordobj.Open "RobertBerry.txt",
"URL=http://www.anywebsite.com"
%>
```

The last example can also be opened using the `Record` object's `Active Connection` property and the `Open` method. The `ActiveConnection` property will be set to http://www.anywebsite.com, while the `Open` method will use only the source `RobertBerrry.txt` and not an active connection argument.

```
<%
```

```
Dim Recordobj
Set Recordobj = Server.CreateObject("ADODB.Record")
Recordobj.ActiveConnection = "http://www.anywebsite.com"
Recordobj.Open "RobertBerry.txt"
%>
```

ActiveConnection   Record Object Property

Purpose

Use this property to either get or set the active connection for the Record object.

Syntax

```
RecordObject.ActiveConnection
```

Example

The earlier example for the Record object's Open method (p. 179) shows how to use the ActiveConnection property to associate a file or directory with a Record object. For the purposes of this example, the directory http://www. anywebsite.com/Myfiles/ is attached to the Record object. The active connection is http://www.anywebsite.com.

```
<%
Dim RecordObject
Set RecordObject = Server.CreateObject("ADODB.Record")
RecordObject.ActiveConnection = "http://www.anywebsite.com"
RecordObject.Open "Myfiles"
%>
```

Mode   Record Object Property

Purpose

Use this property to find or set the available permissions for the files or directory associated with the Record object. This property requires a ConnectMode enumerated constant. The default value for this property is read access or the ConnectMode enumerated constant of adModeRead.

● CROSS-REFERENCE

The ConnectMode enumerated constants are available at the URL noted in the Preface.

Syntax

```
RecordObject.Mode
```

Example

The following example associates the file JeremyBeaver.txt to the Record object. This file is in the directory http://www.myfriends.com. The access permission to this file will be Read/Write; thus, the Mode property will be set to adModeReadWrite. The value for adModeReadWrite is 3.

```
<%
Dim RecordObject
Set RecordObject = Server.CreateObject("ADODB.Record")
RecordObject.ActiveConnection = "http://www.myfriends.com"
RecordObject.Source = "JeremyBeaver.txt"
'You can put either the enumerated constant adModeReadWrite or
'its value 3 as the value for RecordObject.Mode.
RecordObject.Mode = 3
RecordObject.Open
%>
```

ParentURL   Record Object Property

Purpose

Use this property to determine the parent URL of the current record. If no parent exists, a null value is returned. In plain English, the parent URL is the next file level above the present file or directory.

Syntax

```
RecordObject.ParentURL
```

Example

The following code shows the example from the Record object's Active Connection property. The active connection for this Record object is http://www.anywebsite.com and the Record object is associated with the directory Myfiles. Thus, the structure is www.anywebsite.com/Myfiles. The parent directory of Myfiles is www.anywebsite.com. Therefore, the property ParentURL will return www.anywebsite.com for the Record object.

```
<%
Dim RecordObject
Set RecordObject = Server.CreateObject("ADODB.Record")
RecordObject.ActiveConnection = "http://www.anywebsite.com"
RecordObject.Open "Myfiles"
Response.Write "The parenturl is "
Response.Write RecordObject.ParentURL
%>
```

ASP Core Reference

RecordType   Record Object Property

Purpose

Use this property to determine the type of Record object. This is a read-only property. A RecordType enumerated constant is returned. Only three types of records can be returned: simple, collection, or COM-structured.documents.

Syntax

```
RecordObject.RecordType
```

Example

The following example associates a directory with a Record object. The directory is http://www.myfriends.com/CarmenBurgessDir/.

```
<%
Dim RecordObject
Set RecordObject = Server.CreateObject("ADODB.Record")
RecordObject.ActiveConnection = "http://www.myfriends.com/"
RecordObject.Open "CarmenBurgessDir/"
Response.Write "The RecordType is "
Response.Write RecordObject.RecordType
%>
```

Source   Record Object Property

Purpose

Use this property to either get or set the source for the Record object. You can use this property to set the Source property instead of setting the property as one of the options in the Record object's Open method (p. 179).

Syntax

```
RecordObject.Source
```

Example

The following example sets the Source property for a Record object before the Record object is opened. The source for this example is the file TimBurgess.txt. The file TimBurgess.txt is part of the URL http://www.myfriends.com. Look at the examples given in the Record object's Open method (on p. 179). The Source property is set as part of the method, but in this example, its value is set by using this property.

```
<%
Dim RecordObject
Set RecordObject = Server.CreateObject("ADODB.Record")
RecordObject.ActiveConnection = "http://www.myfriends.com"
```

```
RecordObject.Source = "TimBurgess.txt"
RecordObject.Open
Response.Write "The Source is "
Response.Write RecordObject.Source
%>
```

State   Record Object Property

Purpose

Use this property to determine whether the Record object is open or closed.
You can only get the value of this property; you cannot set the property. This
property is best used to determine the execution of a Record object opened in
an asynchronous method. The property returns an ObjectState enumerated
constant.

●—CROSS-REFERENCE

The list of ObjectState enumerated constants is available at the URL
noted in the Preface.

Syntax

```
RecordObject.State
```

Example

The following example opens a Record object to the directory KarlaBeaverDir.
This source is part of the URL http://www.myfriends.com/KarlaBeaverDir/.
The Record object attempts to open using the asynchronous option. The code
will wait eight seconds to determine if the state
of the Record object is open.

```
<%
Dim RecordObject, Tm

Set RecordObject = Server.CreateObject("ADODB.Record")
RecordObject.ActiveConnection = "http://www.myfriends.com"
RecordObject.Source = "KarlaBeaverDir"
Tm = Second(Time())
RecordObject.Open

Do while (Second(Time()) < Tm + 8)
    'waits 8 seconds to test whether Record object opened
Loop

If Not (RecordObject.State = adStateOpen) then
    RecordObject.Cancel
```

ASP Core Reference

```
End
Set RecordObject = nothing
%>
```

RecordSet Object

Purpose

Use the RecordSet object to interact with a resultset from a database. This interaction can include adding, deleting, or updating a record. In addition to these features, you can sort and search on a recordset.

Syntax

```
RecordSet.Method
RecordSet.Property
```

AddNew	RecordSet Object Method

Purpose

Use this method to create a new row in an existing recordset.

Syntax

```
RecordSetObject.AddNew( FieldList , values)
```

Table 55 lists the arguments associated with the AddNew method.

Table 55 *Arguments for the AddNew Method*

Value	Required	Type	Description
FieldList	No	Variant	A single name or an array of names or ordinal positions of the field in the new recordset
Values	No	Variant	A single value or an array of values for the fields in the new record. If Fieldlist is an array, Values must also be an array with the same number of elements.

Examples

The following two examples show you how to use the AddNew method.

To add one record to a recordset:

```
'Assume the DataConn is the Connection object
Set RecordSetObj = Server.CreateObject("ADODB.Recordset")
SqlStm = "Select College From Colleges"
RecordSetObj = DataConn.Execute(SqlStm)
RecordSetObj.AddNew "College","Auburn University"
```

To add a row but put several values into different columns:

```
RecordSetObj.AddNew Array("College","Nickname","State"), Array
( "Auburn
University","Tigers","Alabama")
```

Cancel	**RecordSet Object Method**

Purpose
Use this method to cancel a pending asynchronous open operation.

Syntax
```
RecordSetObject.Cancel
```

Example
This script ensures that after 300 milliseconds the attempt to get a recordset is canceled:

```
Set RecordSetObj = Server.CreateObject("ADODB.Recordset")
SqlStm = "Select College From Colleges"
'if the Connection object has disappeared then
'cancel the Open connection
Dim T
T = True
'while T is true continue looping
While T
    RecordSetObj = DataConn.Execute(SqlStm)
    ToCount = ToCount + 1

    If ToCount > 300 then
        RecordSetObject.Cancel
        T = False
    End if

WEnd
```

ASP Core Reference

CancelBatch — RecordSet Object Method

Purpose

Use this method to cancel a pending batch update when in batch mode. Don't use this method unless you absolutely need to. Using this method can lead to leaving the record pointer at an unknown position.

Syntax

```
RecordSet.CancelBatch (AffectRecords)
```

Table 56 lists the argument associated with the CancelBatch method.

Table 56 *Argument for the CancelBatch Method*

Value	Required	Type	Description
AffectRecords	Yes	AffectEnum	Determines how many records will be affected. Defaults to adAffectAll.

● CROSS-REFERENCE

The AffectRecords enumeration constants are available at the URL noted in the Preface.

Example

The following example shows you how to cancel all the records that are waiting to be inserted into the recordset in a batch mode.

```
Set DataConn = Server.CreateObject("ADODB.Connection")
Set RS = Server.CreateObject("ADODB.Recordset")
SqlStm = "Select CollegeName From Colleges"
RS.Open SqlStm, DataConn, adOpenDynamic
RS.AddNew "CollegeName","UCLA"
RS.AddNew "CollegeName","Arizona"
RS.AddNew "CollegeName","Maine"
RS.CancelBatch(3)
```

CancelUpdate — RecordSet Object Method

Purpose

Use this method to cancel any changes made to the current record or to a new record prior to calling the Update method.

Syntax

```
RecordSetObject .CancelUpdate
```

Example

The following example cancels any updates to a current record:

```
'Assume the DataConn is the Connection object
Set RecordSetObj = Server.CreateObject("ADODB.Recordset")
SqlStm = "Select College From Colleges"

RecordSetObj = DataConn.Execute(SqlStm)
'move to the 6th row in Recordset
RecordSetObj.Move 6
RecordSetObj.Update "Auburn College","Auburn University"
RecordSetObj.CancelUpdate
```

Clone	RecordSet Object Method

Purpose

Use this method to create a duplicate Recordset object from an existing RecordSet object. You need to specify a LockType enumeration constant with this method.

● NOTE

Two recordsets are not created here, but rather, two RecordSet objects that point at the same recordset.

So why would you want to clone a recordset? Cloning a recordset enables you to change one object while keeping a copy of the original recordset.

Syntax

```
Recordset_Clone_Object = RecordSetObject.Clone(LockTypeEnum)
```

The clone method takes one argument: a LockTypeEnum constant.

● CROSS-REFERENCE

The LockType enumeration constants are are available at the URL noted in the Preface.

Example

The following example creates a clone that contains all the same locks as the original Recordset object:

```
'Assume the DataConn is the connection object
Set RecordSetObj = Server.CreateObject("ADODB.Recordset")
```

ASP Core Reference

```
SqlStm = "Select College From Colleges"

RecordSetObj = DataConn.Execute(SqlStm)
'make a copy of the original recordset before any 'changes are
made.
NewRS = RecordSetObj.clone
```

Close   RecordSet Object Method

Purpose

Use this method to close an open recordset.

Syntax

```
RecordSetObject.Close
```

Example

The following code closes an open recordset.

```
'Assume the DataConn is the Connection object
Set RecordSetObj = Server.CreateObject("ADODB.Recordset")
SqlStm = "Select College From Colleges"

RecordSetObj = DataConn.Execute(SqlStm)
'move to the 6th row in Recordset
RecordSetObj.Move 6
RecordSetObj.Update "Auburn College","Auburn University"
'close the open recordset
RecordSetObj.Close
Set RecordSetObj = nothing.
```

Remember that even though you have closed the RecordSet object, it still
exists in memory. Therefore, you must destroy the object:

```
Set RecordSetObject = nothing.
```

CompareBookmarks   RecordSet Object Method

Purpose

Using this method compares two bookmarks and returns a CompareEnum constant indicating their relative value.

●—CROSS-REFERENCE

The list of Compare enumeration constants is available at the URL
noted in the Preface.

Syntax

```
CompareEnum =
RecordSetObject.CompareBookmarks(Bookmark1,Bookmark2)
```

Table 57 lists the arguments associated with the CompareBookMarks method.

Table 57 *Arguments for the CompareBookMarks Method*

Value	Required	Type	Description
Bookmark1	Yes	Variant	The bookmark for the first row to be compared
Bookmark2	Yes	Variant	The bookmark for the second row to be compared

Example

The following code compares two bookmarks, and then returns a message indicating which one is greater:

```
Set DataConn = Server.CreateObject("ADODB.Connection")
Set RS = Server.CreateObject("ADODB.Recordset")
SqlStm = "Select CollegeName From Colleges"
RS.Open SqlStm, DataConn, adOpenDynamic
'Move to 6th record
RS.Move 6
Bookmark1 = RS.BookMark
'Move to 4th record
RS.Move 4
Bookmark2 = RS.BookMark
If CompareBookmarks(Bookmark1,Bookmark2) = adCompareGreaterThan
then
    Response.Write "Bookmark1 greater than bookmark2"
Else
    Response.Write "Bookmark2 greater than bookmark1"
End if
```

Delete   RecordSet Object Method

Purpose

Use this method to remove the current record from the recordset. This method gives you the option to delete a single record or a group of records by using an AffectRecords enumeration constant. The actual removal occurs when you call the Update method.

Syntax

```
RecordSetObject.Delete( AffectRecordEnum)
```

Table 58 lists the argument associated with the Delete method.

Table 58   *Argument for the Delete Method*

Value	Required	Type	Description
AffectRecords	No	AffectEnum	Determines how many records will be affected. Defaults to adAffectAll.

●—CROSS-REFERENCE

The list of AffectRecords enumeration constants is available at the URL noted in the Preface.

Examples

This script shows you how to delete a record from a recordset:

```
'Assume the DataConn is the Connection object
Set RecordSetObj = Server.CreateObject("ADODB.Recordset")
SqlStm = "Select College From Colleges"

RecordSetObj = DataConn.Execute(SqlStm)
'move to the 6th row in Recordset
RecordSetObj.Move 6
RecordSetObj.Delete(1)
RecordSetObj.Update
```

If you wanted to delete four records starting with the sixth record, the script would appear as follows:

```
RecordSetObj.Move 6
RecordSetObj.Delete(4)
RecordSetObj.Update
```

Find	RecordSet Object Method

Purpose

Use this method to search through a recordset to find a matching record.

Syntax

The Criteria argument is the only argument required for this
method.

```
RecordSetObject.Find (Criteria, SkipRecords,
SearchDirection ,Start)
```

Table 59 lists the arguments associated with the Find method.

Table 59   *Arguments for the Find Method*

Value	Required	Type	Description
Criteria	Yes	String	The string that narrows the search
SkipRecords	No	Long	Skips over a certain number of records from the current row to begin the search
SearchDirection	No	SearchDirection Enum	If you have supplied a cursor that allows backward movement, you can initiate the search in a backward direction from the current record. The default direction is forward.
Start	No	Variant	The record number you want the search to begin with

● CROSS-REFERENCE

The SearchDirection enumerated constants are available at the
URL noted in the Preface.

Examples

The following example details use of the Find method. If the criteria are
True, the record pointer will move to the matched record.

```
'Assume the DataConn is the Connection object
Set RecordSetObj = Server.CreateObject("ADODB.Recordset")
SqlStm = "Select College From Colleges"

RecordSetObj = DataConn.Execute(SqlStm)
'if this criteria is true then record pointer
```

ASP Core Reference

```
'will move to the record that matches Auburn
'University
RecordSetObj.Find "College = "Auburn University"
```

You can only use single value searches. In other words, you cannot do searches that use an OR or an AND. A search like the following will generate an error:

```
RecordSetObj.Find "College = Yale" and "College = UNLV"
```

If you need to search on multiple items, use the RecordSet object's Filter property (p. 214).

GetRows	RecordSet Object Method

Purpose

This method enables you to put an entire recordset into an array, which is faster to process than a recordset.

Syntax

```
Array = RecordSetObject.GetRows( Rows, Start, Fields)
```

Table 60 lists the arguments associated with the GetRows method.

Table 60 *Arguments for the GetRows Method*

Value	Required	Type	Description
Rows	No	Long	The records to be retrieved from the recordset. The default value is all the rows. If you use this argument, the default value is adGetRowRest.
Start	No	Variant	The first record that the method should start getting records from. Use the BookMarkEnum constant as the value.
Fields	No	Variant	A single field name, an ordinal position, an ordinal array of field names, or an array of ordinal values representing the fields that should be fetched

CROSS-REFERENCE

The BookMark enumeration constants are listed at the URL noted in the Preface.

Examples

The following scripts show you how to use the GetRows method.

Use the following if you want to put all the retrieved rows in a recordset into an array:

```
Dim ArrayName1
ArrayName1 = RecordSetObject.GetRows()
```

Use the next script if you want to put only the first three rows into the array:

```
ArrayName1 = RecordSetObject.GetRows(3,adBookmarkFirst, )
```

Use the following if you want to put three rows into the array starting at the ninth row:

```
ArrayName1 = RecordSetObject.GetRows(3,9, )
```

Use this if you want to put three rows into the array starting at the ninth row, but only the column named City:

```
ArrayName1 = RecordSetObject.GetRows(3,9, "City")
```

Use the following if you want all the retrieved rows, but only the columns City and State:

```
ArrayName1 = RecordSetObject.GetRows( , , Array("City","State"))
```

After you call GetRows, the next unread record becomes the current record.

GetString   RecordSet Object Method

Purpose

Using this method returns a recordset as a string. Not all database providers support this method.

Syntax

```
RecordSetObject.GetString (StringFormat, NumRows,
ColumnDelimeter, RowDelimiter, NullExpr)
```

Table 61 lists the arguments associated with the GetString method.

Table 61   *Arguments for the GetString Method*

Value	Required	Type	Description
StringFormat	No	StringFormat Enum	The format type that the recordset will be returned as. The default is adClipString.
NumRows	No	Long	The number of rows that will be returned. If you don't indicate this value, all rows will be returned.
Column Delimeter	No	String	The delimiter to use between columns. The Tab is the default.
RowDelimeter	No	String	The delimiter to use between rows. The carriage return is the default.
NullExpr	No	String	The value you want in place if there is a NULL. The default is an empty string.

●—CROSS-REFERENCE

The StringFormat enumerated constants are available at the URL noted in the Preface.

Example

Use this script to discover the value returned by the GetString method:

```
'Assume the DataConn is the connection object
Set RSetObj = Server.CreateObject("ADODB.Recordset")
SqlStm = "Select College From Colleges"
'Open a connection
RSetObj.Open SqlStm , DataConn , adOpenKeyset , adLockOptimistic
'display the RecordSet object as a string using
'the GetString method
Response.Write RsetObj.GetString
```

Move

Purpose

Use this method to move the record pointer a given number of records, based on certain arguments you supply to the method.

Syntax

```
RecordSetObject.Move (NumberOfRecords, Start)
```

Table 62 lists the arguments associated with the Move method.

Table 62 *Arguments for the Move Method*

Value	Required	Type	Description
NumberOfRecords	Yes	Long	The number of rows you want the record pointer to move
Start	No	Long	The record number that you want the record pointer to move from

Example

This example shows you how to move the current record pointer back three rows. In order to move backward and forward, you need to open the record-set with a cursor type that allows full movement, such as dynamic.

```
Set DataConn = Server.CreateObject("ADODB.Connection")
Set RS = Server.CreateObject("ADODB.Recordset")
SqlStm = "Select * From AnyTable"
'Open with a dynamic cursortype
RS.Open SqlStm, DataConn, adOpenDynamic
RecordSetObj = DataConn.Open(SqlStm)
'move to the 6th row in Recordset
RecordSetObj.Move 6
RecordSetObj.Delete(adAffectCurrent)
RecordSetObj.Update
'move back 3 rows
RecordSetObject.Move(-3)
```

MoveFirst

Purpose

Use this method to move the current record pointer to the first record in the RecordSet object.

Syntax

```
RecordSetObject.MoveFirst
```

Example

The next example moves the current record pointer back to the first row. You can only use this method if you have specified a cursor type other than forward-only.

```
Set DataConn = Server.CreateObject("ADODB.Connection")
Set RS = Server.CreateObject("ADODB.Recordset")
SqlStm = "Select * From AnyTable"
'Open with a dynamic cursortype
RS.Open SqlStm, DataConn, adOpenDynamic
RS.MoveFirst
```

MoveLast   RecordSet Object Method

Purpose

Use this method to move the record pointer to the last record in the RecordSet object. You can use this method without having to open a cursor type that allows backward and forward movement. Remember that the default cursor type when opening a recordset is forward-only.

Syntax

```
RecordSetObject.MoveLast
```

Example

The following script shows you how to use the MoveLast method:

```
Set DataConn = Server.CreateObject("ADODB.Connection")
Set RS = Server.CreateObject("ADODB.Recordset")
SqlStm = "Select * From AnyTable"

RS.Open SqlStm, DataConn, adOpenDynamic
RS.MoveLast
```

MoveNext   RecordSet Object Method

Purpose

Use this method to move the current record pointer to the next record in the RecordSet object. You can use this method without having to open a cursor type that allows backward and forward movement. Remember that the default cursor type when opening a recordset is forward-only.

ASP Core Reference

Syntax

```
RecordSetObject.MoveNext
```

Example

The following example moves the record pointer to the next record in the recordset:

```
Set DataConn = Server.CreateObject("ADODB.Connection")
Set RS = Server.CreateObject("ADODB.Recordset")
SqlStm = "Select * From AnyTable"
RS.Open SqlStm, DataConn, adOpenDynamic
'move to next record in recordset
RS.MoveNext
```

MovePrevious   RecordSet Object Method

Purpose

Use this method to move the current record pointer to the previous record in the RecordSet object. In order to use this method, you must open a cursor type that allows backward movement — the dynamic or keystone cursor types.

Syntax

```
RecordSetObject.MovePrevious
```

Example

This script shows you how to move the record pointer back one to the previous record:

```
Set DataConn = Server.CreateObject("ADODB.Connection")
Set RS = Server.CreateObject("ADODB.Recordset")
SqlStm = "Select * From AnyTable"
'open with a adDynamic which is 3.
RS.Open SqlStm, DataConn, 3, 1
'move backwards to previous record.
RS.MovePrevious
```

NextRecordSet   RecordSet Object Method

Purpose

Using this method clears the current recordset and returns the next recordset. This method is best used with multiple recordsets that are returned from a stored procedure.

Syntax

```
Set Recordset = RecordsetObject.NextRecordset (RecordsAffected)
```

ASP Core Reference

Table 63 lists the argument associated with the NextRecordSet method.

Table 63 *Argument for the NextRecordSet Method*

Value	Required	Type	Description
RecordsAffected	No	Variant	A number variable into which the database provider returns the number of records that the operation affected.

Example

The following example shows you how to use the NextRecordSet method on two different recordsets returned from a stored procedure:

Suppose you have a stored procedure that looks something like the following code:

```
CREATE PROCEDURE sp_getColleges
AS
Begin
 SELECT CollegeName From Colleges
 SELECT CollegeName,Region, State From Colleges
End
```

This stored procedure returns two recordsets. If you want to call this stored procedure, use the following code:

```
Const adCmdStoredProc = 4
Const adOpenDyanamic = 2
Set DataConn = Server.CreateObject("ADODB.Connection")
Set RS = Server.CreateObject("ADODB.Recordset")
SqlStm = "sp_getColleges"
RS.Open SqlStm, DataConn, adOpenDyanamic, adCmdStoredProc
'The first recordset returns
Response.Write "From the first recordset<BR>"
Response.Write "The First Row's CollegeName is "
Response.Write RS("CollegeName")
'switch to the second recordset
RS.NextRecordSet
Response.Write "From the second recordset<BR>"
Response.Write "The First Row's College Region is "
Response.Write RS("Region")
```

Open
RecordSet Object Method

Purpose
This method opens a recordset.

Syntax

```
Recordset.Open (Source, ActiveConnection, CursorType, LockType,
Options)
```

Table 64 lists the arguments associated with the Open method.

Table 64 *Arguments for the Open Method*

Value	Required	Type	Description
Source	No	Variant	The name of the command object or sql string that allows the recordset to be opened
ActiveConnection	No	Variant	Any connection object or connection string
CursorType	No	Cursonr TypeEnum	The type of cursor returned
LockType	No	LockType Enum	The type of lock to be applied to the recordset
Options	No	Long	A value that indicates how the database provider should interpret the source argument

●—CROSS-REFERENCE

The CursorType and LockType enumerated constants are available on-line.

Examples
The following examples show you different ways to open a recordset.

To open a recordset with a dynamic cursor Type, use this code:

```
Const adOpenDynamic = 2
Set DataConn = Server.CreateObject("ADODB.Connection")
Set RS = Server.CreateObject("ADODB.Recordset")
```

ASP Core Reference

```
SqlStm = "Select * From AnyTable"
RS.Open SqlStm, DataConn, adOpenDynamic , 1
```

You can also open a recordset by using the Connection object's Execute method (p. 58):

```
Set DataConn = Server.CreateObject("ADODB.Connection")
SqlStm = "Select * From AnyTable"
RS = DataConn.Execute(SqlStrm)
'Assume the DataConn is the connection object
Set RSetObj = Server.CreateObject("ADODB.Recordset")
SqlStm = "Select College From Colleges"
'Open a connection
'if you don't have adOpenKeyset enum constant then use '1
'if you don't have adLockOptimistic enum. Constant the 'use 1
RSetObj.Open SqlStm , DataConn , 1 , 1
```

Requery   RecordSet Object Method

Purpose

Use this method to update a recordset after changes have been made. The difference between Requery and the RecordSet object's Update method (p. 206) is in the approach to the updating of the recordset. The Requery method updates the recordset by executing again the query on which the object is based. The Update method changes the recordset without executing the query on which the recordset is based.

Syntax

```
RecordsetObject.Requery (Options)
```

Table 65 lists the argument associated with the Requery method.

Table 65 *Argument for the Requery Method*

Value	Required	Type	Description
Options	No	Long	Indicates the options to be used when requerying the recordset. The default value is −1.

Example

The following example shows you how to requery a recordset using the Requery method:

```
Set DataConn = Server.CreateObject("ADODB.Connection")
Set RS = Server.CreateObject("ADODB.Recordset")
```

```
SqlStm = "Select CollegeName From Colleges"
RS.Open SqlStm, DataConn, adOpenDynamic
RS.AddNew "CollegeName" "Georgia Tech"
RS.Requery
```

Resync   RecordSet Object Method

Purpose

Use this method to refresh the data in the current recordset without having to requery. The data refreshed is from the underlying values in the recordset.

Syntax

```
RecordsetObject.Resync (AffectRecords , ResyncValues )
```

Table 66 lists the arguments associated with the Resync method.

Table 66 *Arguments for the Resync Method*

Value	Required	Type	Description
AffectRecords	No	AffectEnum	Determines how many records will be affected. Defaults to adAffectAll.
ResyncValues	No	ResyncEnum	Specifies whether the values are overwritten. The default is adResyncAllValues.

●—CROSS-REFERENCE

The AffectRecords and Resync enumerated constants are listed at the URL noted in the Preface.

Example

The following example shows you how to resync the recordset to its underlying value of the RecordSet object RS:

```
Set DataConn = Server.CreateObject("ADODB.Connection")
Set RS = Server.CreateObject("ADODB.Recordset")
SqlStm = "Select CollegeName From Colleges"
RS.Open SqlStm, DataConn, adOpenDynamic
RS.AddNew "CollegeName" "Georgia Tech"
RS.Requery
'to get the underlying values restored use the resync 'method
RS.Resync
```

Save

RecordSet Object Method

Purpose

Use this method to save the recordset to a file.

Syntax

```
RecordsetObject.Save (FileName , PersistFormat )
```

Table 67 lists the arguments associated with the Save method.

Table 67 *Arguments for the Save Method*

Value	Required	Type	Description
FileName	No	String	The complete path of the file where the recordset is to be saved
PersistFormat	No	PersistFormat Enum	The format in which you want the recordset saved

●—CROSS-REFERENCE

The PersistFormat enumerated constants are available at the URL noted in the Preface.

Example

The following example shows you how to save a recordset using the Save method:

```
'use the scripting object to create a file
Dim Sfile,SfileContents
SFile = Server.CreateObject("Scripting.FileSystemObject")
'create a file that will hold the contents of the recordset
Sfile = CreateTextFile("c:\myRSet.txt",true)
'assume DataConn is the Connection object
SqlStm = "Select CollegeName From Colleges"
RS = DataConn.Execute("SqlStm")
'this saves the recordset to the file c:\myRSet.txt
RS.Save "c:\myRSet.txt"
Sfile.close
Set Sfile = nothing
```

Supports	**RecordSet Object Method**

Purpose

Use this method to determine what functionality a RecordSet object supports. The method returns a Boolean type.

●─CROSS-REFERENCE─────────────────────

The CursorOption enumeration constants are available at the URL noted in the Preface.

Syntax

```
Boolean =
RecordSetObject.Supports(CursorOptionsEnum)
```

Example

This example shows you how to determine whether the recordset supports the AddNew method:

```
Set DataConn = Server.CreateObject("ADODB.Connection")
Set RS = Server.CreateObject("ADODB.Recordset")
SqlStm = "Select F_Name,L_Name From Customers"
RS.Open SqlStm, DataConn, adOpenDynamic
    If RS.Supports(adAddNew) then
RS.AddNew ("Peggy","Allison")
RS.Update
Else
SqlInsert = "Insert Into Customers ('F_Name','L_Name')
Values('Peggy','Allison')"
DataConn.BeginTrans
DataConn.Execute(SqlInsert)
If DataConn.Errors.Count > 0 then
    For each error in DataConn.Errors
        Response.Write Error.number
    Next
    DataConn.RollbackTrans
Else
    DataConn.CommitTrans
End if
End if
```

ASP Core Reference

Update
RecordSet Object Method

Purpose

Use this method to save any changes made to the current RecordSet object.

Syntax

```
RecordsetObject.Update( Fields, Values )
```

Table 68 lists the arguments associated with the Update method.

Table 68 *Arguments for the Update Method*

Value	Required	Type	Description
Fields	No	Variant	A field name or an array of field names, or an array of ordinal positions of the fields to be modified
Values	No	Variant	A single value or an array of values to match the array field in the first argument

Examples

The following examples show you how to update a recordset using any of these scripts:

```
Set DataConn = Server.CreateObject("ADODB.Connection")
Set RS = Server.CreateObject("ADODB.Recordset")
SqlStm = "Select F_Name,L_Name,City,State From Names"
RS.Open SqlStm, DataConn, adOpenDynamic
RS("F_Name").Value = "Tommy"
RS("L_Name").Value = "Erwin"
RS("City").Value = "Chiefland"
RS("State").Value = "Florida"
RS.Update
```

Another way to add a record to the object is by directly using the Update method:

```
RS.Update "Jane" ,"Erwin", "Chiefland" , "Florida"
```

The last way to use the Update method is by using an array:

```
RS.Update Array("F_Name" ,"L_Name","City","State"),
Array("Gigi","Buckner","Hinesville","Georgia")
```

UpdateBatch

RecordSet Object Method

Purpose

Use this method to write all pending batch updates to disk.

Syntax

```
RecordsetObject.UpdateBatch (AffectRecords)
```

Table 69 lists the argument associated with the UpdateBatch method.

Table 69 *Argument for the UpdateBatch Method*

Value	Required	Type	Description
AffectRecords	No	AffectEnum	Determines how many records will be affected. Defaults to adAffectAll.

● CROSS-REFERENCE

The AffectRecords enumeration constants are available at the URL noted in the Preface.

Example

The following example shows you how to update all the items that were added to the recordset using the RecordSet object's Addnew method (p. 186) in a batch:

```
Set DataConn = Server.CreateObject("ADODB.Connection")
Set RS = Server.CreateObject("ADODB.Recordset")
SqlStm = "Select CollegeName From Colleges"
RS.Open SqlStm, DataConn, adOpenDynamic
RS.AddNew "CollegeName","UCLA"
RS.AddNew "CollegeName","Arizona"
RS.AddNew "CollegeName","Maine"
RS.UpdateBatch(3)
```

ASP Core Reference

Absolute Page
RecordSet Object Property

Purpose

Use this property to set or get the page on which the current record resides. This property returns a PositionEnum constant.

●—CROSS-REFERENCE

The Position enumeration constants are available on-line.

Syntax

```
RecordSetObject.AbsolutePage
```

Examples

The following example shows you how to get and set the AbsolutePage property.

Use the following to get the AbsolutePage property:

```
PositionEnum = RecordSetObject.AbsolutePage
```

Use this script to set the AbsolutePage property:

```
RecordSetObject.AbsolutePage = PositionEnum
```

Absolute Position
RecordSet Object Property

Purpose

Use this property to set or get the current position of the record pointer. It returns a Position enumeration constant.

●—CROSS-REFERENCE

The Position enumeration constants are available on-line.

Syntax

```
RecordsetObject.AbsolutePosition
```

Examples

The following two examples show you how to get and set the RecordSet object's AbsolutePosition property.

To get the absolute position, use the following code:

```
PositionEnum = RecordsetObject.AbsolutePosition
```

To set the absolute position, use this code:

```
RecordSetObject.AbsolutePosition
```

ActiveCommand   RecordSet Object Property

Purpose
Use this property to determine the Command object associated with the
RecordSet object.

Syntax
```
RecordSetObject.ActiveCommand
```

Example
The following example shows you how to find the active Command object associated with a recordset.

```
Set Command = RecordSetObject.ActiveCommand
Set DataConn = Server.CreateObject("ADODB.Connection")
Set CommObj = Server.CreateObject("ADODB.Command")
SqlStm = "Select F_Name,L_Name,City,State From Names"
CommObj.CommandText = SqlStm
CommObj.ActiveConnection = DataConn
RS = CommObj.Execute
Response.Write "The ActiveCommand for RS is " &RS.ActiveCommand
```

ActiveConnection   RecordSet Object Property

Purpose
Use this property to get or set an active connection for the recordset.

Syntax
```
RecordSetObject.ActiveConnection
```

Examples
The following scripts show you how to get and set the ActiveConnection
property.

To get the ActiveConnection property, use this script:

```
Set Sconnection = RecordsetObject.ActiveConnection
```

To set the ActiveConnection property, use the following:

```
'assume that DataConn is an active connection object
RecordsetObject.ActiveConnection = Dataconn
```

BOF   RecordSet Object Property

Purpose

Use this property to determine whether you are at the beginning of a recordset.

Syntax

```
Boolean = RecordsetObject.BOF
```

Example

The following script uses the BOF property to check the position of the record pointer for the beginning of the recordset.

```
Set DataConn = Server.CreateObject("ADODB.Connection")
Set CommObj = Server.CreateObject("ADODB.Command")
SqlStm = "Select F_Name,L_Name,City,State From Names"
RS.Open SqlStm, DataConn, adOpenDynamic
'check to see if recordset is null
If Not RS.BOF and Not RS.EOF then
    'move to top of recordset
    Rs.MoveFirst
    'check to make sure at beginning of file
    If RS.BOF then
        Response.Write "First record is "&RS(0).Name
    End if
End if
```

EOF   RecordSet Object Property

Purpose

Use this property to determine whether you are at the end of the recordset.

Syntax

```
Boolean = RecordsetObject.EOF
```

Example

The following script uses the EOF property to check the position of the record pointer for the end of recordset.

```
Set DataConn = Server.CreateObject("ADODB.Connection")
Set CommObj = Server.CreateObject("ADODB.Command")
SqlStm = "Select F_Name,L_Name,City,State From Names"
RS.Open SqlStm, DataConn, adOpenDynamic
'check to see if recordset is null
If Not RS.BOF and Not RS.EOF then
```

```
'move to top of recordset
While Not EOF
     'check to make sure at beginning of file
     Response.Write "F_Name is "&RS("F_Name").value
     RS.MoveNext
  Wend
End if
```

Bookmark   RecordSet Object Property

Purpose

Using this property returns a bookmark that identifies the current record in a RecordSet object, or sets the record identified.

Syntax

```
RecordSetObject.Bookmark
```

Example

The following example shows you how to set and identify a bookmark associated with a recordset:

```
Set DataConn = Server.CreateObject("ADODB.Connection")
Set CommObj = Server.CreateObject("ADODB.Command")
SqlStm = "Select F_Name,L_Name,City,State From Names"
RS.Open SqlStm, DataConn, adOpenDynamic
'check to see if recordset is null
RS.Move 8
'set the bookmark
Bookmark = RS.Bookmark
'move to another record
RS.Move 2
'if you now want to move back to the record bookmarked
RS.Move Bookmark
```

CacheSize   RecordSet Object Property

Purpose

Use this property to determine the number of records from a recordset that can be cached in memory. The default is 1. The property returns a datatype of Long.

Syntax

```
RecordsetObject.CacheSize
```

ASP Core Reference

Example

The following script shows you how to check the RecordSet object for the cache size:

```
Set DataConn = Server.CreateObject("ADODB.Connection")
Set CommObj = Server.CreateObject("ADODB.Command")
SqlStm = "Select F_Name,L_Name,City,State From Names"
RS.Open SqlStm, DataConn, adOpenDynamic
'check to see what is the cachesize
Response.Write RS.CacheSize
```

CursorLocation   RecordSet Object Property

Purpose

Use this property to set or return the location of the cursor engine. The property returns or is set by the CursorLocationEnum constant. Generally, the CursorLocation will return an adUseServer value.

● CROSS-REFERENCE

The list of CursorLocation enumeration constants can be found at the URL noted in the Preface.

Syntax

```
RecordsetObject.CursorLocation
```

Example

The following example shows you how to check the cursor location values:

```
'DataConn is the Connection object
Set DataConn = Server.CreateObject("ADODB.Connection")
Set RS = Server.CreateObject("ADODB.Recordset")
SqlStm = "Select CollegeName From Colleges"
'open with a adDynamic which is 3.
RS.Open SqlStm, DataConn, 3, 1
'get the cursorlocation
Response.Write "Cursor Location is "
Response.Write RS.CursorLocation
```

CursorType   RecordSet Object Property

Purpose

Use this property to either determine the cursor type or set the cursor type.

CROSS-REFERENCE

The CursorType enumerated constants are available at the URL noted in the Preface.

Syntax

```
RecordsetObject.CursorType = CursorTypeEnum
```

Example

The following script shows you how to determine what cursor type the RecordSet object uses:

```
'DataConn is the Connection object
Set DataConn = Server.CreateObject("ADODB.Connection")
Set RS = Server.CreateObject("ADODB.Recordset")
SqlStm = "Select CollegeName From Colleges"
'open with a adDynamic which is 3.
RS.Open SqlStm, DataConn, 3, 1
'get the cursorlocation
 Select Case RS.CursorType
Case 0
Response.Write "Cursor Type is ForwardOnly"
Case 1
Response.Write "Cursor Type is Open Keyset"
Case 2
Response.Write "Cursor Type is Dynamic"
Case 3
Response.Write "Cursor Type is Static"
Case -1
Response.Write "Cursor Type is Unspecified"

End Selection
```

EditMode   RecordSet Object Property

Purpose

Use this property to determine the editing status of the current record. An EditMode enumerated constant is returned from the property.

CROSS-REFERENCE

The EditMode enumerated constants are available at the URL noted in the Preface.

Syntax

```
EditModeEnum = RecordsetObject.EditMode
```

Example

The following code finds the value of the EditMode property:

```
'the EditModeEnum constants
Const adEditNone = 0
Const adEditInProgress = 1
Const adEditAdd = 2
Const adEditDelete = 4
'DataConn is the Connection object
Set DataConn = Server.CreateObject("ADODB.Connection")
Set RS = Server.CreateObject("ADODB.Recordset")
SqlStm = "Select CollegeName From Colleges"
'open with a adDynamic which is 3.
RS.Open SqlStm, DataConn, 3, 1
RS.AddNew "CollegeName", "Georgia Southern University"
'get the editmode
 Select Case RS.EditMode
Case adEditNone
Response.Write "EditMode is None"
Case adEditInProgress
Response.Write "EditMode is InProgress"
Case adEditAdd
Response.Write "EditMode is Add"
Case adEditDelete
Response.Write "EditMode is Delete"
End Selection
'update the add to the recordset
RS.Update
```

Filter   RecordSet Object Property

Purpose

Use this property to either set or get the filter on a recordset. You can think of this property as a Where clause in a SQL Select statement. The Filter property can be set to a string, an array of bookmarks, or a FilterGroup enumeration constant.

●—CROSS-REFERENCE

The FilterGroup enumeration constants are available at the URL noted in the Preface.

Syntax

```
RecordsetObject.Filter
```

Example

The following example filters out all records with 'Auburn' in the RecordSet object:

```
'DataConn is the Connection object
Set DataConn = Server.CreateObject("ADODB.Connection")
Set RS = Server.CreateObject("ADODB.Recordset")
SqlStm = "Select CollegeName From Colleges"
'open with a adDynamic which is 3.
RS.Filter = "CollegeName = 'Auburn'"
RS.Open SqlStm, DataConn, 3, 1
```

Index   RecordSet Object Property

Purpose

Use this property to determine the name of the database index currently used by the RecordSet object. If no index is being used, a blank string is returned.

Syntax

```
RecordSetObj.Index
```

Example

The following example will obtain the name of the database index being used by the RecordSet object. If there is no index, a blank will be returned.

```
'DataConn is the Connection object
Set DataConn = Server.CreateObject("ADODB.Connection")
Set RS = Server.CreateObject("ADODB.Recordset")
SqlStm = "Select CollegeName From Colleges"
'open with a adDynamic which is 3.
RS.Filter = "CollegeName = 'Auburn'"
RS.Open SqlStm, DataConn, 3, 1
Response.Write "<BR>The Index being currently used by "
Response.Write "the RecordSet object RS is "
Response.Write RS.Index
```

LockType | RecordSet Object Property

Purpose

Use this property to set or get the type of lock placed on the recordset. A LockType enumeration constant sets or returns from this property.

● CROSS-REFERENCE

The LockType enumeration constants are available on-line.

Syntax

```
LockTypeEnum = Recordset.LockType
RecordsetObject.LockType = LockTypeEnum
```

Examples

The following example shows you how to get the value of the LockType property. The code uses a VBScript function to accomplish this goal.

```
Function LockType(strFieldName)
    LockType = strFieldName.LockType
End Function
```

Use the following VBScript Sub to set the LockType property:

```
Sub SetLockType(strFieldName)
    Const adLockUnspecified = -1
    Const adLockReadOnly = 1
    Const adLockPessimistic = 2
    Const adLockOptimistic = 3
    Const adLockBatchOptimistic = 4
    strFieldName.LockType = adLockReadOnly
End Sub
```

MarshalOptions | RecordSet Object Property

Purpose

Use this property to determine which records will be sent back to the server. The only time you use this property is on a disconnected, client-side recordset — which is never going to happen. Thus, if you are using Netscape, you won't have client-side recordsets. We include it here because it is one of Microsoft's properties. This property returns a MarshalOptions enumeration constant.

CROSS-REFERENCE

The MarshalOptions enumeration constants are available at the URL noted in the Preface.

Syntax

```
MarshalOptionsEnum = RecordSetObject.MarshalOptions
RecordSetObject.MarshalOptions = MarshalOptionsEnum
```

Example

The following example shows you how to use the MarshalOptions property:

```
Set DataConn = Server.CreateObject("ADODB.Connection")
Set RS = Server.CreateObject("ADODB.Recordset")
SqlStm = "Select * From AnyTable"
'set the number of records to be display on page
RS.Open SqlStm, DataConn, 2 , 1
'check to see what the value of the MarshalOptions 'property is
Response.Write RS.MarshalOptions
```

MaxRecords   RecordSet Object Property

Purpose

Use this property to determine the maximum number of records to return to a Recordset object from a query. This property can only be set before a recordset opens.

Syntax

```
Long = RecordsetObject.MaxRecords
RecordsetObject.MaxRecords = Long
```

Example

The following script uses the MaxRecords property to set the number of records to be displayed to 10 per page:

```
Set DataConn = Server.CreateObject("ADODB.Connection")
Set RS = Server.CreateObject("ADODB.Recordset")
SqlStm = "Select * From AnyTable"
'set the number of records to be display on page
RS.MaxRecords = 10
RS.Open SqlStm, DataConn, 2 , 1
```

ASP Core Reference

PageCount   RecordSet Object Property

Purpose

Use this property to determine how many pages of data the RecordSet object contains. However, you must set the RecordSet object's PageSize property (p. 218) before you request this property; otherwise, –1 returns.

Syntax

```
Long = RecordsetObject.PageCount
```

Example

This script finds out if there is more than one page of records. The PageSize property is set to 10 before the code retrieves the RecordSet object. The script tests the record counts to see if there is more than one page of data by using the PageCount property.

```
Set DataConn = Server.CreateObject("ADODB.Connection")
Set RS = Server.CreateObject("ADODB.Recordset")
SqlStm = "Select * From AnyTable"
'set the number of records to be display on page
RS.PageSize = 10
RS.Open SqlStm, DataConn, adOpenDynamic
'check to see how many pages that the recordset
'will display
if RS.PageCount > 0 then
    Response.Write "There are more than 1 page of records"
end if
```

PageSize   RecordSet Object Property

Purpose

Use this property to set the number of records that will be displayed on one page in the RecordSet object. You must set this property before you call the recordset.

Syntax

```
Long = RecordsetObject.PageSize
RecordsetObject.PageSize = Long
```

Example

This script shows you how to set the page size for the RecordSet object. Notice that the page size is set before the RecordSet object is called.

```
Set DataConn = Server.CreateObject("ADODB.Connection")
Set RS = Server.CreateObject("ADODB.Recordset")
```

```
SqlStm = "Select * From AnyTable"
'set the number of records to be display on page
RS.PageSize = 10

RS.Open SqlStm, DataConn, 3, 1
'move to next record in recordset
```

RecordCount   RecordSet Object Property

Purpose

Use this property to determine how many records are contained in a
RecordSet object. It only works with dynamic or linkset cursor types. Use
the RecordSet object's GetRows method (p. 194) to determine the number of
records in a recordset.

Syntax

```
Long = RecordSetObject.RecordCount
```

Example

The following example determines the number of records that the RecordSet
object contains. Notice that the RecordSet object is opened with a dynamic
cursor type.

```
Set DataConn = Server.CreateObject("ADODB.Connection")
Set RS = Server.CreateObject("ADODB.Recordset")
SqlStm = "Select * From AnyTable"
'set the number of records to be display on page
RS.PageSize = 10
RS.Open SqlStm, DataConn, 3, 1
'Check the record count
Response.Write "Recordcount is "
Response.Write RS.RecordCount
```

Sort   RecordSet Object Property

Purpose

Use this property to sort a RecordSet object.

Syntax

```
String = RecordSetObject.Sort
RecordSetObject.Sort = String
```

Use the string *Desc* to indicate descending sort order.

Use the string *Asc* to indicate ascending sort order.

ASP Core Reference

Example

The following code uses the Sort property to initiate a sort on a recordset:

```
Set DataConn = Server.CreateObject("ADODB.Connection")
Set RS = Server.CreateObject("ADODB.Recordset")
SqlStm = "Select CollegeName,Nicknames From Colleges"
'set the number of records to be display on page
RS.PageSize = 10
RS.Open SqlStm, DataConn, 3, 1
'Check the record count
RS.Sort = "Nicknames Desc"
While Not RS.Eof
    Response.Write RS("CollegeName")
Response.Write ", "&RS("Nicknames")
Response.Write "<BR>"
Wend
```

Source   RecordSet Object Property

Purpose

Use this property to determine the command or SQL statement that was the source of the RecordSet object.

Syntax

```
String = RecordsetObject.Source
RecordsetObject.Source = String
Set RecordsetObject.Source = Variant
```

Example

The following code shows you how to get the source of the SQL statement that created the RecordSet object:

```
Set DataConn = Server.CreateObject("ADODB.Connection")
Set RS = Server.CreateObject("ADODB.Recordset")
SqlStm = "Select CollegeName,Nicknames From Colleges"
'set the number of records to be display on page
RS.PageSize = 10
'open a dynamic cursor
RS.Open SqlStm, DataConn, 3, 1
'Check the source
Response.Write "Source of sql is "
Response.Write RS.Source
```

State	RecordSet Object Property

Purpose

Use this property to determine whether a recordset is open, closed, or executing an asynchronous operation. This property returns an ObjectState enumeration constant.

●—CROSS-REFERENCE

The ObjectState enumeration constants are available at the URL noted in the Preface.

Syntax

```
ObjectStateEnum = RecordsetObject.State
```

Example

The following code enables you to determine whether the recordset is still open by using the State property.

```
'___- ObjectState Enum Values ___-
Const adStateClose = 0
Const adStateOpen = 1
Const adStateConnection = 2
Const adStateExecuting = 4
Const adStateFetching = 8

Set DataConn = Server.CreateObject("ADODB.Connection")
Set RS = Server.CreateObject("ADODB.Recordset")
SqlStm = "Select CollegeName,Nicknames From Colleges"
'set the number of records to be display on page
RS.PageSize = 10
'open a dyanamic cursor
RS.Open SqlStm, DataConn, 3, 1
'Check the source
Response.Write "Source of sql is "
Response.Write RS.Source

If (RS.State And adStateOpen) = adStateOpen Then
    'close the recordset
    RS.Close
End If
```

Status	RecordSet Object Property

Purpose

Use this property to determine the status of the current record with respect to match updates or other operations. A RecordStatus enumeration constant is returned from this property.

● CROSS-REFERENCE

The RecordStatus enumeration constants are available at the URL noted in the Preface.

Syntax

```
RecordStatusEnum = RecordSetObject.Status
```

Example

The same example that determined the RecordSet object's State property (p. 221) for a recordset also can determine the status of a RecordSet object. The following code shows you how to use the Status property to determine the status of the recordset:

```
'___- Some of the RecordStatusEnum Values ___-
Const adRecDeleted = 4
Const adRecDBDeleted = 262144
Const adRecInvalid = 16
Const adRecUnmodified = 8
Const adRecOk = 0

Set DataConn = Server.CreateObject("ADODB.Connection")
Set RS = Server.CreateObject("ADODB.Recordset")
SqlStm = "Select CollegeName,Nicknames From Colleges"
'set the number of records to be display on page
RS.PageSize = 10
'open a dyanamic cursor
RS.Open SqlStm, DataConn, 3, 1
'Move to the 5th record
RS.Move 5
RS.Delete
RS.Update
'check to see if delete occurred
If (RS.Status And adRecDeleted) = adRecDeleted Then
    'close the recordset
    Response.Write "Record 5 is deleted"
End If
```

ASP Core Reference

StayinSync   RecordSet Object Property

Purpose

Use this property to indicate whether a reference to the child row should change when the parent record changes. This property returns a Boolean value.

Syntax

```
Boolean = RecordsetObject.StayinSync
RecordSetObject.StayinSync = Boolean
```

Example

This code shows you how to determine the value of the StayinSync property:

```
Set DataConn = Server.CreateObject("ADODB.Connection")
Set RS = Server.CreateObject("ADODB.Recordset")
SqlStm = "Select CollegeName,Nicknames From Colleges"
'open a dyanamic cursor
'the value for setting a dyanamic cursor is 2
RS.Open SqlStm, DataConn, 2, 1
'display the
If RS.StayinSync = True then
    Response.Write "StayinSync is True"
Else
    Response.Write "StayinSync is False"
End if
```

Fields   RecordSet Object Collection

Purpose

Use this collection to contain zero or more Field objects, each representing a field in the recordset. The collection enables you to look at different methods and properties of each field in the collection, such as the value, count, or type.

Syntax

```
Recordset.Fields
```

Example

This code finds the value and type of each field in the Fields Collection object:

```
'assume DataConn is the Connection object
SqlStm = "Select CollegeName From Colleges"
RS = DataConn.Execute("SqlStm")
```

ASP Core Reference

```
'open a recordset with the connection object execute 'method
RS = DataConn.Execute(SqlStm)
For Each oFld in RS.Fields
    Response.Write oFld.Name
    Response.Write oFld.Value
Next
DataConn.close
Set DataConn = nothing
```

Properties | RecordSet Object Collection

Purpose

This collection contains Property objects of the RecordSet object.

Syntax

```
RecordsetObject.Properties
```

Example

This script enables you to identify all the properties that your recordset contains:

```
'assume DataConn is the Connection object
SqlStm = "Select CollegeName From Colleges"
RS = DataConn.Execute("SqlStm")
'open a recordset with the connection object execute 'method
RS = DataConn.Execute(SqlStm)
For Each oFld in RS.Properties
    Response.Write oFld.Name
Next
DataConn.close
Set DataConn = nothing
```

Request Object

Purpose

Use the Request object to obtain any standard HTTP information sent to a Web server. You will use this object extensively when obtaining information sent to the server via an HTML form.

Syntax

```
Request.Collection
Request.Method
Request.Property
```

ClientCertificate — Request Object Collection

Purpose

Use this collection to retrieve the client certification fields from a request issued by the Web browser. A client certificate is an encrypted number stored in a file on the user's computer. This number is sent to the Web server in a request for an ASP. The ClientCertificate collection can then be used to review the certification fields issued by the Web browser.

The ClientCertificate collection is referenced in the X.509 standard. When a Web browser uses the SSL3.0/PCT1 protocol (an URL starting with https:// instead of http://) to connect to a server and the server requests certification, the browser will send the certification fields. The ClientCertificate collection returns EMPTY if no certificate is sent. You must configure your Web server to request client certificates prior to using the ClientCertificate collection.

Syntax

```
Request.ClientCertificate(CertField[SubType] )
```

Table 70 lists the argument associated with the ClientCertificate method.

Table 70 *Argument for the ClientCertificate Method*

Value	Required	Type	Description
CertField	Yes	String	Indicates which of the certification fields to retrieve The list of these fields are listed in Table 71.

Table 71 *Client Certificate Fields*

Value	Required	Type	Description
Certificate	No	Stream	This is a binary stream that contains the certificate contents. The stream is in the ASN.1 format.

Continued

Table 71 *Continued*

Value	Required	Type	Description
Flags	No	String	This is a set of flags that provides you with more information about the certificate:
			ceCertPresent: Tells you if the certificate is present
			ceUnrecognizedIssuer: Tells you there is an unknown issuer for the last certificate in this chain.
			Microsoft states the following about the Flags field: To use the preceding flags, you must include the client-certificate include file in your ASP page. If you are using VBScript, include cervbs.inc. If you are using JScript, include cerjavas.inc. These files are installed in the \Inetpub\ASPSamp\Samples directory.
Issuer	No	String	This field is a list of SubTypes telling you about the issuer of the certificate. Each SubType value in the list is separated by a comma. Items in the list would include country of origin or issuing organization, such as Verisign.
SerialNumber	No	String	This string tells you the certification serial number. The serial number is in ASCII form, with the values represented by hexadecimal bytes; for example, F5-10-AA-AB.
Subject	No	String	This field has information on the subject of the certificate. Each SubType value in the list is separated by a comma. Items in the list would include country of origin or issuing organization, such as Verisign.

ASP Core Reference

Value	Required	Type	Description
ValidFrom	No	Date (in the form of a String)	The date that this certificate becomes valid
ValidUntil	No	Date (in the form of a String)	The date when the certificate expires. The year is in the for mat yyyy, such as 2000 or 1999.

Table 72 lists the values of the SubType parameter that can be specified with the ClientCertificate method.

Table 72 *SubType Parameter Values*

Value	Required	Type	Meaning
C	No	String	The name of the country of origin
CN	No	String	The common name of the issuer of the certificate. This value can only be used on the Subject field.
GN	No	String	The given name of the issuer of the certificate
I	No	String	A set of initials identifying who issued the certificate
L	No	String	The locality of the issuer
O	No	String	The name of the organization that issued the certificate
OU	No	String	The organizational unit that issued the certificate
S	No	String	The state or province
T	No	String	The title of the organization that issued the certificate

Examples

The following example uses the Subject key to determine whether a client certificate is presented on the server:

```
<%
If Len(Request.ClientCertificate("Subject")) = 0 then
    Response.Write("No client certificate is here")
```

```
End if
%>
```

The next example first determines if there is a certificate. If there is a certificate, the serial number,issuing organization and subject name are listed. The
subfield O, which represents the company or organization name, is listed on
the issuing organization attribute.

```
<%
If Len(Request.ClientCertificate("Subject")) = 0 then
Response.Write "<BR>SSN is "
Response.Write Request.ClientCertificate ("SerialNumber")
Response.Write "<br>"
Response.Write "Issuing org is "
Response.Write Request.ClientCertificate("IssuerO")
Response.Write "Subject name"
Response.Write Request.ClientCertificate("Subject")
End if
%>
```

BinaryRead   Request Object Method

Purpose

Use this method to retrieve data sent from the client to the server as a portion of a POST request. This method retrieves the data from the client and
stores it in a *Saf eArray*. A Safe Array is an array that contains information
regarding the number of dimensions and the bounds of its dimensions. The
BinaryRead method is used for low-level access to this data. This contrasts to
using the Request.Form collection to view form data sent in a POST request.

Syntax

```
Request.BinaryRead(count)
```

Examples

The following example shows how to use the BinaryRead method. This
example has an HTML form that passes information put into a textbox to
MyBinaryRead.asp. Once MyBinaryRead.asp receives the information, it displays each byte in a browser. This first section of code is the HTML page.

```
<HTML>
<Body>
<Form Name="Form1" Action = "MyBinaryRead.asp" Method="POST">
FirstName
<Input Type="Text" Name="FirstName">
```

```
LastName
<Input Type="Text" Name="LastName">
<Input Type="Submit" Value="Submit">
</Form>
</body>
</HTML>
```

The next script is the code for MyBinaryRead.asp. In order to get the correct number of bytes from the POST information, you need to use the Request object's TotalBytes method (p. 229). In addition, to output each byte to the browser, you need to use the VBScript function MidB.

```
<HTML>
<BODY>
<%
dim s,d
s = Request.TotalBytes
d = Request.BinaryRead(n)
For i = 1 to n
    Response.Write MidB( d, i, 1 )
Next
%>
</BODY>
</HTML>
```

This example uses the BinaryRead method to place the contents of a request into a SafeArray.

TotalBytes	**Request Object Properties**

Purpose

Use this property to determine the total number of bytes that the body of a client's request contains.

Syntax

```
Request.TotalBytes
```

Example

The following example counts the number of bytes received by an ASP:

```
<%
    Response.Write Request.TotalBytes
%>
```

Cookies   Request Object Collection

Purpose

Use this collection to get the values of the cookies sent in an HTTP request. You can include a value for the key to get the subkeys of a cookie dictionary. If you access a cookie dictionary without specifying the key, all keys will be returned as a single query string. If the client browser sends two cookies with the same name, the Request object's Cookies collection returns the one with the more extensive path.

Syntax

```
Request.Cookies(NameOfCookie)(NameofKey.NameOfAttribute)
```

Table 73 lists the arguments associated with the Cookies collection. Table 74 lists the attributes associated with the Cookies collection.

Table 73 *Arguments for the Cookies Collection*

Value	Required	Type	Description
NameOfCookie	Yes	String	The name of the cookie from which you want to obtain information
NameofKey	No	String	The name of the key in the Cookie that has the information.

Table 74 *Attributes for the Cookies Collection*

Value	Required	Type	Description
Expires	No	String	When the cookie expires
Domain	No	String	Indicates that only individuals with this domain will receive the cookie
Path	No	String	The delivery path of the cookie
Secure	No	String	Indicates whether the cookie is secure
HasKey	No	String	Indicates whether the cookie has any keys with it

Example

This example displays the value of the cookie that is named "YourCookie" in a browser:

```
<%= Request.Cookies("YourCookie") %>
```

Form   Request Object Collection

Purpose

Use the Form collection to obtain the values of form elements posted to the HTTP request body by a form using the POST method.

Syntax

```
Request.Form(element)[(index)|.Count]
```

Table 75 lists the argument associated with the Form Collection.

Table 75 *Arguments for the FormCollection Method*

Value	Required	Type	Description
Element	Yes	String	This is a string representing the name of the element in the Form Collection.
Index	No	Number	Every element in the Form Collection contains a number associated with it. The Index ranges from 1 to the Count.
Count	No	Number	The number of elements that this Form collection contains

Examples

The following script shows an HTML page that contains a form with two text boxes. This form enables users to type in their last and first names. However, both text boxes possess the same Name property-YourName. After filling in the first name and last name fields, the user presses the Submit button. The information is sent via the POST method to YourName.asp. Once the information is passed to YourName.asp, the Request object's Form Collection method is used to obtain the information. But because we used the same name for both text boxes, the Count attribute is used to output the values.

```
<HTML>
<Body>
<Form Name="Form1" Action = "YourName.asp" Method="POST">
```

```
FirstName
<Input Type="Text" Name="YourName">
LastName
<Input Type="Text" Name="YourName">
<Input Type="Submit" Value="Submit">
</Form>
</body>
</HTML>
```

The next script is YourName.asp. It obtains the values passed via the POST method and outputs the multiple values of YourName by using the Count attribute.

```
<%
  For i = 1 To Request.Form("YourName").Count
    Response.Write Request.Form("YourName")(i) & "<BR>"
  Next
%>
```

QueryString   Request Object Collection

Purpose

Use this collection to retrieve the values of the variables in the HTTP query string. The HTTP query string is specified by the values subsequent to the question mark (?). A query string can be generated by several different processes. With it, you can retrieve the QUERY_STRING variable by name. The value of Request.QueryString(parameter) is an array of all the parameter values that occur in QUERY_STRING. The Request.QueryString.Count property enables you to determine the number of values of a parameter.

Syntax

```
Request.QueryString(variable)[(index)|.Count]
```

Table 76 lists the arguments associated with the QueryString collection.

Table 76 *Arguments for the QueryString Collection*

Value	Required	Type	Description
Variable	Yes	String	The variable in the HTTP query string you need to retrieve

ASP Core Reference

Value	Required	Type	Description
Index	No	Number	This is an optional parameter that enables you to retrieve one of multiple values for variable. It can be any integer value in the range 1 to Request.QueryString(variable).Count.
Count	No	Number	The number of items in the QueryString Collection

Examples

The following example shows you how to use the QueryString collection to obtain information passed via a Get method to an ASP. In this example, the HTML page uses an anchor tag to pass a team name to the page YourTeam.asp.

```
<HTML>
<Body>
<A HREF= "YourTeam.asp?team=Hawks">Your Team </A>
</body>
</HTML>
```

The following is the code for YourTeam.asp. The Request object's QueryString collection is used to get the team variable from the URL string.

```
<%
Dim tname
Tname = Request.QueryString("team")
Response.Write "Team Name passed to this page is "
Response.Write Tname
%>
```

Now let's look at using QueryString to get information passed from an HTML form that uses a Get in the method property. Following is the code for an HTML page that contains a form with one element, lastname. The value of the Action property is YourTeam.asp. The method property is set to Get. When a user fills in the last name field and then presses the Submit button, the information is passed to YourTeam.asp via a Get header.

```
<HTML>
<Body>
<Form Name="Form1" Action = "YourTeam.asp" Method="Get">
<Input Type="Text" Name="LastName">
<Input Type="Submit" Value="Submit">
</Form>
</body>
</HTML>
```

Once the information from the preceding HTML page is sent to YourTeam.asp, the following code obtains the value sent:

```
<%
Dim laname
laname = Request.QueryString("LastName")
Response.Write "The LastName is "
Response.Write laname
%>
```

The next bit of code finds the number of items in a QueryString collection:

```
<%
Dim lcnt
lcnt = Request.QueryString("LastName").Count
Response.Write "The number of items in LastName is "
Response.Write lcnt
%>
```

ServerVariables	Request Object Collection

Use this collection to obtain the values of environment variables.

Syntax

```
Request.ServerVariables (server environment variable)
```

Table 77 lists the argument associated with the ServerVariable collection.

Table 77 *Argument for the ServerVariable Collection*

Value	Required	Type	Description
server environment variable	Yes	String	This argument indicates the name of the server environment variable to retrieve.

Table 78 shows the list of all the server environmental variables that existed at the time of this book.

Table 78 *ServerVariable Values*

Variable	Required	Type	Purpose
ALL_HTTP	Yes	String	Retrieves all the headers that are sent by the requesting client.
ALL_RAW	Yes	String	Gets all the headers that are sent by the client.
APPL_MD_PATH	Yes	String	Gets the metabase path for the ISAPI DLL; it will appear something like the following: /LM/W3SVC/1/ROOT.
APPL_PHYSICAL_PATH	Yes	String	Gets the actual physical path to the APPL_MD_PATH server variable. It will appear something like the following: C:\Inetpub\wwwroot\.
AUTH_PASSWORD	Yes	String	The value entered in the client's authentication dialog. Available only if basic authentication is used.
AUTH_TYPE	Yes	String	The authentication method used by the server to validate users who attempt to access a protected script.
AUTH_USER	Yes	String	Indicates the raw authenticated user name.
CERT_COOKIE	Yes	String	The unique ID for the client certificate.

Continued

ASP Core Reference

Table 78 *Continued*

Variable	Required	Type	Purpose
CERT_FLAGS	Yes	String	Here, bit0 is set to 1 if the client certificate is present. bit1 is set to 1 if the Certification Authority of the client certificate is not in the list of recognized CAs on the server.
CERT_ISSUER	Yes	String	This is the SubType value of the client certificate mentioned in the Request.Client Certificate SubType table.
CERT_KEYSIZE	Yes	String	The size (in bits) of the Secure Sockets Layer connection key size; normally it is (128).
CERT_SECRETKEYSIZE	Yes	String	The number of bits in the server certificate private key.
CERT_SERIALNUMBER	Yes	String	The serial number of the client's certificate.
CERT_SERVER_ISSUER	Yes	String	The values for the client certificate Issuer field.
CERT_SERVER_SUBJECT	Yes	String	The values for the client certificate Subject field.
CERT_SUBJECT	Yes	String	The value of the Subject field for the client certificate.
CONTENT_LENGTH	Yes	String	The length in bytes of the contents received from the requesting client.

Variable	Required	Type	Purpose
CONTENT_TYPE	Yes	String	The MIME type of the data received from the requesting client. Normally, Text/Plain is the MIME type.
GATEWAY_INTERFACE	Yes	String	Gets the version of the CBI specification used by the server. Returns a value that will appear something like the following: CGI/1.1
HTTP_<HeaderName>	Yes	String	The value for any HTTP server variable such as HTTP_Connection that is stored in the HeaderName field.
HTTP_ACCEPT	Yes	String	Generally, this value will be */*, meaning all HTTP headers are accepted.
HTTP_ACCEPT_LANGUAGE	Yes	String	The language that a user want to see a Web page in, such as Japanese.
HTTP_USER_AGENT	Yes	String	The name of the browser that sent out the request.
HTTP_COOKIE	Yes	String	Returns the cookie string that was included with the request.
HTTP_REFERER	Yes	String	The name of the URL that made the request before a redirect happened.

Continued

Table 78   *Continued*

Variable	Required	Type	Purpose
HTTPS	Yes	String	Indicates whetherTells you if the request came through a HTTPS. If True, then the value returned will be "ON". If False, then the value will be "OFF".
HTTPS_KEYSIZE	Yes	String	The number of bits in the Secure Sockets Layer connection key. For example, 128 indicates the size—in bits—of the Secure Sockets Layer connection key. It is normally 128.
HTTPS_SECRETKEYSIZE	Yes	String	This returns the number of bits in the certificate's private key. A number returned could be 1024.
HTTPS_SERVER_ISSUER	Yes	String	This servervariable returns the name of the company or person who issued the certificate.
HTTPS_SERVER_SUBJECT	Yes	String	The value of the Subject field in the server certificate.
INSTANCE_ID	Yes	String	This is the value of the IIS textual format.
INSTANCE_META_PATH	Yes	String	This is the metabase path to the IIS that responded to the client's request. This value will return something like LM/W3SVC/1. A metabase is a hierarchical database that is used to store configuration information about the IIS server.

Variable	Required	Type	Purpose
LOCAL_ADDR	Yes	String	Returns the server address on which the request came in. This is important on machines with multiple IP addresses when you want to find out which address the request used.
LOGON_USER	Yes	String	The Windows account that the user is logged into.
PATH_INFO	Yes	String	This is the relative path of the executing ASP. Normally, this value looks something like \thecode.ASP.
PATH_TRANSLATED	Yes	String	This is the absolute path of your ASP or HTML. This value will look something like c:\inetpub\www-root\myproject\the-code.
QUERY_STRING	Yes	String	The values sent by a client via the Get method from a hyper-link or a form. Multiple values are separated by commas.
REMOTE_ADDR	Yes	String	The IP address of the requesting client
REMOTE_HOST	Yes	String	The IP address of the remote host. If you are running a personal Web server, this address will be 127.0.0.1.

Continued

ASP Core Reference

Table 78 *Continued*

Variable	Required	Type	Purpose
REMOTE_USER	Yes	String	This is the unmapped user-name string that is actually sent by the user, as opposed to the names that are modified by any authentication filter on the server.
REQUEST_METHOD	Yes	String	This indicates what method the client used to make their request to the server. The value will be a Get, a Post, a Put, and so on.
SCRIPT_NAME	Yes	String	The name of the ASP or HTML that is executing when you called this servervariable
SERVER_NAME	Yes	String	The DNS name of the server that runs the IIS that executes your ASP code.
SERVER_PORT	Yes	String	The port number to which this request was sent. Normally, it's 80.
SERVER_PORT_SECURE	Yes	String	A string that contains either 0 or 1. If the request is being handled on the secure port, this will be 1. Otherwise, it will be 0.
SERVER_PROTOCOL	Yes	String	This value will usually be either HTTP or HTTPS.
SERVER_SOFTWARE	Yes	String	The version and name of the HTTP server
URL	Yes	String	The base portion of the URL.

ASP Core Reference

Example

The following example uses the ServerVariables "REQUEST_METHOD" to determine if an ASP was accessed via a POST or GET method:

```
<%
Dim cr
cr = Request.ServerVariables("REQUEST_METHOD")

If cr = "POST" then
    Response.Write "Accessed by POST "
end if

If cr = "GET" then
    Response.Write "Accessed by GET "
End if
%>
```

Response Object

Purpose

Use the Response object to send information from the Web server to a client. The client is normally a browser, but could be a wireless device like a PDA.

Syntax

```
ResponseObject.Collection
ResponseObject.Method
ResponseObject.Property
```

Cookies	Response Object Collection

Purpose

Use this collection to set the value of a cookie. If that particular cookie does not exist, it will be created. If the cookie exists, it will take on the new value and the old value will be erased.

Syntax

```
Response.Cookies(cookie)[(key)|.attribute] = value
```

Table 79 lists the argument associated with the Cookies collection. Table 80 lists the attributes associated with the Cookies collection.

Table 79   *Arguments for the Cookies Collection*

Value	Required	Type	Description
Cookie	Yes	String	The name of the cookie
Key	No	String	If key is specified, cookie is a dictionary, and key is set to value
Attribute	No	String	Contains information about the cookie itself, where the attribute parameter can be one of the following
Value	Yes	String	Specifies the value to assign to the key or attribute

Table 80   *Attributes for the Cookies Collection*

Value	Required	Type	Description
Expires	No	String	Sets the date when the cookie will expire
Domain	No	String	Set this property to specify only those users on a domain who will receive the cookie
Path	No	String	The name of the delivery path
Secure	No	String	Indicates whether the cookie is secure or not
HasKeys	No	String	Indicates whether the cookie contains multiple values

Examples

The following example shows you how to create a cookie. The cookie is called "MyKids". It will be assigned a value of "Eric Chesser". This cookie has neither a key value nor an attribute. This is the basic syntax to create a cookie.

```
<% Response.Cookies("MyKids") = "Eric Chesser"%>
```

The preceding script is great if you only want to store one item in a cookie. But if you want to store many values in the cookie "MyKids", you need to create a Cookies Collection that uses a key. The following code shows you how to create a Cookies Collection that stores many items by assigning a key to each value:

```
<%
Response.Cookies("MyKids")("Child1") = "Chris Barker"
```

```
Response.Cookies("MyKids")("Child2") = "Rick Barker"
Response.Cookies("MyKids")("Child3") = "Mellisa Chesser"
Response.Cookies("MyKids")("Child4") = "Kyle Chesser"
Response.Cookies("MyKids")("Child5") = "Eric Chesser"
Response.Cookies("MyKids")("Child6") = "Hanna Allison"
%>
```

You are allowed to overwrite the value of a cookie. The following code over-writes the value of the key "Child6" in the "MyKids" cookie:

```
<% Response.Cookies ("MyKids")("Child6") = "Kitty Boo"%>
```

If for some reason you wanted to change "MyKids" for a multiple-value cookie to a single-value cookie, use code that specifies the cookie but without the keys. The following code destroys the multiple-value cookie "MyKids" and gives the cookie only one value. Once this script is executed, the only value in "MyKids" is "Bunny Boo".

```
<% Response.Cookies ("MyKids") = "Bunny Boo"%>
```

To have a cookie exist for a specified about of time, use the Expires attribute. The following code will set the "MyKids" Cookies collection to expire after Jan 25, 2002:

```
<%
Response.Cookies("MyKids")("Child1") = "Chris Barker"
Response.Cookies("MyKids")("Child2") = "Rick Barker"
Response.Cookies("MyKids")("Child3") = "Mellisa Chesser"
Response.Cookies("MyKids")("Child4") = "Kyle Chesser"
Response.Cookies("MyKids")("Child5") = "Eric Chesser"
Response.Cookies("MyKids")("Child6") = "Hanna Allison"
Response.Cookies("MyKids").Expires = "January 25, 2002"
%>
```

If you want "MyKids" to specify that this cookie can only be delivered over a secure connection such as HTTPS, then set the Secure attribute to True. The following code specifies that the cookie "MyKids" can only be delivered via a secure connection:

```
<%
Response.Cookies("MyKids")("Child1") = "Chris Barker"
Response.Cookies("MyKids")("Child2") = "Rick Barker"
Response.Cookies("MyKids")("Child3") = "Mellisa Chesser"
Response.Cookies("MyKids")("Child4") = "Kyle Chesser"
Response.Cookies("MyKids")("Child5") = "Eric Chesser"
Response.Cookies("MyKids")("Child6") = "Hanna Allison"
Response.Cookies("MyKids").Secure = True
%>
```

ASP Core Reference

The HasKey attribute specifies whether or not a cookie has multiple values. You don't need to set this value, because when the Request object retrieves a cookie, you can use a loop to determine the values in it. However, it's good programming practice to set this value. The following code shows you how to set the HasKey attribute for the cookie "MyKids":

```
<% Response.Cookies("MyKids").HasKeys %>
```

AddHeader	Response Object Method

Purpose

Use this method to create a new header. The header can be either one already supplied for HTTP or you can make up a new one using your own items. Every header must have two parameters: the name of the header and the contents of the header. If you are not going to use a standard HTTP header, then do not use an underscore character (_) in the name of your header. This is because the ServerVariables collection thinks that an underscore character is a dash. When you attempt to retrieve your header with the Request object's ServerVariable method (p. 234), the header will not recognized because the ServerVariable Collection thought the underscore was a dash.

Syntax

```
Response.AddHeader (name, contents)
```

Table 81 lists the attributes associated with the AddHeader method.

Table 81 *Arguments of the AddHeader Method*

Value	Required	Type	Description
Name	Yes	String	The name of the header you want to add
Contents	Yes	String	The content of the header

Examples

The following example creates a new header named "DavidMooreAuburnGrad". The contents for this header will be "David Loves Joy his wife".

```
<%
Response.AddHeader "DavidMooreAuburnGrad", "David Loves Joy his
wife"
%>
```

The following code retrieves the header named "DavidMooreAuburnGrad":

```
<% Request.servervariables("DavidMooreAuburnGrad") %>
```

If you want to set a standard HTTP header such as "Content-Disposition", use the following code:

```
<% Response.AddHeader
("Content-Disposition","attachment;filename="
"c:\yourfile.txt""")%>
```

AppendToLog   Response Object Method

Purpose
Use this method when you want to add a message to the log file. Normally, the best time to use this method is when an error occurs or when you want to keep a log for some special event. The log will be on your server.

Syntax
```
Response.AppendToLog(your message)Example
```

The following example writes a message to the log file if an error occurred during a database transaction:

```
<%
Dim DataConn
Dim TransNestLevel
Dim SqlString
Set DataConn = Server.CreateObject ("ADODB.Connection")
DataConn.ConnectionString = connString
DataConn.Open
TransNestLevel = DataConn.BeginTrans
SqlString = "Delete * From AnyTable"
DataConn.Execute (Sql)
If DataConn.Errors.Count > 0 then
    For each error in DataConn.Errors
      Response.Write Error.number
      'write error to log file
      Response.Write  AppendToLog("Error Number "+Error.number)
    Next
    DataConn.RollbackTrans
Else
    DataConn.CommitTrans
End if
%>
```

ASP Core Reference

BinaryWrite   Response Object Method

Purpose

Use this method to send the actual data to a browser. Normally, when data is sent via HTTP, the data is cleaned up before being output. In some cases, however, such as when you have images stored in databases, you do not want the clean-up process to occur.

Syntax

```
Response.BinaryWrite(bytes)
```

Table 82 lists the argument associated with the BinaryWrite method.

Table 82 *Argument for the BinaryWrite Method*

Value	Required	Type	Description
Bytes	Yes	Number	The actual binary data sent to the browser

Example

The following example shows an HTML file that uses an IMG tag to point to myPage.asp as the source for an image. Once myPage.asp is called, a database connection is made and the BinaryWrite method sends the retrieved image information back to the HTML page.

```
<HTML>
<IMG SRC="myPage.asp?Month='June'">
</HTML>
```

The following script is the code for myPage.asp. This page retrieves an image from a database, and then uses the BinaryWrite method to output the binary data to the HTML page that called this page. The Response object's Flush method (p. 249) is used to force the image to the client. In this case, the client is the HTML page.

```
<%
Dim theImg,sql,DataConn,MonthName,Result
MonthName = request.querystring("Month")
Set DataConn = Server.CreateObject("ADODB.Connection")
DataConn.Open Application("dbConnectionString"),
Session("DataConn_RuntimeUserName"),
Session("DataConn_RuntimePassword")

set Result = server.createobject("ADODB.Recordset")
```

```
sql = "SELECT myImage FROM AllImages WHERE Month ='" & MonthName
&""

Result.Open sql, DataConn, 3
if not (Result.eof and Result.bof) then
   theImg = Result("myImage").GetChunk(1024000)
   Response.Buffer = true
   Response.ContentType = "image/gif"
   Response.BinaryWrite Image
   Response.Flush
   Response.Clear
else
    Response.Write "The image not found in table."
end if
Result.Close
DataConn.Close
'destroy the objects when finished
Set Result = nothing
Set DataConn = nothing
Response.End
%>
```

Clear   Response Object Method

Purpose

Use this method to clear any data that has been buffered by the server. If the Response object's Buffer property (p. 250) is set to True, use this method.

Syntax

```
Response.Clear
```

Example

The following example retrieves the text of Scott Horne's graduation speech at Auburn University from the database table Speeches. The data is retrieved into the variable theSpeech. It is then sent to a client via the Response object's Write method (p. 250). The output is buffered. When the contents of theSpeech is output, the buffer is flushed and the data is cleared from the buffer via the Clear method.

```
<%
Dim theSpeech,sql,DataConn,MonthName,Result
MonthName = request.querystring("Month")
Set DataConn = Server.CreateObject("ADODB.Connection")
DataConn.Open Application("dbConnectionString")
```

```
set Result = server.createobject("ADODB.Recordset")
sql = "SELECT mySpeech FROM Speeches WHERE Speaker ='Scott
Horne'"

Result.Open sql, DataConn, 3
if not (Result.eof and Result.bof) then
    theSpeech = Result("mySpeech")
    Response.Buffer = true
    Response.ContentType = "plain/text"
    Response.Write theSpeech
    Response.Flush
    Response.Clear
else
    Response.Write "The image not found in table."
end if
Result.Close
DataConn.Close
'destroy the objects when finished
Set Result = nothing
Set DataConn = nothing
Response.End

%>
```

End Response Object Method

Purpose

Use this method to manage any data that is in the buffered server's output.
This method gets any data that is stored in the buffer up to the point where
this method is called. When this method is called, then that data is output to
the browser.

Syntax

```
Response.End
```

Example

The following example stops the processing of the code if the Session
object's Timeout property (p. 274) is exceeded:

```
<%
dim Dt
Response.buffer = true
Dt =  Date()
Second = Second(Dt)
```

```
Response.Write "Jon Sansom, Eat at the Grill"
Response.Write "Get a job, no a real job"
If  Second(Date()) > Second+5 then
'stop the processing of the ASP if process took longer than 5
seconds
Response.End
Else
    Response.Write "It took less than 5 seconds"
End if
Response.Flush
Response.Clean
%>
```

Flush   Response Object Method

Purpose

Use this method to clear out any data in the buffer and send it to the browser.
The Response object's Clear method is similar to the Flush method, except
that the Clear method does not send the data in the buffer to the browser.

Syntax

```
Response.Flush
```

Example

The following example writes the line "Mike Falcone is a friend of mine"
to the buffer, and then uses the Flush method to clear out the buffer and
send the text to the browser:

```
<%
Response.Buffer = true
Response.Write "Mike Falcone is a friend of mine."
Response.Flush
%>
```

Redirect   Response Object Method

Purpose

Use this method to change control of your application from one ASP to a different ASP.

Syntax

```
Response.Redirect( "name of your asp or HTML page that will
receive the control ")
```

Example

The following script uses the `Redirect` method to change control to "MyErrorPage.asp" if the `Connection` object is not created:

```
<%
'DataConn is the Data Connection
Dim DataConn
DataConn = Server.CreateObject("ADODB.Connection")
'check to see if the Connection object was created
If Not IsObject(DataConn) then
    Response.Redirect("MyErrorPage.asp")
End if
%>
```

Write   Response Object Method

Purpose

Use this method to output content to the browser. This method outputs a string, which can also be HTML code enclosed in quotes, such as "<HTML>".

Syntax

```
Response.Write string
```

Example

The following example sends output to the browser of an HTML page in quotes:

```
<%
Response.Write "<HTML>"
Response.Write "<BODY>"
Response.Write "Hickory Knob State Resort Park is the greatest
place"
Response.Write "</Body>"
Response.Write "</HTML>"
%>
```

Buffer   Response Object Property

Purpose

Use this property to indicate whether or not you want to buffer your page output. Buffering the page output means the server waits for all of the server scripts on the current page to be processed before sending a response to the client, or until the `Response` object's `Flush` (p. 249) or `End` (p. 248) methods are called. Most ASPs have the `Buffer` property set to False.

Syntax

```
Response.Buffer = flag
```

The Flag property specifies whether or not to buffer page output. Table 83 lists the values of the Flag property.

Table 83   *Values of the Flag Property*

Value	Required	Type	Purpose
FALSE	Yes	Boolean	A value of False means that the output sent to the browser or any client is not buffered. False is the default value for IIS 4.0 and earlier.
TRUE	Yes	Boolean	A value of True means that the output is not sent to the browser until one of the following three events occurs: (1) all the ASP script on your ASP page is processed (2) the Flush method executes (3) the End method executes. True is the default value for IIS 5.0 and later.

● NOTE

You must place the Buffer property near the top of the code. This property must be set before any information is sent to the browser.

Example

The following example shows you how to enable the Buffer property. If this property is set to True, the Web server will cache all the ASP code until a Flush property is issued by the Reponse object. The code is not sent to the browser until the Response.Flush is executed.

```
<%
Dim num
Response.Buffer = True
Response.Write "<HTML><Body>"
For num = 1 to 10
    Response.Write "<BR>Num is :"
    Response.Write num
```

```
Next
Response.Write "</Body></HTML>"
Response.Flush
%>
```

CacheControl   Response Object Property

Purpose

Use this property to enable a proxy server to cache the output from an ASP. If you are in an environment that contains a proxy server, this is a very useful property. The property can be set to either True or False. If True, the proxy server will cache the output of the ASP. If the CacheControl property is set to False, the proxy server passes the results of the ASP without caching the page.

Syntax

```
Response.CacheControl = Cache Control Item
```

Table 84 lists the values associated with the CacheControl property.

Table 84 *Values for the CacheControl Header*

Value	Required	Type	Description
CacheControl Item	Yes	String	Public will cache the output of a user's request. Private will pass the results through a proxy server without caching the users request.

Example

The following example sets the CacheControl property to allow the proxy server to cache a user's request. Whenever a user requests this ASP, the proxy server will cache the output.

```
<% Language="VBScript" %>
<%
'set the CacheControl value to Public to allow the proxy
'server to cache a user's request
Response.CacheControl = Public
Response.Write "My Name is Dr. Cecil Allison"
Response.Write "I was born and raised in Tippo, Mississippi."
Response.write "My cousin is the famous jazz musician Mose
```

```
    Allison"
    %>
```

Charset   Response Object Property

Purpose
Use this property to append the name of the character set to the content-type header in the Response object.

Syntax
```
Response.Charset(CharsetName)
```

Table 85 lists the argument associated with the CharSet property.

Table 85   *Argument for the Charset Property*

Value	Required	Type	Description
CharsetName	Yes	String	This is the name of the character set that you want the text ofyour ASP to be displayed in. This property will added to the content-type header of the Response object.

Example
The following example shows you how to set the Charset property to "us-ascii":

```
<% Response.Charset = "us-ascii" %>
```

The content-type header that is sent with the Response object to the browser will contain the following information about the character set:

```
content-type:text/html; charset=US-ASCII
```

ContentType   Response Object Property

Purpose
Use this property to set the type of content you will be sending to the browser. The browser will recognize the content type and act accordingly. An example of an action the browser might take is to execute a program on the user's desktop such as Microsoft Word or Adobe's Acrobat Reader for .PDF documents. If you are sending a .PDF document to the browser, you will set this property to the value of"application/pdf". However, most of the time you will be sending HTML or text; thus, set this property to "text/HTML".

ASP Core Reference

Syntax

```
Response.ContentType = MIME-Type
```

Example

The following example shows you how to set the ContentType property for the MIME type of "text/HTML":

```
<%
Response.ContentType = "text/HTML"
Response.Write "<HTML><BODY>My School is Warner Robins High
School </BODY></HTML>"
%>
```

Expires	**Response Object Property**

Purpose

Use this property to determine the length of time a cached page on a browser has before the page expires. When the user returns to the same page before it expires, the cached version is displayed. When your ASP file calls the Response object's Expires property, IIS creates an HTTP header showing the time on the server. If the value of this property is set to 0, the browser is forced to request a new page and cannot retrieve the page from the cache.

Syntax

```
Response.Expires = number
```

Table 86 lists the argument associated with the Expires property.

Table 86 *Argument for the Expires Property*

Value	Required	Type	Description
Number	Yes	Number	The number of minutes before the ASP that you specify expires in the browser cache.

Example

The following code sets the Expires property to five minutes:

```
<%Response.Expires = 5 %>
```

The next bit of code sets the page so that it is not cached, but expires immediately:

```
<%Response.Expires = 0 %>
```

ExpiresAbsolute — Response Object Property

Purpose

Use this property to indicate the date and time at which a cached page on a browser expires. If the user returns to the same page before that date and time, the cached version is displayed. The page expires at midnight of the current day if the time is not specified. If a date is not specified, the page expires at the given time on the day that the script is run. The earliest expiration date or time is used when this property is set more than once on a page.

Syntax

```
Response.ExpiresAbsolute #[date] [time]#
```

Table 87 lists the argument associated with the ExpiresAbsolute property.

Table 87 *Argument for the ExpiresAbsolute Property*

Value	Required	Type	Description
Date time	Yes	String	Specifies the time at which the page will expire. This value is converted to GMT before an Expires header is sent. The value sent in the Expires header conforms to the RFC-1123 date format; for example, #August 13,1977 10:00:00#

Example

The following code sets the ExpiresAbsolute property to October 19, 2000 at eleven o'clock in the morning:

```
<% Response.ExpiresAbsolute=#October 19,2000 11:00:00# %>
```

IsClientConnected — Response Object Property

Purpose

Use this property to indicate whether or not the client has disconnected from the server. With this property, you have greater control over circumstances in which the client may have disconnected from the server. If a long period of time has elapsed between when a client request was made and when the server responded, you may want to make sure that the client is still connected before processing the script. It is a read-only property.

ASP Core Reference

Syntax

```
Response.IsClientConnected ()
```

Example

The following code determines if you are connected to a browser. If you are connected, then the message "Client is Connected" will be displayed in the browser.

```
<%
if Response.IsClientConnected() then
    Response.Write "Client is Connected"
else
    Response.Write "Client is Not Connected"
end if
%>
```

Status   Response Object Property

Purpose

Use this property to change the status line Response object property returned by the server. The Status property specifies the value of the status line returned by the server. Status values are defined in the HTTP specification.

Syntax

```
Response.Status = StatusString
```

Table 88 lists the argument associated with the Status property.

Table 88 *Argument for the Status Property*

Value	Required	Type	Description
StatusString	Yes	String	A string that consists of a three-digit number indicating a status code, and a brief explanation of that code; for example, 200 OK, 400 Bad Request, 404 Not Found, or 406 Not Acceptable

Example

This code in this example will change the normal status line of "200 OK" to "200 Auburn is Great, Your page is OK" You must set this property before any Response.Write occurs in your code. Otherwise, a run-time error will be generated.

First run this code:

```
<%@ Language=VBScript %>
<HTML>
<HEAD>
</HEAD>
<BODY>
<%
    Response.Write "<BR>Status is "
    Response.Write Response.Status
    Response.Write "<BR>"
%>
</Body>
</HTML>
```

When you run the preceding code, the output will be "Status is 200 OK."

Now add into the code the line Response.Status = "200 Auburn is Great, Your page is OK":

```
<%@ Language=VBScript %>
<%    Response.Status = "200 Auburn is Great, Your page is OK"
%>
<HTML>
<HEAD>
</HEAD>
<BODY>
<%
    Response.Write "<BR>Status is "
    Response.Write Response.Status
    Response.Write "<BR>"
%>
</Body>
</HTML>
```

The output for this code will be "Status is 200 Auburn is Great, Your page is OK".

PICS   Response Object Property

Purpose

Use the Platform for Internet Content Selection (PICS) property to add a value to the pics-label response header. The PICS property enables you to add a rating that is defined by the Recreational Software Advisory Council on the Internet (RSACi). The goal of this organization is to define ratings for use with Web sites. This property enables you to supply a rating for the ASP.

Your browser's content filter will pick up the value of the PICS header and filter the content accordingly.

The PICS property inserts any string in the header, whether or not it represents a valid PICS label. When a page contains multiple tags containing Response.PICS, each instance of the tag will replace the PICS label set by the foregoing one. As a result, the PICS label will be set to the value specified by the last instance of Response.PICS in the page.

Syntax

```
Response.PICS(PICSLabel)
```

Table 89 lists the argument associated with the PICS property.

Table 89   *Argument for the PICS Property*

Value	Required	Type	Description
PICSLabel	Yes	String	This is a properly formatted PicsLabel string. This becomes part of the response header. When the client's browser sees this portion of the head, the browser checks this header against the browser's rating system.
			On IE 4.0 and later browsers, the Content Rating settings are located in the Contents section of the Tools menu on your browser.

● NOTE

In order to get a rating from RSACi, you must have the PICS property set for every page in your ASP. Go to http://www.icra.org/ to find out more information. To see the format to create a PICSLabel, go to http://www.w3.org/TR/REC-PICS-labels.

Example

The following example is a PICS label that identifies a safe rating for children (meaning there is no nudity in the site). You specify the subject in the label as 0.

```
<%
Dim lab
label = "(PICS-1.1 ""http://www.gcf.org/v2.5"""
```

```
        by ""Tim Eden""
        labels on ""1994.11.05T08:15-0500""
        until "1995.12.31T23:59-0000"
        for ""http://www.anypage.com/My.asp""
        by ""Tim Eden""
        ratings (subject 0 density 1 color/hue 1))"
Response.PICS (label)


%>
```

Server Object

This section lists the methods and properties associated with the Server object.

Purpose

Use the Server object to gain access to methods and properties on the server. Most of these methods and properties serve as utility functions.

Syntax

```
Server.property|method
```

CreateObject	Server Object Method

Purpose

Use this method to create an instance of a server component. Every server component has a prodID. The prodID is a string such as the one used for the Connection object — "ADODB.Connection".

Syntax

```
Server.CreateObject( prodID)
```

Table 90 lists the argument associated with the CreateObject method.

Table 90   *Argument for the CreateObject Method*

Value	Required	Type	Description
ProdID	Yes	String	The name of the object to be created. Specifies the type of object to create. The format for prodID is [Vendor.] Component[.Version].

Examples

The following example uses the CreateObject method to create an instance of the ActiveX Data object (ADO). The variable DataConn becomes the Connection object, and this object can be used to deliver all the methods and properties to your ASP applications. Normally, this is the script that you will use in an ASP page.

```
<%
Dim DataConn
Set DataConn = Server.CreateObject("ADODB.Connection")
%>
```

You can also use the CreateObject method to create objects in the global.asa file. The following code is an example of a global.asa file in which the CreateObject method is used to create an instance of the FileSystemObject in the Session object's Session_OnEnd (p. 269) event.

```
<SCRIPT LANGUAGE=VBScript RUNAT=Server>

Sub Session_OnStart
    Session("userid") = ""
    Session("password) = ""
End Sub

Sub Session_OnEnd
    Set Tfile =
Server.CreateObject("Scripting.FileSystemObject")
    Tfile.CreateTextFile("c:\NameOfFile.txt",true)
    Tfile.WriteLine("We are in the Session_OnEnd event")
    Tfile.WriteLine("The user is  "&Session("userid"))
    Tfile.Close
    'destroy the object to free resource on your server
    Set Tfile = nothing
End Sub

</Script>
```

The following example shows you how to create an object at the application level using the CreateObject method. Creating an object at the application level means the object will reside in memory for as long as the application is running.

```
<SCRIPT LANGUAGE=VBScript RUNAT=Server>

Sub Application_OnStart
    Set Application("Tfile") =
Server.CreateObject("Scripting.FileSystemObject")
```

```
       Tfile.CreateTextFile("c:\NameOfFile.txt",true)

   End Sub

   </Script>
```

HTMLEncode
Server Object Method

Purpose

Use this method to apply HTML encoding to a specific string.

Syntax

```
Server.HTMLEncode( Astring )
```

Table 91 lists the argument associated with the HTMLEncode method.

Table 91   *Argument for the HTMLEncode Method*

Value	Required	Type	Description
Astring	Yes	String	Specifies the string to encode

Example

The following script encodes a string using the HTMLEncode method:

```
<%= Server.HTMLEncode("The BreakLine Code: <BR>") %>
```

The string in the header sent to the browser for the preceding code is given below. Notice that the "<BR>" portion of the string is output as <BR;&gt. The &gt is the HTML equivalent to the greater than (>) character.

```
The BreakLine Code: &lt;P&gt;
```

Once the browser receives the encoded string, it is output. The following string is output by the browser:

```
The BreakLine Code: <P>
```

A better use for this method is to encode strings containing symbols that confuse the Web server, such as the # character.

MapPath
Server Object Method

Purpose

Use this method to map the specified relative or virtual path to the corresponding physical directory on the server. You can use the MapPath method to map a path to a physical directory structure, and subsequently pass on that path to a component that creates the specified directory or file on the server. The MapPath method indicates the relative or virtual path to map to a physical directory.

Syntax

```
Server.MapPath( Path )
```

Table 92 lists the argument associated with the MapPath method.

Table 92 *Argument for the MapPath Method*

Value	Required	Type	Description
Path	Yes	String	Use this to return a path. If Path starts with either a forward slash (/) or a backward slash (\), the MapPath method returns a path as if Path were a full virtual path. You can use the relative path syntax for the Path parameter if the AspEnable ParentPaths property is set to True. You can accomplish this with either the Internet Information Services snap-in or a script.

Examples

The following example uses the MapPath method to obtain the virtual directory in which your ASP application is located.

```
<%
Response.Write "The virtual directory is "
Response.Write Server.MapPath("\")
%>
```

The value returned by the Server object's MapPath method will beC:\Inetpub\ wwwroot. You can also use the MapPath method in conjunction with the Request object's ServerVariables collection (p. 234) to determine the complete path of the page being displayed.

```
<%
Response.Write
server.mappath(Request.ServerVariables("PATH_INFO"))<BR>
%>
```

The preceding script will return the value C:\Inetpub\wwwroot\Test3.asp.

URLEncode	Server Object Method

Purpose

Use this method to apply URL encoding rules, including escape characters, to a specific string. Remember that only ASCII-based characters can be sent over HTTP. Thus, if an URL contains blanks or there is any punctuation in the URL, strange results can occur.

Syntax

```
Server.URLEncode( this string )
```

Table 93 lists the argument associated with the URLEncode method.

Table 93 *Argument for the URLEncode Method*

Value	Required	Type	Description
This String	Yes	String	Specifies the string to encode

Example

The following script sends the string "I love Auburn's #1 Electrical Engineering Program". via a Get method in an HREF link. As you can see, the string contains the apostrophe (') character and the pound (#) character. A Web server has problems decoding these characters properly. But by using the URLEncode method, the Web server can recognize these characters without any problem.

```
<HTML>
<Body>
<%dim str
str = "I love Auburn's #1 Electrical Engineering Program"
%>
<a href = "mypage.asp?MyString=<%=Server.URLEncode(str) %>Send to
the Server</a>
</Body>
</HTML>
```

Transfer | Server Object Method

Purpose

Use this method to send all of the data collected for processing by one .ASP file to a second .ASP file. This method is more efficient than the Response object's Redirect method (p. 249).

When you call theTransfer method, the state information for all the built-in objects will be included in the transfer. Therefore, any variables or objects that have been assigned a value in session or application scope will be preserved. In addition, all of the current contents for the request collections will be available to the .ASP file in the transfer.

If you specify the path in the input parameter for an .ASP file in another application, the .ASP file will execute as if it were in the application that contains the Server.Transfer method. Therefore, all variables and objects that have been given application scope will be available to the called .ASP file.

Syntax

```
Server.Transfer (path)
```

Table 94 lists the argument associated with the Transfer method.

Table 94 *Argument for the Transfer Method*

Value	Required	Type	Description
Path	Yes	String	This value is the path of the .ASP file where control is transferred.

Example

The following example shows you how to transfer control to another page if the year portion of the date is equal to 2000. If the year portion is not equal to 2000, control is transferred to "TheOtherYears.asp".

```
<HTML>
<BODY>
<%
dim a
a = Date()
if Year(a) = 2000 then
    Server.Transfer("TheYear2000.asp")
Else
    Server.Transfer("TheOtherYears.asp")
End if
```

```
%>
</BODY>
</HTML>
```

GetLastError   Server Object Method

Purpose

Use this method to return an ASPError object relating any error condition
that occurs. This method can be used only before the .ASP file has sent the
client content. When an error occurs during the running of an .ASP file
within the application, the server will automatically transfer to this ASP
page via the Server object's Transfer method (p. 264).

Syntax

```
Server.GetLastError ()
```

●—CROSS-REFERENCE

Coverage of the ASPError object begins on page 42.

Example

The following code changes the 500-100.asp to process the error received
from the run-time error '800a01a8':

```
<%
Dim LastErrObj
Dim Desc
Dim Cater
Dim File
Dim Number
'Get the Last Error sent to 500-100.asp

LastErrObj = Server.GetLastError

%>
<HTML>
<BODY>
<Form Action="anypage.asp" Method="Post">

<%
If LastErrObj.ASPCode = '800a01a8'
    Response.Write "You have typed in the wrong syntax"
    Response.Write "<BR>The error is "&LastErrObj.Description
    Response.Write "<BR>The error is on line number "
```

```
        Response.Write LastErrObj.Line
    End if
    %>
    <input type="submit" value="Go To Another Page">
    </Form>
    </Body>
    </HTML>
```

Execute   Server Object Method

Use this method to call and process an ASP as if it were part of the calling ASP script. This method is the new way of doing an include file. Instead of having an include file that is separate from the ASP, the Execute method now makes it a part of the file.

The Execute method is related to a procedure call in many programming languages. This method provides a way to divide a complex application into modules. If you use the Server.Execute method, you can develop a library of .ASP files that you can call as needed. This usage is an alternative to server-side includes.

Syntax

```
    Server.Execute( Path )
```

Table 95 lists the argument associated with the Execute method.

Table 95   *Argument for the Execute Method*

Value	Required	Type	Description
Path	Yes	String	A string specifying the location of the .ASP file you want to execute. This parameter must be specified for an .ASP file within the same application space.

● CROSS-REFERENCE

Coverage of the ASPError object starts on page 42.

Examples

The following code shows you an old way of adding an include file into an ASP. For the purposes of this example, we'll call the include file "/includes/myfile.asp".

This is what is inside of "/includes/myfile.asp":

```
<%
Response.Write Date()
%>

<HTML>
<Body>
<!-#include virtual="/includes/myfile.asp" -->
</Body>
</HTML>
```

Now, using the Server object's.Execute method instead of the include file, the code will look like this:

```
<HTML>
<BODY>
<% Server.Execute("/includes/myfile.asp")%>
</BODY>
</HTML>
```

ScriptTimeout   Server Object Property

Purpose

Use this property to indicate the maximum amount of time allowed for a script to run before it terminates. A default ScriptTimeout property can be set for a Web service or Web server by using the ScriptTimeout property in the metabase. The ScriptTimeout property cannot be set to a value less than that specified in the metabase.

Syntax

```
Server.ScriptTimeout = NumSeconds
```

Table 96 lists the argument associated with the QueryString collection.

Table 96 *Argument for the Value ScriptTimeout Property*

Value	Required	Type	Description
NumSeconds	Yes	Number	This indicates the maximum number of seconds that a script can run before the server terminates it. The default value is 90 seconds.

Example

The following example sets the ScriptTimeout property to 50 seconds. If this value is exceeded, then the Web server will stop processing the pages.

```
<% Server.ScriptTimeout = 50 %>
```

Session Object

Purpose

Use the Session object when you want to save information to be used in a particular user session. When the user jumps between pages in the application, variables deposited in the Session object are not erased. These variables are kept in memory for the entire session.

When a user who does not already have a session requests a Web page from the application, the Web server automatically creates a Session object. The server will destroy the Session object when the session is abandoned or expires. One typical use for the Session object is storing user preferences. Session state is not maintained unless the browser supports cookies.

Syntax

```
Session.collection|property|method
```

Session_OnStart	Session Object Event

Purpose

This event is triggered when the server starts a new session. The server will handle this script before executing the page requested. You should set session-wide variables at the Session_OnStart event, so that they are set before any pages are accessed. All the built-in objects (Application, ObjectContext, Request, Response, Server, and Session) are available and can be referenced in the Session_OnStart event script. Even though the Session object persists if the Session_OnStart event includes a call to the Redirect or End methods, the server will stop processing the script in both the Global.asa file and in the file that triggered the Session_OnStart event.

You can call the Redirect method in the Session_OnStart event to ensure that users always start a session at a specific Web page. When the user enters the application, the server creates a session for that user and processes the Session_OnStart event script.

Syntax

```
<SCRIPT LANGUAGE=ScriptLanguage RUNAT=Server>
Sub Session_OnStart
. . .
```

```
End Sub
</SCRIPT>
```

Example

The following example sets two session variables inside the `Session_OnStart` event in the global.asa file. Thus, whenever a user requests this application, these two variables will be set for the duration of the session.

```
<SCRIPT RUNAT=Server LANGUAGE=VBScript>
Sub Session_OnStart
    Session("ImagePath") = "/pages/images/"
    Session("College") = "Delta State"

End Sub
</SCRIPT>
```

Session_OnEnd   Session Object Event

Purpose

This event is started when a session is abandoned or expires. Only the `Application`, `Server`, and `Session` objects are available from the server built-in objects. You cannot call the `Server` object's `MapPath` method (p. 262) in the `Session_OnEnd` script.

Syntax

```
<SCRIPT LANGUAGE=ScriptLanguage RUNAT=Server>
Sub Session_OnEnd

. . .
End Sub
</SCRIPT>
```

Example

This example writes to a file when the `Session_OnEnd` event is triggered by either the `Session.Abandon` method (p. 270) or the `Session.Timeout` property (p. 274):

```
<SCRIPT RUNAT=Server LANGUAGE=VBScript>
Sub Session_OnEnd

  'the code you want if the web server goes down. Maybe
  'writing to a log file.
Set Tfile = Server.CreateObject("Scripting.FileSystemObject")
Tfile.CreateTextFile("c:\NameOfLogFile.txt",true)
Tfile.WriteLine("We are in the Application_OnEnd event")
```

```
Tfile.WriteLine("Time is "&time())
Tfile.Close

End Sub
</SCRIPT>
```

Abandon   Session Object Method

Purpose

Use this method to remove all the objects retained in a Session object and release their resources. If you do not explicitly call the Abandon method, the server removes these objects when the session ends.

Syntax

```
Session.Abandon
```

Example

The following example abandons a session if the ASP fails to create the Connection object's DataConn variable:

```
<%
Dim DataConn
DataConn = Server.CreateObject("ADODB.Connection")
If Not IsObject(DataConn) then
    Session.Abandon
End if
%>
```

Contents.Remove   Session Object Method

Purpose

Use this method to delete a specific item from the Session object's Contents collection.

Syntax

```
Session.Contents.Remove( Item|Index )
```

Table 97 lists the arguments associated with the Contents.Remove method.

Table 97 *Arguments for the Remove Method*

Value	Required	Type	Description
Item	No	String	The name of the item to delete from the Session object's Contents collection
Index	No	Number	The index number of the item to delete from the Session object's Contents collection

Example

The following example adds and removes a variable called UrName to the Session.Contents collection:

```
<%
   Session("UrName") = " "
   Session.Contents.Remove("UrName")
%>
```

Contents.RemoveAll   Session Object Method

Purpose

Use this method to remove all the session variables that are in the Session object's Contents collection.

Syntax

```
Session.Contents.RemoveAll ()
```

Example

This example shows you the one line of code you need to remove all the elements from the Session object's Contents collection.

```
<%Session.Contents.RemoveAll()%>
```

CodePage   Session Object Property

Purpose

Use this property to establish the language in which you want an ASP to output content. This property is used to change the character map of the ASP to a different language. You set this value at the top of the page.

Syntax

```
Session.CodePage =Codepage value
```

Table 98 lists the argument associated with the CodePage property.

Table 98   *Argument for the CodePage Property*

Value	Required	Type	Description
Codepage value	Yes	Number	An unsigned integer representing a valid language that the ASP supports; for example, 951 Japanese, 1253 Greek, or 1255 Hebrew

●─CROSS-REFERENCE────────────────

The list of values for CodePage can be found at the URL noted in the Preface.

Example

The following example establishes an ASP to accept Japanese. Remember to place the code page at the top of an ASP.

```
<% Session.CodePage(950) %>
```

LCID   Session Object Property

Purpose

Use this property to set output for time, date, and currency to a different location. The formatting of time, date, and currency varies from country to country. This property enables you to specify the format of time, dates, and currency for whatever country you choose. Every country will have an LCID number of its own.

Syntax

```
Session.LCID(LCID Number)
```

Table 99 lists the argument associated with the LCID property.

Table 99   *Argument for the LCID Property*

Value	Required	Type	Description
LCID Number	Yes	Number	The number that represents the local identifier property; for example, 1041 Japanese or 1039 Icelandic

Example

The following example sets the locale to France using the VBScript Format Currency method to display the value 125 as currency with the pound (£) symbol.

```
<%
Session.LCID = 2057
Dim curntNum
curntNum = FormatCurrency(125)
Response.Write (curntNum)
%>
```

●—CROSS-REFERENCE

The FormatCurrrency method is covered in the VBScript Syntax Reference section (p. 421).

SessionID	Session Object Property

Purpose

Use this property to return the session identifier. The session identifier is a unique identifier that is generated by the server when the session is created. The session ID is returned as a Long data type.

Syntax

```
Session.SessionID
```

Example

The following example will display the session ID in a browser:

```
<%
Session("AmyEdenCat") = "The Cat"
Response.Write "SessionID is "
Response.Write Session.SessionID
%>
```

This is what might appear in your browser:

```
SessionID is 650565320
```

Timeout
Session Object Property

Purpose

Use this property to specify the timeout period allotted to the Session object for an application. If a page is not refreshed or requested within the timeout period, the session ends.

Syntax

```
Session.Timeout [  NumMinutes]
```

Table 100 lists the argument associated with the Timeout property.

Table 100   *Argument for the Timeout Property*

Value	Required	Type	Description
NumMinutes	Yes	Number	The number of minutes you want to set the Timeout property to. The default is 10 minutes.

Contents
Session Object Collections

Purpose

Use this collection to determine the value of a specific session item, or to loop through the collection and retrieve a list of all session items. The Session object's Contents collection contains all of the items that have been established for a session without using the <OBJECT> tag.

Syntax

```
Session.Contents( KeyValue )
```

Table 101 lists the argument associated with the Contents collection.

Table 101   *Argument for the Contents Collection*

Value	Required	Type	Description
KeyValue	Yes	String	The name of the item in the session's Contents collection.

Example

This following example creates a Session object — in this case, the MyInfo object. Then the Contents collection is used to retrieve the name of this object.

In the global.asa file the following objects are created:

```
</OBJECT>
<SCRIPT LANGUAGE=VBScript RUNAT=Server>
Sub Session_OnStart
    Session("UserId") = "Mr.AuburnTigerTimEden"
    Session("Wife") = "AmyEden"
End Sub

</Script>
```

In a separate ASP in the application, let's output the names of the items in the Session object's Contents collection:

```
<%
For each item in Session.Contents
    Response.Write "Item is "
    Response.Write item
Next
%>
```

Following is the browser's output after executing the preceding code:

```
Item is UserId
Item is Wife
```

StaticObjects	Session Object Collections

Purpose

Use this collection to find the name to all the Session objects created using the <OBJECT> tag.

Syntax

```
Session.StaticObjects( NameOfObject )
```

Table 102 lists the argument associated with the StaticObjects collection.

Table 102 *Argument for the StaticObjects Collection*

Value	Required	Type	Description
NameOfObject	Yes	String	The name that you supplied to the session object when you created it

Example

The following example first creates a Session object — in this case, the MyInfo object. Then the StaticObjects collection is used to retrieve the name of those objects.

In the global.asa file, the following objects are created:

```
<OBJECT RUNAT=Server SCOPE=Session ID=TheConn
PROGID="ADODB.Connection">

<SCRIPT LANGUAGE=VBScript RUNAT=Server>
Sub Session_OnStart
    Session("UserId") = "Mr.AuburnTigerTimEden"
    Session("Wife") = "AmyEden"
End Sub
</Script>
```

In a separate ASP in the application, let's output the names of the items in the Session object's Contents collection.

```
<%
For each Key in Session.StaticObjects
    Response.Write "Key is "
    Response.Write Key
Next
%>
```

Following is the browser's output after executing the preceding code:

```
Key is TheConn
```

Stream Object

Purpose

Use the Stream object to manipulate a stream of data. The data will either be in binary or text format.

Syntax

```
Set StreamObject = Server.CreateObject("ADODB.Stream")
```

Cancel	**Stream Object Method**

Purpose

Use this method to end the execution of an asynchronous call. By itself, the Stream object does not have a way to open in an asynchronous manner. But in conjunction with the Record object (p. 172), the Stream object can be opened asynchronously.

●─NOTE

Microsoft defines an asynchronous operation as one that returns control to the calling program without waiting for the operation to complete. Before the operation is complete, code execution continues.

Syntax

```
StreamObject.Cancel
```

Example

The following example opens both a Record object and a Stream object. The Record object will open the file www.friends.com/DavidWebb.txt in an asynchronous method call. The code will wait nine seconds to determine if the state of the Record object is open, and then wait another seven seconds to determine if the Stream object is open. If both objects are open, the file will be read. If the Stream object is not opened in seven seconds, the asynchronous call will be canceled using the Cancel method.

```
<%
Dim RecordObject,StreamObject, Tm

Set StreamObject = Server.CreateObject("ADODB.Stream")
StreamObject.Open "
","URL=http://www.myfriends.com/DavidWebb.txt", , , adOpenAsync
Tm = Second(Time())
RecordObject.Open

Do while (Second(Time()) < Tm + 7)
    'waits 7 seconds to test whether Stream object opened
Loop

If Not (RecordObject.State = adStateOpen) then
    RecordObject.Cancel
```

ASP Core Reference

```
Else
   'set the new seconds for variable Tm
   Tm = Second(Time())
   Do while (Second(Time()) < Tm + 7)
    'wait 7 seconds to test the State of Stream object
   Loop

   If Not (StreamObject.State = adStateOpen) then
      StreamObject.Cancel
   Else
      'do what ever you need to code here
   End if
End
Set StreamObject = nothing
%>
```

Close	Stream Object Method

Purpose

Use this method to undo the association between the Stream object and its file.

Syntax

```
StreamObject.Close
```

Example

The following example opens a Stream object to the file www.timeden.com/mycollegegrades.txt. Once the file is opened, the Stream object's ReadText method is used to read the file. The Response object will write the contents of the file to the browser. After all of these actions are finished, the Stream object is closed.

```
<%
Dim MyStrObj
Set MyStrObj = Server.CreateObject("ADODB.Stream")
MyStrObj.Open "URL=http://www.timeden.com/mycollegegrades.txt"
Response.Write MyStrObj.ReadText
'close the Stream object
MyStrObj.Close
'Destroy the object
Set MyStr = nothing
%>
```

CopyTo

Stream Object Method

Purpose

Use this method to copy the contents of one Stream object to a second Stream object.

Syntax

```
Stream.CopyTo SecOpenStreamObject, NumChars
```

Table 103 lists the arguments associated with the CopyTo method.

Table 103 *Arguments for the CopyToMethod*

Value	Required	Type	Description
SecOpenStreamObject	No	Stream object	This is a second Stream object into which you plan to copy the contents of your first Stream object.
NumChars	No	Number	This is the number of bytes or characters that you plan to copy into the second Stream object. The default value is −1.

Example

The following example opens two Stream objects. One Stream object comes from a record in the database table named GreatSpeeches. The contents of this Stream object will be copied into a second Stream object called CopyofSpeeches.txt. We will use the Connection object to open a connection to the table, and then an SQL statement will retrieve the single record from the table GreatSpeeches. The record contains the Gettysburg Address.

```
<%
Dim MyStrObj,MyStrObj2,Str

Set MyStrObj = Server.CreateObject("ADODB.Stream")
Set MyStrObj2 = Server.CreateObject("ADODB.Stream")
'open with option of read
MyStrObj.Open "URL=http://www.GreatSpeeches.com/Gettysburgtxt", 1

'open with option of Read/Write
```

```
MyStrObj2.Open "URL=http://www.myfriends.com/CopyofSpeechestxt",
3

'Copy the contents to CopyofSpeeches.txt
MyStrObj.CopyTo MyStrObj2

'when data is finished writing close object
MyStrObj.Close
MyStrObj2.Close
'Destroy all objects
Set MyStrObj2= nothing
Set MyStrObj = nothing

%>
```

LoadFromFile	Stream Object Method

Purpose

Use this method to load the data from an existing file into a Stream object.

Syntax

```
Stream.LoadFromFile FileName
```

Table 104 lists the argument associated with the LoadFromFile method.

Table 104 *Argument for the LoadFromFile Method*

Value	Required	Type	Description
FileName	Yes	String	The name of the file you want to load into the Stream object

Example

The following example associates the file TrishaOgletree.txt with a Stream object. The file is then loaded into the Stream object via the LoadFromFile method.

```
<%
Dim MyStrObj
```

```
Set MyStrObj = Server.CreateObject("ADODB.Stream")
MyStrObj.LoadFromFile "c:\ TrishaOgletree.txt"
%>
```

Open   Stream Object Method

Purpose

Use this method to associate the contents of a file or binary data with a Stream object.

Syntax

```
StreamObject.Open Source , Mode, OpenStreamOptions, UserName ,
Password
```

Table 105 lists the arguments associated with the Open method.

Table 105   *Arguments for the Open Method*

Value	Required	Type	Description
Source	No	String	The name of the file or directory that will be the source for the Stream object. If you are using a Record object and leave this blank, the source becomes the source from the Record object.
			The source can be an absolute URL, a relative URL, or a RecordSet object that has already been opened.

Continued

Table 105   *Continued*

Value	Required	Type	Description
Mode	No	ConnectionMode enumeration constant	Values determined during the ConnectMode enumeration constants. The four most useful values are given below. Also note the Cross-Reference following this table.
			adModeUnknown (the default) – 0
			adModeRead – 1
			adModeWrite – 2
			adModeReadWrite - 3
OpenStreamOptions	No	StreamOpen Options enumerated constant	This value deter mines the option for opening a stream to receive the data. This value is a StreamOpen Options enumer-ated constant.
			The default value is adOpenStreamUnsp ecified — 1.
UserName	No	String	The user name that a Web site needs if a user name is required in order to authenticate
Password	No	String	The password that a Web site needs if a password is required in order to authenticate

●─CROSS-REFERENCE─────────────────

The `ConnectMode` and `StreamOpenOptions` enumerated constants are available on-line.

Examples

The following example associates the file "KarlaBeaver.txt" with a `Stream` object. This file is located in the URL www.myfriends.com/KarlaBeaver.txt. The file will be opened for reading.

```
<%
Dim MyStrObj
Set MyStrObj = Server.CreateObject("ADODB.Stream")
MyStrObj.Open "URL=http://www.myfriends.com/KarlaBeaver.txt", 1
%>
```

The following example ties the file www.highschoolpeople.com/JackSowers. txt to a `Stream` object. However, www.highschoolpeople.com needs a user name and password. The user name is "Football" and the password is "Auburn".

```
<%
Dim MyStrObj
Set MyStrObj = Server.CreateObject("ADODB.Stream")
'open the a stream to the file
MyStrObj.Open
"URL=http://www.highschoolpeople.com/JackSowers.txt", 1 ,
,"Football","Auburn"
%>
```

Read	Stream Object Method

Purpose

Use this method to read a binary file that is associated with a `Stream` object once the `Stream` object processes its `Open` method (p. 281).

Syntax

```
StreamObject.Read NumberOfBytes
```

Table 106 lists the argument associated with the `Read` method.

Table 106 *Argument for the Read Method*

Value	Required	Type	Description
NumberOfBytes	No	Number	A value that specifies how many bytes to read from the file; or the Stream ReadEnum value adReadAll, which is the default

Example

The following example reads in the file c:\GettysburgAddress.txt. Once the Stream object is created and opened, we need to determine the size of the Stream object in order to know the number of bytes to read. When the number of bytes is found, we use the Read method to read the bytes into the variable StorageBytes.

```
<%
Dim MyStrObj,NumOfBytes,ByteArray,J
Set MyStrObj = Server.CreateObject("ADODB.Stream")
'open the a stream to the file
MyStrObj.Open "URL=c:\\GettysburgAddress.txt", 1
'get the numOfBytes
NumOfBytes = MyStrObj.Size
'read in the file into byte array
Set StorageBytes = MyStrObj.Read(NumOfBytes)
'Now we are going to write out the first 15 bytes of
'the ByteArray
For J = 0 to 15
    Response.Write ByteArray[J]
Next
%>
```

ReadText

Stream Object Method

Purpose

Use this method to read a text file that is associated with a Stream object once the Stream object processes its Open method (p. 281).

Syntax

```
StreamObject.ReadText
```

Example

The following example associates the file KarlaBeaver.txt with a Stream object. This file is located in the URL www.myfriends.com/KarlaBeaver.txt. The file is a text file and will be opened for reading only.

```
<%
Dim MyStrObj
Set MyStrObj = Server.CreateObject("ADODB.Stream")
MyStrObj.Open "URL=http://www.myfriends.com/KarlaBeaver.txt", 1
Response.Write MyStrObj.ReadText
%>
```

SaveToFile	Stream Object Method

Purpose

Use this method to save the Stream object's binary contents as a file.

Syntax

```
StreamObject.SaveToFile FileName, SaveOptions
```

Table 107 lists the arguments associated with the SaveToFile method.

Table 107 *Arguments for the SaveToFile Method*

Value	Required	Type	Description
FileName	Yes	String	The name of the file you want to load into the Stream object
SaveOptions	No	SaveOption Enum	This is an SaveOption enumerated constant.

●─CROSS-REFERENCE

The SaveOption enumerated constants are available at the URL noted in the Preface.

Example

The following example associates the file JoeWilliams.txt with a Stream object. The file is then loaded into the Stream object via the LoadFromFile method. Then the file is saved to AudreyWilliams.txt using the SaveToFile method.

```
<%
Dim MyStrObj
Set MyStrObj = Server.CreateObject("ADODB.Stream")
MyStrObj.LoadFromFile "c:\JoeWilliams.txt"
'Then the file is saved to AudreyWilliams
MyStrObj.SaveToFile "c:\AudreyWilliams.txt"
%>
```

SetEOS   Stream Object Method

Purpose

Use this method to set the current position to the end of the Stream object's contents.

Syntax

```
StreamObject.SetEOS
```

Example

The following example shows you how to use the SetEOS method. This example associates the file BobBarker.txt with a Stream object. This file is located in the URL www.myfriends.com/BobBarker.txt. The file will be opened for reading/writing to a text file. When the file is opened we will use the Position property to set the Stream object's current position to 0. Then we will use the SetEOS method to move the current position to the end of the stream. By setting the current position to 0, and then using the SetEOS method, you get rid of the contents of the Stream object and consequently clear out the file. After you run this code, the file BobBarker.txt is empties. The Stream object's EOS property is used to test that the end of the stream is reached.

```
<%
Dim MyStrObj
Set MyStrObj = Server.CreateObject("ADODB.Stream")
MyStrObj.Open "URL=http://www.myfriends.com/BobBarker.txt",1
'set position to 0
'empty out the contents of the file
MyStrObj.Position = 0
'send current position to end of stream
MyStrObj.SetEOS
If EOS then
    Response.Write "We are at the end of stream"
Else
    Response.Write "We are not at the end of stream"
End if
%>
```

SkipLine

Purpose

Use this method to skip a complete line from being read from a text stream. Text preceding and including the next line separator will be not be read.

Syntax

```
SteamObject.SkipLine
```

Example

The following code associates the file c:\PhilMetzer.txt with a Stream object. Once the Stream object is opened, the Stream object's ReadText method (p. 284) is used to read the contents of the file one byte at a time. The binary character that represents the line separator is found and placed in the variable TheLineSep. When the file is being read, each character is tested against the line separator character. If there is a match, the next line of text is completely skipped. Therefore, you are only going to get every other line of text from c:\PhilMetzger.txt.

```
<%
Dim MyStrObj,str,Thesize,TheLineSep,Counter,temp
Set MyStrObj = Server.CreateObject("ADODB.Stream")
MyStrObj.Open "URL=c:\PhilMetzer.txt"
Counter = 0
Thesize = MyStrobj.size
TheLineSep = MyStrobj.LineSeparator
MyStrobj.Position = 0
Do while not EOF
    Str = MyStrObj
       'read one character at a time
       temp = MyStrobj.ReadText(1)
    If temp = TheLineSep then
      MyStrObj.SkipLine
      End if

    Str = Str & temp
       'increase the current position by 1
       MyStrObj.Position = Counter + 1
Loop

'get rid of all the data in the buffer
MyStrobj.Flush
'when untie the association between the file and the 'Stream
object
MyStrObj.Close
```

```
'after closing file then destroy the object
Set MyStrObj = nothing
%>
```

Write

Purpose

Use this method to write binary data to a Stream object. You write a specified amount of bytes to the Stream object, with no intervening spaces between each byte.

Syntax

```
Stream.Write BinaryData
```

Example

The following example shows you how to obtain a photo stored in a database and place the binary data of that photo into a file using the Stream object's Write method. The Connection object will open a connection to a database, and then a SQL statement will be issued that retrieves the photo into bytes. The bytes are then written to a file called AmyEdenPhoto.gif using the Write method.

```
<%
Dim MyStrObj,J,Str
Dim DataConn,Rset,sqlstm,RSBinary
set DataConn = Server.CreateObject("ADODB.Connection")
DataConn.Open Application("db_ConnectionString")

sqlstm = "Select Photo From TeamPhotos"

Set Rset = DataConn.Execute(sqlstm)
'Make Chucks large enough to hold the data
'100000 is an educated guess.
'The object RSBinary is an array of binary data
Set RSBinary = Rset("Photo").GetChucks(100000)

Set MyStrObj = Server.CreateObject("ADODB.Stream")
MyStrObj.Open "URL=http://www.myfiles.com/AmyEdenPhoto.gif", 2

MyStrObj.Write RSBinary

'when data is finished writing close object
MyStrObj.Close
DataConn.Close
'Destroy all objects
```

```
Set DataConn = nothing
Set MyStrObj = nothing
Set RSBinary = nothing
Set Rset = nothing
%>
```

WriteText   Stream Object Method

Purpose

Use this method to write text data to a file that is associated with a Stream object.

Syntax

```
StreamObject.WriteText StringText, Options
```

Table 108 lists the arguments associated with the WriteText method.

Table 108 *Arguments for the WriteText Method*

Value	Required	Type	Description
StringText	No	String	The string that contains the text you want written into the file
Options	No	StreamWrite enumerated constant	This is a StreamWrite enumerated constant that determines if a line separator character must be written at the end of the specified text.
			There are only two options for this argument:
			adWriteChar – 0 (the default)
			adWriteLine – 1

ASP Core Reference

●—CROSS-REFERENCE

The StreamWrite enumerated constants are available at the URL noted in the Preface.

Example

The following example shows you how to open the file www.anywebsite.
com/Myfiles.txt, and then write the text "My name is Amy Eden" to the file.
The file is opened with the Mode property set to 2, which indicates that the
file is to be written to.

```
<%
Dim MyStrObj,str
Set MyStrObj = Server.CreateObject("ADODB.Stream")
MyStrObj.Open "URL=http://www.anywebsite.com/ Myfiles.txt", 2
Str = "My name is Amy Eden"
MyStrobj.WriteText Str,0
'when untie the association between the file and the 'Stream
object
MyStrObj.Close
'after closing file then destroy the object
Set MyStrObj = nothing
%>
```

Flush	Stream Object Method

Purpose

Use this method to get rid of any data that is still in the Stream object's
buffer. It's a good idea to use the Flush method after calling any of the
Stream object's methods (such as the WriteText method) that write data.

Syntax

```
StreamObject.Flush
```

Example

The following code associates the file c:\PhilMetzer.txt with a Stream object.
Once the Stream object is opened, the Stream object's ReadText method
(p. 284) is used to read the contents of the file one byte at a time. When the
EOS is True, the Flush method is executed to ensure that all the data is out
of the buffer.

```
<%
Dim MyStrObj,str,Thesize,ThelineSep,Counter,temp
Set MyStrObj = Server.CreateObject("ADODB.Stream")
MyStrObj.Open "URL=C:\PhilMetzger.txt"
Counter = 0
Thesize = MyStrobj.size
ThelineSep = MyStrobj.LineSeparator
MyStrobj.Position = 0
Do while not EOF
```

```
      Str = MyStrObj
      'read one character at a time
      temp = MyStrobj.ReadText(1)
       If temp = ThelineSep then
          MyStrObj.SkipLine
       End if

      Str = Str & temp
      'increase the current position by 1
      MyStrObj.Position = Counter + 1
Loop

'get rid of all the data in the buffer
MyStrobj.Flush
'when untie the association between the file and the 'Stream
object
MyStrObj.Close
'after closing file then destroy the object
Set MyStrObj = nothing
%>
```

Charset	Stream Object Property

Purpose

Use this property to indicate the character set into which the text in the Stream object should be translated. Most of the time, you will set this property to ascii. This property can only be used if the stream of data is text. There is a list of character sets you can use in the Registry HKEY_CLASSES_ ROOT\MIME\Database\Charset. Note two prerequisites to using this property: First, the position of the stream must be set to 0 — the beginning; and second, the Steam object must be open.

Syntax

```
StreamObject.Charset
```

Example

The following example opens the file www.anywebsite.com/Myfiles.txt and then writes the text "My name is Amy Eden" to the file. The file is opened with the Mode property set to 2, which indicates that the file is to be written to. The Charset property is set to iso-8859-1. The default setting for the Position property, which is the starting position of the character to be written, is 0. Therefore, we don't have to include the property in the code.

```
<%
Dim MyStrObj,str
```

```
Set MyStrObj = Server.CreateObject("ADODB.Stream")
MyStrObj.Open "URL=http://www.examples.com/ Myfiles.txt", 2
Str = "My name is Amy Eden"
MyStrobj.Mode = 2
MyStrobj.Charset = "iso-8859-1"
MyStrobj.WriteText Str,0
'when untie the association between the file and the 'Stream
object
MyStrObj.Close
'after closing file then destroy the object
Set MyStrObj = nothing
%>
```

EOS   Stream Object Property

Purpose

Use this property to indicate if the end of the stream (EOS) is. This property returns either a True or False value.

Syntax

```
StreamObject.EOS
```

Example

The following example shows you how to use the EOS property to check if the end of the stream has been reached. This example associates the file KarlaBeaver.txt with a Stream object. This file is located in the URL www.myfriends.com/KarlaBeaver.txt. The file is opened for reading/writing to a text file. When the file is opened, we use the Position property to set the Stream object's current position to 0. Then we use the Stream object's SetEOS method (p. 286) to move the current position to the end of the stream. By setting the current position to 0 and then using the SetEOS method, you get rid of the contents of the Stream object. This clears out the file. After you run this code, the file KarlaBeaver.txt will be empty. The EOS is used to test if the end of the stream has been reached.

```
<%
Dim MyStrObj
Set MyStrObj = Server.CreateObject("ADODB.Stream")
MyStrObj.Open "URL=http://www.myfriends.com/KarlaBeaver.txt",1
'set position to 0
'empty out the contents of the file
MyStrObj.Position = 0
'send current position to end of stream
MyStrObj.SetEOS
'check to see the End of Stream(EOS) property is True
```

ASP Core Reference

```
If EOS then
    Response.Write "We are at the end of stream"
Else
    Response.Write "We are not at the end of stream"
End if
%>
```

LineSeparator   Stream Object Property

Purpose

Use this property to determine which binary character the Stream object is
using as a line separator. There are three options:carriage return, line feed, or
line feed and carriage return.

Syntax

```
StreamObject.LineSeparator
```

Example

The following example opens a Stream object to the file c:\anyfile\myfile.txt.
Once the file is opened, the LineSeparator property indicates which character is used for a line separator in the file.

```
<%
Dim MyStrObj
Set MyStrObj = Server.CreateObject("ADODB.Stream")
MyStrObj.Open "URL=c:\anyfile\myfile.txt"
Response.Write "The Line Separator of the Stream object is "
Response.Write MyStrObj.LineSeparator
%>
```

Mode   Stream Object Property

Purpose

Use this property to find or set the available permissions for the files or
directory associated with the Stream object. This property requires a
ConnectMode enumerated constant. The default for this property is read
access or the ConnectMode enumerated constant of adModeRead.

●—CROSS-REFERENCE

The ConnectMode enumerated constants are available at the URL
noted in the Preface.

ASP Core Reference

Syntax

```
StreamObject.Mode
```

Example

The following example associates the contents of the file "JeremyBeaver.txt" to the Stream object. This file is in the directory http://www.myfriends.com. The access permission to this file is read/write; thus, the Mode property will be set to adModeReadWrite. The value for adModeReadWrite is 3.

```
<%
Dim RecordObject,StreamObject
Set RecordObject = Server.CreateObject("ADODB.Record")
Set StreamObject = Server.CreateObject("ADODB.Stream")
RecordObject.ActiveConnection = "http://www.myfriends.com"
RecordObject.Source = "JeremyBeaver.txt"
RecordObject.Mode = 3
RecordObject.Open
StreamObject.Mode = 3
StreamObject.Open
Response.Write StreamObject.ReadFromText

%>
```

Position	Stream Object Property

Purpose

Use this property to determine the current position of the pointer in the Stream object. The Stream object's EOS (p. 292) and Size (p. 295) properties work well this property when reading in the contents of a file.

Syntax

```
Streamobject.Position
```

Example

The following code associates the file c:\GigMetzer.txt with a Stream object. Once the Stream object is opened, the Stream object's ReadText method (p. 284) is used to read the contents of the file one byte at a time. The Position property is used to move the current position forward by one character in the Stream object.

```
<%
Dim MyStrObj,str,Thesize,ThelineSep,Counter,temp
Set MyStrObj = Server.CreateObject("ADODB.Stream")
MyStrObj.Open "URL=c:\ GigMetzger.txt"
Counter = 0
```

```
Thesize = MyStrobj.size
ThelineSep = MyStrobj.LineSeparator
MyStrobj.Position = 0
Do while not EOF
    Str = MyStrObj
    'read one character at a time
    temp = MyStrobj.ReadText(1)
    If temp = ThelineSep then
        MyStrObj.SkipLine
    End if

    Str = Str & temp
    'increase the current position by 1
    MyStrObj.Position = Counter + 1
Loop

'get rid of all the data in the buffer
MyStrobj.Flush
'when untie the association between the file and the 'Stream
object
MyStrObj.Close
'after closing file then destroy the object
Set MyStrObj = nothing
%>
```

Size   Stream Object Property

Purpose

Use this property to determine the number of bytes in the Stream object.

Syntax

```
StreamObject.Size
```

Example

The following example duplicates the example for the Stream object's Write method (p. 288), but with one twist. This time, you will know how many bytes are in the Stream object after the photo data is written to the Stream object.

This example obtains a photo stored in a database and places the binary data of that photo into a file using the Stream object's Write method. The Connection object opens a connection to a database, and then a SQL statement is issued that retrieves the photo into bytes. The bytes will then be written to a file called SamfordHallAuburn.gif using the Write method.

```
<%
Dim MyStrObj,J,Str
Dim DataConn,Rset,sqlstm,RSBinary
set DataConn = Server.CreateObject("ADODB.Connection")
DataConn.Open Application("db_ConnectionString")

sqlstm = "Select Photo From TeamPhotos"

Set Rset = DataConn.Execute(sqlstm)
'Make Chucks large enough to hold the data
'100000 is an educated guess.
'The object RSBinary is an array of binary data
Set RSBinary = Rset("Photo").GetChucks(100000)

Set MyStrObj = Server.CreateObject("ADODB.Stream")
MyStrObj.Open
"URL=http://www.myfiles.com/SamfordHallAuburn.gif"
, 2

MyStrObj.Write RSBinary

'find the number of bytes in the Stream object
Response.Write "Number of bytes in Stream object is "
Response.Write MyStrObj.Size

'when data is finished writing close object
MyStrObj.Close
DataConn.Close
'Destroy all objects
Set DataConn = nothing
Set MyStrObj = nothing
Set RSBinary = nothing
Set Rset = nothing
%>
```

State   Stream Object Property

Purpose

Use this property to determine if the Stream object is opened or closed. You can only get the value of this property, you cannot set the property. The property returns an ObjectState enumerated constant.

CROSS-REFERENCE

The list of `ObjectState` enumerated constants are available at the URL noted in the Preface.

Syntax

```
StreamObject.State
```

Example

The following example opens both a Record object and a Stream object. The Record object will open the file www.friends.com/DavidWebb.txt in an asynchronous method call. The code will wait seven seconds to determine if the state of the Record object is open, and then wait another seven seconds to determine if the Stream object is open. If both objects are opened, the file will be read. If the Stream object is not opened in seven seconds, the asynchronous call will be canceled.

```
<%
Dim RecordObject,StreamObject, Tm

Set StreamObject = Server.CreateObject("ADODB.Stream")
StreamObject.Open " ","URL=http://www.friends.com/DavidWebb.txt",
, , adOpenAsync
Tm = Second(Time())
RecordObject.Open

Do while (Second(Time()) < Tm + 7)
    'waits 7 seconds to test whether Stream object opened
Loop

If Not (RecordObject.State = adStateOpen) then
    RecordObject.Cancel
Else
    'set the new seconds for variable Tm
    Tm = Second(Time())
    Do while (Second(Time()) < Tm + 7)
        'wait 7 seconds to test the State of Stream object
    Loop

    If Not (StreamObject.State = adStateOpen) then
        StreamObject.Cancel
    Else
        'do what ever you need to code here
```

ASP Core Reference

```
        End if
    End
Set StreamObject = nothing
%>
```

Type   Stream Object Property

Purpose

Use this property to obtain the type of data included in the stream. The values returned will be a `StreamType` enumeration constant. The default value is `adTypeText`. The `Type` property will be changed to `adTypeBinary` if binary data is first written to a new and empty stream.

●—CROSS-REFERENCE

The `StreamType` enumeration constants are available at the URL noted in the Preface.

Syntax

```
StreamObject.Type
```

Example

The following example opens a `Stream` object to the file c:\anyfile\myfile.txt. Once the file is opened, the `Response` object's `Write` method (p. 288) will show you the `Stream` object type.

```
<%
Dim MyStrObj
Set MyStrObj = Server.CreateObject("ADODB.Stream")
MyStrObj.Open "URL=c:\anyfile\myfile.txt"
Response.Write "The Type of the Stream object is "
Response.Write MyStrObj.Type
%>
```

TextStream Object

Purpose

Use the `TextStream` object to get access to sequential text files.

Syntax

```
Set TextStreamObject = FileSystemObject.CreateTextFile( file
, OverWriteExisting)
```

Close

Purpose
Use this method to close an open text stream file.

Syntax
```
TextStreamObject.Close
```

Example
The following example closes an open text stream file c:\Auburn.txt using the Close method. First the file auburn.txt is opened, and then all the contents are placed into a strings — file_content. The string is then output to the browser through the Response.Write method.

```
<%

  Dim myfileobj, Auburn,s_file_content
  Set myfileobj = CreateObject("Scripting.FileSystemObject")
  Set Auburn = myfileobj.CreateTextFile("c:\Auburn.txt", True)
'read the entire file into string

s_file_content = Auburn.ReadAll
'write to browser
Response.Write s_file_content
'close the file
'
Auburn.Close
'destroy the file object myfileobj
Set myfileobj = nothing
%>
```

Read

Purpose
Use this method to read a specified number of characters from a text stream file and return the string obtained.

Syntax
```
TextStreamObject.Read(characters)
```

Table 109 lists the argument associated with the Read method.

Table 109 *Argument for the Read Method*

Value	Required	Type	Description
characters	Yes	Number	characters is required. It consists of the number of characters you want to read from the file.

Example

The following example illustrates how to use the Read method to read seven characters from a file and return the resulting string:

```
Function ReadTextFileTest
   Const ForReading = 1, ForWriting = 2, ForAppending = 8
   Dim myfileobj, f, Msg
   Set myfileobj = CreateObject("Scripting.FileSystemObject")
   Set f = myfileobj.OpenTextFile("c:\WarnerRobinsHighSchool.txt",
ForWriting, True)
   f.Write "Phillip is a quantum mechanic!"
   Set f = fso.OpenTextFile("c:\test.txt",
1)
   ReadTextFileTest =  f.Read(7)
End Function
```

ReadAll   TextStream Object Method

Purpose

Use this method to read an entire text stream file and return the obtained string. When you are accessing large files, using the ReadAll method wastes memory resources. Other techniques should be used to input a file.

Syntax

```
TextStreamObject.ReadAll
```

Example

The following example uses the ReadAll method to read in the entire contents of the file auburn.txt. The contents are placed into a s_file_content string and the string is then output to the browser through the Response.Write method.

```
<%
```

```
  Dim myfileobj, Auburn,s_file_content
  Set myfileobj = CreateObject("Scripting.FileSystemObject")
  Set Auburn = myfileobj.CreateTextFile("c:\auburn.txt", True)
'read the entire file into string

s_file_content = Auburn.ReadAll
'write to browser
Response.Write s_file_content
'close the file
'
Auburn.Close
'destroy the file object myfileobj
Set myfileobj = nothing

%>
```

ReadLine   TextStream Object Method

Purpose

Use this method to read an entire line and return the resulting string (up to
the newline character) from a text stream file.

Syntax

```
TestStreamObject.ReadLine
```

Example

The following example reads in a file "WarnerRobinsHighSchool1977.txt"
one line at a time. When the line is read, it is output to the browser.

```
<%
Dim myfileobj, Auburn,s_file_content
Set myfileobj = CreateObject("Scripting.FileSystemObject")
Set Auburn =
myfileobj.CreateTextFile("c:\WarnerRobinsHighSchool1977.txt",
True)
'read the each line of file and output to browser
While NOT Auburn.AtEndOfStream
    Response.Write Auburn.ReadLine
Wend

'close the file
'
Auburn.Close
'destroy the file object myfileobj
```

```
Set myfileobj = nothing

%>
```

Skip   TextStream Object Method

Purpose

Use this method to skip a precise number of characters when reading a text stream file. Skipped characters will be erased.

Syntax

```
TextStreamObject.Skip(characters)
```

Table 110 lists the argument associated with the Skip method.

Table 110 *Argument for the Skip Method*

Value	Required	Type	Description
Characters	Yes	Number	characters is required. It consists of the number of characters you want to skip when you read from the file.

Example

The following example opens a file for reading, and then uses the Skip method to jump to the tenth character in the file. Once the first 10 characters are skipped, the file is read.

```
<%
   Dim myfileobj, Auburn,s_file_content
   Set myfileobj = CreateObject("Scripting.FileSystemObject")
   Set Auburn =
myfileobj.CreateTextFile("c:\WarnerRobinsHighSchool1977.txt", 1)

'skip over the first 10 character
Auburn.Skip(10)
'Read in the first line
str = Auburn.ReadLine
'output line to browser
Response.Write str

'close the file
'
```

```
Auburn.Close
'destroy the file object myfileobj
Set myfileobj = nothing

%>
```

SkipLine   TextStream Object Method

Purpose

Use this method to skip the next line when reading a text stream file.
Skipping a line requires reading and ignoring all characters in a line up to
and including the next newline character. If the file is not open for reading,
an error will occur.

Syntax

TextStreamObject.SkipLine

Example

The following code skips over the first line of the file JesseMetzger.txt:

```
<%
   Dim myfileobj, Auburn,s_file_content,j

   Set myfileobj = CreateObject("Scripting.FileSystemObject")
   Set Auburn = myfileobj.CreateTextFile("c:\ JesseMetzger.txt",
True)
'read the each line of file and output to browser
'initialize j to 1
'if j = 1 then skip over first line
While NOT Auburn.AtEndOfStream
    If j = 1 then
        Auburn.SkipLine
        j = j+1
    else
        Response.Write Auburn.ReadLine
    End if
Wend

'close the file
'
Auburn.Close
'destroy the file object myfileobj
Set myfileobj = nothing

%>
```

Write   TextStream Object Method

Purpose
Use this method to write a particular string to a text stream file.

Syntax

```
TextStreamObject.Write(string)
```

Table 111 lists the argument associated with the Write method.

Table 111 *Argument for the Write Method*

Value	Required	Type	Description
String	Yes	String	String is required. It consists of the text you want to write to the file.

Example
The following example writes the line "Phillip Metzger is married to Gigi Metzger." to a file named TrudyMetzger.txt. For the sake of simplicity, we are going to use the VBScript *Const* to establish constants in this example. The constants in this case are ForReading =1 and ForWriting =2.

```
<%
   Dim myfileobj, Auburn,s_file_content,j
  Const ForReading = 1
  Const ForWriting = 2
   Set myfileobj = CreateObject("Scripting.FileSystemObject")
   Set Auburn = myfileobj.CreateTextFile("c:\ TrudyMetzger.txt",
ForWriting, True)

Auburn.Write "Phillip Metzger is married to Gigi Metzger."
'close the file
'
Auburn.Close
'destroy the file object myfileobj
Set myfileobj = nothing
%>
```

WriteLine	**TextStream Object Method**

Purpose
Use this method to write a specified string and newline character to a text stream file.

Syntax

```
TextStreamObject.WriteLine([string])
```

Table 112 lists the argument associated with the WriteLine method.

Table 112 *Argument for the WriteLine Method*

Value	Required	Type	Description
String	Yes	String	String is required. It consists of the text you want to write to the file. If omitted, a newline character is written to the file.

Example
The following example writes the line "What Quarter is it David Webb?" to a file named JonSansom.txt. using the WriteLine method. Again, we are going to use the VBScript *Const* to establish constants in this example. The constants we state in the code below are as follows: ForReading =1 and ForWriting =2.

```
<%
  Dim myfileobj, Auburn,s_file_content,j
  Const ForReading = 1
  Const ForWriting = 2
  Set myfileobj = CreateObject("Scripting.FileSystemObject")
  Set Auburn = myfileobj.CreateTextFile("c:\ JonSansom.txt",
ForWriting, True)

Auburn.WriteLine "What Quarter is it David Webb?"
'close the file
'
Auburn.Close
'destroy the file object myfileobj
Set myfileobj = nothing
%>
```

WriteBlankLines   TextStream Object Method

Purpose

Use this method to write a specified number of blank lines to a text stream file.

Syntax

```
TextStreamObject.WriteBlankLines (lines)
```

Table 113 lists the argument associated with the WriteBlankLines method.

Table 113 *Argument for the WriteBlankLines Method*

Value	Required	Type	Description
lines	Yes	Number	Lines is required. It indicates the number of newline characters you want to write to the file.

Example

The following example illustrates the use of the WriteBlankLines method. It writes the following lines into the file c:\CarmenBurgress.txt. The code first writes a header to the file, and then separates the header from the rest of the text via a blank line.

```
<%
Dim myfileobj, Auburn,s_file_content,j
Const ForReading = 1
Const ForWriting = 2
Set myfileobj = CreateObject("Scripting.FileSystemObject")
   Set Auburn = myfileobj.CreateTextFile("c:\ CarmenBurgress.txt",
ForWriting, True)

Auburn.WriteLine "%%%%%%%%%%%%%%%%%%%%%%"
Auburn.WriteLine "%%   Jacob Burgess %%"
Auburn.WriteLine "%%%%%%%%%%%%%%%%%%%%%%"
Auburn.WriteBlankLines 2
Auburn.WriteLine "Is the Son of Tim Burgess"
Auburn.WriteBlankLines
'close the file
'
Auburn.Close
```

```
'destroy the file object myfileobj
Set myfileobj = nothing
%>
```

AtEndOfLine   TextStream Object Property

Purpose

Use this property to return True when at the end of a line, and False when
not at the end of a line. The end of the line is reached if the file pointer
comes before the end-of-line marker in a text stream file. The AtEndOfLine
property applies only to text stream files that are open for reading; otherwise, an error occurs. This is read-only.

Syntax

```
TextStreamObject.AtEndOfLine
```

Example

The following example reads in a file one character at a time. When the file
reaches the end of a line in the file is closed.

```
<%
Const ForReading = 1
Dim fso, theFile, retstring
Set fso = CreateObject("Scripting.FileSystemObject")
Set theFile = fso.OpenTextFile(filespec, ForReading, False)
Do While theFile.AtEndOfLine <> True
    retstring = theFile.Read(1)
Loop
theFile.Close
ReadEntireFile = retstring
%>
```

AtEndOfStream   TextStream Object Property

Purpose

Use this to property to return True if the file pointer is at the end of a text
stream file, or to return False if not. The AtEndOfStream property applies
only to text stream files that are open for reading, otherwise, an error occurs.
This is read-only.

Syntax

```
TextStreamObject.AtEndOfStream
```

ASP Core Reference

Example

The following example uses the AtEndofStream property to read in the file c:\TrishaAllison.txt one line at a time. When the line is read in, it is output to the browser.

```
<%
Dim myfileobj, Auburn,s_file_content
Set myfileobj = CreateObject("Scripting.FileSystemObject")
Set Auburn = myfileobj.CreateTextFile("c:\ TrishaAllison.txt",
True)
'read the each line of file and output to browser
While NOT Auburn.AtEndOfStream
     Response.Write Auburn.ReadLine
Wend

'close the file
'
Auburn.Close
'destroy the file object myfileobj
Set myfileobj = nothing
%>
```

ASP Core Reference

Column	TextStream Object Property

Purpose

Use this property to return the column number of the current character position in a text stream file. Column is a read-only property.

Syntax

```
TextStreamObject.Column
```

Example

The following example reads in the file c:\JoeMaxberry.txt, and then locates the column number after the first line is read. That column number is then output to be displayed in the browser.

```
<HTML>
<BODY>
<%
Const ForReading = 1
Const ForWriting = 2
Dim myobj, f, Str
Set myobj = CreateObject("Scripting.FileSystemObject")
Set f = myobj.OpenTextFile("c:\JoeMaxberry.txt", ForReading,
True)
```

```
Str = f.ReadLine
'get the column number
GetColumn = f.Column
Response.Write "the column number for the end of file"
Response.Write GetColumn
%>
</Body>
</HTML>
```

Line	TextStream Object Property

Purpose

Use this property to return the current line number in a text stream file.
After a file is initially opened and before any data is written to the
TextStream object, the value of the Line property is equal to 1. The Line
property is a read-only.

Syntax

```
TextStreamObject.Line
```

Example

The following example uses the Line property to find the current line being
read. The example uses the VBScript reserve word *Const* to set the constant
ReadTheFile.

```
<HTML>
<BODY>
<%
Const ReadTheFile = 1
Dim fso, f, ra
Set fso = CreateObject("Scripting.FileSystemObject")
Set f = fso.OpenTextFile("c:\testfile.txt", ReadTheFile)
ra = f.ReadAll
GetLine = f.Line
Response.Write "the Line number is "
Response.Write GetLine
%>
</Body>
</HTML>
```

ASP Core Reference

ASP Languages Used with ASP Reference

The ASP Reference part contains the following reference sections:

IN THIS PART

- HTML by Category
- HTML Reference
- VBScript by Category
- VBScript Reference
- SQL by Category
- SQL Reference

HTML by Category

The HTML tag categories tags represent the formatting and definition functions of each tag. For example, Header and Title tags are used for Headers of various sizes and fonts, and the Title tag is used to display the title of the HTML page. Table tags refer to those tags used in and for table definition. Form tags are used in and for forms. Some tags uniquely identify parts of the page, such as the Main tag category (<BODY> and <HEAD>). Also, some are primarily used to format characters (<SMALL> and <STRONG>) or lines and paragraphs (<ADDRESS>).

Keyword	Category	Page Number in HTML Reference Section
<A></A>	Link	320
<ADDRESS></ADDRESS>	Line and Paragraph Formatting	322
<APPLET></APPLET>	Image, Sound, and Other Media	322
<AREA>	Image, Sound, and Other Media	324
<B></B>	Character Formatting	324
<BASE>	Main	325
<BASEFONT>	Character Formatting	326
<BGSOUND>	Image, Sound, and Other Media	327
<BIG></BIG>	Character Formatting	327
<BLINK></BLINK>	Other Element	328
<BLOCKQUOTE></BLOCKQUOTE>	Line and Paragraph Formatting	328
<BODY></BODY>	Main	329

	Line and Paragraph Formatting	330
<BUTTON></BUTTON>	Form	331
<CAPTION></CAPTION>	Table	332
<CENTER></CENTER>	Line and Paragraph Formatting	333
<CITE> </CITE>	Line and Paragraph Formatting	333
<CODE></CODE>	Character Formatting	334
<COL></COL>	Table	335
<COLGROUP></COLGROUP>	Table	336
<DD>	List	336
<DFN></DFN>	Line and Paragraph Formatting	337
<DIR></DIR>	List	337
<DIV></DIV>	Line and Paragraph Formatting	338

Keyword	Category	Page Number in HTML Reference Section
<DL></DL>	List	339
<DT>	List	340
<EM></EM>	Character Formatting	340
<EMBED>	Image, Sound, and Other Media	341
<FIELDSET></FIELDSET>	Line and Paragraph Formatting	342
<FONT></FONT>	Character Formatting	342
<FORM></FORM>	Form	343
<FRAME>	Frame	345
<FRAMESET></FRAMESET>	Frame	346
<H1>through <H6>	Header and Title	348
<HEAD></HEAD>	Main	347
<HR>	Line and Paragraph Formatting	349
<HTML></HTML>	Main	350
<I></I>	Character Formatting	350
<IMG>	Image, Sound, and Other Media	351
<INPUT>	Form	352
<ISINDEX>	Main	354
<ISINDEX></ISINDEX>	Form	354
<KBD></KBD>	Character Formatting	355
<LABEL></LABEL>	Form	356
<LEGEND></LEGEND>	Line and Paragraph Formatting	357
<LI>	List	357
<LINK>	Main	358
<MAP></MAP>	Image, Sound, and Other Media	359
<MENU></MENU>	List	360
<META>	Main	360

Continued

HTML by Category

Keyword	Category	Page Number in HTML Reference Section
<NOBR></NOBR>	Line and Paragraph Formatting	361
<NOFRAME></NOFRAME>	Frame	361
<OBJECT>	Image, Sound, and Other Media	362
<OL></OL>	List	364
<OPTION>	Form	365
<P>	Line and Paragraph Formatting	366
<PARAM>	Image, Sound, and Other Media	367
<PRE></PRE>	Character Formatting	367
<RT></RT>	Character Formatting	368
<RUBY></RUBY>	Character Formatting	369
<SAMP></SAMP>	Character Formatting	370
<SCRIPT>	Image, Sound, and Other Media	370
<SELECT></SELECT>	Form	371
<SMALL></SMALL>	Character Formatting	372
<SPAN></SPAN>	Line and Paragraph Formatting	373
<STRIKE></STRIKE>	Character Formatting	374
<STRONG></STRONG>	Character Formatting	374
	Character Formatting	375
	Character Formatting	376
<TABLE>	Table	376
<TBODY></TBODY>	Table	378
<TD></TD>	Table	379
<TEXTAREA></TEXTAREA>	Form	380
<TH></TH>	Table	381
<THEAD></THEAD>	Table	383

Keyword	Category	Page Number in HTML Reference Section
<TITLE></TITLE>	Header and Title	384
<TR></TR>	Table	384
<TT></TT>	Line and Paragraph Formatting	386
<U></U>	Character Formatting	386
<UL></UL>	List	387
<VAR></VAR>	Character Formatting	388
<WBR>	Line and Paragraph Formatting	388
Special Character Sets	Character Entity	389

HTML Reference

HyperText Markup Language (HTML), the standard language for content on the Internet, uses text files containing tags to indicate formatting specifics. As of December 1999, HTML Version 4.01 was available, primarily as a bug fix for HTML Version 4.0. Many of the changes are reflected in this document. Generally, some media types have been added; and there is more flexibility in the attributes descriptors. Many of the new specifications refer to Desktop Documents Types (DDT) and style sheets, which are not covered here. In addition, some of the following tags are being deprecated, or phased out, in 4.01, although they can still be used. You can check the validity of the HTML code on any Web site at: http://validator.w3.org.

The HTML tags are arranged hierarchically in order to determine the characteristics of the document. They allow you to specify the typeface, style, and color of the Web content. These tags are set off from the content of the HTML page by less than and greater than symbols surrounding the tags. A beginning tag consists of a less than symbol, the tag name, and then a greater than symbol. HTML tags are to be distinguished from HTML elements. The tags are interpreted by the browser, parsed, and then converted into elements. The tag is the code and the element is its function. HTML uses formatting symbols to indicate what element is being formatted on a page. HTML is page centered and each page constitutes a file with the .htm or. html extension. The embedded commands provide instructions as to how the Web page will be organized. The HTML page is made up of elements, or tags, and is divided into three parts: HTML, HEAD, and BODY. The page is organized so that there are elements specific to each part of a page, as follows:

```
<HTML>
<HEAD>
<TITLE>    </TITLE>
</HEAD>
<BODY>
</BODY>
</HTML>
```

This code centers the page with slashes indicating that a specific element has ended. The entire page is contained within the <HTML> tags, and the <TITLE> tag is contained within the <HEAD> tags. The main portion of the page is encapsulated in the <BODY> tags. Finally, the <HTML> tag ends the page.

The <BODY> tags can contain many other tags as well. For example, HTML contains tables, forms, alignment, font, and data commands. Images are indicated with the <IMG> tag. You can specify many attributes, such as text and background color, style, and pattern. You can have background images, quotes, and hyperlinks to Web sites.

This HTML Tag Syntax reference section lists all the HTML tags in alphabetical order. The tags are categorized into 11 tag types. The tag types are: Header and Title Tags; Main Tags; Links; Lists; Character Formatting; Line and Paragraph Formatting; Images, Sounds, and Other Media; Forms; Tables; Frames; Other Elements and Character Entities. The tag type is noted next to each tag.

<A> </A>   Link Tag

Purpose

Use this tag as an anchor to signify the start or destination of a hypertext link. This tag requires that the href or the Name property be specified. The anchor may include both text and images. If a link has been selected, images will show a border with a changed color. The <A> tag is an inline element and requires a closing tag. This tag is available in HTML and script as of Internet Explorer 3.0.

Syntax

```
<A
ACCESSKEY=keyCLASS=classname
COORDS = coordinates [CN]

  DATAFLD=colname
    DATASRC=#ID
    HREF=url
HREFLANG = langcode [CI]
   ID=value
    LANG=language
    LANGUAGE=JAVASCRIPT | JSCRIPT | VBSCRIPT  | VBS
    METHODS=http-method
    NAME=name
    REL="stylesheet"
    REV="stylesheet"
SHAPE = default|rect|circle|poly [CI]

    STYLE=css1-properties
    TABINDEX=n
    TARGET=window_name | _blank | _parent | _search | _self |
_top
TYPE=Type
    TITLE=text
    URN=urn
    event = script
 >
```

Example

This example uses the A anchor with the href property to display an image.
The border width and the dimensions are also defined.

```
<A href="http://www.compumaxcomputers.com"><img border="0"
src="compumaxweb.gif" width="100" height="70"></A>
```

The A tag

<ADDRESS> </ADDRESS>	Line and Paragraph Formatting Tag

Purpose

Use this tag to indicate information, such as address, authorship, or other details in the current document. Internet Explorer displays the contents of an <ADDRESS> tag in italics. The <ADDRESS> tag is a block element and requires a closing tag. This tag is available in HTML as of Internet Explorer 3.0, and in script as of Internet Explorer 4.0.

Syntax

```
<ADDRESS
    CLASS=classname
    ID=value
    LANG=language     LANGUAGE=JAVASCRIPT | JSCRIPT | VBSCRIPT |
VBS
    STYLE=css1-properties
    TITLE=text
    event = script
>
```

Example

The following example will result in a display of large italicized text:

```
<ADDRESS>Fruita Hogmeyer</ADDRESS>
<ADDRESS>Hogmeyer's Hog Farm</ADDRESS>
```

```
Fruita Hogmeyer
Hogmeyer's Hog Farm
```

Using the Address tag

<APPLET> </APPLET>	Image, Sound, and Other Media Tag

Purpose

Use this tag to insert an executable script onto the page. The <APPLET> tag is a block element and requires a closing tag. To use executable content specified by the <APPLET> tag, a user's computer must have the Microsoft virtual machine installed. This tag is available in HTML as of Internet Explorer 3.0, and in script as of Internet Explorer 4.0. However, it has been depreciated in HTML Version 4.01. Furthermore, only subdirectories are now searched for the codebase.

Syntax

```
<APPLET
ALIGN=ABSBOTTOM | ABSMIDDLE | BASELINE | BOTTOM | LEFT |
MIDDLE | RIGHT | TEXTTOP | TOPALT=text
ARCHIVE = uri-list [CT]

  CLASS=classname
    CODE=filename
    CODEBASE=url
    DATAFLD=colname
    DATASRC=#ID
    HEIGHT=n
    HSPACE=n
    ID=value
    NAME=name
  OBJECT = cdata [CS]

    SRC=url
    STYLE=css1-properties
    TITLE=text
    VSPACE=n
    WIDTH=n
    event = script
>
```

Example

This example shows an <APPLET> tag that describes a hover button available in Microsoft FrontPage. The <APPLET> tag creates a rectangular button that appears to glow when the mouse is passed over it. The "color" and "hover-color" values determine each color in the glow. Font information is also included, in addition to a hyperlink to another document.

```
<APPLET code="fphover.class" codebase="./" width="70"
height="24">
        <param name="text" value="Email List">
        <param name="color" value="#FFFFFF">
        <param name="hovercolor" value="#FF0000">
        <param name="textcolor" value="#000000">
        <param name="effect" value="glow">
        <param name="font" value="Dialog">
        <param name="fontstyle" value="bold">
        <param name="fontsize" value="14">
        <param name="url" valuetype="ref" value="links.htm">
    </APPLET>
```

<AREA> | Image, Sound, and Other Media Tags

Purpose

Use AREA to define the shape, coordinates, and connected URL of one hyperlink region within a client-side image MAP (see the <MAP> tag on p. 359). There is no limit on the number of <AREA> tags that can be contained within the same MAP element. The format of the COORDS value depends on the value of the SHAPE attribute. The AREA element is not rendered and requires a closing tag. This tag is available in HTML as of Internet Explorer 3.0, and in script as of Internet Explorer 4.0.

Syntax

```
<AREA
  ACCESSKEY = character [CN]

    ALT=text
    CLASS=classname
    COORDS=coordinates
    HREF=url
    ID=value
    LANG=language
    LANGUAGE=JAVASCRIPT | JSCRIPT | VBSCRIPT | VBS
    NOHREF
    SHAPE=CIRC | | POLY | RECT | STYLE=css1-properties
    TABINDEX=n
    TARGET=window_name | _blank | _parent | _search | _self |
_top
    TITLE=text
    event = script
>
```

Example

See the example for the <MAP> tag (p.359). This also displays a case in point regarding the <AREA> tag.

<B> </B> | Character Formatting Tag

Purpose

Use this tag to specify that the text should be bold. The <B> tag is an inline element and requires a closing tag. This tag is available in HTML as of Internet Explorer 3.0, and in script as of Internet Explorer 4.0.

Syntax

```
<B
    CLASS=classname
    ID=value
    LANG=language
    LANGUAGE=JAVASCRIPT | JSCRIPT | VBSCRIPT | VBS
    STYLE=css1-properties
    TITLE=text
    event = script
>
```

Example

The following example of the use of the <B> tag is similar to the <STRONG> tag (see p. 374).

```
<p><B>The B tag causes text to be shown in bold.</B>
```

> **The B tag causes text to be shown in bold.**

HTML using the < B > tag

<BASE>   Main Tag

Purpose

Use this tag to provide a reference URL for a Web page. The URL or folder that is given as a <BASE> tag will remain in effect for use when providing links to subdirectories of the base URL. The <BASE> tag does not require a closing tag.

Syntax

```
<BASE
    HREF=url
    TARGET=window_name | _blank | _parent | _search | _self |
_top
>
```

Example

This example establishes a base URL for the Web site where the executable files reside. These files can be run at various points in the document. Because the BASE address has already been established, only the names of the files to be executed need to be referenced in each instance. Here, the time and date on the Web server will be displayed.

```
<BASE HREF="http://www.hitekdesigns.com/">
</HEAD>

<BODY bgcolor="#CCFFCC">
<BODY bgcolor="#CCFFCC">
Click <A HREF="mall2/welcome.asp">here</A> to get the time and
date.
```

<BASEFONT> Character Formatting Tag

Purpose

Use this tag to determine a base font to be used as the default font when rendering text. This tag can be used only within the <BODY> tag (see p.329) *see body* or the <HEAD> tag (see p. 347). The <BASEFONT> tag should appear before any displayed text in the BODY of the document. The <BASEFONT> tag does not require a closing tag. This tag is available in HTML as of Internet Explorer 3.0, and in script as of Internet Explorer 4.0. This tag was deprecated in HTML Version 4.01.

Syntax

```
<BASEFONT
     CLASS=classname
     COLOR=color
     FACE=font
     ID=value
     LANG=language
     SIZE=n
STYLE = style [CN]

TITLE = text [CS]

>
```

Example

In this example, the first line shows no BASEFONT size specified. The second line shows a BASEFONT specified. The third line shows a FONT SIZE specified to override the BASEFONT. The fourth line shows the BASEFONT size continued.

```
At this point, there is no BASEFONT size specified yet.
<P><BASEFONT SIZE=6> Set the BASEFONT size.
<P><FONT SIZE=3> Override the BASEFONT size just
set.</FONT><P>Now resume the BASEFONT size.
```

At this point, there is no BASEFONT size specified yet.

Set the BASEFONT size.

Override the BASEFONT size just set.

Now resume the BASEFONT size.

The < BASEFONT > tag

<BGSOUND>   Image, Sound, and Other Media Tags

Purpose

Use this tag to attach a background sound or soundtrack to a Web page. The <BGSOUND> tag can be used only within the HEAD tag (see p. 347). The <BGSOUND> tag does not require a closing tag. This tag is available in HTML as of Internet Explorer 3.0, and in script as of Internet Explorer 4.0.

Syntax

```
<BGSOUND
    BALANCE=n
    CLASS=classname
    ID=value
    LANG=language
    LOOP=n
    SRC=url
    TITLE=text
    VOLUME=n
>
```

Example

The example attaches the Passport midi file to the document and plays the music when the page is previewed in the browser.

```
<BGSOUND src="file:///c:/windows/media/Passport.mid" loop="-1">
```

<BIG> </BIG>   Character Formatting Tag

Purpose

Use this tag to reformat the enclosed text so that it is displayed larger than the current font. The <BIG> tag is an inline element and requires a closing tag. This tag is available in HTML as of Internet Explorer 3.0, and in script as of Internet Explorer 4.0.

Syntax

```
<BIG
    CLASS=classname
    ID=value
    LANG=language
    LANGUAGE=JAVASCRIPT | JSCRIPT | VBSCRIPT | VBS
    STYLE=css1-properties
    TITLE=text
    event = script
>
```

Example

This example shows how to switch the text font size within a line. It is similar, in this sense, to the examples shown for the <CITE> tag (see p. 333) and the <VAR> tag (see p.388).

```
<BIG>Using the BIG tag, this text is larger</BIG> than the rest
of the text on this line.</BODY>
```

> **Using the BIG tag, this text is larger** than the rest of the
> text on this line.

Changing to and from the <Big> tag

<BLINK> </BLINK>   Other Element Tag

Purpose

Use this tag to cause the text between the <BLINK> tags to flicker off and on, depending upon the browser. This tag requires a closing tag. It does not operate with Internet Explorer.

Example

When viewed in Netscape Navigator 4.5, the HI There text will alternate off and on like a neon sign.

```
<BLINK> HI There </BLINK>
```

<BLOCKQUOTE> </BLOCKQUOTE>   Line and Paragraph Formatting Tag

Purpose

Use this tag to set off a quotation in text. The <BLOCKQUOTE> tag is a block element and requires a closing tag. This tag is available in HTML as of Internet Explorer 3.0, and in script as of Internet Explorer 4.0.

Syntax

```
<BLOCKQUOTE
    CLASS=classname
    ID=value
    LANG=language
    LANGUAGE=JAVASCRIPT | JSCRIPT | VBSCRIPT | VBS
    STYLE=css1-properties
    TITLE=text
    event = script
>
```

Example

The following example causes the "Hello Beeg Boyee!" text to drop down a line and to be indented from the margin.

```
<P>She Said,
<BLOCKQUOTE>"Hello Beeg Boyee!"</BLOCKQUOTE>
```

> She Said,
>   "Hello Beeg Boyee!"

Using the <BLOCKQUOTE> tag

<BODY<BODY </BODY>   Main Tag

Purpose

Use this tag to specify the body of a document. The BODY block is the heart of the document. The <BODY> tag requires a closing tag. It falls inside the HTML block and contains a host of attributes, methods, behaviors, styles, properties, and events. References, copyright notices, background color, tables, and links are some of the elements the BODY block can contain. The <BODY> tag contains formatting information, references to external and internal links, as well as additional script code, such as VBScript (see VBScript Reference Section on p. 399) Java, and Active Server Pages. Many attributes have been deprecated in this tag in HTML 4.01.

Syntax

```
<BODY
    ALINK=color
    BACKGROUND=url
    BGCOLOR=color
    BGPROPERTIES=FIXED
    BOTTOMMARGIN=pixels
    CLASS=classname
    ID=value
```

```
LANG=language
LANGUAGE=JAVASCRIPT | JSCRIPT | VBSCRIPT  | VBS
LEFTMARGIN=pixels
LINK=color
RIGHTMARGIN=pixels
SCROLL=YES|NO
STYLE=css1-properties
TEXT=color
TITLE=string
TOPMARGIN=n
VLINK=color
event = script
>
```

Example

The following example creates a page with a pale green background with no
other elements visible. The document title does not display. The information
within the BODY block simply displays the bgcolor property specified. Of
course, usually many other attributes are to be specified as well.

```
<HTML>
<HEAD> <TITLE>Wild Country Rottweilers</TITLE></HEAD>
<body bgcolor="#CCFFCC">
</BODY>
</HTML>
```


                      Line and Paragraph Formatting Tag

Purpose

Use this tag to insert a line break wherever the <BR> tag occurs on a line. The

 tag does not require a closing tag. This tag is available in HTML as of
Internet Explorer 3.0, and in script as of Internet Explorer 4.0.

Syntax

```
<BR
    CLASS=classname
    CLEAR=ALL |LEFT | RIGHT| NONE
    ID=value
    LANGUAGE=JAVASCRIPT | JSCRIPT | VBSCRIPT  | VBS
    STYLE=css1-properties
    TITLE=text
>
```

Example

In this example, the <BR> tag causes the sentence to be shown on two lines, being broken after the words "stands for."

```
<DFN>ASP stands for <BR>Active Server Pages.</DFN>
```

> 'ASP stands for
> Active Server Pages.

The <BR> tag

<BUTTON> </BUTTON>

Form Tag

Purpose

Use this tag to identify a container for rich HTML. When the <BUTTON> tag is submitted in a form, Internet Explorer 5 and later submits the VALUE attribute, if it exists. Otherwise, the innerText property is submitted. In Internet Explorer 4.0, only the innerText property value is submitted. The <BUTTON> tag is an inline element and requires a closing tag. This tag is available in HTML and script as of Internet Explorer 4.0.

Syntax

```
<BUTTON
    ACCESSKEY=string
    CLASS=classname
    DATAFLD=colname
    DATAFORMATAS=HTML | TEXT
    DATASRC=#ID
    DISABLED=true | false
    ID=value
    LANG=language
    LANGUAGE=JAVASCRIPT | JSCRIPT | VBSCRIPT | VBS
    NAME=name
    STYLE=css1-properties
    TITLE=text
    TYPE=BUTTON | RESET | SUBMIT
    VALUE=value
    event = script
>
```

Example

The following code creates a simple button:

```
<BUTTON type = Button> </BUTTON>
```

<CAPTION> </CAPTION>   Table Tag

Purpose

Use this tag to give a specific description for a <TABLE> tag (see p. 376). The <CAPTION> tag should be a child of the <TABLE> tag. The <CAPTION> tag is a block element and requires a closing tag. This tag is available in HTML as of Internet Explorer 3.0, and in script as of Internet Explorer 4.0.

Syntax

```
<CAPTION
    ALIGN=BOTTOM | | LEFT | RIGHT | TOP (depreciated)
    CLASS=classname
    ID=value
    LANG=language
    LANGUAGE=JAVASCRIPT | JSCRIPT | VBSCRIPT  | VBS
    STYLE=css1-properties
    TITLE=text
    VALIGN=BOTTOM | TOP
    event = script
>
```

Example

Here, the <CAPTION> tag is added to the code for the <TABLE> tag. In that event, the caption would display under the table used in that example.

```
<TABLE>
<CAPTION VALIGN=BOTTOM> Whatever you write will display below the
table. </CAPTION>
</TABLE>
```

The caption below the table

<CENTER> </CENTER> — Line and Paragraph Formatting Tag

Purpose

Use this tag to cause subsequent text and images to be centered. The <CEN-TER> tag is a block element and requires a closing tag. This tag is available in HTML as of Internet Explorer 3.0, and in script as of Internet Explorer 4.0.

Syntax

```
<CENTER
    CLASS=classname
    ID=value
    LANG=language
    LANGUAGE=JAVASCRIPT | JSCRIPT | VBSCRIPT | VBS
    STYLE=css1-properties
    TITLE=text
    event = script
>
```

Example

Here, the text between the <CENTER> tags will be set in the middle of the page:

```
<CENTER>Center this text on the page, Please.</CENTER>
```

Center this text on the page, Please.

Centering the text on the page

<CITE> </CITE> — Line and Paragraph Formatting

Purpose

Use this tag to specify a citation by changing text to italic. This is for references to books, articles, or other published material. The <CITE> tag is an inline element and requires a closing tag. This tag is available in HTML as of Internet Explorer 3.0, and in script as of Internet Explorer 4.0.

Syntax

```
<CITE
    CLASS=classname
    ID=value
    LANG=language
    LANGUAGE=JAVASCRIPT | JSCRIPT | VBSCRIPT | VBS
```

```
STYLE=css1-properties
TITLE=text
event = script
>
```

Example

In this example, The Iliad is shown in italic and is differentiated from the word Homer's.

```
<P><strong>Homer's<strong/> <CITE>The Iliad.</CITE>
```

Homer's *The Iliad.*

Using the < CITE > tag

<CODE> </CODE>   Character Formatting Tag

Purpose

Use this tag to set off a code sample. This is similar to using a special font in a word processor to set aside code segments. The <CODE> tag is an inline element and requires a closing tag. This element is available in HTML as of Internet Explorer 3.0, and in script as of Internet Explorer 4.0.

Syntax

```
<CODE
CLASS=classname
    ID=value
    LANG=language
    LANGUAGE=JAVASCRIPT | JSCRIPT | VBSCRIPT | VBS
    STYLE=css1-properties
    TITLE=text
    event = script
>
```

Example

In this example, the words between the <CODE> tags are displayed as code:

```
<CODE>If you wish to display programming code, this is how to do
it.</CODE>
```

If you wish to display programming code, this is how to do
it.

Displaying code

<COL>   **Table Tag**

Purpose

Use the Col tag to set defaults for the table properties that are based on the column(s). The <COL> tag is a block element and does not require a closing tag. This tag is available in HTML as of Internet Explorer 3.0, and in script as of Internet Explorer 4.0.

```
<COL
ALIGN=CENTER | LEFT | RIGHT |JUSTIFY|CHAR [CI]
CHAROFF = length [CN]

    CLASS=classname
    ID=value
    SPAN=n
    STYLE=css1-properties
    TITLE=text
    VALIGN=BASELINE | BOTTOM | MIDDLE | TOP
    WIDTH=n
>
```

Example

In this example, the two columns are aligned left and right, respectively:

```
<TABLE width="470">
<COLGROUP><COL ALIGN=left></COLGROUP>
<COLGROUP><COL ALIGN=right></COLGROUP>
<TBODY>
<TR>
<TD width="140">The first column in the group and it is aligned
left.</TD>
<TD width="140">The second column represents a new group and it
is aligned right.</TD>
</TR>
</TABLE>
```

The first column in the group and it is aligned left.	The second column represents a new group and it is aligned right.

Lining up columns

<COLGROUP>   Table Tag

Purpose

Use this tag to enclose a collection of columns. The <COLGROUP> tag is a block element and requires a closing tag if the COLGROUP has <COL> tag (see p. 335) elements nested within it; otherwise, it does not require a closing tag. This tag is available in HTML as of Internet Explorer 3.0, and in script as of Internet Explorer 4.0.

```
<COLGROUP
ALIGN=CENTER | LEFT | RIGHT|JUSTIFY|CHAR
CHAROFF = length [CN]

    CLASS=classname
    ID=value
    SPAN=n
    STYLE=css1-properties
    TITLE=text
    VALIGN=BASELINE | BOTTOM | MIDDLE | TOP
    WIDTH=n
>
```

Example

See the example shown for the <COL> tag (p. 335).

<DD>   List Tag

Purpose

Use this tag to provide the definition in the definition list. Here the definition is indented. The <DD> tag is a block element and does not require a closing tag. This tag is available in HTML as of Internet Explorer 3.0, and in script as of Internet Explorer 4.0

Syntax

```
<DD
CLASS=classname
    ID=value
    LANG=language
    LANGUAGE=JAVASCRIPT | JSCRIPT | VBSCRIPT  | VBS
    NOWRAP
    STYLE=css1-properties
    TITLE=text
    event = script
>
```

Example

See the example shown for the <DL> tag (p. 339).

<DFN> </DFN>   Line and Paragraph Formatting

Purpose

Use this tag to designatethe defining instance of a term. The <DFN> tag is an
inline element and requires a closing tag. This tag is available in HTML as of
Internet Explorer 3.0, and in script as of Internet Explorer 4.0.

Syntax

```
<DFN
     CLASS=classname
     ID=value
     LANG=language
     LANGUAGE=JAVASCRIPT | JSCRIPT | VBSCRIPT | VBS
     STYLE=css1-properties
     TITLE=text
     event = script
>
```

Example

Compare the following example with other examples of text-modifying tags
(<EM> (p. 340), <CODE> (p. 334), <KBD> (p. 355), <STRONG> (p. 374), etc.): DFN is
simply a formatting tag to emphasize a defining term in text. (Each one of the
refs is preceded by the correct ref.)

```
<DFN>ASP stands for Active Server Pages.</DFN>
```

<DIR> </DIR>   List Tag

Purpose

Use this tag to designate a directory list. The <DIR> tag is a block element
and requires a closing tag. This tag is available in HTML as of Internet
Explorer 3.0, and in script as of Internet Explorer 4.0.

Syntax

```
<DIR
     CLASS=classname
     ID=value
     LANG=language
     LANGUAGE=JAVASCRIPT | JSCRIPT | VBSCRIPT | VBS
     STYLE=css1-properties
     TITLE=text
```

```
      TYPE=DISC | CIRCLE | SQUARE
      event = script
>
```

Example

This example produces a bulleted list that looks similar to the one shown for the < MENU> tag (see p. 360):

```
<DIR>
<LI>Sales
<LI>Marketing
<LI>Accounting
<LI>Personnel
<LI>Research
</DIR>
```

- Sales
- Marketing
- Accounting
- Personnel
- Research

Making a directory list

<DIV> </DIV>   Line and Paragraphing Formatting Tag

Purpose

Use this tag to identify a container for the < HTML> tag (p. 350). The <DIV> tag is a block element that requires a closing tag. This tag is available in HTML as of Internet Explorer 3.0, and in script as of Internet Explorer 4.0.

Syntax

```
<DIV
      ALIGN=CENTER | LEFT | RIGHT | JUSTIFY
      CLASS=classname
      DATAFLD=colname
      DATAFORMATAS=HTML | TEXT
      DATASRC=#ID
      ID=value
      LANG=language
      LANGUAGE=JAVASCRIPT | JSCRIPT | VBSCRIPT | VBS
      STYLE=css1-properties
      TITLE=text
      event = script
>
```

Example

In this example, the text is centered and represented as a block separate from the rest of the page:

```
<DIV ALIGN=CENTER>
This delineates one section, and centers its text.
</DIV>
```

<DL> </DL>   List Tag

Purpose

Use the DL tag to differentiate a definition list. The <DL> tag is a block element and requires a closing tag. This tag is available in HTML as of Internet Explorer 3.0, and in script as of Internet Explorer 4.0.

Syntax

```
<DL
    CLASS=classname
    COMPACT
    ID=value
    LANG=language
    LANGUAGE=JAVASCRIPT | JSCRIPT | VBSCRIPT | VBS
    STYLE=css1-properties
    TITLE=text
    event = script
>
```

Example

This example shows how to nest categories using the <DD> tag (p. 336) and <DT> tag (p. 340). They are used here to create a definition list.

```
<DL>
<DT>Rottweiler
<DD>A large, strong, determined dog.
<DT>Malamute
<DD>A working dog, accustomed to cold climates.
</DL>
```

Rottweiler
   A large, strong, determined dog.
Malamute
   A working dog, accustomed to cold climates.

Nesting categories with the <DD>, <DL> and <DT> tags

<DT> List Tag

Purpose

Use this tag to identify a definition term within a definition list. The <DT> tag is a block element and does not require a closing tag. This tag is available in HTML as of Internet Explorer 3.0, and in script as of Internet Explorer 4.0.

Syntax

```
<DT
    CLASS=classname
    ID=value
    LANG=language
    LANGUAGE=JAVASCRIPT | JSCRIPT | VBSCRIPT | VBS
    STYLE=css1-properties
    TITLE=text
    event = script
>
```

Example

See the example shown for the <DL> tag (p. 339).

<EM> </EM> Character Formatting Tag

Purpose

Use this tag to emphasize text. This is usually done by changing the style of the text to italic. The <EM> tag is an inline element and requires a closing tag. This tag is available in HTML as of Internet Explorer 3.0, and in script as of Internet Explorer 4.0.

Syntax

```
<EM
    CLASS=classname
    ID=value
    LANG=language
    LANGUAGE=JAVASCRIPT | JSCRIPT | VBSCRIPT | VBS
    STYLE=css1-properties
    TITLE=text
    event = script
>
```

Example

This example shows you how to call attention to your text by italicizing it:

```
<EM>You can use this (EM) tag to emphasize text, most of the time
in italic style. </EM>
```

You can use this (EM) tag to emphasize text, most of the time in italic style.

Emphasizing text with the <EM> tag

<EMBED>   Image, Sound, and Other Media Tags

Purpose

Use this tag to embed documents. The <EMBED> tag must appear inside the
<BODY> tag (see p. 329) of the document. You must have an application that
can view the data installed on your computer. The <EMBED> tag is a block element and does not require a closing tag. This tag is available in HTML as of
Internet Explorer 3.0, and in script as of Internet Explorer 4.0.

```
<EMBED
    ALIGN=ABSBOTTOM | ABSMIDDLE | BASELINE | BOTTOM | LEFT |
        MIDDLE | RIGHT | TEXTTOP | TOP
    ALT=text
    CLASS=classname
    CODE=filename
    HEIGHT=n
    HSPACE=n
    ID=value
    NAME=name
    SRC=url
    STYLE=css1-properties
    TITLE=text
    UNITS=value
    VSPACE=n
    WIDTH=n
>
```

Example

In this example, a waveform sound WAV is played. The Autostart property
is set to true so that the sound plays when the page is loaded. Height and
width parameters do not need to be set.

```
<EMBED SRC="blackhol.wav" HIDDEN="TRUE" AUTOSTART="TRUE"
width="128" height="128">
```

<FIELDSET> </FIELDSET>	Line and Paragraph Formatting Tag

Purpose

Use this tag to draw a box around the text and other elements contained in the field set. It is helpful for grouping elements in a form and for uniquely marking text in a document. The <FIELDSET> tag has the same behavior as a window frame. Because window frames do not have scrollbars, assigning the Overflowproperty a value of scroll will render it as if the value were hidden. Align is deprecated in HTML Version 4.01. The <FIELDSET> tag is a block element and requires a closing tag. This tag is available in HTML and script as of Internet Explorer 4.0.

Syntax

```
<FIELDSET
    ALIGN= LEFT | CENTER | RIGHT
    CLASS=classname
    ID=value
    LANG=language
    LANGUAGE=JAVASCRIPT | JSCRIPT | VBSCRIPT  | VBS
    STYLE=css1-properties
    TITLE=text
    event = script
>
```

Example

In this example, When the words are viewed in the browser, a box will be drawn around the words:

```
<FIELDSET>
<INPUT NAME="CHOICE 1" TYPE="BUY" VALUE="YES">
<INPUT NAME="CHOICE 1" TYPE="BUY" VALUE="NO">
</FIELDSET>
```

<FONT> </FONT>	Character Formatting Tag

Purpose

Use this tag to specify a new font, size, and color to be used for showing the enclosed text. The <FONT> tag requires a closing tag. This tag is available in HTML as of Internet Explorer 3.0, and in script as of Internet Explorer 4.0. This tag is deprecated in HTML Version 4.01.

Syntax

```
<FONT
    CLASS=classname
```

```
        COLOR=color
        FACE=font
        ID=value
        LANG=language
        LANGUAGE=JAVASCRIPT | JSCRIPT | VBSCRIPT | VBS
        SIZE=n
        STYLE=css1-properties
        TITLE=text
        event = script
    >
```

Example

This example illustrates the font definition as well as the size of the font:

```
<FONT face="Courier New, Courier" size=3></pre>
<P>Hey you, I'm Courier, size 3.
</FONT>
```

```
Hey you, I'm Courier, size 3.
```

Setting the typeface and font size

<FORM> </FORM>   Form Tag

Purpose

Use this tag to indicate that the contained controls (<INPUT> and <SELECT> tags) are part of a form. Forms are used to collect data from client-side users and submit the data to a server in a standard format. The creator of a form designs the form to collect the required data using many types of controls, such as INPUT (see p. 352) or SELECT (see p. 371). Clicking the Submit button sends the data to the server, where a script on the server then processes the data.

Each control element's NAME attribute must be defined if the data is to be submitted with the form. An element in a form can be referenced by the NAME property or the ID property, or through the elements collection.

The onsubmit event fires when the user presses ENTER. The dark border indicates that the user pressed ENTER to submit the form. The <FORM> tag is a block element and requires a closing tag. This tag is available in HTML and script as of Internet Explorer 3.0.

Syntax

```
    <FORM
    Accept=Contenttype
    ACTION=url
```

```
        CLASS=classname
        ENCTYPE=encoding
        ID=value
    LANG=language
        LANGUAGE=JAVASCRIPT | JSCRIPT | VBSCRIPT | VBS
        METHOD=GET | POST
        NAME=name
        STYLE=css1-properties
        TARGET=window_name | _blank | _parent | _search | _self |
    _top
        TITLE=text
        event = script
    >
```

Example

In this illustration, the <FORM> tag is set up to collect data on Name, Address, City, and State fields. The HTML code draws a form on the page, outlining and captioning the fields in which the user will enter data. Once the data entry is completed, the user presses the Submit button and the data is e-mailed to the Webmaster at the e-mail address specified.

```
<FORMMETHOD="POST" ACTION="/cgi-bin/sendmail.asp">
  <input type="hidden" name="recipient"
value="webmaster@mymall.com"><input type="hidden" name="subject"
value="request"><div align="center"><center><TABLEBORDER="5"
CELLPADDING="5" ALIGN="center">
    <TR>
      <TD>Name </TD>
      <TD><input TYPE="text" SIZE="25" NAME="NAME" VALUE> </TD>
    </TR>
    <TR>
      <TD>Address: </TD>
      <TD><input TYPE="text" SIZE="45" NAME="address" VALUE>
</TD>
    </TR>
    TR><TR>
      <TD>City: </TD>
      TD><TD><input TYPE="text" SIZE="20" NAME="city" VALUE>
</TD>
    </TR>
    <TR>
      <TD>State: </TD>
      <TD><input TYPE="text" SIZE="12" NAME="state" VALUE> </TD>
    </TR>
    </TABLE>
```

```
    </center></div>
    </center></div><div align="center"><center><p><input
TYPE="submit" VALUE="Submit"> <input TYPE="reset" VALUE="Reset
Form"> </p>
    </center></div><p><br>
      </FORM>
```

Name	
Address:	
City:	
State:	

Submit | Reset Form

Creating a form

<FRAME>   FRAME Tag

Purpose

Use this tag to isolate a particular area within a page that has control over subsequently selected areas. The <FRAME> tag refers to an individual frame within a <FRAMESET> tag (see p.346). If a user opens a Web folder inside a frame by selecting a link, the new window will appear inside the original FRAME. For example, if a page contains a frame pointing to a particular Web site, and a user clicks on a link that goes to a second Web site, the frame in the first Web site takes control of the entire window. The <FRAME> tag is a block element and does not require a closing tag. This tag is available in HTML and script as of Internet Explorer 3.0.

Syntax

```
<FRAME
    BORDERCOLOR=color
    CLASS=classname
    DATAFLD=colname
    DATASRC=#ID
    FRAMEBORDER=NO | YES | 0 | 1
    HEIGHT=n
    ID=value
    LANG=language
    LANGUAGE=JAVASCRIPT | JSCRIPT | VBSCRIPT | VBS
  LONGDESC = uri [CT]
```

```
      MARGINHEIGHT=pixels
      MARGINWIDTH=pixels
      NAME=window_name | _blank | _parent | _self | _top
      NORESIZE=NORESIZE | RESIZE
      SCROLLING=AUTO | NO | YES
      SRC=url
   STYLE = style [CN]

      TITLE=text
      WIDTH=n
      event = script
   >
```

Example

In this example, "leftframe.htm" is the name of the document that comprises the frame. The frame attributes are scrolling, target, marginheight, and marginwidth:

```
<FRAME name="contents" target="main" src="leftframe.htm"
scrolling="no" marginwidth="10" marginheight="16">
```

<FRAMESET> </FRAMESET>   Frame Tag

Purpose

Use this tag to specify a frameset, which is used to organize multiple frames (see <FRAME> tag on p. 345 and nested framesets. If a user opens a Web folder inside a frame and then clicks something in the Web folder, the file or folder that the user clicks takes over the entire window. For example, if a page contains a frame pointing to a particular Web site and a user clicks on a link that goes to a second Web site, the frame in the first Web site takes control of the entire window. The <FRAMESET> tag is a block element and requires a closing tag. This tag is available in HTML as of Internet Explorer 3.0, and in script as of Internet Explorer 4.0.

Syntax

```
<FRAMESET
     BORDER=pixels
     BORDERCOLOR=color
     CLASS=classname
     COLS=col-widths
     FRAMEBORDER=NO | YES | 0 | 1
     FRAMESPACING=spacing
     ID=value
     LANG=language
     LANGUAGE=JAVASCRIPT | JSCRIPT | VBSCRIPT | VBS
```

HTML Reference

```
    ROWS=row-heights
 STYLE = style [CN]
    TITLE=text
>
```

Example

Here, the border width and frame spacing are set to zero pixels, and the column width is 120 pixels:

```
<FRAMESET framespacing="0" border="0" cols="120,*"
frameborder="0">
</FRAMESET>
```

<HEAD> </HEAD>   Main Tag

Purpose

Use this tag to provide information to the browser, excluding the layout and attributes of the page. It requires a closing tag. This tag became available in HTML as of Microsoft Internet Explorer 3.0. The following tags can be used when located within the <HEAD> tag:

- <BASE> (see p. 325). This explicitly identifies a base URL to resolve links. It can be used to link and reference external sources for particular files. It does not need to have an ending element.
- <BASEFONT> (see p. 326). This causes the document to contain one basic font throughout, but it can be temporarily overridden by inserting the FONT command. It is used within the <BODY> tags and should be placed before any displayed text. Attributes are Color, Face, ID and Size.
- <BGSOUND> (see p. 327). This must be used within the <HEAD> tag. It causes a sound file (.WAV, .MID, etc.) to be played while that page is in the browser.
- <LINK> (see p. 358). This is used to provide a link to an external document. It does not require a closing tag.
- <META> (see p. 360). This is used to provide information used by search engines. This information is hidden on the page, so it is not displayed to users. It does not require a closing tag.
- <NEXTID> This creates unique identifiers to be read by text editing programs; it does not require a closing tag.
- <SCRIPT> (see p. 370). This enables the page to run an external script. It is a block command and requires a closing tag.
- <STYLE> This refers to a style sheet, and does require a closing tag.
- <TITLE> (see p. 384). This is used only within the HEAD block; it states the title of the page.

Syntax

```
<HEAD

LANG = language-code [CI]

PROFILE = uri [CT]

>
```

Example

Here, the HEAD block (see p. 347) is used to create <META> tags (p. 360), which will be used by search engines to categorize and index the Web site. The CONTENT in the description area of the META NAME tells what the site is about and what services it offers. The keywords section contains words that the designer determines are most likely to be entered by a prospective visitor at a search site to find a Web site similar to the current one; for example, one that offers similar services. The <TITLE> tag (see p. 384) also falls into the HEAD block and is often used by searching and indexing services to access the Web site.

```
<HTML>
<HEAD>
<meta NAME="description" CONTENT="Hi-Tek Mall provides Free web
page design with low cost, reliable web hosting. ">
<meta NAME="keywords" CONTENT="web page design, free web design,
webpage design, web hosting, hosting">
<TITLE>web page design and hosting</TITLE>
</HEAD>
<BODY  bgcolor="#CCFFCC">
</BODY>
</HTML>
```

<H*n*> (H1 through H6)   Header and Title Tag

Purpose

Use the <H*n*> tags to represent Headers 1 through 6. The first header tag is written as H1, the second as H2, and so on. They are used with style sheets to designate font sizes, colors, styles, and typefaces. The <H*n*> tag is a block element and requires a closing tag. This tag is available in HTML code as of Internet Explorer 3.0, and in script as of Internet Explorer 4.0.

Syntax

```
<Hn
    ALIGN=CENTER | LEFT | RIGHT | JUSTIFY
    CLASS = classname
    ID = value
```

```
   LANG = language
   LANGUAGE = JAVASCRIPT | JSCRIPT | VBSCRIPT  | VBS
   STYLE = css1-properties
   TITLE = text
   event  = script
></Hn>
```

Example

In this example, the header (H2) utilizes the style designated by the default style sheet in use by the HTML editor (in this case, Microsoft FrontPage) as H2. Here, H2 has been defined in the style sheet as the Arial typeface, font size 4 (point size 14). The <STRONG> tag means strongly emphasized and represented as bold.

```
<H2 align="left"><font face="Arial" size="4"><strong>Visit our
clients' sites:</strong></font><H2/>
```

<HR>   Line and Paragraph Formatting Tag

Purpose

Use this tag to draw a horizontal rule. The <HR> tag is a block element and does not require a closing tag. This tag is available in HTML as of Internet Explorer 3.0, and in script as of Internet Explorer 4.0.

Syntax

```
<HR
    ALIGN=CENTER | LEFT | RIGHT
    CLASS=classname
    COLOR=color
    ID=value
    LANG=language
    LANGUAGE=JAVASCRIPT | JSCRIPT | VBSCRIPT  | VBS
    NOSHADE
    SIZE=n
    STYLE=css1-properties
    TITLE=text
    WIDTH=n
    event = script
>
Remarks
```

Example

The following line of HTML code causes a horizontal line to be displayed above the text (just as it says). The <HR> tag by itself draws a line with no text.

```
<HR>This tag will draw a horizontal line above this text.
```

> This tag will draw a horizontal line above this text.

Drawing a horizontal line above text

<HTML> </HTML> — Main Tag

Purpose

Use this tag to identify the HTML document. The <HTML> tag requires a closing tag (<HTML/>) denoted by a slash / inside the right bracket. As shown in the example, the <HTML> tag is the first tag on an HTML document. In this context, the <HTML> tag is the parent of the other tags, but the < HTML> tag is the child of the parent document. This tag is available in HTML as of Internet Explorer 3.0, and in script as of Internet Explorer 4.0.

Syntax

```
<HTML
LANG = language
VERSION = cdata [CN]


>
```

Example

The following example shows that the <HTML> tag must be the first and last tag on a document page:

```
<HTML>
<BODY>
<P> The HTML tag specifies that the document is HTML.</P>
</BODY>
</HTML>
```

<I> </I> — Character Formatting Tag

Purpose

Use this tag to ensure that text is displayed as italic, when available. The <I> tag is an inline element and requires a closing tag. This tag is available in HTML as of Internet Explorer 3.0, and in script as of Internet Explorer 4.0.

Syntax

```
<I
    CLASS=classname
    ID=value
    LANG=language
```

```
    LANGUAGE=JAVASCRIPT | JSCRIPT | VBSCRIPT | VBS
    STYLE=css1-properties
    TITLE=text
    event = script
>
```

Example

The <I> tag is similar to the <CITE> (see p. 333), <DFN> (see p. 337), <VAR> (see p. 388), and <EM> (see p. 340) tags.

```
<P><I>This how to show text in italic.</I>
```

> *This how to show text in italic.*

Italicizing text

<IMG>	Image, Sound, and Other Media Tags

Purpose

Use this tag to embed images and video clips in documents. This tag does not initiate the onfocus event when it receives the input focus, unless it has been associated with a <MAP> tag. The <IMG> tag is an inline element and does not require a closing tag. This tag is available in HTML as of Internet Explorer 3.0, and in script as of Internet Explorer 4.0.

Syntax

```
<IMG
    ALIGN=ABSBOTTOM | ABSMIDDLE | BASELINE | BOTTOM | LEFT |
        MIDDLE | RIGHT | TEXTTOP | TOP
    ALT=text
    BORDER=n
    CLASS=classname
    DATAFLD=colname
    DATASRC=#ID
    DYNSRC=url
    HEIGHT=n
    HSPACE=n
    ID=value
    ISMAP
    LANG=language
    LANGUAGE=JAVASCRIPT | JSCRIPT | VBSCRIPT | VBS
    LONGDESC=Long Description
    LOOP=n
    LOWSRC=url
```

```
     NAME=name
     SRC=url
     STYLE=css1-properties
     TITLE=text
     USEMAP=url
     VSPACE=n
     WIDTH=n
     event = script
  >
```

Example

This example will load a bitmap onto the Web page. The path specified must be correct, or a rectangle with an X inside will be displayed instead.

```
<IMG SRC=c:\herbs.gif>
```

Inserting a bitmap onto a Web page

<INPUT> Form Tag

Purpose

Use this tag to create an assortment of input controls for forms. The TYPE attribute for the <INPUT> tag is used to denote form input controls (button, checkbox, hidden, file, image, password, radio, submit, text, and reset). The <INPUT> tag controls are inline elements and do not require a closing tag.

Syntax

```
<INPUT
ACCESSKEY=key
    ALIGN=LEFT | CENTER | RIGHT
    ALT=text
CHECKED [CI]

    CLASS=classname
    DISABLED
```

```
      DYNSRC=url
      ID=value
   ISMAP=IsMap
      LANG=language
      LANGUAGE=JAVASCRIPT | JSCRIPT | VBSCRIPT | VBS
      LOWSRC=url
      MAXLENGTH=n
      NAME=name
      READONLY
      SIZE=n
      SRC=url
      STYLE=css1-properties
      TABINDEX=n
      TITLE=text
      TYPE=BUTTON | CHECKBOX | FILE | HIDDEN | IMAGE | PASSWORD |
          RADIO | RESET | SUBMIT | TEXT
   USEMAP = uri [CT]

      VALUE=value
      event = script
   >
```

Example

The following example shows how to accept input from a Password field, a radio button, a single-line text field, and a checkbox:

```
<FORM METHOD="POST" ACTION="/cgi-bin/sendmail.asp">
  <input type="hidden" name="recipient"
value="webmaster@mymall.com"><input type="hidden" name="subject"
value="request">
<P>Name</P>
<BR><INPUT TYPE="PASSWORD" NAME="CONTROL2"> <P>Color</P>
<BR><INPUT TYPE="RADIO" NAME="CONTROL3" VALUE="0" CHECKED>Red
<INPUT TYPE="RADIO" NAME="CONTROL3" VALUE="1">Green <INPUT
TYPE="RADIO" NAME="CONTROL3" VALUE="2">Blue <P>Comments</P>
<BR><INPUT TYPE="TEXT" NAME="CONTROL4" SIZE="20,5"
MAXLENGTH="250"> <P><INPUT NAME="CONTROL5" TYPE=CHECKBOX
CHECKED>Send receipt</P> <P><INPUT TYPE="SUBMIT"
VALUE="OK"><INPUT TYPE="RESET" VALUE="Reset"></P> </FORM>
```

Name

Color

○ Red ○ Green ○ Blue

Comments

☑ Send receipt

OK Reset

Using input to accept user input

<ISINDEX>   Main Tag

Purpose

Use this tag to initiate the display of a dialog window that prompts the user
to enter a line of input. Currently, use of the <INPUT> tag (see p. 352) is rec-
ommended over that of <ISINDEX>. This tag does not require a closing tag.
This element is available in HTML as of Internet Explorer 3.0. This tag is
depreciated in version 4.01.

Syntax

```
<ISINDEX
   CLASS = classname
   ID = value
   LANG = language
   LANGUAGE = JAVASCRIPT | JSCRIPT | VBSCRIPT  | VBS
   PROMPT = text
   STYLE = css1-properties
   event  = script
TITLE = text

></ISINDEX>
```

Example

This example will replace the default prompt and the user will be prompted
to enter some text:

```
<HTML>
<HEAD>
</HEAD>
<BODY>
```

```
<ISINDEX PROMPT="Enter a line to find:">
</BODY>
</HTML>
```

Enter a line to find:

Using the Isindex prompt

<KBD> </KBD>   **Character Formatting Tag**

Purpose

Use this tag to display text in a fixed-width font. The <KBD> tag is an inline
element and requires a closing tag. This tag is available in HTML as of
Internet Explorer 3.0, and in script as of Internet Explorer 4.0.

Syntax

```
<KBD
    CLASS=classname
    ID=value
    LANG=language
    LANGUAGE=JAVASCRIPT | JSCRIPT | VBSCRIPT  | VBS
    STYLE=css1-properties
    TITLE=text
    event = script
>
```

Example

This example is similar to the examples shown in the <EM> (see p. 340),
<STRONG> (see p. 374), and <CODE> (see p. 334) tag sections in that it modifies
the font used in the text:

```
<p><KBD>This shows your text as a fixed-width font with a new
paragraph.</KBD>
```

This shows your text as a fixed-width font with a new
paragraph.

Displaying text in a fixed-width font

<LABEL> </LABEL>   Form Tag

Purpose

Use this tag to identify a label for a different element on the page. It allows you to use a control key sequence to move the focus into a specific area.

You set the FOR attribute of the <LABEL> tag equal to the ID of the control in order to bind label to another control. To submit a form, you specify a NAME on the control to which the <LABEL> tag is being bound. Use the rich text support in the label to wrap the U element around the character in the label text specified by the ACCESSKEY property. Alternatively, you can use cascading style sheets (CSS) to apply style formatting, enclose the designated character in a SPAN, and set the style to "text-decoration: underline."

If the user clicks the label, the onclick event goes to the label and then bubbles to the control specified by the htmlFor property. Pressing the access key for the label is the same as clicking the label. The <LABEL> tag is an inline element and requires a closing tag. Labels cannot be nested. This tag is available in HTML and script as of Internet Explorer 4.0.

Syntax

```
<LABEL
    ACCESSKEY=key
    CLASS=classname
    DATAFLD=colname
    DATAFORMATAS=HTML | TEXT
    DATASRC=#ID
    FOR=ID
    ID=value
    LANG=language
    LANGUAGE=JAVASCRIPT | JSCRIPT | VBSCRIPT | VBS
    STYLE=css1-properties
    TITLE=text
    event = script
>
```

Example

The following example uses a control key sequence to move the focus to the text box for entering input:

```
<LABEL FOR="oCtrlID" ACCESSKEY="1">
    #<U>1</U>: Press Alt+1 to set focus to textbox
</LABEL>
<INPUT TYPE="text" NAME="TXT1" VALUE="Type here"
        SIZE="20" TABINDEX="1" ID="oCtrlID">
```

<LEGEND> </LEGEND>   Line and Paragraphing Formatting

Purpose

Using this tag enables you to insert a caption into the <FIELDSET> box (see p. 342). It must be the first element in the <FIELDSET> tag. The <LEGEND> tag is a block element and requires a closing tag. This tag is available in HTML and script as of Internet Explorer 4.0.

Syntax

```
<LEGEND
ACCESSKEY=Key
ALIGN=BOTTOM | | LEFT | RIGHT | TOP
    CLASS=classname
    ID=value
    LANG=language
    LANGUAGE=JAVASCRIPT | JSCRIPT | VBSCRIPT | VBS
ACCESSKEY = character

    STYLE=css1-properties
    TITLE=text
    event = script
>
```

Example

See the example for the <FIELDSET> tag (see p. 342).

<LI>   List Tag

Purpose

Use this tag to code each item in a list. The TYPE attribute values disc, circle, and square apply to unordered lists; the values 1, a, A, i, and I apply to ordered lists. The <LI> tag is an inline element and does not require a closing tag. This tag is available in HTML as of Internet Explorer 3.0, and in script as of Internet Explorer 4.0.

Syntax

```
<LI
    CLASS=classname
    ID=value
    LANG=language
    LANGUAGE=JAVASCRIPT | JSCRIPT | VBSCRIPT | VBS
    STYLE=css1-properties
```

```
          TITLE=text
          TYPE=1 | a | A | i | I | DISC | CIRCLE | SQUARE
          VALUE=value
          event = script
     >
```

Example

See the example used for the <DIR> tag (see p. 337) for uses of the <LI> tag.

<LINK>   Main Tag

Purpose

Use this tag to establish an external link to other documents. This tag is used only within the <HEAD> tag (see p. 347) and does not require a closing tag. It is available in HTML as of Internet Explorer 3.0, and in script as of Internet Explorer 4.0.

Syntax

```
     <LINK
     CHARSET = charset

     DISABLED
          HREF=url
     HREFLANG = langcode
          ID=value
          MEDIA=SCREEN | PRINT | ALL
          REL=STYLESHEET
          REV=STYLESHEET
          TITLE=text
     TARGET = frame-target
     TYPE = content-type

     >
```

Example

The following example illustrates the application of the <LINK> tag to apply an external style sheet to the document:

```
<LINK REL=stylesheet
HREF="file:///c:/word/personal/cook/_themes/arcs/color0.css">
```

| <MAP> </MAP> | Image, Sound, and Other Media Tags |

Purpose

Use this tag to set up coordinates for regions inside a bitmap image. Defining the coordinates creates an image with predefined regions. The regions of the image map contain links to other documents or anchors. For example, you could create an image of the menu items containing links that the user can click to navigate to individual pages for a Web site. The MAP object is referenced with the USEMAP attribute in an <IMG> tag (see p. 351) as follows. The <MAP> tag requires a closing tag.

This tag is available in HTML as of Internet Explorer 3.0, and in script as of Internet Explorer 4.0.

Syntax

```
<MAP
      CLASS=classname
      ID=value
      LANG=language
      NAME=name
      STYLE=css1-properties
      TITLE=text
      event = script
>
```

Example

In this instance, the map coordinates are set for the home page, the news page, the feedback page, and another Web site. The x and y coordinates are given for each corner of the rectangle being defined. This outlines an area in which a mouse click will take the user to a different page. The <USEMAP> tag references the USEMAP attribute in an IMG element.

```
<map name="MYMAP">
<area href="../default.htm" shape="rect" coords="1, 108, 99,
155">
<area href="../news.htm" shape="rect" coords="0, 165, 96, 209">
<area href="../feedback.htm" shape="rect" coords="2, 214, 99,
257">
<area href="http://www.hi-tekmall.com/default.htm" coords="2,
263, 99, 318" shape="rect">
</map>
<img border="0" src="left2.jpg" usemap="#MYMAP" width="100"
height="400">
</p>
```

<MENU> </MENU>   List Tag

Purpose

Use this tag to create an unordered list of items. The <MENU> tag is a block element and requires a closing tag. It is available in HTML as of Internet Explorer 3.0, and in script as of Internet Explorer 4.0.

Syntax

```
<MENU
     CLASS=classname
     ID=value
     LANG=language
     STYLE=css1-properties
     TITLE=text
     TYPE=DISC | CIRCLE | SQUARE
     event = script
>
```

Example

This example creates a bullet-style menu with three options:

```
<MENU>
<LI>This is number one on the menu.
<LI>And this is number two.
<LI>And this is number three.
</MENU>
```

- This is number one on the menu.
- And this is number two.
- And this is number three.

Using menu to display selections

<META>   Main Tag

Purpose

Use this tag to include information about a Web site that will be accessed and processed by World Wide Web search engines. This item can be used only within the <HEAD> tag (see p. 347). The <META> tag does not require a closing tag. It is available in HTML as of Internet Explorer 3.0, and in script as of Internet Explorer 4.0.

Syntax

```
<META
     CONTENT=description
```

```
    HTTP-EQUIV=response
    NAME=text
SCHEME = cdata

    TITLE=text
>
```

Example

This <META> tag will not be displayed on the page, but will be found by search engines and categorized for keyword searches:

```
<HEAD>
<meta name="description" content="the Aardvark Company
specializes in selling birds.">
</head>
```

<NOBR> </NOBR>   Line and Paragraph Formatting

Purpose

Use this tag to display text without line breaks. The <NOBR> tag requires a closing tag. This tag is available in HTML and script as of Internet Explorer 4.0.

Syntax

```
<NOBR
    ID = value
    STYLE = css1-properties
    TITLE=text
>
```

Example

Here, the <NOBR> tag at the beginning and the </NOBR> tag at the end of the line ensure that the text between the tags will not break in the middle.

```
<NOBR>This line should not be broken . . .
So you use the NOBR tag.</NOBR>
```

This line should not be broken . . . So you use the NOBR tag.

Preventing a line from being broken into two lines

<NOFRAMES> </NOFRAMES>   Frame Tag

Purpose

Use this tag to accommodate users with browsers that do not support the <FRAMESET> tag (see p. 346). It allows a disclaimer or explanation to be displayed for users with such browsers. The <NOFRAMES> tag is a block element and requires a closing tag. This tag is available in HTML as of Internet Explorer 3.0, and in script as of Internet Explorer 4.0. In HTML Version 4.01, text was added to the description.

Syntax

```
<NOFRAMES
CLASS = cdata-list

ID = value
LANG = language-code
STYLE = style
TITLE = text

></NOFRAMES>
```

Example

This example provides the user with a message explaining why there is a problem with the display, in case the user's browser doesn't show frames:

```
<NOFRAMES>
     <p>This page uses frames, but your browser doesn't support
them.
</NOFRAMES>
```

<OBJECT> </OBJECT>
Image, Sound, and Other Media Tags

Purpose

Use this tag to place an object into the Web page. An object can appear in the <HEAD> tag (see p. 347) or the <BODY> tag (see p. 329) of a document. Possible return values generated by the DHTML object model properties on the <OBJECT> tag depend on the content of the object and how the object is implemented. For example, the readyState property returns null or error if the object does not implement a readyState property. For information about supported properties, consult the documentation for the individual object.

Events are sent directly to the <OBJECT> tag. If the embedded object returns the event, it bubbles accordingly. If the event is not returned, it does not bubble. The OBJECT event handlers also can be defined in script (see the example for this tag.)

The OBJECT element is a block element and requires a closing tag. The PARAM attribute was added in HTML 4.01 for use instead of the DATA and CLASSID attributes. This tag is available in HTML as of Internet Explorer 3.0, and in script as of Internet Explorer 4.0.

Syntax

```
<OBJECT
ACCESSKEY=key
    ALIGN=ABSBOTTOM | ABSMIDDLE | BASELINE | BOTTOM | LEFT |
        MIDDLE | RIGHT | TEXTTOP | TOP
ARCHIVE = uri-list

    CLASS=classname
    CLASSID=id
    CODE=filename
    CODEBASE=url[#version=a,b,c,d]
    CODETYPE=media-type
    DATA=url
    DATAFLD=colname
    DATASRC=#ID
  DECLARE

    HEIGHT=n
    ID=value
    LANG=language
    LANGUAGE=JAVASCRIPT | JSCRIPT | VBSCRIPT  | VBS
    NAME=name
STANDBY = text

    STYLE=css1-properties
    TABINDEX=n
    TITLE=text
    TYPE=MIME-type
USEMAP = uri

    WIDTH=n
    event = script
>
```

Example

The following example uses the <OBJECT> tag to embed the Macromedia Flash movie into a document. The codebase is referenced and the HEIGHT and WIDTH parameters are given. The plug-in is downloaded when the document is previewed in the browser (assuming that there is Internet access when the document is previewed). The codes for the preceding documents have been changed and are not valid.

```
<OBJECT classid="clsid:0000"
 codebase="http://active.macromedia.com/flash2/#version=4,0,0,0"
 ID=left WIDTH=140 HEIGHT=450>
 <PARAM NAME=movie VALUE="left.swf"> <PARAM NAME=quality
VALUE=high> <PARAM NAME=bgcolor VALUE=#FFFFFF> <EMBED
src="leftmall.swf" quality=high bgcolor=#FFFFFF  WIDTH=140
HEIGHT=450 TYPE="application/x-shockwave-flash"
PLUGINSPAGE="http://www.macromedia.com/shockwave/download/index.
cgi?P1_Prod_Version=ShockwaveFlash"></EMBED>
</OBJECT>
```

<OL> </OL>   List Tag

Purpose

Use this tag to draw lines of text as a numbered list. You set the list type for all subsequent lists using the TYPE attribute. The <OL> tag is a block element and requires a closing tag. This tag is available in HTML as of Internet Explorer 3.0, and in script as of Internet Explorer 4.0.

Syntax

```
<OL
CLASS=classname
    ID=value
    LANG=language
    LANGUAGE=JAVASCRIPT | JSCRIPT | VBSCRIPT  | VBS
    START=n
    STYLE=css1-properties
    TITLE=text
    TYPE=1 | a | A | i | I
    event = script
>
```

Example

Here, the <OL> tag numbers each line of text according to the order in which the lines appear. The <LI> tag (see p. 357) delineates the lines.

```
<OL> <LI>This is the first item in the list. <LI>And this is the
second item in the list. </OL>
```

> 1. This is the first item in the list.
> 2. And this is the second item in the list.

Making a numbered list

| **<OPTION>** | Form Tag |

Purpose

Use this tag to represent an option in a <SELECT> tag (see p. 371). This will appear as a drop down list. Except for background color and color, style settings applied through the style object for the <OPTION> tag are ignored. In addition, style settings applied directly to individual options override those applied to the containing <SELECT> tag as a whole. The <OPTION> tag does not require a closing tag. This tag is available in HTML and script as of Internet Explorer 3.0.

Syntax

```
<OPTION
CLASS=classname
DISABLED
    ID=value
LANG =language-code

    LANGUAGE=JAVASCRIPT | JSCRIPT | VBSCRIPT | VBS
    SELECTED
STYLE = style
TITLE = text

    VALUE=value
    event = script
>
```

Example

Here the options are ranges of numbers in categories of home sizes, measured in square feet:

```
<H4>How many square feet do you want?
<SELECT NAME="Square_Feet">
<OPTION VALUE="Select below"><FONT SIZE=+0>Select below
<OPTION VALUE="Less than 1600">Less than 1600
<OPTION VALUE="1600 - 2000">1600 - 2000
<OPTION VALUE="2000 - 2500">2000 - 2500
<OPTION VALUE="2500 - 3000">2500 - 3000
<OPTION VALUE="More than 3000">More than 3000
</FONT></SELECT></H4>
```

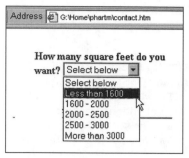

Setting up a drop-down list

<P> | **Line and Paragraph Formatting**

Purpose

Use this tag to act as if the Enter key were pressed and creates a paragraph from the <P> tag in the HTML code. The <P> tag is a block element and does not require a closing tag. This tag is available in HTML as of Internet Explorer 3.0, and in script as of Internet Explorer 4.0.

Syntax

```
<P
ALIGN=CENTER | LEFT | RIGHT | JUSTIFY
    CLASS=classname
    ID=value
    LANG=language
    LANGUAGE=JAVASCRIPT | JSCRIPT | VBSCRIPT  | VBS
    STYLE=css1-properties
    TITLE=text
    event = script
>
```

Example

The <P> tag used here will drop the text down one line as if the Enter key is pressed:

```
<BODY>
<p><font face="Arial" size="3">You describe your needs, and give
us your ideas for a Web
Page.</font>
</BODY>
```

You describe your needs and give us your ideas for a Web page.

Beginning a new paragraph

<PARAM>   Image, Sound, and Other Media Tags

Purpose

Use this tag to determine the property value for a specific object. The <PARAM> tag is valid within the <APPLET> (see p. 322), <EMBED> (see p. 341), and <OBJECT> (see p. 362) tags. The <PARAM> tag does not require a closing tag. This tag is available in HTML as of Internet Explorer 3.0.

Syntax

```
<PARAM
DATAFLD=colname
    DATAFORMATAS=HTML | TEXT
    DATASRC=#ID
ID=name

    NAME=name
    VALUE=value
VALUETYPE = data|ref|object

>
```

Example

See the example for the <APPLET> tag (see p. 322) for the uses of <PARAM>.

<PRE> </PRE>   Character Formatting

Purpose

Use this tag to display text in a preformatted fixed-width font. Text within the <PRE> tag is formatted. Spaces and carriage returns are preserved. The <PRE> tagt is a block element and requires a closing tag. This tag is available in HTML as of Internet Explorer 3.0, and in script as of Internet Explorer 4.0.

Syntax

```
<PRE
CLASS=classname
    ID=value
    LANG=language
    LANGUAGE=JAVASCRIPT | JSCRIPT | VBSCRIPT | VBS
    STYLE=css1-properties
    TITLE=text
    event = script
>
```

Example

This example shows how to preserve the formatting of your text exactly as you wish, without regard for reformatting concerns that usually come into play in HTML:

```
<PRE>
You can Format your
            text just
                    as
                    you
              like
            it.
</PRE>
```

```
You can Format your
            text just
                    as
                    you
              like
            it.
```

Preformatting text as typed in HTML

<RT>   Character Formatting Tag

Purpose

Use this tag to assign the ruby text for the <RUBY> tag (see p. 369). The string of text annotated with a ruby is referred to as the *base*. The ruby text specified by the <RT> tag is positioned above or inline with the rubyPosition property. Browsers that do not support the <RT> tag render the ruby text inline with the base text. The <RT> tag is an inline element and does not require a closing tag. This tag is available in HTML and script as of Internet Explorer 5.0

Syntax

```
<RT
      CLASS=classname
      DIR=LTR | RTL
      ID=value
      LANG=language
      LANGUAGE=JAVASCRIPT | JSCRIPT | VBSCRIPT | VBS
      NAME=name
      STYLE=css1-properties
      TITLE=text
      event = script
>
```

Example

Please refer to the example for <RUBY tag (see p. 369).

<RUBY> </RUBY>   **Character Formatting Tag**

Purpose

Use this tag to identify a notation or pronunciation guide to be placed above or inline with a string of text, which is referred to as the *base*. The only object allowed within the <RUBY> tag is the ruby text object (<RT> tag (see p. 368). Any wording outside the < RT> tag is understood to be a part of the base. The <RUBY> tag is an inline element and requires a closing tag. This tag is available in HTML and script as of Internet Explorer 5.0.

Syntax

```
<RUBY
    CLASS=classname
    DIR=LTR | RTL
    ID=value
    LANG=language
    LANGUAGE=JAVASCRIPT | JSCRIPT | VBSCRIPT | VBS
    NAME=name
    STYLE=css1-properties
    TITLE=text
    event = script
>
```

Example

This example shows that the <RUBY> tag displays ruby text above the base text:

```
<RUBY>
    This is the Base Text
    <RT>Now you see the Ruby Text
</RUBY>
```

Now you see the Ruby Text
This is the Base Text

Using ruby text

<SAMP> </SAMP>	Character Formatting Tag

Purpose

Use this tag to specify a code sample. The <SAMP> tag is an inline element and requires a closing tag. This tag is available in HTML as of Internet Explorer 3.0, and in script as of Internet Explorer 4.0.

Syntax

```
<SAMP
CLASS=classname
    ID=value
    LANG=language
    LANGUAGE=JAVASCRIPT | JSCRIPT | VBSCRIPT  | VBS
    STYLE=css1-properties
    TITLE=text
    event = script
>
```

Example

This example displays the message in the fixed-width font format:

```
<SAMP>This shows text in a small fixed-width font.</SAMP>
```

```
This shows text in a small fixed-width font.
```

Using SAMP to create fixed-width text

<SCRIPT> </SCRIPT>	Image, Sound, and Other Media Tags

Purpose

Use this tag to identify a script that needs to be interpreted by a script engine. Code within the SCRIPT block that is not contained within a function is executed immediately as the page is loaded. To keep scripts from being displayed on down-level browsers, nest the SCRIPT block within a COMMENT block. Script appearing after a <FRAMESET> tag is ignored. The <SCRIPT> tag is a block element and requires a closing tag. This tag is available in HTML as of Internet Explorer 3.0, and in script as of Internet Explorer 4.0.

Syntax

```
<SCRIPT
CHARSET = charset

DEFER
    LANGUAGE=JAVASCRIPT | JSCRIPT | VBSCRIPT  | VBS | XML
```

```
    SRC=url
    TITLE=text
    TYPE=MIME-type
>
```

Example

The following example indicates that a block of JavaScript code follows in the block. This script acts to clear frames from other Web sites so that this document will not be displayed inside another document's frame.

```
<SCRIPT language="JavaScript">
<!-- hide
//Clear inherited frames
if (top.frames.length!=0)
    top.location=self.document.location;
// unhide -->
</SCRIPT>
```

<SELECT> </SELECT>   Form Tag

Purpose

Use this tag to provide a way for the user to select from a list box or drop-down list. The <SELECT> tag is an inline element and requires a closing tag. This tag is available in HTML and script as of Internet Explorer 3.0.

Syntax

```
<SELECT
ACCESSKEY=key
    ALIGN=ABSBOTTOM | ABSMIDDLE | BASELINE | BOTTOM | LEFT
|
        MIDDLE | RIGHT | TEXTTOP | TOP
    CLASS=classname
    DATAFLD=colname
    DATASRC=#ID
    DISABLED
    ID=value
    LANG=language
    LANGUAGE=JAVASCRIPT | JSCRIPT | VBSCRIPT | VBS
    MULTIPLE
    NAME=name
    SIZE=n
    STYLE=css1-properties
    TABINDEX=n
    event = script
>
```

Example

Here, the user sees a box with an arrow on the right side. The option Rottweiler is shown as selected. When the user clicks on the arrow, the other options can be viewed.

```
<SELECT NAME="Dogs" SIZE="1">
<OPTION VALUE="1">Poodle
<OPTION VALUE="2">Labrador retriever
<OPTION VALUE="3" SELECTED>Rottweiler
</SELECT>
```

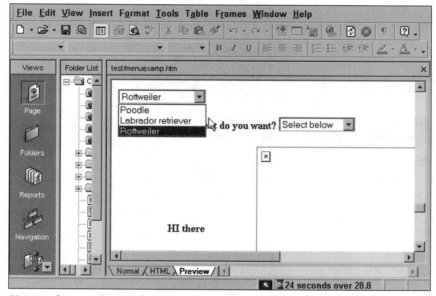

Using select to show a default option

<SMALL> </SMALL>   Character Formatting Tag

Purpose

Use this tag to show the enclosed text in a smaller font. The <SMALL> tag is an inline element and requires a closing tag. This tag is available in HTML as of Internet Explorer 3.0, and in script as of Internet Explorer 4.0.

Syntax

```
<SMALL
CLASS=classname
    ID=value
    LANG=language
```

```
LANGUAGE=JAVASCRIPT | JSCRIPT | VBSCRIPT | VBS
STYLE=css1-properties
TITLE=text
event = script
>
```

Example

The first example uses only the <SMALL> tag to show that the SMALL text is smaller than the rest of the text, which is displayed as normal size. The second line uses the < SMALL> in combination with the <BIG> tag (see. p. 327) to create a greater contrast in size.

```
<SMALL>Using the SMALL tag, this text is smaller</SMALL> than the
rest of the text on this line.
<SMALL>Using the SMALL tag, this text small</SMALL> <BIG>Wow!
this text is big.<BIG/>
```

> Using the SMALL tag, this text is smaller than the rest of the text on this line.
> Using the SMALL tag, this text small Wow! this text is big.

Changing sizes in text

<SPAN> </SPAN>   Line and Paragraph Formatting Tag

Purpose

Use this tag to identify an inline text container. This tag is especially useful for applying cascading style sheets (CSS) styles. The <SPAN> tag is an inline element and requires a closing tag. This tag is available in HTML as of Internet Explorer 3.0, and in script as of Internet Explorer 4.0.

Syntax

```
<SPAN
CLASS=classname
    DATAFLD=colname
    DATAFORMATAS=HTML | TEXT
    DATASRC=#ID
    ID=value
    LANG=language
    LANGUAGE=JAVASCRIPT | JSCRIPT | VBSCRIPT | VBS
    STYLE=css1-properties
    TITLE=text
    event = script
>
```

Example

The following line of code temporarily changes the base color. In this case, it's just for one word.

```
<P>This line contains one <SPAN STYLE="color: gray">gray</SPAN>
word.
```

This line contains one gray word.

Changing text within the line

<STRIKE> </STRIKE>   Character Formatting Tag

Purpose

Use this tag to convert text to strikethrough type. The <STRIKE> tag is an inline element and requires a closing tag. This tag is available in HTML as of Internet Explorer 3.0, and in script as of Internet Explorer 4.0.

Syntax

```
<STRIKE
CLASS=classname
    ID=value
    LANG=language
    LANGUAGE=JAVASCRIPT | JSCRIPT | VBSCRIPT  | VBS
    STYLE=css1-properties
    TITLE=text
    event = script
>
```

Example

This shows how the <STRIKE> tag is used to change text to strikethrough:

```
<STRIKE>This text is converted to Strikethrough.</STRIKE>
```

~~This text is converted to strikethrough.~~

Producing strikethrough text

<STRONG> </STRONG>   Character Formatting Tag

Purpose

Use this to present text as bold. The <STRONG> tag is an inline element and requires a closing tag. This tag is available in HTML as of Internet Explorer 3.0, and in script as of Internet Explorer 4.0.

Syntax

```
<STRONG
CLASS=classname
    ID=value
    LANG=language
    LANGUAGE=JAVASCRIPT | JSCRIPT | VBSCRIPT  | VBS
    STYLE=css1-properties
    TITLE=text
    event = script
>
```

Example

This example shows how to use this tag to bold (see the <B> tag on p. 324) any text in your document:

```
<STRONG>You can BOLD this text using the STRONG tag. <STRONG/>
```

You can BOLD this text using the STRONG tag.

Using STRONG to bold text

Character Formatting Tag

Purpose

Use this tag to display text as subscript by using a font smaller than the default in the rest of the document. The <SUB> tag is an inline element and requires a closing tag. This tag is available in HTML as of Internet Explorer 3.0, and in script as of Internet Explorer 4.0.

Syntax

```
<SUB
CLASS=classname
    ID=value
    LANG=language
    LANGUAGE=JAVASCRIPT | JSCRIPT | VBSCRIPT  | VBS
    STYLE=css1-properties
    TITLE=text
    event = script
>
```

Example

When previewed, the following code will display the numbers 1 and 2 as subscripts, so that this looks like two different references being noted:

```
(REF<SUB>1</SUB>,REF<SUB>2</SUB>)
```

$$(REF_1, REF_2)$$

Using a subscript with text

Purpose

Use this tag to display the enclosed text as superscript, using a font smaller than the default in the rest of the document. The <SUP> tag is an inline element and requires a closing tag. This tag is available in HTML as of Internet Explorer 3.0, and in script as of Internet Explorer 4.0.

Syntax

```
<SUP
CLASS=classname
    ID=value
    LANG=language
    LANGUAGE=JAVASCRIPT | JSCRIPT | VBSCRIPT | VBS
    STYLE=css1-properties
    TITLE=text
    event = script
>
```

Example

This example uses the zero as a stand-in for the degree symbol, just to demonstrate the superscript function:

```
<P>(212<SUP>0</SUP>F. and 250<SUP>0</SUP>F.)
```

$$(212^0F. \text{ and } 250^0F.)$$

Creating a superscript display

Purpose

Use this tag to organize content into a table format with rows and columns. The following tags are valid within a table: <CAPTION> (see p. 332), <COL> (see p. 335), <COLGROUP> (see p. 336), <TBODY> (see p. 378), <TD> (see p. 379), <TH> (see p. 381), <THEAD> (see p. 383), and <TR> (see p. 384). The TABLE object model is read-only for data-bound tables. For example, script used to remove a table row works correctly on an unbound table, but not on a data-bound table. The properties of a table object are still available, but changes to the bound data in a table must be made to the data source.

The properties of a table are distinct from the properties of cells contained within the table. For example, the offsetLeft property of a multicolumn table is not the same as the offsetLeft property of the leftmost cell in the table. Refer to the appropriate object when writing scripts involving table and/or cell objects. The <TABLE> tag is a block element and requires a closing tag. This tag is available in HTML as of Internet Explorer 3.0, and in script as of Internet Explorer 4.0.

Syntax

```
<TABLE
ALIGN=CENTER | LEFT | RIGHT
    BACKGROUND=url
    BGCOLOR=color
    BORDER=n
    BORDERCOLOR=color
    BORDERCOLORDARK=color
    BORDERCOLORLIGHT=color
    CELLPADDING=n
    CELLSPACING=n
    CLASS=classname
    COLS=n
    DATAPAGESIZE=n
    DATASRC=#ID
    FRAME=ABOVE | BELOW | BORDER | BOX | INSIDES | LHS | RHS |
        VOID | VSIDES
    HEIGHT=n
    ID=value
    LANG=language
    LANGUAGE=JAVASCRIPT | JSCRIPT | VBSCRIPT | VBS
    RULES=ALL | COLS | GROUPS | NONE | ROWS
SUMMARY = text

    STYLE=css1-properties
    TITLE=text
    WIDTH=n
    event = script
>
```

Example

Tables are often used to organize images on a page. In this example, four pictures are to be displayed in two rows and two columns. Some of the pictures have captions placed below the pictures.

```
<TABLEBORDER="0" CELLSPACING="2" CELLPADDING="2" ALIGN="DEFAULT"
WIDTH="100%">
```

```
   <TR>
     <td ALIGN="LEFT" VALIGN="TOP"><h4><img border="0"
src="flo2.gif" width="275" height="231"></h4>
     </TD>
     <td ALIGN="LEFT" VALIGN="TOP"><h5><img border="0"
src="4genz2.jpg" width="300" height="188"><br>
        Circa 1998.</h5>
     </TD>
   </TR>
   <TR>
     <td ALIGN="LEFT" VALIGN="TOP">
       <h5><br>
       <img border="0" src="3gens2.jpg" width="206"
height="250"><br>
        Circa 1979.</h5>
     </TD>
     <td ALIGN="LEFT" VALIGN="TOP"><h5><img border="0"
src="kbd6.jpg" width="250" height="205"><br>
        Circa 1997</h5>
     </TD>
   </TR>
</TABLE>
```

Creating a table to hold pictures

<TBODY> </TBODY>   Table Tag

Purpose

Use this tag to identify rows in the body of the table. Allowable tags within the <TBODY> tag include: <TD> (see p. 379), <TH> (see p. 381), and <TR> (see p. 384), and <THEAD> (see p. 383). This tag is available for all tables, even if the

HTML Reference

table does not designate a <TBODY> tag. The TBODY tag is a block element and requires a closing tag. This tag is available in HTML as of Internet Explorer 3.0, and in script as of Internet Explorer 4.0.

```
<TBODY
ALIGN=CENTER | LEFT | RIGHT|JUSTIFY|CHAR
     BGCOLOR=color
CHAR = character
CHAROFF = length


     CLASS=classname
     ID=value
     LANG=language
     LANGUAGE=JAVASCRIPT | JSCRIPT | VBSCRIPT  | VBS
     STYLE=css1-properties
     TITLE=text
VALIGN= TOP| MIDDLE| BOTTOM | BASELINE | |


     event = script
>
```

Example

See the example shown for the <THEAD> tag (p. 383).

<TD> </TD>
Table Tag

Purpose

Use this tag to refer to a cell inside a table. The <TD> tag is a block element and requires a closing tag. This tag is available in HTML as of Internet Explorer 3.0, and in script as of Internet Explorer 4.0.

Syntax

```
<TD
ALIGN= LEFT | CENTER | RIGHT |JUSTIFY |CHAR
     BACKGROUND=url
     BGCOLOR=color
     BORDERCOLOR=color
     BORDERCOLORDARK=color
     BORDERCOLORLIGHT=color
CHAR=Character
CHARSET=Length
     CLASS=classname
     COLSPAN=n
     HEIGHT=height
```

```
     ID=value
     LANG=language
     LANGUAGE=JAVASCRIPT | JSCRIPT | VBSCRIPT | VBS
     NOWRAP
     ROWSPAN=n
     STYLE=css1-properties
     TITLE=text
 VALIGN=BASELINE | BOTTOM | MIDDLE | TOP
     WIDTH=width
 event = script
 >
```

Example

In this example, taken from the example for <TABLE> (see p. 376), the <TD> tag is used to align the picture in the cell. In this case, it is aligned to the left and top.

```
<TR>
    <td ALIGN="LEFT" VALIGN="TOP">
      <h5><br>
      <img border="0" src="3gens2.jpg" width="206"
height="250"><br>
      Circa 1979.</h5>
    </TD>
```

<TEXTAREA> </TEXTAREA>   Form Tag

Purpose

Use this tag to define a multi-line text input control. It is much like the < INPUT> tag (see p.352), but allows a scrolling box for input. The default font is fixed pitch. The <TEXTAREA> tag is an inline element and requires a closing tag. This tag is available in HTML and script as of Internet Explorer 3.0.

Syntax

```
<TEXTAREA
    ACCESSKEY=key

    CLASS=classname
    COLS=n
    DATAFLD=colname
    DATASRC=#ID
    DISABLED
    ID=value
    LANG=language
```

```
LANGUAGE=JAVASCRIPT | JSCRIPT | VBSCRIPT  | VBS
NAME=name
READONLY
ROWS=n
STYLE=css1-properties
TABINDEX=n
TITLE=text
WRAP=OFF | HARD | SOFT
event = script
>
```

Example

In this example, the <TEXTAREA> size is specified using the Rows and Cols attributes:

```
<textarea name="Message" rows="8" cols="52"></textarea></p>
  <p>Email :
<input type="text" name="email" size="40"></p>
  <p>Phone:
<input type="text" name="phone" size="12"></p>
  <p><input type="submit" value="Submit ">
<input type="reset" value="Clear "><br>
  <br>
```

Specifying a text area for data input

<TH> </TH>   Table Tag

Purpose

Use this tag to identify a header column. The header columns are bold and centered within cells. The <TH> tag is a block element and requires a closing tag. This tag is available in HTML as of Internet Explorer 3.0, and in script as of Internet Explorer 4.0.

Syntax

```
<TH
ALIGN=CENTER | LEFT | RIGHT|JUSTIFY|CHAR
    BACKGROUND=url
    BGCOLOR=color
```

```
      BORDERCOLOR=color
      BORDERCOLORDARK=color
      BORDERCOLORLIGHT=color
   CHAR=Character
   CHARSET=Length

      CLASS=classname
      COLSPAN=n
      HEIGHT=height
      ID=value
      LANG=language
      LANGUAGE=JAVASCRIPT | JSCRIPT | VBSCRIPT  | VBS
      NOWRAP
      ROWSPAN=n
      STYLE=css1-properties
      TITLE=text
   VALIGN=BASELINE | BOTTOM | MIDDLE | TOP
      WIDTH=width
      event = script
   >
```

Example

In this example, the text for header column TH is displayed in the center of the cell. Add this code to the table used in the example for the <TABLE> tag (see p. 376).

```
<TR>
  <th>HI there</th>
    <td ALIGN="LEFT" VALIGN="TOP"><h4><img border="0"
src="flo2.gif" width="275" height="231"></h4>
    </TD>
```

Creating header columns for tables

<THEAD> </THEAD>   Table Tag

HTML Reference

Purpose

Use this tag to assign rows for the body of the table. This element is exposed for all tables, even if the table does not explicitly define a <TBODY> tag. Valid tags within the <TBODY> tag include <TD> (see p. 379), <TH> (see p. 381), and <TR> (see p. 384) .

The <THEAD> tag is a block element and requires a closing tag. This tag is available in HTML as of Internet Explorer 3.0, and in script as of Internet Explorer 4.0.

Syntax

```
<THEAD
ALIGN=CENTER | LEFT | RIGHT|JUSTIFY|CHAR
    BGCOLOR=color
CHAR=Character
  CHAROFF=Length

    CLASS=classname
    ID=value
    LANG=language
    LANGUAGE=JAVASCRIPT | JSCRIPT | VBSCRIPT | VBS
    STYLE=css1-properties
    TITLE=text
VALIGN=BASELINE | BOTTOM | MIDDLE | TOP
    event = script
>
```

Example

In this example, there is a HEAD and BODY to the table. The <THEAD> tag is designated here as distinguished from the <TBODY> tag (see p. 378).

```
<TABLE>
<THEAD>
<TR>
<TD>
Place THEAD text here.
</TD>
</TR>
</THEAD>
<TBODY>
<TR>
<TD>
Place TBODY text here.
```

```
</TD>
</TR>
</TBODY>
</TABLE>
```

```
Place THEAD text here.
Place TBODY text here.
```

Creating Head and body elements in a table

<TITLE> </TITLE>   Header and Title Tag

Purpose

Use this tag to denote the title of a document. This tag can be used only within the < HEAD> tag (see p. 347). Any text between the opening and closing <TITLE> tags is displayed in the browser title bar and in the Microsoft Windows taskbar. In HTML applications, by contrast, only the specified title appears. The <TITLE> tag is a block element and requires a closing tag. This tag is available in HTML as of Internet Explorer 3.0, and in script as of Internet Explorer 4.0.

Syntax

```
<TITLE
ID=value
LANG = language-code

    TITLE=string
>
```

Example

This example shows how the title is placed between the <TITLE> tags:

```
<TITLE>web page design and web hosting</TITLE>
```

<TR> </TR>   Table Tag

Purpose

Use this tag to identify a row in a table. The <TD> tag (see p. 379) and <TH> tag (see p. 381) are valid within a row. The <TR> tag does not explicitly support the HEIGHT attribute. To change the HTML in the <TR> tag, use the table object model. For example, use the rowIndex property or the rows collection to retrieve a reference to a specific table row. The insertRow and deleteRow methods add or delete rows. To find a reference to a specific cell, use the cellIndex property or the cells collection. You can add or delete rows using the insertCell and deleteCell methods. To change the content of a particular cell, use the innerHTML or innerText property. The <TR> tag is a block element and requires a closing tag. This tag is available in HTML as of Internet Explorer 3.0, and in script as of Internet Explorer 4.0.

Syntax

```
<TR
ALIGN=CENTER | LEFT | RIGHT|JUSTIFY|CHAR
    BGCOLOR=color
    BORDERCOLOR=color
    BORDERCOLORDARK=color
    BORDERCOLORLIGHT=color
CHAR=Character
CHAROFF=Length
    CLASS=classname
    HEIGHT=height
    ID=value
    LANG=language
    LANGUAGE=JAVASCRIPT | JSCRIPT | VBSCRIPT | VBS
    STYLE=css1-properties
    TITLE=text
VALIGN=BASELINE | BOTTOM | MIDDLE | TOP
    WIDTH=width
    event = script
>
```

Example

In this instance, the Number one row will appear within the boundaries of the first row, and the words Number two row will be in the second row:

```
<TABLE>
<TR>
<TD>Number one row.</TD>
</TR>
<TR>
<TD>Number two row.</TD>
</TR>
</TABLE>
```

Placing text in table cells based upon row position

HTML Reference

<TT> </TT>   Line and Paragraph Formatting Tag

Purpose

Use the TT tag to display text in a fixed-width font. This is an inline element and requires a closing tag. This tag is available in HTML as of Internet Explorer 3.0, and in script as of Internet Explorer 4.0.

Syntax

```
<TT
CLASS=classname
    ID=value
    LANG=language
    LANGUAGE=JAVASCRIPT | JSCRIPT | VBSCRIPT  | VBS
    STYLE=css1-properties
    TITLE=text
    event = script
>
```

Example

This tag is very similar to <SAMP> (see p. 370) or <KBD> (see p. 355),as it formats text in a fixed width:

```
<TT>This is an example of plain text.</TT>
```

> This is an example of plain text.

Setting text in Fixed Width Font

<U> </U>   Character Formatting Tag

Purpose

Use this tag to underline text. The <U> tag is an inline element and requires a closing tag. This tag is available in HTML as of Internet Explorer 3.0, and in script as of Internet Explorer 4.0.

```
<U
CLASS=classname
    ID=value
    LANG=language
    LANGUAGE=JAVASCRIPT | JSCRIPT | VBSCRIPT  | VBS
    STYLE=css1-properties
    TITLE=text
    event = script
>
```

Example

Use the <U> tag to surround the text you want underlined:

```
<U>Let's see how we can underline this text.</U>
```

Let's see how we can underline this
text.

Underlining text

<UL> </UL>

Purpose

Use this tag to display lines of text as a bulleted list. The TYPE attribute sets the list type for all subsequent lists unless a different type value is set. The <UL> tag is a block element and requires a closing tag. This tag is available in HTML as of Internet Explorer 3.0, and in script as of Internet Explorer 4.0.

Syntax

```
<UL
CLASS=classname
    ID=value
    LANG=language
    LANGUAGE=JAVASCRIPT | JSCRIPT | VBSCRIPT | VBS
    STYLE=css1-properties
    TITLE=text
    TYPE=DISC | CIRCLE | SQUARE
    event = script
>
```

Example

The <UL> tag example for the <OL> tag (see p. 364) is similar in the sense that they both format lists. The <UL> tag displays the list prefaced by a bullet, rather than numbering it.

```
<UL> <LI>This is first in the list. <LI>And this is second in the
list. <LI>Guess what? This is third.</UL>
```

- This is first in the list.
- And this is second in the list.
- Guess what? This is the third.

Formatting a bulleted list with UL

<VAR> </VAR>   Character Formatting Tag

Purpose

Use this tag to represent text in a small fixed-width font. The <VAR> tag is an inline element and requires a closing tag. This tag is available in HTML as of Internet Explorer 3.0, and in script as of Internet Explorer 4.0.

Syntax

```
<VAR
CLASS=classname
    ID=value
    LANG=language
    LANGUAGE=JAVASCRIPT | JSCRIPT | VBSCRIPT | VBS
    STYLE=css1-properties
    TITLE=text
    event = script
>
```

Example

Here, only the text you want emphasized or set apart is shown in a different font. Compare <VAR> with the <EM> tag (see p. 340).

```
<p>Type your <VAR>Response</VAR> in the box.
```

Type your *Response* in the box.

Changing inline text

<WBR>   Line and Paragraph Formatting Tag

Purpose

Use this tag to introduce a soft line break into a block of NOBR text (see p. 361). The <WBR> tag does not require a closing tag. This tag is available in HTML as of Internet Explorer 3.0, and in script as of Internet Explorer 4.0.

Syntax

```
<WBR
    ID=value
>
```

Example

In this example, the line will break if the user makes the window smaller by clicking and dragging the window border, or if some action (such as using a search engine) causes the window housing the text to shrink in width:

```
<NOBR>This line though,<WBR> will break after the word "though,"
when the window shrinks enough.</NOBR>
```

> **This line though,**
> **will break after the word "though," when the window shrink**

Creating a soft line break

Character Sets

Purpose

The bytes that represent the contents of your HTML document are translated to readable characters by *character sets*. Browsers such as Microsoft Internet Explorer or Netscape Navigator interpret the characters in your document according to the applied character set translations. They interpret numeric or hex character references ("〹" or "ሴ") as ISO10646 code points, consistent with the Unicode standard, Version 2.0. They are independent of the chosen character set. Named entities such as the ampersand are displayed independently of the chosen character set. In order to display a random numeric character, a font that is consistent with the specific character must exist on the system in question. Because some systems may not contain the essential fonts, the content display may not be consistent on all systems.

Character sets supported by HTML are as follows:

- ISO Latin-1
- Additional Named Entities for HTML
- Character Entities for Special Symbols and BIDI Text
- Character Set Recognition

ISO Latin-1 Character Set

Table 1 shows some examples of characters in the ISO Latin-1 character set. This character set corresponds to the first 256 entries of the Unicode character collection in Internet Explorer 4.0 and later. The table includes the characters, the decimal codes, the HTML named entity reference, and a brief description.

Table 1 *HTML Character Codes for ISO Latin-1*

Character	Decimal Code	HTML Named Entity	Description
___	&#13;	___	Carriage Return
A	&#65;	___	Capital A
B	&#66;	___	Capital B
1/4	&#188;	&frac14;	Fraction one-fourth
1/2	&#189;	&frac12;	Fraction one-half

VBScript by Category

The following table helps you locate the page number of the most common VBScript keywords in the VBScript Reference section. The keywords are grouped into the following categories:

- Function
- Statement
- Operator
- Constant
- Object
- Method
- Date/Time Function
- Literal
- Property

Keyword	Category	Page Number in the VBScript Reference Section
Abs	Function	400
Addition	Operator	400
And	Operator	401
Array	Function	401
Class	Statement	404
Class	Object	404
Clear	Method	405
Color	Function	406
Concatenation	Operator	406
Const	Statement	407
CreateObject	Function	407
Date Format	Constant	408
DateSerial	Date/Time Function	411
DateValue	Date/Time Function	412
Dictionary	Object	413
Dim	Statement	413
Division	Operator	414
Do...Loop	Statement	414
Erase	Statement	415
Err	Object	415
Eval	Function	416
Exit	Statement	417
FileSystemObject	Object	418
Filter	Function	419
For Each...Next	Statement	419
For...Next	Statement	420
FormatCurrency	Function	421

VBScript by Category

Keyword	Category	Page Number in the VBScript Reference Section
FormatDateTime	Function	421
FormatNumber	Function	422
FormatPercent	Function	423
Function	Statement	423
GetObject	Function	424
Hex	Function	424
Hour	Date/Time Function	425
If...Then...Else	Statement	425
InputBox	Function	426
InStr,	Function	427
Int	Function	427
Is	Operator	428
IsArray	Function	428
IsEmpty	Function	429
IsNull	Function	430
IsNumeric	Function	430
IsObject	Function	431
Join	Function	431
Lbound	Function	432
Lcase, UCase	Function	432
Left	Function	433
Len	Function	433
LoadPicture	Function	434
Log	Function	434
Mid	Function	435

Continued

Keyword	Category	Page Number in the VBScript Reference Section
Modulus arithmetic	Operator	436
MonthName	Function	436
MsgBox	Function	437
Not	Operator	438
Nothing	Literal	438
Number	Property	439
On Error	Statement	439
Option Explicit	Statement	440
Or, Xor	Operator	441
Private	Statement	441
Public	Statement	442
Raise	Method	442
Randomize	Function	443
ReDim	Statement	444
Replace	Function	444
RGB	Function	445
Right	Function	445
Rnd	Function	446
Round	Function	446
ScriptEngine	Function	447
Select Case	Statement	448
Set	Statement	449
Sgn	Function	449
Sin	Function	450
Space	Function	450
Sqr	Function	451
StrComp	Function	451
String	Function	452
StrReverse	Function	452
Sub	Statement	453

Keyword	Category	Page Number in the VBScript Reference Section
Subtraction	Operator	453
Tan	Function	454
TimeSerial	Function	454
TimeValue	Function	455
Trim	Function	455
UBound	Function	456
VarType	Function	457
WeekDay	Function	457
WeekdayName	Function	458
While...Wend	Statement	458
Year	Function	459

VBScript Reference

A fairly new addition to the Visual Basic programming languages, Microsoft Visual Basic Scripting Edition (VBScript) is an elementary form of Visual Basic that enables you to integrate VBScript commands with HTML documents. VBScript is interpreted and executed along with the HTML commands.

VBScript takes active scripting to different environments, including Web client scripting in Microsoft Internet Explorer and Web server scripting in Microsoft Internet Information Server. Most browsers do not support it. Netscape, for example, is compatible only with a plug-in. Currently, only Internet Explorer supports VBScript. VBScript provides ways for developers to link and automate many types of objects in Web sites. Generally, Active Server Pages are constructed using VBScript. But VBScript is server-side scripting, rather than client-side.

Constants are built into VBScript. They provide an expedient means to reference particular values without knowing the actual value. Because the constants are defined within VBScript, you can use them without using declarations up front. For example, you use the keyword for a color constant, rather than entering the hex or decimal value, for the color you want to use as a background or font color.

This section does not contain a complete reference for VBScript. It provides definitions, syntax, and examples of many of the keywords commonly used.

Abs — Array Handling Function

Purpose

Use this function to return the absolute value of a number.

Syntax

```
Abs(number)
```

This argument is a numeric expression. The value returned will be exactly the same as that entered in the expression, unless the number entered is negative. If the number is negative, it will be returned unsigned.

Example

In this example, the data returned will be a whole number whether or not the original value was negative or positive:

```
Dim MyExample
MyExample = Abs(10.5)   ' Returns10.5. It is 10.5.
MyExample = Abs(-10.5) ' Returns 10.5.
```

Returning an absolute number with Abs

Addition(+) — Operator

Purpose

Sums two numbers. This operator's (+) syntax consists of an expression + expression = a sum. Strings can be concatenated using the addition operator, but the & operator is preferred for concatenation because of its better documentation.

Syntax

```
One expression + one expression = Result
```

Example

This example shows how to sum two numbers:

```
1 + 1 = 2
```

And   Operator

Purpose

Use this operator to perform a logical conjunction with two expressions. The result is True only if both expressions evaluate to True. The result is False if either expression evaluates to False.

Syntax

```
One expression And One expression = result
```

Example

In this example, the result will be 2:

```
B = 2
C = 3
A = B and C
```

Array   Array Handling Function

Purpose

Use this function to return a variant that contains an array.

Syntax

```
Array(elementlist)
```

The elementlist argument is a list of values delimited by commas. Each of the values in the list is designated as an element in an array contained in the variant type. Typically, the first element is zero.

Example

In this example, the first statement sets the value of the ThisY2k array to month abbreviations. The value of the second element in the array (ThisY2k (2)) is "Mar," as the array begins with zero.

```
<%
Dim AArray(3), AString
AArray(0) = "Ms."
AArray(1) = "Sasha "
AArray(2) = "Von "
```

VBScript Reference

```
AArray(3) = "Angel"
AString = Join(AArray)
Response.Write "aarray = " & AString
%>

Dim Mymonth, ThisY2k
ThisY2k = Array("Jan", "Feb", "Mar", "Apr", "May",
 "Jun", "Jul", "Aug", "Sep", "Oct", "Nov", "Dec")
Mymonth = ThisY2k(2)
<% Response.Write ("Mymonth = " & Mymonth) %>
```

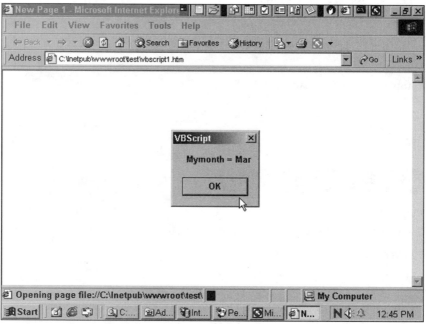

Using an array to store and retrieve string values for the month

Asc   String Function

Purpose

Use this function to return the ASCII character code representing the first
letter in a string.

Syntax

```
Asc(string)
```

Use the string argument to refer to a valid string expression.

Example

In the following example, Asc returns the ANSI or ASCII character code of the first letter of each string:

```
<%
Dim MyAsc1, MyAsc2, MyAsc3
  MyAsc1 = Asc("X") 'Returns 88 MyAsc2 =  Asc("Y") 'Returns 89
  MyAsc3 =  Asc("y") 'Returns 121
  Response.write MyAsc1 &" " & MyAsc2 & " " & MyAsc3
%>
```

Returning ASCII values with Asc

Call   Procedure Statement

Purpose

Use this statement to shift control to a new procedure. You do not have to use the Call keyword when calling a procedure.

Syntax

```
[Call] name [argumentlist]
```

Example

In this example, Somefunction is called and control is passed to SomeFunction to perform the intended task. When completed, control is passed back to the calling procedure.

```
Call SomeFunction ("display a line of text here")
Function SomeFunction(text)
End Function
```

Chr   String Function

Purpose

Use this function to return the particular character associated with the individual ANSI character code.

Syntax

```
Chr(charcode)
Can I just make up something for the syntax? I don't get it.
```

A character is identified in the `charcode` argument by a number.

Example

This example returns the ASCII or ANSI character associated with the numbers between 60 and 70. On each pass through the loop, the counter is incremented, and a different code will be displayed in the message box.

```
<%
For i=60 to 70:
myasc=chr(i):
Response.Write myasc
next
%>
```

Class   Object

Purpose

Use this object to manipulate the events of a class that you create. It will not work to make a variable of the type `Class`. The `Class` object refers to an object defined using the `Class` statement. You can create a specific instance of that class when you define a class using the `Class` statement.

Example

Here, you must use the `Dim` statement (p. 413) and the `Set` statement (p. 449) to refer to the class. In this example, a class is being created using the `Dim` and `Set` statements.

```
Dim pdq
Set pdq = some classname
```

Class   Statement

Purpose

Use this statement to identify a class. You can also determine the methods and properties, as well as the variables, comprising a class. You can make class members private or public.

Syntax

```
Class name
statements
End Class
```

The Class statement syntax consists of a class name and statements to be carried out. The name is based on standard variable nomenclature. The statements are used to define methods, variables, and properties.

Example

Please see the example for the Class object (p. 404) in the preceding section.

Clear Method

Purpose

Use this method to clear the property settings of the Err object (p. 415). You use Clear to clear the Err object after an error is handled. A typical use would be for deferred error handling with the On Error Resume Next statement.

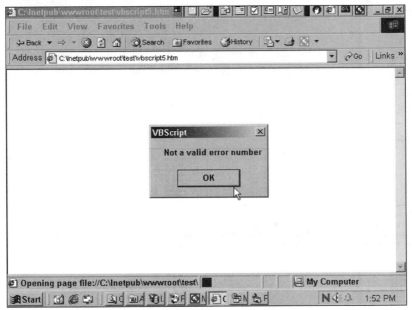

Raising and clearing an error with On Error Resume Next

Syntax

```
object.Clear
```

Example

This example shows the use of the Clear method when an Err object (p. 415) is raised:

```
On Error Resume Next
    b = Val(Text1.Text)
```

```
Err.Clear
Err.Raise b
If b > 0 And b < 65535 Then
   Msg = "Error # " & Str(Err.Number) & " you tried a " _
         & Chr(13) & Err.Description
   MsgBox Msg, , "Error", Err.HelpFile, Err.HelpContext
Else
MsgBox "Not a valid error number"
End If
Err.Clear
```

Color   Constant

Purpose

Use these constants to apply color in applications. You don't have to define these constants to use them, as they are built into VBScript. Color constants can be used in your code to represent the hex values. The constants are as follows: vbBlack (Black), vbRed (Red), vbGreen (Green), vbYellow (Yellow), vbBlue (Blue), vbMagenta (Magenta), vbCyan (Cyan), and vbWhite (White).

Syntax

```
Object.property = ColorConstant
```

Example

In this example, the background color of a form is set to the red color constant. When the procedure runs, the form becomes red.

```
Formfirst.BackColor = vbRed
```

Concatenation   Operator

Purpose

Use the concatenation operator to concatenate two string expressions. An expression is converted to a string type whenever an expression is not a string.

Syntax

```
result = expressiona & expressionb
```

Example

In this example, C will be displayed as "Hi there" on the screen:

```
<%
Dim A, B, C
A = "Hi"
```

```
b = " there"
c = a & b
Response.Write c
%>
```

Const   Declaration

Purpose

Use this statement to declare constants instead of literal values. Constants are public statements (p. -public page--) by default, but are always private statements (see Private Statement p. 441) within procedures. You can't define variables or user functions because they aren't constants. You can use constants similarly to variable expressions.

Syntax

```
[Public | Private] Const anyname = expression
```

Example

This example will display "The constant is Hi There."."

```
<%

Private Const HiString1 = "Hi"
Const HiString2 = " There"
Response.Write ("The constant is " & " " " & _
Histring1 & Histring2)
%>
```

The constant is Hi There

Programming with constants

CreateObject   Function

Purpose

Use this object to create and return a reference to an Automation object. Automation servers provide different types of objects. Word-processing applications might provide application objects and a document object. A spreadsheet application could offer a sheet and cells.

Syntax

```
CreateObject(servername.typename [, location])
```

Example

To create an Automation object, assign the object returned by CreateObject to an object variable. Here, the object variable is WordDoc.

```
Dim WordDoc
Set WordDoc = Nothing
 Set WordDoc = CreateObject("Word.Application")
 WordDoc.Visible = TRUE  WordDoc.Document.open =
("c:\temp\test.doc")
```

Or,

```
Dim Web
Set Web = CreateObject("InternetExplorer.Application")
 Web.Visible = TRUE
 Web.Navigate "www.idgbooks.com"
```

An error occurs if the specified remote server does not exist or cannot be found.

Using CreateObject to launch Internet Explorer and navigate to a Web site

Date and Time   Constants

Purpose

The date and time constants enable you to use days and time in applications. These constants do not need to be defined, as they are built into VBScript. You can use date and time constants in your code to represent hex values.

The day of the week Constants are vbSunday (Sunday), vbMonday (Monday), vbTuesday (Tuesday), vbWednesday (Wednesday), (Thursday), vbFriday (Friday), and vbSaturday (Saturday). Table 1 describes the other date and time constants.

Table 1 *Additional Date and Time Constants*

Constant	Value	Description
vbUseSystem	0	Applies the date format from your computer's regional settings

Constant	Value	Description
vbUseSystemDayOfWeek	0	Applies the day of the week from your system's settings for the first day of the week
vbFirstJan1	1	Applies the week in which January 1 occurs (default)
vbFirstFourDays	2	Applies the first week that has at least four days in the new year
vbFirstFullWeek	3	Applies the first full week of the year

Example

This code will display the number of the week in which the first of January falls in the current year:

```
A = vbFirstJan1
    Print A
```

Date · Date/Time Function

Purpose

Use this function to return the current system date.

Syntax

```
Date
```

Example

This example uses the Date function to return the current system date:

```
Dim ThisDate
ThisDate = Date      ' ThisDate contains the current system date
```

DateAdd · Date/Time Function

Purpose

Use this function to return a date with a time interval. You can use the DateAdd function to add or subtract a specified time interval from a date. You can also use DateAdd to calculate a date a given number of days from yesterday, or a time a specified number of minutes from now. Adding days to a specific date requires using the Day of Year ("y") function, the Day ("d") function (p. 412), or the WeekDay ("w") function (p. 457).

Syntax

```
DateAdd(interval, number, date)
```

VBScript Reference

Table 2 lists the values for the DateAdd Function.

Table 2 *Values for DateAdd Function*

Value	Description
yyyy	Year
q	Quarter
m	Month
y	Day of year
d	Day
w	Weekday
ww	Week of year
h	Hour
n	Minute
s	Second

Example

In this example, the variable A adds a quarter (three months) to the value of the current date:

```
Dim thisdate
Thisdate = DateAdd("q", 1, Now)
Response.Write thisdate
```

Address	http://www.mytest.com/memo/testdate.asp
2/17/01 6:54:09 PM	

Adding a quarter to the date entered

DateDiff   Date/Times Function

Purpose

Use this function to return the number of specified intervals between two dates. You could use DateDiff to calculate the number of days between two dates, or the number of weeks between today and the end of the year.

Syntax

```
DateDiff(interval, date1, date2 [,firstdayofweek[,
firstweekofyear]])
```

Table 3 lists and describes the arguments used with the DateDiff function.

Table 3 *DateDiff Function Syntax*

Arguments	Purpose
Interval	Use this string expression to identify an interval to be used to calculate the differences between the first and second date. Required.
date1, date2	Use this argument to identify dates to be used in the calculation. Required.
firstdayofweek	Use this constant to select the day of the week. Optional.
firstweekofyear	Use this constant to select the first week of the year. The first week is assumed to be the week in which January 1 occurs, if not specified. Optional.

Example

The following example subtracts a date entered in a text box from today's date:

```
Label1.Caption = DateDiff("d", Now, Text1.Text)
```

Subtracting the number of days from today's date

DateSerial

Conversion and
Date/Time Function

Purpose

Use this function to return a variant data type for the Date function (p. 409) for a particular year, month, and day. To identify a date, such as December 31, 1999, the range of numbers for each DateSerial argument should be in the accepted range for the unit; that is, 1–31 for days and 1–12 for months. However, you can also specify relative dates for each argument using any numeric expression that represents some number of days, months, or years before or after a certain date.

Syntax

```
DateSerial(year, month, day)
```

Example

The code in this example will return a date of 6/29/2000:

```
Dim AnyDate
AnyDate = DateSerial(2001 - 1, 9 - 2, 1 - 2)    '
```

DateValue

Purpose

Use this function to return a Variant for the Date function (p. 409). The date argument is customarily a string expression signifying a date from January 1, 100 through December 31, 9999. If a date includes invalid time information, an error is produced.

The short date format defined for your system is recognized by DateValue in terms of the order of month, day, and year when a date is given as a string that includes only numbers separated by valid date separators. The DateValue function can distinguish between full month names and abbreviations.

Syntax

```
DateValue(date)
```

Example

This example converts a string to a date:

```
Dim ThisDate
ThisDate = DateValue("September 8, 1998")
```

Day

Date/Time Function

Purpose

Use this function to return an integer between 1 and 31, which denotes the day of the month. The argument is any expression that could possibly represent a date.

Syntax

```
Day(date)
```

Example

This example uses the Day function to find the twentieth of July from the full text date entered:

```
Dim AnyDay
AnyDay = Day("July 20, 2000")
Response.Write AnyDay
```

Dictionary   Object

Purpose

Use this object to maintain keys and items associated with the keys in an array. Items are linked to a unique key.

Example

This code shows how you can create a Dictionary object that can be used as an array to associate items that are related to one another:

```
Dim x                      ' Create a variable.
Set x = CreateObject("Scripting.Dictionary")
x.Add "1", "Akita"    ' Add keys and items.
x.Add "2", "Bulldog"
x.Add "3", "Rottweiler"
```

Dim   Statement

Purpose

Use this statement to declare variables. The Dim statement creates the variable and allocates storage space. In Visual Basic, there are different data types and correspondingly differing amounts of storage space allocated for each. In VBScript, there is only the Variant type. Variables declared with Dim are available to all procedures inside the script and only within the procedure at the procedure level. You also can declare a dynamic array using the Dim statement.

Syntax

```
Dim varname[([subscripts])][, varname[([subscripts])]] . . .
```

Example

Here, an array is dimensioned to represent the first six months of the year. The variable, Mymonth, is set to the third value of This6mo, which is "Mar.".

```
Dim Mymonth, This6mo
This6mo = Array("Jan", "Feb", "Mar", "Apr", "May", "Jun")
   Mymonth = This6mo(3)    ' Mymonth is "Mar."
```

Division   Operator

Purpose

Use this operator to divide one number by another. The number to the left of the division symbol (/) will be divided by the number on the right side of the symbol.

Syntax

```
Number / Number = Result
```

Example

The following example shows that dividing the number 4 by the number 2 results in the value of 2:

```
4 / 2 = 2
```

Do..Loop   Control Flow Statement

Purpose

Use this statement to continue testing for a condition while the condition is True or until the condition becomes True.

Syntax

```
Do [ {While| Until} some state of affairs]
 [some words]
[Exit Do]
[some words]
Loop
Do [{While | Until} condition]
[statements]
[Exit Do]
[statements]
Loop
```

Or,

```
Do
[statements]
[Exit Do]
[statements]
Loop [{While | Until} condition]
```

Example

Here, i represents a counter variable that is incremented on each pass through the loop. The variable i stands for each of the six months dimensioned in the example for the Dim statement (p. 413).

```
Do While i < 7
        Print This6mo(i): i = i + 1
Loop
```

Erase	**Array Handling Statement**

Purpose

Use this statement to re-initialize elements in fixed-size arrays and eliminate the storage space allocation for dynamic arrays (see Array Function on p. 401). You need to know whether an array is fixed-size (ordinary) or dynamic.

Syntax

```
Erase thisarray
```

The thisarray argument is the name of the Array variable to be erased.

Example

In the subsequent example, the array This6mo is defined as containing six elements, then the elements will be erased (eliminated).

```
Dim This6mo()
ReDim This6mo(6)
Erase This6mo
```

Err	**Object**

Purpose

Use this object to store run-time error information. The Err object also accepts the Raise and Clear methods for generating and clearing run-time errors. The Err object has global scope. The Err object's properties are set to zero or null after the On Error Resume Next statement (p. 439).

VBScript Reference

Syntax

```
Err.Property
Err.Method
```

Example

See also the example shown for the Clear method (p. 405).

```
On Error Resume Next
Err.Raise 13 ' Raise a type mismatch error.
MsgBox ("Error # " & CStr(Err.Number) _ & " " &
Err.Description)
Err.Clear ' Clear the error
```

Eval   Function

Purpose

Use this function to calculate an expression and deliver the result. In VBScript, setting one variable to the value of another variable can be interpreted in two ways. Two values are compared to see if they are identical.

Syntax

```
[result = ]Eval(expression)
```

Example

This example creates a form with a Submit button "Click me". When the button is clicked, it launches a dialog box prompting you to "Enter your guess:". If you guess correctly (a one in five chance), you get the message "Congratulations! You guessed it!" ; and if you don't, you see "Sorry! Try again".

```
<form NAME="YourForm">
 <p><input TYPE="TEXT" NAME="txtNameText" size="1"> <input
TYPE="BUTTON" NAME="cmdSubmit"
 VALUE="click me"> </p>
</form>
<script language="vbscript">

Sub cmdSubmit_OnClick
Dim MyForm
Set Myform=Document.YourForm
Dim WhatNum, RndNum
RndNum = Int((5) * Rnd(1) + 1)
WhatNum = CInt(InputBox("Enter your guess:",,0))
 Do
```

```
   If Eval("WhatNum = RndNum") Then
      Response.Write "Congratulations! You guessed it!"
Exit Sub
   Else
      WhatNum = CInt(InputBox("Sorry! Try again.",,0))
End If
 Loop Until WhatNum = 0
End Sub
</script>
```

Congratulations! You guessed it!

Using Eval to compare input

Exit
Statement

Purpose

Use this statement to exit a block of Do...Loop, For...Next, Function, or Sub code.

Syntax

The following lists show the correct syntax for Exit Statements:

- Use Exit Do to exit a Do...Loop statement (p. -see Do--). Use it only inside a Do...Loop statement. Control is transferred to the statement following the Loop statement.
- Use Exit For to exit a For loop. Use only in a For...Next statement (p. 420)or a For...Each (p. 419) loop. The Exit For control statement transfers control to the statement following the Next statement. (It transfers control to the statement immediately after the Next statement.) In nested structures, control is transferred to the loop, one level above the loop where the Exit...For statement appears.
- Use the Exit function to exit a function procedure. Execution will continue with the statement immediately following the statement calling the Function.
- Use Exit property to exit the property procedure where it appears. Execution will continue with the statement after the statement that originally called the procedure.
- Use Exit Sub to exit a Sub procedure. Execution continues with the statement following the calling statement.

Example

This example illustrates the use of the Exit statement by exiting a function:

```
Function Division(xnum, yden) As Variant
    Const myDivByZero = 11
```

VBScript Reference

```
      On Error GoTo MathFix
Division = xnum / yden
      Exit Function
End Function
```

FileSystemObject   Object

Purpose
Use this object to retrieve files on a computer's file system.

Syntax
For example, the FileSystemObject using the Drive property has the following syntax:

```
FileSystemObjectname.Drives
Scripting.FileSystemObject
```

Example
In the following code, the see CreateObject function (p. 407) returns the FileSystemObject (fso). The DrColl refers to the Drive collection. The For...Each (p. 419) loop enables you to examine each of the elements in a collection. You can use this method to read each drive name and type and to append a dash and the volume name to the drive letter designation. The variable, Sname, contains the text of the drive letter and adds each new drive letter on each pass through the loop. For each drive in the collection, the loop will execute as many times as necessary until all the system drives have been appended to the Sname variable.

```
Dim fso, Drv, DrColl, Sname, DrName, Msg
Set fso = CreateObject("Scripting.FileSystemObject")
    Set DrColl = fso.Drives
    For Each Drv In DrColl
    On Error Resume Next
        Sname = Sname & Drv.DriveLetter & " - "
        If Drv.DriveType = Remote Then
            DrName = Drv.ShareName
        Else
            DrName = Drv.VolumeName
        End If
        Sname = Sname & DrName & vbCrLf
        Text1.Text = Sname
        Next
        XS = Sname
```

The list of drives

Filter   Function

Purpose

Use this function to return a zero-based array containing a subset of a string array based on specified filter criteria. If there are no matches of Value within InputStrings, the function returns an empty array.

Syntax

```
Filter(InputStrings, Value[, Include[, Compare]])
```

Example

This example uses the Filter function to return the month beginning with the letter "F":

```
Dim ThisY2k, ThisIndex
ThisY2k = Array("Jan", "Feb", "Mar", "Apr", "May", "Jun")

ThisIndex = Filter(ThisY2k, "F") ' ThisIndex(0)
Print ThisIndex(0)
```

For...Each   Control Flow Statement

Purpose

Use this block to repeat a set of statements for each element in an array or collection. The For Each block is entered if there is at least one of the elements in the group. Once the loop is begun, all the statements in the loop are executed for the first element in the group. As long as there are more elements in the group, the statements in the loop continue to execute for each element. When there are no more elements in the group, the loop is exited and execution continues with the statement following the Next statement.

Syntax

```
For Each element In group
[statements]
[Exit For]
[statements]
Next [element]
```

Example

The following command block is similar to a For...Next (p. 420) loop. It is responsible for bringing each one of the selected files into the Textbox. The BringFilz function is called to index the files. The For...Each loop is used to pass through a series of elements in a collection or array. The routine exits when there are no more elements in the group. The vRC variable is a counter for the file elements in the array.

```
For Each vRC In Data.Files
BringFilz Text1, vRC
Next vRC
End If
```

For...Next   Control Flow Statement

Purpose

Use this statement to repeat a group of statements the number of times indicated. The counter is incremented once the loop starts and all statements in the loop have executed the step. Finally, the statements in the loop execute again or the loop is exited and execution continues with the statement following the Next statement.

Syntax

```
For counter = start To end [Step step]
[statements]
[Exit For]
[statements]
Next
```

Example

The following code will cause the word "Hello" to be printed on the form 10 times, each time with an additional space in front of the word "Hello." When loops are nested, subsequent variables must be named, designated as Next X, Next Y, and so on.

```
<%
Dim I, word
For I = 1 to 10
```

```
Word = "Hello"
Response.Write space(I) & Word
Next
%>
```

FormatCurrency | Formatting String Function

Purpose

Use this function to return a value using a currency symbol as set up on your system. The definition of the currency format resides in your computer's regional settings.

Syntax

```
FormatCurrency(Expression[,NumDigitsAfterDecimal
[,IncludeLeadingDigit [,UseParensForNegativeNumbers
[,GroupDigits]]]])
```

Example

This example illustrates the use of the FormatCurrency function. The number is formatted with the dollar sign and zeros are added to the right of the decimal point.

```
Dim ThisCurrency
    ThisCurrency = FormatCurrency(2500)   ' MyCurrency contains
$2500.00.
   ("This big buck = " & ThisCurrency)
```

Formatting and displaying currency

FormatDateTimeFunction

Purpose

This function returns a value that has a date or time format.

Syntax

```
FormatDateTime(Date[, NamedFormat])
```

Example

This example shows the date in long format. For example, if the current date is 05/31/2000, the value shown for GetCurrentDate will be Thursday, May 31, 2000.

```
<%
GetCurrentDate = FormatDateTime(Date, 1)
Response.Write ("long date "& GetCurrentDate)
%>
```

long date Wednesday, May 31, 2000

Formatting and displaying the long date

FormatNumber   Formatting String Function

Purpose

Use this function to format numbers. The format for numbers in the regional settings of your computer determines how the numbers will be displayed.

Syntax

```
FormatNumber(Expression [,NumDigitsAfterDecimal
[,IncludeLeadingDigit [,UseParensForNegativeNumbers
[,GroupDigits]]]])
```

Example

In this example, the number (ThisNum) is formatted with two places to the right of the decimal point.

```
<%
Dim ThisNum, MyNumber
ThisNum = 12.5
MyNumber = FormatNumber(ThisNum, 2)
Response.Write MyNumber
%>
```

12.50

Formatting and displaying decimal values

FormatPercentFunction

Purpose

Use this function to reformat a number so that it is displayed as a percentage (multiplied by 100) with a trailing % character. The format for numbers in the regional settings of your computer determines how the numbers will be displayed.

Syntax

```
FormatPercent(Expression[,NumDigitsAfterDecimal
[,IncludeLeadingDigit [,UseParensForNegativeNumbers
[,GroupDigits]]]])
```

Example

Here, the dividend is formatted as 50%, rather than as a fraction (.5):

```
Dim ThisPercent
    ThisPercent = FormatPercent(12 / 24)
' MyPercent is 50%
    Response.Write  ThisPercent
```

```
50.00%
```

Formatting and displaying numbers as percentages

Function Statement

Purpose

Use this statement to set up a procedure that will carry out a specific task and /or do calculations when parameters are passed to it.

Syntax

```
[Public [Default] | Private] Function name [(arglist)]
[statements]
[name = expression]
[Exit Function]
[statements]
[name = expression]
End Function
```

Example

This function includes the On Error GoTo statement, and variables are declared for the numerator and denominator. A constant contains the

error number of the Division by Zero error. The Err object has a Number
property, which is a numeric code evaluating to an error. If the error number is the same as the constant, a message box is displayed to the user.

```
Function Division(xnum, yden) As Variant
     Const myDivByZero = 11
On Error GoTo MathFix
     Division = xnum / yden
Exit Function
MathFix:
   If Err.Number = myDivByZero Then
        Response.Write "DIVIDE BY ZERO ERROR"
        Resume Next
   End If
End Function
```

DIVIDE BY ZERO ERROR

Generating the Divide by Zero error

GetObject   Function

Purpose

Use this function to use an Automation object by launching a file. The Set
statement assigns an object variable to the object.

Syntax

```
GetObject([pathname] [, class])
```

Example

In this example, the object to be obtained is a Windows bitmap in a specific
folder.

```
Dim CObject
Set CObject = GetObject("C:\art\cove001.bmp")
```

Hex   Conversion Function

Purpose

Use this function to return a string that shows the hexadecimal value of a
number. Before being evaluated, the number is rounded to the nearest whole
number.

Syntax

```
Hex(number)
```
The number argument is any valid expression.

Example

This illustrates the decimal/hex conversion. When the figure 100 is placed in the parentheses, the hex equivalent is 64.

```
Dim ThisHex
ThisHex = Hex(100)    ' Returns 64.
Print ThisHex
```

Hour   Date/Time Function

Purpose

Use this function to return a whole number between 0 and 23 that indicates the hour of the day.

Syntax

```
Hour(time)
```

Example

The hour (on 24-hour basis), date, and time (complete hour and minutes) are displayed.

```
Dim ExampleTime, ExampleHour
    ExampleTime = Now
    ExampleHour = Hour(ExampleTime)
            Response.Write ExampleHour & " " & ExampleTime
```

If...Then...Else   Control Flow Statement

Purpose

Use this statement to set up conditions to be tested so that certain functions are performed. The statements are first evaluated, the condition immediately following the If is tested, and if the condition exists (is True), the statements following are then executed. In the event that the condition does not exist (is False), the ElseIf conditions are evaluated. Under the ElseIf conditions, each condition is tested to see if it exists (is True). If none of these conditions is found to be true, then the testing moves on to the Else statements. Finally, after each process is completed, in a top-down manner, the program execution continues with statements following the End if statement. Single-line statements must not contain the keyword Else.

Syntax

```
If condition Then statements [Else elsestatements ]
Or, you can use the block form syntax:
If condition Then
[statements]
[ElseIf condition-n Then
[elseifstatements]] . . .
[Else
[elsestatements]]
End If
```

Example

Here, a counter (Bc) is incremented when Newname is the same as Oldname. If Newname and Oldname are not the same, a different counter (X) is incremented.

```
Dim Oldname As String, Newname As String, Bc As Integer, X As
Integer
If Newname = Oldname Then
        Bc = Bc + 1
Else
        X = X + 1
End if
```

InputBox   Input/Output Function

Purpose

Use this function to display a prompt in a dialog box, wait for text input or a button click, and then return the value entered. When the user clicks OK or presses Enter, the InputBox function returns whatever is in the text box. If the user clicks Cancel, the function returns a zero-length string ("").

Syntax

```
InputBox(prompt[, title][, default][, xpos][, ypos][, helpfile,
context])
```

Example

In this example, the InputBox function is used to display an input box and assign the string to the variable Input:

```
Dim YourInput
YourInput = InputBox("Enter your email address")
Response.Write ("You entered: " & YourInput)
```

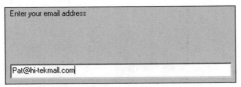

Creating an input box

You entered: Pat@hi-tekmall.com

Providing confirmation of input with MsgBox

InStr   Function

Purpose

Use this function to return the position of the first occurrence of one string contained inside another.

Syntax

```
InStr([start, ]string1, string2[, compare])
```

Example

This example demonstrates how you can use InStr to search a string:

```
Search ="Roses are Red" ' String to search in.
SChar="s"
ThisPos = Instr(5, Search, SChar, 1)
' compares text starting at position 5 Returns s.
Response.Write ("It is:" & ThisPos)
```

The search for 1st s in 5th place is: 5

Searching a string and displaying the result

Int   Function

Purpose

Use this function to return the whole portion of a number. The Int function is like Fix, except that negative numbers cause Int to return the first negative integer less than or equal to the number, whereas Fix returns the first negative integer greater than or equal to the number.

VBScript Reference

Syntax

```
Int(number)
Fix(number)
```

Example

This example demonstrates the difference in results between Int and Fix:

```
ThisNumber = Int(98.8) ' Returns 98.
ThatNumber = Fix(97.2) ' Returns 97.
Response.Write ("Int is: " & ThisNumber)
Response.Write ("Fix is: " & ThatNumber)
```

Is   Operator

Purpose

Use this operator to compare two object reference variables. If each object reference variable refers to the same object, the result will be True. If not, the result will be False.

Syntax

```
result = objecta Is objectb
```

Example

This example sets X to take the same value as:

```
Set X = Y
```

IsArray   Function

Purpose

Use this variant to return a Boolean value indicating whether the object is an array variable. True is returned when the variable is an Array variable (p. 401), and False is returned when it is not.

Syntax

```
IsArray(varname)
The varname argument can be any variable.
```

Example

The IsArray variant is used here to test for the status of the variable:

```
ThisY2k = Array("Jan", "Feb", "Mar", "Apr", _
"May", "Jun", "Jul", "Aug", "Sep", "Oct", "Nov", "Dec")
Mymonth = IsArray(ThisY2k) ' it contains "True."Response.Write
("mymonth " & Mymonth)IsDateFunction
```

Purpose

Use this function to return a Boolean value that indicates whether an expression can be converted to a date. True is returned if the value can be converted to a date. If not, False is returned. All dates from January 1, 100 A.D. through December 31, 9999 A.D are valid.

Syntax

```
IsDate(expression)
```

The expression argument can be any date expression or string expression recognizable as a date or time.

Example

This illustration tests the date validity of the ThisCheck strings:

```
Dim ThisDate, YourDate, NoDate
Dim ThisCheck1, ThisCheck2, ThisCheck3
ThisDate = "October 19, 1962": YourDate = 10199222: NoDate =
"Hello"
ThisCheck1 = IsDate(ThisDate) ' Returns True.
ThisCheck2 = IsDate(YourDate) ' Returns False.
ThisCheck3 = IsDate(NoDate)   ' Returns False.
Response.Write ("Thisdate = " & ThisCheck1)
Response.Write ("YourDate = " & ThisCheck2)
Response.Write ("NoDate = " & ThisCheck3)
```

```
Thisdate = True
```

Displaying the value returned for ThisDate

IsEmpty   Variant Function

Purpose

Use this function when you want a returned value to show that the variable has been initialized. True is returned if the variable is not initialized and False if it is.

Syntax

```
IsEmpty(expression)
```

The expression argument can be any expression. However, because the IsEmpty function is used to determine if individual variables are initialized, the expression argument is most often a single variable name.

Example

The message box displays True for the ThisCheck variable and shows nothing for ThisVar, as it has no value (Null).

```
Dim ThisVar, ThisCheck
ThisCheck = IsEmpty(ThisVar) ' Returns True.
ThisVar = Null               ' Assign Null.
Response.Write ("thischeck = " & ThisCheck)
Response.Write ("thisvar = " & ThisVar)
```

IsNull   Variant Function

Purpose

Use this function when you want a returned Boolean value to show that a given expression does not contain valid data. The IsNull function returns True when the expression is Null and False if there is valid data.

Syntax

```
IsNull(expression)
```

The expression argument can be any expression.

Example

The empty assignment in the preceding example will return False.

```
ThisVar = Empty                ' Assign Empty.
ThisCheck = IsNull(ThisVar)    ' Returns False.
```

IsNumericFunction

Purpose

Use this function when you need a returned Boolean value to indicate whether an expression can be used as a number. True is returned when the whole value can be evaluated as a number and False when it cannot.

Syntax

```
IsNumeric(expression)
```

The expression argument can be any expression.

Example

In this case, Bozo is not a numeric value, even though "439" is, so IsNumeric returns False:

```
Dim ThisVar, ThisCheck
ThisVar = "Bozo 439"              ' Assign a value.
ThisCheck = IsNumeric(ThisVar)    ' Returns False.
```

IsObjectFunction

Purpose

Use this function when you need a returned Boolean value to indicate that the reference made is to an Automation object. True is returned if the reference is made to a valid object and False if it is not.

Syntax

```
IsObject(expression)
```

The expression argument can be any expression.

Example

Here, because Thisobject has been given a value, the statement will evaluate to True:

```
Dim ThisCheck, ThisObject
Set Thisobject = Me
ThisCheck = IsObject(Thisobject)  ' Returns True.
Response.Write ("ThisCheck is " & ThisCheck)
```

ThisCheck is True

Displaying the return value for ThisCheck

JoinFunction

Purpose

Use this function to return a string created by joining a number of substrings contained in an array.

Syntax

```
Join(list[, delimiter])
```

Example

Once joined, the elements in the array will consist of "Ms. Sasha Von Angel":

```
Dim AString
Dim AArray(4)
AArray(0) = "Ms."
AArray(1) = "Sasha "
AArray(2) = "Von "
AArray(3) = "Angel"
AString = Join(AArray)
Response.Write ("Aarray = " & AString)
```

VBScript Reference

> **aarray = Ms. Sasha Von Angel**

Joining strings in an array

Lbound · Array Handling Function

Purpose

Use this function when you want to return a value for the lowest subscript defined for an Array function (p. 401). The Lbound function is used with the UBound function (p. see ubound 456) to determine the size of an array. Use the UBound function to find the upper limit of an array dimension. The lower bound for any dimension is always zero.

Syntax

```
LBound(arrayname[, dimension])
```

Example

In this example, the value of lowest is zero:

```
Dim Aarray (3)
Dim lowest
lowest = LBound(AArray, 1)
Response.Write lowest
```

Finding the lower limit in an array

LCaseFunction

Purpose

Use this function to return a string that has been converted to lowercase. This can be used only to convert uppercase letters to lowercase. Lowercase letters and other characters are not changed.

Syntax

```
LCase(string)
```

The string argument is any valid string expression. Null is returned if the string contains Null.

Example

Here, the word "HELP!" will be changed to "help!":

```
Dim TheString
Dim LCaseExamp
TheString = "HELP!"
LCaseExamp = LCase(TheString) ' LcaseExamp
```

Left   String Function

Purpose

Use this function to return a specified number of characters from the left-most portion of a string.

Syntax

```
Left(string, length)
```

Example

This example demonstrates the Left function. When the code is run, the value of LeftExamp will be "HE."

```
Dim LeftExamp, TheString
TheString = "HELP!"
LeftExamp = Left(TheString, 2)
Response.Write LeftExamp
```

Displaying the value of LeftExamp

Len   String Function

Purpose

Use this function to return the number of characters in a string. In addition, you can use it to obtain the number of bytes of storage required by a variable.

Syntax

```
Len(string | varname)
```

Example

This example exemplifies the use of the Len function to measure the length of a string in characters and bytes:

```
Dim LenExamp, TheString
TheString = "All hope is gone."
LenExamp = Len(TheString) ' LenExamp
```

Displaying the length of a string

LoadPicture   Input/Output Function

Purpose

Use this function to load a picture. The graphics formats acknowledged by the LoadPicture function include bitmap (.bmp) files, icon (.ico) files, run-length encoded (.rle) files, metafile (.wmf) files, enhanced metafiles (.emf), GIF (.gif) files, and JPEG (.jpg) files. It is available only on 32-bit platforms.

Syntax

```
LoadPicture(picturename)
```

The picturename argument is a string expression that indicates the name of the picture file to be loaded.

Example

In this example, the path location of the graphic files must be given, as well as the actual file names associated with the pictures.

```
Dim clouds, rose
Set rose = LoadPicture("c:\vb\rose.wmf")
Set clouds = LoadPicture("c:\vb\clouds.gif")
```

Log   Math Function

Purpose

Use this function in order to return the *natural logarithm* of a number. The natural logarithm is the logarithm to the base "e." The constant e is approximately 2.718282.

Syntax

```
Log(number)
```

The number argument can be any valid numeric expression greater than zero.

Example

The code in this example will return a value of 2. If X were equal to 10, the value returned would be 1.

```
X = 100
   Log10 = Log(X) / Log(10)
```

Displaying the value returned by the Log example

Mid   Function

Purpose

Use this function to display or use the number of characters from a string that you specify.

Syntax

```
Mid(string, start[, length])
```

Example

Here, the word love is parsed from the sentence by specifying the display of four characters in the middle of the string beginning at the third character:

```
Dim URVar
URVar = Mid("I love VBScript", 3, 4) ' URVar ="love."
Response.Write ("what do I do?" & URVar)
```

Extracting a word from a string

Minute   Date/Time Function

Purpose

Use this function to display a whole number between 0 and 59 that represents the minute of the hour (p. 425).

Syntax

```
Minute(time)
```

The time argument is any expression that can represent a time. If time contains Null, Null is returned.

Example

The minute (numbered from 0 to 59) will depend upon the exact minute within the hour on the system in use.

```
UrVar = Minute(Now)
Response.Write ("Minute " & Urvar)
```

Minute 7

Finding the minute in the current time

Mod   Operator

Purpose

Use this operator in order to divide two numbers and return what remains. The modulus, or remainder, operator divides *number1* by *number2* (rounding floating-point numbers to integers) and returns only the remainder as the result.

Syntax

```
Result = number1 Mod number2
```

Example

This example will display the answer (2), because 20 divided by 9 = 2.222 and the Mod operator removes the fractional digits.

```
A = 20 Mod 9
Response.Write (A)
```

Month   Date/Time Function

Purpose

Use this function when you need to obtain an integer between 1 and 12 that represents the number of the month of the year.

Syntax

```
Month(date)
```

The date argument is an expression that represents a date. If date contains Null, Null is returned.

Example

This syntax is similar to that of the Minute function in the sense that the time frame is changed from minute to month. That is, the portion of the Now variable is the number of the month in the year.

```
UrVar = Month(Now)
Response.Write ("Month " & Urvar)
```

MonthName Function

Purpose

Use this function to return the name of the month in the form of a string indicating the month in question. (See Month Function on p. 436).

Syntax

```
MonthName(month[, abbreviate])
```

Example

This example shows the name of the month based upon the numerical sequence of the month. Here, requesting the fifth month will display May as the MonthName.

```
UrVar = MonthName(5)
Response.Write ("Month " & Urvar)
```

Month May

Displaying May, the name of the fifth month

MsgBox   Function

Purpose

Use this function to show a dialog box containing a message specified in the code. The MsgBox function will wait for user input and return a value indicating which button the user clicked. The constants determine the options for the message box format and what is displayed on its title bar.

Syntax

```
MsgBox(prompt[, buttons][, title][, helpfile, context])
```

Example

The following example shows how to use a MsgBox function:

```
Dim UrVar
UrVar = MsgBox ("Hello World!", 6, "MsgBox Example")
```

Not   Operator

Purpose

Use this operator when you want to make a logical expression negative. The Not operator inverts the bit values of any variable and sets the associated bit in the result. You can use the Not operator in searches to exclude members of certain categories.

Syntax

```
result = Not expression
```

Example

Here, the result will be –5. If x and y were both 1, the result would be –3.

```
X = 3:y = 1:z = not x + y
Response.Write ("z " & z)
```

Now   Date/Time Function

Purpose

Use this function to return the current date and time (p. 408) according to your computer's setting of system date and time.

Syntax

```
Now
```

Example

This is intuitively simple. The Now function displays the exact date and time.

```
Response.Write Now
```

Nothing   Literal Keyword

Purpose

Use this keyword in VBScript to clear from memory an object variable from any actual object. Use the Set statement to assign Nothing to an object variable.

Syntax

```
Set Variable = Nothing
```

Example

The object variable UrObject has been cleared, or set to nothing.

```
Set UrObject = Nothing
```

Number   Property

Purpose

Use this property to return or set a numeric value in order to indicate an error. The Number property is the Err object's (p. 415) default property.

Syntax

```
object.Number [= errornumber]
```

Example

In this example, an error number is entered into a text box and the message box displays the textual representation of the error. See the Err object (p, 415) and On Error Resume Next statement (p. 439) for illustrations.

```
If b > 0 And b < 65535 Then
Msg = "Error # " & Str(Err.Number) & " you tried a " _
        & Chr(13) & Err.Description
    Response.Write Msg, , "Error", Err.HelpFile, _
Err.HelpContext
Else
    Response.Write "Not a valid error number"
End If
```

On Error Resume Next   Error Handling Statement

Purpose

Use this statement to enable error handling. Failing to use the On Error Resume Next statement will result in fatal errors. That is, execution stops when the error message is displayed.

With On Error Resume Next, you can continue execution with the statement immediately following the statement that caused the run-time error, or with the statement immediately following the On Error Resume Next statement.

Syntax

```
On Error Resume Next
```

Example

In this scenario, a routine has been built to raise an error, printing the message when the corresponding error number has been entered in the text box. If the number entered is out of the specified range, the message box shows that the number does not indicate a valid error.

```
On Error Resume Next
    b = Val(Text1.Text)
Err.Clear
Err.Raise b
If b > 0 And b < 65535 Then
 Msg = "Error # " & Str(Err.Number) & " you tried a " _
        & Chr(13) & Err.Description
   Msgbox Msg, , "Error", Err.HelpFile, Err.HelpContext
 Else
    Msgbox "Not a valid error number"
End If
```

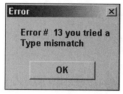

Raising an error and displaying a message

Option Explicit   Option

Purpose

Use this option to constrain variables to be declared. The Option Explicit statement must appear in a procedure prior to other statements. When you use the Option Explicit statement, you must explicitly declare all variables using the Dim (p. 413), Private (p. 441), Public (p. 442), or ReDim (p. 444) statements. You will not be allowed to create variables on the fly.

Syntax

```
Option Explicit
```

Example

In this illustration, ThisVar was not declared, so any reference to it will result in an error message:

```
Option Explicit
    Dim Urvar
Urvar = 15
    ThisVar = 15
```

Or   Operator

Purpose

Use this operator to stipulate a logical either/or action that takes place on two expressions. That is, if either 1 or 2 exists, then some action takes place.

Syntax

```
result = expression1 Or expression2
```

Example

Here, a counter (x) is being incremented on each pass through the loop. On each pass, there is a test to see if x equals either 1 or 2. If it does, then another variable (y) = 2. This is a simple example of the Or operator, but Or can also be used in very complex calculations.

```
For x = 1 To 6
    If x = 1 Or x = 2 Then
        y = 2
    End If
Next x
```

Private   Statement

Purpose

Use this statement when you want to create private variables and designate storage. Private variables can be used only in the script of declaration. Public variables can be used throughout a program. Private is also used to declare arrays.

Syntax

```
Private varname[([subscripts])][, varname[([subscripts])]] . . .
```

Example

This statement creates a private variable of the variant type:

```
Private UrNumber ' Private variable
```

In the following example, a Private array is created, which is really multiple declarations of each of the nine variables:

```
Private UrArray(9)   'Private array
```

Public   Statement

Purpose

Use this statement when you want to create public variables and designate storage. Private variables can be used only in the script of declaration. Public statement variables are available to all procedures in all scripts.

Syntax

```
Public varname[([subscripts])][, varname[([subscripts])]] . . .
```

Examples

This statement creates a public variable of the variant type:

```
Public UrNumber ' Public variable
```

In the following example, a Public array is created, which is really multiple declarations of each of the nine variables:

```
Public UrArray(9)   'Public array
```

Raise   Method

Purpose

Use this method when you want to raise a run-time error. Raising an error means that you reveal and display the error that interferes with the execution of the program. If you use Raise without specifying some arguments, however, and the property settings of the Err object (p. 415) contain values that have not been cleared, those values become the values for your error.

Syntax

```
object.Raise(number, source, description, helpfile, helpcontext)
```

Example

Here, a subroutine has been built in order to raise an error, showing the message when the corresponding error number has been entered in a text box.

VBScript Reference

If the number entered is out of the specified range, the message box shows that the number does not indicate a valid error. See the illustration shown with the On Error Resume Next statement (p. 439).

```
On Error Resume Next
    b = Val(Text1.Text)
Err.Clear
Err.Raise b
If b > 0 And b < 65535 Then
    Msg = "Error # " & Str(Err.Number) & " you tried a " _
& Chr(13) & Err.Description
    MsgBox Msg, , "Error", Err.HelpFile, Err.HelpContext
  Else
      Msgbox "Not a valid error number"
End If
```

Randomize   Math Statement

Purpose

Use this statement when you want to utilize the random-number generator. The Rnd function's random-number generator is used by the Randomize statement to give it a new seed value. The seed value is the starting point for the number generation. If you omit number, the new seed value will be the value returned by the system timer. When Randomize is not used, the Rnd function (no arguments) seeds with the same number the first time it is called, and then uses the last generated number as a seed value.

Syntax

```
Randomize [number]
```

The number argument can be any valid numeric expression.

Example

Here, you can create a random number effect that operates each time you press the Refresh button. At first, nothing shows on the screen in the browser window. When you click Refresh, a new number is displayed; and each time you Refresh the window, a new number will appear.

```
Dim Randumm
randomize
Randumm = int(Rnd* 10) + 1
```

Displaying the random number generated

ReDim   Statement

Purpose

Use this statement to declare dynamic array (see Array function on p. 401) variables, and to allocate or change the storage space required. The ReDim statement is used to size and resize an already declared dynamic array when it has been declared using no subscripts. You also can use the ReDim statement repeatedly to change the number of elements and dimensions in an array.

Syntax

```
ReDim [Preserve] varname(subscripts) [, varname(subscripts)]
 . . .
```

Example

This example illustrates how you can increase the size of the last dimension of a dynamic array without erasing any existing data held in the array:

```
ReDim Z(9, 9, 9)
ReDim Preserve Z(9, 9, 10)
```

Replace   String Function

Purpose

Use this function to return a string with a replaced substring. The return value of the Replace function is a string that begins at the position specified by start and concludes at the end of the expression string, with substitutions made. It is not a copy of the original string from beginning to end.

Syntax

```
Replace(expression, find, replacewith[, start[, count[,
compare]]])
```

Example

In this example, the message box will display the new string as "This is a Pest," because the "Te" was replaced with "Pe."

```
dim Anyvar
    Anyvar = Replace("This is  a  Test ",
```

```
"T", "P")
    Response.Write ("new string " & Anyvar)
```

new string This is a Pest

Changing "Test" to "Pest" with Replace

RGB   Miscellaneous Function

Purpose

Use this function to manipulate color values. You can return a whole number
representing an RGB color value. The RGB color values specify the relative
intensities of red, green, and blue, causing a color to be displayed in corre-
spondence with the relative numerical values for R, G, or B. The low-order
byte contains the value for red; the middle byte contains the value for green;
and the high-order byte contains the value for blue.

Syntax

```
RGB(red, green, blue)
```

Example

In this illustration, random numbers are being generated for each R, G, or
B value. The Xspot sets the horizontal position of a spot. The Yspot sets the
vertical position of a spot. A star is drawn at Xspot, Yspot.

```
Dim R, G, B
    R = 255 * Rnd
    G = 255 * Rnd
    B = 255 * Rnd
' bit to a random location on the form.
    Xspot = Rnd * ScaleWidth
' bit to a random location on the form.
    Yspot = Rnd * ScaleHeight
' bit a random color.
    PSet (Xspot, Yspot), RGB(R, G, B)
```

Right   Function

Purpose

Use this function to return the number of characters you specify from the
right side of a string.

Syntax

```
Right(string, length)
```

VBScript Reference

Example

This routine displays a dialog box proclaiming "I am fantastic!", which is quite different from the original string.

```
    Dim UrString
UrString = "His story was totally fantastic!"
UrString = Right(UrString,10)
Response.Write ("I am " & UrString)
```

> **I am fantastic!**

Changing the meaning of a string with Right

Rnd   Math Function

Purpose

Use this function with the Randomize statement (p. 443) to initialize the random-number generator with a seed based on the system timer. The same number sequence is generated for any given initial seed because each successive call to the Rnd function uses the previous number as a seed for the next number in the sequence.

Syntax

```
Rnd[(number)]
```

The number argument can be any valid numeric expression.

Example

Here, you set the values of the RGB variables to 255 times the Rnd function. These color variables can have values from 0 to 255, so each will stand for the Red, Green, or Blue values.

```
R = 255 * Rnd
G = 255 * Rnd
B = 255 * Rnd
```

Round   Math Function

Use this function to return a number rounded to the number of decimal places you specify.

Syntax

```
Round(expression[, numdecimalplaces])
```

Example

In this example, the result in this routine will be 357:

```
Dim MyVar, numb
numb = 356.9999
MyVar = Round(numb, 2)
```

ScriptEngine
Script Engine Identification Function

Purpose

Use this function to return a string that represents the scripting language in use.

Syntax

```
ScriptEngine
```

Example

The result will be the scripting engine version number.

```
<%
Dim pdq
pdq=scriptengine & scriptenginemajorversion
Response.Write pdq
%>
```

Second
Date/Time Function

Purpose

Use this function similarly to the Minute (p. 435) and Hour (p. 425) functions, to return a whole number between 0 and 59, inclusive, representing the second of the minute.

Syntax

```
Second(time)
```

The time argument is any expression that can represent a time. If time contains Null, Null is returned.

Example

In this example, a dialog box will display the current second on the system clock:

```
UrVar = Second(Now)
Response.Write ("Second " & Urvar)
```

VBScript Reference

Second 29

The current second on the system

Select Case   Control Flow Statement

Purpose

Use this statement to enable a multiple choice in which the first case that matches the criterion is performed. In Select Case, a number of conditions are tested for one object; whereas the If command block can have nested If statements (see If...Then...Else statement on p. 425), Else statements, and Else if statements.

The Select Case statement structures test one expression, comparing the result of this expression with the values for each Case statement in the structure. A block of code is executed if there is a match. If there is no match, the execution falls to the next Case statement.

A common use of Select Case is to provide menu options. For example, you might have a menu with ten options. Rather than using a series of If statements to test for each of the ten conditions, you could more easily code the menu using the Case structure. Select Case statements can be nested. Each nested Select Case statement must have a matching End Select statement.

Syntax

```
Select Case testexpression
[Case expressionlist-n
[statements-n]] . . .
[Case Else expressionlist-n
[elsestatements-n]]
End Select
```

Example

The Select Case code allows testing for a number of options; in this example, six options. Using If statements would require much more code.

```
Select Case Index
  Case 1
    Text1.text = "One"
  Case 2
    Text2.text = "Two"
  Case 3
```

```
      Text3.text = "Three"
   Case 4
      Text4.text = "four"
    Case 5
      Text5.text = "Five"
    Case 6
      Text6.text = "Six"
   End Select
```

Set   Assignment Statement

Purpose
Use this statement to assign an object reference to a variable or property, or to link a procedure reference to an event. You must use the Set statement because the Dim (p. 413), Private (p. 441), Public (p. 442), ReDim (p. 444) statements will only declare a variable with reference to an object.

Syntax
```
Set objectvar = {objectexpression | New classname | Nothing}
Set object.eventname = GetRef(procname)
```

Example
See the LoadPicture function (p. 434) for an example of the use of a Set statement.

Sgn   Conversion Function

Purpose
Use this function to return a whole number that shows the sign of a number.

Syntax
```
Sgn(number)
```

The number argument can be any valid numeric expression.

Example
As the following example shows, Sgn will return a 1 for Var1, and a negative 1 for Var2.

```
Dim Var1, Var2
   Var1 = 10: Var2 = -5
   Ursign = Sgn(Var1)
```

```
    Response.Write ("Var1 = " & Ursign)
Ursign = Sgn(Var2)
    Response.Write ("Var2 = " & Ursign)
```

Sin   Math Function

Purpose

Use this function in order to return the sine of an angle. The Sin function returns the relationship between two sides of a right triangle. The length of the side opposite the angle divided by the length of the hypotenuse is the ratio.

Syntax

```
Sin(number)
```

The number argument can be any valid numeric expression that expresses an angle in radians.

Example

This example returns the sine of an angle:

```
Dim UrAngle, UrCosecant
    UrAngle = 1.3
    'angle in radians.
UrCosecant = 1 / Sin(UrAngle)
Response.Write ("" & UrCosecant)
```

Space   String Function

Purpose

Use this function to return a string that displays the requested number of spaces.

Syntax

```
Space(number)
```

The number argument is the number of spaces you want in the string.

Example

This example shows that the words "Hi" and "There" are now separated by five spaces.

```
Dim MyString
Something = Space(5)
Something = "Hi" & Space(9) & "There"
Response.Write (Something)
```

```
Hi    There
```

Displaying the five-character separation between "Hi" and "There"

Sqr
Math Function

Purpose
Use this function to return the square root of a number.

Syntax
```
Sqr(number)
```

The number argument can be any valid numeric expression greater than or equal to zero.

Example
The following example will return the value of the square root of nine, which is 3:

```
Dim UrSquare
    UrSquare=Sqr(9)
    Response.Write("square of 9 = " & UrSquare)
```

```
square of 9 = 3
```

Displaying the returned value for the square root of nine

StrComp
Function

Purpose
Use this function when you need to see a value that shows the consequence of a string comparison.

Syntax
```
StrComp(string1, string2[, compare])
```

A numeric value indicates the kind of comparison to use when evaluating strings. If omitted, a binary comparison is performed. The compare value is optional.

Example
Because the compare value has been omitted, a binary compare is carried out, resulting in a value of 1.

```
Dim MyStr1, MyStr2, UrComp
UrStr1 = "ABCDE": UrStr2 = "abcd"
```

```
UrComp = StrComp(UrStr1, UrStr2, 1)
Response.Write("comparison = " & UrComp)
```

comparison = 1

The message box shows the value of the binary string comparison

String   Constant Function

Purpose

Use this function when you want to return a repeating character string of a length you indicate.

Syntax

```
String(number, character)
```

The character code (p. 403) specifies the character or string expression whose first character is used to construct the return string.

Example

Here, the resulting message box displays five number sixes, because the string "65" is led by a 6.

```
Dim UrString
UrString = String(5, "65")
Response.Write("string = " & UrString)
```

string = 66666

The repeating character "65"

StrReverse   Function

Purpose

Use this function to return a string in reverse order of the characters in a given string.

Syntax

```
StrReverse(stringa)
```

The string to be reversed is the stringa parameter (see String function on p. 452).

Example

In this example, the string "dim" will be displayed in the message box as "mid."

```
UrStr = StrReverse("dim")
Response.Write("string = " & UrStr)
```

> string = mid

Reversing a string with StrReverse

Sub   Statement

Purpose
Use this statement in order to identify a procedure. A Sub statement declares the name, arguments, and code that form the body of a Sub procedure. Subs may be public or private. A public Sub statement is one in which the procedure can be used by all other scripts. Private procedures are available only to the particular procedure where declared.

Syntax
```
[Public [Default]| Private] Sub name [(arglist)]
[statements]
[Exit Sub]
[statements]
End Sub[ByVal | ByRef] varname[( )]Example
```

Example
The For..Next loop in this procedure is executed as the result of a button click, so it is a Click procedure.

```
Private Sub Cmdhello_Click()
    For I = 1 To 10
    <% Response.Write ("HELLO") %>
    Next
End Sub
```

Subtraction (–)   Operator

Purpose
Use this operator in order to obtain the difference between two numbers, or to designate the negative value of a numeric expression.

Syntax
```
result = number1-number2
```

or

```
-number
```

Example

This example is the same as saying 2–1 = 1:

```
Dim MyMinus
MyMinus = 2-1
```

Tan   Math Function

Purpose

Use this function in order to return the tangent of an angle. The Tan function takes an angle and returns the ratio of two sides of a right triangle. The length of the side opposite the angle divided by the length of the side adjacent to the angle is the ratio.

Syntax

```
Tan(number)
```

The number argument can be any valid numeric expression that expresses an angle in radians.

Example

Please see the example for the Sin function (p. 450).

Time   Date/Time Function

Purpose

Use this function to display the current system time.

Syntax

```
Time
```

Example

This example is similar to the Now function (p. 438), except that Time returns only the time and not the date.

```
Dim UrTime
UrTime = Time
```

TimeSerial   Date/Time Function

Purpose

Use this function in order to display or return a date (see Date function p. 409) containing the time for a specific hour, minute, and second.

Syntax

```
TimeSerial(hour, minute, second)
```

Example

In this example, the TimeSerial function returns a time for 20 minutes before (–20) six hours after noon (12 + 6), or 5:40:00 P.M.

```
Dim UrTime1
UrTime1 = TimeSerial(12 + 6, -20, 0)
Response.Write("TimeSerial = " & UrTime1)
```

```
TimeSerial = 5:40:00 PM
```

Returning a serial time value

TimeValue   Date/Time Function

Purpose

Use this function when you want to return a Date (see Date function p. 409) including the time. You can enter valid times using either a 12-hour or 24-hour clock. Both 1:30 P. M. and 13:30 are valid. The TimeValue function doesn't return date information, but an invalid date will cause an error.

Syntax

```
TimeValue(time)
```

Example

Here, the example uses the TimeValue function to convert a string to a time:

```
UrTime1 = TimeValue("4:35:17 PM")
Response.Write("TimeValue = " & UrTime1)
```

```
TimeValue = 4:35:17 PM
```

Converting a string to a time value

Trim   Function

Purpose

Use this function when you want to remove leading spaces (LTrim), trailing spaces (RTrim), or both leading and trailing spaces (Trim) from a string.

VBScript Reference

Syntax

```
LTrim(string)
RTrim(string)
Trim(string)
```

The string argument is any valid string expression. If string contains Null, Null is returned.

Example

When previewed in a browser or online, the preceding will display "Oh Boyee" in a dialog box, showing the left blank spaces trimmed, the right blank spaces trimmed, and both left and right blanks removed.

```
Dim ThisTrim
    ThisTrim = LTrim(" Oh Boyee ")
    Response.Write ("show" & ThisTrim)
    ThisTrim = RTrim(" Oh Boyee ")
    Response.Write ("show" & ThisTrim)
    ThisTrim = Trim(" Oh Boyee ")
    Response.Write ("show" & ThisTrim)
```

Ubound   Array Handling Function

Purpose

Use this function when you want to find the largest available subscript for the array in question. The UBound function is used with the LBound function (p. 432) to determine the size of an array.

Syntax

```
UBound(arrayname[, dimension])
```

Example

In an array with three elements, element 1 will have a Ubound value of 50, element 2 a value of 33, and element 3 a value of 4. See the example for the Lbound function (p. 432).

```
Dim Sasha(50,33,4)
```

UCase   String Function

Purpose

Use this function to convert a string to uppercase. Only lowercase letters are converted to uppercase. Non-alphabetic characters remain unchanged.

Syntax

```
UCase(string)
```

The string argument is any valid string.

Example

Once the code is executed, "HI THERE" will be displayed in the message box.

```
UrWord = UCase("Hi There")
Response.Write("Upper Case = " & UrWord)
```

> Upper Case = HI THERE

Converting a string to uppercase

VarType   Function

Purpose

Use this function to obtain a value indicating the subtype of a variable. The VarType function doesn't return an array value alone. The array (p. 401) value is combined with another value that indicates a specific array type.

Syntax

```
VarType(varname)
```

The varname argument can be applicable to any variable.

Example

The value returned by MyCheck in this case is 5. The value 5 represents the constant (vbDouble) for a double-precision floating-point number.

```
Dim MyCheck
MyCheck = VarType(30.00)
Response.Write("variable type = " & MyCheck)
```

> variable type = 5

Returning a value representing the variable subtype

WeekDay   Function

Purpose

Use this function to return an integer associated with a day of the week. The constants standing for each day of the week are as follows: vbSunday (1 Sunday), vbMonday (2 Monday), vbTuesday (3 Tuesday), vbWednesday (4 Wednesday), vbThursday (5 Thursday), vbFriday (6 Friday), vbSaturday (7 Saturday).

Syntax

```
WeekDay(date, [firstdayofweek])
```

Example

Here, the constant value of 6 will be returned by MyWeekDay, as 6 is the code
for vbFriday, the constant representing that day:

```
Dim MyDate, MyWeekDay
MyDate = #May 19, 2000#
MyWeekDay = WeekDay(MyDate)
Response.Write("day constant = " & MyWeekday)
```

WeekDayName   Function

Purpose

Use this function to return a name in the form of a string showing the specified day of the week.

Syntax

```
WeekDayName(weekday, abbreviate, firstdayofweek)
```

Example

Here, the message box will display "Thu", as that is the value for
vbThursday:

```
MyDate = WeekDayName(5, True)
Response.Write("day name = " & MyDate)
```

day name = Thu

The WeekDayName value for Thursday

While...Wend   Control Flow Statement

Purpose

Use this statement to execute code within a block of statements that continues executing as long as a given condition is True.

Syntax

```
While condition
[statements]
Wend
```

Example

As long as X is less than 2000, A will continue to be incremented by 1 each
time execution continues through the loop.

When X = 2000, the Wend statement is encountered and execution falls to the next statement.

```
While X < 2000
A = A + 1
Wend
```

Xor   Operator

Purpose
Use this operator when you want to logically exclude a value in two expressions. If one, and only one, of the expressions evaluates to True, the result is True. However, if either expression is Null, the result is also Null.

Syntax
```
result = expression1 Xor expression2
```

Example
In the following example, the first line of code evaluates to True because the first expression is true. The second line of code is false because both expressions are true.

```
Urexample = 2 > 1 Xor 2 > 3 ' Returns True.
Urexample = 5 > 4 Xor 10 > 9  ' returns False.
```

Year   Function

Purpose
Use this function to return an integer associated with the year.

Syntax
```
Year(date)
```

Any expression that can represent a date (p. date 401) is a valid argument.

Example
Here, the year is extracted from the complete date:

```
MyDate = #May 19, 2000#
MyYear = Year(MyDate)
Response.Write("Year = " & MyYear)
```

Year = 2000

The value of the year in an expression

SQL by Category

Every programmer who works with Active Server Page (ASP) technology deals with the creation, change, and deletion of information from a database with the use of Structured Query Language (SQL). The following table helps you locate the page number of the most common SQL commands and methods. The common commands and methods are grouped into the following categories: Data Definition Language, Data Manipulation Language, Data Control Language, Logical Connectors, Comparison Operators, Aggregate Functions, Joins, Subquery, the Where Clause, Non-Standard functions, and Relational Operators. Because Alias is a special situation in SQL, we placed this item in a category of its own.

The SQL categories are described as follows:

- Data Definition Language covers SQL commands that create and destroy database tables.
- Data Manipulation Language covers SQL commands that create, change, or destroy the information in a database table or the structure of the table.

- Data Control Language covers protection of the database, such as granting access to the tables.
- Logical Connectors cover those items that add logic to an SQL statement, such as And or Or.
- Comparison Operators cover those operators that allow for the comparison between two items.
- Aggregate Functions deal with those standard SQL functions that allow programmers to narrow a search of a database.
- Joins category covers those items that allow information from two or more tables to be related.
- Subquery category covers items that allow a programmer to extend the search of a database to include an SQL Select statement.
- Where Clause category deals with predicates that narrow the scope of an SQL Select statement that retrieves data.
- Non-Standard functions covers functions that database providers, such as Oracle, provide.
- Relational Operators cover items that allow programmers to write an SQL statement that either includes rows of a table or excludes rows of a table from a database search.

Keyword	Category	Page Number in SQL Reference Section
Abs	Nonstandard Numeric Function	470
Alias	Alias	471
And	Logical Connector	472
Avg	Aggregate Function	473
Basic Subquery	Subquery	468
Between	Where Clause	475
Ceiling	Nonstandard Numeric Function	476
Concatenation	Nonstandard String Function	478
Conditional Join	Join	478
Count	Aggregate Function	480
Create Index	Data Definition Language	481

Keyword	Category	Page Number in SQL Reference Section
Create Table	Data Definition Language	481
Create View	Data Definition Language	482
Delete	Data Manipulation Language	481
Drop Index	Data Definition Language	483
Drop Table	Data Definition Language	483
Equal (=)	Comparison Operator	483
Except	Relational Operator	484
Exists/Not Exists	Subquery	485
Floor	Nonstandard Numeric Function	487
Grant	Data Control Language	489
Greater Than (>)	Comparison Operator	490
Greater Than or Equal to (>=)	Comparison Operator	491
Group by	Other Clause	492
Having	Relational Clause	494
In/Not In	Where Clause	495
Inner Join	Join	497
Insert	Data Manipulation Language	499
Intersect	Relational Operator	500
Is Null/Is Not Null	Where Clause	502
Left	Nonstandard String Function	503
Length	Nonstandard String Function	504
Less Than (<)	Comparison Operator	505
Less Than or Equal to (<=)	Comparison Operator	506

Continued

SQL by Category

Keyword	Category	Page Number in SQL Reference Section
Like/Not Like	Where Clause	507
Lower	Nonstandard String Function	510
Max	Aggregate Function	511
Min	Aggregate Function	511
Not	Logical Connector	511
Not Equal (<>)	Comparison Operator	512
Or	Logical Connector	512
Order by	Relational Operator	513
Outer Join	Join	514
Power	Nonstandard Numeric Function	517
Revoke	Data Control Language	518
Right	Nonstandard String Function	518
Select	Data Manipulation Language	519
Select [Distinct]	Data Manipulation Language	519
Sign	Nonstandard Numeric Function	521
Sqrt	Nonstandard Numeric Function	521
Substr	Nonstandard String Function	522
Sum	Aggregate Function	522
Truncate	Data Definition Language	523
Union	Relational Operator	523
Update	Data Manipulation Language	525
Upper	Nonstandard String Function	526
Where	Where Clause	527

in plain english in pla
sh in plain english in
glish in plain english
in plain english in pla
sh in plain english in
glish in plain english
in plain english in pla
glish in plain english
in plain english in pla
sh in plain english in
glish in plain english
in plain english in pla
sh in plain english in
glish in plain english
in plain english in pla
lish in plain english
in plain english in pla
sh in plain english in
glish in plain english
in plain english in pla
sh in plain english in
lish in plain english
in plain english in pla
glish in plain english

SQL Reference

This reference section does not include every possible function that exists for every database vendor. Instead, it provides you with the basic syntax for the most commonly used SQL statements. You may be using Oracle, Sybase, or Microsoft MS SQL Server as your database. Some of these databases use a certain syntax for items such as Clustered Indexes. You can consult the the vendors for further information.

As an ASP developer, sometimes you must look up the syntax to different SQL commands. Many times, you are asked to perform simple database administration tasks like creating and dropping tables. This reference section is written with this in mind. Common SQL commands, such as `Insert`, `Update`, `Select`, and `Delete`, are covered in this chapter. In addition, data command language commands, such as `Create` and `Drop Table`, `Grant`, and `Revoke`, are also covered.

A Basic Subquery   Subquery

Purpose

Use a subquery when the criteria in a Where clause needs to use another Select statement.

Syntax

```
Select * From TableA Where [Condition] [Select * From Table]
```

Examples

Suppose you wanted to know the last name of all the customers who purchased an item in the month of May from you. The Customers and PurchasedItem tables (see Tables 1 and 2) show the data. In order to get this information, retrieve all the customers from the Customers table. Then compare those customers with the buyer id from the PurchasedItem table. The SQL statement to accomplish these actions follows:

```
Select LastName From Customers Where CustomerId =
(Select BuyerId From PurchasedItem Where Month =
'May')
```

The ASP code to accomplish this SQL command is as follows:

```
<%
Dim DataConn,SQL
Set DataConn = Server.CreateObject("ADODB.Connection")
DataConn.Open Application("db_ConnectionString")

SQL = " Select LastName From Customers "
SQL = SQL & "Where CustomerId =  "
SQL = SQL & " (Select BuyerId From PurchasedItem "
SQL = SQL & " Where Month = 'May')"

Set Recdset = DataConn.Execute(SQL)
Response.Write "<BR>LastName"
Do while Not Recdset.Eof
    Response.Write Recdset(0)
  Response.Write "<BR>"
Loop
%>
SelectWhereSelectWhere
```

The results of this SQL statement are in Table 3.

Table 1 *Tables Customers*

CustomerId	FirstName	LastName
1	Melissa	Chesser
2	Kitty	Boo
3	Rick	Barker
4	Kathleen	Neel

Table 2 *Table PurchasedItem*

ItemId	Item	BuyerId	Month
1	Chair	3	June
1	Table	3	May
2	Lamp	1	May
3	Sofa	2	October

Table 3 *Results of a Basic Subquery SQL Statement*

LastName
Barker
Chesser

Another way that an SQL statement can be written is to use the In predicate to find the customers who brought in the month of May. This is shown below:

```
Select * From Customers Where 'May' In (Select Month From
PurchasedItem)
```

The ASP code to accomplish this SQL command is as follows:

```
<%
Dim DataConn,SQL
Set DataConn = Server.CreateObject("ADODB.Connection")
'the connection string is in Application variable
DataConn.Open Application("db_ConnectionString")
```

```
    SQL = " Select * From Customers "
SQL = SQL & "Where 'May' IN  "
SQL = SQL & " (Select Month From PurchasedItem )"

Set Recdset = DataConn.Execute(SQL)
Response.Write "<BR>LastName"
Do while Not Recdset.Eof
  Response.WriteRecdset(0)
  Response.Write "<BR>"
Loop
%>
```

Abs

Purpose

Use the Abs function to get the absolute value of a column in a Select statement.

Syntax

```
Abs (number)
```

Example

The following SQL statement returns the absolute value of the column temp1 from the table ChemistryReadings.

```
Select Abs (temp1) From ChemistryReadings
```

The ASP code to accomplish this SQL command is as follows:

```
<%
Dim DataConn,SQL
Set DataConn = Server.CreateObject("ADODB.Connection")
'the connection string is in Application variable
DataConn.Open Application("db_ConnectionString")

SQL = " Select Abs(temp1) From ChemistryReadings "
Set Recdset = DataConn.Execute(SQL)
Response.Write "<BR>Absolute Value of Readings"
Do while Not Recdset.Eof
    Response.Write Recdset(0)
Response.Write "<BR>"
Loop
%>
```

Alter Table

Data Definition Language

Purpose

Use this command to alter the structure of an existing table. The Syntax below shows a simple syntax to what in reality is a complex SQL command. However, be careful not to use the Modify option to change a table that already contains data. For instance, let's say that you have a column specified as varchar2(100), but really want the column to be varchar2(50). Most databases will not allow you to change the column's specification if data exists in the column. Syntax:

```
Alter Table [Add|Modify] TableName
[Condition]
```

Example

If you wanted to add a column named Players to a table named TEAMS, use this statement:

```
Alter Table TEAMS Add (Players VarChar (50)
Not Null)
```

If you want to modify the Players column that was just added to the Teams table, then use this statement. Remember, to modify a column in Oracle you must not have any data in the table.

```
Alter Table TEAMS Modify (Players VarChar (20)
Not Null)
```

Alias

Basic Use of Alias

Purpose

Use an alias to assign a synonym to a table or a column in a Select statement. An alias is useful with tables that are labeled with many characters.

Syntax

```
SelectColumnname As Alias From
Tablename
Select
```

Example

The following SQL statement shows how to use an alias to label a table. The table Student has an alias of Stu, and the table School has an alias of Sch. The two tables are linked together by a column named SchoolID. The Where clause gives this SQL statement an inner join.

```
Select Stu.FirstName,Stu.LastName,Sch.SchoolName From Student
Stu, School Sch Where Stu.SchoolID = Sch.SchoolID
```

Not only can you give a table an alias, but also a column. The following SQL statement indicates that the column FirstName will be displayed with the alias "First Name of Student" in those rows that are returned when this statement is executed.

```
Select FirstName As "First Name of Student" From Students
```

And   Logical Connector

Purpose

Use the And connector to specify that two or more conditions must be met in order for this statement to be true.

Syntax

```
Select* From TableName Wherecondition1 AND
condition2
```

Example

The following example uses the And logical connector to find all the students in Table StudentClasses (see Table 4) that made an **A** in English and a **B** in Math. In order to accomplish this task, use the And connector in the Where clause. The following statement could be read this way: "Find those rows in table StudentClasses in which the student made an A in English and an A in Math."

```
Select * From StudentClasses Where English = 'A' And
Math = 'B'
```

The ASP code to accomplish this SQL command is as follows:

```
<%
Dim DataConn,SQL
Set DataConn = Server.CreateObject("ADODB.Connection")
'the connection string is in Application variable
DataConn.Open Application("db_ConnectionString")
SQL = " Select * From StudentClasses "
SQL = SQL & " Where English = 'A' AND Math = 'B' "
Set Recdset = DataConn.Execute(SQL)
%>
<TABLE Border = 1 ><TR>
<%For I = 0 to Recdset.Fields.Count -1%>
<TD><B><%= Recdset(I).Name %></B></TD>
<%Next%>
<TR>
<% For I = 0 to Recdset.Fields.Count - 1 %>
```

```
<%= Recdset(I) %></TD>
</TR>
<% Recdset.MoveNext      Loop
%>
< /Table>
```

Table 4 *Table StudentClasses*

Student	English	Math	Science
Andy	C	A	B
Beth	A	A	A
Tim	A	B	Null
Cara	A	B	D
Manda	A	C	C

The results of this SQL statement are shown in Table 5.

Table 5 *Returned Rows from And SQL Statement*

Student	English	Math	Science
Tim	A	B	C
Cara	A	B	D

Avg   Aggregate Function

Purpose

Use the Avg function to calculate the average of the values in a specified column. The column must be a number field.

Syntax

```
Select Avg ([All|Distinct] Column) From
TableName [Whereclause]
```

Examples

The following example shows an SQL statement that uses the Avg function to get the average of the box weights from column Box_Weight in table Groceries (see Table 6). The result for the SQL statement is given in Table 7.

```
Select Avg(Box_Weight) As Avg1 From Groceries
```

The ASP code to accomplish this SQL command is as follows:

```
<%
Dim DataConn,SQL
Set DataConn = Server.CreateObject("ADODB.Connection")
'the connection string is in Application variable
DataConn.Open Application("db_ConnectionString")
SQL = "Select Avg(All Box_Weight) As Avg1 "
SQL = SQL & "From Groceries "
Set Recdset = DataConn.Execute(SQL)
%>
<TABLE Border = 1 ><TR>
<%For I = 0 to Recdset.Fields.Count −1%>
<TD><B><%= Recdset(I).Name %></B></TD>
<%Next%>
<TR>
<% For I = 0 to Recdset.Fields.Count − 1 %>
<%= Recdset(I) %></TD>
</TR>
<% Recdset.MoveNext
       Loop
%>
< /Table>
```

Table 6 *Table Groceries*

Item	Box_Weight (lbs)	Brand_Name	Fat (gms)
Cereal	1.4	Ken's Rice Cakes	0.05
Cereal	1.25	OH's	1.67
Cereal	0.97	Jay's Oats	Null
Cereal	0.99	Needy Squares	2.34
Cereal	1.29	MegNut Cereal	1.87

Table 7 *Results from Avg SQL Statement*

AVG1
1.18

The next SQL statement shows how to get the average for all box weights over 1 lb. A Where clause is added to the statement to narrow the search of rows to those over 1 lb. As you can see in Table 6, only three rows meet this criterion. The result is shown in Table 8.

```
Select Avg (Box_Weight) As AVG_OVER_1 From Groceries
Where
Box_Weight > 1
```

Table 8   *Results of Avg Weight Over 1 lb.*

AVG_OVER_1

1.313

Between   Where Clause

Purpose

Use the Between predicate in the Where clause when you want to set a condition to return rows only if conditions exist between two items.

Syntax

```
SelectColumn From TableName [Where condition
Between
item1 AND item2]
```

Example

The following SQL statement shows how to return those rows from TableA (see Table 9) that have an order date between January 1, 2000, and January 31, 2000.

```
Select * From TableA Where OrderDate Between '1/1/2000'
And
'1/31/2000'
```

The ASP code to accomplish this SQL command is as follows:

```
<%
Dim DataConn,SQL
Set DataConn = Server.CreateObject("ADODB.Connection")
'the connection string is in Application variable
DataConn.Open Application("db_ConnectionString")
SQL = " Select * From TableA "
SQL = SQL & "Where OrderDate Between  "
SQL = SQL & "'1/1/2000' AND '1/31/2000' "
Set Recdset = DataConn.Execute(SQL)
%>
```

```
<TABLE Border = 1 ><TR>
<%For I = 0 to Recdset.Fields.Count —1%>
<TD><B><%= Recdset(I).Name %></B></TD>
<%Next%>
<TR>
<% For I = 0 to Recdset.Fields.Count — 1 %>
<%= Recdset(I) %></TD>
</TR>
<% Recdset.MoveNext
      Loop
%>
< /Table>
Select
```

Table 9   *TableA*

Item	Quantity	OrderDate
Chairs	10	3/3/2000
Sofa	2	1/10/2000
Tables	20	2/2/2000
Sofa	3	1/20/2000
Sofa	5	1/22/2000

Table 10 shows the results of this query.

Table 10   *Results of Between SQL Statement*

Item	Quantity	OrderDate
Sofa	2	1/10/2000
Sofa	3	1/20/2000
Sofa	5	1/22/2000

Ceiling

**Nonstandard
Numeric Function**

Purpose

Use the Ceiling function to return the rounded-up-to-the-next-highest-integer value of a single column's decimal data type.

Syntax

```
Ceiling(decimal)
```

Example

The following SQL statement gets the ceiling value of the column testavg from the table School. See Table 11 for the School Table.

```
Select Ceiling (testavg) As "TEST AVG" From School
```

The ASP code to execute this SQL statement is as follows:

```
<%
Dim DataConn,SQL
Set DataConn = Server.CreateObject("ADODB.Connection")
'the connection string is in Application variable
DataConn.Open Application("db_ConnectionString")
SQL = " Select Ceiling (testavg) "
SQL = SQL & "As "TEST AVG" From School "
Set Recdset = DataConn.Execute(SQL)
%>
<TABLE Border = 1 ><TR>
<%For I = 0 to Recdset.Fields.Count −1%>
<TD><B><%= Recdset(I).Name %></B></TD>
<%Next%>
<TR>
<% For I = 0 to Recdset.Fields.Count − 1 %>
<%= Recdset(I) %></TD>
</TR>
<% Recdset.MoveNext
    Loop
%>
< /Table>
```

Table 11 *Table School*

ClassID	testavg
1	89.3
2	75.8
3	92.77

Table 12 shows the results of the using the Ceiling function.

Table 12 *Results of Ceiling SQL Statement*

TEST AVG

90

76

93

Concatenation (+)(||) | Nonstandard String Function

Purpose

Use the concatenation operator (||) or (+) whenever you need to combine two strings of text into one. You can only use this function with data types that are string-related, such as char, varchar, and so on. Oracle uses the (||) operator to do concatention, while MS SQL 7.0 uses the (+) operator.

Syntax

```
String1+String2 depending on the database
provider.
```

```
String1 || String2 if Oracle is the database provider.
```

Example

The following SQL statement shows the concatenation of the contents of the FirstName column with the contents of the column LastName from the table Students. This example is good for a MS SQL database.

```
Select FirstName+","+LastName From Students
```

The example below is good for an Oracle database:

```
Select FirstName || " " || LastName From Students
```

Conditional Join | Join

Purpose

Use a conditional join when a criterion must be true in the Where clause in order for a recordset to be returned.

Syntax

```
SelectTableA.Column From TableA,TableB Where
TableA.ColumnA =
TableB.ColumnA And condition
```

Example

The following SQL statement returns from the table Student (see Table 13) those students who attend school in District 1. The SQL statement joins the column from table Student and table District (see Table 14).

```
Select* From Student, District Where Student.
DistrictID = District.DistrictID And District.District
= 1


<%
Dim DataConn,SQL
Set DataConn = Server.CreateObject("ADODB.Connection")
'the connection string is in Application variable
DataConn.Open Application("db_ConnectionString")
SQL = " Select * From Student, District "
SQL = SQL & "Where Student.DistrictID = District.DistrictID "
SQL = SQL & " And District.District = 1 "
Set Recdset = DataConn.Execute(SQL)
%>
<TABLE Border = 1 ><TR>
<%For I = 0 to Recdset.Fields.Count —1%>
<TD><B><%= Recdset(I).Name %></B></TD>
<%Next%>
<TR>
<% For I = 0 to Recdset.Fields.Count — 1 %>
<%= Recdset(I) %></TD>
</TR>
<% Recdset.MoveNext
    Loop
%>
< /Table>
```

Table 13 *Table Student*

FirstNam	LastNam	DistrictID
Elaine	Smith	1
Jim	Newly	1
Rick	Barker	2
Jon	Sansom	4

Table 14 *Table District*

DistrictID	SchoolName
1	Barn High School
2	Eden High School
3	Sam Hendrix Junior High School

Table 15 gives the results of the SQL statement.

Table 15 *Results of Conditional Join SQL Statement*

FirstNam	LastNam	SchoolName	District
Elaine	Smith	Barn High School	1
Jim	Newly	Barn High School	1

Count	**Aggregate Function**

Purpose

Use the Count function to get the number of rows in a table. This function is useful when you need to know how many rows are in a table.

Syntax

```
SelectCount (*) From TableName
SelectCount (All | Distinct Column) From TableName
```

Examples

The SQL statement uses the Count function to return the number of rows in the Groceries table.

```
Select Count(*) From Groceries
```

The following SQL statement finds the number of items in the Groceries table that have a box weight over 1 lb.

```
Select Count(*) From Groceries Where Box_Weight > 1
```

You can supply the Count function with a column name instead of the * character. The * character means all columns when used in the Select statement. However, because any rows containing a NULL are not counted, it is better to use the * character when counting rows of a table.

The following SQL statement shows the syntax for counting rows in the table using the column `fat` as the argument supplied to the function. Thus, the SQL statement will count only those rows from `fat` that are not null.

```
Select Count (All fat) From Groceries
```

Create Index   Data Definition Language

Purpose

Use `Create Index` to create an index on a column in a table. The index allows for quicker access to rows in a table. Without an index on databases with millions of records — such as the IRS's database — it could take days to locate a record. You normally want to create an index on the primary key of a table. Some database providers have unique, clustered, or nonclustered indexes. Consult their documentation to learn how to create these types of indexes.

Syntax

```
CREATE INDEX IndexName ON TableName (Column to be indexed)
```

The SQL statement creates a new index named `PLAYER_IDX`. The index is created on the column `Players` of table Teams.

```
Create Index PLAYER_IDX On Teams (Players)
```

Create Table   Data Definition Language

Purpose

Use the `Create Table` statement to create a table. When creating a table, you must supply at least one column of the table.

Syntax

```
Create Table TableName (
Column Name1    Data Type   Null or Not Null  Primary Key,
Column Name2    Data Type    Null or Not Null
Constraint  Name_FK Foreign Key (Columnname ) References Table
(Columnname) );
```

Example

The following SQL statement will create the table BaseBallTeams. This table will contain three columns, of which `TeamName` will be the primary key.

The primary key to a table is very important. This marker gives each row in the table a unique signature. A primary key can consist of one column or multiple columns, but the primary key for each row must be different from every other row. In this case, `TeamName` will be unique, which is why it is the primary key.

```
Create Table BaseBallTeams (
TeamName          VarChar(25)      Not Null PRIMARY KEY,
City              VarChar(50)   Not Null,
State             VarChar(100)  Not Null) ;
```

Create View   Data Definition Language

Purpose

Use the Create View command to assign the results of a query to a new personal-use table, which you can use in other queries. This new table is given the view name in your From clause.

Syntax

```
Create View ViewName As Select* From TableName
```

Example

Suppose you need to use the data from all Auburn and Clemson baseball players who pitched for their universities between 1964 and 1977. You plan to use the retrieved data with other SQL statements later in your program. This is a good situation for creating a view. The following code will create the view you need:

```
Create View  AUBURNBASEBALL AS
Select* Auburn_Pitchers, Clemson_Pitchers From Auburn,Clemson
Where Year Between 1964 and 1977
```

Delete   Data Manipulation Language

Purpose

Use the Delete command in an SQL statement when you want to remove rows from a table.

Syntax

```
Delete ColumnName From TableName [Where
clause]
Delete * From TableName
```

Example

The following SQL statement uses a Delete to remove from the Cities table all the rows whose column State contains the string "Alabama":

```
Delete * FROM Cities WhereState = "Alabama"
```

The next example shows you how to delete all the rows in the table Cities:

```
Delete * FROM Cites
```

Drop Index   Data Definition Language

Purpose

Use the Drop Index command in your SQL statement to remove an existing index from a database.

Syntax

```
Drop Index   IndexName
```

Example

The following SQL statement deletes the index named PLAYER_IDX:

```
Drop Index PLAYER_IDX
```

Drop Table   Data Definition Language

Purpose

Use the Drop Table statement to remove a table from a database.

Syntax

```
Drop Table TableName
```

Example

The following SQL statement deletes the table BaseballTeams from the database:

```
Drop Table BaseBallTeams
```

Equal (=)   Comparison Operator

Purpose

Use the equal (=) comparison operator to compare two items to determine if they are equal in value.

Syntax

```
Select* From TableName Where column = item
```

Example

The following SQL statement uses the = operator in the Where clause to find in the table HighSchoolLeague1956 those rows whose column Losses contain the value 4.

```
Select * From HighSchoolLeague1956 Where Losses = 4
```

Except   Relational Operator

Purpose

Use the Except clause to find all the rows that do not intersect two tables. The two tables must have the same structure. The All option in the syntax allows this command to return all the records that meet the criterion including duplicates. One word of warning: the Except operator is not accepted by all database providers.

Syntax

```
Select * From Table1 Except
[All][Corresponding] Select * From
Table2
```

Example

If you want to know which students from the tables Students1964 and Students1965 are not in both tables (see Tables 16 and 17), use the following SQL statement:

```
Select * Students1964 Expect All Select * Students1965
```

This SQL statement will return all the students in the Students1964 table (see Table 16) who are not in the Students1965 table.

The ASP code to accomplish this SQL command is as follows:

```
<%
Dim DataConn,SQL
Set DataConn = Server.CreateObject("ADODB.Connection")
'the connection string is in Application variable
DataConn.Open Application("db_ConnectionString")
SQL = " Select * Students1964 "
SQL = SQL & "All Select * Students1965 "
Set Recdset = DataConn.Execute(SQL)
%>
<TABLE Border = 1 ><TR>
<%For I = 0 to Recdset.Fields.Count -1%>
<TD><B><%= Recdset(I).Name %></B></TD>
```

```
<%Next%>
<TR>
<% For I = 0 to Recdset.Fields.Count - 1 %>
<%= Recdset(I) %></TD>
</TR>
<% Recdset.MoveNext
    Loop
%>
</Table>
```

Table 16 *Table Students1964*

First_Name	Last_Name
Bob	Barker
Mary	Barker
Sam	Anderson

Table 17 *Table Students1965*

First_Name	Last_Name
Bob	Barker
Mary	Barker

You can see from the preceding two tables that all the students are the same except Sam Anderson. Thus, Sam Anderson is the row returned in Table 18.

Table 18 *Results of Except SQL Statement*

First_Name	Last_Name
Sam	Anderson

Exists/Not Exists   Subquery

Purpose
Use the Exists predicate in a subquery to determine if there are any rows that match the condition the subquery condition.

Syntax

```
Select * From TableName Where Exists
[Subquery Condition]
```

Example

Suppose you want to find out what products exist in the inventory of the Georgia warehouse at this time. The Products and Inventory tables (see Tables 19 and 20) list the inventory and products. Use the following SQL statement to find the Georgia inventory:

```
Select ProductName From Products Where Exists (Select * From
Inventory Where WareHouseState = 'Georgia')
```

The ASP code to execute this SQL statement is as follows:

```
<%
Dim DataConn,SQL
Set DataConn = Server.CreateObject("ADODB.Connection")
'the connection string is in Application variable
DataConn.Open Application("db_ConnectionString")
SQL = "Select ProductName From Products "
SQL = SQL & "Where Exists (Select * From Inventory "
SQL = SQL & "Where WareHouseState = 'Georgia')
   "
Set Recdset = DataConn.Execute(SQL)
%>
<TABLE Border = 1 ><TR>
<%For I = 0 to Recdset.Fields.Count -1%>
<TD><B><%= Recdset(I).Name %></B></TD>
<%Next%>
<TR>
<% For I = 0 to Recdset.Fields.Count - 1 %>
<%= Recdset(I) %></TD>
</TR>
<% Recdset.MoveNext
    Loop
%>
< /Table>
```

Table 19   *Table Products*

ProductId	ProductName
1	Blue Hats
2	Red Hats
3	Green Hats
4	Sofas

Table 20   *Table Inventory*

WareHouseId	WareHouseState	ProductId	NumbInStock
1	Florida	2	15
1	Florida	4	100
2	Georgia	1	1000
2	Georgia	2	75

Table 21 shows the results of the SQL statement.

Table 21   *Results of Exists SQL Statement*

ProductName
Red Hats
Blue Hats

If you wanted to determine the inventory that did *not* exist in the Georgia warehouses, then execute this statement:

```
Select ProductName From Products Where Not Exists (Select * From
Inventory Where WareHouseState = 'Georgia')
```

Floor	Nonstandard Numeric Function

Purpose

Use the Floor function to return the rounded-down value of a column that has a decimal data type.

Syntax

```
Floor (decimal)
```

Example

The SQL statement uses the Floor function to round down the value of the column testavg in table School (see Table 22). The table shows the contents of the School table.

```
Select Floor (testavg) As "Floor of avg" From School
The ASP code to execute the preceding SQL statement is as
follows:<%
Dim DataConn,SQL
Set DataConn = Server.CreateObject("ADODB.Connection")
'the connection string is in Application variable
DataConn.Open Application("db_ConnectionString")
SQL = "Select Floor (testavg) As "
SQL = SQL & """"Floor of avg"" From School "
Set Recdset = DataConn.Execute(SQL)
%>
<TABLE Border = 1 ><TR>
<%For I = 0 to Recdset.Fields.Count -1%>
<TD><B><%= Recdset(I).Name %></B></TD>
<%Next%>
<TR>
<% For I = 0 to Recdset.Fields.Count - 1 %>
<%= Recdset(I) %></TD>
</TR>
<% Recdset.MoveNext
    Loop
%>< /Table>
```

Table 22 *Table School*

SchoolId	testavg
1	98.4
2	78.3
3	83.7

Table 23 shows the results returned from executing the SQL statement.

Table 23   *Results of the Floor SQL Statement*

Floor of avg

98

78

83

Grant   Data Control Language

Purpose

Use the Grant command to give different levels of access to tables in a database.

Syntax

```
Grant [Fill in From list of privileges]  On [Object to
grant access to ]To user list [With Grant Option]
```

Table 24 shows the syntax for privileges granted by the database administrator.

Table 24   *Privileges that Can be Granted*

Privileges that can be filled into GRANT

ALL PRIVILEGES

Select Delete

Select Insert [(Columnname1, Columnname2, etc.)]

Select Update [(Columnname1, Columnname2, etc.)]

Select References [(Columnname1, Columnname2, etc.)]

Usage

Examples

The following SQL statement uses the Grant command to allow a user list known as clerks to be able to insert records into table Inventory:

```
Grant Insert On Inventory To Clerks
```

If you wanted to allow the public to only read the table Inventory, then use this SQL command:

```
Grant Select On Inventory To Public
```

If you wanted to grant the clerks permission to update only the column named ProductId in the table Inventory, then use the following SQL command:

```
Grant Update (ProductId) On Inventory To Clerks
```

Greater Than (>)   Comparison Operator

Purpose

Use the greater than (>) comparison operator to compare two items to determine which is greater.

Syntax

```
Select * From TableName Where Column > item
```

Example

If you wanted to determine which teams in table HighSchoolLeague1956 (see Table 25) won more than six football games, use the following SQL statement:

```
Select * From HighSchoolLeague1956 Where Wins > 6
```

The ASP code to execute the preceding SQL statement is as follows:

```
<%
Dim DataConn,SQL
Set DataConn = Server.CreateObject("ADODB.Connection")
'the connection string is in Application variable
DataConn.Open Application("db_ConnectionString")
SQL = "Select * From HighSchoolLeague1956 "
SQL = SQL & " Where Wins > 6 "
Set Recdset = DataConn.Execute(SQL)
%>
<TABLE Border = 1 ><TR>
<%For I = 0 to Recdset.Fields.Count -1%>
<TD><B><%= Recdset(I).Name %></B></TD>
<%Next%>
<TR>
<% For I = 0 to Recdset.Fields.Count - 1 %>
<%= Recdset(I) %></TD>
</TR>
<% Recdset.MoveNext
    Loop
%>
< /Table>
```

Table 25 *Table HighSchoolLeague1956*

Team	Wins	Loses
A	3	7
B	9	1
C	6	4
D	7	3

Table 26 shows the rows returned from the SQL statement.

Table 26 *Rows Returned from the Greater Than (>) SQL Statement*

Team	Wins	Loses
B	9	1
D	7	3

Greater Than or Equal (>=) | Comparison Operator

Purpose

Use the greater than or equal (>=) comparison operator to compare two items to determine which is greater than or equal to an item.

Syntax

```
Select * From TableName Where column >= item
```

Example

If you wanted to determine which teams in table HighSchoolLeague1956 (see Table 27) won six or more football games, use the following SQL statement:

```
Select * From HighSchoolLeague1956 Where Wins >= 6
```

The ASP code to execute the preceding SQL statement is as follows:

```
<%
Dim DataConn,SQL
Set DataConn = Server.CreateObject("ADODB.Connection")
'the connection string is in Application variable
DataConn.Open Application("db_ConnectionString")
SQL = "Select * From HighSchoolLeague1956 "
```

SQL Reference

```
SQL = SQL & " Where Wins >= 6 "
Set Recdset = DataConn.Execute(SQL)
%>
<TABLE Border = 1 ><TR>
<%For I = 0 to Recdset.Fields.Count —1%>
<TD><B><%= Recdset(I).Name %></B></TD>
<%Next%>
<TR>
<% For I = 0 to Recdset.Fields.Count — 1 %>
<%= Recdset(I) %></TD>
</TR>
<% Recdset.MoveNext
    Loop
%>< /Table>
```

Table 27   *Table HighSchoolLeague1956*

Team	Wins	Loses
A	3	7
B	9	1
C	6	4
D	7	3

Table 28 shows the results of the SQL statement.

Table 28   *Results of the Greater Than or Equal to (> =) SQL Statement*

Team	Wins	Loses
B	9	1
C	6	4
D	7	3

Group By   Other Clause

Purpose

Use the Group By clause to sort retrieved rows from a table into groups of data.

Syntax

```
Select * From Table1 Where condition Group By Columnname
```

Example

The following SQL statement uses the Group By clause to sort table Cities (shown in Table 29) into groups by state name:

```
Select * From Cities Group By State
```

The ASP code to execute the preceding SQL statement is as follows:

```
<%
Dim DataConn,SQL
Set DataConn = Server.CreateObject("ADODB.Connection")
'the connection string is in Application variable
DataConn.Open Application("db_ConnectionString")
SQL = "Select * From Cities Group By state "
Set Recdset = DataConn.Execute(SQL)%>
<TABLE Border = 1 ><TR>
<%For I = 0 to Recdset.Fields.Count −1%>
<TD><B><%= Recdset(I).Name %></B></TD>
<%Next%>
<TR>
<% For I = 0 to Recdset.Fields.Count − 1 %>
<%= Recdset(I) %></TD>
</TR>
<% Recdset.MoveNext
    Loop
%>< /Table>
```

Table 29 *Table Cities*

RecordId	City	State
1	Auburn	Alabama
2	Jacksonville	Florida
3	Detroit	Michigan
4	Orlando	Florida
5	Mobile	Alabama

Table 30 shows the results of this statement.

Table 30 *Rows Retrieved from the Group By SQL Statement*

RecordId	City	State
1	Auburn	Alabama
5	Mobile	Alabama
2	Jacksonville	Florida
4	Orlando	Florida
3	Detroit	Michigan

Having   Relational Clause

Purpose

Use the Having clause as a filter on retrieved rows that use the Group By clause. Think of using the Having clause in the same manner as the Where clause is used — as a filter on existing data.

Syntax

```
Select * From Table1 Group By Columnname Having condition
```

Example

The following SQL statement returns from table Cities, shown in Table 31, those rows that are grouped by the contents from the State column having the value of "Alabama." The Having clause acts just like the Where clause with the Group By clause, narrowing the search for records.

```
Select * From Cities Group By State Having State = "Alabama"
```

The ASP code to execute the preceding SQL statement is as follows:

```
<%
Dim DataConn,SQL
Set DataConn = Server.CreateObject("ADODB.Connection")
'the connection string is in Application variable
DataConn.Open Application("db_ConnectionString")
SQL = "Select * From Cities Group By "
SQL = SQL & "State Having State = ""Alabama"""

Set Recdset = DataConn.Execute(SQL)%>
<TABLE Border = 1 ><TR>
<%For I = 0 to Recdset.Fields.Count -1%>
<TD><B><%= Recdset(I).Name %></B></TD>
<%Next%>
<TR>
```

```
<% For I = 0 to Recdset.Fields.Count — 1 %>
<%= Recdset(I) %></TD>
</TR>
<% Recdset.MoveNext
    Loop
%>< /Table>
```

Table 31   *Table Cities*

RecordId	City	State
1	Auburn	Alabama
2	Jacksonville	Florida
3	Detroit	Michigan
4	Orlando	Florida
5	Mobile	Alabama

The returned rows from executing the SQL statement are shown in Table 32.

Table 32   *Rows Returned from Having SQL Statement*

RecordId	City	State
1	Auburn	Alabama
5	Mobile	Alabama

In/Not In   Where Clause

Purpose

Use the In or Not In predicates when you want to set a condition to return rows only if certain items are either in a list of items or not in a list of items.

Syntax

```
Select COLUMNS From TableName [Wherecondition In condition]
Select COLUMNS From TableName [Wherecondition Not In condition]
```

Examples

The following SQL statement retrieves only those stores in TableB in Table 33 that are located in Alabama and Michigan:

```
Select * From TableB Where State In ('ALA', 'MICH')
```

The ASP code to execute the preceding SQL statement is as follows:

```
<%
Dim DataConn,SQL
Set DataConn = Server.CreateObject("ADODB.Connection")
'the connection string is in Application variable
DataConn.Open Application("db_ConnectionString")
SQL = "Select * From TableB Where State In ('ALA', 'MICH') "
Set Recdset = DataConn.Execute(SQL)%>
<TABLE Border = 1 ><TR>
<%For I = 0 to Recdset.Fields.Count -1%>
<TD><B><%= Recdset(I).Name %></B></TD>
<%Next%>
<TR>
<% For I = 0 to Recdset.Fields.Count - 1 %>
<%= Recdset(I) %></TD>
</TR>
<% Recdset.MoveNext
    Loop
%>< /Table>
```

Table 33 *TableB*

Item	City	State
Store1	Ayden	NC
Store2	Auburn	ALA
Store3	Jacksonville	FLA
Store4	Mobile	ALA
Store5	Detroit	MICH

Table 34 shows the results of using the In statement.

Table 34 *Rows Retrieved from In SQL Statement*

Item	City	State
Store4	Mobile	ALA
Store5	Detroit	MICH

The following SQL statement finds those stores in TableB that are not located in Alabama. The results of executing this SQL statement are shown in Table 35.

```
Select * From TableB Where State Not In ('ALA')
```

Table 35 *Rows Retrieved from the Not In SQL Statement*

Item	City	State
Store1	Ayden	NC
Store3	Jacksonville	FLA
Store5	Detroit	MICH

Inner Join   Join

Purpose

Use an Inner Join clause when you want to discard all rows in a table that do not match the criteria between two tables. You can use two syntaxes to achieve an inner join. In one of the syntaxes, you use the actual words inner join. The other syntax uses a Where clause to achieve the inner join.

Syntax

```
Select * From TableA Inner Join TableB On [column to be joined]
Select * From TableA,TableB WhereTableA.Column1 = TableB.Column1
```

Examples

The following SQL statement uses the Inner Join clause to determine how many home runs Tommy Allison hit in 1930. Table 36 and Table 37 show two tables: PlayerInfo and YearStats. Using these tables, the following SQL statement will return the number of home runs Tommy Allison hit in 1930:

```
Select A.HR From PlayerInfo A Inner Join YearStats B On PlayerNUM
WhereB.Year = 1930 And A.PlayerNum = 103
```

Table 36 *Table PlayerInfo*

PlayerNum	Player
101	Trisha Allison
102	Tim Eden
103	Tommy Allison
104	Hanna Banna

Table 37 *Table YearStats*

Year	PlayerNum	HR	RBI	Avg.
1930	103	6	45	.301
1930	102	7	34	.278
1930	104	17	66	.209

Following is another way you can construct the SQL statement to give an inner join. This SQL statement finds the number of home runs Tommy Allison hit in 1930 by using the Where clause to create the inner join on tables PlayerInfo and YearStats.

```
Select YearStats.HR From PlayerInfo, YearStates Where
PlayerInfo.PlayerNum = YearStats.PlayerNum And
YearStats.PlayerNum = '101' And YearStats.Year = 1930
```

The ASP code to execute the first inner join statement is as follows:

```
<%
Dim DataConn,SQL
Set DataConn = Server.CreateObject("ADODB.Connection")
'the connection string is in Application variable
DataConn.Open Application("db_ConnectionString")
SQL = "Select A.HR From PlayerInfo A Inner Join "
SQL = SQL & "YearStats B On PlayerNUM Where "
SQL = SQL & "B.Year = 1930 And A.PlayerNum = 103
Set Recdset = DataConn.Execute(SQL)%>
<TABLE Border = 1 ><TR>
<%For I = 0 to Recdset.Fields.Count -1%>
<TD><B><%= Recdset(I).Name %></B></TD>
<%Next%>
<TR>
<% For I = 0 to Recdset.Fields.Count - 1 %>
<%= Recdset(I) %></TD>
</TR>
<% Recdset.MoveNext
    Loop
%>< /Table>
```

The results for both inner join SQL statements are given in Table 38.

Table 38   *Results from Both Types of Inner Joins*

HR

6

| Insert | Data Manipulation Language |

Purpose

Use the Insert statement to add new rows to a table.

Syntax

```
Insert Into TableName ( Column1, Column2, Column 3 ...) Values
( Value1, Value2, Value 3)
```

Example

The following SQL statement adds a new record to the Cities table found in Table 39:

```
Insert Into Cities (RecordId, City, State) Values
(6,"Atlanta","Georgia")
```

The ASP code to insert the record and then retrieve the updated table is as follows:

```
<%
Dim DataConn,SQL,Recdset
Set DataConn = Server.CreateObject("ADODB.Connection")
'the connection string is in Application variable
DataConn.Open Application("db_ConnectionString")
SQL = "Insert Into Cities (RecordId, City, State) "
SQL = SQL & "Values (6,"Atlanta","Georgia") "
DataConn.Execute(SQL)
'After the insert get the updated table
SQL = "Select * From Cities "
Set Recdset = DataConn.Execute(SQL)%>
<TABLE Border = 1 ><TR>
<%For I = 0 to Recdset.Fields.Count -1%>
<TD><B><%= Recdset(I).Name %></B></TD>
<%Next%>
<TR>
<% For I = 0 to Recdset.Fields.Count - 1 %>
<%= Recdset(I) %></TD>
</TR>
```

```
<% Recdset.MoveNext
    Loop
%>< /Table>
```

Table 39 *Table Cities*

RecordId	City	State
1	Auburn	Alabama
2	Jacksonville	Florida
3	Detroit	Michigan
4	Orlando	Florida
5	Mobile	Alabama

The results of executing this statement are found in Table 40. The new record appears as RecordId 6.

Table 40 *Results of the Insert SQL Statement*

RecordId	City	State
1	Auburn	Alabama
2	Jacksonville	Florida
3	Detroit	Michigan
4	Orlando	Florida
5	Mobile	Alabama
6	Atlanta	Georgia

Intersect   Relational Operator

Purpose

Use the Intersect relational operator to find those rows in two tables that are the same. The two tables that you use this SQL statement with must have the same data structure.

Syntax

```
Select * From Table1 Intersect [All][Corresponding] Select * From
Table2
```

Examples

The following SQL statement uses the Intersect clause to determine which students in table Students1964 and table Students1965 are common to both tables. Tables 41 and 42 show you the contents of tables Students1964 and Students1965. As you can see, three students intersect the two tables.

```
Select * FROM Students1964 Intersect All Select * Students1965
```

The ASP code to execute the preceding SQL statement is as follows:

```
<%
Dim DataConn,SQL
Set DataConn = Server.CreateObject("ADODB.Connection")
'the connection string is in Application variable
DataConn.Open Application("db_ConnectionString")
SQL = "Select * From Students1964 Intersect All Select *
Students1965 "
Set Recdset = DataConn.Execute(SQL)%>
<TABLE Border = 1 ><TR>
<%For I = 0 to Recdset.Fields.Count −1%>
<TD><B><%= Recdset(I).Name %></B></TD>
<%Next%>
<TR>
<% For I = 0 to Recdset.Fields.Count − 1 %>
<%= Recdset(I) %></TD>
</TR>
<% Recdset.MoveNext
    Loop
%>< /Table>
```

Table 41   *Table Students1964*

First_Name	Last_Name
Hanna	Bannana
Cecil	Allison
Peggy	Allison
Trisha	Allison

Table 42 *Table Students1965*

First_Name	Last_Name
Trisha	Allison
Peggy	Allison
Chris	Barker
Hanna	Bannana

The results to the SQL statement are given in Table 43.

Table 43 *Returned Rows of the Intersect SQL Statement*

First_Name	Last_Name
Hanna	Bannana
Peggy	Allison
Trisha	Allison

Suppose you want to narrow the search for students from both Students1964 and Students1965 to just the first name. Next, you want to use the corresponding keyword with the Intersect clause. The following SQL statement uses the INTERSECT CORRESPONDING clause to narrow the search to those students in both tables whose value in the column First_Name is the same. The results of the following SQL statement are the same as those in Table 43.

```
Select * FROM Students1964 Intersect Corresponding
(First_Name) Select *
Students1965
```

Is Null/Is Not Null   WhereClause

Purpose
Use the Is Null or Is Not Null predicates to find all rows in selected columns that do or do not contain null values.

Syntax
```
Select Columns From TableName [Where condition Is Null ]
Select Columns From TableName [Where condition Is Not Null]
```

Example

The following SQL statement finds the rows in the Customer table whose values in the column LastName contain a NULL value:

```
Select * From Customer Where LastName Is Null
```

If you wanted to find the rows in the Customer table whose values in the column LastName did not contain a NULL value, use the following SQL statement:

```
Select * From Customer Where LastName Is Not Null
```

Left   Nonstandard String Function

Purpose

Use the Left function to find the leftmost number of character in a column that is defined as a char or varchar data type. You can use this function on returned columns or in a Whereclause.

Syntax

```
Left (string, number of character from left)
```

Example

The following SQL statement gets the three leftmost characters from the column LastName in the Students table listed in Table 44:

```
Select Left (LastName, 3) As "Left Name" From Students
```

The ASP code to execute the preceding SQL statement is as follows:

```
<%
Dim DataConn,SQL
Set DataConn = Server.CreateObject("ADODB.Connection")
'the connection string is in Application variable
DataConn.Open Application("db_ConnectionString")
SQL = "Select Left (LastName,3) As "Left Name" From Students"
Set Recdset = DataConn.Execute(SQL)%>
<TABLE Border = 1 ><TR>
<%For I = 0 to Recdset.Fields.Count —1%>
<TD><B><%= Recdset(I).Name %></B></TD>
<%Next%>
<TR>
<% For I = 0 to Recdset.Fields.Count — 1 %>
<%= Recdset(I) %></TD>
</TR>
```

```
<% Recdset.MoveNext
     Loop
%>< /Table>
```

Table 44 *Table Students*

FirstNam	LastName	SchoolName	District
Kitty	Boo	Barn High School	1
Jane	Erwin	Barn High School	1
Amy	Eden	Han High School	2
Tim	Chesser	Abe High School	3

The results of executing the SQL statement are given in Table 45.

Table 45 *Results of the Left SQL Statement*

Left Name

Boo

Erw

Ede

Che

Length   Nonstandard String Function

Purpose

Use the Length function to find the length of a column with a char or var-char data type.

Syntax

```
Length (char or varchar datatype)
```

Example

The following SQL statement finds all the students in Table 44 whose last name is greater than seven characters.

```
Select * From Students Where Length (LastName) > 7
```

Since there are no rows in the Students table that have a LastName column containing more than seven characters, no data will be returned when you execute the above SQL statement.

Less Than (<) | Comparison Operator

Purpose

Use the less than (<) comparison operator to compare two items to determine which is less than an item.

Syntax

```
Select * From TableName Wherecolumn < item
```

Example

The following SQL statement finds the teams in table HighSchoolLeague1956 (shown in Table 46) that had less than seven wins. The Where clause uses the less than comparison operator to limit the search to only those rows whose column Wins contains less than seven wins.

```
Select * From HighSchoolLeague1956 Where Wins < 7
```

The ASP code to execute the preceding SQL statement is as follows:

```
<%
Dim DataConn,SQL
Set DataConn = Server.CreateObject("ADODB.Connection")
'the connection string is in Application variable
DataConn.Open Application("db_ConnectionString")
SQL = "Select * From HighSchoolLeague1956 Where Wins < 7 "
Set Recdset = DataConn.Execute(SQL)%>
<TABLE Border = 1 ><TR>
<%For I = 0 to Recdset.Fields.Count —1%>
<TD><B><%= Recdset(I).Name %></B></TD>
<%Next%>
<TR>
<% For I = 0 to Recdset.Fields.Count — 1 %>
<%= Recdset(I) %></TD>
</TR>
<% Recdset.MoveNext
    Loop
%>< /Table>
```

Table 46 *Table HighSchoolLeague1956*

Team	Wins	Loses
A	3	7
B	9	1
C	6	4
D	7	3

Table 47 shows the results of using the SQL less than statement.

Table 47 *Results of the Less Than (<) SQL Statement*

Team	Wins	Loses
A	3	7
C	6	4

Less Than or Equal to (<=)	Comparison Operator

Purpose

Use the less than or equal to (<=) comparison operator to compare two items to determine if one item is less than or equal to the second item.

Syntax

```
Select * From TableName Wherecolumn <= item
```

Example

The following SQL statement finds the teams in table HighSchoolLeague1956 (shown in Table 48) that had less than or equal to seven wins. The Where clause uses the less than comparison operator to limit the search to only those rows whose column Wins contain seven or less wins.

```
Select * From HighSchoolLeague1956 Where Wins <= 7
```

The ASP code to execute the preceding SQL statement is as follows:

```
<%
Dim DataConn,SQL
Set DataConn = Server.CreateObject("ADODB.Connection")
'the connection string is in Application variable
```

```
DataConn.Open Application("db_ConnectionString")
SQL = "Select * From HighSchoolLeague1956 Where Wins <= 7"
Set Recdset = DataConn.Execute(SQL)%>
<TABLE Border = 1 ><TR>
<%For I = 0 to Recdset.Fields.Count −1%>
<TD><B><%= Recdset(I).Name %></B></TD>
<%Next%>
<TR>
<% For I = 0 to Recdset.Fields.Count − 1 %>
<%= Recdset(I) %></TD>
</TR>
<% Recdset.MoveNext
    Loop
%></Table>
```

Table 48   *Table HighSchoolLeague1956*

Team	Wins	Loses
A	3	7
B	9	1
C	6	4
D	7	3

Table 49 shows the results of using the SQL less than or equal to statement.

Table 49   *Results of the Less Than or Equal to (< =) SQL Statement*

Team	Wins	Loses
A	3	7
C	6	4
D	7	3

Like/Not Like

Where Clause

Purpose

Use the Like and Not Like predicates to specify a search condition in the WhereWhere clause that is more general than the In or Not In clauses. If you want a set of conditions to be true if a string of characters exists or does not exist, then use the Like or Not Like predicates. You use the percent (%) and underscore (_) symbols to set the conditions to true.

Syntax

```
Select Columns From TableName  [Wherecondition Like condition]
Select Columns From TableName [Wherecondition Not Like condition]
The Like or Not Like condition can contain % or _ symbols.
```

The percent (%) symbol stands for any string of characters. The underscore (_) symbol stands for any single character.

Examples

The following SQL statement finds all the customers in the Customer table (shown in Table 50) whose column LastName value contains the letter e.

```
Select * From Customer Where LastName Like '%e%'
```

The ASP code to execute the preceding SQL statement is as follows:

```
<%
Dim DataConn,SQL
Set DataConn = Server.CreateObject("ADODB.Connection")
'the connection string is in Application variable
DataConn.Open Application("db_ConnectionString")
SQL = "Select * From Customer Where LastName Like '%e%' "
Set Recdset = DataConn.Execute(SQL)%>
<TABLE Border = 1 ><TR>
<%For I = 0 to Recdset.Fields.Count -1%>
<TD><B><%= Recdset(I).Name %></B></TD>
<%Next%>
<TR>
<% For I = 0 to Recdset.Fields.Count - 1 %>
<%= Recdset(I) %></TD>
</TR>
<% Recdset.MoveNext
Loop
%>< /Table>
```

Table 51 shows the results of the SQL Like statement.

Table 50   *Table Customer*

CustomerNum	FirstName	LastName
1	Hanna	Bannana
2	Peggy	Allison

CustomerNum	FirstName	LastName
3	Tommy	Erwin
4	Timothy	Eden
5	Kelly	NULL
6	Tim	Chesser
7	Anderson	The%Under

Table 51   *Results of the Like SQL Statement*

CustomerNum	FirstName	LastName
3	Tommy	Erwin
4	Timothy	Eden
6	Tim	Chesser
7	Anderson	The%Under

If you want to find those customers whose last name begins with the character e, use the following SQL statement. The difference between finding customers whose last name contains the character e and finding customers whose last name starts with e is the way you use the percent (%) wildcard.

```
Select * From Customer Where LastName Like '%e'
```

If you are trying to filter out a string that has a percent (%) character in it, use #%% as the Like statement. The following SQL statement finds any values in the column LastName that contain the character '%'. Table 52 shows the results of executing the following SQL statement:

```
Select * From Customer Where LastName Like '#%%'
```

Table 52   *Results of the Like SQL Statement with '#%%' characters*

CustomerNum	FirstName	LastName
7	Anderson	The%Under

If you want to find those customers who have a first name beginning with the letter a and three letters in their first name is l, use the following SQL statement. Table 53 shows the result returned.

```
Select * From Customer Where FirstName Like 'A_l'
```

Table 53   *Results of the Like SQL Statement with an Underscore (_)*
Character

CustomerNum	FirstName	LastName
1	Albert	Smith

If you want to find those customers whose first name doesn't begin with the
letter B and whose third letter is not the letter n, use the Not Like clause in
the SQL statement. The following SQL statement finds all the rows in Table
50 in which the first character and third character in the last name are not
like the characters B and n. The results of the following SQL statement are
shown in Table 54.

```
Select * From Customer Where LastName Not Like 'B_n'
```

Table 54   *Results of the Not Like SQL Statement with an Underscore (_)*
Character

CustomerNum	FirstName	LastName
2	Peggy	Allison
3	Tommy	Erwin
4	Timothy	Eden
5	Kelly	NULL
6	Tim	Chesser
7	Anderson	The%Under

Lower   Nonstandard String Function

Purpose
Use the Lower function to convert the value returned in an SQL statement
from a column with a string, char, or varchar data type to all lowercase letters. The Lower function can be used in a Where clause to narrow the search
for records.

Syntax
```
Lower (string)
```

Example
The following SQL statement returns all the values of the column LastName
displayed in lowercase letters:

```
Select Lower (LastName) From Students.
```

The next SQL statement shows you how to return records from the Students table where the LastName is 'albers'.

```
Select * From Students Where Lower(LastName) = 'albers'.
```

Max   Aggregate Function

Purpose

Use the Max function to find the maximum value in a column. The value passed to this function can be either a numeric data type or a column that contains one of the string types (string, char, or varchar).

Syntax

```
Select Max(Column) From TableName [Where clause]
```

Example

The following SQL statement finds the maximum value of an individual item in the Groceries table:

```
Select Max (Box_Weight) From Groceries
```

Min   Aggregate Function

Purpose

Use the Min function to find the minimum value in a column. The value passed to this function can be either a numeric data type or a column that contains one of the string types (string, char, or varchar).

Syntax

```
Select Min(Column) From TableName [Whereclause]
```

Example

The following SQL statement uses the Min function to look at all the values of the column Box_Weight in the table Groceries to find the minimum value.

```
Select Min (Box_Weight) From Groercies
```

Not   Logical Connector

Purpose

Use the Not logical connector to retrieve from an SQL statement those rows that don't meet the criteria in the Where clause.

Syntax

```
Select * From TableName WhereColumn1 Not condition
```

Example

The following SQL statement returns from table StudentClasses all the rows for which the column Science does not contain a Null value:

```
Select * From StudentClasses Where Science Not Null
```

Not Equal (<>)   Comparison Operator

Purpose

Use the not equal (<>) comparison operator to compare two items to determine if they are not equal in value.

Syntax

```
Select * From TableName Wherecolumn <> item
```

Example

The following SQL statement uses the not equal operator to determine those rows in table WaterBills that are not equal to 17 dollars. The statement returns the columns BillNo, Address, and MonthofBill.

```
Select BillNo, Address, MonthofBill From WaterBills Where Amount <> 7
```

Or   Logical Connector

Purpose

Use the Or logical connector to specify two or more conditions for which only one of the conditions must be true.

Syntax

```
Select * From TableName Wherecondition1 Or condition2
```

Example

The following SQL statement finds all the students in table StudentClasses (shown in Table 55) who received an A in English or a B in Math.

```
Select * From StudentClasses Where English = 'A' Or Math = 'B'
```

The ASP code to execute the preceding SQL statement is as follows:

```
<%
Dim DataConn,SQL
Set DataConn = Server.CreateObject("ADODB.Connection")
'the connection string is in Application variable
DataConn.Open Application("db_ConnectionString")
SQL = "Select * From StudentClasses Where English = 'A' Or Math =
'B' "
Set Recdset = DataConn.Execute(SQL)%>
```

```
<TABLE Border = 1 ><TR>
<%For I = 0 to Recdset.Fields.Count -1%>
<TD><B><%= Recdset(I).Name %></B></TD>
<%Next%>
<TR>
<% For I = 0 to Recdset.Fields.Count - 1 %>
<%= Recdset(I) %></TD>
</TR>
<% Recdset.MoveNext
    Loop
%>< /Table>
```

Table 55 *Table StudentClasses*

Student	English	Math	Science
Beth	A	A	A
Hanna	C	C	C
Tim	A	B	null
Cara	A	B	D
Manda	A	C	C

Table 56 shows the rows returned from the execution of the SQL statement.

Table 56 *Results of the Or SQL Statement*

Student	English	Math	Science
Beth	A	A	A
Tim	A	B	null
Cara	A	B	D
Manda	A	C	C

Order By   Relational Operator

Purpose

Use the Order By clause to sort retrieved rows in either a descending or ascending order. However, one important rule exists for the Order By clause: You can only use this clause on columns that you reference in the Select clause.

Syntax

```
Select * From Table1 Where condition Order By
ColumnName1,ColumnName2) [Asc | Desc]
```

Example

The following SQL statement would be incorrect, because the Order By clause is attempting to sort on a column that was not stated in the Select clause:

```
Select City From Cities Order By State
```

In order for this statement to be correct, the following SQL statement needs to be used:

```
Select City, State From Cities Order By State
```

Outer Join   Join

Purpose

A join that *does not care* if there are matching rows is known as an *outer join*. This *does not care* situation is the difference between an *inner join* and an *outer join*. When an outer join is executed, the rows that do not match are returned as NULL. Furthermore, there are three different types of outer joins: left outer joins, right outer joins, and full outer joins. One drawback to using outer joins is that the syntax can vary between database providers.

Syntax

```
Normal Syntax for Left Outer Join:
Select * From TableA A Left Outer Join TableB B On A.Column =
B.Column
```

Normal syntax for a right outer join:

```
Select * From TableA A Right Outer Join TableB B On A.Column = B.Column
```

Normal syntax for a full outer join:

```
Select * From TableA A Full Outer Join TableB B On A.Column = B.Column
```

Sybase left outer join:

```
Select * FROM TableA , TableB Where TableA.Colum *= TableB
```

Sybase right outer join:

```
Select * FROM TableA , TableB Where TableA.Colum =* TableB
```

Oracle left outer join:

```
Select * FROM TableA, TableB Where TableA.Column += TableB
```

Oracle right outer join:

```
Select * FROM TableA, TableB Where TableA.Column =+ TableB
```

Examples

The following SQL statement creates a left outer join on tables PlayerInfo and YearStats, shown in Tables 57 and 58, respectively. For no other reason than the purpose of this example, the PlayerInfo table will be the table on the left side of the join. Notice in the SQL statement that the Oracle syntax for a left outer join is used. When this join statement begins to execute, the table on the left side of the Where clause starts with the first row of PlayerInfo and attempts to match the join column (in this case, PlayerNum) with the table on the right side of the statement — YearStats. If no row exists in the table on the right side of the statement, NULL values are returned for those columns in the Select clause. As you can see from Table 58, there exists a record for each playernum in PlayerInfo except for Tommy Allison.

```
Select * From PlayerInfo, YearStates Where PlayerInfo.PlayerNum
+= YearStats.PlayerNum
```

The ASP code to execute this outer join SQL statement is as follows:

```
<%
Dim DataConn,SQL
Set DataConn = Server.CreateObject("ADODB.Connection")
'the connection string is in Application variable
DataConn.Open Application("db_ConnectionString")
SQL = "Select * From PlayerInfo, YearStates Where "
SQL = "PlayerInfo.PlayerNum += YearStats.PlayerNum "
Set Recdset = DataConn.Execute(SQL)%>
<TABLE Border = 1 ><TR>
<%For I = 0 to Recdset.Fields.Count -1%>
<TD><B><%= Recdset(I).Name %></B></TD>
<%Next%>
<TR>
<% For I = 0 to Recdset.Fields.Count - 1 %>
<%= Recdset(I) %></TD>
</TR>
<% Recdset.MoveNext
    Loop
%></Table>
```

Table 57 *Table PlayerInfo*

PlayerNum	Player
101	Bob Smith
102	Tim Eden
103	Tommy Allison
104	Ken Toms

Table 58 *Table YearStats*

Year	PlayerNum	HR	RBI	Avg
1930	101	6	45	.301
1930	102	7	34	.278
1930	104	17	66	.209

Thus, in the results in Table 59, Tommy Allison has nulls returned for columns Year, HR, RBI, and Avg.

Table 59 *Returned Rows from the Left Outer Join SQL Statement*

PlayerNum	Player	Year	HR	RBI	Avg
101	Bob Smith	1930	6	45	.301
102	Tim Eden	1930	7	34	.278
103	Tommy Allison	Null	Null	Null	Null
104	Ken Toms	1930	17	66	.209

The following SQL statement shows a right outer join. In the case of a right outer join, the table on the right side of the statement is the joiner of the two tables. In the case of the following SQL statement, the table PlayerInfo is joined to YearStats. In the case of the left outer join, the table YearStats is joined to the PlayerInfo table. When the right outer join statement is executed, each row in table YearStats matches its PlayerNum against the PlayerNum in PlayerInfo. In this example, all the rows in YearStats contain a match. Therefore, no Null values are returned.

```
Select * FROM YearStates Z1 Right Outer Join PlayerInfo TR1 On
Z1.PlayerNum = TR1.PlayerNum
```

The ASP code to execute the preceding SQL statement is as follows:

```
<%
Dim DataConn,SQL
Set DataConn = Server.CreateObject("ADODB.Connection")
'the connection string is in Application variable
DataConn.Open Application("db_ConnectionString")
SQL = "Select * From YearStates Z1 Right Outer Join "
SQL = "PlayerInfo TR1 On Z1.PlayerNum = TR1.PlayerNum "
Set Recdset = DataConn.Execute(SQL)%>
<TABLE Border = 1 ><TR>
<%For I = 0 to Recdset.Fields.Count -1%>
<TD><B><%= Recdset(I).Name %></B></TD>
<%Next%>
<TR>
<% For I = 0 to Recdset.Fields.Count - 1 %>
<%= Recdset(I) %></TD>
</TR>
<% Recdset.MoveNext
    Loop
%>< /Table>
```

Table 60 shows the results of executing the SQL right outer join statement.

Table 60 *Returned Rows from the Right Outer Join SQL Statement*

PlayerNum	Player	Year	HR	RBI	Avg
101	Bob Smith	1930	6	45	.301
102	Tim Eden	1930	7	34	.278
104	Ken Toms	1930	17	66	.209

Power	Nonstandard Numeric Function

Purpose

Use the Power function to return X to the Y power of a column with a numeric data type.

Syntax

```
Power (X, Y)
```

Example

The following SQL statement uses the Power function to find those rows in the table ChemistryReading where the value of the Measurement column raised to the exponential value of the Temp column is greater than 43.

```
Select temp From ChemistryReadings Where Power (Measurement,
Temp) > 43
```

Revoke   Data Control Language

Purpose

Use the Revoke command to remove a user's granted permissions on a database. Whereas the DBA gives access to the data through the command Grant, the DBA removes the granted permission with the command Revoke.

Syntax

```
Revoke [Grant permission] On object From user list [Restrinct |
Cascade ]
```

Example

If you want to revoke the update permission given to the Clerks group on the column ProductId in the Inventory table, then use this following SQL command:

```
Revoke Update On Inventory (ProductId) From Clerks
```

Right   Nonstandard String Function

Purpose

Use the Right function to return the rightmost number of characters that you specify in a string.

Syntax

```
Right (string, number of character from right or end of string)
```

Examples

The following SQL statement gets the three rightmost characters in a student's last name.

```
Select Right (LastName, 3) From Students
```

The next SQL statement returns only those rows that match the three right-most characters in column LastName that equal 'ing':

```
Select * From Students Where Right(LastName, 3) = 'ing'
```

Select   Data Manipulation Language

Purpose

Use a Select to retrieve rows from a database. The Select statement includes several options that enable you to narrow the search on a database. The Where clause is the most useful.

Syntax

```
Select [Distinct|All] [Columnname1, Columnname2,etc.] From
Table_Name [Where clause] [Group By][Having clause][Order By]
```

Examples

The following SQL statement retrieves all the rows from a table named States:

```
Select * From States
```

The next SQL statement retrieves rows but only displays the columns State and City from a table named Location:

```
Select State, City From Location
```

If you want to retrieve rows from Location, but no duplicates can exist, then use the Distinct keyword. The following SQL statement gets only those rows with Distinct values:

```
Select Distinct * From Location
```

Select [Distinct]   Data Manipulation Language

Purpose

Use the keyword Distinct to eliminate duplicates when attempting to join two tables together.

Syntax

```
Select Distinct Column1, Column2 ETC From Table1, Table2 Where
Table1.Column1 = Table2.Column3
```

Examples

The following example uses the keyword Distinct in the Select statement to eliminate duplicate rows from being returned. The StudentYears table in Table 61 contains four rows. However, two of the rows contain duplicate values in the columns LastName and FirstName: Amy Eden and Lori Chesser. If you execute the following Select statement on table StudentYears, multiple rows of the same data will be returned:

```
Select LastName, FirstName From StudentYears
```

The ASP code to execute the preceding SQL statement is as follows:

```
<%
Dim DataConn,SQL
Set DataConn = Server.CreateObject("ADODB.Connection")
'the connection string is in Application variable
DataConn.Open Application("db_ConnectionString")
SQL = "Select LastName, FirstName From StudentYears "
Set Recdset = DataConn.Execute(SQL)%>
<TABLE Border = 1 ><TR>
<%For I = 0 to Recdset.Fields.Count -1%>
<TD><B><%= Recdset(I).Name %></B></TD>
<%Next%>
<TR>
<% For I = 0 to Recdset.Fields.Count - 1 %>
<%= Recdset(I) %></TD>
</TR>
<% Recdset.MoveNext
    Loop
%>< /Table>
```

Table 61   *Table StudentYears*

StudentID	SchoolYear	LastName	FirstName
1	1990	Amy	Eden
1	1991	Amy	Eden
2	1993	Lori	Chesser
2	1994	Lori	Chesser

If you use the Distinct keyword with this SQL statement, however, you will get the results shown in Table 62.

```
Select Distinct LastName, FirstName From StudentYears
```

Table 62 *Results from Using a Distinct in a Select Statement*

LastName	FirstName
Amy	Eden
Lori	Chesser

Sign

Nonstandard
Numeric Function

Purpose

Use the Sign function if you want to know whether a column with a numerical data type is positive or negative. The function returns a minus if the number is less than 0.

Syntax

```
Sign (number)
```

Example

Suppose you wanted to find only those golf scores that were below par at last year's golf championship. The following SQL statement returns only those rows in which the Sign value for the column Score is negative. In golf, a negative score indicates a below-par status — which is very good. One of the authors wishes his golf score were below par at least once.

```
Select * From Master_Golf_Scores Where Sign (Score) < 0
```

Sqrt

Nonstandard
Numeric Function

Purpose

Use the Sqrt function to return the square root of a number.

Syntax

```
Sqrt (number1)
```

Examples

The following code shows you how to obtain the square root on a column named numOfStudents from the table School. Because no Where clause is specified in the following statement, all the rows from the table School are returned with their square root value.

```
Select Sqrt (numOfstudents) From School
```

The Sqrt function also can be used in the Where clause to specify a search condition. The SQL statement finds all the boxes of apples for which the weight of the box is less than 2.5 lbs.

```
Select BoxOfApples From Groceries
Where Sqrt(weightofboxes) < 2.5
```

Sum   Aggregate Function

Purpose

Use the Sum function to find the sum of a column with a numerical data type.

Syntax

```
Select SUM(Column) From TableName [Where clause]
```

Example

The following SQL statement gets the sum of all the values for column Box_Weight from table Grogercies. The statement will return 1 value for all the rows.

```
Select SUM (Box_Weight) From Groceries
```

Substr   Nonstandard String Function

Purpose

Use the Substr function to create a substring of a string.

Syntax

```
Substr (string, startpostion, number of chars of substring)
```

Examples

Suppose you want the first four chars displayed from the last name of a student in a school. The following SQL statement uses the Substr function to display the first four characters of the last name for all rows in the Students table. The SQL statement returns all rows because no Where clause is specified.

```
Select Substr (LastName, 1,4), FirstName From Students
```

You can also use the Substr function to specify conditions for a search. The following SQL statement finds all the rows in the Students table whose column FirstName contains the first three characters equal to 'Tim'.

```
Select * From Students Where Substr (FirstName, 1,3)=
'Tim'
```

Truncate   Data Definition Language

Purpose

Use the Truncate command to delete all the data in a table. The Truncate command removes the data from the table but leaves the structure of the table intact.

Syntax

```
Truncate Table Tablename
```

Example

The following SQL statement deletes all the rows from the table Students.

```
Truncate Table Students
```

Union   Relational Operator

Purpose

Use the Union clause to combine the data from two tables under the following two conditions: First, both tables must contain the same number of rows; and second, at least one column in each table must be the same.

Syntax

```
Select * From Table1 Union [All] Select * From Table2
```

Example

The following SQL statement will combine the information from table A and table B in Tables 63 and 64. Notice that table A and table B both contain the same number of rows, and both contain a column that is the same — TeamID. For this example, you can assume that both columns have identical data types – varchar.

```
Select * From TableA Union All Select * From TableB
```

The ASP code to execute the preceding SQL statement is as follows:

```
<%
Dim DataConn,SQL
Set DataConn = Server.CreateObject("ADODB.Connection")
'the connection string is in Application variable
DataConn.Open Application("db_ConnectionString")
SQL = "Select * From TableA Union All Select * From TableB "
Set Recdset = DataConn.Execute(SQL)%>
<TABLE Border = 1 ><TR>
<%For I = 0 to Recdset.Fields.Count —1%>
<TD><B><%= Recdset(I).Name %></B></TD>
<%Next%>
<TR>
<% For I = 0 to Recdset.Fields.Count — 1 %>
<%= Recdset(I) %></TD>
</TR>
<% Recdset.MoveNext
    Loop
%></Table>
```

Table 63   *TableA*

TeamId	TeamName	City
1	Sharks	Boston
2	StreamRollers	Atlanta

Table 64   *TableB*

TeamId	TicketPrices	Stadium
1	30	Fenway Park
2	29.50	Turner Field

The results of the SQL statement are shown in Table 65.

Table 65 *Results of a Union SQL Statement*

TeamId	TeamName	City	TicketPrices	Stadium
1	Sharks	Boston	30	Fenway Park
2	StreamRollers	Atlanta	29.50	Turner Field

Update   Data Manipulation Language

Purpose
Use the Update command to change the data in existing rows in a table.

Syntax
```
Update TableName Set Column1 = Data1, Column2 = Data2   [Where
clause]
```

Example
The following SQL statement updates any record in Table 66 in the Cities table whose column City is equal to "Orlando" and whose column State is equal to "Florida":

```
Update Cities Set City = "Richmond", State="Virginia" Where City
"Orlando" And State = "Florida"
```

The ASP code to execute the update and return the new results is as follows:

```
<%
Dim DataConn,SQL
Set DataConn = Server.CreateObject("ADODB.Connection")
'the connection string is in Application variable
DataConn.Open Application("db_ConnectionString")
SQL = "Update Cities Set City = ""Richmond"", "
SQL = "State = ""Virginia"" "
SQL = SQL & "Where City = ""Orlando"" "
SQL = SQL & "And State = ""Florida"" "

DataConn.Execute(SQL)
'Get the Updated results
SQL = "Select * From Cities "
Set Recdset = DataConn.Execute(SQL)%>
<TABLE Border = 1 ><TR>
```

```
<%For I = 0 to Recdset.Fields.Count -1%>
<TD><B><%= Recdset(I).Name %></B></TD>
<%Next%>
<TR>
<% For I = 0 to Recdset.Fields.Count - 1 %>
<%= Recdset(I) %></TD>
</TR>
<% Recdset.MoveNext
    Loop
%>< /Table>
```

Table 66 *Table Cities*

RecordId	City	State
1	Auburn	Alabama
2	Jacksonville	Florida
3	Detroit	Michigan
4	Richmond	Virginia
5	Mobile	Alabama
6	Atlanta	Georgia

The result of the SQL statement is shown in Table 67.

Table 67 *Results of the Update SQL Statement*

RecordId	City	State
2	Jacksonville	Florida
3	Detroit	Michigan
4	Richmond	Virginia
6	Atlanta	Georgia

Upper   Nonstandard String Function

Purpose

Use the Upper function to convert a string to all uppercase letters.

Syntax

```
Upper (string)
```

Example

The following SQL statement retrieves all the rows in the table Students and displays the returned column LastName in uppercase characters:

```
Select Upper (LastName) From Students.
```

Where Clause

Where Clause

Purpose

Use the Where clause to define what criteria to use in searching rows.

Syntax

Select * From Tablename Where [condition]

Example

The following SQL statement finds those rows in Table 68 in which the column State is equal to "Florida." The Where clause allows the search on the table Location to be narrowed to just those rows that contain the string "Florida."

```
Select * From Location Where State = "Florida"
```

The ASP code to execute the preceding SQL statement is as follows:

```
<%
Dim DataConn,SQL
Set DataConn = Server.CreateObject("ADODB.Connection")
'the connection string is in Application variable
DataConn.Open Application("db_ConnectionString")
SQL = "Select * From Location Where State = ""Florida"" "
Set Recdset = DataConn.Execute(SQL)%>
<TABLE Border = 1 ><TR>
<%For I = 0 to Recdset.Fields.Count -1%>
<TD><B><%= Recdset(I).Name %></B></TD>
<%Next%>
<TR>
<% For I = 0 to Recdset.Fields.Count - 1 %>
<%= Recdset(I) %></TD>
</TR>
<% Recdset.MoveNext
    Loop
%>< /Table>
```

Table 68 *Table Location*

RecordId	City	State
1	Auburn	Alabama
2	Jacksonville	Florida
3	Detroit	Michigan
4	Orlando	Florida
5	Mobile	Alabama

The results of the SQL statement are provided in Table 69.

Table 69 *Rows Retrieved from the SQL Where Clause*

RecordId	City	State
2	Jacksonville	Florida
4	Orlando	Florida

The Tutorial

The tutorial part contains the following chapters:

IN THIS PART

Chapter 1 Getting Started with Active Server Pages

Chapter 2 VBScript and Active Server Pages

Chapter 3 Objects Used for ASP Applications

Chapter 4 Working with the Database: The ADO Object

Chapter 5 Creating Server-Side ActiveX COM Objects

Chapter 6 Visual Basic and Active Server Pages

Getting Started with Active Server Pages

1

Creating dynamic content on the Internet is the primary objective of many Web developers. This chapter provides you with the fundamentals of dynamic Web development using Active Server Pages. Whether you want to create an application that interacts with a database, or replace a cgi script, Active Server Pages (ASP) enables you to create server-side programs that will accomplish these tasks. Active Server Pages is a Microsoft technology that uses server-side ActiveX components known as Component Object Model (COM) objects. We are not getting into the details of COM object architecture in this chapter. But in layperson's terms, COM is Microsoft's architecture for creating reusable objects using Microsoft-platform Windows.

The chapter talks about the beginnings to creating Active Server Pages. From installing the Internet Information Server to the objects that allow you to create the dynamic content, the pages below show you an overview of getting started in the world of ASP. We have included a discussion about the elements to creating some of your very first pages — Response, Request, and Server objects.

CROSS-REFERENCE

Chapter 5 gives you an overview of ASP and COM objects.

As you start to program with ASP, you will notice that you use four COM objects more than all the rest — the ActiveX Data Objects (ADO), the Response object, and the Request and the Server objects. These four objects will become the foundation for all of your ASP projects. This chapter covers the Response, Request, Server objects, but not the ADO. Because the ADO allows you to connect to a database, we felt this object should be covered in a chapter on its own. In addition to the server objects provided by Microsoft, you can create your own ActiveX server components. Some of these components are listed later in this chapter.

CROSS-REFERENCE

Chapter 5 of the tutorial section shows you how to create your own objects.

Let's get started with the beginning piece of the puzzle — the Internet Information Server.

Installing the Internet Information Server

What do you need to do to get started programming ASP? In order to run ASP, you must have the Internet Information Server (IIS) installed on your computer. IIS comes via five ways: Personal Web Server for Windows 98, Windows NT 4.0 Option Pack, Visual Studio 6, Windows 2000 Professional, and Windows 2000 Server. The following sections cover how to install the IIS in the three most common ways: with Windows 98, Windows NT, and Windows 2000 Server version. Although Visual Studio is a great product, we are not covering it in this book. Since it is a graphical development environment for creating ASP projects, it is not a topic for this book. As for Windows 2000, both the Professional and Server versions come with a Web server that contains IIS. The Professional version is a personnel Web server; the Server version is a full-blown Web server.

IIS and Windows 98

If you are running Windows 98, use the following instructions to install IIS on your computer. First, place the Windows CD into your

CD reader on your computer. Next, go to the Windows98\add-ons\ PWS directory on the CD and run the setup.exe program. This action installs the Personnal Web Server (PWS) so you can run Active Server Pages through Windows 98. The PWS will be installed on your hard drive in the c:\inetpub\wwwroot directory. For the sake of the examples in the rest of this chapter, go ahead and create a directory under wwwroot called MyExamples. The complete directory name will be c:\inetpub\wwwroot\MyExamples.

Once the PWS is installed, a small icon should appear in the lower right-hand corner of your computer screen — right next to the time setting. You find out if the PWS is running by placing your mouse over the icon. A small yellow message tag will appear indicating whether the PWS is running or not. If the PWS is not running, then right-click on the icon to bring up the PWS menu. When the menu appears, click on the choice that says "Start Service."

Any of the ASP or HTML pages that you run from your PWS will have the URL of http://localhost/.

IIS and Windows NT 4.0 Option Pack

Setting up IIS on Windows NT is a little different from setting up IIS on Windows 98. First, if you do not have NT 4.0 Option Pack, you need to download it from http://www.microsoft.com/ntserver/ nts/downloads/default.asp.

●—NOTE

We assume that you already have the Windows NT Server installed. After all, it doesn't make sense to install NT 4.0 Option Pack if you don't have Windows NT 4.0 Server installed.

Before you install the Option Pack, the following list of software needs to be installed, and installed in this order for Windows NT Server to run properly:

1. Windows NT 4.0 Server
2. NT 4.0 Service Pack 3
3. Internet Explorer 4.01 or later
4. NT 4.0 Option Pack
5. NT 4.0 Service Pack 6a

●—NOTE

There is information on installing the NT Option pack at http://www. microsoft.com/TechNet/winnt/deploy.asp.

1

If you are running Windows 2000, don't worry about installing Windows NT and the preceding list of software — just install the Windows 2000 Server. Of course, if you're running Windows 2000, you've already installed it.

Once Windows NT Option Pack 4 is installed, you need to set up a virtual directory on your default Web server to house your ASP code. To accomplish this task, go to the Windows Start menu and select "Windows NT 4.0 Option Pack 4." When you highlight this option, a list of programs that go with the 4.0 Option Pack will appear. The associated menu choices that appear when you highlight the Windows NT 4.0 Option Pack 4 are Microsoft Internet Information Server, Microsoft Transaction Server, Product Documentation, Release Notes, and Windows NT 4.0 Option Pack Setup. Figure 1-1 shows what you should see on a Windows NT machine when these options appear.

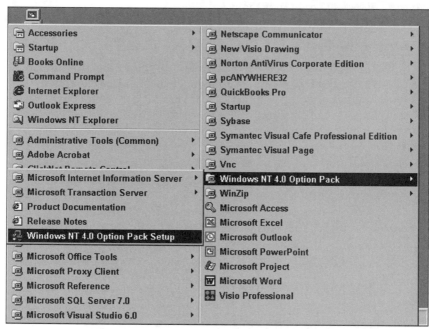

Figure 1-1   *The programs available with the Windows NT 4.0 Option Pack*

Highlight from this list the menu option Microsoft Internet Information Server. A window will appear with two options: FrontPage Server Administrator and Internet Service Manager (see Figure 1-2).

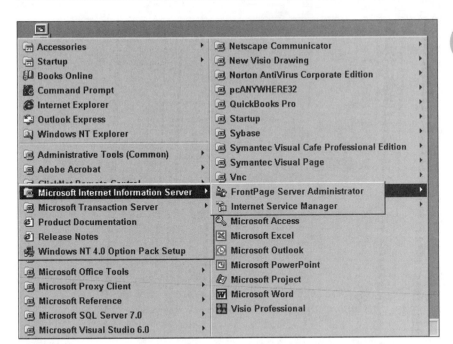

Figure 1-2 *Highlighting the IIS lets you select the Internet Service Manager.*

Click on the Internet Service Manager menu option to bring up the Microsoft Management Console (MMC) window. MMC provides you with wizards to set up either Web sites or virtual directories on a Web site. For the example in this chapter, you will create a virtual directory under your default Web server named MyExample. The default Web server for Windows NT is the c:\inetput\wwwroot directory. Figure 1-3 shows you what your default Web server directory tree looks like and how to get to the virtual directory wizard.

After you select the virtual directory wizard, a window will appear asking you the name of your virtual directory. Type in the name *"MyExample"* and press the Next button. A new window will appear asking you to enter the name of the directory in which your virtual directory will go. For this example, you use the default Web server or c:\inetput\wwwroot. Once you type in this path to the default Web server, press the Next button. A final window will appear asking you "What access permissions do you want to set for this virtual directory?" You should set at least read, write, and script access. Once you have given the permissions, click the Finish button. Congratulations! You have created the MyExample virtual directory under the default Web server.

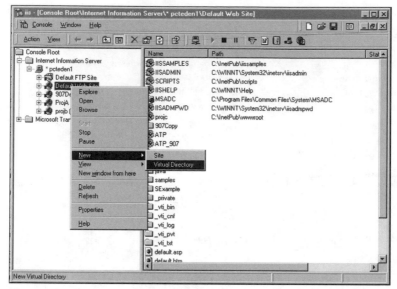

Figure 1-3 *Setting up the Virtual Directory wizard using the MMC*

IIS and Windows 2000 Server

Microsoft has made creating a virtual Web site easier in Windows 2000. All you have to do is go to the Start menu, click on the Programs menu, then click the menu option labeled Administrative Tools. When you select the Administrative Tools option a window appears (see Figure 1-4).

Once this window appears, double-click on Internet Services Manager. The Internet Information Services window will appear.

Within this window, you will see a tree view of items such as Default FTP Site and Default Web Site. Highlight the Default Web Site menu option. Once this selection is highlighted, press the right button on your mouse. A list of menu options appears. Select the New option. This option enables you to create a new virtual Web site. Figure 1-5 shows you how this window appears on your screen.

Next, you have to create a new virtual directory. To do this, double-click on the Virtual Directory menu option, and then follow the wizard that appears. This wizard is a program that Microsoft incorporated into Windows 2000 server in order to guide you through a step-by-stop process to creating a new virtual directory on the server. Follow the instructions to create a new virtual directory. Name the virtual directory MyExample.

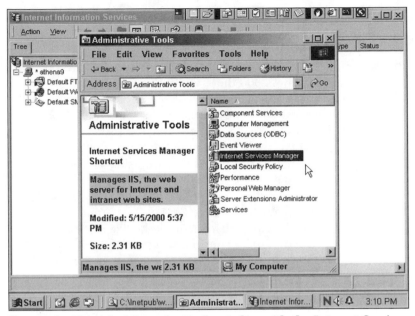

Figure 1-4 *The Administrative Tools window with the Internet Services Manager highlighted*

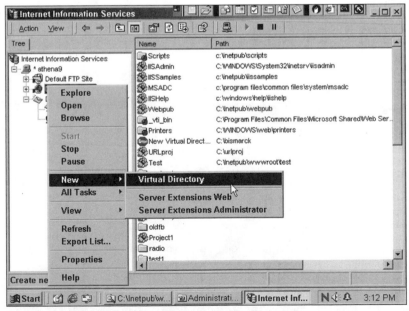

Figure 1-5 *Selecting the New option in the Windows 2000 Internet Information Services window*

Creating Your First Active Server Page

If you have read the discussions on installing IIS on Windows 98, Windows NT, or Windows 2000 there will be a virtual directory on Windows NT or Window 2000 called MyExample. If you're running Windows 98, there should be a directory at c:\inetpub\wwwroot\ MyExamples. If you have skipped over reading the installation, then create a virtual directory. If you're running the Windows NT or Windows 2000 server, call it MyExample. If you are using Windows 98, call it c:\inetpub\wwwroot\MyExamples.

With the "MyExample" directory created on your web server, it is now time to create your first Active Server Page. Your first ASP will be called HelloWorld.asp. This page uses the Response object to send the message "Hello World" from the server to the browser. The Response object is discussed in more detail later in this chapter.

Learning the Syntax of ASP

Type the following code into Notepad. First is the code to HelloWorld.asp.

```
<%@ Language=VBScript %>
<HTML>
<Body>
<% Response.Write "Hello World" %>
</Body>
</HTML>
```

●—**TIP**———————————————————————

Instead of writing Response.write "Hello World", you can use `<%= "Hello World" %>`.

When you are done typing, save the file as c: \inetpub\wwwroot\ MyExample\HelloWorld.asp.

●—**NOTE**———————————————————————

It is assumed here that IIS is located on your c: drive.

After you place the code into the virtual directory, open a browser and type in the following URL: http://localhost/ MyExample/HelloWorld.asp. Figure 1-6 shows you the result of executing this URL in your browser. You now have your first ASP page.

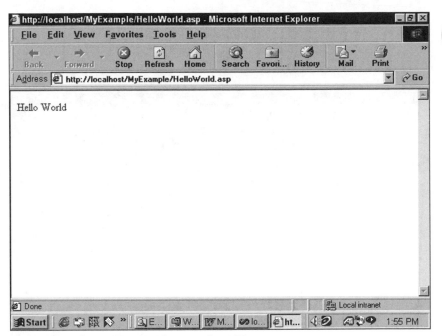

Figure 1-6   *The Hello World example ASP page*

Notice the <% %> tag in your ASP code. IIS interprets any code inside the tag as server-side script. Anytime you need to use server-side programming, such as connecting to a database, you need to place this tag around your code.

Using VBScript with an ASP

Now that you have created your first ASP, the next step is to create an ASP that uses VBScript. Type the following script into Notepad and save the file as GetTime.asp. This code is going to use the VBScript function Time(), which gets the time from your computer and displays it in the browser.

```
<%@ Language=VBScript %>
<HTML>
<Body>
<% Response.Write "The Time is "
    Response.Write Time()
%>
</Body>
</HTML>
```

After you save the file, place it in your virtual directory "http://localhost/MyExample/," open a browser, and type the following: http://localhost/GetTime.asp. Figure 1-7 shows you what the page looks like in a browser.

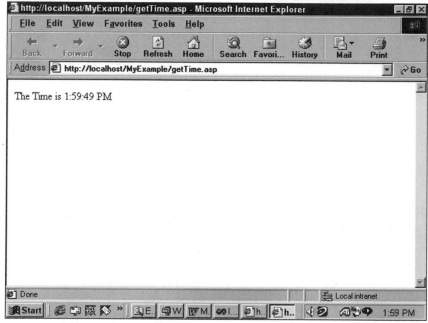

Figure 1-7   *The GetTime example ASP with VBScript*

Getting Started with ASP Components

You've now created your first ASP. The next step to your education is to give more detail about the three of the four objects we mentioned at the beginning of this chapter — the Response, Request, and Server objects. Remember, we're not going to cover the ADO in this chapter. Some people refer to these as ASP components. You can call them either objects or components, both references are correct.

Through the process of learning to create the HelloWorld.asp, you have used one of these objects — the Response object. So let's begin the discussion with this object.

The Response Object

Anytime you need to send output from the server to the browser or any requesting object, use the Response object. There are two methods that you will use more than the rest: write and redirect.

●—CROSS-REFERENCE

The ASP Core Reference section on page (p. 241) lists the methods and attributes of the Response object.

The Write Method

You use the Response object to send information to the browser. In creating the HelloWorld.asp, you've seen how you can use the Response object's Write method to send a message or the results of a VBScript function to the browser. Well, you can also send HTML tags written as a string to the browser. The following code is the "HelloWorld" example but with a twist. All of the HTML tags from the HelloWorld example are sent to the browser via the Response object's write method. Therefore, you can write an entire HTML page, including all the tags, with the Response object. The second line of code, response.write "<HTML>", is a good example of how to write the HTML tag as a string.

```
<%@ Language=VBScript %>
<%Response.Write "<HTML>"
   Response.Write "<Body>"
   Response.Write "Hello World"
   Response.Write "</Body>"
   Response.Write "</HTML>"
%>
```

●—NOTE

Notice the top line of the code, <@ Language=VBScript>. This is known as the *Language tag,* and it must be the first line of code on any Active Server Page.

The ability to enable the Response object to create an HTML page will be a benefit when you start to format data retrieved via the ActiveX Data Objects (ADOs).

●—CROSS-REFERENCE

The ADO is the object you are going to use to connect to, and bring back information from, a database. Chapter 4 (p. 611) discusses the ADO.

The Redirect Method

The `Redirect` method gives you the capability to divert to another ASP or HTML page based on logic in your program. You can accomplish this task by using the `Response` object's `Redirect` method. The following code shows you how to redirect to a page called nextpage.html. The line of code `Response.redirect("nextpage.html")` is where the redirection occurs.

```
<%@ Language=VBScript %>
<% myvar = 5
    if myvar = 5 then
        Response.Redirect("nextpage.html")
    end if
%>
```

If you want to pass information to the next page using the `Redirect` method, then use this code. The following ASP will pass the variable `college` in the URL:

```
<%@ Language=VBScript %>
<%
School = "Auburn University"
myvar = 5
if myvar = 5 then
    Response.Redirect ("nextpage.asp?College="& School)
end if
%>
```

● **NOTE**

If you use a `Response.Write` before a `Response.redirect` in an ASP under IIS 4.0, the following error message will be displayed in your browser: Under Windows 2000 running IIS 5.0, this error will not appear.

```
Response object error 'ASP 0156 : 80004005'
Header Error
The HTTP headers are already written to the client browser.
Any HTTP header modifications must be made before writing
page content.
```

Integrating the Response.ContentType with an Excel Spreadsheet

One of the best ways to integrate the Internet with desktop applications, such as Microsoft's Excel SpreadSheet program, is to use the `Response` object's `Response.ContentType` method.

CROSS-REFERENCE

You can find additional information about the `Response.ContentType` property in the ASP Core Reference section (p. 253).

The key to creating the Excel spreadsheet is using the MIME type of "application/x-msexcel" and placing the information in an HTML format. Listing 1-1 shows you how to create a three-column, two-row Excel spreadsheet.

Listing 1-1 *Creating an Excel spreadsheet with the Response. ContentType method*

```
<%
Response.ContentType="application/x-msexcel"
Response.Write "<Table>"
'the title cells
Response.Write "<Tr>"
Response.Write "<Td>"
Response.Write "First Name"
Response.Write "</Td>"
Response.Write "<Td>"
Response.Write "Middle Name"
Response.Write "</Td>"
Response.Write "<Td>"
Response.Write "Last Name"
Response.Write "</Td>"
Response.Write "</Tr>"
'the cells with a Name
Response.Write "<Tr>"
Response.Write "<Td>"
Response.Write "Amy"
Response.Write "</Td>"
Response.Write "<Td>"
Response.Write "The Bun"
Response.Write "</Td>"
Response.Write "<Td>"
Response.Write "Eden"
Response.Write "</Td>"
Response.Write "</Tr>"
'make sure all the information is flushed out of buffers to
browser
Response.Flush

%>
```

1

When you execute the above code in an ASP, the Response object sends the browser a header with the ContentType indicating that the data about to be received is a Microsoft Excel document. Once the browser detects this as an Excel document, then as long as Microsoft's Excel program is installed on the user's computer, the user's browser will open the Excel program and write the data as a spreadsheet. The <TR> and <TD> HTML tags indicate to the Excel program the spreadsheet's rows and cells, integrating the Response.ContentType with the Acrobat Reader.

One of the fastest-growing aspects of the Internet is the use of Portable Document Format (PDF) to send documents. The Response object's Response.ContentType method can also be used to create PDF documents on the server and send them to the browser. Of course, users must have Adobe's Acrobat Reader installed on their computer in order for the PDF document to be seen. This chapter does not discuss the structure of a PDF document. However, as with the Excel spreadsheet, you use the MIME type "application/pdf." The following code will give you a good start to putting together a PDF document.

```
<%
Response.ContentType = "application/pdf"
Response.write "%PDF-1.3"
Response.write "1 0 obj"
Response.write "<<"
Response.write "/Type /Catalog"
Response.write "/Pages 3 0 R"
Response.write "/Outlines 2 0 R"
Response.write "/PageMode /UseOutlines"
Response.write ">>"
%>
```

●—CROSS-REFERENCE

Understanding the preceding code is only the beginning of creating a PDF document with ASP. Several examples in the PDF technical reference pages (located at www.pdfzone.com/resources/pdfspec13.html) will give you a better understanding.

The Request Object

You use the Request object to retrieve any information sent from a browser to the server. The browser passes information to the server primarily through either a Get or Post method. You use a Get method in an HTML link or with the Response object's redirect method. You use the Post method in an HTML form. Thus, you will use the

QueryString and the Form collection more than any other request method or collection in the Request object's arsenal. (A collection is a group of objects or attributes.) First let's look at an example using the Request object's QueryString collection.

●─CROSS-REFERENCE───────────────

The rest of the methods and properties for the Request object are listed in the ASP Core Reference Material on page 224.

The QueryString Collection

You use the Request.QueryString collection to retrieve information from a URL formed through a Get. Table 1-1 describes the options of the Request.QueryString collection. The syntax for the QueryString is as follows:

```
Request.QueryString (variable)(index)
```

Table 1-1 *Request.QueryString Collection Options*

Name	Type	Required	Description
Variable	String	Yes	A string enclosed in quotes, specifying the name of the variable in the HTTP query string to be retrieved.
Index	Integer	No	Enables access to multiple values contained in the variable. The range that can be obtained is 1 to Request.QueryString(variable).

The best way to understand how to use the QueryString collection is by understanding the following example. The following HTML page contains a URL link to mypage.asp. This link will send the key value pair University and TeamName to mypage.asp. All the key value pairs behind the ? symbol in the link are what is passed to mypage.asp.

```
<HTML>
<BODY>
<a
href="mypage.asp?University=Auburn&TeamName=Tigers">Team</a>
</BODY>
<HTML>
```

1

The following code is mypage.asp. As you can see, the QueryString collection gathers the values from UniversityName and TeamName, and then displays their values in an HTML page.

```
<%@ Language=VBScript %>
<%
'initialize these variables with the DIM statement
Dim UniName,Tname
UniName = Request.QueryString ("UniversityName")
Tname = Request.QueryString ("TeamName")
'Use the Response Object's Write method to send results to an
HTML page
%>
<HTML>
<BODY>
The University Name Passed to this ASP is <%=UniName%>
<BR>
The Team Name of the University is <%=Tname%>
</BODY>
</HTML>
```

If you want to send multiple college names to mypage.asp, use the following code:

```
<a
href="mypage.asp?UniversityName=Auburn&UniversityName=
Princeton">myColleg</a>
```

In order to obtain the multiple options from the preceding URL, change mypage.asp to the following code:

```
<%@ Language=VBScript %>
<%
'initialize these variables with the DIM statement

Dim,m
IF Request.QueryString("UniversityName").Count < 1 then
    Response.write "No UniversityName choosen "
Else
    For m  = 1 To Request.QueryString("UniversityName").Count
        Response.write Request.QueryString("UniversityName")(m)
        Response.write "<BR>"
    Next
End if
%>
```

The Form Collection

Any time an HTML form submits information using a Post method, you need to use the Form collection to retrieve the information. The Form collection contains several options you can use, as shown in Table 1-2. The syntax for the Forms collection is shown here:

```
Request.Form(Element)(Index)
Request.Form(Element).Count
Request.Form(Num)
```

Table 1-2 *Form Collection Options*

Name	Type	Required	Description
Element	String	Yes	A string specifying the name of the form element.
Index	Integer	No	Enables access to multiple values, such as checkbox values passed. The range of multiple values can go from 1 to Request.Form(element).Count.
Num	Integer	No	Uses a number to specify the form element instead of a string.
Count	Property	No	Returns the number of elements in a form.

Consider the following HTML page. Using the POST method, this HTML page will pass the form elements "LASTNAME" and "FIRSTNAME" to MyASPFORM.asp.

```
<HTML
<BODY>
<FORM NAME="FORM1" Action="MyASPFORM.asp" Method="Post">
LastName:
<INPUT TYPE=TEXT NAME="LASTNAME"
<BR>
FirstName:
<INPUT TYPE=TEXT NAME="FIRSTNAME"
<BR>
<INPUT TYPE=SUBMIT VALUE="CLICK">
</FORM>
</BODY>
</HTML>
```

The following code is for `MyASPFORM.asp`. Because the form passed to this page is a `Post` method, the page uses the `Request.Form` collection to retrieve the values from "LASTNAME" and "FIRSTNAME".

```
<%@ Language=VBScript %>
<%
'initialize these variables with the DIM statement
Dim LNAME,FNAME
LNAME = Request.Form("LASTNAME")
FNAME = Request.Form("FIRSTNAME")
Response.Write "The LastName passed to this page is "
Response.Write LNAME
Response.Write "<BR>"
Response.Write "The FirstName passed to this page is "
Response.Write FNAME
%>
```

If you want to know how many elements are contained in the form that is passed to the preceding code, use the `Count` property. The following code shows you the syntax for using the `Request` object's Form collection. This code is going to use the Count property to find out how many elements in the HTML form contain the name "LAST-NAME". The number returned should be 1 because there is only one item in that form element.

```
'get the number of elements in the form
intcount = Request.Form("LASTNAME").count
```

The `Form` collection also enables you to retrieve multiple values, such as those in HTML checkboxes. The following code illustrates how to obtain multiple values from an HTML form. This HTML page contains three checkboxes; therefore, multiple values can occur for this HTML page.

```
<HTML
<BODY>
<FORM NAME="FORM1" Action="MyASPFORM.asp" Method="Post">

<INPUT TYPE=CHECKBOX  NAME="STATE" VALUE="GEORGIA">Georgia
<BR>
<INPUT TYPE=CHECKBOX  NAME="STATE" VALUE="FLORIDA">Florida

<BR>
<INPUT TYPE=CHECKBOX  NAME="STATE" VALUE="ALABAMA">Alabama
<INPUT TYPE=SUBMIT VALUE="CLICK">
</FORM>
```

```
</BODY>
</HTML>
```

Following is the ASP page to capture the multiple values. Notice the line of code IF Request.Form("State").Count < 1 then. When we ran the code in the preceding example to count the number of items in the HTML form element ("LASTNAME"), we got a value of 1. For the case of the HTML form element ("State"), we will get 3.

```
<%@ Language=VBScript %>
<%
'initialize these variables with the DIM statement
Dim STATE,m
IF Request.Form("State").Count < 1 then
    Response.write "No state choosen "
Else
    For m  = 1 To Request.Form("State").Count
          Response.Write Request.Form("State")(m)
          Response.Write "<BR>"
    Next
End if
%>
```

Instead of using the VBScript For...Next, you can loop through the multiple values using the For each item in script. For instance, the following code loops through the Form element "State" to get the multiple values:

```
<%
For each item in Request.Form("State")
    Response.write item & "<BR>"
Next
%>
```

If all three values from the preceding code are chosen, then the output returned to the browser will be as follows:

```
GEORGIA
FLORIDA
ALABAMA
```

The ServerVariables

One of the properties of the Request object that is very helpful in building Web applications is the ServerVariables collection. Any time you need to find out information about your server, this is the collection to use. Let's look at how to use the ServerVariables.

●—CROSS-REFERENCE————————————————————

The list of the `ServerVariables` collection is provided in the ASP Core Reference Material on page 234.

With the growing trend in e-commerce, developers need to track who is coming to a Web site. The ServerVariables `REMOTE_ADDR` and `REMOTE_HOST` provide you with the information to track incoming "clicks" to your site. The following script shows you how to track who is coming to your site:

```
<%@ Language=VBScript %>
<%
Dim In_coming_addr
Dim In_coming_host
Dim In_coming_port
In_coming_addr = Request.ServerVariables("REMOTE_ADDR")
In_coming_host = Request.ServerVariables("REMOTE_HOST")
In_coming_host = Request.ServerVariables("SERVER_PORT")
Response.Write "The Remote Address is "
Response.Write In_coming_addr
Response.Write "<br>"
Response.write "The Remote Host is "
Response.Write In_coming_host
Response.Write "<br>"
Response.Write "The Remote Host is "
Response.Write In_coming_host
Response.Write "<br>"
Response.Write "The Port on my server that received the HTTP
request is "
Response.Write In_coming_host
Response.Write "<br>"

%>
```

If you want to list out all the ServerVariables in an HTML page, use the following script:

```
<%@ Language=VBScript %>
<HTML>
<Body>
<Table border="1">
<tr>
<td valign="top">
Variable Name
</td>
<td>
Value of Variable
```

```
</td>
</tr>
<% For Each Item in Request.ServerVariables %>
   <tr>
   <td>
       <% Response.Write Item %>
   </td>
   <td>
      <%Response.Write Request.ServerVariables(Item)%>
      </td>
      </tr>
   <% Next %>
   </Table>

   </Body>
</HTML>
```

Using the "REQUEST_METHOD" Server Variable with VBScript

Sometimes an Active Server Page is accessed via a Get and a Post method from different ASPs or HTML pages. When this occurs, use the "REQUEST_METHOD" ServerVariable to determine what request method is invoked. Let's look at an example to see how to use the "REQUEST_METHOD" variable.

Suppose you want to redirect to another page when your ASP receives a Get method, or execute a function if your page receives a Post method. The following example below achieves this goal. If a Get request method is detected, the user is redirected to MyRedirect.asp. However, if a Post is detected, the VBScript function Add executes.

```
<%@ Language=VBScript %>
<%
Function Add(v1, v2)
    Add = v1 + v2
End Function

Dim myMethod,AddAnswer
MyMethod =
UCase(Request.ServerVariables("REQUEST_METHOD"))

If MyMethod = "GET" then
    Response.Redirect("MyRedirect.asp")
End if

If MyMethod = "POST " then
```

```
AddAnswer = Add( 19, 10)
Response.write "The Add Answer is "
Response.write AddAnswer
End if
%>
```

The Server Object

The Server object allows you to control the creation of components, the direction that code in your ASPs take, the encoding of information in an http response, and how to obtain information about errors that occur during the execution of an ASP. Microsoft has improved the Server object with some methods. So let's begin our discussion of the Server object with these new methods.

New Methods in IIS 5.0

With the release of IIS 5.0, Microsoft includes three new methods for the Server Object: execute, transfer, and etLastError.

● **CROSS-REFERENCE**

The ASP Core Reference Material on age (p. 264) covers these methods in more detail. Also, an article at www.4guysfromrolla.com/ ASPScripts/PrintPage.asp?REF=/webtech/010700-1.2.shtml provides additional information.

The Transfer Method   The Transfer method allows you to transfer control to another ASP. The Response object's redirect method also allows you to redirect control to another ASP. The difference lies in how IIS 4.0 and IIS 5.0 implement a redirect.

When a redirect occurs in IIS 4.0, the server first sends a message to the browser to load a new URL. The browser loads the new URL, and then sends a request to the server for the new URL. At least three calls across the network make this process happen. Figure 1-8 shows the redirect process for IIS 4.0.

With the new Transfer method, the server does all the work before actually sending the new URL to the browser; therefore, only one network message is sent. For this reason, use the Transfer method when you can. Figure 1-9 displays the process that executing the Transfer uses to redirect to a new page.

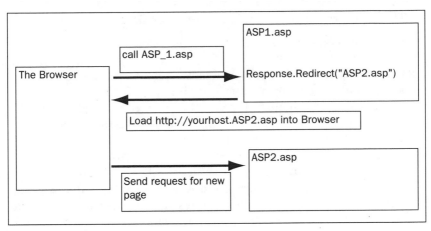

Figure 1-8 *IIS 4.0 method of redirection*

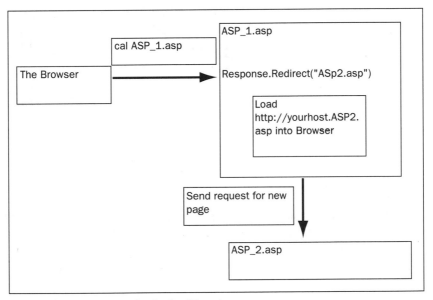

Figure 1-9 *IIS 5.0 method of redirection*

●—CROSS-REFERENCE

You can find additional information about the Transfer method at msdn.microsoft.com/library/psdk/iisref/vbob9waa.htm.

The following script is an example of doing a redirect in IIS 4.0:

```
<% Response.Redirect "/myotherpage.asp" %>
```

The next script is an example of doing a redirect in IIS 5.0:

```
<% Server.Transfer "/myotherpage.asp" %>
```

The Execute Method   The Server object's Execute method gives you an alternative to using a server-side include file. The difference between a server-side include file and the Execute method is how code is executed. With a server-side include file, the file executes as part of one page. When the ASP encounters the Server object's Execute method, control is transferred to another ASP that then executes its script. When the ASP that gained control is finished executing its code, control is sent back to the ASP that contains the Execute method. Thus, the Execute method allows you to break up tasks in an ASP into small modules. Figure 1-10 shows you how the redirection process works in IIS 5.0.

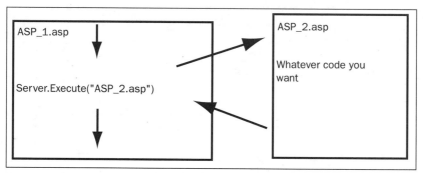

Figure 1-10   *The redirection process of the execute method*

● **CROSS-REFERENCE**

More information on the Server.Execute method can be found at msdn.microsoft.com/library/psdk/iisref/vbob9pid.htm.

Let's look at an example to see how this method works. When the following ASP executes the *"Server.Execute MyASPPage.ASP"* code, control is redirected to MyASPPage.ASP. When MyASP2Page.ASP gets control, the VBScript function Now() is sent to the browser. Then control is sent back to the calling page.

```
<%
Response.Write "<HTML>"
Response.Write "<BODY>"
```

```
Server.Execute "MyASP2Page.ASP"
Response.Write "</BODY>"
Response.Write "</HTML>"
%>
```

Following is MyASP2Page.ASP, which outputs the time:

```
<%
Response.Write Now()
%>
```

The GetLastError Method   Error handling in IIS 4.0 was virtually non-existent. But Microsoft introduces a new object in IIS 5.0, the ASPError object, that allows you to handle errors generated by COM objects or ASPs. You use the Server object's GetLastError method to return an ASPError Object. This returned object contains information about the last error occurring in your application.

●**—CROSS-REFERENCE**————————————————————

The methods and properties for the ASPError object are shown in the ASP Core Reference section on page 42.

An ASP can generate three types of errors: pre-processing, script, or run-time. The following code generates a run-time error:

```
<% Response.Write "My Name is Tim" %>
```

The following message is generated for this code:

```
Microsoft VBScript runtime error '800a01a8'
Object required: 'Response'
```

IIS 5.0 configures your default Web site to process errors to the file \iishelp\common\500-100.asp. The name of the page really is "500-100.asp", no joke. Whenever an error occurs, the server automatically transfers control to this ASP by using the Server. Transfer method. (From 500-100.asp you can write logic to process any errors.) This default error-processing page is where you use the Server object's GetLastError method. Figure 1-11 shows how this process works.

The diagram in Figure 1-11 shows that when an error occurs in an ASP, the Transfer method automatically redirects the processing of that error to the ASP called 500-100.asp. Once in the page 500-100. asp, this page uses the Server object's GetLastError method to process the error.

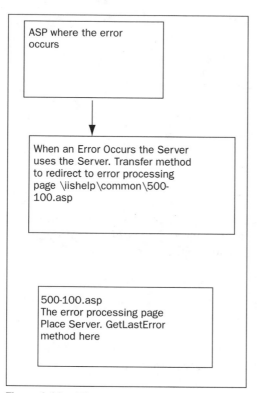

Figure 1-11 *The error-processing procedure*

● NOTE

If you don't like the file that IIS 5.0 defaults error processing to, then go into the IIS and change the properties on the default Web site to another ASP — maybe something like ErrorProcessingPage.ASP.

The following code shows you how to change the 500-100.asp to process the error received from the preceding example's run-time error 800a01a8.

```
<%
Dim LastErrObj
Dim Desc
Dim Cater
Dim File
Dim Number
'Get the Last Error sent to 500-100.asp
LastErrObj = Server.GetLastError
%>
```

```
<HTML>
<BODY>
<Form Action="anypage.asp" Method="Post">
<%
If LastErrObj.ASPCode = '800a01a8'
    Response.Write "You have typed in the wrong syntax"
Response.Write "<BR>The error is "&LastErrObj.Description
Response.Write "<BR>The error is on line number "
Response.Write LastErrObj.Line
End if
%>
<input type="submit" value="Go To Another Page">
</Form>
</Body>
</HTML>
```

Additional ASP Server Objects

Most of the components mentioned in this chapter are located in the \Winnt\System32\InetSrv directory in Windows NT. The scripting objects, NextLink and MyInfo, are located in \Winnt\Inetsrv. However, not all components discussed here come installed with IIS. Five objects are installed with IIS: Browser Capabilities, Ad Rotator, NextLink, MyInfo, and FileSystemObject (or scripting object). The rest of the components mentioned in this chapter can be purchased from Microsoft through the Microsoft SDK.

Looking at the Available Sever-Side Objects   Table 1-3 lists the available server-side objects and their corresponding .dll files in the aforementioned directories. It also lists the program ID name.

Table 1-3   *Available Server-Side Objects*

Component Name	Installed with IIS	PROGID Name	DLL name
Browser Capabilities	Yes	MSWC. BrowserType	BROWSCAP.dll
Ad Rotator	Yes	MSWC.AdRotator	Adrot.dll
Content Linking List	Yes	MSWC.NextLink	NextLink.dll
MyInfo	Yes	MSWC.MyInfo	MyInfo.dll
Scripting Objects	Yes	Scripting. FileSystemObjects	Scrrun.dll

Continued

Table 1-3 *Continued*

Component Name	Installed with IIS	PROGID Name	DLL name
Logging Utility	Yes	MSWC.IISLog	Logscript.dll
Dictionary	Yes	Scipting.Dictionary	Scrrun.dll
Tools	No	MSWC.Tools	Tools.dll
Content Rotator	No	MSWC.ContentRotator	ContRot.dll
Page Counter	No	MSWC.PageCounter	PageCnt.dll
Counter	No	MSWC.Counters	Counters.dll
Permission Checker	No	MSWC.PermissionChecker	Permchk.dll

Creating an Object   In order to use an object in ASP, you must create an instance of the object. When you create a instance of an object, you are really just creating a reference to the object. You could think of it as creating a personalized copy of the object.

There are two ways to create an instance of an object. One way is through the global.asa file using the <Object> tag. Another way is using the Server object.

●─CROSS-REFERENCE─────────────────────────

Although the global.asa file hasn't been discussed yet, you can find information about this file in the ASP Core Reference section (p. 269) and in Chapter 3 (p. 593).

For instance, if you want to create the Tools object using the <Object> tag in the global.asa, use the following code:

```
<Object RUNAT= Server Scope= Session Id=Tools PROGID =
"MSWC.Tools" >
```

If you want to create the Tools object with the Server object in an ASP, use this script:

```
Set myToolObj = Server.CreateObject ("MSWC.Tools")
```

Using Server-Side Include Files

Whenever you need to reuse the same code in several Active Server Pages, use a server-side include file. These lines of script can be HTML code, JavaScript code, or VBScript. This include file can be placed anywhere on the page, and IIS acts as though the file is a part of your page. The following code to an HTML page contains JavaScript:

```
<HTML>
<Head>
<title> The Title to This Page is Example </Title>
</Head>
<Script Language="JavaScript">
function open_hello()
{
    alert("hello");
    return true;
}
</script>

<Body onLoad="open_hello()">
This is an Example
</Body>
</HTML>
```

Suppose you want to use the JavaScript in the preceding example in several ASPs, but you don't want to type the JavaScript into every page. A server-side include file solves this problem. To create a server-side include file, open a text editor such as Notepad, and copy the following code into a file. Then save the file as *"MyJavaScript.inc"*, and place the code in the virtual directory *"MyExample."*

```
<Script Language="JavaScript">
function open_hello()
{
    alert("hello");
    return true;
}
</script>
```

Now it's time to integrate the include file into the HTML page. The following code shows the syntax for using an include file in either HTML or ASP (discussed in the next section) if the file is at the root directory:

```
<!--#include
virtual="/MyExample/includes/your_include_file_name.inc"-->
```

You can also give the physical location of the file by using this syntax:

```
<!--#include
file=c:\inetpub\wwwroot\MyExample\includes\your_include_file_
name.inc"-->

<HTML>
    <Head>
    <title> The Title to This Page is Example </Title>
    </Head>
<! --#include virtual="/your_include_file_name.inc"-->

<Body onLoad="open_hello()">
This is an Example
</Body>
</HTML>
```

Using ASP as Server-Side Include Files

You can also use ASPs as server-side include files. The following code shows a typical ASP with two VBScript functions: Add and Subtract. The code calls the Add function in the line a_answer = Add(10, 5), passing two arguments to the function. Then the answer is output to the browser.

```
<%@ Language=VBScript %>
<%
    Function Add(num1,num2)
        Add = num1 + num2
    End Function

    Function Subtract(num1,num2)
        Subtract = num2 — num1
    End Function

    %>
    <HTML>
    <BODY>
    <%Dim a_answer
        a_answer = Add(10,5)
      Response.Write "Add returned "
    Response.write a_answer
    %>
    </Body>
    </HTML>
```

However, if you want to reuse the Add and Subtract VBScript functions, create an ASP that looks like the following code:

```
<%
    Function Add(num1,num2)
        Add = num1 + num2
    End Function

    Function Subtract(num1,num2)
        Subtract = num2 - num1
    End Function
%>
```

Once you create this ASP, save it as *"UtilFunctions.asp"* and place it in the *"MyExample"* virtual directory. Now let's add your ASP include file back into the original page:

```
<%@ Language=VBScript %>
    <!-- #Include virtual="/MyExample/UtilFunctions.asp" -->
    <HTML>
    <BODY>
    <%Dim a_answer
    a_answer = Add(10,5)
    Response.Write "Add returned "
        Response.Write a_answer
    %>
    </Body>
    </HTML>
```

Using VBScript Subs and Functions

Subs and functions are the first pieces of reusable code you encounter with Active Server Pages. The most frequently asked question is "What is the difference between a Sub and a Function?" Well, a Sub is a Function that executes VBScript but doesn't return a value, whereas a Function is a Sub that returns a value. That may sound confusing, so in order to make things a little clearer, let's look at an example.

The following function calculates the future value of $100 for a period of 11 years and returns the answer. In a VBScript Function, using the name of the function returns the answer. In the case of the following example, the return value is sent via the variable FutureValue, which is the name of the function:

```
<%
Function FutureValue( numOfPeriods, interest,
PresentValueOfMoney)
```

```
Dim Int
Int = interest / 100
FutureValue = PresentValueOfMoney * ( ( 1 + Int ) ^
numOfPeriods)
End Function
```

```
%>
```

The next example shows a Sub. As you can see, the Sub doesn't
return a value, it only executes an action — in this case, outputting a
MessageBox based on logic inside the Sub.

```
<%
Sub MyMessBox( Num )
If Num = 15 then
    MessageBox("You are from Auburn University")
Else
    MessageBox("You are from Warner Robins High School")
End if
End Sub
%>
```

If you want to change the Sub MyMessBox into a Function, then
you need to provide a return value. Of course, you also need to
change Sub to Function. Look at the following code to see this occur:

```
<%
Function MyMessBox( Num )
  If Num = 15 then
      MessageBox("You are from Auburn University")
  Else
      MessageBox("You are from Warner Robins High School")
  End if

 'returns a value in this case a true
  MyMessBox = true
End Function
%>
```

Now that you understand the difference between a Sub and
Function, look at Listing 1-2, which integrates the "REQUEST_METHOD"
ServerVariables with a Sub and a Function. Listing 1-2 should be
labeled "*Example.asp.*"

Listing 1-2 *Example.asp integrates the REQUEST_METHOD ServerVariables with a Sub and Function.*

```
<%@ Language=VBScript %>
<%
Dim N
N = 0
Sub GoToAnotherPage()
   Response.Redirect("PageA.asp")
End Sub
Function MyFavoriteBand(num)
   MyFavoriteBand = "The Dave Clark " & Cstr(num)
End Function
If  Request.ServerVariables("REQUEST_METHOD") = "GET" then
   Call GoToAnotherPage
Else
   N = Request.Form("NumbOfBand")
   If N <> 0 then
     Response.write  MyFavoriteBand (N)
   End if
   Response.Write "<HTML>"
   Response.Write "<Body>"
   Response.Write "<Form Action=""Example.asp"" Method=""POST"
   Response.Write "Put in a Number"
   Response.Write "<Input Type=Text Name=""Numb"">"
   Response.Write "<BR>"
   Response.Write "<Input Type=Submit Value=Submit>"
   Response.Write "</Form>"
   Response.Write "</Body>"
   Response.Write "</HTML>"
End if
%>
```

Here is the code for PageA.asp, which the above code redirects to if the ServerVariable ("REQUEST_METHOD") equals "Get".

```
<%
Response.Write "<HTML><BODY>"
Response.Write "Mrs. Terri Eden is my Mom"
Response.Write "Her Mom is from Ireland"
Response.Write "My Dad is Mr. Roger Eden"
Response.Write "He grew up in Olive Hill Kentucky"
Response.Write "</BODY></HTML>"
%>
```

The first example above checks to see what the value of the ServerVariable ("REQUEST_METHOD") is. If a value of Get is found, then the code calls the GoToAnotherPage sub. However, if the value

1

of the ServerVariable is not Get, then the code obtains the value of the request object variable NumOfBand. If the value found for NumOfBand is greater than zero, then the function MyFavoriteBand returns a string. (Oh by the way, the Dave Clark 5 is my favorite band.) However, for this example the number supplied in the NumOfBand variable could return the string The Dave Clark 12.

The whole purpose of the above example is to show you the difference between a sub and a function. The sub doesn't return a value. The function returns a value.

In this chapter, you learned what you need to do to begin working with ASP. This chapter is not a detailed guide to every method and propety of the Request, Response, or Server object. We show you how to get started because ASPs offer a great opportunity to program applications for the Web.

VBScript and Active Server Pages

Microsoft Visual Basic Scripting Edition (VBScript) is a relatively recent addition to the Visual Basic programming language. It brings active scripting to a wide variety of milieus, including Web client scripting in Microsoft Internet Explorer and Web server scripting (which is supported by Active Server Pages) in Microsoft's Internet Information Server (IIS). For small-scale publishing, the Personal Web Server (PWS) is a desktop Web server. It enables you to test and publish Web applications and script ASP. It is the desktop counterpart of Internet Information Services.

This chapter discusses VBScript and provides documentation for many key terms. You learn how to use VBScript to do both clientside scripting that executes in Internet Explorer and server side scripting that executes on the PWS and the IIS. It also shows you how to install the PWS and IIS.

What Is VBScript?

If you already know Visual Basic, VBScript will be very familiar. VBScript is a simplified form of Visual Basic that allows you to include VBScript commands with HTML documents. VBScript is an interpreted language and executes along with the HTML commands. VBScript provides ways for developers to link and automate many types of objects in Web sites.

VBScript uses ActiveX Scripting to communicate with host applications. With ActiveX Scripting, browsers and other host applications don't require special integration code for each scripting component. ActiveX Scripting enables language developers to create standard language run times for scripting. Microsoft intends to provide run-time support for VBScript, and is cooperating with some Internet entities to define an ActiveX Scripting standard. Such a standard is intended to make the scripting engines interchangeable. ActiveX Scripting is used in Internet Explorer and in Internet Information Server (IIS).

VBScript can be obtained from Microsoft as source code or as compiled binary. This has the advantage that your users can always download the latest version of VBScript from the Microsoft Web site. You also can integrate VBScript with Jscript or any scripting technology for which the ActiveX scripting engine is available. The beauty of using the VBScript binary is that you can take care of licensing merely by acknowledging Microsoft in your application's About box.

Browser Support

Not all browsers support VBScript. Currently, only Internet Explorer supports VBScript. Netscape is compatible only when a plug-in is added. Netscape Navigator does not support DHTML or ActiveX controls either, so you must devise other ways to enable Netscape Navigator to receive script events. One way is to use a simple JavaScript function. Because both Internet Explorer and Netscape Navigator support plug-ins and JavaScript functions, these can be utilized.

●—**NOTE**———————————————————————————

> You can find examples of code that enable the functionality of the Windows Media Player for Netscape Navigator on the Microsoft Web site: `http://msdn.microsoft.com/workshop/imedia/windowsmedia/crcontent/cross-browser.asp`.

You can then capture script events that activate other ActiveX controls and plug-ins. In Figure 2-1, you use a plug-in for Netscape that responds to events and also controls another plug-in.

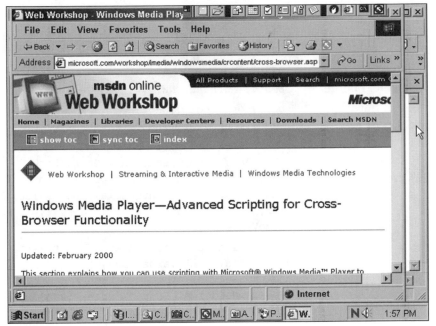

Figure 2-1 *Cross-browser functionality scripts*

Support Considerations

All development in VBScript is procedural. There is no support for
classes, as there is in Visual Basic. Nor is there any support for Object
Linking and Embedding (OLE). There is no support for control arrays,
data access or file operations, debugging tools, Multiple Document
Interface (MDI) forms, or built-in predefined constants. Furthermore,
there is no access to the Windows Help system. However, the Microsoft Script Debugger will help you track down errors in other ActiveX
scripting languages, as well as VBScript. Debugging with the Script
Debugger is similar to using the Debug menu in the Visual Basic
Integrated Development Environment. The Script Debugger is discussed later in this section.

There is support in VBScript for forms using the <FORM> </FORM>
tags. In addition, modules are supported through the <SCRIPT>
</SCRIPT> tags. VBScript supports only the Variant variable type.

VBScript Features

VBScript syntax comes in the following categories. The corresponding VBScript code is next to each category.

Array Handling	Array, Dim, Private, Public, ReDim, IsArray, Erase, LBound, UBound
Assignments	Set
Comments	Comments using ' or Rem
Constants/Literals	Empty, Nothing, Null, True, False
Control flow	Do...Loop, For...Next, For Each...Next,If...Then...Else Select Case,While...Wend
Conversions	Abs, Asc, AscB, AscW, Chr, ChrB, ChrW, CBool, CByte, CCur, CDate, CDbl, CInt, CLng, CSng, CStr, DateSerial, DateValue, Hex, Oct, Fix, Int, Sgn, TimeSerial, TimeValue
Dates/Times	Date, Time, DateAdd, DateDiff, DatePart, DateSerial, DateValue, Day, Month, MonthName,Weekday, WeekdayName,Year,Hour, Minute, Second, Now, TimeSerial, TimeValue
Declarations	Const, Dim, Private, Public, ReDim, Function, Sub
Error Handling	On Error, Err
Formatting strings	FormatCurrency, FormatDateTime, FormatNumber, FormatPercent
Input/Output	InputBox, LoadPicture, MsgBox
Literals	Empty, False, Nothing, Null, True
Math	Atn, Cos, Sin, Tan, Exp, Log, Sqr, Randomize, Rnd
Miscellaneous	RGB Function
Objects	CreateObject, Err Object, GetObject
Operators	Addition, Subtraction, Exponentiation, Modulus arithmetic, Multiplication, Division, Integer Division Negation, String concatenation, Equality, Inequality,Less Than, Less Than or Equal To, Greater Than, Greater Than or Equal To,Is, And, Or, Xor, Eqv, Imp
Options	Option Explicit
Procedures	Call, Function, Sub
Rounding	Abs, Int, Fix, Round, Sgn

Strings	Asc, AscB, AscW, Chr, ChrB, ChrW,Filter, InStr, InStrB, InStrRev, Join, Len, LenB, LCase, UCaseLeft, LeftB, Mid, MidB, Right, RightB, Replace, Space, Split, StrComp, String, StrReverse, LTrim, RTrim, Trim
Variants	IsArray, IsDate, IsEmpty, IsNull, IsNumeric, IsObjectTypeName,VarType
Script Engine Identification	ScriptEngine, ScriptEngineBuildVersion, ScriptEngineMajorVersion, ScriptEngineMinorVersion

Using VBScript for Client Scripting

Essentially, VBScript is used to develop applications on the Web. Internet applications can be developed in HTML, DHTML, Java, JScript, or several other options, depending upon the kind of application you need to develop. You can write applications in HTML using Microsoft Word or even NotePad. That is because HTML is made up of text. You can create a Web site using only HTML. However, you may not be able to create the kind of Web site you want using only HTML.

While you get a lot of debugging help in Visual Basic you don't get any help from the Visual Basic environment with VBScript.

●─CROSS-REFERENCE ──────────────────────────
See Chapter 6 for a discussion of Visual Basic (p. 699).

Visual Basic provides you with the pop-up context menus, syntax checking, prompting, the Immediate window, and other debug windows. VBScript, on the other hand, provides only an error message when the application runs.

The difficulty is that you do not use the Visual Basic IDE to create VBScript applications. You must use an HTML editor and use Internet Explorer to test them. This involves a two-step process, unless you can use a product such as Microsoft FrontPage or Corel Web Designer, which let you preview your work in the browser as a single step. Again, if you test your work in Netscape or other browsers, you will find that some or all of the features don't work.

You do, however, have solutions to the problem of debugging. The Script Debugger is a debugging environment that extends Internet Explorer and IIS by allowing Web developers to browse, edit, and debug scripted HTML pages (.htm, .html, and .asp files). The

Microsoft Script Debugger, as shown in Figure 2-2, is the first environment that allows users to debug scripted HTML, and gives developers a seamless way to combine HTML and script development.

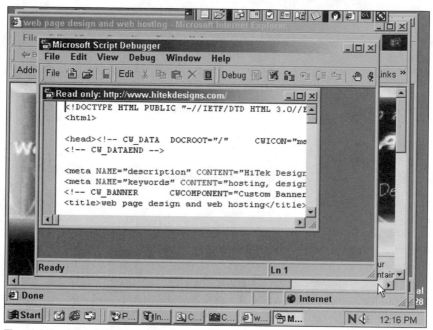

Figure 2-2 *The Script Debugger*

Using the Script Debugger, you can debug your Web scripts dynamically from your HTML page. To do this, you select Script Debugger from the View menu in Internet Explorer. You cannot edit the scripts directly in the Script Debugger, but you can open a document in the Script Debugger and then edit it.

Building Applications with VBScript

You can build some powerful Internet applications with VBScript. The most immediately handy ones are those that simply enhance an existing HTML document, or those in which a VBScript procedure will save steps if attempted in HTML.

When programming on the Internet with HTML, the HTML commands can be complex, but they are pretty basic when you are creating a simple page.

●—CROSS-REFERENCE—————————————————————————
HTML commands can be found in the HTML Syntax Reference section
(p. 319).

For example, <HTML> begins each page and </HTML> ends each
page. The hierarchy of required commands falls in the order of the
following:

```
<HTML>
<HEAD>
</HEAD>
<TITLE> </TITLE>
<BODY>
<FORM> </FORM>
</BODY>
</HTML>
```

You can see that the pattern is symmetrical, and most of the commands (not shown here) fall between the body tag block. The VBScript
tag block goes in between the body block as well.

```
<BODY>
<VBSCRIPT> </VBSCRIPT>
</BODY>
```

The VBScript code usually appears in Sub or Function procedures.
These procedures are called when your code initiates execution. You
can write VBScript outside of the procedures as long as it is within a
Script block.

```
<SCRIPT> </SCRIPT>
```

The preceding code will be executed when the HTML page loads.

Integrating VBScript into HTML Documents

You can use any script editor to draft your HTML page. Even Windows NotePad works. However, if you have Microsoft Visual InterDev,
Microsoft FrontPage, or another HTML editor, your job will be a great
deal easier. Microsoft Word 97 and Word 2000 come with the capability of editing HTML. A plug-in is available for previous versions of
Word. If you do use NotePad as an editor, be sure to use Save As to
name the file with the htm extension, or rename it after saving.

Let's do an exercise that includes only a form with a button that
you can press to see a dialog box. In your editor, create an HTML
document named vbtest.htm.

First write the HTML tags, using:

```
<HTML>
<HEAD>
 <TITLE>Fruit Crate Art</TITLE>
</HEAD>.
```

Next begin the <BODY> block. Set up a Form block as well and name the form "Form1":

```
<form NAME="Form1">
  <p><input TYPE="button" NAME="Button1" VALUE="Click Me">
<script FOR="Button1"
  EVENT="onClick" LANGUAGE="VBScript">
MsgBox "You pressed my button!"
</script> </p>
</form>
```

When you have finished writing the page, save it as vbtest.htm, launch Internet Explorer, and select Open from the File menu to open this file. Now you can test your work.

For some additional interest, insert an image file (bitmap) using the following:

```
<p><img border="0" src="fall.gif"
width="159" height="88">
</p>
```

Add this code to the end of the "Form" code and view again. If you used the image pictured, you should now see a fruit crate art poster below the Click Me button, as shown in Figure 2-3.

Although most scripting code will be in the HEAD area, where the code can be organized, you can place SCRIPT blocks anywhere in the HTML page. The SCRIPT blocks can be placed in both the BODY and HEAD sections if you wish. If your SCRIPT will be called from the BODY section, you should keep your code in the HEAD section where it can be read before it is called.

However, if you are embedding a SCRIPT in a form, you need to keep the code there. In the Fruit Crate example, this is exactly what you have done. Your script is placed within the form because it is responding to the button click.

In the Fruit Crate example, you are creating Form and Button objects and an event to which the VBScript will respond. Thus, the script FOR is a variation of the <SCRIPT> tag, because it is written to respond to the onClick event. The code spells it out. The script is FOR =Button1 in the onClick event, using the language VBScript.

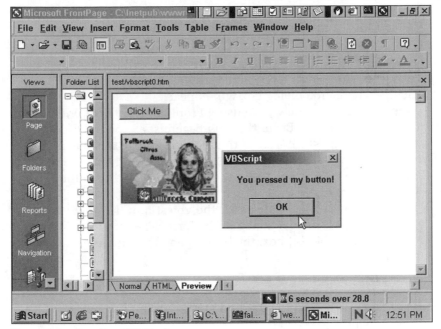

Figure 2-3 *Result of VBScript*

The message box fires upon the event. Finally, you ended the script block and the form block with the closing tags. You added the bitmap mainly as an afterthought, although an image dresses up the plain page.

View your Web page in your browser by typing the local path for your page in the address box. For example, if the location of your HTML file is C:\programs\vbtest.htm, type in that path.

More Client-Side VBScript Examples

The following examples illustrate some simple ways of incorporating VBScript into your Web pages. The first uses a text box to collect user input, and the second accesses the History List (a list of URLs previously visited).

Validating Entries with VBScript

Here, the user is prompted to enter a name. If the text box is left empty, there will be a different response than if something were typed into the box. The VBScript in this exercise demonstrates a practical application.

2

As in the previous example, there will be a form. This time, the form is used to capture the text input. The text box is examined to determine if any text was entered. If it was, a corresponding message is displayed. If no text was entered, the message will indicate that a name must be entered. If any characters were entered in the form's text field, a Thank-You dialog box will appear.

Prepare to create a new page using FrontPage, Notepad, Word, or your editor of choice. Begin the new page just as you did the previous one. Place the <HTML> tag at the top, with the <HEAD> tag next. If you wish, enter a beginning <TITLE> and ending </TITLE> as well. Add the </HEAD> ending tag. Begin the BODY block, and then the <NAME="YourForm">.

The code is much the same as for the vbtest.htm. However, in this case, the VBScript is not contained in the form. The form is strictly an HTML form, with the text box, the button, and the submit value for the button.

```
<TITLE>Enter Name</TITLE>
</HEAD>
<BODY><FORM NAME="YourForm">
  <p><input TYPE="TEXT"
NAME="txtNameText" SIZE="25">
<input TYPE="BUTTON" NAME="cmdSubmit"
  VALUE="Submit"> </p>
</FORM>
```

This produces a text box (form field) to the left of the Command button. The command button has the caption "Submit." At that point, the SCRIPT block begins. Because the objective is not to respond to an event like the button click, the SCRIPT block can be placed outside the form.

The button name is cmdSubmit, so the VBScript procedure is cmdSubmit_onClick. Here, just as in Visual Basic and other languages, you can declare variables. The difference with VBScript is that there is only one data type, the Variant data type, so you do not need to be concerned about the data type. The data types used in Visual Basic (string, integer, currency, and so on) do not pertain to VBScript.

Declare the MyForm variable to stand for the YourForm form. Then, use the Set statement to set MyForm equal to the document in the YourForm form.

```
<script LANGUAGE="VBScript">
Sub cmdSubmit_OnClick
   Dim MyForm
   Set MyForm = Document.YourForm
```

You want to determine if the user entered some text, so you check to see if the text field is empty.

```
If Myform.txtNameText.Value = "" Then
   MsgBox "Please enter your name."
     Else
   MsgBox "Thank You."
     End If
   End Sub
</script>
```

If the field is empty (signified by a null response), a message box is displayed asking the user to "Please enter your name." (This is shown in Figure 2-4.) If that is not the case (if there is something in the field), the message box thanks the user. The If...Then command block is ended and the procedure is ended. Save your file as Vbtest2.htm.

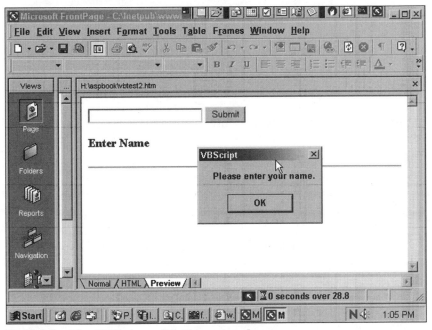

Figure 2-4 *The VBScript validation example*

Referencing the History List with VBScript

The next exercise offers a different twist. In this VBScript application, you create a Go Backward button that displays the History list retained in the browser. By default, the History list is set to 50 URLs. If you press the Back arrow, you will go back to the last URL you visited. Pressing the Back arrow subsequent times returns you to each URL recorded in the History list. Each URL is retained in the order in which it was accessed. Therefore, each time the Back arrow is pressed, the next-to-last URL is displayed. This method performs the same action as a user choosing the Back button in the browser. The go Backward method is the same as history.go(-1). Trying to go past the beginning of the History list does not generate an error. Instead, you are left at the current page.

Write your HTML code beginning the same way you did in the previous two exercises. Make the title read "Using History List." After the <BODY BODY> tag, make a < form> tag.

Then set up your form with a button to move backward to the previous URL (or file in this case), as follows:

```
<title>Using History List</title>
</HEAD>
<BODY>
<form>
<input TYPE="button" NAME="Go Backward!"
VALUE="Back Button" LANGUAGE="VBScript"
   OnClick="call window.history.back(1)">
```

This will cause the browser to display the last item in the History list when the button is clicked.

Add another line to create another button containing a Go Forward caption:

```
<input TYPE="Button" NAME="Go Forward"
VALUE="Forward Button"
LANGUAGE="VBScript"
onClick="Call window.history.forward(1)">
</script>
```

At this point, you can add the ending tags for form, BODY, and HTML.

```
</form>
</BODY>
</HTML>
```

When you launch your browser or Internet Explorer to display your page, vbtest3.htm, you should open another of the three files you created (vbtest.htm or vbtest2.htm). Use File Open on the Browser menu to open the files. Figure 2-5 shows how "Using History List" looks when viewed in the browser. Next, load the remaining file, so that you have a Back and Forward on your History list. Now press

the Go Backward button and retreat to your previously loaded file.
Press the Go Forward button and advance to the next file.

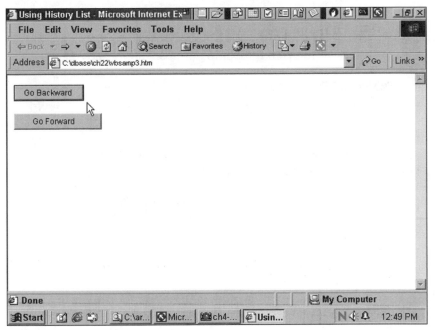

Figure 2-5 *The History list example*

Once you have loaded your HTML pages containing VBScript into
the browser and pressed the Go Backward button, you will then view
the previous file you accessed in the History list. You won't be able to
press the Go Forward button because the vbtest3.htm file is no longer
displayed in the browser window. You must click the forward arrow
on your browser to return to vbtest3.htm. Then you can press the forward arrow to move to the file you loaded after vbtest3.htm.

Installing the Personal Web Server and IIS

In the previous VBScript examples, the client-side functions that
were carried out (for example, entering text and moving back and
forth through the History list) were all performed in the browser.
Client-side applications may not be completely effective because they
do not work in all browsers. You will find the solution to this problem in the next section, which covers server-side scripting. However,

before you move on to actual server-side scripting, you need to know how to install the Personal Web Server (PWS) and the IIS, both of which are needed for server-side scripting.

2 Installing the Personal Web Server

The PWS is set up for Web publishing on a smaller scale.

●—CROSS-REFERENCE

See Chapter 1 (p. 533), for more information regarding IIS and PWS installation.

It provides many of the same services and features as the IIS, a strong Web server designed to carry out large-scale Web publishing services. You can use the PWS to develop and test your Web applications, and then upload them to a Web server that is running IIS.

Either the IIS or the PWS uses Active Server Pages. The IIS is available only with Windows NT 4.0 and Windows 2000 Professional and Server editions. The Personal Web Server is for use with Windows 95/98. It is shipped on the installation CD, but does not install with the typical installation.

First, you must have the Windows 95 or 98 CD. You need to open the Control Panel and double-click the Add/Remove Programs icon. The Windows Add/Remove Programs Setup window is then displayed (see Figure 2-6).

Click the Windows Setup tab. Select Internet Tools from the list of Windows Programs as shown in Figure 2-7. To view the options, you can click on the Details button. In the next window, the Personal Web Server will be displayed. There must be a checkmark next to this item. When you click OK, the installation will begin.

You also can install the PWS that ships with FrontPage 97, FrontPage 98, and FrontPage 2000. The installation will take place automatically except that you will be prompted to configure the location of files, including the home directory. Usually, the Personal Web Server creates a root directory at the location C:\Webshare\WWWroot\ or C:\Inetpub\ WWWroot. You also can usually use the address http://localhost/ directoryofchoice to launch your scripts for browser preview.

When you install the Personal Web Server, it should be placed in your Startup folder so that it loads and remains running in the background. While running, its icon is visible on the Windows Taskbar. You can read its documentation in Internet Explorer. To do so, right click on the PWS icon on the Taskbar, select Properties, then select any of the options on the Help Menu for more information. Figure 2-8 shows the PWS option highlighted.

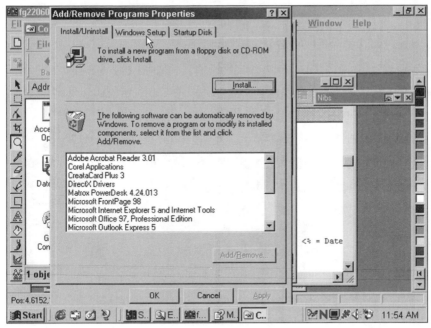

Figure 2-6   *The Windows Add/Remove Programs Setup window*

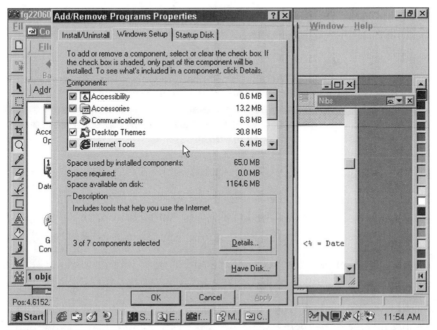

Figure 2-7   *The Internet Tools option*

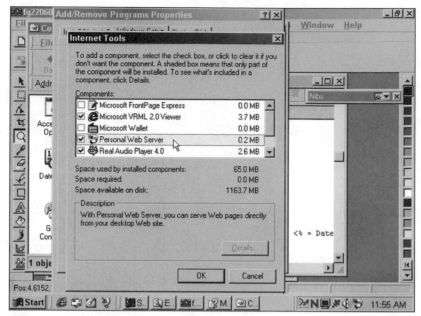

Figure 2-8 *The Personal Web Server option*

● **CAUTION** ———————————————————————————

The PWS uses your computer's name (the name entered when Windows was installed) after the `http://` prefix. For example, if your computer's name were Max, the home page would be located at `http://max`. This part of the installation is confusing because knowing operating system commands does not help much in figuring out where your files are. If the home directory that PWS uses is located at C:\Webshare\WWWroot, it may not be apparent when you open files to edit from `http://max` or `http://localhost`.

Installing IIS

If you are running Windows NT or Windows 2000 Professional or Server, you should install the IIS. IIS ships with Windows NT and Windows 2000. IIS looks much like the PWS. The IIS will locate files under the Inetpub directory. When you view your work in Internet Explorer, you must reference the location of your files as localhost or the computer's name, whichever you used to configure the Web server.

You access the IIS in Windows 2000 Internet Services Manager or the Windows 2000 Personal Web Manager under Administrative Tools on the Control Panel. The Administrative Tools window is then displayed, as shown in Figure 2-9.

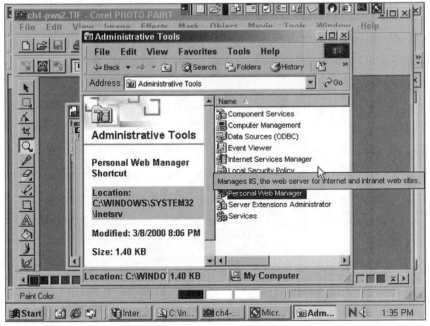

Figure 2-9 *The Windows 2000 Administrative Tools window*

Windows 2000 will also install FrontPage 2000 extensions when you select the Internet Information Services (IIS) component. In addition, you get FTP Server, IIS Snap-In, Personal Web Manager, SMTP Service, and Visual InterDev RAD Remote Deployment Support. You select the options under Administrative Tools from the Control Panel to manage IIS.

Another option under Administrative Tools, Personal Web Manager, looks similar to the Personal Web Server in Windows 95/98, but it works with IIS to help you publish your personal Web pages and/or share documents on your computer with others on a network. The Personal Web Manager interface looks similar to the Windows 95/98 Personal Web Server. The Windows 2000 Personal Web Manager (see Figure 2-10) works in conjunction with IIS to let you create virtual directories for sharing Web content, helps you create forms for your Web site, and tests your site before you post it to an intranet or the Internet and share documents across platforms via HTML. In short, it functions much like the older Personal Web Server, except that it works with the more robust IIS to assist you in Web publishing.

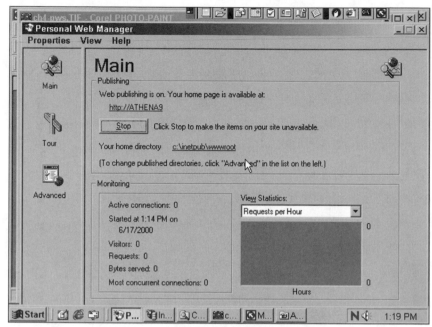

Figure 2-10   *The Windows 2000 Personal Web Manager*

Using VBScript and Active Server Pages for Server-Side Scripting

Client-side scripts execute on the client, rather than on the server. A page is downloaded into the user's (client's) browser and executes there. As previously noted, the problem with writing only client-side scripts is that they will not execute in many browsers. That is, if you try running some scripts using Netscape or AOL's browser, they are viewable in most cases, but they will not perform the functions for which you programmed them.

In order to use VBScript on the client side, you must test to see what browser is being used. Generally, Java script will work on Netscape, but without developing a test for each visitor, you won't know which technique to apply.

On the other hand, if you use server-side scripting, you need not worry about the individual browsers accessing your site, as the scripts all execute on the server, not the client's browser.

Active Server Pages offers support for the use of existing scripting languages, such as third-party languages (PERL, and so on), as well as Microsoft VBScript in HTML pages. Active Server Pages is also compatible with ActiveX scripting languages, and ActiveX components can be created in effectively any language.

The advantage of Active Server Pages is that you can customize your Web pages for each user on the fly. You can arrange to have one type of page for one visitor type and another for a different type of visitor.

Active Server Pages is part of the Windows NT and Windows 2000 packages, but it can be implemented using the Personal Web Server. The chief benefit is using any one of a number of different scripting languages while targeting any browser.

Active Server Pages scripts run upon the request of a file with an .ASP extension from a browser. The Web server calls Active Server Pages. Active Server Pages reads the entire file and executes commands. The page is then sent to the browser. Your ASP file is simply a file that can contain HTML and scripting, as well as calls to components. Once a change is made to an ASP file on the server and the changes are saved, the script will automatically be compiled the next time the Web page is loaded. This works because the ASP technology is integral to Microsoft Web servers (Windows 95/98 Personal Web Server and Internet Information Server).

Because the scripts all run directly on the server, rather than on individual browsers, the Web server serves the Web pages to the browser. Thus, it does not matter which browser a client has, as the browser receives the processed page from the server. Standard HTML is returned to the browser. Also, because only the results of the process are sent to the browser, users can't see the commands that generated the Web pages they view.

An important aspect of Active Server Pages technology is its independence of programming languages. VBScript and JScript are supported automatically. Support for other scripting languages, such as PERL, is also available. Regardless of the scripting language you use, you can simply enclose script statements in special delimiters for ASP. Active Server Pages use a command-block syntax in which commands are embedded within the less than symbol and percent symbol (<%), and the reverse to end the block (%>).

If you would like to create an HTML page from which to link to the Active Server Pages, you can do so by entering the following simple code:

```
<a href="http://localhost/asptest2.asp"> </a>
```

Again, determine your machine's name from the Network icon on the Windows Control Panel. Click the Identification tab to see what your system was named. This was done either by you or by those who initially set it up. After coding the Web page, name it default.htm and save it in the location for your home page. You can also check the Personal Web Server Manager to determine the home page and home directory locations. Double-click the Personal Web Server icon in the area to the right of the Start menu. The Main button will display the information.

There are a number of quite sophisticated applications for Active Server Pages. For example, ASP is often used to detect and accommodate the individual client browser. This way, the server responds differently to users depending upon the capabilities of the browser being used. You probably won't want to tackle the most difficult applications at first. Some simple practice exercises include obtaining the date and time from the Web server.

Creating a Random Number Effect

When you create your Active Server Pages application, you begin with an ordinary HTML page, and then embed the ASP command block within it:

```
<HTML>
<HEAD>
<title>Pick a Number</title>
</HEAD>
<BODY>
<center>
</center>
```

Using VBScript, You can use the Rnd function to create the effect:

```
VarX = Int( 4 * Rnd +1)
```

Everything in the Active Server Pages command block must be placed within the characters <% and %>. The following code creates a random number effect that operates each time you click the Refresh button. At first, nothing shows on the screen in the browser window. When you click Refresh a new number is displayed, and each time you refresh the window, a new number will appear.

```
<% Dim Randumm
randomize
Randumm = int(Rnd* 10) + 1
%>
<% = Randumm %>
```

Notice that you do not need to use a command to print or display the result of the number generated on the screen. That occurs by default. Finally, finish with the ending HTML tags:

```
</BODY>
</HTML>
```

The important part of this exercise is naming your ASP file with an .ASP file extension. Active Server Pages files have the .ASP file extension so that the server identifies the page and processes the code.

Requesting Server Information

To make effective use of Active Server Pages technology, ideally you should put the Web server to work finding information to display in the user's browser. There are many different kinds of tasks. You can invoke other processes from Active Server Pages, such as Microsoft Transaction Server components. If you decide to do this, you need to modify your system's Registry. Another thing you can do with Active Server Pages is set the values in "Cookies." A cookie is a tiny text file placed on your computer's hard drive by a Web server in order to recognize you as a user on future visits.

In carrying out the requesting task, the ASP objects request information from the user, respond by sending information to the user, control the Internet Information Server, maintain the user's current session, and share application information and settings.

The next example involves requesting and displaying the date and time from the server. Actually, one command can do both functions. You simply use the WeekdayName function, which requests both the current date and time. Of course, that is the date and time on the server where the process is running. For example, if you place your file on a Web site and then execute it, you will get the date and time on that server. This can be substantially different from your time zone if your Web site is far away.

Create your HTML code to start the page:

```
<HTML>
<HEAD>
<title>Hi There</title>
</HEAD>
<BODY>
<font size="4">
<p align="center">Hello </font></p>
</BODY>
</HTML>
```

Next, set up the function using Active Server Pages:

```
<h3>It is <% =WeekdayName(Weekday(Date)) %>, <% = Date %>.
```

You can write the prompt in HTML, but the Now must be
encased in the less than and percent sign symbols that operate as
brackets in ASP. Save your file with the .ASP extension. Open your
file in the browser and check it out. The WeekdayName(Weekday
(Date)) will request the name of the day as well as the date from
the server. Finally, provide the ending HTML tags and save the
file as ASPtest2.ASP (or whatever pleases you). Open the file in
your browser. Figure 2-11 shows the date and time displayed.

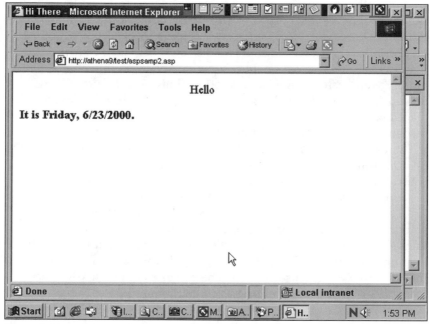

Figure 2-11 *The server time and date*

This tutorial introduced you to the world of VBScript and ASP.
It showed you how to use VBScript to do clientside scripting that
executes in Internet Explorer. You also learned how to do server-
side scripting that executes on the PWS and the IIS.

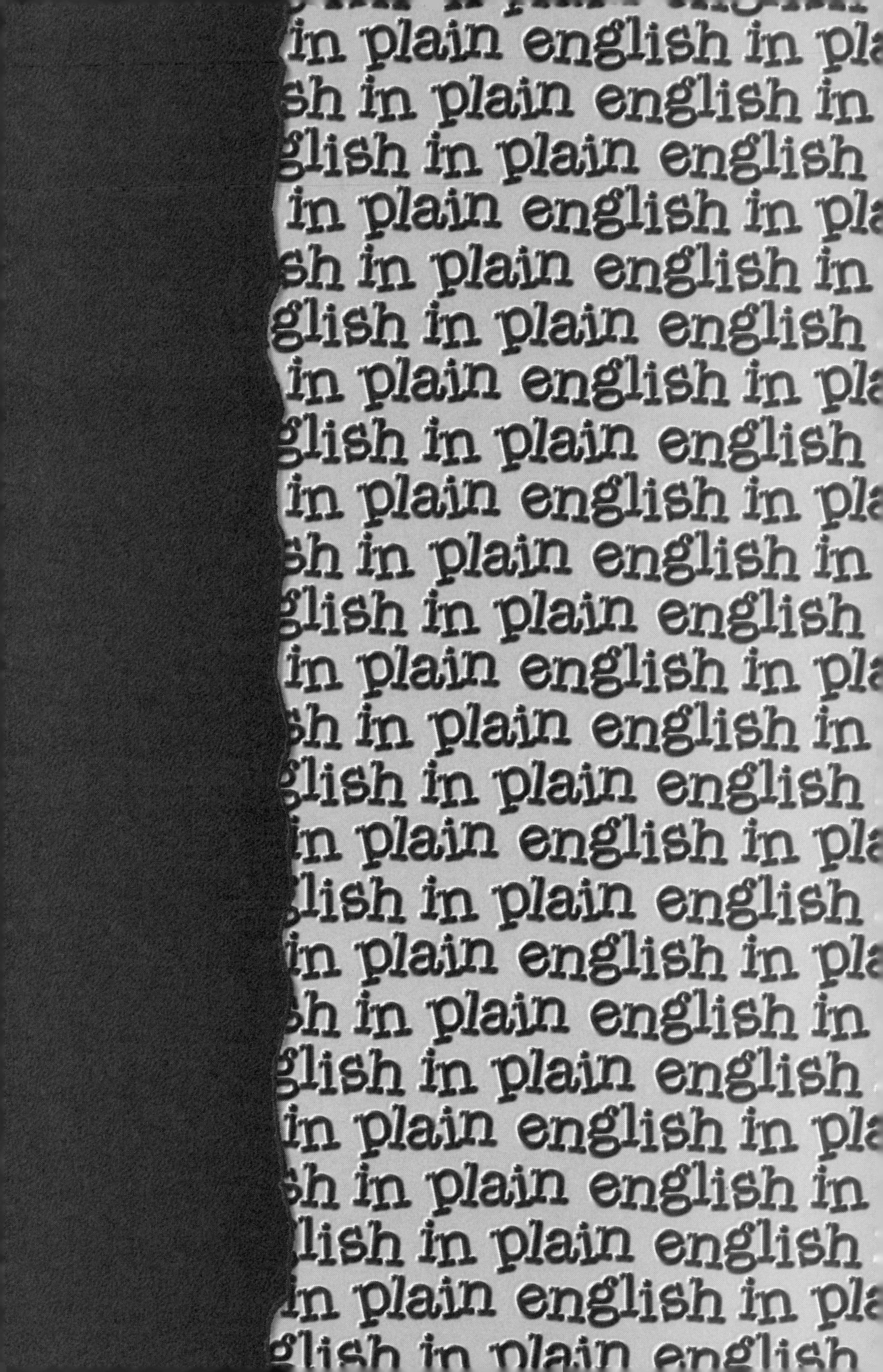
in plain english in
sh in plain english in
glish in plain english
in plain english in
sh in plain english in
glish in plain english
in plain english in
glish in plain english
in plain english in
sh in plain english in
glish in plain english
in plain english in
sh in plain english in
glish in plain english
in plain english in
glish in plain english
in plain english in
sh in plain english in
glish in plain english
in plain english in
sh in plain english in
glish in plain english
in plain english in

Objects Used for
ASP Applications

All Active Server Pages (ASP) applications need certain objects in order to work. These objects can provide the one capability that static HTML pages cannot — maintaining state. This chapter explains how to start and set up an ASP application. It then covers two objects — the Application object and the Session object — and how they work with ASP to maintain state on the Internet.

However, before you learn how to set up an application, a few words need to be said about what "maintaining state" means.

Maintaining State on the Internet

The Internet is a *stateless* environment. That means that if you enter any information on Web page A, and then go to Web page B, the information entered on Web page A is forgotten. The stateless environment of the Web presents a problem if you're trying to write business applications that need to remember information input on previous pages. One way that Web engineers get around this problem is to pass all the information through a URL address or a Common Gateway Interface (CGI).

Microsoft presented their solution to the "stateless" problem through two ASP objects: the `Application` and the `Session`. Both of these objects are covered in this chapter. But, let's first take a look at what you need to get started building an application.

Starting an ASP Application: The Global.asa File

Anytime you call any ASP page in your browser, the global.asa attached to that Web site is fired off first. That is, whenever an application is started, the global.asa is placed into memory. The asa extension stands for Active Server Application. This file contains the beginning events, objects, and variables that a programmer assigns to an application. From the user's point of view, the file keeps track of the "state" of those events, objects, and variables as the user moves through the application. The global.asa is always located in the inetpub\wwwroot\yourwebsite directory.

Following is an example of a global.asa file. Notice the four events in the file: `Application_OnStart`, `Application_OnEnd`, `Session_OnStart`, and `Session_OnEnd`. The `Application_OnStart` and `Session_OnStart` events are where the majority of your code for the global.asa will be located.

```
<OBJECT RUNAT=Server SCOPE=Session ID=MyTools
PROGID="MSWC.Tools">
</OBJECT>

<SCRIPT LANGUAGE=VBScript RUNAT=Server>

Sub Application_OnStart
    '--Project Data Connection
    Application("db_ConnectionString") =
"DSN=eTransDev;User Id=sa;PASSWORD=;SERVER=Star
Technology;UID=sa;WSID=STAR TECHNOLOGY;DATABASE=my_Dev"
    Application("db_ConnectionTimeout") = 15
    Application("db_CommandTimeout") = 30
    Application("db_CursorLocation") = 3
    Application("db_RuntimeUserName") = "sa"
    Application("db_RuntimePassword") = ""
End Sub

Sub Application_OnEnd
```

```
        Set MyTools = nothing

End Sub


Sub Session_OnStart
    Session("UserId") = ""
    Session.Timeout = 15
    Session("Password") = ""
    Session("CompanyId") = ""
End Sub

Sub Session_OnEnd

End Sub

</SCRIPT>
```

Notice at the top of the global.asa that an instance of the Tools component is created. Creating an instance of an object in the global.asa with an application scope makes that object global to the entire application. The advantage to creating the object in the global.asa file is that you only have to create the object once for all users. The disadvantage to creating the object in the global.asa file is that the object resides in memory, eating up resources.

●─NOTE

There can be only one global.asa file per ASP application.

●─TIP

A web farm is a Web architecture that has two or more Web servers to handle the traffic coming into a Web site. If you are going to use a Web farm in an ASP application for e-commerce, do not create any objects in the global.asa file. Nor should you create application variables in Web farms. (A variable set through Application("variable") is the same as a global variable for ASPs). So how do you store global variables for ASP applications in a Web farm? By storing any global variable information in a database, and then recalling that information through an SQL SELECT statement in a stored procedure.

Part of what you need to understand about ASP applications is the *scope* of an object. The next few pages will define what the scope of an object is and how to create scope for Application and Session variables and objects.

Scope of Applications: Application and Session Objects

The *scope* in Active Server applications defines the level at which an object, variable, or event occurs. In ASPs, there are two levels of scope: the Application level and the Session level. The objects that correspond to these levels are the Application object and the Session object.

Application-Level Scope: The Application Object

A variable or object that is accessible by all users is known as an application variable or object. Use the application-level variables for items that will be used by all individuals throughout the application, such as a connection string to a DSN. The following code shows you the syntax for creating an application variable:

```
Application("My_ConnectionString") = "DSN=myConn;User
Id=sa;PASSWORD=;SERVER=MyServer;UID=sa;WSID=MyServer;DA
TABASE=my_Dev"
```

Although application variables are primarily set in the global.asa, you can set them anywhere in your application. Two events happen when the application starts and ends: Application_OnStart and Application_OnEnd. You can assign application variables inside these events or in the global.asa.

Look at the following code; some application variables are assigned inside the Application_OnStart event, while some are assigned outside the event in the global.asa. The Application_OnEnd event is triggered when the Web server shuts down.

```
<SCRIPT LANGUAGE=VBScript RUNAT=Server>

Sub Application_OnStart
    '--Project Data Connection
    Application("db_ConnectionString") =
"DSN=eTransDev;User Id=sa;PASSWORD=;SERVER=Star
Technology;UID=sa;WSID=STAR TECHNOLOGY;DATABASE=my_Dev"
    Application("db_ConnectionTimeout") = 15
    Application("db_CommandTimeout") = 30
    Application("db_CursorLocation") = 3
    Application("db_RuntimeUserName") = "sa"
    Application("db_RuntimePassword") = ""
```

```
End Sub



'upon a application shutting down write a note to a log
'file.

Sub Application_OnEnd
     'the code you want if the web server goes down.
Maybe
     'writing to a log file.
    Set Tfile =
    Server.CreateObject("Scripting.FileSystemObject")
    Tfile.CreateTextFile("c:\NameOfLogFile.txt",true)
    Tfile.WriteLine("We are in the Application_OnEnd
event")
    Tfile.WriteLine("Time is "&time())
    Tfile.Close
End Sub

'set two application variables outside the
Application("MyFavoriteSister") = "Lori Chesser"
Application("MyBunny") = "Amy Eden"
</Script>
```

●─**NOTE**───────────────────────

The Response and Request objects do not work in the Application_
OnEnd event. You can find out more about the Response and Request
object in Chapter 1 (p. 533).

Session-Level Scope: The Session Object

The opposite of the application-level variable is the session-level variable, which can only be accessed by an individual user. Anytime you
want to create variables or objects that can only be accessed by an
individual user, assign that user a session-level or Session object variable. Items such as user IDs and passwords are good candidates for
session-level variables. The following code shows you the syntax to
assign a session-level variable:

```
Session("userid") = ""
Session("password") = ""
```

As with the application level, the session level also has two events
that occur when you start and stop a session: Session_OnStart and

Session_OnEnd. The following code shows you an example of assigning a blank character to Session variables.

```
<SCRIPT LANGUAGE=VBScript RUNAT=Server>

Sub Session_OnStart
    Session("userid") = ""
    Session("password") = ""
End Sub

</Script>
```

Notice that no variables were assigned outside of the Session_OnStartevent. If any variables are assigned outside of any event in the global.asa file, they are considered global. The Session_OnEnd is fired off when the Session.Timeout expires or the Session.abandon property is set to true.

● **NOTE**

You can't use Response.Write in the Session_OnEnd event.

The following script is a good template to copy for your first global.asa file. Most ASP programmers have a set of templates such as this in order to speed up the development of an application.

```
<SCRIPT LANGUAGE=VBScript RUNAT=Server>

Sub Session_OnStart
    Session("userid") = ""
'Set the session timeout to 5 minutes
    Session("password") = ""Session.Timeout = 5

End Sub

Sub Session_OnEnd
    Set Tfile =
Server.CreateObject("Scripting.FileSystemObject") Tfile.
CreateTextFile("c:\NameOfFile.txt",true)
    Tfile.WriteLine("We are in the Session_OnEnd
event")
    Tfile.WriteLine("The user is
"&Session("userid"))
    Tfile.Close
End Sub

</Script>
```

●—**NOTE**—————————————————————————————

> Session variables die after the `Session_OnEnd` event has finished. Furthermore, the `Request` and `Response` objects do not work with the `Session_OnEnd` event.

Now that you've seen how the global.asa file is constructed, let's take a detailed look at the Session and Application objects.

●—**CROSS-REFERENCE**———————————————————————

> The ASP Core Reference section covers the methods, events, and properties of the `Application` (p. 36) and `Session` (p. 268) objects.

Session Object Properties and Methods

The Session object contains four properties that enable you to control the session environment: `SessionID`, `TimeOut`, `CodePage`, and `LCID`.

●—**CROSS-REFERENCE**———————————————————————

> These four `Session` object properties are covered in the ASP Core Reference section (pgs. 273, 274, 271, and 272).

The Session object has only three methods: `Abandon`, `Contents.Remove`, and `Contents.RemoveAll`. The `Contents.Remove` and `Contents.RemoveAll` methods are contained inside the `Contents` Collection.

●—**CROSS-REFERENCE**———————————————————————

> The `Session` object's method and properties can be found in the ASP Core Reference section, beginning on page (p. 268).

SessionID Property

Any time a new session is started, the server generates a `SessionID`. As long as the `Session.TimeOut` or `Session.Abandon` method have not been called, the `SessionID` exists. The syntax to use this property is as follows:

```
Session.SessionId
```

TimeOut Property

The TimeOut property goes into action if a page of your application has remained idle for a certain amount of minutes. The default is 10 minutes, but with this property you can set the time. The syntax to use this property is as follows:

```
Session.TimeOut
```

LCID Property

If you are writing an ASP application for a locale other than the United States, the LCID property is very useful. This property allows you to set the local identifier used in the dates, currency, or time for places other than the United States. The syntax to use this property is as follows:

```
Session.LCID
```

CodePage Property

In association with the LCID property is the CodePage property. The CodePage property sets the text to a language, such as Japanese. If your application is going to be used by Far Eastern users, you want the time to be set by the LCID property, and you want the language for the text of your application to be in Japanese. The syntax to use this property is as follows:

```
Session.CodePage
```

Abandon Method

If you leave a page idle for a certain amount of time, the Session.Timeout property will end the session. But if you want to end a session before the time set by the TimeOut property, use the Abandon method. When this method is executed, the Session_OnEnd event is fired off. The syntax to use this method is as follows:

```
Session.Abandon
```

Session.Contents.Remove Method

When you create a Session variable, that variable is added to the Session Content collection. If you want to later remove that or any Session variable from the collection, then use the Contents.Remove method. Look at the following example. It adds a Session variable called "FamousTippoMississippiPeople".

```
Session("FamousTippoMississippiPeople") =
"Dr. Cecil Allison"
```

The Contents collection for the Session object now shows one entry. To delete that entry from the collection, use the Contents. Remove method:

```
Session.Contents.Remove("FamousTippoMississippiPeople")
```

Session.Contents.RemoveAll Method

Because the Contents.Remove method will delete a single entry, the Contents.RemoveAll method deletes all the entries in the Session Contents collection. The following code shows two entries added to the Content collection for the Session object. Then the Contents. RemoveAll method is used to delete the two entries from the collection.

```
Session("HinesvilleGaPeople1") = "GladysBuckner"
Session("OliveHillKyPeople") = "Roger Eden-my Father"
Session("LandmarkAtAuburnUniv") = "SanfordHall"
Session.Contents.RemoveAll()
```

Application Object Methods

The Application Object does not have properties associated with it. However, there are four Application object methods: -Lock, UnLock, Contents.Remove, and Contents.RemoveAll. Contents.Remove and Contents.RemoveAll are methods contained inside the Application collection. These two methods act exactly as the Session.Contents. Remove and Session.Contents.RemoveAll methods work, except at the application level.

Lock Method

Sometimes it is necessary to prevent several users from changing an application variable at the same time. This is the problem of concurrent users. However, the Microsoft engineers provide ASPs with an application-level method to solve the concurrent user situation: the Lock method. This method allows the programmer to tightly control the modification of any application variable. The following code shows you how to implement this method. If you need to find the maximum number of records from table PlayersNumber, you can assign the value

to an "MaxNumofRec" application variable. The Lock method allows
only one user to change the application ("MaxNumofRec").

```
<%

Dim DataConn
Dim RS
Dim Sqlstm
Dim MaxNum
Set DataConn =
Server.CreateObject("ADODB.Connection")
Application.Lock
Sqlstm = "Select Max(Num) from PlayersNumber"
RS = DataConn.Execute(Sqlstm)
'get the maximum number from recordset RS
if Not RS.EOF and RS.BOF then
    Application("MaxNumofRec") = Sqlstm(0)
End if
Application.UnLock
%>
```

As you can see from the example, the Lock method will not allow
any other user to use that piece of code until the Application.UnLock
is set. If you didn't place the Application.Unlock in the code, the
ASP would release the lock when the page was finished processing.

UnLock Method

Because the Lock method locks the application to other users for a time,
the UnLock method releases that lock. For every lock, you must have an
unlock. The following code provides the syntax to release a lock:

```
Application.UnLock
```

Application.Contents.Remove Method

When you create an Application variable, that variable is added to
the Application Content collection. If you want to later remove that
or any Application variable from the collection, use the Contents.
Remove method. Consider the following example, which adds an
Application variable called "MyFavoriteGaPeople":

```
Application("MyFavoriteGaPeople") = "Terri Eden"
```

The Contents collection for the Application object now shows
one entry. To delete that entry from the collection, use the Contents.
Remove method:

```
Application.Contents.Remove("MyFavoriteGaPeople")
```

Application.Contents.RemoveAll Method

Whereas the `Contents.Remove` method deletes a single entry from the Application collection, the `Contents.RemoveAll` method deletes all the entries in the Application Content collection. The following code shows three entries added to the `Contents` collection for the Application object. Then the `Contents.RemoveAll` method is used to delete the three entries from the collection.

```
Application("HinesvilleGaPeople2") = "Robert Hendry"
Application("TeacherWhoChangedMylife") = "Margie Pyle
Land-Auburn 66"
Application("GoodPeople") = "Robert Futrell"
Application("GoodGirl") = "Micailah Burgress"
Application.Contents.RemoveAll()
```

One of the nice features of ASP is the ability to use the `Application` or `Session` objects to store global information in an array. The following pages discuss how you can store global information in an array through either the `Application` or `Session` objects.

Application and Session Object Collections

The `Application` and `Session` objects have collections associated with them: Contents and `StaticObjects`. These collections store all the variables, arrays, and objects assigned to either object.

Contents Collection

Microsoft states, "The `Contents` collection contains all the items that have been added to the application through a script command." What that means in plain English is that anything you put in the `Application_onStart` event or in an application variable in your code is now part of the `Contents` collection. To understand this a little better, look at the following example code, which is a typical script that you would find in the global.asa file.

Contents Collection Application Object Example

The following code shows you typical code for any `Application_OnStart` event. Three application variables are assigned values in the code. The example following this code shows how to use the `Contents` collection to obtain all the application variable names. There are three

Application variable in the code below: Application("UserId"),
Application("Name"), and Application("db_ConnectionString").

```
<SCRIPT LANGUAGE=VBScript RUNAT=Server>

Sub Application_OnStart
    Application("UserId") = ""
    Application("Name") = "Timothy Eden"
    Application("db_ConnectionString") =
"DSN=eTransDev;User Id=sa;PASSWORD=;SERVER=Star
Technology;UID=sa;WSID=STAR
TECHNOLOGY;DATABASE=eTransport_Dev"


End Sub

</Script>
```

The following code lists all the "key" names of the variables in
the application Contents collection:

```
<%
For each Key in Application.Contents
    Response.write "Key is "
    Response.write  Key
    Response.write "<BR>"
Next
%>
```

The preceding code returns the following values:

```
UserId
Name
db_ConnectionString
```

Contents Collection Session Object Example

Just as with the Contents collection for the Application object, the
Session object also has a Contents collection. The Session object's
collection contains all the functionality of the Application object collection, except at the session level. The following code demonstrates
this functionality:

```
<SCRIPT LANGUAGE=VBScript RUNAT=Server>

Sub Session_OnStart
 Session("UserId") = ""
 Session("Name") = "Timothy Eden"
    Session("db_ConnectionString") =
```

```
"DSN=eTransDev;User Id=sa;PASSWORD=;SERVER=Star
Technology;UID=sa;WSID=STAR
TECHNOLOGY;DATABASE=eTransport_Dev"

End Sub

</Script>
```

The following code lists all the key names of the variables in the Session Contents collection:

```
<%
For each Key in Session.Contents
Response.write "Key is "
Response.write  Key
Response.write "<BR>"
Next
%>
```

The preceding code returns the following values:

```
UserId
Name
db_ConnectionString
```

Storing Global Information in Arrays

Arrays are used to store information. They are a valuable tool to use with any ASP application. But arrays created at the application level behave differently from arrays created at the session level. The following sections examine the different syntax involved in using arrays at the two levels.

Storing Global Information in Arrays at the Application Level

If you need to store several pieces of information that all users will use, use an array in the Application_onStart event. The array method of storing information enables you to change information at any time in a central location, rather than in several ASPs. Besides, arrays are a more efficient way to store static information than placing the information in a database and then doing an sql call. The following code shows you how to store information in an array in the Application_onStart event:

```
<SCRIPT LANGUAGE=VBScript RUNAT=Server>

Sub Application_OnStart
```

```
Dim ProgDetails(3)
ProgDetails(0) = "Version 1.0"
ProgDetails(1) = "Author – Peggy Allison"
ProgDetails(2) = "Company Location – Jacksonville,Fla"
Application("ProgD") = ProgDetails
End Sub

</Script>
```

To use the array in your application, use the following code:

```
<%
Dim MyArray
MyArray = Application("ProgD")
Response.write "The version is " & MyArray(0)
%>
```

The variable MyArray will automatically match the size of the array ProgDetails.

Storing Global Information in Arrays at the Session Level

The process for storing an array in a Session object is the same as that for storing in an Application object.

```
<SCRIPT LANGUAGE=VBScript RUNAT=Server>

Sub Session_OnStart
 Dim ProgDetails(3)
 ProgDetails(0) = "Version 1.0"
 ProgDetails(1) = "Author – Peggy Allison"
 ProgDetails(2) = "Company Location – Jacksonville,Fla"
 Session("ProgD") = ProgDetails
End Sub

</Script>
```

To use the session object variable "ProgD" containing the array in your application, use the following code:

```
<%
Dim MyArray
MyArray = Session("ProgD")
Response.write "The version is " & MyArray(0)
%>
```

Just as with the Application object, the variable MyArray will automatically match the size of the array ProgDetails with the Session object.

StaticObjects Collection

This collection is the same as the Contents collection except that the collection is for objects created through the <OBJECT> tag in the Application_onStart event. Let's look at some code to understand the StaticObjects collection. In the following script, notice that the Browser Capabilities, Tools, and ADO objects are created at the application level.

●—CROSS-REFERENCE———————————————————————

The <OBJECT> tag is covered in the HTML Reference section (p. 362).

StaticObjects Application Object Example

The following example shows three objects being created in the global.asa file: myBrowser, DataConn, and myTools. Just as the Application object's Content collection contained the "key" names to all the application variables, the StaticObjects collection for the application level contains all the objects created with the application scope.

```
<OBJECT RunAt = Server Scope=Application ID = myBrowser
PROGID = "MSWC.BrowserType"></OBJECT>
<OBJECT RunAt = Server Scope=Application ID = DataConn
PROGID = "ADODB.Connection"></OBJECT>
<OBJECT RunAt = Server Scope=Application ID = myTools
PROGID = "MSWC.Tools"></OBJECT>
<SCRIPT LANGUAGE=VBScript RUNAT=Server>

Sub Application_OnStart
    Application("UserId") = ""
    Application("Name") = "Jon Sansom"
End Sub

</Script>
```

●—**NOTE**————————————————————

As you can see, you need to place the <OBJECT> tag before the <SCRIPT> tag in the global.asa file. The <SCRIPT> tag is covered in the HTML Reference section (p. 370).

You can use the following script to determine the key names of the objects in the application-level StaticObjects collection:

```
<%
For each Key in Application.StaticObjects
    Response.Write  "Key is -> "
    Response.Write  Key
    Response.Write  "<Br>"
Next
%>
```

The results to running the preceding code are as follows:

```
Key is -> myBrowser
Key is -> DataConn
Key is ->  myTools
```

StaticObjects Session Object Example

The Session object StaticObjects collection is the nearly the same as the Application object's StaticObjects collection, except for the scope assignment. The following example shows you objects being created at the session level, and the next example shows you how to determine the "key" names of those objects.

```
<OBJECT RunAt = Server Scope=Session ID = myBrowser
PROGID = "MSWC.BrowserType"></OBJECT>
<OBJECT RunAt = Server Scope=Session ID = DataConn
PROGID = "ADODB.Connection"></OBJECT>
<OBJECT RunAt = Server Scope=Session ID = myTools
PROGID = "MSWC.Tools"></OBJECT>

<SCRIPT LANGUAGE=VBScript RUNAT=Server>Sub
Session_OnStart
    Application("UserId") = ""
    Application("Name") = "Tim Burgess"
End Sub

</Script>
```

You can use the following script to determine the key names of the objects in the session level collection:

```
<%
For each Key in Session.StaticObjects
     Response.Write  "Key is -> "
     Response.Write  Key
     Response.Write "<Br>"
Next
%>
```

The results to running the preceding code are as follows:

```
Key is -> myBrowser
Key is -> DataConn
```

You've now learned the basics of what is needed to start an ASP application. You'll need a global.asa file and the use of events at either the application level or the session level. Remember not to use too many application variables, because each variable resides in memory for as long as the application is running.

Working with the Database: The ADO Object

4

In this chapter, you enter the world of connecting to a database. In order to accomplish this task, Microsoft provides an ActiveX server-side component named the *ActiveX Data Objects (ADO)*. And, as a server-side ActiveX component, it's a Component Object Model (COM) object. COM objects are Microsoft's version of compiled reusable objects. The advantage to using COM objects is that they can be used with all Microsoft-based architecture applications, such as Visual Basic.

ADO is based on Microsoft's data access technology, called Object Linking and Embedding for Databases (or OLE DB). OLE DB is a defined set of interfaces that enables you to connect to any type of data source. ADO lets you communicate with the data source, whether that source is a comma-delimited text file or a relational database such as Oracle. This chapter does not present a detailed explanation of the ADO, as that's not the purpose of this book. You need to know how to use the methods (also called functions) and attributes of each of the objects that come with the ADO. A brief explanation of the OLE DB will aid you in understanding the ADO.

What is OLE DB?

If you have been connecting to a database through Open Database Connectivity (ODBC), then you are familiar with the technology. However, Microsoft couldn't leave a good thing alone; they have improved it with OLE DB. One drawback to ODBC is that you can only connect to row-based databases such as Access or Oracle. But the world's data isn't always stored in an SQL-compliant database. OLE DB enables you to connect to the rest of the data world that stores information in low-level text files, such as an e-mail data store or a comma-delimited text file.

The ADO Model

The ADO contains several objects, including those in the following list. Each object has its own methods, properties, and collections. But the heart and soul of the ADO is the Connection object. The Datacontrol, Datafactory, and Dataspace objects belong to the Remote Data Services. A complete discussion of the Remote Data Services is beyond the scope of this book. However, you'll learn a little about the Remote Data Services later in the chapter.

- Connection
- Error
- Command
- Parameter
- Property
- RecordSet
- Field
- Record
- Datafactory
- Datacontrol
- Dataspace
- Stream

All of these objects are discussed in further detail in the following sections. You are going to read a lot about objects and collections in this chapter. To avoid confusion, take a minute to go over the difference between the two:

- An object contains methods and attributes.
- A collection is a group of these objects.

The best way to illustrate the difference between an object and a collection is with the Error collection and Error object. When an error occurs during the execution of an SQL statement, the ADO generates one or several errors. The group of errors is known as the Error collection. The individual errors in the collection are the Error objects. Tables 4-1 through 4-8 and Table 4-12 list the methods, properties, and collections for each ADO objects covered in the ASP Core Reference section. Tables 4-9 through 4-11 list the objects dealing with the Remote Data Services. The page numbers are not given for these objects because they are not covered in this book.

4

Table 4-1 *Connection Object Methods and Properties*

Connection Object	Name	Page Number
Methods	BeginTrans	57
	Cancel	58
	CommitTrans	60
	RollBackTrans	64
	Close	59
	Execute	58
	OpenSchema	63
	Open	61
Properties	Attributes	65
	CommandTimeout	66
	ConnectionString	67
	ConnectionTimeout	68
	CursorLocation	68
	DefaultDatabase	69
	Errors	74
	IsolationLevel	70
	Mode	70
	Properties	75
	Provider	72
	State	72
	Version	73

Table 4-2 *Error Object Methods, Properties, and Collections*

Error Object	Name	Page Number
Properties	Description	92
	NativeError	92
	Number	93
	Source	94
	SQLState	94
Collection Methods	Clear	95
	Refresh	96
Collection Properties	Count	96
	Item	97

Table 4-3 *Command Object Methods and Properties*

Command Object	Name	Page Number
Methods	Cancel	47
	CreateParameter	47
	Execute	48
Properties	ActiveConnection	49
	CommandText	50
	CommandTimeout	51
	CommandType	51
	Name	52
	Parameters	53
	Prepared	52
	Properties	54
	State	53

Table 4-4 *Parameter Object Methods, Properties, and Collections*

Parameter Object	Name	Page Number
Methods	AppendChunk	156

Parameter Object	Name	Page Number
Properties	Attributes	157
	Direction	158
	Name	159
	NumericScale	159
	Precision	159
	Size	160
	Type	161
	Value	162
Collection Properties	Count	163
	Item	164
Collection Methods	Append	162
	Delete	162
	Refresh	163

4

Table 4-5 *Property Object Methods, Properties, and Collections*

Property Object	Name	Page Number
Properties	Attributes	164
	Inherited	165
	Name	166
	Type	167
	Value	168
Method	Refresh	170
Properties	Count	171
	Item	171

Table 4-6 *Recordset Object Methods and Properties*

RecordSet Object	Name	Page Number
Methods	AddNew	186
	Cancel	187

Continued

Table 4-6 *Continued*

RecordSet Object	Name	Page Number
Methods	CancelBatch	188
	CancelUpdate	188
	Clone	189
	Close	190
	CompareBookmarks	190
	Delete	191
	Find	192
	GetRows	194
	GetString	195
	Move	197
	MoveFirst	197
	MoveLast	198
	MoveNext	198
	MovePrevious	199
	NextRecordSet	199
	Open	201
	Requery	202
	Resync	203
	Save	204
	Supports	205
	Update	206
	UpdateBatch	207
Properties	AbsolutePage	208
	AbsolutePosition	208
	ActiveCommand	209
	ActiveConnection	209
	BOF, EOF	210
	Bookmark	211
	CacheSize	211
	CursorLocation	212
	CursorType	212

RecordSet Object	Name	Page Number
Properties	EditMode	213
	Fields	223
	Filter	214
	Index	215
	LockType	216
	MarshalOptions	216
	MaxRecords	217
	PageCount	218
	PageSize	218
	Properties	224
	RecordCount	219
	Sort	219
	Source	220
	State	221
	Status	222
	StayInSync	223

Table 4-7 *Field Collection Object, Methods, and Properties*

Field Object	Name	Page Number
Methods	AppendChunk	98
	GetChunk	99
Properties	ActualSize	100
	Attributes	100
	DefinedSize	101
	Name	102
	NumericScale	102
	OriginalValue	103
	Precision	103
	Status	104
	Type	105

Continued

Table 4-7 *Continued*

Field Object	Name	Page Number
Methods	UnderlyingValue	106
	Value	107
Fields Collection Methods	Append	108
	CancelUpdate	109
	Delete	110
	Refresh	111
	Update	112
Properties	Count	113
	Item	113

Table 4-8 *Record Object Methods and Properties*

Record Object	Name	Page Number
Methods	Cancel	172
	Close	173
	CopyRecord	174
	DeleteRecord	176
	GetChildren	177
	MoveRecord	177
	Open	179
Properites	ActiveConnection	182
	Mode	182
	ParentURL	183
Properites	Source	184
	State	185
	RecordType	184

Table 4-9   *DataFactory Object Methods*

DataFactory Object	Name
Methods	ConvertToString
	CreateRecordset
	Query
	SubmitChanges

Table 4-10   *DataControl Object Methods and Properties*

DataControl Object	Name
Methods	Cancel Method
	CancelUpdate
	CreateRecordset
	MoveFirst
	MoveLast
	MoveNext
	MovePrevious
	Refresh Method
	Reset Method
	SubmitChanges
Properties	Connect Property
	ExecuteOptions
	FetchOptions
	FilterColumn
	FilterCriterion
	FilterValue
	InternetTimeout
	ReadyState
	Recordset

Continued

Table 4-10   *Continued*

DataControl Object	Name
Properties	SourceRecordset
	Server
	SortColumn
	SortDirection
	SQL
	URL

4

Table 4-11   *DataSpace Object Methods and Properties*

DataSpace Object	Name
Method	CreateObject
Property	InternetTimeout

Table 4-12   *Stream Object Methods and Properties*

Stream Object	Name	Page Number
Methods	Cancel	277
	Close	278
	CopyTo	279
	Flush	290
	LoadFromFile	280
	Open	281
	Read	283
	SaveToFile	285
	SetEOS	286
	SkipLine	287
	Write	288
	WriteText	289
Properties	Charset	291
	EOS	292
	LineSeparator	293

Stream Object	Name	Page Number
Properties	Mode	293
	Position	294
	Size	295
	State	296
	Type	298

General Overview of Getting a Connection

It is important for you to understand the Connection object before getting into the other objects. If you're going to do any database interaction using ASP, you definitely need to become familiar with the Connection object (which is covered in more detail in the next section) and its associated methods and properties. First, let's look at creating a connection to a data source with the use of the Connection object.

Creating a Connection to a Datasource

To get a connection to a data source, you always need a connection string. The following line of code is an example of a typical connection string to a Microsoft Access database named IceCompany.mdb:

```
connString = "DSN=
IceCompany;DBQ=c:\IceCompany.mdb;DriverId=281;FIL=MS
Access;MaxBufferSize=2048;PageTimeout=5;"
```

After you set up your connection string, create a Connection object and open a connection to a data source. The following code shows you how to use the connection string variable connString that was created in the preceding code in order to open a connection to the database IceCompany.mdb. The line of code DataConn.Open creates the connection to the database that's listed in the connection string connString.

```
Dim DataConn
Set DataConn = Server.CreateObject ("ADODB.Connection")
DataConn.ConnectionString = connString
'Open a connection to the datasource through the
'connection string connString
DataConn.Open
```

The preceding code uses the Connection object ConnectionString property to store the connection string. You can also open a connection to a data source by just supplying the connection string as an argument to the Connection object Open method. The following code uses an example of a possible Oracle connection string:

```
Dim DataConn
Set DataConn = Server.CreateObject ("ADODB.Connection")
ConnString = "DSN=MyOracleDB; UID=MYID; PWD=MYPWD"
DataConn.Open connString
```

If you want users to always be prompted for their user ID and password before getting a connection to a data source, use the Connection object Properties property. Use the string"Prompt" with the Properties property to cause a prompt to appear when a user needs to enter a user ID and password. The following code shows the code needed to use the ("Prompt") string:

```
Dim DataConn
Set DataConn = Server.CreateObject ("ADODB.Connection")
ConnString = "DSN=MYDSN_MAIN"
DataConn.Properties ("Prompt") = adPromptAlways
DataConn.Open connString, userid, password
```

These were just basic examples to show you the fundamentals of creating a connection. Now let's get into the details.

Creating a DSN with the ODBC

Part of the connection string is the Data Source Name (DSN). All ASP applications that interact with a database must have a DSN or the elements that make-up the DSN. You can supply the name of the ODBC database driver and location of the data source on your network or hard drive in the connection string without creating a DSN. This is known as a DSN-less connection string. We'll cover a DSN-less connection string in the next section. But, here, we'll show you how to create a DSN. We know from experience that it is better to use a DSN rather that a DSN-less connection string.

The DSN notifies your server of the data source's name, the ODBC driver, and the location of the database on your network or local hard drive. If you aren't already familiar with the function of an ODBC driver, it is a piece of software that a database provider, such as Sybase, uses to enable a proper connection to its data and to enable the information in the datasource to be returned. The Windows operating system comes with a standard set of ODBC drivers. The administration software for ODBC is odbcad32.exe, and it can be found in your c:\windows\systems directory. This file is the application that creates your ODBC DSN.

● **NOTE**

In order for ADO to work in ASP, the DSN must be set up as a system DSN, and not as a user DSN or file DSN.

To create a DSN in your Windows operating system, go to the Program Manager by clicking the Start button at the lower left-hand part of the screen, and then follow the series of steps given here:

1. Go to the Control Panel under the Program Manager's Settings option, and then double-click on the Control Panel option (see Figure 4-1).

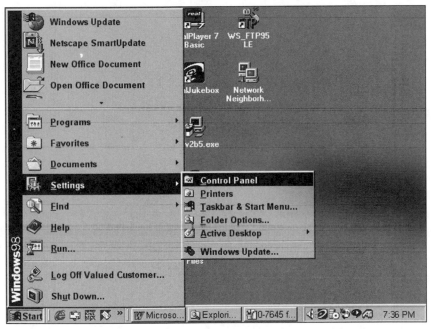

Figure 4-1 *Getting to the Windows Control Panel*

2. In the Control Panel window, click on the ODBC Administrator icon (see Figure 4-2). The icon in the Control Panel window is labeled ODBC Data Sources (32bit). If you do not have the OBDC Administrator icon on your Control Panel, look for the odbcad32.exe file in your directories and then click on the OBDC32 icon.

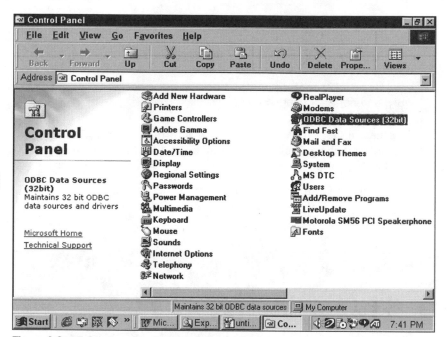

Figure 4-2 *Selecting the ODBC driver Administrator icon on the Control Panel*

3. The ODBC Data Source Administrator window will appear (see Figure 4-3). Select the window tab labeled System DSN, and then click the Add button.

4. After clicking the Add button, the Create New Data Source window will appear (see Figure 4-4). A list of ODBC database drivers will be shown. Highlight the name of the ODBC driver that matches the database to which you are trying to connect. For example, if you are trying to make a connection to an Oracle database, select the ODBC driver labeled Microsoft ODBC for Oracle. After you have chosen the ODBC driver, click the Finish button.

5. The window named ODBC Microsoft Access Setup will appear next (see Figure 4-5). The name of this window varies from data provider to data provider. Type in the name of the data source and any other information, such as user ID and password, and then click the OK button.

6. A window prompting you for the name and location of your database appears next (see Figure 4-6).

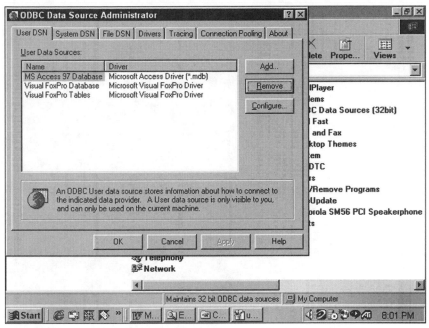

Figure 4-3 *Opening the ODBC Data Source Administrator window*

Figure 4-4 *The Create New Data Source window*

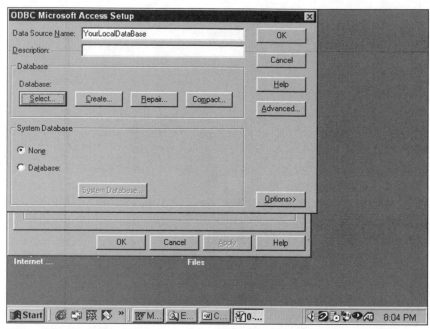

Figure 4-5 *The ODBC Microsoft Access Setup window*

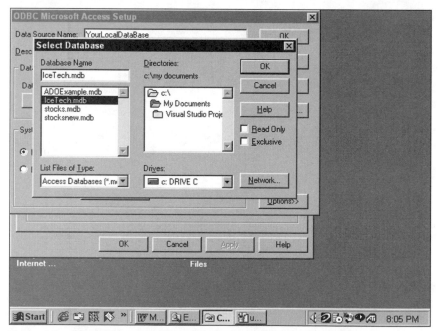

Figure 4-6 *The Select Database window, asking for the database name and location*

7. After you have supplied the name and location of the database, the window entitled ODBC Microsoft Access Setup returns. When the window appears now, the name of the database is labeled. Look at Figure 4-7 to see "IceTech.mdb" next to the database label.

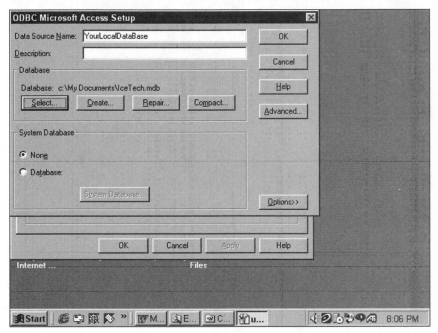

Figure 4-7   *Name of the data source in the Access Setup window*

8. The ODBC Data Source Administrator window now appears with the new DSN inserted into the System DSN list (see Figure 4-8). Now you can use the DSN you created. Figure 4-8 shows what the ODBC Data Source Administration window will look like when the window appears. As you can see, the User Dsn tab appears initially. You will have to click on the System DSN tab to see your new DSN.

Now that you know how to create a System DSN entry, the following section will show you how to use this DSN with the Connection object.

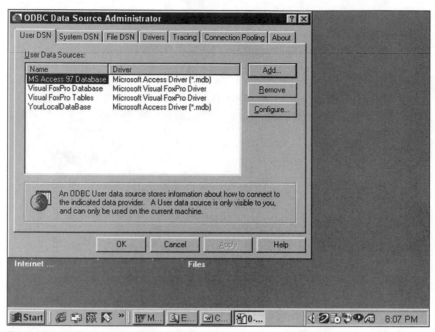

Figure 4-8 *The ODBC Data Source Administrator window*

The Connection Object

The previous section gave you an overview of how to connect to a data source with the Connection object. The Connection object enables you to open a connection to a data source. However, first a few words about the terms database and data source. A *data source* can be any source that contains information — from a comma-delimited text file to an Oracle database. In layperson's terms, a database is the information stored in row-organized sets, such as Oracle, Sybase, SQL Server, Informix, Progress, or any of your favorite database providers. For the purposes of the Connection object, it doesn't matter if you use the term data source or database. If you have an ODBC driver to that data source, the Connection object can get to it.

Establishing a Connection with the Connection Object

In order to establish a Connection object, you create an instance of the ADO. The code to create a Connection object is as follows:

```
Set DataConn = Server.CreateObject ("ADODB.Connection")
```

The Connection object needs to know the name of the data source in order to connect. The ConnectionString property contains the necessary information to make the connection. The connection string can be just the Data Source Name (DSN), or it can be DSN-less. A DSN-less connection string contains the name of the database driver.

Following is an example of a DSN in which the user ID and password are in the DSN connection string:

```
Dim connString
ConnString = "DSN=MYDSN_MAIN; UID=MYID; PWD=MYPWD"
```

This next example is of a DSN-less connection string to a Microsoft Access ODBC driver:

```
ConnString = "Driver={Microsoft Access Driver (*.mdb)};"
ConnString = ConnString & "Dbq=\somepath\mydb.mdb;"
ConnString = ConnString & "Uid=Admin;"
ConnString = ConnString & "Pwd=;"
```

Once you have the connection string, all you need to do is open a connection. You can do this in two ways: This first example shows you how to open a connection using a variable that contains a connection string:

```
'for purposes of this example we will assume the
'variable ConnString contains the connection string.
'use the ConnectString attribute
DataConn.ConnectString = ConnString
DataConn.Open
```

Another way to open a connection is by placing the entire connection string as an argument to the Connection object's Open method. The following code gives you an example of a connection string, user ID, and password as arguments to the Connection object's Open method. Note that the Connection object's ConnectString property is not used.

```
'not using the ConnectString attribute
Userid = "tim"
Password = "eden"
DataConn.Open "DSN=MYDSN_MAIN", Userid, Password
```

It is possible to provide the user ID and password in the DSN. The following example shows a DSN that already contains the user ID and password:

```
'if the DSN already contains the userid and password
DataConn.Open "DSN=MSDSN_MAIN"
```

Executing Transactions Against a Data Source with the Connection Object

Now you know how to create a `Connection` object and open a connection to a data source. The next step is to learn to execute transactions against a data source using the `Connection` object. What is a transaction? Any change (insert, update, delete, and so on) to a data source is a transaction. The `Connection` object has three methods you will use during the execution of any transaction: `BeginTrans`, `RollbackTrans`, and `CommitTrans`. In addition to these methods, you are going to incorporate the `Connection` object's error collection. If an error occurs, you will rollback the transaction; otherwise, you will commit the transaction.

The following code shows you an example of using the `BeginTrans`, `RollbackTrans`, and `CommitTrans` methods:

```
'assume DataConn is your Connection object
DataConn.Open "DSN=MYDSN_MAIN", Userid, Password
SqlString = "Delete * From A_Table_In_THE_DSN"
DataConn.BeginTrans()
DataConn.Execute (SqlString)
If DataConn.Errors.Count > 0 then
    'We know that an error has occurred therefore
    'you will need to rollback the transaction
for each error in DataConn.Errors
    Response.W("Number is "&Error.Number)
    Response.W("Description is " &
Error.Description)
Next
    'Rollback Transaction
    DataConn.RollbackTrans ()
Else
    'Commit Transaction
    DataConn.CommitTrans ()
End if
'close the connection
' use the Connection object's state property ,
'adStateOpen is one of the
'ObjectStateEnum constants
if DataConn.State = adStateOpen then
    DataConn.close
end if
```

Freeing Resources with the Connection Object

The Connection object method Close only closes a data connection.
The data connection still resides in memory. In order to free resources
in your computer, you need to provide the following code when you
are finished using the Connection object:

```
Set DataConn = nothing
```

● NOTE

Remember that once the data connection is made, you cannot set a
Connection object property for that connection.

Once you have established a connection to a database, the next
step is to get information from that database. The Recordset object
takes care of that task.

The RecordSet Object

Once your Connection object establishes a connection to a database,
the next step is retrieving data into a *recordset*. A *recordset* is all the
rows that a query against a data source retrieves. A RecordSet object
is that recordset plus the methods and properties that enable you to
do things to the recordset.

Following is the syntax for creating a RecordSet object. This line
of code returns the RecordSet object MyRS, but it doesn't return a
recordset. You need to run an SQL statement against a database to
a recordset.

```
Set MyRS = Server.CreateObject ("ADODB.RecordSet")
```

If you want to create a RecordSet object and a recordset at the
same time — OK, not exactly the same time, but pretty close — then
look at the next example. The following code shows you how to use
the Connection object's Execute method to create a recordset and a
RecordSet object at the same time. Notice that the example doesn't
use the Server.CreateObject("ADODB.Recordset") method to create
a RecordSet object. That's because the DataConn.Execute method
creates the RecordSet object for you.

```
Set DataConn = Server.CreateObject ("ADODB.Connection")
Sqlstring = "Select * From AnyTable"
DataConn.ConnectionString =  "DSN= IceCompany;"
DataConn.Open
'creates a recordset no need to use server.createobject
MyRecSet = DataConn.Execute (Sqlstring)
```

Now, if you want to use the `Server.CreateObject` (`"ADODB.`
`Recordset"`) method to create the `RecordSet` object, but don't want
the `Connection` object to create your recordset, examine the following
code. Notice that the `RecordSet` object `Source` property contains the
SQL statement. To get the recordset, all you have to do is use the
`Open` method of the recordset. The following code shows you how
to create the recordset using that method:

```
'DataConn is the Connection object
Set MyRecSet = Server.CreateObject ("ADODB.Recordset")
MyRecSet.ActiveConnection = DataConn
MyRecSet.Source = "SELECT * From AnyTable"
MyRecSet.Open
```

The `Command` object, discussed later in this chapter, also enables
you to create a recordset and `RecordSet` object at the same time
from a stored procedure. The following code uses the `Command` and
`Parameter` objects. You'll learn about these objects later. For now,
look at the line of code that says `DataCommand.Execute`. This code is
where the recordset and `RecordSet` object are created. The following
code returns a recordset and `RecordSet` object from the stored procedure "`sp_mystoredProcedure`":

```
Set DataCommand = Server.CreateObject ("ADODB.Command")
'DataConn is the Connection object in use
DataCommand.AcitveConnection = DataConn
DataCommand.CommandText = "Call sp_mystoredProcedure"
Set ParaObject = DataCommand.CreateParameter
ParaObject.Name = "AnyParaName"
ParaObject.Type = adVarChar
ParaObject.Direction = adParamInput
ParaObject.Size = 25
ParaObject.Value = '7899884'
DataCommand.Parameters.Append ParaObject
'return a recordset from the stored procedure
Set MyRS = DataCommand.Execute
```

Understanding Isolation, Locking, and Cursor Types

Before continuing our discussion of the recordset, you need to be
familiar with three concepts: isolation, locking, and cursor types.
All three play an important role in the integration of data retrieval
in the `Recordset` object.

Isolation Level of the Transaction

Two terms deal with the retrieval of bad data: *dirty reads* and *phantom records*. A phantom record occurs when you retrieve data that no longer exists. A dirty read occurs when the data you retrieve is in the process of being changed. How do these events occur? Part of the answer is found in the isolation level of the transaction. What does that mean?

If your bank totally isolated every transaction from one another, unacceptable things would happen. Suppose a married couple has a joint checking account with $1,000 in the account. In transaction A, the husband is withdrawing $600. At the same time, the wife (creating transaction B) is checking the balance in the account. Because each transaction is totally isolated from the other, transaction A is not completed before transaction B checks the balance. The wife will see $1,000 in the account instead of $400. Obviously, this is not good!

The Connection object enables you to set the isolation level for transactions. You set the Connection object's IsolationLevel property with a IsolationLevelEnum constant.

●—CROSS-REFERENCE————————————————

The IsolationLevel enumerated constants are available at the URL noted in the Preface.

Locking

Locking gives the developer the ability to tell the recordset at what level the data retrieved in a recordset can be accessed by other recordsets.

Suppose you have a table in a database that allows only one transaction at a time to go against it, such as buying stock on an open bid system. The price of the stock is open for bid. If someone accepts that bid, while the information is being entered into the computer, that table must have a lock on it. That is, no one else can change the table. The locking of the table ensures the integrity of the data. You can supply a LockTypeEnum constant to the Recordset object's Open method.

●—CROSS-REFERENCE————————————————

The LockType enumerated constants are available at the URL noted in the Preface.

Cursor Types

A cursor enables you to navigate through the recordset. However, depending on the cursor type you choose, certain methods in the recordset will not work. The forward-only cursor is the default cursor for a recordset. This cursor does not allow you to use the MovePrevious method. The RecordSet object provides four types of cursors, each of which is described in Table 4-13.

Table 4-13 *Cursor Types*

Cursor-Type	Actual Value for CursorType	Description
Forward-Only	0	This is the default cursor. It provides for forward-only and read-only movement.
KeySet	1	This cursor enables you to move both forward and backward. It is read/write enabled. However, you cannot see additions or deletions from the recordset.
Dynamic	2	This cursor enables you to move both forward and backward. It is read/write enabled. You can also see additions or deletions. It is the slowest of the cursors.
Static	3	This cursor enables you to move both forward and backward. It is read/write enabled. However, additions or deletions by other users to this database are not visible.

The forward-only cursor is the default cursor for a recordset. If you are going to add or delete rows from a recordset, you have to use the dynamic cursor. But you need to integrate either a locking specification or an isolation level with your cursor in order to achieve the highest level of data integrity. When opening a recordset, you can use a CursorTypeEnum constant to specify the cursor type.

●—CROSS-REFERENCE

The list of CursorType enumerated constants are available at the URL noted in the Preface.

Integrating the IsolationLevel, Locking, and Cursor Type on a Recordset

The following code shows you how to avoid the dirty read and phantom record pitfalls. This code shows you — by setting the Connection object IsolationLevel property to the enumerated constant adXactChaos — how you can ensure that the recordset returned from the Connection object will not allow overwrites of pending transactions.

```
Set DataConn = Server.CreateObject ("ADODB.Connection")
Sqlstring = "Select * From AnyTable"
DataConn.ConnectionString = =  "DSN= IceCompany;"
'set to not allow overwrites of pending transactions
DataConn.IsolationLevel = adXactChaos
DataConn.Open
SetMyRS = DataConn.Execute (Sqlstring)
```

Let's look at the syntax you will follow to open a RecordSet object with a defined cursor and lock type. You may have noticed from the earlier example of getting a recordset that using the RecordSet object's Open method uses no arguments. That's because we used the Recordset object's Source property to specify the SQL statement. However, any time you use the RecordSet object'sOpen method that includes the cursor type and lock type as arguments, you must use a Command object to specify the SQL statement.

```
RecordsetObject.open CommandObject, ConnectionObject,
CursorTypeEnum, LockTypeEnum
```

The following code shows you how to open a recordset with a defined cursor type and lock type. In this case, the example opens a recordset with a forward-only cursor type and a lock type of adLockOptimistic. The locktype adLockOptimistic tells the provider to lock the record when it's being updated.

```
Set DataConn = Server.CreateObject ("ADODB.Connection")
Set DataCommand = Server.CreateObject ("ADODB.Command")
Set MyRS = Server.CreateObject ("ADODB.Recordset")
'DataConn is the Connection object in use
DataCommand.ActiveConnection =
DataConn
DataCommand.CommandText = "Select * From AnyTable"
MyRS.Open DataCommand, DataConn, adOpenForwardOnly,
adLockOptimistic
```

Navigating the Recordset

Navigation of a RecordSet object recordset is done via a record-pointer. Various methods and properties move the recordpointer to the desired record. The following sections examine using some of these methods and properties so you can start using them in your ASP application.

Finding the Beginning or End of a File

After you have retrieved a recordset, you need to know how to find the beginning or the end of the recordset. After all, you may need to go through the recordset to find one piece of information. How are you going to know when you have reached the end of the recordset? The BOF (Beginning of File) method or EOF (End of File) property gives you the needed information. In addition to determining the position of the record pointer, these two properties can determine if an SQL statement returns any records into a recordset.

By checking to see if the End of File and Beginning of File properties are true, you can determine if any records exist in the recordset:

```
If MyRS.Bof and MyRS.Eof then
    Response.write "No rows in recordset"
End if
```

Moving the Recordpointer

In order to move a recordset backward, you must choose a Dynamic or KeySet cursor type. To navigate to a certain record, use the AbsolutePosition property.

The following line of code shows you how to place the record-pointer at the third record in the recordset:

```
RecordSetObject.AbsolutePosition = 3
```

Figure 4-9 illustrates moving the recordpointer to a record in a recordset using the AbsolutePosition property.

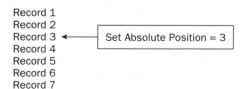

Record 1
Record 2
Record 3 ← Set Absolute Position = 3
Record 4
Record 5
Record 6
Record 7

Figure 4-9 *The absolute position of a record in a recordset*

The RecordSet object enables you to specify how many records you want to appear in an ASP. Because an ASP turns into HTML code, the capability to limit the number of records on an ASP means the user is not forced to use a scrollbar to view records on the browser. The PageSize property in conjuction with the AbsolutePage property gives you the capability to not only control the number of records on an ASP, but also to move the recordpointer in large increments at one time.

The PageSize property lets you divide a recordset into groups of records. The AbsolutePage property lets you navigate the recordset in a size set by the Pagesize property. To understand this concept a little better, look at Figure 4-10. The page size in Figure 4-10 has been set to 4, and the absolute page has been set to 3. Therefore, the recordpointer will position itself at the ninth record in the recordset.

RecordSetObject.Pagesize = 4

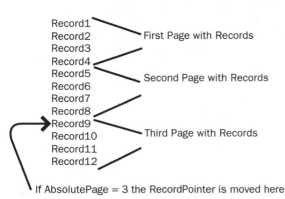

If AbsolutePage = 3 the RecordPointer is moved here

Figure 4-10 *The Pagesize and AbsolutePage properties in action*

The following code shows you the syntax for setting the Pagesize property to six records:

```
RecordSetObject.PageSize = 6
```

The following code sets the AbsolutePage property to display two records:

```
RecordSetObject.AbsolutePage = 2
```

To move to the last record in the recordset, use this code:

```
RecordSetObject.MoveLast
```

To move to the first record in the recordset, use this code:

```
RecordSetObject.MoveFirst
```

To move to the next record, use this code:

```
RecordSetObject.NextRecord
```

To move to the previous record, use this code:

```
RecordSetObject.MovePrevious
```

To move the current record pointer six rows from the current record, use this code:

```
RecordSetObject.Move 6
```

Adding, Updating, and Deleting a Recordset

If you want to add a new record to a recordset, use the AddNew method. The following code shows you how to add a new record to the MyRS recordset:

```
Set DataConn = Server.CreateObject ("ADODB.Connection")
Set DataCommand = Server.CreateObject ("ADODB.Command")
Set MyRS = Server.CreateObject ("ADODB.Recordset")
'DataConn is the Connection object in use
DataCommand.ActiveConnection = DataConn
DataCommand.CommandText = "Select College,Nickname From
UniversityTable"
'open a recordset with Dynamic cursor
MyRS.Open DataCommand, DataConn, adOpenDynamic,
adLockOptimistic

'add new recordRS.AddNew
MyRS ("College") = "Auburn University"
MyRS ("Nickname") = "WarEagles"
MyRS.Update
```

●—**NOTE**—————————————————————————

Always use `RecordsetObject.Update` method to complete the addition of a record to the recordset.

If you want to update the current record, use this code:

```
MyRS.Update Nickname,"Tigers"
```

If you want to delete the current record, use this code:

```
MyRS.Delete
```

● **TIP**

Even if you have set the cursor type to dynamic, not all database providers allow you to use the RecordSet object properties to modify the recordset. So how can you determine if a database provider supports changing a recordset? Easy, with the Support property:

```
If MyRS.Supports (adAddNew) then
  'database provider supports the addNew method
  MyRS.AddNew
  MyRS("College") = "Amy Eden University"
  MyRS("Nickname") = "Kitty Boos"
  MyRS.Update
End if
```

Viewing Recordset Changes with Resync and Requery

You can use the Requery and Resync methods to view changes made to a recordset. If you want to view all the changes made to the recordset, use the Requery method:

```
RecordSetObject.Requery
```

With the Requery method, the original SQL statement that created the recordset is executed again.

With the Resync method, you don't re-execute the SQL statement. Instead, the values that other users have changed in the recordset will be visible. The following code uses the Resync method:

```
MyRS.Resync adAffectCurrent
```

The Resync method can have two arguments: AffectEnum and ResyncEnum. The AffectEnum method is an enumerated constant that indicates which records are affected by the Resync method. The ResyncEnum is also an enumerated constant, which enables you to overwrite existing data and cancel pending updates when a Resync is done. The syntax for using these methods is as follows:

```
RecordSet.Resync AffectEnum, ResyncEnum
```

● **CROSS-REFERENCE**

The AffectEnum and Resync enumerated constants are available at the URL noted in the Preface.

Checking the Status of a RecordSet Action

Sometimes you need to check whether a record has been successfully added to a recordset. In order to check the status of an update, Microsoft provides one of the best properties of the RecordSet object: the Status property. With this property, you can find out whether any changes you attempted to make to a recordset failed or were successful.

The following example shows you the status of adding a new record by testing the Status property. If the line of code MyRS.Status = adRecNew is true, the record was successfully added. Notice that the RecordStatus enumeration constant adRecNew is used to check the value of the Status property.

```
'add new recordRS.AddNew
MyRS ("College") = "Auburn University"
MyRS ("Nickname") = "WarEagles"
MyRS.Update
'test the Status of a new Record with the RecordStatus
'Enum constant adRecNew
If MyRS.Status = adRecNew then
     Response.Write "New Record was successfully
added"
Else
     Response.Write "New Record was not added"
End if
```

●─CROSS-REFERENCE───────────────

The RecordStatusEnum constants are available at the URL noted in the Preface.

Turning a Recordset into an Array

One of the most useful methods that the RecordSet object supplies is the GetRows method. This method takes any recordset and turns it into an array. Using an array is a much faster way to navigate through a recordset. The following code shows you the technique for placing the records in a recordset into an array. You must always initialize the array before attempting to use it. Note the line Dim avarArray, which initializes the array.

```
<%
'You must initialize the array
Dim avarArray
'Assume the Connection Object is DataConn
Set MyRS = DataConn.Execute ("Select City, State From
```

```
AnyTable")
'if there are records in the recordset then use the
'GetRows method to put records into an array
If NotMyRS.Eof and Not MyRS.Bof then
    avarArray =MyRS.GetRows( )
End if  %>
```

●—**NOTE**————————————————————————————————————

As you begin to work with the `GetRows` method, you will notice a slight difference in the way that it creates an array. Normally, an array is specified in Rows, Columns, but the `GetRows ( )` method turns a recordset into an array that is Columns, Rows.

Once you have put the records from your recordset into an array, you can control how the rows and columns of the array are used. The following code shows how to go through each element of the array to display in an HTML page:

```
'output columns
<Table>
<%' UBound tells you how many rows are in array %>
<%    for irow = 0 to UBound(avarArray,2) %>
    <TR>
        <% for jcol = 0 to 1 %>
        <TD>
        <!-2 columns City,State-->
        <%=avarArray(jcol,irow) %>
        </TD>
    <%next%>
    </TR>
<% next %>
```

Displaing a Recordset in an HTML Page

Listing 4-1 is an example of retrieving a recordset, placing the record-set in an array, and then displaying the elements of that array in an HTML page.

Listing 4-1 *Placing a Recordset in an HTML Page*

```
<%@ LANGUAGE = "VBSCRIPT" %>
<% 'CREATING THE CONNECTION OBJECT

Set DataCommand = Server.CreateObject ("ADODB.Command")
Set MyRS = Server.CreateObject ("ADODB.Recordset")
'DataConn is the Connection object in use
```

Continued

Listing 4-1 *Continued*

```
DataCommand.ActiveConnection =
DataConn
DataCommand.CommandText = "Select City,State From
Location"
 'open recordset with dynamic cursor
MyRS.Open DataCommand, DataConn, adOpenDynamic,
adLockOptimistic
'check the error object
IF DataConn.Errors.Count > 0 THEN
    For each dbError in DataConn.Errors
        IF dbError.Number <> 0 THEN
        Response. Write "<BR>" & Cstr (dbError.Number)  &
"<BR>"
        Response. Write  "<BR>" & dbError. Description &
"<BR>"
    END IF
    NEXT

ELSE
    'Find out if there is any records
    if MyRS.Eof and MyRS.Bof then
     ' we have no records

    else
     'lets print out records to HTML
%>
    <Table Border=1>
    <%Do while not MyRS.EOF%>
    <TR>
    <%For k = 0 to MyRS.Fields.Count —1 %>
    <TD><B>
    <%Response.Write MyRS(k).Name%>
    </TD>
     <TD><B>
    <%Response.write MyRS(k).Value%>
    </TD>
    <%Next%>
    <%MyRS.MoveNext%>
    </TR>
    <% Loop %>
    </Table>

    <%end if%>

<%End If %>
```

Filling in a Drop Down List Box with a Recordset

Listing 4-2 takes the records from a recordset and fills an HTML dropdownlist box with the contents of that recordset.

Listing 4-2 *Placing Contents of a Recordset in a Drop Down List Box*

```
<%@ LANGUAGE = "VBSCRIPT" %>
<% 'CREATING THE CONNECTION OBJECT
Set DataCommand = Server.CreateObject ("ADODB.Command")
Set MyRS = Server.CreateObject ("ADODB.Recordset")
'DataConn is the Connection object in use
DataCommand.ActiveConnection = DataConn
DataCommand.CommandText = "Select City,State From
Location"


MyRS.Open DataCommand, DataConn, adOpenDynamic,
adLockOptimistic

IF DataConn.Errors.Count > 0 THEN
    For each dbError in DataConn.Errors
      IF dbError.Number <> 0 THEN
         Response.Write "<BR>" & Cstr (dbError.Number)
& "<BR>"
         Response.Write  "<BR>" & dbError. Description &
"<BR>"
       END IF
     NEXT

ELSE
     'Find out if there is any records
     if MyRS.Eof and MyRS.Bof then
     'we have no records

    else
'lets print out records to HTML
%>
<Table Border=1>
<TR>
<TD>
<Form action="anypage.asp" method="post">
<Select Name="anyname" >
    <%Do while not MyRS.EOF%>

    <OPTION VALUE="<%Response. Write
```

Continued

Listing 4-2 *Continued*

```
MyRS(k).Name%>"<%Response. Write
MyRS(k).Name%></OPTION>

    <%MyRS.MoveNext%>
    <% Loop %>

    </SELECT>
</Form>
</Table>

<%End If %>
```

The preceding section dealt with the records returned in a record-set, but what about the individual fields in each record? How can you retrieve and use information about the fields in a recordset? That's where the `Field` object comes into play, the subject of the next section.

The Field Object

The `Field` object and the `RecordSet` object are tightly bound together. The `Field` object is the interface in the ADO that represents a single column of data in a recordset. The best way to get to know the `Field` object is by using the properties. So let's get to it.

The `Field` object enables you to identify a field (another name for field is *column*) in a record through the field's ordinal number in the recordset or by the field's name. The following line of code shows you the syntax for using the first field of a record from the recordset MyRS:

```
'MyRS is the RecordSet
MyRS.Fields (0)
```

●—NOTE

The first ordinal of a field or column in a record is 0. If you want to find the sixth field in a recordset (provided there is a sixth field), then use the number 5 as the ordinal.

You can also identify a field in a record by stating the name of the field (using the `Field` object and then the actual name of the field), or by supplying the ordinal number of the field in the recordset. The next four lines of code show you three ways to obtain the value of a field from a recordset:

```
MyRS("CompanyName")
MyRS.Fields("CompanyName")
'this returns the first field of the recordset
 MyRS(0)
```

The next line of code shows you how to find the name of the second field in a record of the recordset MyRS by using the ordinal number syntax:

```
MyRS.Fields (1). Name
```

The following code shows you how to identify the data type of the fourth column in a record from the recordset MyRS:

```
MyRS.Fields (3). Type
```

● NOTE

The Type property will return a DataTypeEnum constant. You can find the entire list of DataTypeEnum constants on-line.

The next line of code shows you how to access properties of a field. The example uses the field named "MyFirstName". The property being investigated is ActualSize.

```
MyRS.Fields ("MyFirstName"). ActualSize
```

You can also find out the current value of this column by investigating the UnderlyingValue property:

```
MyRS.Fields ("MyFirstName"). UnderlyingValue
```

Obtaining information on a recordset and the fields associated with a record is very useful. However, during the course of retrieving information from a data source, errors can occur. You need to be able to do error handling if events dictate the need. The Error object and Error collection provide you with the capability to do error handling.

The Error Object and Error Collection

The Error object contains information about a specific error that was generated during an ADO transaction. But an ADO transaction can generate several Error objects. Thus, the Error collection is used to check the Error objects. The Error collection is exactly what it suggests, a collection of the error objects.

The Error object has no methods, just properties. To help you understand how to use the Error object properties, consider the following code. This code shows how to check for errors in a Connection object after an SQL statement executes:

```
DataConn.ConnectionString = "DSN=OracleDSN;"
DataConn.Open
Sqlstatement = "Select * From MyTable"
DataConn.Execute (Sqlstatement)


'This is the Error Collection using the Count Property
If DataConn.Errors.Count > 0 then
 'This is the Error Collection check for each Error
 'Object that occurred during the Connection objects
 'transactions.
 For each error in DataConn.Errors
   Response.W("Number is "&Error.Number)
   Response.W("Description is " &
Error.Description)
   Response.W("SQLState is
"&Error.SQLState)
  Next
Else
     'Complete the code

End if
```

If you want to get really fancy with your error detection, then try using some of the ErrorValueEnum constants. For example, if you wanted to check for a wrong datatype error, you could use the following code:

```
If DataConn.Errors.Count > 0 then
    'This is the Error Collection check for each Error
    'Object that occurred during the Connection objects
    'transactions.
    For each error in DataConn.Errors


    if adErrDataConverion then
Response.Write "You have a wrong datatype"
```

```
End if
Response.Write "Number is "&Error.Number
Response.Write ("Description is " & Error.Description)
     Next
Else
      'Complete the code

End if
```

●—**CROSS-REFERENCE**————————————————

The `ErrorValue` enumerated constants are available at the URL noted in the Preface.

You've now been introduced to the `Connection`, `RecordSet`, `Field`, and `Error` objects. That leaves the last two: the `Command` and `Parameter` objects. These two objects, covered in the following sections, deal with the use of stored procedures with the ADO.

The Command Object

You really don't need to use the `Command` object unless you are going to work with a stored procedure. The `Command` object's main function is to pass a parameter to a stored procedure. The `Command` object let's you set the active connection. But you can use the `Command` object to pass queries to your database. The following code shows the syntax used to create a `Command` object:

```
Set DataCommand = Server.CreateObject ("ADODB.Command")
```

The `Command` object `Execute` method returns a `RecordSet` object. This method also gives you the opportunity to use several options, as shown in the following syntax:

```
Set Recordsetobject = Commandobject.Execute
numberOfRecordsAffected,
parameter_array, options
```

Table 4-14 describes the arguments you can use with the `Execute` method. This table also notes each argument type and whether or not the argument is required.

Table 4-14 *Arguments for Executing a Command Object*

Argument	Required	Type	Description
numberOfRecords Affected	No	Long	This argument is a variable that you can use to tell you how many rows were affected by executing the sql statement in the CommandText property.
parameter_array	No	Variant	This argument is an array of parameter values to send to the Command object. This array is not needed if you pass the parameters in the CommandText property.
options	No	Long	This is the CommandType Enum constant that tells the provider what type of command you are going to execute.

Passing Parameters to a Stored Procedure via the CommandText Property

The following code demonstrates how to use the numberOfRecords Affected option. The CommandTypeEnum constant adCmdText is used to tell the database provider that the command is a text command. Notice that the parameter_array argument in the code line Set MyRS = DataCommand.Execute nVarRec,,adCmdText is blank. That's because the parameters are passed via the SQL CommandText property. You'll learn how to pass these parameter via the parameter_array argument in the next example.

```
'create instance of Command object
Set DataCommand = Server.CreateObject ("ADODB.Command")
'DataConn is the Connection object in use
DataCommand.Active = DataConn
'Place sql statement
DataCommand.CommandText = "call sp_storedProcedure 124
,'TotalNumber'"
'create instance of RecordSet
Set MyRS = Server.CreateObject ("ADODB.RecordSet")
'Initialize nVarRec variable
```

```
nVarRec = 0
'execute the commandtext – use the CommandTypeEnum
constant adCmdText
'nVarRec is the variable that will contain the
'number of records affected by the executing the
'stored procedure
Set MyRS = DataCommand.Execute nVarRec,,adCmdText
Response.W, "number of records affected by SQL "
Response.WWrite nVarRec
```

Passing Parameters via the parameter_array Argument

We promised you an example of passing the two parameter values 124 and 'TotalNumber' from the last piece of code via the parameter_ array. In the next listing, look at the line of code that contains the DataCommand.Execute method. Note that the syntax Array(124, 'TotalNumber') is passed as the parameter_array argument.

```
'create instance of Command object
Set DataCommand = Server.CreateObject ("ADODB.Command")
'DataConn is the Connection object in use
DataCommand.ActiveConnection =
DataConn
'Place sql statement
DataCommand.CommandText = "call sp_storedProcedure "_
'create instance of RecordSet
Set MyRS = Server.CreateObject ("ADODB.RecordSet")
'Initialize nVarRec variable
nVarRec = 0
'execute the commandtext – use the CommandTypeEnum
constant adCmdText
'nVarRec is the variable that will contain the
'number of records affected by the executing the
'stored procedure
Set MyRS = DataCommand.Execute
nVarRec,Array(124,'TotalNumber'),adCmdText
Response.W"number of records affected by SQL is "
Response.WnVarRec
```

● **NOTE**

You only need to create a RecordSet object if your stored procedure is returning a value from the database.

Using Other Command Object Properties

This section covers other properties associated with the Command object, in particular the ActiveConnection and CommandType properties. It also covers the CommandText property in more detail.

Using the ActiveConnection Property

This preceding code shows how to use the Command object to set the active connection. Anytime you use a Command object, it's a good idea to use the ActiveConnection property. In the following code, the ActiveConnection tells the Command object which Connection object to use:

```
'create instance of Command object
Set DataCommand = Server.CreateObject ("ADODB.Command")
'DataConn is the Connection object in use
DataCommand.ActiveConnection =
DataConn
'Place sql statement
DataCommand.CommandText = "Select * From AnyTable"
'create instance of RecordSet
Set MyRS = Server.CreateObject ("ADODB.RecordSet")
'execute the commandtext
MyRS = DataCommand.Execute
```

Using the CommandText Property

The next bit of code calls a stored procedure named sp_mystored procedure. The code passes a string 'myarg' into the stored procedure through the CommandText property.

```
'create instance of Command object
Set DataCommand = Server.CreateObject ("ADODB.Command")
'DataConn is the Connection object in use
DataCommand.ActiveConnection =
DataConn
'Place call to stored procedure passing in one argument
DataCommand.CommandText = "call sp_mystoredprocedure
'myarg'"
'create instance of RecordSet
Set MyRS = Server.CreateObject
("ADODB.RecordSet")
'execute the commandtext to return a recordset from the
'stored procedure
MyRS = DataCommand.Execute
```

Using the CommandType Property

Suppose you knew that your stored procedure would not return any values. This is a good place to use the CommandType property. This property lets you tell the database provider what kind of command you have. In the case of a stored procedure, use the CommandTypeEnum constant adCmdStoredProc. The following example shows you how to use the CommandType property:

```
'create instance of Command object
Set DataCommand = Server.CreateObject ("ADODB.Command")
'DataConn is the Connection object in use
DataCommand.ActiveConnection =
DataConn
'Place call to stored procedure passing in one argument
DataCommand.CommandText = "call sp_mystoredprocedure
'myarg'"
'tell the provider that the command is a stored
'procedure
DataCommand.CommandType = adCmdStoredProc
'create instance of RecordSet
Set MyRS = Server.CreateObject
("ADODB.RecordSet")
'execute the commandtext to return a recordset from the
'stored procedure
MyRS = DataCommand.Execute
```

For a sql string, the CommandType property uses adCmdText, as follows:

```
DataCommand.CommandText = "Select * From AnyTable"
DataCommand.CommandType = adCmdText
```

The following code shows you the syntax to using the Command object's Execute method. The method uses the variable nRowsAffected to return the number of rows deleted. The CommandTypeEnum constant adCmdText notifies the database provider that this is a sql statement, not a stored procedure.

```
DataCommand.CommandText = "Delete * From AnyTable"
DataCommand.Execute nRowsAffected,   , adCmdText

If nRowsAffected > 0 then
    Response.W"Number of Rows Deleted is "
    Response.WnAffected
End if
```

●─**CROSS-REFERENCE**─────────────────────────────────

All the values for the `CommandTypeEnum` and `ObjectStateEnum` constants can be found on-line.

Storing a Procedure from a SQL Server

Let's put all the information about the `Command` object from the last few sections into an example. The following code shows you an example of a stored procedure that was created in the database Microsoft MS SQL server. This stored procedure reads in one parameter: the telephone number. It then returns the records from the SQL statement.

```
CREATE PROCEDURE sp_mystoreProcedure
@PhoneNumber varchar(10)

AS
Begin
    Select Name,Address
    From Phone_Table
    Where PhoneNumber = @PhoneNumber
End
```

Look at the next example to see how to use the `Command` object to pass in the parameter to this stored procedure. Notice the `Command` object's `CommandText` property. This is where you pass in the parameters to the stored procedure "sp_mystoredProcedure. In this case, you can pass the telephone number and name to the store procedure using the following code:

```
'DataConn is the Connection object
Set DataCommand = Server.CreateObject ("ADODB.Command")
'DataConn is the Connection object in use
DataCommand.ActiveConnection=
DataConn
DataCommand.CommandText = "Call sp_mystoredProcedure
'7899999', thereturnedName "
'place the returned record from stored procedure
'into recordset MyRS
Set MyRS = DataCommand.Execute
```

Now that you've learned how to pass parameters directly to a stored procedure, let's look at how to pass parameters to a stored procedure through a `Parameter` object.

The Parameter Object and Collection

The Command object is best used to pass parameters to a stored procedure. However, the engineers at Microsoft who designed the ASP technology, give you an additional way to pass parameters to a stored procedure — the Parameter object and Parameter collection. The use of the Command object verus the Paramater object/Parameter collection deals with what type of stored procedure you are using.

There are two types of stored procedures:

- Parameterized stored procedures are stored procedures that expect arguments.

- Non-parameterized stored procedures are stored procedures that do not expect arguments.

The previous section on the Command object showed you how to execute non-parameterized stored procedures. This section shows you how to use parameterized stored procedures. The code to create a parameter object is provided in the next section. You can create a parameter object in two ways, both of which are discussed in the next two sections.

Passing Values to the CreateParameter Method

The first way to create a parameter object is to pass values to the CreateParameter method. The syntax to accomplish this task is as follows:

```
Set parameterObject = commandObject. CreateParameter
(Name, Type, Direction,
Size, Value)
```

The preceding line of code shows you the needed arguments for the Parameter object's CreateParameter method. You supply to this method the Name, Type, Direction, Size, and Value of the parameter. Now you will see an example in which the arguments to the CreateParameter method are filled in. We are going to pretend that these parameters will be used on a stored procedure that requires a string of up to 25 characters passed in. The value of the string to be passed to the stored procedure is "My Value." We've named this Parameter object "AnyParaName." The five arguments that the CreateParameter method uses are really Parameter object properties. Thus, the argument "AnyParaName" is setting the Name property. The second argument in the following example, which uses adVarChar, is setting the Type property.

```
'assume that the Command object DataCommand has already
'been created.
'we are going to name this parameter object
'"AnyParaName"
Set ParaObject =
DataCommand.CreateParameter("AnyParaName", adVarChar,
adParamInput,25,"My Value")
DataCommand.Execute
```

Table 4-15 describes the list of arguments that can be added to a Parameter object.

4

Table 4-15 *Parameter Object Arguments*

Argument	Required	Type	Description
Name	No	String	Defines the name of the parameter to be created.
Type	No	DataType enumerated constant	Defines the variant type of the parameter being passed, such as adBigInt, adBoolean, adCurrency, and so on. Values come from the DataTypeEnum constants.
			The DataTypeEnum constants can be found on-line.
Direction	No	Parameter Direction enumerated constant	A stored procedure can accept a parameter that is provided, can output a parameter, or both. The Direction argument sets the direction in which the parameter is going. The values supplied come from the ParameterDirectione numerated constants.
			The ParameterDirection enumerated constants can be found at the URL in the Preface.
Size	No	long	The size of the variant
Value	No	A value you assign	The value you assign to the Parameter object. This can be omitted.

Assigning Properties Before Calling the Execute Method

You can also pass parameters to the Command object using the Parameter object by assigning the properties before you call the Execute method. The following code shows you how to set the arguments of a Parameter object by assigning the value directly to the property, instead of using the CreateParameter method. This example passes the phone number parameter to the stored procedure covered in the Command object section: sp_mystoredProcedure. This time, however, we are passing the parameter via the Parameter object.

```
'DataConn is the Connection object
Set DataCommand = Server.CreateObject ("ADODB.Command")
'DataConn is the Connection object in use
DataCommand.ActiveConnection =
DataConn
DataCommand.CommandText = "sp_mystoredProcedure"
Set ParaObject = DataCommand.CreateParameter
ParaObject.Name = "AnyParaName"
ParaObject.Type = adVarChar
ParaObject.Direction = adParamInput
ParaObject.Size = 10
ParaObject.Value = '7899999'
DataCommand.Parameters.Append ParaObject
'place the returned record from stored procedure
'into recordset MyRS
Set MyRS = DataCommand.Execute
```

The Property Object and Collection

The Property collection is used by the Connection, Command, Record Set, and Field objects to store a set of Property objects for these four objects. We can tell you from experience that the Property object confuses most developers because of the word "Property." The Connection object contains a set of properties; for example, State, Version, and so on. But the Connection object also has properties such as "Catalog Usage," "Connection Status," and "Driver Version." The Field object has additional properties such as "OCTETLENGTH," "BASETABLENAME," and "OPTIMIZE." Each of the properties in quotes is a Property object and can be found by using the Properties collection.

The Connection, Command, RecordSet, and Field objects all contain a Properties collection. The property called Properties (which is listed with the other properties at the beginning of this chapter) retrieves this Property collection. If all this sounds confusing, looking at some code should help clarify things.

The Property object has four properties: Attributes, Name, Type, and Value. The Attributes property will return a PropertyAttributes enumeration constant. The value returned will be either a single value or a combination of these enumerated constants. Let's look at some script to clarify this last sentence. The following code finds out the value for the property labeled "Hold Rows":

```
<%
set DataConn = Server.CreateObject("ADODB.Connection")
DataConn.Open Application("db_ConnectionString")
    sqlstm = "Select SchoolName From Schools"
    'Open a connection
    Dim RSetObj
    Set RSetObj =
server.CreateObject("ADODB.Recordset")
RSetObj.Open SqlStm , DataConn , 1 , 1
Response.Write "<BR>ATTRIBUTE ->"

Response.Write RsetObj.Properties("Hold
Rows").Attribute
%>
```

The value returned could be

```
ATTRIBUTE ->513
```

The 513 represents a combination of the Required and Read property constants.

●─CROSS-REFERENCE─────────────────

The list of PropertyAttribute enumerated constants is available on-line.

The next example creates a Connection object to a database. Then, once the Connection object is established, the code uses the Properties property to get the name and value of each Property object in the Properties collection.

```
<%
set DataConn = Server.CreateObject("ADODB.Connection")
DataConn.Open Application("db_ConnectionString")
    For each item in DataConn.Properties
        Response.Write "<BR>"&item.Name&"->"
        Response.Write item.Value
    next
%>
```

When you run this code, you will get a list of numerous Property objects. The following list is just an example of what the output for the preceding script might be:

```
Active Sessions->0
Asynchable Commit->False
Catalog Location->1
Catalog Term->database
Catalog Usage->7
Column Definition->1
NULL Concatenation Behavior->0
Data Source Name->eTransDev
Read-Only Data Source->False
DBMS Name->Microsoft SQL Server
DBMS Version->07.00.0623
GROUP BY Support->2
```

Heterogeneous Table Support- > 0. Let's look at a possible list for the Properties collection for the RecordSet object. The next bit of code shows you how to connect to a data source, get a recordset, and then use the Properties collection to list out the Property object for that recordset. In this script, we will output the four properties of a Property object: Name, Value, Type, and Attributes.

```
set DataConn = Server.CreateObject("ADODB.Connection")
DataConn.Open Application("db_ConnectionString")

    sqlstm = "Select SchoolName From Schools"
    'Open a connection
    Dim RSetObj
    Set RSetObj =
server.CreateObject("ADODB.Recordset")
RSetObj.Open SqlStm , DataConn , 1 , 1
    'output the 4 properities of Property object
    For each item in RSetObj.Properties
        Response.Write "<BR>"&item.Name&"->"
        Response.Write item.Value
        Response.Write "    ATTRIBUTE ->"
        Response.Write item.Attributes
        Response.Write "    TYPE -> "
        Response.Write item.type
    next
%>
```

Following is some of the long output of `Property` objects for the `RecordSet` object that you will see when you run the preceding script:

```
Preserve on Abort->False ATTRIBUTE ->513 TYPE -> 11
Blocking Storage Objects->True ATTRIBUTE ->513 TYPE->11
Use Bookmarks->True ATTRIBUTE ->1537 TYPE -> 11
Skip Deleted Bookmarks->False ATTRIBUTE ->513 TYPE ->11
Bookmark Type->1 ATTRIBUTE ->513 TYPE -> 3
Fetch Backwards->True ATTRIBUTE ->1537 TYPE -> 11
Hold Rows->True ATTRIBUTE ->1537 TYPE -> 11
Scroll Backwards->True ATTRIBUTE ->1537 TYPE -> 11
Column Privileges->True ATTRIBUTE ->513 TYPE -> 11
Command Time Out->30 ATTRIBUTE ->1537 TYPE -> 3
Preserve on Commit->False ATTRIBUTE ->513 TYPE -> 11
```

Run the following scripts for the `Field` and `Command` objects, and you'll be able to see the `Property` objects in their `Property` collection for these two objects.

```
<%
set DataConn = Server.CreateObject("ADODB.Connection")
DataConn.Open Application("db_ConnectionString")

    sqlstm = "Select SchoolName From Schools"
    'Open a connection
    Dim RSetObj
    Set RSetObj =
server.CreateObject("ADODB.Recordset")
RSetObj.Open SqlStm , DataConn , 1 , 1

    For each item in RSetObj(0).Properties
        Response.Write "<BR>"&item.Name&"->"
        Response.Write item.Value
        Response.Write "    ATTRIBUTE ->"
        Response.Write item.Attributes
        Response.Write "    TYPE -> "
        Response.Write item.type
    Next
%>


<%
set DataConn = Server.CreateObject("ADODB.Connection")
DataConn.Open Application("db_ConnectionString")
```

```
Set CmdObj = server.CreateObject("ADODB.Command")
CmdObj.ActiveConnection = DataConn
For each item in CmdObj.Properties
    Response.Write "<BR>"&item.Name&"->"
    Response.Write item.Value
    Response.Write "    ATTRIBUTE ->"
    Response.Write item.Attributes
    Response.Write "    TYPE -> "
    Response.Write item.type
Next
%>
```

The Record Object

Most of the data that you have seen in the preceding sections comes to the ADO through a database. The examples in the above sections that show you how to connect to a database always bring back a recordset from a relational database such as Oracle or Microsoft SQL Server. But the ADO can also handle nonrelational data sources such as files, directories, and mail systems. The Record object is how ADO handles these other data sources.

Because the Record object is new to ADO 2.5, there aren't many uses for it yet. One use is with the OLE DB Provider for Internet Publishing. Let's now look at how you can use the Record object.

First let's look at the syntax to create a Record object:

```
Dim Recordobj
Set Recordobj = Server.CreateObject("ADODB.Record")
```

In the examples below, you will use the Record object's Open method to obtain data that is stored in a text format in a file. This data source could include a mainframe VSAM report that has been output into a text file. If you're asking what is VSAM, then you have never dealt with the mainframe world so don't worry about it. We just thought we would give you another idea of how to use the Record object.

Once you create the Record object, you open a nonrelational data source using the Open method. In the case of the code below, you will supply the name of the external text file that is the data source and the location of that external data source. The syntax to open a directory as a record follows. However, if you'll read Table 4-16, you will see that all the arguments can be optional. For the purposes of using an external text file as the data source, you will need to supply data for the "datasourcename" and the "url location of directory" arguments.

```
Recordobj.Open "datasourcename","url location of
directory",connection mode, file options, userid,
password
```

If you wanted to open a text file as a Record object, use the following: Notice you only need to supply the "datasourcename" and "url location of directory" arguments.

```
Recordobj.Open "anyfile.txt","URL =
"http://www.anyname.com/"
```

If you wanted to open a directory as a Record object, use this code:

```
Recordobj.Open "wwwroot","URL =
"http://www.anyname.com/"
```

Table 4-16 describes the Record object Open method.

Table 4-16 *Open Method Arguments*

Argument	Required	Type	Description
Datasourcename	No	String	The name of the directory; for example, "wwwroot" (you don't have to specify the c:\").
Url location of directory	No	String	This is the URL of the directory or the location of a file. For a directory on a Web site, the syntax is always URL = http://directory.
Connection mode	No	ConnectionMode enumeration constant	This argument tells you the connection mode to be used.
			The ConnectionMode enumerated constants can be found at the URL in the Preface.

Argument	Required	Type	Description
File options	No	RecordCreate Options enumerated constant	This argument tells you if an existing file should be opened or a new file created.
			The RecordCreate Options enumerated constants can be found at the URL noted in the Preface.
File open options	No	RecordOpen options enumerated constant	This argument tells you how the record can be opened.
			The RecordOpen Options enumerated constants can be found at the URL noted in the Preface.
UserId	No	String	If a userid is needed for authorizing access to the data source.
Password	No	String	If a password is needed for authorizing access to the data source.

Note one thing about dealing with directories with respect to the Record object and the RecordSet object: The Record object is the main directory, the top of the hierarchy; the RecordSet object is all the subdirectories under the main directory. See Figure 4-11 for a visual picture of this explanation. The big arrow in the figure points at the web directory FriendsFromAuburn. The little arrows point at the subdirectories PhilMetzger, JonSansom, DavidWebb, JoeRaley, MikeFalcone, ScottHorne, and DavidMoore; these would be the RecordSet object. Note that the subdirectory DavidMoore has a file in it named WarEagle.txt. We'll get the contents of this file in the Stream object.

This is the Record object

These subdirectories make up the Recordset object

Figure 4-11   *The directory structure*

Let's create a `Record` object from the directory shown in
Figure 4-11. The example below uses a directory named "Friends
FromAuburn." This directory resides on a local computer's hard
drive rather than a network hard drive. The directory is located
at c:\inetpub\wwwroot.

```
<%
Dim Recordobj
Set Recordobj = Server.CreateObject("ADODB.Record")
Recordobj.Open "FriendsFromAuburn","URL =
c:\inetpub\wwwroot\"
%>
```

The Web site that this particular directory is on is http:\
localhost, which is the url of a Personnel Web Server (PWS). Thus,
you could also use the following code to achieve the same results:

```
<%
Dim Recordobj
```

```
Set Recordobj = Server.CreateObject("ADODB.Record")
Recordobj.Open "FriendsFromAuburn","URL =
"http://localhost/"
%>
```

We have now created a `Record` object — recordobj — that represents the `FriendFromAuburn` directory. As you can see in Figure 4-11, FriendsFromAuburn has six subdirectories. Many methods and properties are associated with the `Record` object, but `GetChildren`, `Copy Record`, `MoveRecord`, and `DeleteRecord` need to be explained further.

●—CROSS-REFERENCE

The methods and properties of the `Record` object are covered in the ASP Core Reference section (p.172).

4

GetChildren Method

The `Record` object contains a method that enables you to access the six subdirectories shown in Figure 4-11: the `GetChildren` method. You can think of the FriendsFromAuburn directory as being the parent of the PhilMetzger directory. The subdirectories under the `Record` object are not only childern, they are also a `RecordSet` object. This `RecordSet` object has a `Field` and `Properties` collection, just like a recordset pulled from an Oracle database. Thus, the `GetChildren` method returns a `RecordSet` object. The syntax for using the `Get Children` method is as follows:

```
<%
Dim recordobj,ChildRecordSet
Set recordobj = Server.CreateObject("ADODB.Record")
Recordobj.Open "FriendsFromAuburn","URL =
"http://www.anyanme.com/"
Set ChildRecordSet = recordobj.GetChildren()
%>
```

Remember that `GetChildren` returns a `RecordSet` object containing a `Field` collection, just like a regular relational database. The code to use the `Field` collection with the `RecordSet` object for this `Record` object is as follows:

```
<%
Dim recordobj,ChildRecordSet,j
Set recordobj = Server.CreateObject("ADODB.Record")
Recordobj.Open "FriendsFromAuburn","URL =
"http://www.anyname.com/"
Set ChildRecordSet = recordobj.GetChildren()
Response.Write "number of Fields in RecordSet is"
```

```
Response.Write ChildRecordSet.Fields.Count
For j = 0 to ChildRecordSet.Fields.Count-1
    Response.Write "<BR>"
    Response.Write "Name is "
    Response.Write ChildRecordSet.Fields(j).Name
    Response.Write "Value is "
    Response.Write ChildRecordSet.Fields(j).Value
    ChildRecordSet.MoveNext
Next
%>
```

4 CopyRecord, MoveRecord, and DeleteRecord Methods

The CopyRecord, MoveRecord, and DeleteRecord methods live up
to their name. The CopyRecord method copies a Record object from
one location to another. The MoveRecord method moves a Record
object from one location to another. The DeleteRecord deletes a
Record object.

The following code shows you how to use these methods, using
the WarEagle.txt file located under the DavidMoore directory shown
in Figure 4-11 as the Record object. This example opens the Record
object and then copies the object to c:\inetpub\wwwroot\AnotherDir\
(or, in URL terms, this directory is http://localhost/AnotherDir).
We rename the Record object to WarEagle2.txt when we copy it.
After we have copied the Record object to this location, we use the
MoveRecord method to move the Record object to http://localhost/
DougBurris. Once the Record object has been moved to the URL
http://localhost/DougBurris, it is deleted from AnotherDir using
the DeleteRecord object.

```
<%
Dim RecObj
RecObj = Server.CreateObject("ADODB.Record")
RecObj.Open
"WarEagle.txt","URL=http://localhost/FriendsFromAuburn/
DavidMoore/WarEagle.txt
'Copy Record object From DavidMoore to AnotherDir
RecObj.CopyRecord
"","http://localehost/AnotherDir/WarEagle2.txt"
'Move Record object from DavidMoore to DougBurris
RecObj.MoveRecord
"","http://localhost/DougBurris/WarEagle.txt"
'Delete Record from FriendsFromAuburn/DavidMoore
RecObj.DeleteRecord
%>
```

The Stream Object

The Stream object is another new object to ADO 2.5. This object accesses the contents of anything in a directory structure, such as the files shown in Figure 4-11. The syntax to create a Stream object is as follows:

```
Dim streamobj
Set streamobj = Server.CreateObject("ADODB.Stream")
```

In order to access any data using the Stream object, you will need to use the Open method. This method has five arguments. Notice from Table 4-17 that all the arguments are optional. The examples below will get the contents of a file as the data for the Stream object; therefore, we are supplying the location of the file, how the file is to be accesssed, and type of source from which the file.

For the purposes of this example, use the following code to get the contents of a file into the Stream object:

```
streamobj.Open "file location",access
mode,TypeofSource,userid,passwordTim
```

Table 4-17 describes the arguments for the Stream object Open method.

Table 4-17   *Open Method Arguments*

Value	Required	Type	Description
File location	No	String	The location of the file, whether URL or c:\.
Access mode	No	ConnectMode enumerated constant	This is how the Stream object is to be accessed. It is a ConnectionMode enumerated constant. Following are three access modes: adModeRead — 1 adModeReadWrite — 3 adModeWrite — 2

Continued

Table 4-17 *Continued*

Value	Required	Type	Description
TypeofSource	No	StreamOpen Options enumerated constant	This argument describes type of source the file is from. Whether a asynchronous, record, or url source.
			StreamOpenOptions enumerated constant
			adOpenStream Async — 1
			adOpenStreamFrom Record — 4
			adOpenStreamFrom URL —8
UserId	No	String	If a userid is needed for authorizing access to the data source.
Password	No	String	If a password is needed for authorizing access to the data source.

●—CROSS-REFERENCE

The methods and properties to the `Stream` object can be found in the ASP Core Reference section (p. 276).The `StreamOpenOptions` and `ConnectionMode` enumerated constants can be found at the URL noted in the Preface.

We are going to use the `Stream` object to read the contents of WarEagle.txt, listed under the DavidMoore subdirectory shown in Figure 4-11. Then output the contents to an HTML `textarea` component.

```
<%
Dim StreamObj
Set StreamObj = Server.CreateObject("ADODB.Stream")
'Open the Stream
StreamObj.Open
"URL=http://localhost/FriendsFromAuburn/DavidMoore/WarE
agle.txt", 3 ,8
'specify what type of character are in file to be
streamed
```

```
StreamObj.Charset = "ascii'
%>
<HTML>
<BODY>
<TABLE>
<TR>
<TD FONTSIZE=4 FONTCOLOR=BLUE>
<%Response.Write StreamObj.ReadText %>
<%
'close stream object and destroy the object to free up
resources.
StreamObj.Close
Set StreamObj = nothing
%>
</TD>
</TR>
</BODY>
</HTML>
```

The Remote Data Services

When ASP technology was first introduced, Microsoft began looking for a way to enable users to interact with a data source. The ADO is that evolving solution. The ADO works great as long as the Web server, data server, router, or any other network component is up and running. When these components work, ADO is a beautiful thing. But any of these components can go down. If you are a network administrator, you know the headaches of delivering a reliable Web service. Microsoft sought to give users access to data in an unreliable Internet setting. The solution Microsoft came up with is Remote Data Services (RDS).

In a normal ADO setting, a user can connect many times to the data server to access information. In this situation, the Web server does all the work of data retrieval. Anytime a user needs to retrieve the data, another SQL Select statement is issued. With RDS, the user issues an initial SQL Select, and then caches the results on the client-side browser. The user can then manipulate the recordset as he or she pleases. The majority of the work is then transferred from the Web server to the browser.

In order to manipulate the cached data, Microsoft created three new objects: DataFactory, DataControl, and DataSpace. A complete discussion of creating an RDS application is beyond the scope of this book; several books on the market cover this subject in far greater detail.

In order for the RDS to work, there must be two components: one to send the data to the browser, and one to receive the data on the browser. If this sounds to you like fat client server, you're right. Isn't that a step backward from the promise of the Internet to deliver thin client? Yes, it is. As Internet technology matures, Microsoft and other companies have found that the promise of delivering data totally on the server doesn't always meet every customer's demand for data delivery. That's why fat client server technology is never going to go away — it works.

Sending the data from the server to the client is called "marshaling the data." The server-side RDS component that marshals the data to the browser is the DataFactory. Think of this component as a factory that builds the data. Two other components need to be installed on your browser: the DataControl and DataSpace objects. These components create the communication channel to the browser, and then allow manipulation of the data once it's on the browser. With this information in hand, let's look at these components in a little more detail.

● — **NOTE** ————————————————————

Currently, you can only use the Internet Explorer browser to implement this technology. Remember: We are using ActiveX controls on the browser, so the folks at Netscape won't be helping out any.

DataFactory Object

The DataFactory object is a COM object that is installed with the server-side RDS components. This object handles retrieving the data from the database and sending the data to the browser. Once this component is installed, it will communicate with the DataSpace object, which will be on the browser. So now you need to install the Remote Data Services on your server.

Perform the following steps to install the RDS:

1. Go to Start Program and select the Windows NT Option Pack 4.0. A list of menu options will appear.

2. Select Windows NT Option Pack 4.0 Setup.

3. After you select this menu option, a window will appear with the message "Setup is initializing. Please wait," If you don't get this message, you have a very fast computer. Lucky you!

4. The Windows NT Option Pack 4 Setup window will appear. Click the Next button. A window will appear that contains two buttons: Add/Remove and Remove All.

5. Click the button labeled Add/Remove.

6. A window will appear that contains a list of components, with a checkbox next to each. Find the component labeled Microsoft Data Access Component 1.5. Highlight this menu option and then click the button labeled Show Subcomponents. Figure 4-12 shows you what this window looks like.

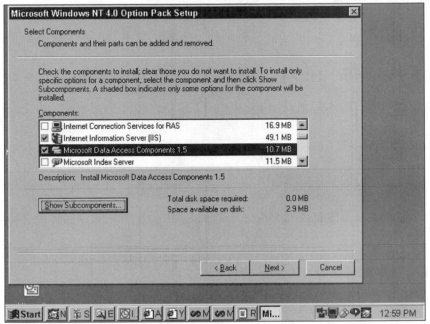

Figure 4-12   *Installing the Remote Data Services on Windows NT*

7. After you have clicked the Show Subcomponents button, a window labeled Microsoft Data Access Components 1.5 appears. In this window, you should see a list of at least three options. One of the options is labeled Remote Data Services 1.5 (RDS/ADS). Figure 4-13 shows what this window looks like.

8. Click the checkbox next to Remote Data Services and click OK. Once the OK button is clicked, you will return to the window entitled Windows NT 4.0 Option Pack Setup. When this window appears, click the button labeled Next. Windows NT will install the RDS, and with it the DataFactory component.

● **NOTE**

You can get the latest version of the RDS from http://www. microsoft.com/data.

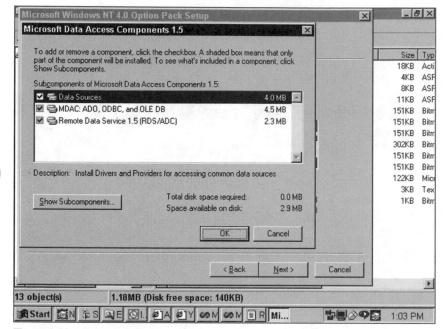

Figure 4-13 *Selecting Remote Data Services*

DataSpace Object

The DataSpace object is a COM object that acts like a conduit, allowing data to flow between the browser and the DataFactory object. The DataSpace object contains one method, CreateObject; and one property, InternetTimeout. The following code shows you the syntax to create the client-side RDS DataSpace object.

```
<OBJECT ID='dsoDataSpace" CLASSID="CLSID:DB96C556-65A3-
11D0-983A-00C04FC29E36">
```

DataControl Object

The DataControl object is a client-side (meaning browser) ActiveX object that stores and manipulates data once it arrives on the browser. In other words, the object attaches a recordset to one of the ActiveX controls that Microsoft has (a text box, grid control, or combo box) to display the recordset data on a Web page. You can use several Data Control ActiveX objects to manage data. Following is a list of several of these objects. All of these DataControl objects actually fall under the Data Source objects.

- Tabular Data Control
- Microsoft HTML Control (MSHTML)
- XML Data Source Object

RDS References

Because this book is not intended to cover the RDS in detail, you may want to check out the following articles and URLs.

The following five links give you a detailed overview of the RDS:

- http://www.asptoday.com/articles/19990326.htm
- http://www.asptoday.com/articles/19990607.htm
- http://www.aspwatch.com/c/199928/dAFF3AD262B4511D38 67500902730270D.asp
- http://www.asp101.com/ado/18350701.asp
- http://www.asptoday.com/articles/20000225.htm

The next two links show you how to create a remote recordset using RDS:

- http://www.asptoday.com/articles/19990813.htm
- http://www.asp101.com/ado/18350704.asp

This link will show you how to create a list for HTML using RDS:

- http://www.microsoft.com/mind/0599/picklists/ picklists.htm

The next link is great at describing different DataControl objects:

- http://msdn.microsoft.com/workshop/author/databind/ datasources.asp

The following link provides details about the DataControl object:

- http://msdn.microsoft.com/library/psdk/dasdk/ mdao1hyk.htm

This following link is from Microsoft support catalog giving details on using ASP with a RDS Data Control

- http://support.microsoft.com/support/kb/articles/ q259/5/33.asp

This chapter provided you with a brief overview of the objects that are a part of the Active Data Object (ADO). If you're going to create any database ASP applications, we recommend studying this chapter several times. Also, check the web sites www.15seconds.com or www.ASPToday.com for examples on ADO code.

4

in plain english in pl
sh in plain english in
glish in plain english
in plain english in pl
sh in plain english in
glish in plain english
in plain english in pl
glish in plain english
in plain english in pl
sh in plain english in
glish in plain english
in plain english in pl
sh in plain english in
glish in plain english
in plain english in pl
lish in plain english
in plain english in pl
sh in plain english in
glish in plain english
in plain english in pl
sh in plain english in
lish in plain english
in plain english in pl
glish in plain english

Creating Server-Side ActiveX COM Objects

As noted in the earlier tutorial chapters, COM stands for Component Object Model, and is a product of Microsoft COM object technology. COM is a software architecture that enables applications to be built from binary software components. In fact, COM is a binary standard for software object interaction. It is the underlying architecture that forms the foundation for high-level software services, such as those provided by Object Linking and Embedding (OLE). OLE services cover various aspects of system functionality, including compound documents, custom controls, inter-application scripting, data transfer, and other software interactions.

COM creates a way for software components to communicate with one another. The COM standard combines both binary and networking to enable any two components to communicate no matter what machine they're running on, what operating systems the machines are running, or what language the components are written in.

This feature operates within certain guidelines. COM capability depends upon the computers being connected and the operating systems and languages supporting COM. COM also enables you to deploy your components without regard to location. When you write your components, you don't need to know whether the other components are in process DLLs or local EXEs, or are components located on some other machine.

This chapter covers Microsoft COM object technology (including the Component Object Model and Classes), using Visual Basic 6 to create an ActiveX Com object, creating a COM object with Visual Basic 6, registering the object, running the Com object, and using the COM object in server-side scripting.

5 Understanding the COM Object and ActiveX Objects

Reduced to the simplest terms, the basic unit of COM is the object, which is created by COM itself. A COM object is not the same as an object in Visual programming. The concept of the COM object goes deeper. The COM object is more similar to a component than to the object in object-oriented programming. A COM object cannot be accessed without an interface. The interface in this case is, in a sense, a contract between the object and its clients for how the interaction will take place and which objects will be involved. This interface is a set of methods and an agreement about what those methods do.

An example of how to provide an interface to the COM object is via OLE Automation. OLE provides a way to define an interface to a COM object, an interface that can be called by any software that understands the interface description.

COM+ and TIP

COM+ is a set of additional services for COM-based applications. COM+ adds to COM a set of transaction services. It enables you to set attributes for transactions on your components.

Another addition to COM is Transaction Internet Protocol (TIP). Currently, TIP is a proposed standard. TIP provides a way to receive requests for transactions over the Internet. TIP, combined with Bring Your Own Transactions (BYOT), integrates transactions and allows transaction management. BYOT offers a set of interfaces that can be combined with COM+.

Objects and Classes

Objects include both code and data. They have properties, events, and methods. Properties are characteristics of the object. Events are the things the objects actually do. Methods are used to cause the objects to do something. However, objects must first be created from classes. Objects are always specific occurrences of a class, and every object has a class. Visual Basic stores an internal identification number for each and every object defined in an application. Classes combine data and procedures into one unit. Descriptions of classes are stored in type libraries and can be viewed with object browsers.

Uses of ActiveX Objects

ActiveX is a set of technologies that is based upon the COM model. This technology is platform-independent, so resellers and vendors not affiliated with Microsoft can use it and distribute their products. ActiveX objects can be developed without using Microsoft tools and run on non-Windows operating systems such as Unix and Macintosh.

There are different uses of ActiveX objects. These include ActiveX controls, code components, and documents. ActiveX controls are, in fact, COM objects. An ActiveX control is a control that you install by adding it to your Visual Basic ToolBox. The controls are compiled into files with an .OCX extension. If you develop several ActiveX controls and compile all the controls in a project, the .OCX file you build will include all the controls you developed. This means that you can build an ActiveX (COM) control and Web developers can use it on Web pages and trigger it via scripting language.

ActiveX documents enable you to create interactive Internet applications. While ActiveX documents are not contained in forms, they can link to forms. These documents and forms can be displayed in Internet Explorer. ActiveX documents can contain ActiveX controls. These documents can also act as code components. When you complete your document, it is compiled into a .VBD file.

ActiveX objects, including controls, code components, and documents, represent the ActiveX COMl. An ActiveX component includes In-Process and Out-of-Process servers. The In-Process servers use files with a .DLL extension. Those that are .EXE files are called Out-of-Process servers. A good reason to use ActiveX controls is that they add power to your Web pages. You can use ActiveX controls (COM objects) to add menus, moving words, and animation to your Web site.

Using Visual Basic to Create an ActiveX COM Object

If you are familiar with Visual Basic, you have already used the ActiveX controls shipped with Visual Basic. You may even have created your own ActiveX controls. Creating an ActiveX COM object is similar to creating a Visual Basic ActiveX control, except that it is easier. It is easier to create an ActiveX COM object because a control requires a means of implementation, such as a form on which to access and use the control. However, these entities also have much in common, as you will see in the following sections, which outline the steps for creating an ActiveX COM object.

The ActiveX DLL Project

You can create an in-process ActiveX COM object in Visual Basic that can be distributed and used on the Web. To create an in-process ActiveX object, begin by creating a folder directly under the root directory under C:\. Name this folder "test." The path will be C:\test\. This is important, as the ActiveX .DLL (Dynamic Link Library) file must reside directly under the root.

Creating an ActiveX object is a way of carrying out some function that is not dependent upon the user's browser type. Following are the steps for creating a server component:

1. Launch Visual Basic.

2. Once in Visual Basic, the New Project window is launched. If you are already running Visual Basic you can select New Project from the File menu or click on the New icon on the toolbar at the top of the window.

3. From the New Project window, select ActiveX DLL by clicking on the icon (see Figure 5-1). Click OK.

4. Once you have clicked OK, a new Project window labeled "Project1 — Class1 (Code)" appears. Select Components from the Project menu. The Components window appears.

5. Select the Controls tab. You will see a list of component files. Click the Selected Items Only checkbox. The list should disappear. This is illustrated in Figure 5-2. Click OK.

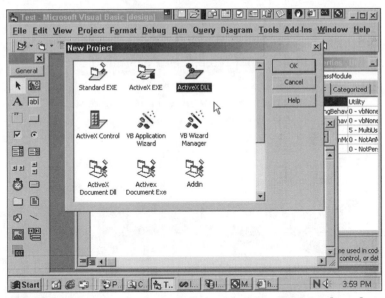

Figure 5-1 *The New Project window with ActiveX DLL selected*

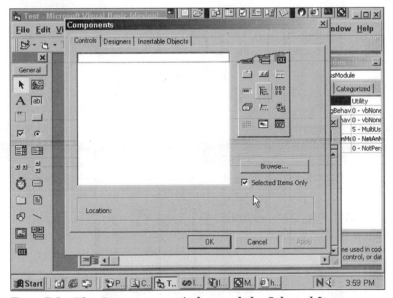

Figure 5-2 *The Components window and the Selected Items
Only checkbox*

6. You are now back at the Project Window. Select References from the Project menu. The list of available references will be displayed in the window (see Figure 5-3). Make sure that only the following four references are checked:

a. Visual Basic For Applications

b. Visual Basic runtime objects and procedures

c. Visual Basic objects and procedures

d. OLE Automation

7. Deselect any other items if their checkboxes are checked. Click OK.

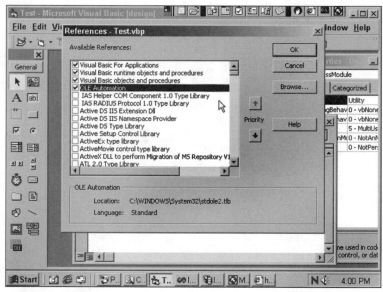

Figure 5-3 *The References list with correct boxes checked*

Changing the Name of the Project and Class Module

When you selected the ActiveX DLL icon in the first step in the preceding section, you created a class module. Now you must change the names of the Project and the Class module.

Select the Project Explorer from the View menu. You should now see the files comprising the project. Double-click the Class module displayed under the project. Now you should see the Class module code window. When you create an ActiveX DLL project, Visual Basic automatically assigns it a single class. The function code will be placed in the class module. The class module appears exactly like that of any Visual Basic code window.

You must name the class module and the project. To change the name of the project, select the Properties window from the View menu if it is not already displayed. In the Properties window, click on the name shown opposite the Name property and rename it Utility. Select Properties from the Project menu, and then change the name of the project in the Project Name box to Test. Click OK. Figure 5-4 shows the Properties window with the new project name.

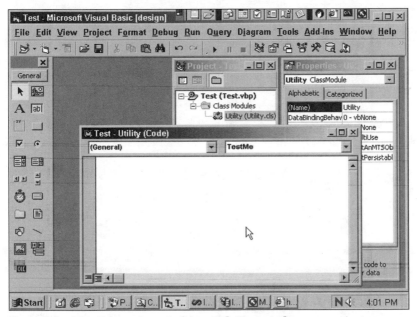

Figure 5-4 *The Properties window, with Test as the new project name*

To change the name of the procedure, select Add Procedure from the Tools menu. (If the code window is active, Add Procedure is the only option available on the Tools menu.) The Add Procedure window appears (see Figure 5-5). In the Name field, type **TestMe** and select Function as the Type of procedure. Leave the Scope as Public. Click OK.

Select the File menu and save both the class module (Utility.cls) and the project, (Test.vbp) in the "test" folder you just created, as shown in Figure 5-6.

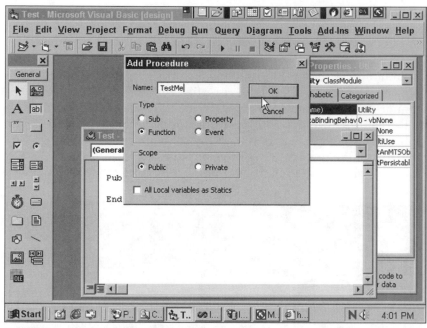

Figure 5-5 *The Add Procedure window*

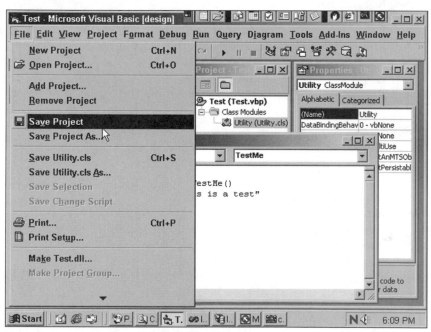

Figure 5-6 *Saving the Test project*

Creating a Function in the Class Module

The next step in creating an ActiveX COM object is to create a function in the Utility class module. The purpose of the function is to return a value that can be utilized from an ASP page. In the TestMe function for the Utility class module code window, type the following code (see Figure 5-7):

```
TestMe   = "This is a test"
```

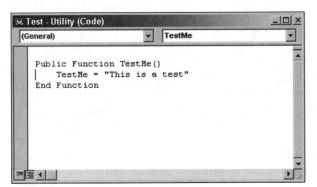

Figure 5-7 *Entering the TestMe function code in the function procedure*

Save the project again and select Make Test.DLL from the File menu. Select the C:\Test folder to save the file.

The following steps for completing the ActiveX COM object can be done in any HTML editor. Examples are given for using Microsoft Visual Interdev and Microsoft FrontPage.

Completing and Running Your ActiveX Com Object

In order to run your ActiveX object, you must use ASP scripting. If you choose to use Visual Interdev to write the ASP code, you will notice that the programming environment looks almost exactly like that of Visual Basic. The major differences lie in the area of Web site design, with Visual Basic having less to offer than Visual Interdev.

Using Microsoft Visual Interdev to Write ASP Code

The first step is to launch the Interdev program. Then select New Project from the File menu, as shown in Figure 5-8.

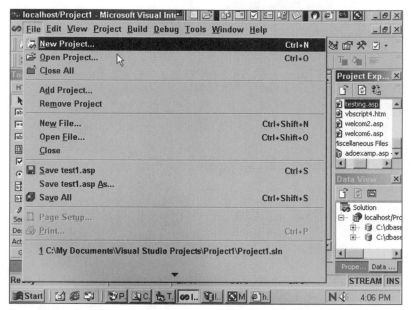

Figure 5-8 *Starting a New Project in Visual Interdev*

Choose New Web Project in the New Project window. Figure 5-9 illustrates this step.

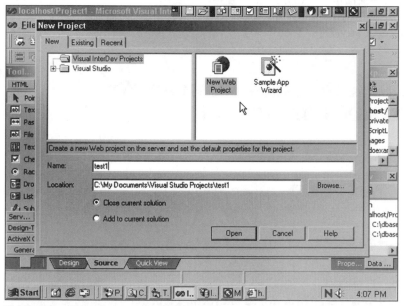

Figure 5-9 *Selecting a new Web project*

When the Web Project Wizard starts, select the correct server for either the Personal Web Server or the Internet Information Server (IIS). This will depend on the name of the root of the Web server residing on your system. Select the Master mode, and then click Next. Finally, click Finish. This is illustrated in Figure 5-10.

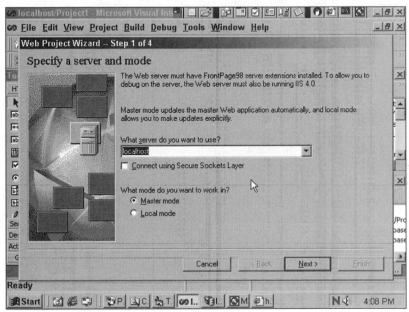

Figure 5-10   *Selecting the server and mode*

●─**CROSS-REFERENCE**

The IIS is covered in Chapter 2 (p. 581) and Chapter 1 (p.534).

When you have finished creating the new project, you can name it Test1, and then do the following:

1. Click the Project menu and select Add Item from the list.

2. From the Add Item window, select ASP Page.

3. In the Name field, name the page Testing.asp.

You can now view the file in the Project Explorer window. The Project Explorer is virtually the same as that in Visual Basic. Double-click the file Testing.asp and you will be able to view it in the code window. Interdev will create the ASP and VBScript tags for you at the top of the page. Add the following lines of code:

```
<%set r = Server.CreateObject("Test.Utility")%>
my first test
<br>
<%Response.Write r.TestMe%>
```

The preceding code is shown in Figure 5-11. The CreateObject function is used here to create the ActiveX COM object Test. Utility. This is represented in the Utility class in the Test project. The Response.Write function simply enables you to see the actual value returned; otherwise, without Response.Write, the variable value would exist within the ASP project, (for some purpose other than display). In the VBScript Syntax Reference section and in other VBScript examples, you could use the message box to achieve the same result. You cannot use the message box (MsgBox) here because VBScript will execute on the client browser, rather than the server. You must use ASPs in order to execute your code on the server and have it be browser-independent. The objective here is to make use of the ActiveX COM object independently of the client's browser.

●—CROSS-REFERENCE

The VBScript Syntax reference section begins on page 399.

Once you have completed entering the code, save the Testing. asp file. Select View in Browser from the View menu, as shown in Figure 5-12.

If the Web server is configured correctly, in your browser you will be able to view the value returned by the TestMe function. You should see my first test and, immediately under that phrase, the value set for the TestMe function, This is a test. This is illustrated in Figure 5-13.

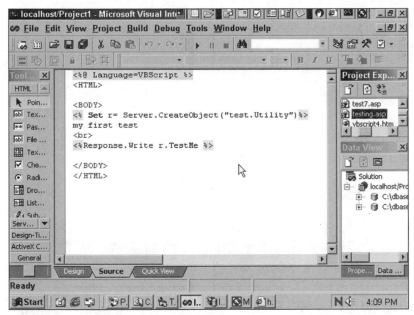

Figure 5-11   *Testing.asp ASP code*

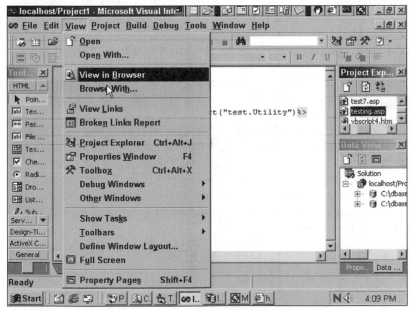

Figure 5-12   *Selecting View in Browser from the View menu*

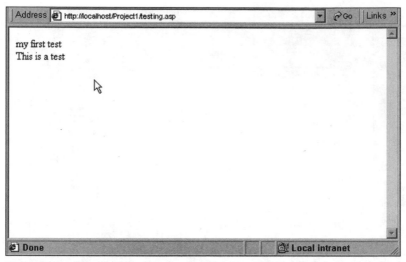

Figure 5-13 *The returned value for the TestMe function*

Using Microsoft FrontPage to Write ASP Code

You do not need to use a programming environment such as Visual
Interdev in order to test your new ActiveX COM object. You can use
any editor (even Windows NotePad). FrontPage makes a handy HTML
and ASP editor. If you have this, you can follow the approximate steps
detailed in the previous section to test your ActiveX COM object.

Assuming that you are using FrontPage, launch the editor from
the Start menu. Select the HTML tab at the bottom of the screen to
view the HTML code rather than the Normal page. Enter the code
shown in the previous Interdev example and in Figure 5-14.

Once you have completed entering the code, save the Testing.asp
file. Select Preview in Browser from the File menu. This is shown in
Figure 5-15.

You will be able to view the value returned by the TestMe function in your browser. You should see my first test and, immediately
under that phrase, the value set for the TestMe function, This is a
test (see Figure 5-16).

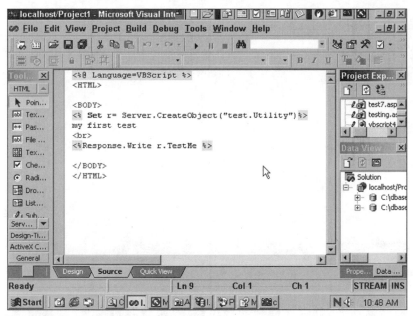

Figure 5-14   *Testing.asp ASP code*

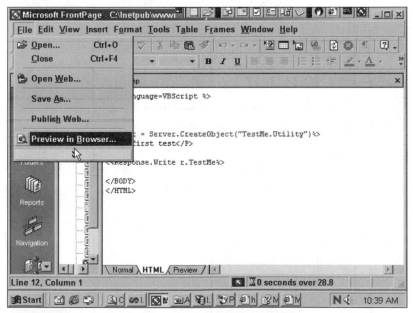

Figure 5-15   *Selecting the Preview in Browser option*

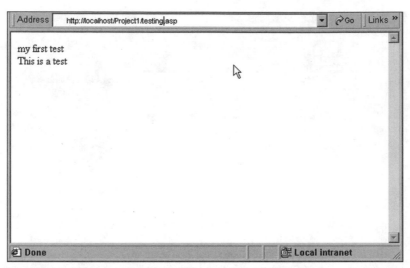

Figure 5-16   *The returned value for the TestMe function*

Registering the ActiveX COM Object

Once you have written your Testing.asp code, tested, and saved it,
you are ready to register the component. An ActiveX DLL component
must be properly registered in the system Registry before it can be recognized or used by any Windows program, including Visual Basic. All
ActiveX DLLs created with Visual Basic export the DllRegisterServer
and DllUnregisterServer functions. The ActiveX/COM objects must
be entered in the Registry so that the COM (Component Object Model)
knows how to instantiate the object servers from the appropriate
executable file.

The process of compiling the component in Visual Basic automatically registers it on your system, but anyone who intends to use your
add-in on another system must register it there before they can use
it. This means that if you have an in-process component (.DLL file),
you (or your user) must use a utility such as RegSvr32.exe to register
it on your (or their) system. To make this easy for the customer, you
could do this in the component's setup program.

When the component reference is written to the system Registry, the registered name is the programmatic ID. That is, it is made up of the name of your project (as shown in the Project Name box on the General tab of the Project Properties dialog box), plus the name of the class module that contains the function code. For example, if you create a component using the Visual Basic default names (Project1 for the project name and Class1 for the class module name), the registered name will be Project1.Class1.

Compiling the DLL will automatically register it on the development computer. After the DLL is created, it must be moved to the Web server and registered manually. Registering a DLL means that the system knows how to find it when an application creates an object using the DLL's ProgID. In our case, the ProgID is the name of the Visual Basic project combined with the name of the class.

If the DLL is compiled on the Web server where the object resides, Visual Basic automatically registers it for you. However, we advise you to separate client and server, and recommend that you not use client development tools on a production server. To register a DLL on the Web server, follow these five steps:

1. Create a directory called greetings under the %systemroot%\system32 directory.

2. Copy test.dll to the test directory.

3. Copy the file msvbvm60.dll to the system32 directory on the Web server.

4. From a command prompt in the test directory on the Web server, type the following:

   ```
   RegSvr32 test.dll
   ```

5. To complete the registration, select Run from the Start menu. In the Open field, type the following:

   ```
   RegSvr32 c:\test\test.dll
   ```

Click OK to run the regsvr32 program. Figure 5-17 illustrates this step.

If all the steps have been carried out correctly, you will receive a message that the component is registered (see Figure 5-18).

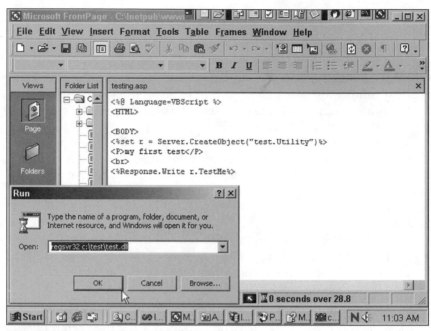

Figure 5-17 *Running the RegSvr32.exe program*

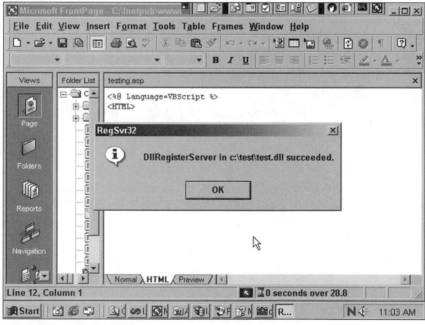

Figure 5-18 *The registration completed message*

Creating an ActiveX COM Object to Divide Numbers

Another kind of ActiveX COM object example uses a Division function to calculate values. Again, create another folder directly under the root directory under C:\. Name this folder Division. The path will be C:\Division\.

Launch Visual Basic and begin a new ActiveX DLL project. Select New Project from the File menu or click on the New icon on the toolbar at the top of the window. Once in the New Project window, select ActiveX DLL by clicking on the icon.

Once again, select Components from the Project menu. Next, select the Controls tab. You will see a list of component files. Click the Selected Items Only checkbox. The list should disappear. Click OK. Select References from the Project menu. Make sure that the following four references are checked:

- Visual Basic For Applications
- Visual Basic runtime objects and procedures
- Visual Basic objects and procedures
- OLE Automation

Deselect any other items if their checkboxes are checked. Click OK.

In the Project Explorer, you can view the project files. Name the class module DivUtil and the project Division.

Now, select Add Procedure from the Tools menu. In the Name field, type **Division** and select Function as the type of procedure. Click OK. Select the File menu and save both DivUtil.cls and Division.vbp in the Division folder you just created.

You are going to create a function in the DivUtil class module. The purpose of the function is to calculate and return a value to an ASP page. In the Division function for the DivUtil class module code window, type the following code, as shown in Figure 5-19.

```
Division = xnum / yden
```

You set up the variables shown as parameters in the Division function (xnum and yden) with xnum representing the numerator and yden the denominator. Thus, when the variables are passed to the function, this action will be carried out on the variables from the Click procedure.

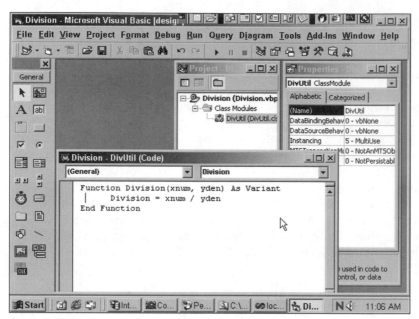

Figure 5-19 *The Division project*

To use this function, a variable will be used to pass the X and Y values to the Division function. Once the variables *X* and *Y* are passed to the Division function, they will represent xnum and yden. The division is done using the *X* value for xnum and the *Y* value for yden. The name of the variable and the values of X and Y do not matter to the Division function. It is built to accept all potential variables and values and calculate the division based on the formula.

Save the project again and select Make Division.DLL from the File menu. Then select the C:\Division folder to save the file.

The following steps to create the ActiveX COM object can be done in your preferred HTML editor. Enter the code shown. Create your server using CreateObject and reference the project and the class (Division.DivUtil). This time, you are going to pass the values you want calculated to the function. In this case, the numerator is 10 and the denominator is 7. Because you have two parameters to pass to the ActiveX DLL, they are separated by a comma, just as are the variables xnum and yden in the Division function. The code is shown in Figure 5-20.

Once you have completed entering the code, save the Division.asp file. Preview the page in your Browser. You will be able to view the value returned by the Division function in your browser (see Figure 5-21). You should see my 2nd test and immediately under that phrase, the value calculated in the Division function, 1.42857142857143.

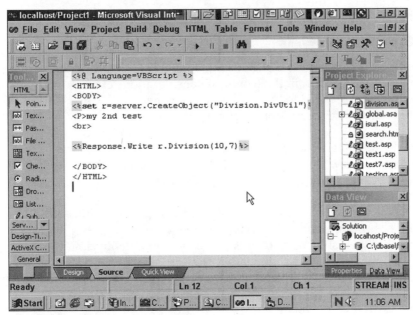

Figure 5-20 *Division.asp Active Server Pages code*

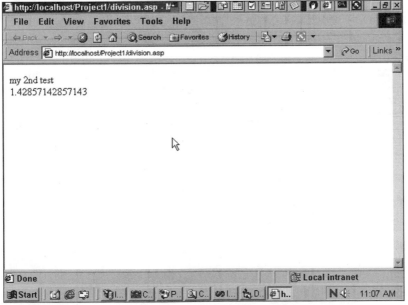

Figure 5-21 *The returned value for the Division function*

Objectives of Component Development

The examples in this tutorial give you a place to start developing server components. Aside from the technical considerations explored only briefly here, you need to be aware of more general objectives that will carry you through the entire development process.

In Visual Basic, it is not difficult to build Component Object Model (COM) components. Without writing code, a programmer can create a new Microsoft ActiveX project. Adding properties and methods is also similarly easy. Not quite so easy is the process of maintaining components and providing versions.

What are your objectives and aspirations in developing and maintaining components? Developing new components as well as maintaining existing components means writing, debugging, modifying, and deploying components that run in business applications. These applications are intended to automate important tasks in businesses. It is costly to redesign these components and even more costly to have them fail.

Because components often need to interact with other components, it is critical to design them with this in mind. The usability and interactivity of components is essential to a large organization.

From the examples in this chapter, you can see how ActiveX COM Objects can be used to carry out calculations and perform other functions that enable you to write powerful Web applications using ASP. Once developed, the COM object is platform independent and can be employed to create dynamic effects.

Visual Basic and Active Server Pages

This chapter covers the areas where Visual Basic and ASP come together. The Component Object Model (COM) is the glue that bridges Visual Basic and ASP. The chapter begins by explaining the relationship between Visual Basic and VBScript. The chapter shows how to create ActiveX controls and documents in Visual Basic. ActiveX data objects are explained as well as the role of Object Linking and Embedding (OLE DB) in uniform data access. A discussion of ASP objects and their functions is also included. Server-side scripting and its relation to Visual Basic is demonstrated and the process of packaging and deploying applications is described and explained.

What is Visual Basic?

Visual Basic is an object oriented, general-purpose language. But it is much more than a Windows migration of MS-DOS versions of the BASIC programming language. As Basic evolved under MS-DOS, it became substantially more sophisticated and developed many more capabilities. Visual Basic began life as a more fully functional language than any version of procedural Basic and has subsequently evolved into an even more complex and varied language.

Elements of Visual Basic

As its name implies, Visual Basic provides you with a visual interface. You are provided with a design window area in which to work. This design window comes complete with a toolbox, toolbars, and menus.

The first thing you do when you launch Visual Basic is either begin a new project or open an existing one. If you have never used Visual Basic, you begin with a new project. When you begin a standard EXE project (a good beginning point), a *form* appears in the design window. It is in this form that you begin your new project, by designing and adding objects to it.

During the process, you use the tools provided on the menus, toolbars, and toolbox. The objects that appear as icons in the ToolBox are called *controls*. These controls can be added to your form to interact with users. The form controls can be buttons to be pressed, picture boxes to display graphics, boxes to hold text user input, lists from which the user can choose items, and many other possibilities.

The first and most important step in the learning process is to master the Integrated Development Environment (IDE). This means becoming familiar with the menus and ToolBox controls. It is worth spending several hours, or even several days, opening and closing windows and dialog boxes, adding new items from the View menu, and checking the properties of different objects you have added to your form. It also means learning about concepts such as *object* and *event*. In previous tutorial chapters (Chapters 2, 4, and 5), you have used VBScript to write some simple scripts, access databases, and create COM objects in Visual Basic.

After you have acquired skill in manipulating the IDE, you will learn about variables, constants, and data types. You will also learn to write procedures, attaching them to forms and modules. You will gain experience in making decisions and selections using code.

Finally, you will gain experience responding to and anticipating events generated by the application and by the application's users. At that point, you will be ready to further enhance your knowledge of forms, menus, and controls.

Visual Basic and VBScript

VBScript is a subset of Visual Basic used primarily to develop applications on the Web. Like Visual Basic, VBScript uses ActiveX and communicates with host applications using ActiveX Scripting. ActiveX Scripting makes it unnecessary for browsers and other host applications to use special integration code for each scripting component.

ActiveX Scripting lets the host manage the namespace available to the developer. Microsoft is working with other groups to define an ActiveX Scripting standard so that scripting engines can be interchangeable. ActiveX Scripting is used in Microsoft Internet Explorer and in Microsoft Internet Information Server.

Scripting an ActiveX Automation Object

ActiveX Scripting is used with HTML to carry out functions beyond what can be done using HTML. Also called an Automation server, an ActiveX component is an application that provides its objects to other applications. You can use any of these objects in a Visual Basic application, but it is not necessary to use Visual Basic to create a simple ActiveX code component to be viewed in a browser.

●—**CROSS-REFERENCE**——————————————————
The ActiveX COM object is covered in Chapter 5 on page 675.

Linking and Embedding Objects

One way to create an ActiveX object to be used on the Internet is to use OLE (Object Linking and Embedding), or Automation. However, you can see how to create a kind of ActiveX object by using the OLE capabilities of Visual Basic. Object Linking and Embedding is the facility that enables you to incorporate components from different programs within an application. Stated in the simplest terms, linking is the act of attaching the objects in an external application. Embedding occurs when you place these objects in a container such as the OLE container.

Though it uses the ActiveX technology, embedding and linking objects from one application to another (OLE) is only one type of ActiveX implementation. Automation enables you to return, edit, and export data by referencing another application's objects, properties, and methods.

In order to construct the example ActiveX object in this exercise, you need to use some type of HTML editor. The editor is a means for you to create your HTML page, which will contain VBScript code for the object's creation. Once completed, the page will be viewed in your Internet browser (Internet Explorer). The page can be placed on the Web or accessed from your PWS (Personal Web Server) or IIS (Internet Information Server).

Editors that you can use run the gamut from Windows NotePad to Visual Interdev 6. Microsoft FrontPage and other Web site construction programs are included in the category of editors. Recent versions of Microsoft Word as well as other word processors often support HTML.

Once you decide on the appropriate editor, you can begin constructing your page. Inside the <HTML> </HTML> tags, place the following code:

```
<HTML>
<HEAD>
</HEAD>
<BODY>
    <SCRIPT LANGUAGE = "vbscript">
```

●─CROSS-REFERENCE

The <HTML> tag is covered in the HTML Reference section on page 350.

The <SCRIPT> language tag lets the browser know that the code immediately following is a script language and, in this case, VBScript. On the next line, declare a new variable:

```
Dim WordApp
```

●─CROSS-REFERENCE

The <SCRIPT> tag is covered in the HTML Reference section on page 370.

Use the Visual Basic CreateObject function with the Word OLE Programmatic Identifier (Word.Application):

```
Set WordApp = CreateObject("Word.Application")
```

Use the GetVersion function to obtain the version of Word running on the machine:

```
GetVersion = WordApp.Version
```

Once the version has been obtained, display it in a message box:

```
MsgBox ("Word Version " & WordApp.version)
</SCRIPT>
</BODY>
</HTML>
```

Select the option on your editor's menu that enables you to view your work in a browser, or whatever action enables you to run

Internet Explorer to view the results. For example, Visual Interdev has a View in Browser option on the View menu; and FrontPage has a Preview panel under the editor window.

When this script is run, the first dialog box to appear is a warning that an ActiveX control is about to run and that it might be unsafe. You have the option of selecting Yes or No to continue as shown in Figure 6-1.

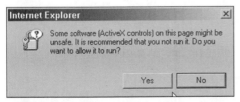

Figure 6-1   *The Internet Explorer ActiveX warning box*

In effect, you have just created an instance of an ActiveX control. Although this object does not require Visual Basic to run (it uses VBScript) and is not a visual control, it is operating. Of course, this script will only function when the client browser is Internet Explorer. As shown in Figure 6-2, you can display the results in a message box to show that the version number is contained in the WordApp.

Figure 6-2   *The VBScript message box displaying the Word Version number*

Next, edit the preceding code by declaring two new variables. This is shown as follows:

```
dim appword
Dim objWord
```

These variables will stand for a Word application and Word document objects, respectively.

Next, use the Visual Basic CreateObject function with the Word OLE Programmatic Identifier (Word.Application or Word.Document):

```
Set objWord = CreateObject("Word.Document")
set appword = Createobject("word.application")
```

Setting the Visible property to True enables you to view the Word session:

```
appword.Visible = true
```

Here, the CreateObject function returns a Word Application object and assigns it to appword. The CreateObject function assigns the Word document object to objWord. Using the objects, properties, and methods of the Word Application object, you can control Word through this variable. Finally, open a copy of a Word file and close the script command block:

```
set objWord = appword.documents.open("c:\word\test.doc")
</script>
```

When this script is run, the file, test.doc, is opened in a Word window, as shown in Figure 6-3.

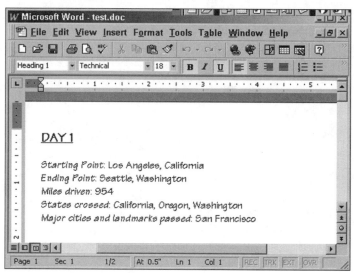

Figure 6-3 *The file test.doc in a separate Word window*

Writing a String Test Function

In addition to OLE Automation, you can create functions that return results. For example, you can write a function that tests a string to see if a particular substring constitutes a legal URL value. If the string contains a possible URL value (www.thiswebsite.com), then the value returned is True; if not, it is False. Because all possible URLs begin with specific characters, you can examine each of those in turn. Table 6-1 describes the commonly used URL protocols on the Internet.

Table 6-1 *Uniform Resource Locator Protocols*

URL Protocol	Description
FILE	Indicates that the file is in the file system of a computer on the network.
FTP	File Transfer Protocol. An Internet client-server protocol for transferring files between computers.
GOPHER	A service that offers access to files and directories on Gopher servers throughout the Internet. The Gopher client presents the individual user with directory lists.
HTTP	Hypertext Transfer Protocol. The Internet protocol that delivers information by way of the World Wide Web. HTTP makes it possible for a user to use a client program to enter a URL, or to click a hyperlink to retrieve text, graphics, sound, and other digital information from a Web server. URLs of files on Web servers begin with `http://`.
HTTPS	The secure Hypertext Transfer Protocol is a communications protocol designed to transfer encrypted information between computers over the World Wide Web. HTTPS is HTTP using a Secure Socket Layer (SSL).
MAILTO	Opens a client's e-mail system.
NEWS	Specifies the full address to a news group.
NNTP	Network News Transfer Protocol. This defines a protocol for the distribution, inquiry, posting, and retrieval of news items between a news server and clients. Messages are stored on a central host server, with clients connecting via a connection stream such as TCP.
TELNET	Telnet is a Windows socket-based application that simplifies TCP/IP terminal emulation with Windows NT. It includes a number of command-line utilities enabling work in a remote character session environment.

The `IsURL` function will parse and test a string to determine if the string begins with the correct syntax for each protocol. First, declare the string variable that will hold the value for the URL:

```
Dim varTemp
varTemp= "http://www.hi-tekmall.com"
```

Next, create the function. The name of the function is `IsURL`, and the value is initially set to True:

```
Function IsURL(varTemp)
  IsURL = True
```

A series of If..Then statements are used to test the string for each possible protocol. The Ucase function is used to covert the string to uppercase, as the comparison string is coded in uppercase. The Left and Trim string functions are used to select only the number of characters needed in varTemp to assess the protocol named in the string:

```
If UCase(Left(Trim(varTemp), 6)) = "HTTP:/" Then Exit Function
If UCase(Left(Trim(varTemp), 6)) = "FILE:/" Then Exit Function
If UCase(Left(Trim(varTemp), 8)) = "MAILTO:/" Then Exit Function
If UCase(Left(Trim(varTemp), 5)) = "FTP:/" Then Exit Function
If UCase(Left(Trim(varTemp), 8)) = "GOPHER:/" Then Exit Function
If UCase(Left(Trim(varTemp), 6)) = "NEWS:/" Then Exit Function
If UCase(Left(Trim(varTemp), 7)) = "HTTPS:/" Then Exit Function
If UCase(Left(Trim(varTemp), 8)) = "TELNET:/" Then Exit Function
If UCase(Left(Trim(varTemp), 6)) = "NNTP:/" Then Exit Function
IsURL = False
```

CROSS-REFERENCE

The Left and Trim functions are covered in the VBScript Reference section on pages 433 and 455, respectively.

Because the number of characters in each protocol differs, a separate If..Then statement is required for each possible protocol. The first six characters are required to test for HTTP:/, but eight are required for MAILTO:/. Finally, if each condition (possible protocol) is tested and all fail the test (exit the function), IsURL is set to False. Thus, False is returned if a match does not cause program execution to exit the function. The function ends and the message box displays True, as the string held in varTemp actually is correct syntax for a URL.

```
End Function
  msgbox ("URL is " & isURL(varTemp))
```

You can try the function using a different, bogus URL and see the result shown in Figure 6-4.

Figure 6-4 *The message box returns the value True because the protocol is valid*

Writing a Conversion Function

The ConvertNull function returns a value based upon string data, makes a substitution of Empty for Null values, and thereby trims leading and trailing spaces from the string. Again, the string is stored in the variable varTemp. This could be a string that is entered in a text box or form field.

```
varTemp = "              between words "
```

Quite a few leading spaces have been inserted before the text in the preceding code in order to demonstrate the change returned by the ConvertNull function.

```
varTemp = "between words    "
Function ConvertNull(varTemp)
    If IsNull(varTemp) Then
        ConvertNull = ""
    Else
        ConvertNull = Trim(varTemp)
    End If
End Function
 msgbox ("There is no space" & varTemp)
```

The text in the varTemp string is passed to the ConvertNull function for processing. The IsNull function causes convertNull to return a null if the string is empty. Otherwise, the text will be trimmed and the function ends. Figure 6-5 shows the message box displaying the words "There is no space" and the string stored by varTemp.

Figure 6-5 *The leading spaces are trimmed from* varTemp

Creating Classes in Visual Basic

The chief difference between classes and standard modules lies in the way the data is stored. There is only one copy of data in a standard module. The advantage of having only one data copy in a standard module is that changing a public variable will result in a correct value for that variable in another part of the application. Conversely, class module data exists separately for each object created from the class. In addition, class module data exists only as long as the life of the object, rather than the life of the program.

In a standard module, public variables are visible throughout your project. However, in a class module, public variables can be used only if there is an object variable that has a reference to the class.

In chapter 5, you created functions in class modules and then accessed the functions from Active Server Pages. Often, for casual Visual Basic users, ActiveX DLL projects seem to differ from standard EXE projects in that standard modules always begin with a form on which to place objects. The code is then attached to the objects on the form. ActiveX DLL projects automatically create a class module. These class modules differ from standard modules in much the same way that ActiveX DLL projects differ from standard EXE projects.

Creating ActiveX Controls in Visual Basic

Visual Basic uses ActiveX code components, documents, and controls. When you create an ActiveX control in Visual Basic, it is often with the intent of placing the control in the Visual Basic Toolbox.

The ToolBox contains an initial set of controls that ships with Visual Basic. You can add more controls from third-party vendors or create new controls on your own and add them to the ToolBox.

The ActiveX controls that you create are just like any other controls in your ToolBox. In fact, once you create one, compile it, and register it, you will see it included in your ToolBox. If you create one or many ActiveX controls and then compile them using Make Control name.ocx on the File menu, all the controls in the project will be compiled into one .OCX file.

When you add controls from the Project Components menu in Visual Basic, you sometimes get a family of controls, and sometimes only one. The Microsoft Common Controls are examples of several controls residing in one .OCX file. The Media Player or Common-Dialog are examples of only one control included in the .OCX file. Thus, you can create multiple ActiveX controls that are related and create one file containing them all.

Some of the ActiveX controls included with Visual Basic (the Professional and Enterprise editions) are as follows: ImageList, Multimedia MCI, PictureClip, ProgressBar, RichTextBox, StatusBar, SysInfo, TabStrip, and Toolbar.

Others can be purchased from vendors who sell ActiveX controls. But the ability to create your own ActiveX controls is a special feature of Visual Basic. There is always some specialized need that only the development of a new control can address. Once you decide on the functions and appearance of your control, you can begin building it. The process begins by selecting ActiveX Control from the New Project dialog box. Then, you can add properties and property procedures and methods to your control.

When you have finished, the resulting file is saved with a .CTL extension. At this point, you can then make the .OCX file. Just as you registered your ActiveX DLL component in Chapter 5, you must register the control with Windows in order to use it in a new project. Once registered, the control is placed on the list of controls in the Components menu on the Project menu.

●—CROSS-REFERENCE

Registering the Active X DLL component is covered in Chapter 5 on page 690.

Creating a control is much the same as creating an ActiveX server component. You can imagine several useful functions, such as a calculator that adds two numbers together, a calculator that subtracts a birth date from today's date to obtain age, a progress bar that performs specific functions, and so on. Making an ActiveX control often means combining other controls with event and procedure code.

In Visual Basic, select a new project, as displayed in Figure 6-6. You can do this by clicking on the File menu or the New icon on the toolbar. In the New Project window, select ActiveX Control. Visual Basic creates a UserControl object, rather than the project and form with which you may be familiar.

Right-click User Control to access the Properties window and name the control CalcContrl. You can leave the project name as Project1 or, in the Project Explorer window, right-click for Properties or select Project Properties from the Project menu and give the project a different name.

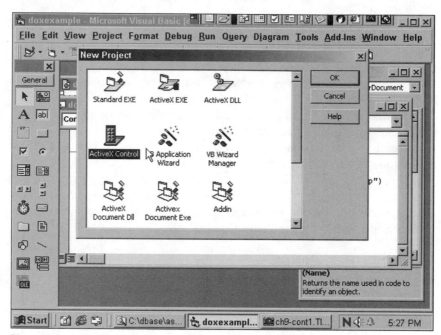

Figure 6-6 *Choosing the ActiveX Control New Project*

Adding Features to the UserControl

At this point, your UserControl object doesn't do anything. To make it do something, you need to add some features.

To add a text box from the ToolBox in the upper left corner of the User Control, double-click the TextBox control in the ToolBox, or click and drag the control onto the User Control object. Add another text box immediately under the first one. Place a label control under the second text box. In the caption area of the label control, place a plus sign. You can enter a caption by typing it in the area to the right of the caption property in the Properties window. Place a third TextBox control under the Label control. Figure 6-7 shows the UserControl with the three text boxes and the label control.

You should now have four controls along the left side of the User Control. Now place a command button to the right of the label control with the plus sign caption. Finally, create a caption on the Command button that displays an equal sign. You place these controls on the User Control as if it were a form. You are going to have this new control display the addition of two numbers entered into each of the first two text boxes when the button is clicked. When you click the button with the equal sign, your browser will fire up and you will see the User Control with the text boxes and the equal and plus signs. When you enter numbers in each of the top text boxes and click the button with the equal sign, the result of the addition of the two numbers will appear in the bottom text box. You have now created a specific function for the `CalcContrl` control.

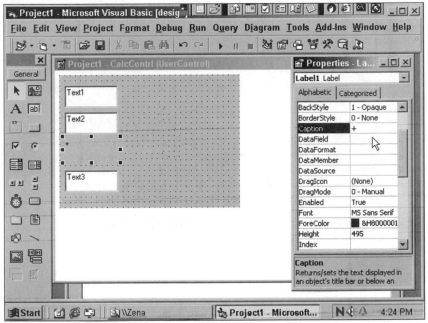

Figure 6-7 *Placing TextBox and Label controls on the UserControl*

You can probably imagine other enhancements for your control. You might add a shape control to present something of interest, or add an image control to display a photo. In addition, you could perform other calculator functions. Figure 6-8 shows the UserControl with the Command button added.

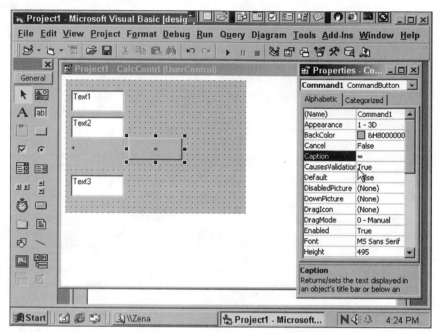

Figure 6-8 *Placing the Command button on the UserControl*

Writing the Code and Testing the Control

Your new ActiveX control has only one procedure, the one that performs the addition of the two numbers entered in the text boxes. You need to attach the code to the Equal button's click procedure, as the button click is the event that triggers the calculation and the display of the result. Double-click the Equal button. In the Command1_Click procedure, enter the following code:

```
Text3.Text = Str(Val(Text1.Text) + Val(Text2.Text))
```

This sets the text in the Text3 control equal to the string of the values entered into the Text1 and Text2 text boxes. That is the only code necessary for this simple control. Because you have not created any form, the default browser will launch when you select Start from the Run menu. You also can test your control by building a form. In this case, you do not need to do that if you have a browser configured. Test your control by running the control and entering numbers in the top text boxes. Click the Equal button to see the result in the bottom text box. In Figure 6-9 you see the UserControl as viewed in the browser.

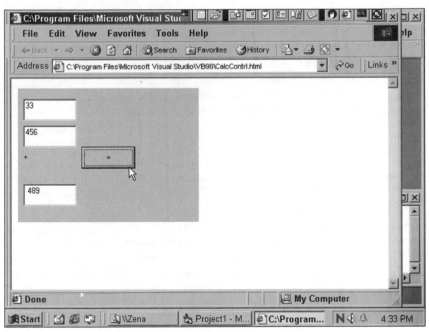

Figure 6-9 *Browsing the UserControl*

Creating ActiveX Documents in Visual Basic

Visual Basic's ActiveX controls and ActiveX documents share some similarities, but they are quite different in other respects. ActiveX documents, like ActiveX controls, must reside in a container object. In spite of these common features, the ActiveX document is more comparable to a form than it is to a control.

Organizing an ActiveX Document

An ActiveX document is organized to include a UserDocument, code, code modules, and the controls that you place on the UserDocument. The UserDocument is like a form in the sense that both are stored in ASCII text files that include source code and the properties of the controls that it contains.

The UserDocument has many of the events found on a Form. Events shared by forms and user documents include: DragDrop, GotFocus, KeyPress, KeyUp, MouseDown, MouseMove, LostFocus, and Click. Activate, Deactivate, LinkClose, LinkError, LinkExecute, LinkOpen, Load, QueryUnload, and Unload are events available on a form but not on a UserDocument. AsyncReadComplete, EnterFocus, ExitFocus, Hide, InitProperties, ReadProperties, Scroll, Show, and WriteProperties events are those available on a UserDocument, but not available for a form.

The .DOB file extension is used by Visual Basic for these files. Bitmaps and other graphic files contained in the UserDocument object are stored separately in files having .DOX extensions.

The .DOB and .DOX files define the properties, events, and methods of the document. The ActiveX document can be compiled into ActiveX, .EXE, or .DLL. ActiveX documents can be built into .EXE or .DLL files. Files with the .EXE extension are know as out-of-process components; whereas, .DLL files are known as in-process components. There also is a file with the .VBD extension, and the browser must navigate to the path of that file.

The .VBD file must be placed in the same directory as the compiled component. Data in the .VBD can be accessed and manipulated via standard OLE interfaces, such as other Microsoft applications.

To help you develop an ActiveX UserDocument, Visual Basic offers the ActiveX Doc Migration Wizard. This wizard will convert a standard EXE project form and controls to an ActiveX UserDocument. This add-in is accessed via the Add-In Manager on the Add-Ins menu.

Once loaded, this wizard will copy the form properties of an existing project to a new UserDocument. It will comment out form code that will not work on the UserDocument. It also will copy the controls from the form. You have the option to create an ActiveX document EXE (out-of-process) project or an ActiveX document DLL (in-process) project. If there is a counterpart to events between the old form and the new UserDocument, the event handlers will be transferred.

Building a UserDocument

You can build a form and then copy the code from the form to work out the differences in events and properties. If you do so, you will have to draw replicas of all the controls on your new UserDocument, as they will not have been copied.

For example, the End command is most likely to be commented out, as UserDocuments terminate, rather than End. The Form_Load procedure is not used with UserDocuments, as there is no form to load. They initialize instead. You can either change the procedure name to UserDocument_Initialize, or add that procedure and call the old Form_Load procedure.

You must not use the ActiveX Doc Migration Wizard to create a new user document on a project that was created as a standard EXE project. If you want to convert a standard project to an ActiveX document, you can either copy the corrected code to the new `UserDocument` object you created or use the Save filename.dob As option to save the converted document in the same directory as your new `UserDocument` object. Figure 6-10 shows the New Project window with the ActiveX Document Dll selected. To create a new document, follow these steps:

Figure 6-10 *Selecting an* `ActiveX` *document Dll in the New Project window*

1. Select the ActiveX Document DLL icon in the New Project window.

2. Select Project Explorer from the View menu.

3. Select the User Document displayed in the Project Explorer window, and then right-click to view the object in the Properties window.

4. To the right of the Name property, rename the document to **Userexample**.

5. Select Properties from the Project menu and overwrite the project name in the Project Name box. Change the name to doxexample as shown in Figure 6-11.

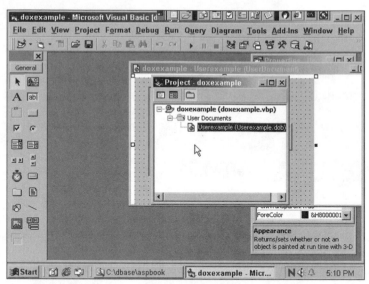

Figure 6-11 *Naming the User Document and Project*

6. Select a PictureBox control and a Command button from the ToolBox and place them on the User Document. Name the caption on the Command button Get Picture" as displayed in Figure 6-12.

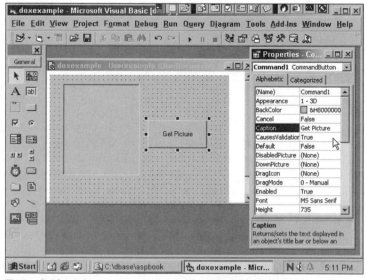

Figure 6-12 *Placing controls on the User Document*

7. Double-click the Get Picture Command button and enter the code shown in Figure 6-13 to enable the click event to load a picture into the PictureBox control.

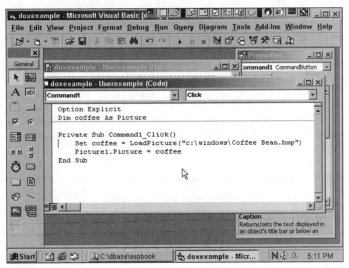

Figure 6-13   *The Command1_Click event code to load a picture*

8. Save the project and test it by selecting Start from the Run menu. When the document is displayed in your browser, click the Get Picture button and view the picture in the PictureBox control displayed in Figure 6-14.

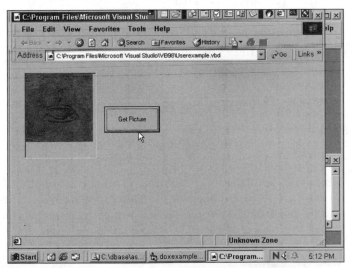

Figure 6-14   *The coffee bean picture shown in the browser*

Data Access in Visual Basic

Multiple data sources are in demand today. Increasingly, SQL data-bases are being used. These databases (such as Oracle and Microsoft SQL Server) are capable of handling huge amounts of data, enabling fast searching. Because not all data exists in one format, an important challenge has been developing engines that enable all kinds of for-mats to be available and easily accessible. Visual Basic has several approaches to data access. The Active Data Object (ADO) is the newest interface, and it simplifies access by using OLE. This enables the ADO to make common forms of data such as e-mail, text, graph-ics, and relational and nonrelational databases (virtually any data source) usable and accessible.

●─CROSS-REFERENCE─────────────────────

The ADO is covered in Chapter 4 on page 611.

The most interesting aspect of ADO is in the development of Internet applications. The ADO data access technology works with OLE DB as the data provider to access both large-scale Internet data-bases and small databases on personal computers.

OLE DB provides uniform access to diverse data and is part of the Component Object Model (COM) interfaces. OLE DB works for multiple environments and types of data storage. OLE DB is a replacement for the ODBC technology that uses specific drivers for each database type. You can determine the drivers installed on your system by clicking the ODBC icon in the Windows Control Panel. These drivers must be used if you access data through the ADO con-trol. The OLE DB data provider accesses data similarly to the older ODBC but enables access to a broader range of data sources.

The COM, Visual Basic, and ASP

As you saw in Chapter 5 the Component Object Model (COM) inter-face is a product of Microsoft object technology. The COM model creates a way for software components to communicate with one another. In fact, COM is a design that provides the foundation for advanced services. Visual Basic is a key development tool and can be used to create cross platform objects that can be accessed via Active Server Pages.

●─CROSS-REFERENCE─────────────────────

COM is covered in Chapter 5 on page 675.

COM

The goal of the COM standard is to allow components to communicate regardless of the hardware, the operating systems, or the language in which the components are written. However, COM technology depends upon the connection between the computers and the operating systems and the languages that support COM. The COM can be seen as a refinement of the Visual Basic model under Active Server Pages.

Visual Basic

As you have seen, Visual Basic provides a number of `ActiveX` controls as part of the standard ToolBox available in the Integrated Development Environment. You can create your own `ActiveX` controls as well. ActiveX and the COM model provide the thread that ties Visual Basic and Active Server Pages together. In Visual Basic, you can create ActiveX objects, including controls that can be run on the Web server as part of ASP.

ASP

ASP scripts run upon the request of a file with a .ASP extension from a browser. The Web server calls ASP. ASP will read the entire file and execute commands. The page is then sent to the browser.

Because the scripts all run directly on the server, rather than on individual browsers, the Web server serves the Web pages to the browser. Thus, it does not matter which browser a client has, as the browser receives the processed page from the server. Standard HTML is returned to the browser. Moreover, because only the results of the process are sent to the browser, users can't see the commands that generated the Web pages they view. ASP use a command-block syntax in which commands are embedded within the less than symbol and percent symbol (<%) to begin the block and the reverse to end the block (%>).

To make effective use of ASP technology, ideally you should put the Web server to work finding information to display in the user's browser. There are many different kinds of tasks. You can invoke other processes from ASP, such as Microsoft Transaction Server components. If you decide to do this, you will need to modify your system's Registry.

Another thing you can do with ASP is to set the values in *cookies*. Cookies are a way of commandeering the user's system to store values that can later be referenced with ASP. Once stored, cookies can be later retrieved from the user's system to provide information about the user. Storage of this information can be helpful to the user as well as to the application. For example, a user might have filled out a form telling the provider about preferences for products available at a Web site. Cookies stored on the client's system enable the user to log on to the site and access data without having to reenter all the original information.

The ASP objects carry out the following functions:

- Request information from the user
- Respond by sending information back to the user
- Control the Internet Information Server (IIS)
- Maintain the user's current session
- Share application information and settings

ActiveX, MAPI, and OLE

ActiveX, Message Application Program Interface (MAPI), and Object Linking and Embedding (OLE) all are technologies built on the COM foundation. You have been exposed to the ActiveX COM model in this chapter, as well as in Chapter 5 and throughout most of the tutorial section. How ActiveX interacts with MAPI and OLE can be found in the following section. MAPI is a messaging service that is used to provide email to users and OLE gives you the ability to incorporate features from a variety of applications into an ActiveX object.

ActiveX

ActiveX is a technology that can be used to create interactive applications. These applications are most valuably applied to the Internet. Because many browsers other than Internet Explorer do not support ActiveX, the method used to work around this lack of support is to execute the applications on the Web server instead of the client's browser. If ActiveX applications are run on the server side, the client's browser is of no consequence in terms of implementing the ActiveX. Of course, the Web server must be Microsoft (NT or Windows 2000). It is much easier, though, to control the server you are using than to control the various browsers all of your clients are using.

MAPI

The Messaging Application Program Interface (MAPI) enables you to write messaging applications, such as mail programs. Visual Basic provides two controls using MAPI: `MAPIMessages` and `MAPISession`. They can be loaded into Visual Basic from (Microsoft MAPI controls) the Controls tab on the Components option on the Visual Basic Project menu.

MAPI provides a set of system components that enable you to connect an e-mail application to MAPI-compliant information services. The MAPI controls are designed to interact with your basic message subsystem. This means that you must install a MAPI-compliant e-mail system such as Microsoft Exchange.

Your Windows\System directory must contain the MAPI DLL files in order to perform MAPI functions. The files installed on most Windows systems are MAPIstub.dll, mapi32x.dll, and mapi32. dll. Windows 2000 adds Mapisp32.exe and Mapisrvr.exe in the Windows\System32 directory, and Mapiu.dll and Mapix.dll in the Windows\System directory. You can check your system to locate these files. Without these files installed correctly, you will not be able to perform `MAPI` functions such as signing on and off. When you `SignOn`, the `SessionID` property returns a value that represents the session handle. This is associated with a messaging session.

The `MAPI` Messages control lets you receive, send, attach, and read messages from your Inbox. The methods attached to these controls include `Compose`, `Copy`, `Delete`, `Fetch`, `Forward`, `Reply`. `ReplyAll`, `Save`, and `Send`. You use the `MAPISession` control to sign in and out of a session. This control will summon the underlying message subsystem on your system.

OLE

Object Linking and Embedding is the facility that enables you to incorporate components from different programs in an application. Stated in the simplest terms, linking is the act of attaching the objects in an external application. Embedding occurs when you place these objects in a container such as the OLE container.

Using the `OLE` container control, you can link or embed objects from any application that supports automation. This includes Microsoft products such as Word and Excel. It also includes Corel products such as Draw and PhotoPaint; MicroGrafx; and many other products as well. You can see what products are supported under Insertable Objects under the Components option on the Project menu. Any products you installed on your system will appear here, and you can select them to be inserted in your applications.

The resulting application using `OLE` is known as *document centered,* because you can import documents from various applications, to be combined and to function together in your new application.

As you learned in the OLE DB section in this chapter, OLE is used to link databases in the newest form of database access technology from Microsoft.

Advantages of ASP and Server-Side Scripting

An IIS (Internet Information Server) application is a Visual Basic application that uses a combination of HTML and compiled Visual Basic code in a dynamic, browser-based application. An IIS application resides on a Web server, where it receives requests from a browser, runs code associated with the requests, and returns responses to the browser.

At its simplest, you can use an IIS application to intercept a user request and return an HTML page to the browser. A few of the things you can do with IIS applications include querying databases, retrieving Web pages, and creating Web page input forms and graphics.

Advantages of ASP

The advantage of ASP is that you can customize your Web pages for each user on the fly. You can arrange to have one type of page for one user and another type of page for a different user. The user types could refer to those with browsers that don't support certain scripting languages, such as VBScript. If the code executes on the Web server instead of the client's browser, then it doesn't matter which browser is accessing the Web site.

Because client-side scripts will not execute in many browsers, there are situations when you cannot rely on detecting the users' browser and programming accordingly. Scripting on the server side enables you to have complete control of the application environment.

A Simple Server-Side Script

You can try out a very simple ASP script by requesting the time on your Personal Web Server or the Internet Information Server. If you have configured your Personal Web Server or if you have Windows 2000 or NT with IIS, you can read and display your system's time and date from your browser. If you have rights to your own domain, you also can run this ASP script from the domain and get the time and date on the remote server. Enter the following code onto an ASP page. That is, enter the code, and then save the page with the .asp extension. Save the page in a folder that is in a virtual directory under the root for your Web server. Then discuss the installation and configuration of the Personal Web Server or IIS. Use any HTML editor or word processor that is capable of saving your work as an HTML file.

●—CROSS-REFERENCE

Chapter 1 (p. 534) covers the installation and configuration of the Personal Web Server and IIS.

```
<HTML>
<HEAD>
<TITLE>Hi There</TITLE>
</HEAD>
<BODY>
<FONT SIZE="4">
<p align="center">Hello </FONT></p>
<h3>It is <% =WeekdayName(Weekday(Date)) %>, <% = Date %>.
</BODY>
</HTML>
```

When you have finished entering and saving the code, you can use the Preview in Browser option to view your page in the browser. You also can launch the browser and type the path of the ASP file you just created. For example, if you have the Personal Web Server installed, you might use http://localhost/welcome.asp. Figure 6-15 shows the result of the ASP code as viewed in the browser.

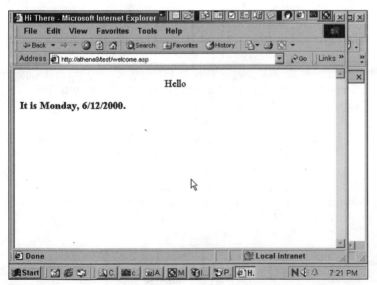

Figure 6-15 *Viewing the Welcome.asp page in the browser*

Packaging and Deploying Applications in Visual Basic

Visual Basic will allow you to package your application using a setup program from which it can be distributed and deployed. Packaging enables you to combine all the necessary files in one package. Deployment is the process a developer goes through to correctly unpack all the files needed by an application and place them in appropriate locations from which they can be used.

When you have finished creating your control, the resulting file is saved with a .CTL extension. At this point, you can then make the .OCX file. The final step is registration. You must register the control with Windows in order to use it in a new project. The registration places the control on the list of Controls in the Components option on the Project menu.

The Package and Deployment Wizard uses the Setup Toolkit at the time your setup program is created. The Setup Toolkit project you create will include all the objects and code that the setup program needs in order to install the files on your user's system. The Setup1.exe file, created by the Package and Deployment Wizard, is your application's major installation file.

The two programs used in the installation process are Setup.exe and Setup1.exe. The Setup.exe program is not modifiable. It carries out specific tasks that include copying the Setup1.exe program as well as the other files required by your application. You can modify the Setup1.exe program via the Setup Toolkit program. It is important to back up the files in the c:\VB98\Wizards\PDWizard\Setup1 directory in case you make changes to any of the files. These are the files used by the Package and Deployment Wizard when you package your applications. Any changes to the Setup1.exe program will be reflected in subsequent programs you package and deploy.

You can modify Setup1.exe by loading the Setup1.vbp project file into Visual Basic. You can then make any changes you want in the way your project looks and functions. This means that you will make the changes in the Setup1.exe file manually, and then compile the Setup1.vbp project into the Setup1.exe file. Finally, you use the Package and Deployment Wizard to do the actual packaging and deploying of your application.

Packaging Your Control

If you are compiling a control, such as the control (CalContrl) in the Project1 project earlier in this chapter, you will compile it into an .OCX file by selecting the Make Project1.ocx from the File menu as shown in

Figure 6-16. Once the OCX file is compiled and registered, you will be able to install it as a component from the Project menu. Thus, it will be available to be installed into the ToolBox and added to your projects.

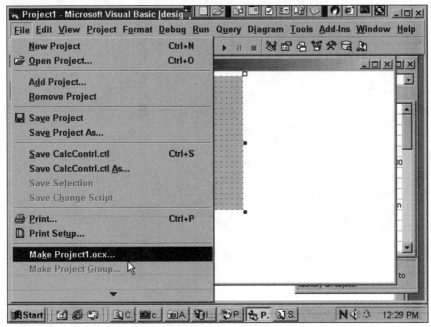

Figure 6-16   *Compiling the CalcContrl Control*

Once you compile the CalcContrl control, you are ready to launch the Package and Deployment Wizard. Select Package and Deployment Wizard from the options on the Add-Ins menu.

Notice that your options are Bundle this project into a distributable package, such as an Internet Cab or setup program; Send one of this project's packages to a distribution site; such as an Internet server; or Rename, duplicate, and delete your packaging and deployment scripts for this project. Select the first option to Bundle this project into a distributable package, such as an Internet cab or a setup program, as shown in Figure 6-17. Next, you can choose a script if you have already created one. If you create a script, you can use it when packaging a later application, and keep the same settings.

Next, you can select the package type. Here you should select the Internet Package as displayed in Figure 6-18. Now choose a directory (folder) in which to assemble your package. If you select the directory where your CalcContrl.ocx file is located, the package will be placed under that in a subdirectory called Package.

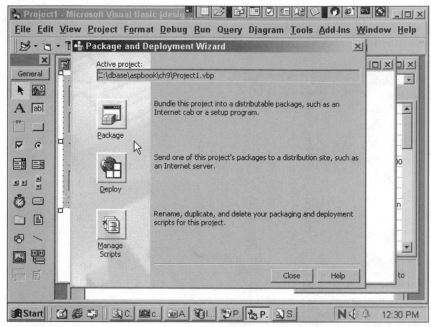

Figure 6-17 *Choosing the Package option*

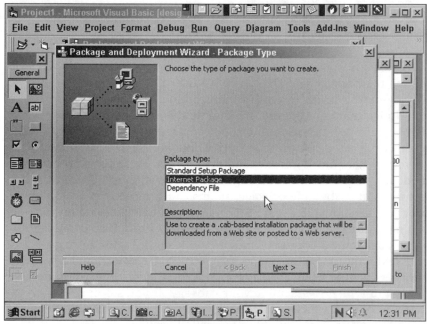

Figure 6-18 *Selecting the Internet Package*

The Included Files List shows the names and locations of each of the files to be included in your package. The executable file you started with when you compiled the project is displayed at the top of the list and selected. Select also MSSTKPRP.DLL and the VB6 Runtime and OLE Automation, as shown in Figure 6-19. If you wish, you can add and remove files from the list by removing the checkmark from the checkbox on the left or by clicking the Add button. If you remove a file with dependencies, you will effectively remove all the files associated with it. You can recheck the box if you inadvertently removed the checkmark.

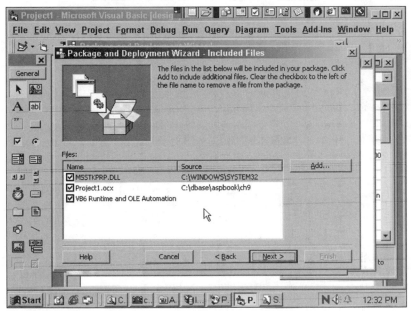

Figure 6-19 *Viewing the Included Files*

The Safety Settings window shown in Figure 6-20 lets you provide information about safety for scripting and initialization. A Yes mark means you claim that the ActiveX object will not harm a user's machine. Once you mark a component safe for scripting, no other component should be able to access code in this object that could change characteristics of files or change system settings. A Yes mark for initializing means that data generated on initialization will not cause the component to modify files or change system settings. Essentially, Yes marks for these items mean that your application won't harm the user's data, programs, or any aspect of the system. In addition, the Cabinet (.CAB) files must be signed in order for these options to have significance.

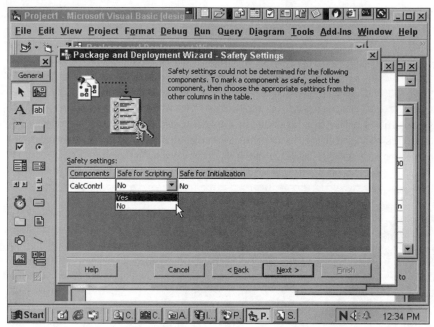

Figure 6-20   *The Safety Settings window*

When you have finished packaging your control, the report will be displayed and you will be prompted to save it.

The .OCX DLL file can contain more than one `ActiveX` control. This simplifies distribution, which may include components downloaded from the Internet. You will need digital signatures to correlate the vendor's name with a particular file. That requires you to provide the vendor name in each control name included.

Deploying the Control

First, decide how you want to deploy the control. Do you want to publish it on the Web or in a local folder (directory)? Select Folder as the place to publish your package.

Open the CalcContrl project. Select Add-In Manager from the Add-Ins menu. Select Package and Deployment Wizard from the Available Add-Ins list. Check the Loaded/Unloaded box under the Load Behavior section. Click OK to close the Add-In Manager. Select Package and Deployment Wizard from the Add-Ins menu. This time, select the `Deploy` option on the first screen. Next, select the Internet Package 1 shown in Figure 6-21 as the package to deploy.

Choose Web Publishing or Folder (in Figure 6-22) as the Deployment method.

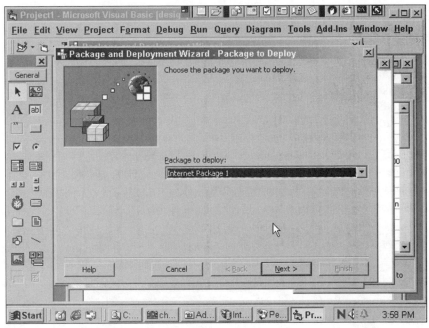

Figure 6-21   *Selecting the package to deploy*

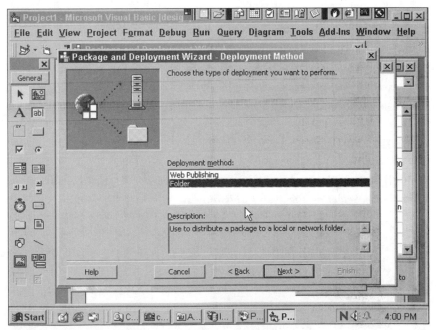

Figure 6-22   *Choosing the Deployment method*

Finish the deployment by accepting the default script name (Folder Deployment 1) in the Finished! window.

When you select the Folder option, your users must copy the files to that same path or the graphics won't be found and an error will be generated. The setup program will not do this. You can place all the files used in your application in the same directory and specify that in the code. All of the files will be deployed in the same directory specified by the user or under the program files directory by default.

You also can deploy to a Web site. Choose Web Publishing instead of Folder as the place to deploy. The next screen has a box where you should enter the destination URL shown in Figure 6-23. A second box allows you to select either HTTP Post or FTP as destinations for the posting.

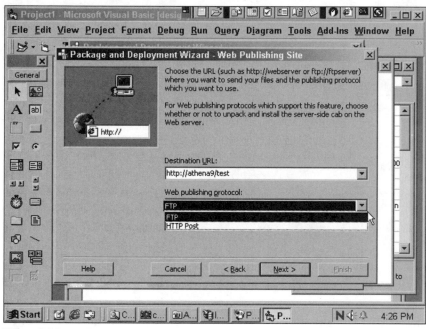

Figure 6-23 *Selecting the Web Publishing site*

Choose FTP and enter the Web site URL, as shown in Figure 6-24. This will be the way most users access the files.

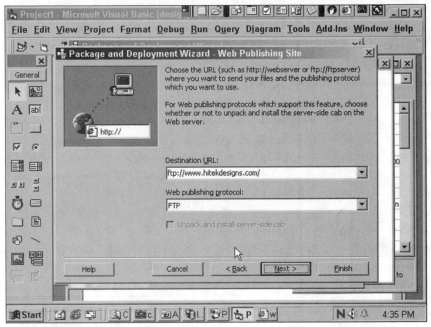

Figure 6-24 *Selecting the FTP site*

After you click the Finish button, you will be prompted to enter your user ID and password for the site. The site can be your personal Web server or an actual Internet site.

Index

A

\<A\> HTML tag, 320–321

Abandon method, Session object, 270, 600

Abs function
  SQL, 470
  VBScript, 400

absolute path name, 129

absolute position, records, 636

Absolute Position method, Recordset object, 208–209

absolute values, numbers, 400, 470

AbsolutePage method, Recordset object, 208, 637

actions, recordsets, 640

ActiveCommand property, Recordset object, 209

ActiveConnection property
  Command object, 49–50, 650
  Record object, 182
  Recordset object, 209

ActiveX, 6, 720
  COM objects
    creating, Visual Basic and, 678–683
    dividing numbers, 693–695
    overview, 676–677
    registering, 690–692
    running, 683–690
    server-side, creating, 675–696
  components, creating, 6
  controls, Visual Basic, 708–713
  documents, in Visual Basic, 713–717

Continued

ActiveX *(continued)*
   organizing, 713–714
   scripting, linking and embedding
      objects, 701–704
   scripts, writing, 6
ActiveX Data Object, 6
ActiveX DLL project, 678–683
ActualSize property, Field object, 100
Add method, Dictionary object, 76–77
AddHeader method, Response object,
   244–245
addition (+) operator, VBScript,
   400–401
AddNew method, Recordset object,
   186–187
< ADDRESS > HTML tag, 322
ADO (ActiveX Data Objects), 534
ADO model, 612–621
ADO object, 611
   Connection object, 612
   DataControl object, 612, 670–671
   DataFactory object, 668–670
   DataSpace object, 612, 670
aggregate functions (SQL), 462
   Count, 480–481
   Max, 511
   Min, 511
   Sum, 522
aliases (SQL), 471–472
Alter Table command (SQL), 471
And connector (SQL), 472–473
And operator, VBScript, 401
Append method, Field object,
   108–109
Append property, Parameter object,
   162

AppendChunk method
   Field object, 98–99
   Parameter object, 156–157
AppendToLog method, Response
   object, 245
< APPLET > HTML tag, 322–323
application building, VBScript and,
   574–575
Application object, 36–41, 596–597
   collections, 603–605
   methods, 601–603
   StaticObjects collection, 607–608
Application.Contents.Remove method,
   Application object, 40, 602
Application.Contents.RemoveAll
   method, Application object, 40,
   603
Application_OnEnd event, 39
Application_OnStart event, 38–39
< AREA > HTML tag, 324
arguments, passing to stored procedures, 47–48
array function, VBScript, 401–402
arrays
   Abs function (VBScript), 400
   Erase statement (VBScript), 415
   global information storage, 605–607
   recordsets, 640–641
Asc function, VBScript, 402–403
ASP (Active Server Pages)
   @index H:advantages, 722–723
   applications, starting, 594–595
   code
      writing with FrontPage, 688–690
      writing with Visual InterDev,
      683–688

editors, 7
syntax, 540-541
ASP objects, 6
AspCode property, 42
AspDescription property, Application
object, 42-43
AspError object, 42-46
AtEndOfLine property, TextStream
object, 307
AtEndOfStream property, TextStream
object, 307-308
Attributes property
Connection object, 65-66
Field object, 100-101
File object, 114-115
Folder object, 145-146
Parameter object, 157
Property object, 164-165
AvailableSpace property, Drive Object,
84-85
averaging values, 473-475
Avg function (SQL), 473-475

B

<B> HTML tag, 324-325
<BASE> HTML tag, 325-326
base names, files, 129-130
<BASEFONT> HTML tag, 326-327
BeginTrans method, Connection object,
57-58
Between clause (SQL), 475-476
<BGSOUND> HTML tag, 327
<BIG> HTML tag, 327-328
binary files, reading, 283-284
BinaryRoad method, Request object,
228-229

BinaryWrite method, Response object,
246
<BLINK> HTML tag, 328
<BLOCKQUOTE> HTML tag,
328-329
<BODY> HTML tag, 329-330
BOF property, Recordset object,
210
bold text, 374
<B> HTML tag, 324-325
Bookmark property, Recordset object,
211
bookmarks, comparing, 190-191

 HTML tag, 330-331
browsers, VBScript support, 570-571
Buffer method, Response object,
250-252
BuildPath method, FileSystem object,
122
<BUTTON> HTML tag, 331
BYOT (Bring Your Own Transactions),
676

C

CacheControl method, Response
object, 252-253
CacheSize method, Recordset object,
211-212
call statement, VBScript, 403
Cancel method
Command object, 47
Connection object, 58-59
Record object, 172-173
Recordset object, 187
Stream object, 277-278
CancelBatch method, Recordset object,
188

CancelUpdate method
  Field object, 108–109
  Recordset object, 188–189
<CAPTION> HTML tag, 332
captions, <LEGEND> HTML tag, 357
categories
  keywords, 10–20
  SQL, 461–464
  VBScript, 393–397, 571–573
Category property, Application object,
  43
Ceiling function (SQL), 476–478
<CENTER> HTML tag, 333
character formatting
  <B> HTML tag, 324–325
  <BASEFONT> HTML tag, 326–327
  <BIG> HTML tag, 327–328
  <CODE> HTML tag, 334
  <EM> HTML tag, 340–341
  <FONT> HTML tag, 342–343
  <KBD> HTML tag, 355
  <PRE> HTML tag, 367–368
  <RT> HTML tag, 368–369
  <RUBY> HTML tag, 369
  <SAMP> HTML tag, 370
  <SMALL> HTML tag, 372–373
  <STRIKE> HTML tag, 374
  <STRONG> HTML tag, 374
  <SUB> HTML tag, 375–376
  <SUP> HTML tag, 376
  <U> HTML tag, 386–387
  <VAR> HTML tag, 388
character sets, HTML, 389–390
Charset method
  Response object, 253
  Stream object, 291–292

Chr function, VBScript, 403–404
<CITE> HTML tag, 333–334
Class object, VBScript, 404
Class statement, VBScript, 404–405
classes
  ActiveX COM objects, 677
  Visual Basic, 707–708
clauses (SQL), 462
  Between, 475–476
  group by, 492–494
  Having, 494–495
  Inner Join, 497–499
  Where, 527–528
  where clauses
    In/Not in, 495–497
    Is Null/Is Not Null, 502–503
    Like/Not Like, 507–510
Clear method
  Response object, 247–248
  VBScript, 405–406
Clear property, Error object, 95–96
client scripting, VBScript and, 573–577
ClientCertificate collection, Request
  object, 225–228
clients, browser, 6
Clone method, Recordset object,
  189–190
Close method
  Connection object, 59–60
  Record object, 173–174
  Recordset object, 190
  Stream object, 278
  TextStream object, 299
<CODE> HTML tag, 334
CodePage property, Session object,
  271–272, 600

<COL> HTML tag, 335
<COLGROUP> HTML tag, 336
collections
    Application object, 603–605
    Connection, 74–76
    Contents, 36–37
    Error, 614, 645–647
    Field, 108–114, 617–618
    Folder, 153–155
    Parameter, 614–615, 653–655
    Property, 170–172, 615, 655–659
    Recordset object
      Properties, 224
    Request object
      ClientCertificate, 225–228
      @index1:Cookies, 230–231
      Form, 231–232, 549–551
      QueryString, 232–234, 546–548
      ServerVariables, 234–241,
        549–553
    Response object, Cookies,
      241–244
    Session object, 603–605
    Contents, 274–275
    StaticObjects, 37–38
    Session object, 275–276
Color constant (VBScript), 406
color (VBScript), RGB function, 445
Column property
    Application object, 43–44
    TextStream object, 308–309
COM+, 676
COM (Component Object Model), 6,
    533
    objects, ADO objects and, 534
    Visual Basic and, 718–720

COM objects
    overview, 676–677
    registering, 6
Command object, 46–56, 647–652
    methods, 614
    properties, 614
commands, executing, 51
commands (SQL)
    Alter Table, 471
    Delete, 482–483
    Drop Index, 483
    Grant, 489–490
    Revoke, 518
    Truncate, 523
    Update, 525–526
CommandText property, Command
    object, 50, 650
    parameter passing, 648–649
CommandTimeout property
    Command object, 51
    Connection object, 66
CommandType property, Command
    object, 51–52, 651–652
CommitTrans method, Connection
    object, 60–61
CompareBookmarks method,
    Recordset object, 190–191
CompareMode property, Dictionary
    object, 81–82
comparison operators, SQL, 462
    greater than (>), 490–491
    greater than or equal to (> =),
      491–492
    less than (<), 505–506
    less than or equal to (< =), 506–507
    Not Equal (< >), 512

component development objects, 696

Component Object Model, 6

components, 542–560

   shipping, 7

concatenation operators

   SQL, 478

   VBScript, 406–407

conditional joins (SQL), 478–480

Connection Collections (Connection

   object), 74–76

Connection object, 6, 56–73

   ADO and, 612

   Connection collections, 74–76

   connections, establishing, 628–629

   methods, 613

   properties, 613

   resources, freeing, 631

   transactions and, 630

connection strings, 622

connections

   Connection object and, 628–629

   creating, 621–622

   databases, creating, 6

   overview, 621–628

ConnectionString property, Connection

   object, 67

ConnectionTimeout property,

   Connection @index1:object, 68

connectors (SQL), And, 472–473

Const statement, VBScript, 407

containers

   < BUTTON > HTML tag, 331

Contents collection

   Application object, 36–37, 603–604

   Session object, 274–275, 604–605

Contents.Remove method, Session

   object, 270–271

Contents.RemoveAll method, Session

   object, 271

ContentType property, Response

   object, 253–254

conversion functions, Visual Basic, 707

Cookies collection

   Request object, 230–231

   Response object, 241–244

Copy method, Folder object, 141–142

CopyFile method, FileSystem object,

   122–123

CopyFolder method, FileSystem object,

   123–124

copying

   directories, 141–142

   files, 122–123

   folders, 123–124

   stream objects, 279–280

CopyRecord method, Record object,

   174–176, 664

CopyTo method, Stream object,

   279–280

Count function (SQL), 480–481

Count property

   Dictionary object, 82–83

   Error object, 95–96

   Field object, 113

   Parameter object, 163–164

   Property object, 171

Create Index (SQL), 381

Create Table (SQL), 481–482

Create View (SQL), 482

CreateFolder method, FileSystem

   object, 124–125

CreateObject function (VBScript), 407–408

CreateObject method, Server object, 259–261

CreateParameter method, Command object, 47–48, 653–654

CreateTextFile method
FileSystem object, 125–126
Folder object, 142–143

cursor types, 634

CursorLocation property
Connection object, 68–69
RecordSet object, 212

CursorType property, Recordset object, 212–213, 635

D

data access in Visual Basic, 718

Data Control Language, 462
Grant command, 489–490
Revoke command, 518

Data Definition Language, 461
Create Index, 481
Create Table, 481–482
Create View, 482
Drop Index command, 483
Drop Table statement, 483
Truncate command, 523

Data Manipulation Language, 461
Delete command, 482–483
Insert statement, 499–500
Select statement, 519
Update command, 525–526

data sources, connecting to
Connection object, 630
overview, 621

databases
connections, creating, 6
retrieving data, 6
tables, joins, 6

DataControl object (ADO), 612, 670–671
methods, 619–620
properties, 619–620

DataFactory Object (ADO), 668–670
methods, 619

DataSpace object (ADO), 612, 670
methods, 620
properties, 620

date and time constants (VBScript), 408–409

Date function, VBScript, 408–409

DateAdd function (VBScript), 408–409

DateCreated property
File object, 115–116
Folder object, 146

DateDiff function (VBScript), 410–411

DateLastAccessed property
File object, 116
Folder object, 146–147

DateLastModified property
File object, 116–117
Folder object, 147

DateSerial function (VBScript), 411

DateValue function (VBScript), 412

Day function (VBScript), 412–413

< DD > HTML tag, 336–337

DDT (Desktop Documents Types), 319

DefaultDatabase property, Connection @index1:object, 69–70

DefinedSize property, Field object, 101

definition lists, 339

Delete command (SQL), 482–483

Delete method
Field object, 110–111
Folder object, 143–144
Parameter object, 162–163
RecordSet object, 191–192

DeleteFile method, FileSystem object, 126

DeleteFolder method, FileSystem object, 126–127

DeleteRecord method, Record object, 176–177, 664

deleting
directories, 143–144
files, 126
folders, 126–127
records from recordsets, 638–639

deploying applications, Visual Basic, 724–731

Description property
Application object, 44
Error object, 92

< DFN > HTML tag, 337

Dictionary object, 76–84
VBScript, 413

Dim statement, VBScript, 413–414

< DIR > HTML tag, 337–338

Direction property, Parameter object, 158

directories
copying, 141–142
deleting, 143–144
parent, 135
paths, adding, 122

dirty reads, 633

Distinct keyword (SQL), 519–521

< DIV > HTML tag, 338–339

dividing numbers with ActiveX COM object, 693–695

Division operator (VBScript), 414

< DL > HTML tag, 339

DLL (Dynamic Link Library), ActiveX DLL project, 678–683

documents, ActiveX, 713–717

Do..Loop statement (VBScript), 414–415

drive names, 131

Drive object, 84–91

Drive property
File object, 117
Folder object, 147–148

DriveLetter property, Drive object, 85

Drives method, Folder object, 153–154

Drives property, FileSystem object, 140

DriveType property, Drive object, 85–86

drop-down list boxes, recordsets and, 643–644

Drop Index command (SQL), 483

Drop Table statement (SQL), 483

DSN (Data Source Name), creating, ODBC and, 622–628

E

EditMode property, Recordset object, 213–214

editors, 7

elements, HTML, 320

< EM > HTML tag, 340–341

< EMBED > HTML tag, 341

emphasized text, 340–341

End method, Response object, 248–249

EOF property, Recordset object, 210–211

EOS property, Stream object, 292–293

Equal (=) operator (SQL), 483–484

Erase statement (VBScript), 415

Err object (VBScript), 415–416

error checking, 6

error codes
  descriptions, 42–43
  line number, 45
  number, 45–46
  returning, 42
  source code, 46

Error collection, 645–647

Error object, 6, 91–97, 645–647
  collections, 614
  methods, 614
  properties, 614

errors
  columns, 43–44
  descriptions, 44, 92
  file names, 44–45

Errors collection, Connection object, 74–75

Eval function (VBScript), 416–417

events
  Application_OnEnd, 39
  Application_OnStart, 38–39
  Session object
    Session_OnEnd, 269–270
    Session_OnStart, 268–269

Except operator (SQL), 484–485

Execute method
  Command object, 48–49, 647
  Server object, 266–267, 556–557

existence of files/folders, 127–128

Exists method, Dictionary object, 76

Exists (SQL subquery), 485–487

Exit statement (VBScript), 417–418

Expires property, Response object, 254

ExpiresAbsolute property, Response object, 255

extension names, files, 132

F

Field object, 97–108, 644–645
  collections, 108–114, 617–618
  methods, 617–618
  properties, 617–618

Fields property, Recordset object, 223–224

<FIELDSET> HTML tag, 342

File object, 114–121

File property, Application object, 44–45

FileExists method, FileSystem object, 127–128

filenames, creating, 125–126

files
  base name, 129–130
  copying, 122–123
  deleting, 126
  existence, 127–128
  extensions, 132
  global.asa, 594–595
  moving, 137
  names, 133–134
  server-side include, 561–566
  temporary, 136–137

Files property, Folder object, 148, 154–155

FileSystem object, 121–140
  VBScript, 418–419

FileSystem property, Drive object, 86–87

Filter function, VBScript, 419

Filter property, Recordset object, 214–215

Find method, RecordSet object, 192–194

flickering text, < BLINK > HTML tag, 328

Floor function (SQL), 487–489

Flush method
  Response object, 249
  Stream object, 290–291

Folder object, 141–153
  collections, 153–155

FolderExists method, FileSystem object, 128

folders
  copying, 123–124
  creating, 124–125
  deleting, 126–127
  existence, 127–128
  moving, 138
  special, 135

Folders property, Folder object, 155

< FONT > HTML tag, 342–343

fonts
  < KBD > HTML tag, 355
  < SMALL > HTML tag, 372–373
  < TT > HTML tag, 386
  < VAR > HTML tag, 388

For...Each statment (VBScript), 419–420

Form collection, Request object, 231–232, 549–551

< FORM > HTML tag, 343–345

FormatCurrency function (VBScript), 421

FormatDateTime function (VBScript), 421–422

FormatNumber function (VBScript), 422

FormatPercent function (VBScript), 423

formatting
  < BUTTON > HTML tag, 331
  character formatting
    < B > HTML tag, 324–325
    < BASEFONT > HTML tag, 326–327
    < BIG > HTML tag, 327–328
    < CODE >, 334
    < EM > tag, 340–341
    < FONT > tag, 342–343
    < KBD > HTML tag, 355
    < PRE > HTML tag, 367–368
    < RT > HTML tag, 368–369
    < RUBY > HTML tag, 369
    < SAMP > HTML tag, 370
    < STRIKE > HTML tag, 374
    < STRONG > HTML tag, 374
    < SUB > HTML tag, 375–376
    < SUP > HTML tag, 376
    < U > HTML tag, 386–387
    < VAR > HTML tag, 388
  < INPUT > HTML tag, 352–354
  < LABEL > HTML tag, 356
  line formatting, 322
    < BLOCKQUOTE > HTML tag, 328–329
    < BR > tag, 330–331
    < CENTER > tag, 333
    < CITE > tag, 333–334

< DFN > tag, 337
< DIV > tag, 338–339
< FIELDSET > tag, 342
< HR > HTML tag, 349–350
< NOBR > HTML tag, 361
< P > HTML tag, 365–366
< SPAN > HTML tag, 373–374
< TT > HTML tag, 386
< WBR > HTML tag, 388–389
< OPTION > HTML tag, 365–366
paragraph formatting, 322
< BR > tag, 330–331
< CENTER > tag, 333
< CITE >, 333–334
< DFN > tag, 337
< DIV > tag, 338–339
< HR > HTML tag, 349–350
< NOBR > HTML tag, 361
< P > HTML tag, 365–366
< SPAN > HTML tag, 373–374
< TT > HTML tag, 386
< WBR > HTML tag, 388–389
< SELECT > HTML tag, 371–372
< TEXTAREA > HTML tag, 380–381
forms, < FORM > HTML tag, 343–345
For...Next statement (VBScript),
420–421
< FRAME > HTML tag, 345–346
frames
< FRAME > tag, 345–346
< FRAMESET > HTML tag,
346–347
< NOFRAMES > HTML tag,
361–362
< FRAMESET > HTML tag, 346–347
FreeSpace property, Drive object, 87

FrontPage, writing ASP code, 688–690
Function statement (VBScript),
423–424
functions
SQL
Abs, 470
aggregate, 462
Avg, 473–475
Ceiling, 476–478
Count, 480–481
Floor, 487–489
Left, 503–504
Length, 504–505
Lower, 510–511
Max, 511
Min, 511
Power, 517–518
Right, 518–519
Sign, 521
Sqrt, 521–522
Substr, 522–523
Sum, 522
Upper, 526–627
VBScript, 563–566
Abs, 400
array function, 401–402
Asc, 402–403
Chr, 403–404
CreateObject, 407–408
Date, 408–409
DateAdd, 408–409
DateDiff, 410–411
DateSerial, 411
DateValue, 412
Day, 412–413

Continued

functions *(continued)*
    Eval, 416–417
    Filter, 419
    FormatCurrency, 421
    FormatDateTime, 421–422
    FormatNumber, 422
    FormatPercent, 423
    GetObject, 424
    Hex, 424–425
    Hour, 425
    InputBox, 426–427
    InStr, 427
    Int, 427
    IsArray, 428–429
    IsEmpty, 429–430
    IsNull, 430
    IsNumeric, 430
    IsObject, 431
    Join, 431–432
    Lbound, 432
    LCase, 432–433
    Left, 433
    Len, 433–434
    LoadPicture, 434
    Log, 434–435
    Mid, 435
    Minute, 435–436
    Month, 436–437
    MonthName, 437
    MsgBox, 437–438
    Now, 438
    Replace, 444
    RGB, 445
    Right, 445–446
    Rnd, 446
    Round, 446–447

    ScriptEngine, 447
    Second, 447–448
    Sgn, 449–450
    Sin, 450
    Space, 450–451
    Sqr, 451
    StrComp, 451–452
    String, 452
    StrReverse, 452–453
    Tan, 454
    Time, 454
    TimeSerial, 454–455
    TimeValue, 455
    Trim, 455–456
    Ubound, 456
    UCase, 456–457
    VarType, 457
    WeekDay, 457–458
    WeekDayName, 458
    Year, 459
  Visual Basic
    conversion, 707
    string test, 704–706

G

GetAbsolutePathName method,
    FileSystem object, 129
GetBaseName method, FileSystem
    object, 129–130
GetChildren method, Record object,
    177, 663–664
GetChunk method, Field object,
    99–100
GetDrive method, FileSystem object,
    130–131
GetDriveName method, FileSystem
    object, 131

GetExtensionName method,
    FileSystem object, 132
GetFile method, FileSystem object,
    132–133
GetFileName method, FileSystem
    object, 133–134
GetFolder method, FileSystem object,
    134
GetLastError method, Server object,
    265–266, 557–559
GetObject function (VBScript), 424
GetParentFolderName method,
    FileSystem object, 135
GetRows method, Recordset object,
    194–195
GetSpecialFolder method, FileSystem
    object, 135–136
GetString method, Recordset object,
    195–196
GetTempName method, FileSystem
    object, 136–137
global information, arrays, 605–607
global.asa files, 594–595
    setup, 6
Grant command (SQL), 489–490
greater than (>) comparison operator
    (SQL), 490–491
greater than or equal to (> =) compari-
    son operator (SQL), 491–492
group by clause (SQL), 492–494

H

Having clause (SQL), 494–495
< HEAD > HTML tag, 347–348
headers
    creating, 244–245
    < Hn > HTML tags, 348–349

    tables, 381–382
    < TITLE > HTML tag, 384
Hex function (VBScript), 424–425
history list, VBScript, 579–581
< Hn > HTML tags, 348–349
Hour function (VBScript), 425
< HR > HTML tag, 349–350
< HTML > HTML tag, 350
HTML (Hypertext Markup Language),
    6
    categories, 313–317
    character sets, 389–390
    documents
        VBScript, 6
        VBScript integration and,
        575–577
    elements, 320
    forms, 6
    links, 320–321
    pages, displaying recordsets,
        641–642
    reference, 313–390
    tags, 313–317
HTMLEncode method, Server object,
    261

I

< I > HTML tag, 350–351
If...Then...Else statement (VBScript),
    425–426
IIS (Internet Information Server), 6
    installation, 6, 534–539
        VBScript and, 584–586
    PWS and, 534
    Windows 2000 Server, 538–539
    Windows NT 4.0 Option Pack,
        535–538

images
    < APPLET > HTML tag, 322–323
    < AREA > HTML tag, 324
    < BGSOUND > HTML tag, 327
    < EMBED > HTML tag, 341
    < IMG > HTML tag, 351–352
    < MAP > HTML tag, 359
    < OBJECT > HTML tag, 362–364
    < PARAM > HTML tag, 367
    < SCRIPT > HTML tag, 370–371
< IMG > HTML tag, 351–352
In/Not In where clause (SQL), 495–497
Index property, Recordset object, 215
indexes, Create Index (SQL), 381
Inherited property, Property object,
    165–166
Inner Join clause (SQL), 497–499
< INPUT > HTML tag, 352–354
InputBox function (VBScript), 426–427
Insert statement (SQL), 499–500
installation
    IIS, 6, 534–539
        VBScript and, 584–586
        Windows 98, 534–535
    PWS, 6
        VBScript and, 582–584
InStr function (VBScript), 427
Int function (VBScript), 427
Intersect operator (SQL), 500–502
Is Null/Is Not Null where clause (SQL),
    502–503
Is operator (VBScript), 428
IsArray function (VBScript), 428–429
IsClientConnected property, Response
    object, 255–256
IsEmpty function (VBScript), 429–430

< ISINDEX > HTML tag, 354–355
IsNull function (VBScript), 430
IsNumeric function (VBScript), 430
ISO Latin-1 Character Set, HTML,
    389–390
IsObject function (VBScript), 431
isolation, 632–633
IsolationLevel property
    Connection object, 70
    Recordset object, 635
IsReady property, Drive object, 87–88
IsRootFolder property, Folder object,
    148–149
italic text, < I > HTML tag, 350–351
Item property
    Dictionary object, 83
    Error object, 97
    Field object, 113–114
    Property object, 171–172
Items method, Dictionary object,
    78–79

J

Join function (VBScript), 431–432
joins (SQL), 6, 462
    conditional, 478–480
    Inner Join clause, 497–499
    outer joins, 514–517

K

< KBD > HTML tag, 355
Key property, Dictionary object, 84
Keys method, Dictionary object, 79–80
keywords
    categories, 10–20
    Distinct (SQL), 519–521
    Nothing (VBScript), 438–439

L

< LABEL > HTML tag, 356
Lbound function (VBScript), 432
LCase function (VBScript), 432–433
LCID property, Session object, 272–273, 600
Left function
    SQL, 503–504
    VBScript, 433
< LEGEND > HTML tag, 357
Len function (VBScript), 433–434
Length function (SQL), 504–505
less than (<) operator (SQL), 505–506
less than or equal to (< =) operator (SQL), 506–507
< LI > HTML tag, 357–358
Like/Not Like where clause (SQL), 507–510
line breaks, <NOBR>, 361
line formatting, HTML, 322
    < BLOCKQUOTE > tag, 328–329
    < BR > tag, 330–331
    < CENTER > HTML tag, 333
    < CITE > tag, 333–334
    < DFN > tag, 337
    < DIV > HTML tag, 338–339
    < FIELDSET > tag, 342
    < HR > HTML tag, 349–350
    < NOBR > HTML tag, 361
    < P > HTML tag, 365–366
    < SPAN > HTML tag, 373–374
    < TT > HTML tag, 386
    < WBR > HTML tag, 388–389

line numbers, error codes, 45
Line property
    Application object, 45
    TextStream object, 309
LineSeparator property, Stream object, 293
< LINK > HTML tag, 358
linking/embedding, ActiveX scripting and, 701–704
links, HTML, 320–321
list boxes, recordsets, 643–644
lists
    < DD > HTML tag, 336–337
    definition lists, 339
    < DIR > HTML tag, 337–338
    < DL > HTML tag, 339
    < LI > HTML tag, 357–358
    < MENU > HTML tag, 360
    < OL > HTML tag, 364
    < UL > HTML tag, 387–388
LoadFromFile method, Stream object, 280–281
LoadPicture function (VBScript), 434
Lock method, Application object, 41, 601–602
locking, 633
LockType property, Recordset object, 216, 635
log files, messages, 245
Log function (VBScript), 434–435
logarithms, 434–435
logical connectors (SQL), 462
    Not, 511–512
    Or, 512–513
Lower function (SQL), 510–511

M

main tags (HTML)

<BODY>, 329-330

<HEAD> tag, 347-348

<HTML> tag, 350

<ISINDEX> tag, 354-355

<LINK>, 358

<META> tag, 360-361

<MAP> HTML tag, 359

MAPI (Messaging Application Program
Interface), 720-721

MapPath method, Server object,
261-262

MarshalOptions property, Recordset
object, 216-217

Max function (SQL), 511

MaxRecords property, Recordset
object, 217

MDI (Multiple Document Interface),
571

media

<APPLET> HTML tag, 322-323

<AREA> HTML tag, 324

<BGSOUND> HTML tag, 327

<EMBED> HTML tag, 341

<IMG> HTML tag, 351-352

<MAP> HTML tag, 359

<OBJECT> HTML tag, 362-364

<PARAM> HTML tag, 367

<SCRIPT> HTML tag, 370-371

<MENU> HTML tag, 360

<META> HTML tag, 360-361

methods

Applications object

Application.Contents.Remove, 40,
602

Application.Contents.RemoveAll,
40, 603

Lock, 601-602

UnLock, 601

calls, canceling, 47

Command object, 614

Cancel, 47

CreateParameter, 47-48, 653-654

Execute, 48-49, 647

Connection object, 613

BeginTrans, 57-58

Cancel, 58-59

Close, 58-59

CommitTrans, 60-61

Open, 61-63

OpenSchema, 63-64

RollbackTrans, 64-65

DataControl object (ADO), 619-620

DataFactory Object (ADO), 619

DataSpace object (ADO), 620

Dictionary object

Add, 76-77

Exists, 76

Items, 78-79

Keys, 79-80

Remove, 80-81

RemoveAll, 81

Error object, 614

Refresh, 96-97

Field object, 617-618

Append, 108-109

AppendChunk, 98-99

CancelUpdate, 108-109

Delete, 110-111

GetChunk, 99-100

Refresh, 111

Resync, 111–112
Update, 112–113
FileSystem object
BuildPath, 122
CopyFile, 122–123
CopyFolder, 123–124
CreateFolder, 124–125
CreateTextFile, 125–126
DeleteFile, 126
DeleteFolder, 126–127
FileExists, 127–128
FolderExists, 128
GetAbsolutePathName, 129
GetBaseName, 129–130
GetDrive, 130–131
GetDriveName, 131
GetExtensionName, 132
GetFile, 132–133
GetFileName, 133–134
GetFolder, 134
GetParentFolderName, 135
GetSpecialFolder, 135–136
GetTempName, 136–137
MoveFile, 137
MoveFolder, 138
OpenTextFile, 139–140
Folder object
Copy, 141–142
CreateTextFile, 142–143
Delete, 143–144
Drives, 153–154
Move, 144
Lock, 41
Parameter object, 614–615
AppendChunk, 156–157
Delete, 162–163

Refresh, 163
Property object, 615
Refresh, 170–171
Record object, 618–619
Cancel, 172–173
Close, 173–174
CopyRecord, 174–176, 664
DeleteRecord, 176–177, 664
GetChildren, 177, 663–664
MoveRecord, 177–179, 664
Open, 179–182
RecordSet object, 615–617
AbsolutePage, 208, 637
AbsolutePosition, 208–209
AddNew, 186–187
CacheSize, 211–212
Cancel, 187
CancelBatch, 188
CancelUpdate, 188–189
Clone, 189–190
Close, 190
CompareBookmarks, 190–191
Delete, 191–192
Find, 192–194
GetRows, 194–195
GetString, 195–196
Move, 197
MoveFirst, 197–198
MoveLast, 198
MoveNext, 198–199
MovePrevious, 199
NextRecordSet, 199–200
Open, 201–202
Requery, 202–203, 639
Resync, 203, 639

Continued

methods *(continued)*
  Save, 204
  Supports, 205
  Update, 206
  UpdateBatch, 207
  Request object, BinaryRoad,
    228–229
  Response object
    AppendToLog, 245
    BinaryWrite, 246–247
    Buffer, 250–252
    CacheControl, 252–253
    Charset, 253
    Clear, 247–248
    Flush, 249
    Redirect, 249–250, 544
    Response.ContentType, 544–546
    Write, 250, 543
  Server object
    CreateObject, 259–261
    Execute, 266–267, 556–557
    GetLastError, 265–266, 557–559
    HTMLEncode, 261
    MapPath, 261–262
    Transfer, 264–265, 554–556
    URLEncode, 263
  Session object
    Abandon, 270, 600
    Contents.Remove, 270–271
    Contents.RemoveAll, 271
    Session.Contents.Remove,
      600–601
  Stream object, 620–621
    Cancel, 277–278
    Charset, 291–292
    Close, 278

    CopyTo, 279–280
    Flush, 290–291
    LoadFromFile, 280–281
    Open, 281–283
    Read, 283–284
    ReadText, 284–285
    SaveToFile, 285–286
    SetEOS, 286
    SkipLine, 287–288
    Write, 288–289
    WriteText, 289–290
  TextStream object
    Close, 299
    Read, 299–300
    ReadAll, 300–301
    ReadLine, 301–302
    Skip, 302–303
    SkipLine, 303
    Write, 304
    WriteBlankLines, 306–307
    WriteLine, 305
  Unlock, 41
  VBScript
    Clear, 405–406
    Raise, 442–443
Mid function (VBScript), 435
Min function (SQL), 511
Minute function (VBScript), 435–436
MMC (Microsoft Management
    Console), 537
Mod operator (VBScript), 436
Mode property
  Connection object, 70–71
  Record object, 182–183
  Stream object, 293–294
Month function (VBScript), 436–437

MonthName function (VBScript), 437

Move method
  Folder object, 144
  Recordset object, 197

MoveFile method, FileSystem object, 137

MoveFirst method, Recordset object, 197–198

MoveFolder method, FileSystem object, 138

MoveLast method, Recordset object, 198

MoveNext method, Recordset object, 198–199

MovePrevious method, Recordset object, 199

MoveRecord method, Record object, 177–179, 664

moving
  files, 137
  folders, 138

MsgBox function (VBScript), 437–438

N

Name property
  Command object, 52
  Field object, 102
  File object, 117–118
  Folder object, 149
  Parameter object, 159
  Property object, 166–167

NativeError property, Error object, 92–93

navigating recordsets, 636–638

Netscape Navigator plug-ins, 570

NextRecordSet method, Recordset object, 199–200

< NOBR > HTML tag, 361

< NOFRAMES > HTML tag, 361–362

Not Equal (< >) operator (SQL), 512

Not logical connector (SQL), 511–512

Not operator (VBScript), 438

Nothing keyword (VBScript), 438–439

Now function (VBScript), 438

Number property
  Application object, 45–46
  Error object, 93
  VBScript, 439

numbers
  absolute value, 400
  dividing with ActiveX COM object, 693–695
  logarithms, 434–435
  random, 446
  rounding, 446–447, 476–478
  sign, 449–450
  square root, 451

numeric functions (SQL)
  Power, 517–518
  Sign, 521
  Sqrt, 521–522

numeric values, precision, 159–160

NumericScale property
  Field object, 102–103
  Parameter object, 159

O

< OBJECT > HTML tag, 362–364

objects
  ActiveX COM objects, 677
  ActiveX Data Object, 6
  Application, 36–41, 596–597
  ASP, 6

Continued

objects *(continued)*
   AspError, 42–46
   COM, registering, 6
   Command, 46–56
   Component Object Model, 6
   Connection, 6
   creating, 560
   Dictionary, VBScript, 413
   Error, 6, 91–97
   File, 114–121
   FileSystemObject, 121–140
     VBScript, 418–419
   Folder, 141–153
   Parameter, 156–164
   Property, 164–172
   Record, 172–186
   recordset, 6
   Recordset object, 186–224
   Request, 224–241
   request, 6
   Response, 241–259, 543–546
   response, 6
   Server, 259–268
   server-side, 559–560
   Session, 6, 268–276, 597–599
   Stream, 276–298
   TextStream, 298–309
   VBScript
     Class, 404
     Err, 415–416
ODBC Data Connection, 6
   DSN and, 622–628
< OL > HTML tag, 364
OLE DB, 612
OLE (Object Linking and Embedding),
   571, 721–722

On Error Resume Next statement
   (VBScript), 439–440
Open method
   Connection object, 61–63
   Record object, 179–182
     arguments, 660–661
   Recordset object, 201–202
   Stream object, 281–283
     arguments, 665–666
opening recordsets, 190, 201–202
OpenSchema method, Connection
   object, 63–64
OpenTextFile method, FileSystem
   object, 139–140
operators
   comparison (SQL), 462
     greater than (>), 490–491
     greater than or equal to (> =),
     491–492
   concatenation (VBScript), 406–407
   relational (SQL), 462
     Union, 523–525
   SQL
     concatenation, 478
     Equal (=), 483–484
     Except, 484–485
     Intersect, 500–502
     less than (<), 505–506
     less than or equal to (< =),
     506–507
     Not Equal (< >), 512
     Order by, 513–514
   VBScript
     addition (+), 400–401
     Division, 414
     Is, 428

Mod, 436

Not, 438

Or, 441

Subtraction, 453–454

Xor, 459

and (VBScript), 401

Option Explicit option (VBScript),
440–441

< OPTION > HTML tag, 365–366

options (VBScript)

Option Explicit, 440–441

Or logical connector (SQL), 512–513

Or operator (VBScript), 441

Order by relational operator (SQL),
513–514

OriginalValue property, Field object,
103

outer joins (SQL), 514–517

P

< P > HTML tag, 365–366

page breaks, < BR > HTML tag,
330–331

PageCount property, Recordset object,
218

PageSize property, Recordset object,
218–219, 637

paragraph formatting, HTML, 322

< BLOCKQUOTE > tag, 328–329

< BR > tag, 330–331

< CENTER > HTML tag, 333

< CITE > tag, 333–334

< DFN > tag, 337

< DIV > tag, 338–339

< FIELDSET > tag, 342

< HR > HTML tag, 349–350

< NOBR > HTML tag, 361

< P > HTML tag, 365–366

< SPAN > HTML tag, 373–374

< TT > HTML tag, 386

< WBR > HTML tag, 388–389

< PARAM > HTML tag, 367

Parameter collection, 653–655

Parameter object, 156–164, 653–655

collections, 614–615

methods, 614–615

properties, 614–615

parameter_array argument, 649

parameters, passing to stored procedures, 46–56, 648–649

Parameters collection, Command
object, 53–56

parent directories, name, 135

ParentFolder property

File object, 118

Folder object, 150

ParentURL property, Record object,
183

Path property

Drive object, 88

File object, 119

Folder object, 150–151

paths

absolute path name, 129

adding, 122

phantom records, 633

PICS (Platform for Internet Content
Selection), 257–259

PICS property, Response object,
257–259

plug-ins, Netscape Navigator and,
570

pointers, recordsets, 197, 636–638

Position property, Stream object,
  294–295
Power function (SQL), 517–518
< PRE > HTML tag, 367–368
Precision property
  Field object, 103–104
  Parameter object, 159–160
Prepared property, Command object,
  52–53
Private statement (VBScript), 441–442
procedures
  control, 403
  VBScript, Sub statement, 453
processing transactions, 6
properties
  Application object
    AspCode, 42
    AspDescription, 42–43
    Category, 43
    Column, 43–44
    Description, 44
    File, 44–45
    Line, 45
    Number, 45–46
    Source, 46
  Command object, 614
    ActiveConnection, 49–50, 650
    CommandText, 50
    CommandText property, 650
    CommandTimeout, 51
    CommandType, 51–52, 651–652
    Name, 52
    Prepared, 52–53
    State, 53
  Connection object, 70–71, 613
    Attributes, 65–66

CommandTimeout, 66
ConnectionString, 67
ConnectionTimeout, 68
CursorLocation, 68–69
DefaultDatabase, 69–70
IsolationLevel, 70
Provider, 72
State, 72–73
Version, 73
DataControl object (ADO), 619–620
DataSpace object (ADO), 620
Dictionary object
  CompareMode, 81–82
  Count, 82–83
  Item, 83
  Key, 84
Drive object
  Available Space, 84–85
  DriveLetter, 85
  DriveType, 85–86
  FileSystem, 86–87
  FreeSpace, 87
  IsReady, 87–88
  Path, 88
  RootFolder, 89
  SerialNumber, 89–90
  ShareName, 89–90
  TotalSize, 90–91
  VolumeName, 91
Error object
  Clear, 95–96
  Count, 95–96
  Description, 92
  Item, 97
  NativeError, 92–93
  Number, 93

Source, 94
SQLState, 94–95
Error object (ADO), 614
Field object, 617–618
　ActualSize, 100
　Attributes, 100–101
　Count, 113
　DefinedSize, 101
　Item, 113–114
　Name, 102
　NumericScale, 102–103
　OriginalValue, 103
　Precision, 103–104
　Status, 104–105
　Type, 105–106
　UnderlyingValue, 106–107
　Value, 107–108
File object
　Attributes, 114–115
　DateCreated, 115–116
　DateLastAccessed, 116
　DateLastModified, 116–117
　Drive, 117
　Name, 117–118
　ParentFolder, 118
　Path, 119
　ShortName, 119–120
　ShortPath, 120
　Size, 120–121
　Type, 121
FileSystem object
　Drives, 140
Folder object
　Attributes, 145–146
　DateCreated, 146
　DateLastAccessed, 146–147

DateLastModified, 147
Drive, 147–148
Files, 148, 154–155
Folders, 155
IsRootFolder, 148–149
Name, 149
ParentFolder, 150
Path, 150–151
ShortName, 151
Size, 151–152
SubFolders, 152
Type, 152–153
IsolationLevel, 635
Parameter object, 614–615
　Append, 162
　Attributes, 157
　Count, 163–164
　Direction, 158
　Name, 159
　NumericScale, 159
　Precision, 159–160
　Size, 160–161
　Type, 161
　Value, 162
Property object, 615
　Attributes, 164–165
　Count, 171
　Inherited, 165–166
　Item, 171–172
　Name, 166–167
　Type, 167–168
　Value, 168–169
Record object, 618
　ActiveConnection, 182
　Mode, 182–183

Continued

properties *(continued)*
ParentURL, 183
RecordType, 184
Source, 184–185
State, 185–186
RecordSet object, 615–617
ActiveCommand, 209
ActiveConnection, 209
BOF, 210
Bookmark, 211
CursorLocation, 212
CursorType, 212–213
EditMode, 213–214
EOF, 210–211
Fields, 223–224
Filter, 214–215
Index, 215
LockType, 216
MarshalOptions, 216–217
MaxRecords, 217
PageCount, 218
PageSize, 218–219, 637
RecordCount, 219
Source, 220
State, 221
Status, 222
StayinSync, 223
Request object
TotalBytes, 229
Response object
ContentType, 253–254
Expires, 254
ExpiresAbsolute, 255
IsClientConnected,
255–256
PICS, 257–259
Status, 256–257

Server object
ScriptTimeout, 267–268
Session object
CodePage, 271–272, 600
LCID, 272–273, 600
SessionID, 273, 599
TimeOut, 600
Timeout, 274
Stream object, 620–621
EOS, 292–293
LineSeparator, 293
Mode, 293–294
Position, 294–295
State, 296–298
Type, 298
TextStream object, 309
AtEndOfLine, 307
AtEndOfStream, 307–308
Column, 308–309
users, on-the-fly setup, 6
VBScript, Number, 439
Properties collection
Command object, 54–56
Connection object, 75–76
Recordset object, 224
Property collection, 655–659
Property object, 164–172, 655–659
collections, 615
methods, 615
properties, 615
Provider property, Connection object,
72
Public statement (VBScript), 442
PWS (Personal Web Server). *See* PWS
IIS and, 534
installation, 6
VBScript and, 582–584

Q

queries, 6
queries (SQL)
    subqueries, 462, 468–470
        Exists, 485–487
QueryString collection , Request
        object, 232–234, 546–548

R

Raise method, VBScript, 442–443
random numbers, 446
    server-side scripting and, 586–590
Randomize statement (VBScript),
        443–444
RDS (Remote Data Services), 667–672
    DataControl object, 670–671
    DataFactory object, 668–670
    DataSpace object, 670
    references, 671–672
Read method
    Stream object, 283–284
    TextStream object, 299–300
ReadAll method, TextStream object,
        300–301
ReadLine method, TextStream object,
        301–302
ReadText method, Stream object,
        284–285
Record object, 172–186, 659–664
    methods, 618–619
    properties, 618–619
RecordCount property, Recordset
        object, 219
recordpointer, moving, 636–638
RecordSet object, 6, 186–224,
        631–644
    creating, 631–632

methods, 615–617
    properties, 615–617
recordsets, 631
    actions, status, 640
    arrays, 640–641
    beginning, 636
    changes, reviewing, 639
    drop-down list boxes, 643–644
    duplicating, 189–190
    end, 636
    HTML pages, 641–642
    navigating, 636–638
    opening, 190, 201–202
    pointer, moving, 197, 636–638
    records
        adding, 638–639
        deleting, 191–192, 638–639
        updating, 638–639
    rows, new, 186–187
    saving, to file, 204
RecordType property, Record object,
        184
ReDim statement (VBScript), 444
Redirect method, Response object,
        249–250, 544
Refresh method
    Error object, 96–97
    Field object, 111
    Parameter object, 163
    Property object, 170–171
registering ActiveX COM object,
        690–692
RegSrv32.DLL, 6
relational operators (SQL), 462
    Order by, 513–514
    Union, 523–525

Remove method, Dictionary object, 80–81

RemoveAll method, Dictionary object, 81

Replace function (VBScript), 444

Requery method, Recordset object, 202–203, 639

Request object, 6, 224–241, 546–554

resources, freeing with Connection object, 631

Response object, 6, 241–259, 543–546

Response.ContentType method, Response object

Excel spreadsheets and, 544–546

Resync method

Field object, 111–112

Recordset object, 203, 639

Revoke command (SQL), 518

RGB function (VBScript), 445

Right function

SQL, 518–519

VBScript, 445–446

Rnd functionVBScript, 446

RollbackTrans method, Connection object, 64–65

RootFolder property, Drive object, 89

Round function (VBScript), 446–447

rounding numbers, 446–447, 476–478

rows, recordsets, 186–187

RSACI (Recreational Software Advisory Council on the Internet, 257–259

< RT > HTML tag, 368–369

< RUBY > HTML tag, 369

S

< SAMP > HTML tag, 370

Save method, Recordset object, 204

SaveToFile method, Stream object, 285–286

saving recordsets to file, 204

< SCRIPT > HTML tag, 370–371

ScriptEngine function (VBScript), 447

scripting

ActiveX

linking and embedding, 701–704

writing, 6

client scripting, VBScript, 573–577

server-side, 6

VBScript and, 586–590

ScriptTimeout property, Server object, 267–268

Second function (VBScript), 447–448

Select Case statement (VBScript), 448–449

< SELECT > HTML tag, 371–372

Select statement (SQL), 519

SerialNumber property, Drive object, 89–90

server information, requesting, 589–590

server installation

IIS, 6

PWS, 6

Server object, 259–268, 554–560

server-side ActiveX COM objects, 675–696

server-side includes, files, 561–566

server-side objects, 559–560

server-side scripting, 6, 722–723

VBScript and, 586–590

ServerVariables collection, Request object, 234–241, 549–553

Session object, 6, 268–276, 597–599
    collections, 604–605
    properties, 599–601
        SessionID, 599
        StaticObjects collection,
            608–609
Session.Contents.Remove method,
    Session object, 600–601
Session.Contents.RemoveAll method,
    Session object, 601
SessionID property, Session object,
    273, 599
Session_OnEnd event, Session object,
    269–270
Session_OnStart event, Session object,
    268–269
Set statement (VBScript), 449
SetEOS method, Stream object, 286
Sgn function (VBScript), 449–450
ShareName property, Drive object,
    89–90
ShortName property
    File object, 119–120
    Folder object, 151
ShortPath property, File object,
    120
Sign function (SQL), 521
Sin function (VBScript), 450
sine, 450
Size property
    File object, 120–121
    Folder object, 151–152
    Parameter object, 160–161
    Stream object, 295–296
Skip method, TextStream object,
    302–303

SkipLine method
    Stream object, 287–288
    TextStream object, 303
<SMALL> HTML tag, 372–373
sound
    <APPLET> HTML tag, 322–323
    <AREA> HTML tag, 324
    <BGSOUND> HTML tag, 327
    <EMBED> HTML tag, 341
    <IMG> HTML tag, 351–352
    <MAP> HTML tag, 359
    <OBJECT> HTML tag, 362–364
    <PARAM> HTML tag, 367
    <SCRIPT> HTML tag, 370–371
Source property
    Application object, 46
    Error object, 94
    Record object, 184–185
    Recordset object, 220
Space function (VBScript), 450–451
<SPAN> HTML tag, 373–374
special folders, 135
SQL Server, stored procedures, 652
SQL (Structured Query Language), 6
    categories, 461–464
    commands (See commands (SQL))
    comparison operators, 462
    Create Index, 481
    Create Table, 481–482
    Create View, 482
    Data Control Language
        Grant command, 489–490
        Revoke, 518
    Data Definition Language
        Drop Index command, 483

Continued

SQL (Structured Query Language)
(continued)
  Drop Table statement, 483
  Truncate command, 523
  Data Manipulation Language
  Delete command, 482-483
  Insert statement, 499-500
  Select statement, 519
  Update, 525-526
SQLState property, Error object, 94-95
Sqr function (VBScript), 451
Sqrt function (SQL), 521-522
square root, 451
state, 593-594
State property
  Command object, 53
  Connection object, 72-73
  Record object, 185-186
  Recordset object, 221
  Stream object, 296-298
statements
  SQL
    Insert, 499-500
    Select, 519
  VBScript
    call, 403
    Class, 404-405
    Const, 407
    Dim, 413-414
    Do...Loop, 414-415
    On Error Resume Next, 439-440
    Exit, 417-418
    For...Each, 419-420
    For..Next, 420-421
    Function, 423-424
    If...Then...Else, 425-426

  Private, 441-442
  Public, 442
  Randomize, 443-444
  ReDim, 444
  Select Case, 448-449
  Set, 449
  Sub, 453
  While...Wend, 458-459
StaticObjects collection
  Application object, 37-38, 607-608
  Session object, 275-276, 608-609
Status property
  Field object, 104-105
  Recordset object, 222
  Response object, 256-257
StayinSync property, Recordset object,
  223
stored procedures
  arguments, passing to, 47-48
  parameters, passing to, 648-649
  passing parameters to Command
    @index1:object, 46-56
  SQL Server and, 652
StrComp function (VBScript),
  451-452
Stream object, 276-298, 665-667
Stream object (ADO)
  methods, 620-621
  properties, 620-621
<STRIKE> HTML tag, 374
String function, VBScript, 452
string functions (SQL)
  Left, 503-504
  Length, 504-505
  Lower, 510-511
  Right, 518-519

Substr, 522–523

Upper, 526–527

string test functions, Visual Basic, 704–706

strings

  comparison, 451–452

  connection strings, 622

  functions

    Chr (VBScript), 403–404

    VBScript, 402–403

    repeating character strings, 452

    replacing with strings, 444

    reverse order, 452–453

    spaces, 450–451

    uppercase, 456–457

    VBScript

      FormatCurrency, 421

      FormatNumber, 422

      Hex function, 424–425

      Left function, 433

      Len function, 433–434

< STRONG > HTML tag, 374

StrReverse function (VBScript), 452–453

< SUB > HTML tag, 375–376

Sub statement (VBScript), 453

SubFolders property, Folder object, 152

subqueries (SQL), 462, 468–470

  Exists, 485–487

subs (VBScript), 563–566

subscript text, 375–376

Substr function (SQL), 522–523

Subtraction operator (VBScript), 453–454

Sum function (SQL), 522

< SUP > HTML tag, 376

superscript text, 376

Supports method, Recordset object, 205

syntax, 540–541

System DSN, creating, 6

T

< TABLE > HTML tag, 376–378

tables

  < CAPTION > HTML tag, 332

  < COL > HTML tag, 335

  < COLGROUP > HTML tag, 336

  Create Table (SQL), 481–482

  joins, 6

  < TABLE > HTML tag, 376–378

  < TBODY > HTML tag, 378–379

  < TD > HTML tag, 379–380

  < TH > HTML tag, 381–382

  < THEAD > HTML tag, 383–384

  < TR > HTML tag, 384–385

Tan function (VBScript), 454

tangent, 454

< TBODY > HTML tag, 378–379

< TD > HTML tag, 379–380

temporary files, 136–137

text

  bold, 324–325

  emphasized, 340–341

  flickering, 328

  italic, 350–351

  ruby text, 369

  strikethrough, 374

  subscript, 375–376

  superscript, 376

  underlined, 386–387

< TEXTAREA > HTML tag, 380–381

TextStream object, 298–309

< TH > HTML tag, 381-382
< THEAD > HTML tag, 383-384
Time function (VBScript), 454
TimeOut property, Session object, 274,
   600
TimeSerial function (VBScript),
   454-455
TimeValue function (VBScript), 455
TIP (Transaction Internet Protocol),
   676
< TITLE > HTML tag, 384
titles
   < Hn > HTML tag, 348-349
   < TITLE > HTML tag, 384
TotalBytes property, Request object,
   229
TotalSize property, Drive object, 90-91
< TR > HTML tag, 384-385
transactions
   BeginTrans method, 57-58
   Connection object and, 630
   isolation level, 633
   processing, 6
Transfer method, Server object,
   264-265, 554-556
Trim function (VBScript), 455-456
Truncate command (SQL), 523
< TT > HTML tag, 386
Type property
   Field object, 105-106
   File object, 121
   Folder object, 152-153
   Parameter object, 161
   Property object, 167-168
   Stream object, 298

U

< U > HTML tag, 386-387
Ubound function (VBScript), 456
UCase function (VBScript), 456-457
< UL > HTML tag, 387-388
underlined text (< U > HTML tag),
   386-387
UnderlyingValue property, Field
   object, 106-107
Union operator (SQL), 523-525
UnLock method, Application object,
   41, 601
Update command (SQL), 525-526
Update method
   Field object, 112-113
   Recordset object, 206
UpdateBatch method, Recordset
   object, 207
updating records, recordsets, 638-639
Upper function (SQL), 526-527
uppercase strings, 456-457
URLEncode method, Server object, 263
URLs (Uniform Resource Locator)
   < BASE > HTML tag, 325-326
UserDocument, ActiveX, 714-717
users properties, on-the-fly setup, 6

V

validation, VBScript and, 577-579
Value property
   Field object, 107-108
   Parameter object, 162
   Property object, 168-169
values
   passing to CreateParameter
      @index1:method, 653-654
   precision, 159-160

< VAR > HTML tag, 388
variable types, 457
VarType function (VBScript), 457
VBScript, 6
   application-building, 574–575
   ASP and, 541–542
   browser support, 570–571
   categories, 393–397, 571–573
   client scripting, 573–577
   entry validation, 577–579
   history list, 579–581
   HTML documents and, 6
     integration, 575–577
   overview, 569–573
   PWS installation, 582–584
   server-side scripting and, 586–590
   subs, 563–566
   Visual Basic and, 700–701
Version property, Connection object, 73
views, Create View (SQL), 482
Visual Basic
   ActiveX COM objects, creating, 678–683
   ActiveX controls, 708–710
     testing, 712–713
     UserControl, 710–712
     writing code, 712–713
   ActiveX documents, 713–717
   classes, creating, 707–708
   COM and, 718–720
   conversion functions, 707
   data access, 718
   deploying applications, 724–731
   overview, 699–701
   packaging applications, 724–731

   string test functions, 704–706
   VBScript, 700–701
Visual Basic Packaging and
   Deployment, 7
Visual InterDev, 7
   ASP code, writing, 683–688
Visual Studio, IIS and, 534
VolumeName property, Drive object, 91

W

< WBR > HTML tag, 388–389
WeekDay function (VBScript), 457–458
WeekDayName function (VBScript), 458
Where clause (SQL), 527–528
where clauses (SQL)
   In/Not in, 495–497
   Is Null/Is Not Null, 502–503
   Like/Not Like, 507–510
While...Wend statement (VBScript), 458–459
Write method
   Response object, 250, 543
   Stream object, 288–289
   TextStream object, 304
WriteBlankLines method, TextStream object, 306–307
WriteLine method, TextStream object, 305
WriteText method, Stream object, 289–290

X

Xor operator (VBScript), 459

Y–Z

Year function (VBScript), 459

Two Books in One!

CONCISE TUTORIALS

Each In Plain English guidebook delivers concise, targeted tutorials—no hand-holding, no coddling, just the skills you need to get up and running fast.

READY-REFERENCE HELP

Each book also features topic-sorted and A-to-Z reference sections that answer your questions quickly and help you get the job done, day after day.

In Plain English. All the tools you need to get up to speed—and get results.

3